The

BEST

of

Uncle John's

BATHROOM

READER

The Bathroom Readers'
Institute

Bathroom Readers' Press

"Why Your Feet Smell," by Teo Furtado, © 1994. Reprinted by permission of the author.

"The Great T.P. Shortage," by Ralph Schoenstein, © 1974. Reprinted by permission of the author.

"King of Farts," excerpted from *It's a Gas: A Study of Flatulence*, by Eric S. Rabkin, Ph.D., and Eugene M. Silverman, M.D. Manticore Books, 3644 Creekside Dr., Ann Arbor, MI 48105. Reprinted by permission of the authors.

"Elvis'sToothbrush" originally appeared in *Meet the Stars*, © 1985, by Missy Laws. Reprinted by permission of Ross Books.

"You Can Collect Toilet Paper," originally appeared in *Antique & Collecting Magazine*, © 1990, by Harry L. Rinker. Reprinted by permission of the author.

"Supermarket Secrets," Copyright 1994, CSPI. Reprinted from Nutrition Action Healthletter (1875 Connecticut Ave., N.W., Suite 300, Washington, D.C. 20009-5728. $24.00 for 10 issues).

"Birth of the Bikini," "Fabulous Flops," "The Miniskirt Saga," "Mustang: Car of the '60s," "How Pantyhose Hatched," originally appeared in *60s!*, © 1983, by John and Gordon Javna. Reprinted by permission of the authors.

"M*A*S*H," "I Love Lucy," "Star Trek," "The Twilight Zone," "Gilligan's Island," "Lost in Space," "Batman on TV," "The Three Stooges" originally appeared in *Cult TV*, © 1985, by John Javna. Reprinted by permission of the author.

"Louie, Louie," "The Magic Dragon," "Layla," "The Monster Mash," "First Hits," "Real-Life Songs" originally appeared in *Behind the Hits*, © 1985, by B. Shannon and J. Javna. Reprinted by permission of the authors.

"The Birds" originally appeared in *Animal Superstars*, © 1985, by John Javna. Reprinted by permission of the author.

"Doo-Wop Sounds" originally appeared in *The Doo-Wop Sing-Along Songbook*, © 1985, by J. Javna. Reprinted by permission of the author.

Selections from *Primetime Proverbs*, © 1989 by Jack Mingo and John Javna. Reprinted by permission of the authors.

"Marilyn," "Elvis Lives" originally appeared in *It's a Conspiracy!* by The National Insecurity Council. Text © 1992 by Michael Litchfield. Published by EarthWorks Press. Reprinted by permission of EarthWorks Press.

THANK YOU!

The Bathroom Readers' Institute sincerely thanks the people whose advice and assistance made this book possible.

John Javna
John Dollison
Lenna Lebovich
Gordon Javna
Erik Linden
Jack Mingo
Melissa Schwarz
Sharilyn Hovind
Susan LaCroix
Larry Kelp
Andy Sohn
Michael Brunsfeld
Sherry Powell
Amber James
Benjamin Brand

Brad Bunnin
Lori Emerson
Gordon Van Gelder
Eric Lefcowitz
Leni Litonjua
Julie Roeming
Gordon Javna
Lonnie Kirk
Paul Stanley
Bennie Slomski
Gordon Javna
Thomas Crapper
Jesse & Sophie, *B.R.I.T.*
…and all the bathroom readers
Hi to Emily and Molly!

P.S. THANKS FOR ALL THE LETTERS!
Here's one of our all-time favorites (No kidding—someone really sent this to us)…

Uncle John,
It was a strain writing, but now that we've started, it's a relief. I'm sure the feeling will pass, so being brief, we'd like to "sit down and be counted"—it has really bowled us over! We were unable to flush out any discrepancies….Well, that about wipes it up.
                    —*Mike and Dan M., Colora, Maryland*

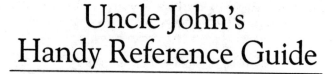

Uncle John's
Handy Reference Guide

Here's a book-by-book list of the chapters in The Best of Uncle John's Bathroom Reader. *It wasn't easy picking our favorites…we hope you like them. If you do…check out* Uncle John's Bathroom Reader *vol.1-7!*

The following articles are from *Uncle John's Bathroom Reader.*
Copyright © 1988, by the Bathroom Readers' Institute.
Reprinted by arrangement with St. Martin's Press.

GROUNDS FOR DIVORCE

In Lynch Heights, Delaware, a woman filed for divorce because her husband "regularly put itching powder in her underwear when she wasn't looking."

Note: There are other selections taken from *Uncle John's Bathroom Reader*, volumes 5–7—but we ran out of room and couldn't list them all.

GROUNDS FOR DIVORCE

In Honolulu, Hawaii, a man filed for divorce from his wife, because she "served pea soup for breakfast and dinner...and packed his lunch with pea sandwiches."

CONTENTS

Note: Because the B.R.I. understands your reading needs, we've
divided the contents by length as well as subject.
Short—A quick read
Medium—1 to 3 pages
Long—For those extended visits, when something
a little more involved is required

★ ★ ★

GROUNDS FOR DIVORCE

• In Frackville, Pennsylvania, a woman filed for divorce because her husband insisted on "shooting tin cans off of her head with a slingshot."

• In Loving, New Mexico, a woman divorced her husband because he made her salute him and address him as "Major" whenever he walked by.

• One Winthrop, Maine, man divorced his wife because she "wore earplugs whenever his mother came to visit."

• A Smelterville, Idaho, man won divorce from his wife on similar grounds. "His wife dressed up as a ghost and tried to scare his elderly mother out of the house."

• One Tarittville, Connecticut, man filed for divorce after his wife left him a note on the refrigerator. It read, "I won't be home when you return from work. Have gone to the bridge club. There'll be a recipe for your dinner at 7 o'clock on Channel 2."

INTRODUCTION

"*There are two kinds of people in the world—people who read in the bathroom, and people who don't.*"

That was how we began *Uncle John's Bathroom Reader* in 1988. It seems like only yesterday that we plunged in...but nearly eight years have passed (so to speak). Back then, when we sat down to go to work, we figured a lot of people would go with the flow when we asked them to "come out of the water closet and say it loud, 'I read in there and I'm proud!' " But we had no idea just how strong the response would be. It bowled us over.

Uncle John's Bathroom Reader was so popular that we wrote a second volume...and then a third...and a fourth...until, today, there are seven volumes in print, with more than a *million* total copies sold. Clearly, we've flushed out a new "silent majority."

Now that we've hit the 1 million mark, we've decided to celebrate by rolling out our biggest book yet, *The Best of Uncle John's Bathroom Reader*, complete with about 350 pages of classic entries from earlier editions, and 150 pages of *new* material.

To tell the truth, it wasn't easy going through seven volumes of *Bathroom Readers* and picking out the best stuff; everyone at the Bathroom Readers' Institute has their own favorite chapters. You probably do, too. Hope we haven't left yours out. (If so, let us know, so we can include it in a future "*Best of.*")

One more thing: We'd like to thank the thousands of loyal *Bathroom Reader* fans who've written us over the years with questions, comments, and suggestions—many of which have ended up as chapters in our books. We couldn't have done it without you.

As we say at the Bathroom Readers' Institute: "Go With the Flow." And for everything so far, tanks a lot.

—*Uncle John & the In-House and Out-House Staff of the Bathroom Readers' Institute*

BATHROOM LORE

It seems appropriate to begin this volume with a little background on the room you're probably sitting in right now.

THE FIRST BATHROOM

The idea of a separate room for the disposal of bodily waste goes back at least 10,000 years (to 8000 B.C.). On Orkney, an island off the coast of Scotland, the inhabitants, who lived in stone huts, created a drainage system that carried the waste directly into a nearby stream.

THE FIRST SOPHISTICATED PLUMBING

• Bathtubs dating back to 2000 B.C. have been found on the island of Crete (where there's also evidence of the first flush toilet). Considering that they were built almost 4,000 years ago, the similarity to modern baths is startling.

• Around 1500 B.C., elite Egyptians had hot and cold running water; it came into homes through a system of copper tubing or pipes.

THE FIRST SOCIAL BATHING

The ancient Romans took their bathing seriously, building public facilities wherever they settled—including London. The more elaborate of these included massage salons, food and wine, gardens, exercise rooms, and in at least one case, a public library. Coed bathing was not uncommon, nor frowned upon.

A STEP BACKWARD

• As Christianity became increasingly powerful, techniques of plumbing and waste disposal—and cleanliness in general—were forgotten; only in monasteries was this knowledge preserved.

• For hundreds of years, people in Europe basically stopped washing their bodies, in large part because nudity—even for reasons of health or hygiene—was regarded as sinful by the Church.

• In some cases, a reverence for dirt arose in its place. St. Francis of Assisi, for example, believed "dirtiness was an insignia of holiness."

• Upper-class citizens tried to cover up the inevitable body odors

First American to have plumbing installed in his home: Henry Wadsworth Longfellow, 1840.

with clothes and perfume, but the rest of the population suffered with the rank smells of filth.

CHAMBER POTS AND STREET ETIQUETTE

• Until the early 1800s, Europeans relieved themselves in chamber pots, outhouses, streets, alleys, and anywhere else they happened to feel like it.

• It was so common to relieve oneself in public that people were concerned about how to behave if they noticed acquaintances "urinating or defecating" on the street. Proper etiquette: Act like you don't see them.

• Chamber pots were used at night, or when it was too cold to go outside. Their contents were supposed to be picked up once a day by a "waste man," who carted the community's leavings to a public cesspool.

• But frequently, the chamber pot was surreptitiously dumped at night, which made it dangerous to go strolling in the evening.

DISEASE AND CHANGE

The lack of bathing took an enormous toll on the European in the Middle Ages, as epidemics caused by unsanitary living conditions became rampant. But in the 1830s, a London outbreak of cholera—a disease the English believed could only be contracted by inferior races—finally convinced the government to put its power behind public sanitation. Over the next 50 years, the British built new public facilities that set the pace for the rest of the world.

THE MODERN FLUSH TOILET

The modern flush toilet was invented by an Englishman named Alexander Cumming in 1775. Cumming's toilet emptied directly into a pipe, which then carried the undesirable matter to a cesspool. Other toilets had done this, too, but Cumming's major improvement was the addition of a "stink trap" that kept water in the pipe and thus blocked odor.

Note: It is widely believed that an Englishman named Thomas Crapper invented the toilet. That's probably a myth. (See page 18.)

HEAD FOR THE JOHN

• In the mid-1500s in England, a chamber pot was referred to as a

---

The first known contraceptive was crocodile dung, used by Egyptians in 2000 B.C.

"Jake." A hundred years later, it became a "John," or "Cousin John." In the mid-1800s, it was also dubbed a "Joe."

• That still may not be the source of the term "John" for the bathroom—it may date to the 1920s, when Men's and Ladies' rooms became common in public places. They were also referred to as "Johns" and "Janes"—presumably after John and Jane Doe.

• The term *potty* comes from the pint-sized chamber pot built for kids.

BATHROOMS

• The bathroom we know—with a combination toilet and bath—didn't exist until the 1850s. And then only for the rich.

• Until then, the term *bathroom*—which came into use in the 1820s or 1830s—meant, literally, a room with a bathtub in it.

A FEW AMERICAN FIRSTS

• First American hotel with indoor modern bathrooms: The Tremont House in Boston, 1880s.

• First toilet in the White House: 1825, installed for John Quincy Adams (leading to a new slang term for toilet—a *quincy*).

• First city with modern waterworks: Philadelphia, 1820.

• First city with a modern sewage system: Boston, 1823.

THE FIRST TOILET PAPER

• In ancient times, there was no T.P. Well-to-do Romans used sponges, wool, and rosewater. Everyone else used whatever was at hand, including sticks, stones, leaves, or dry bones. In the Middle Ages, nobles preferred silk or goose feathers (still attached to the pliable neck).

• Toilet paper was introduced in America in 1857, as a package of loose sheets. But it was too much like the paper Americans already used—the Sears catalog. It flopped.

• In 1879, an Englishman named Walter Alcock created the first perforated rolls of toilet paper. A year later, Philadelphia's Scott Brothers saw the potential in the U.S. for a product that would constantly have to be replaced. They introduced Waldorf Tissue (later Scott Tissue), which was discreetly sold in plain brown wrappers. The timing was right—by then there were enough bathrooms in America to make "toilet tissue" a success.

Starfish have eight eyes—one at the end of each leg.

THOMAS CRAPPER: MYTH OR HERO?

*If our mail was any gauge, the most controversial tidbit in the first
Bathroom Reader was our comment that the widely accepted
notion that Thomas Crapper invented the toilet is a hoax.
Readers sent all kinds of evidence "proving" that Crapper was
real. But was he? Let's take a closer look.*

FLUSHED WITH PRIDE

The name Thomas Crapper appears to have been unknown among bathroom historians until 1969, when English writer Wallace Reyburn published a 99-page book entitled *Flushed with Pride—The Story of Thomas Crapper.*

This biography (which Reyburn's publisher calls "The Little Classic of the Smallest Room") begins this way:

"Never has the saying 'a prophet is without honor in his own land' been more true than in the case of Thomas Crapper. Here was a man whose foresight, ingenuity, and perseverence brought to perfection one of the great boons to mankind. But is his name revered in the same way as, for example, that of the Earl of Sandwich?"

Of course not. Not, anyway, until Reyburn's book was published.

CRAPPER, THE MAN

According to Reyburn:

• Tom Crapper was born in 1837 and died in 1910.

• He is responsible for many toilet innovations—including, as bathroomologist Pat Mitchell puts it, "the toilets that flush in a rush seen in public restrooms today, and the...trap in plumbing that keeps sewer gas from rising into our homes."

• But the most important of Crapper's alleged accomplishments was Crapper's Valveless Water Waste Preventer, an apparatus that made flushing more efficient. *Cleaning Management* magazine calls it "the forerunner of our present-day flush system."

• For this contribution, Crapper was supposedly appointed the Royal Plumber by King Edward VII.

In 1980, the yellow pages accidentally listed a Texas funeral home under Frozen Foods.

• Crapper's name was stenciled on all the cisterns—and later, toilets—his company manufactured: T. Crapper & Co., Chelsea, London. American soldiers stationed in England during World War I began calling a toilet a "crapper."

FACT OR FICTION?

Beats us. But here are a few things to consider:

• The premier bathroom history, an impressive tome called *Clean and Decent*, makes absolutely no mention of Thomas Crapper.

• Reyburn followed *Flushed with Pride* with another social "history," entitled *Bust Up: The Uplifting Tale of Titzling and the Development of the Bra*.

• Charles Panati, in *Extraordinary Origins of Everyday Things*, notes that "the accumulation of toilet-humor puns, double-entendres, and astonishing coincidences eventually reveals...Reyburn's hoax." He offers some examples: "He moved to London and eventually settled on Fleet Street, where he perfected the 'Crapper W.C. Cistern after many dry runs'....The installation of a flushing toilet at the Royal Palace was 'a high-water mark in Crapper's career'.... He was particularly close with his niece, 'Emma Crapper', and had a friend named 'B. S.' "

• On the other hand, Pat Mitchell sent us this information: "It seems that in recent years, a certain Ken Grabowski, researcher at the Field Museum of Natural History in Chicago, has unselfishly, unswervingly, and unrelentingly sought to uncover the truth. His findings? Indeed, there was a Thomas Crapper (1836-1910). And Crapper founded a London plumbing fixture company in 1861. His efforts did produce many improvements in the fixtures he manufactured. His company's products (with his name upon them) were distributed all over Europe. Military barracks included. These were still there during World War I."

CONCLUSION

The Bathroom Readers Institute is stuck; we can't relieve the tension or wipe away the rumors. The legend of Crapper seems to have survived all the stink made about his life. Or, as Pat Mitchell puts it, "I'm not certain the legend can be killed, but if it could, does BRI want to be the executioner?"

The first sound recording ever made was "Mary Had a Little Lamb," by Tom Edison in 1877.

FREE ADVICE

Here are some helpful hints from high-profile heavyweights.
From Friendly Advice, *by Jon Winokur.*

"Never kick a fresh turd on a hot day."
—*Harry S Truman*

"Never say anything on the phone that you wouldn't want your mother to hear at the trial."
—*Sydney Biddle Barrows, the "Mayflower Madam"*

"You can get much further with a kind word and a gun than you can with a kind word alone."
—*Al Capone*

"Never trust a man unless you've got his pecker in your pocket."
—*Lyndon Baines Johnson*

"To succeed with the opposite sex, tell her you're impotent. She can't wait to disprove it."
—*Cary Grant*

"Sleeping alone, except under doctor's orders, does much harm. Children will tell you how lonely it is sleeping alone. If possible you should always sleep with someone you love. You recharge your mutual batteries free of charge."
—*Marlene Dietrich*

"Anything worth doing is worth doing slowly."
—*Gypsy Rose Lee*

"Don't try to take on a new personality; it doesn't work."
—*Richard Nixon*

"There's nothing to winning, really. That is, if you happen to be blessed with a keen eye, an agile mind, and no scruples whatsoever."
—*Alfred Hitchcock*

"Rise early. Work late. Strike oil."
—*J. Paul Getty*

"Don't let your mouth write a check that your tail can't cash."
—*Bo Diddley*

"Never eat at a place called Mom's. Never play cards with a man named Doc. And never lie down with a woman who's got more troubles than you."
—*Nelson Algren*

"What is worth doing is worth the trouble of asking someone to do it."
—*Ambrose Bierce*

Genghis Khan's calvary rode female horses. Why? So soldiers could drink their milk.

MYTH AMERICA

*You've believed these stories since you were a kid. Most Americans
have, because they were taught to us as sacred truths.
Well, sorry. Here's another look.*

SAVAGES

The Myth: Scalping was a brutal tactic invented by the
Indians to terrorize the settlers.

The Truth: Scalping was actually an old European tradition dating
back hundreds of years. Dutch and English colonists were paid a
"scalp bounty" by their leaders as a means of keeping the Indians
scared and out of the way. Finally the Indians caught on and adopted the practice themselves. The settlers apparently forgot its origins
and another falsehood about Indian cruelty was born.

MOTHER OF THE FLAG

The Myth: Betsy Ross, a Philidelphia seamstress, designed and
sewed the first American flag at the behest of the Founding
Fathers.

Background: This story first surfaced in 1870 when Betsy Ross's
grandson told a meeting of the Pennsylvania Historical Society
that his grandmother had been asked to make a flag for the new nation. The tale must have touched a nerve, because it quickly spread
and soon was regarded as the truth.

The Truth: While Betsy Ross did in fact sew flags for the Pennsylvania Navy, there is no proof to back up her grandson's tale. Ironically, no one is sure who designed the flag. The best guess is that
the flag's design is derived from a military banner carried during the
American Revolution.

MIDNIGHT RAMBLER

The Myth: Paul Revere made a solitary, dramatic midnight ride
to warn patriots in Lexington and Concord that the British were
coming.

Background: Revere's effort was first glorified in Henry Wadsworth Longfellow's poem, "The Midnight Ride of Paul Revere."

Longfellow may have written the ode out of guilt—his grandfather had tried to court-martial Revere during the Revolutionary War. The charge: "Unsoldierly behavior tending toward cowardice." (Revere was not convicted.)

The Truth: Paul Revere was actually one of two men who attempted the famous ride...and it was the other one, William Dawes, who made it to Concord. Revere didn't make it—he was stopped by British troops. As for Revere's patriotic motives: According to Patricia Lee Holt, in *George Washington Had No Middle Name*, "Paul Revere billed the Massachusetts State House 10 pounds 4 shillings to cover his expenses for his ride."

AMERICUS THE BEAUTIFUL

The Myth: Amerigo Vespucci, a Florentine navigator, made four trips to the New World from 1497 to 1502. The newly discovered land was named in his honor.

Background: Vespucci wrote an account of his four voyages. An Italian mapmaker was so impressed by it that he put "Americus's" name on the first known map of the New World.

The Truth: America is named after a probable fraud. Scholars doubt Vespucci made those trips at all.

THANKSGIVING

The Myth: The Pilgrims ate a Thanksgiving feast of turkey and pumpkin pie after their first year in the New World, and we've been doing it ever since.

The Truth: Thanksgiving didn't become a national holiday until Abraham Lincoln declared it in 1863, and the Pilgrims ate neither the bird we call turkey, nor pumpkin pie.

TAKING A STAND

The Myth: General George Armstrong Custer's "Last Stand" at Little Bighorn was a heroic effort by a great soldier.

The Truth: It wasn't heroism, it was stupidity. Custer had unwarranted contempt for the American Indians' fighting ability. His division was supposed to be a small part of a major attack, led by General Alfred Terry—who was planning to meet Custer in two days with his troops. Custer was instructed to wait for Terry. Instead, he led his 266 men into battle. They were all slaughtered.

WORD PLAY

What do these familiar phrases really mean? Etymologists have researched them and come up with these explanations.

FLY OFF THE HANDLE
Meaning: Get very angry, very quickly.

Background: Refers to axe heads, which, in the days before mass merchandising, were sometimes fastened poorly to their handles. If one flew off while being used, it was a dangerous situation... with unpredictable results.

HIGH ON THE HOG
Meaning: Luxurious, prosperous.

Background: The tastiest parts of a hog are its upper parts. If you're living high on the hog, you've got the best it has to offer.

PULL THE WOOL OVER SOMEONE'S EYES
Meaning: Fool someone.

Background: "Goes back to the days when all gentlemen wore powdered wigs like the ones still worn by the judges in British courts. The word wool was then a popular, joking term for hair....The expression 'pull the wool over his eyes' came from the practice of tilting a man's wig over his eyes, so he couldn't see what was going on."

HOOKER
Meaning: Prostitute.

Background: Although occasionally used before the Civil War, its widespread popularity can probably be traced to General Joseph Hooker, a Union soldier who was well-known for the liquor and whores in his camp. He was ultimately demoted, and Washington prostitutes were jokingly referred to as "Hooker's Division."

LET THE CAT OUT OF THE BAG
Meaning: Reveal the truth.

Background: Refers to a con game practiced at country fairs in old England. A trickster tried to sell a cat in a burlap bag to an unwary bumpkin, saying it was a pig. If the victim figured out the trick and insisted on seeing the animal, the cat had to be let out of the bag.

The largest painting on earth is a 72,437-square-foot smiley face.

FAMOUS FOR 15 MINUTES

We've included this feature—based on Andy Warhol's comment that "in the future, everyone will be famous for 15 minutes"—in several Bathroom Readers. Here are some of the more memorable stars.

THE HEADLINE: *Man Saves President Ford's Life by Deflecting Assassin's Gun*

THE STAR: Oliver Sipple, an ex-marine living in San Francisco

WHAT HAPPENED: President Gerald R. Ford was visiting San Francisco on September 22, 1975. As he crossed the street, a woman in the crowd, Sara Jane Moore, pulled out a gun and tried to shoot him. Fortunately, a bystander spotted Moore and managed to tackle her just as the gun went off. The bullet missed the president by only a few feet.

Oliver Sipple, the bystander, was an instant hero—which was about the last thing he wanted. Reporters investigating his private life discovered that he was openly gay—a fact he'd hidden from his family in Detroit. Sipple pleaded with journalists not to write about his private life, but they ignored him. The next day, the *Los Angeles Times* ran a front-page story headlined "Hero in Ford Shooting Active Among S.F. Gays."

THE AFTERMATH: The incident ruined his life. When Sipple's mother learned of his sexual orientation, she stopped speaking to him. And when she died in 1979, Sipple's father would not let him attend the funeral. Sipple became an alcoholic. In 1979 he was found dead of "natural causes" in his apartment. He was 37.

THE HEADLINE: *New Jersey Student Makes Vice President Look Like a Foole*

THE STAR: William Figueroa, a 12-year-old student

WHAT HAPPENED: In June 1992, Vice President Dan Quayle visited a Trenton, New Jersey, elementary school where a spelling bee was being held. Quayle took over. Reading from a cue card,

---

There are only 2 places in the world where men outlive women: southern Asia and Iran.

Quayle asked Figueroa, a sixth-grader, to spell the word "potato." The boy spelled the word correctly, but Quayle insisted that he change it, because "potato" was spelled with an 'e' at the end. "I knew he was wrong," Figueroa later told reporters, "but since he's the vice president, I went and put the 'e' on, and he said, 'That's right, now go and sit down.' Afterward, I went to a dictionary and there was potato like I spelled it."

THE AFTERMATH: Figueroa became an instant celebrity. "Late Night with David Letterman" had him on as a guest, and he was asked to lead the pledge of allegiance at the 1992 Democratic National Convention. Afterwards, an AM radio station paid him $50 a day to provide political commentary on the Republican National Convention. He was also hired as spokesperson for a company that makes a computer spelling program.

THE HEADLINE: *Small Man in Big Leagues: A Veeck Stunt*

THE STAR: Eddie Gaedel, a three-foot, seven-inch midget

WHAT HAPPENED: It was a Sunday doubleheader with the Detroit Tigers on August 19, 1951, and the St. Louis Browns were celebrating the 50th anniversary of the American League. Between games, Brown owner Bill Veeck wheeled a huge cake out onto the field, and out jumped Eddie Gaedel, wearing a Browns uniform with the number 1/8 on it. During the first inning of the next game, Gaedel popped out of the dugout and informed the umpire he was pinch hitting. Challenged by the ump, Veeck produced a valid contract. Pitching is difficult as it is, but a batter under four feet tall has a strike zone of about 18 inches. Gaedel walked on four straight pitches. He then left for a pinch-runner.

THE AFTERMATH: Gaedel made a quick $100 for his appearance, and American League president Will Harridge issued a solemn declaration barring midgets from baseball.

THE HEADLINE: *Amateur Captures Assassination on Film*

THE STAR: Abraham Zapruder, president of a ladies' garment company headquartered in Dallas

WHAT HAPPENED: On November 22, 1963, Abraham Zapruder and his secretary took the afternoon off to watch President John

F. Kennedy's motorcade pass through the streets of Dallas. Zapruder climbed up on top of a concrete abutment to wait for the presidential limousine. At 12:29 it finally appeared, and Zapruder began filming. "As they were approaching where I was standing, I heard a shot.... Then I heard another shot. It hit the president in the head and practically opened it up...I was still shooting the picture until he got under the underpass—I don't even know how I did it."

THE AFTERMATH: Zapruder and his unique footage of the assassination instantly became world-famous. The film turned out to be a critical piece of evidence for the Warren Commission. And because it clearly shows Kennedy's head jerking *backward* after the shots were fired, it introduced the possibility that more than one gunman was involved. (If Oswald had fired the fatal shot, the argument goes, JFK's head would have jerked *forward*).

After a round of interviews and appearances, Zapruder sold the original copy of the film for $25,000 to Time-Life, Inc. They turned it over to the National Archives. Zapruder died of cancer in 1970.

THE HEADLINE: *Lucky Fan Hits $1 Million Shot in Chicago*

THE STAR: Don Calhoun

WHAT HAPPENED: On April 14, 1993, Calhoun, a 23-year-old office supply sales rep got a free ticket to an NBA game between the Miami Heat and the Chicago Bulls.

As he headed for his seat, someone told him he'd been picked to take the "Million Dollar Shot" (a promotion sponsored by Coke and a local restaurant chain). He'd get to take one shot from the opposite foul line, 73 feet away, and try to sink a basket. The prize: $1 million. Eighteen people had already tried and failed.

At first he didn't want to do it—he even suggested that his friend make the shot instead. But the Bulls representative insisted. So during a time-out early in the third period, he was brought to the floor. He took one dribble, launched the ball, and...basket!

THE AFTERMATH: Calhoun's Cinderella story was on every sportscast that night. He did radio interviews, TV shows, even NBC's "Today" show. His story got more interesting when it turned out that contest rules stipulated no one who'd played ball in college could participate—and Calhoun had played 11 games of college basketball. But the sponsors, wary of bad publicity, forked over the money anyway. Later, Calhoun joined the Harlem Globetrotters.

Dr. Seuss coined the word "nerd" in his 1950 book *If I Ran the Zoo*.

A FOOD IS BORN

*These foods are common, but you probably don't
know where they came from. Here are the answers.*

BAGELS
According to *The Bagels' Bagel Book*: "In 1683 in Vienna,
Austria, a local Jewish baker wanted to thank the King of Po-
land for protecting his countrymen from Turkish invaders. He made
a special hard roll in the shape of a riding stirrup—*Beugel* in Austrian—commemorating the king's favorite pastime, and giving the bagel its distinctive shape."

MAYONNAISE
Originally brought to France by Duc de Richelieu, who tasted it
while visiting Mahon, a city on the island of Minorca. It was eventually dubbed *Mahonaisse* by French chefs, and was considered a del-
icacy in Europe. In America, it became known as *mayonnaise*, but
for over a century was still regarded as suitable for only the most elegant meals. Finally, in 1912, Richard Hellman, a German immigrant, began packing it and selling it in jars from his New York deli.
This transformed mayonnaise from a carefully prepared treat for the
select few to a mass-merchandised condiment.

GATORADE
According to *60s!*, by John and Gordon Javna: "In 1965, Dr. Robert
Cade was studying the effects of heat exhaustion on football players
at the University of Florida (whose team name is the Gators). He
analyzed the body liquids lost in sweating and within three minutes
came up with the formula for Gatorade. Two years later, Cade sold
the formula to Stokely-Van Camp. Soon, annual sales were well
over $50 million and Gatorade could be found on the training ta-
bles of over 300 college sports teams, 1,000 high school squads, and
all but 2 pro football teams."

7-UP
According to *Parade* magazine: "In October 1929, just before the
stock market crash, St. Louis businessman Charles L. Grigg began
marketing a beverage called Bib-Label Lithiated Lemon-Lime Soda.
His slogan: 'Takes the "Ouch" out of grouch.' The drink was a huge

Where does the word *condom* come from? Dr. Charles Condom (1630-1685).

success during the Depression, perhaps because it contained lithium, a powerful drug now prescribed for manic-depressives. The drink's unwieldy name was later changed to 7-UP. The '7' stood for its 7-ounce bottle, the 'UP' for 'bottoms up,' or for the bubbles rising from its heavy carbonation, which was later reduced. The lithium was listed on the label until the mid-'40s."

TEA BAGS
In 1908, a New York tea importer mailed his customers free samples of tea, which he packaged in tiny silk bags. When customers wrote back asking for more of the bags, the importer realized they were using them to steep the tea…and began packaging all his tea that way.

POPSICLES
Eleven-year-old Frank Epperson accidentally left a mixture of powdered soda mix and water on his back porch one winter night in 1905. The next morning, he found the stuff frozen, with the stirring stick standing straight up in the jar. He pulled it out, and had the first "Epperson icicle"—or "Epsicle." He later renamed it "Popsicle," since he'd made it with soda pop. It was patented in 1923, 18 years later.

THE ICE CREAM CONE
It happened at the 1904 World's Fair in Saint Louis (where the hot dog and the hamburger were also popularized). An ice cream vendor who was selling cups of the frozen dessert had so many customers in the hot weather that he ran out of cups. In desperation, he looked around to see if another nearby vendor might have some spare containers, but all he could find was a waffle concession. He quickly bought some waffles and began selling them wrapped around a scoop of ice cream. The substitute became even more popular than the original, and it spread around the country.

DR. PEPPER
In Virginia in the 1880s, a pharmacist's assistant named Wade Morrison fell in love with his boss's daughter. The pharmacist decided Morrison was too old for his daughter and encouraged him to move on. He did, settling down in Waco, Texas, where he bought his own drugstore. When one of his employees developed a new soft drink syrup, Morrison named it after the man who got him started in the pharmacy business—his old flame's father, Dr. Kenneth Pepper.

PRIMETIME PROVERBS

TV comments about everyday life. From Prime Time Proverbs, *by Jack Mingo and John Javna.*

ON FOOD

"Why am I bothering to eat this chocolate? I might as well apply it directly to my thighs."

–Rhoda Morgenstern,
Mary Tyler Moore Show

Gracie: "The reason I put the salt in the pepper shaker and the pepper in the salt shaker is that people are always getting them mixed up. Now when they get mixed up, they'll be right."

–*Burns and Allen*

"Six years, and you haven't learned *anything*—it's *white wine* with Hershey Bars."

–Harvey Barnes,
Making the Grade

ON THE BATTLE OF THE SEXES

"Early to bed, early to rise, and your girl goes out with other guys."

–Bob Collins,
Love That Bob

"Carmine and I have an understanding. I'm allowed to date other men, and he's allowed to date ugly women."

–Shirley Feeny,
Laverne and Shirley

ON MARRIED LIFE

Edith: "Do you like bein' alone with me?"
Archie: "Certainly I like being alone with you. What's on television?"

–*All in the Family*

ON MONEY

"There are two things [I won't do for money]. I won't kill for it and I won't marry for it. Other than that, I'm open to about anything."

–Jim Rockford,
The Rockford Files

CURRENT EVENTS

"What's this I hear about making Puerto Rico a steak? The next thing they'll be wanting is a salad, and then a baked potato."

–Emily Litella
(Gilda Radner),
Saturday Night Live

The heaviest dog on record was a St. Bernard that weighed 310 pounds.

CR_ _ SW_ _ D
P_ ZZL_ S

*Here's an expanded version of a chapter that appeared
in* Uncle John's Fourth Bathroom Reader.

ORIGIN
Arthur Wynne was a writer for the game page of the *New York World* at the turn of the 19th century. One winter afternoon in 1913, while trying to think up new types of games for the newspaper's special Christmas edition, he came up with a way to adapt the "word squares" his grandfather had taught him when he was a boy. In a word square, all of the words in the square have to read the same horizontally and vertically, like the example below.

But in the new puzzle Wynne came up with, the "across" words were *different* from the "down" words. It was more challenging, since there were more words to work on.

C	I	R	C	L	E
I	C	A	R	U	S
R	A	R	E	S	T
C	R	E	A	T	E
L	U	S	T	R	E
E	S	T	E	E	M

Wynne's puzzle, which he called a "Word-Cross," debuted on Sunday December 21 as planned. And it was well-received. So many people wrote in to praise the puzzle that he put one in the paper the following Sunday, and again on the third Sunday.

Reversal of Fortune

Four weeks after the puzzle first appeared, typesetters at the newspaper inadvertantly transposed the words in the title to read "Cross-Word." For some reason, the name stuck—and so did the puzzle. When the *World* tried to drop it a few months later, readers were so hostile that the paper reversed itself and decided to make it a permanent feature of the puzzle page instead.

Though the puzzles were popular with readers, they were decidedly unpopular with editors. Crosswords were difficult to print and were plagued with typographical and other errors. In fact, no other newspaper wanted any part of them. So for the next 10 years, if you wanted to work on a crossword puzzle, you had to buy the *World*.

ENTER SIMON AND SCHUSTER

According to legend, in 1924 a young Columbia University graduate named Richard L. Simon went to dinner at his Aunt Wixie's house. A *World* subscriber and a cross-word devotee, she asked where she could buy a book of crossword puzzles for her daughter. Simon, who was trying to break into the publishing business with college chum M. Lincoln Schuster, told her there were no such books...and then hit on the idea of publishing one himself.

The next day, he and Schuster went to the *World's* offices and made a deal with the paper's crossword puzzle editors. They would pick the newspaper's best crossword puzzles and pay $25 apiece for the rights to publish them in a book. The pair then used all their money to print *The Cross Word Puzzle Book*.

HOT OFF THE PRESSES

It was literally an overnight success. The *World's* crossword puzzlers flocked to stores to get copies, and by the end of the year more than 300,000 crossword books had been sold.

The book turned Simon & Schuster into a major publisher. (Today it's the largest U.S. publishing house and the second-largest publisher on earth.) It also started a major craze. Crossword puzzles became a way of life in the 1920s. Newspapers started adding them to increase circulation. They inspired a Broadway hit called *Games of 1925* and a hit song called "Crossword Mama, You Puzzle Me." Sales of dictionaries soared, and foot traffic in libraries increased dramatically. Clothes made with black-and-white checked fabric were the rage. The B&O Railroad put dictionaries on all its mainline trains for crossword-crazy commuters.

CROSSWORD CASUALTIES

Some folks were driven over the edge by the craze. In 1924, a Chicago woman sued her husband for divorce, claiming "he was so engrossed in solving crosswords that he didn't have time to work." The judge ordered the man to "limit himself to 3 puzzles a day and devote the rest of his time to domestic duties." In 1925, a New York Telephone Co. employee shot his wife when she wouldn't help with a crossword puzzle. And in 1926, a Budapest man committed suicide, leaving an explanation in the form of a crossword puzzle. (No one could solve it.) Eventually, the craze died down. It took *The New York Times* to revive it. (See page 293 for the story.)

THE FIRST
CROSSWORD PUZZLE

*BRI bonus: Here's the very first crossword puzzle, designed by Arthur
Wynne. It appeared in the New York World on December 21, 1913.*

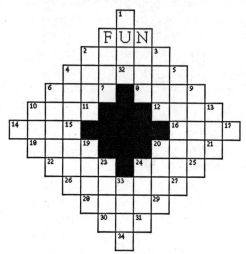

ACROSS

2-3. What bargain hunters enjoy.
4-5. A written acknowledgment.
6-7. Such and nothing more.
10-11. A bird.
14-15. Opposed to less.
18-19. What this puzzle is.
22-23. An animal of prey.
26-27. The close of a day.
28-29. To elude.
30-31. The plural of is.
8-9. Cultivate
12-13. A bar of wood or iron.
16-17. What artists learn to do.
20-21. Fastened.
24-25. Found on the seashore.

DOWN

10-18. The fiber of the gomuti palm.
6-22. What we all should be.
4-26. A day dream.
2-11. A talon.
19-28. A pigeon.
F-7. Part of your head.
23-30. A river in Russia.
1-32. To govern.
33-34. An aromatic plant.
N-8. A fist.
24-31. To agree with.
3-12. Part of a ship.
20-29. One.
5-27. Exchanging.
9-25. To sink in mud.
13-21. A boy.

The Solution:

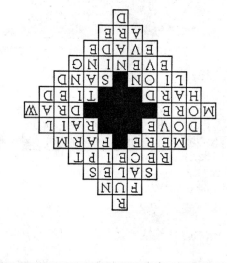

Iceland consumes more Coca-Cola per capita than any other nation on Earth.

GILLIGAN'S ISLAND

Few TV shows have been both as reviled and beloved—sometimes by the same person—as "Gilligan's Island." Two questions remain unanswered about this program: 1) Where did they get all those clothes? 2) How did they last for three years without sex?

HOW IT STARTED

In 1963, veteran TV writer Sherwood Schwartz ("The Red Skelton Show, "I Married Joan") was ready to break away from writing other people's shows and create his own sitcom. A literate man with degrees in zoology and psychology, Schwartz had an idea for a meaningful show: he'd take representative members of American society, strand them on an island (this was inspired by Daniel Defoe's *Robinson Crusoe*), and their interaction would be a microcosm of life in the United States.

How this idea turned into "Gilligan's Island" is anyone's guess. In the end, Sherwood's castaways were more caricatures than characters. He called them "cliches"; "the wealthy, the Hollywood glamour girl, the country girl, the professor, the misfit, and the resourceful bull of a man." He added, "Anybody who is watching can identify with someone." Yes, but would they want to?

Schwartz brought his concept to CBS and United Artists; both agreed to finance a pilot. But after the pilot was filmed, CBS started playing with the premise. Network president Jim Aubrey felt it should be a story about a charter boat that went out on a new adventure every week. "How would the audience know what those guys were doing on the island?" he wanted to know. It looked like Schwartz's original idea was sunk. Then he had a brainstorm— explain the premise in a theme song. He wrote his own tune and performed it at a meeting of CBS brass (probably a first). And on the basis of that song, CBS OK'd the castaways. Now, do we thank them or what?

INSIDE FACTS

Even "Gilligan's Island" wasn't sanitized enough for the censors. Never mind that there wasn't a hint of sex in three years on a de-

---

serted island. CBS censors still objected to Tina Louise's low-cut dresses and Dawn Wells's exposed navel.

• Believe it or not, some viewers took the show seriously. The U.S. Coast Guard received several telegrams from concerned citizens asking why they didn't rescue the Minnow's crew.

• Schwartz picked the name "Gilligan" from out of the Los Angeles phone book.

• Schwartz originally wanted Jerry Van Dyke to play Gilligan. He turned it down in favor of the lead in a different TV series—"My Mother the Car." Another actor wanted to play the Skipper, but was rejected: Carroll "Archie Bunker" O'Connor.

EVERYONE'S A CRITIC

The public loved "Gilligan," but most critics hated it. A sample:

• *Los Angeles Times:* " 'Gilligan's Island' is a show that should never have reached the airwaves, this season or any other."

• *San Francisco Chronicle:* "It is difficult to believe that this show was written, directed, and produced by adults. It marks a new low in the networks' estimation of public intelligence."

THE PILOT FILM

• The pilot was shot in Hawaii, just a few miles from the spot that *South Pacific* was filmed.

• One of the major problems faced by the production crew during the pilot's filming: frogs. Inexplicably, they piled up by the hundreds outside the doors of the on-site cottages.

• Filming of the pilot was completed on November 22, 1963—the day JFK was assassinated.

ABOUT THE ISLAND

• The island used in the series cost $75,000 to build (a bargain, considering how much they made from it).

• It was artifical, located in the middle of an equally artificial lake at CBS's Studio Center in Hollywood, and surrounded by painted landscapes, fake palm trees, and wind machines.

• At one point, the concrete lake bottom leaked and had to be completely drained, repaired, and filled again.

Only about a third of "Gilligan's Island" episodes are actually about getting off the island.

THE TOUGHEST TOWN IN THE WEST

Think of a typical Western town in the 1870s. Saloons with swinging doors…horse manure all over the street…painted ladies waving at passersby…and gunfights. Lots of gunfights. It was such a popular image that Palisades, Nevada, decided to preserve it. Here's the story, with thanks to the People's Almanac.

A LEGEND IS BORN

By the late 1870s, the Wild West era was winding down. But it was such an entrenched part of American lore that many people hated to see it go.

One town, Palisade, Nevada, decided to keep it alive for as long as possible…by staging fake gunfights for unsuspecting train passengers on the Union Pacific and Central Pacific railroads, which regularly pulled into town for brief rest stops.

The idea got started when a train conductor suggested to a citizen of Palisade that "as long as so many easterners were traveling west hoping to see the Old West, why not give it to them?"

COMMUNITY ACTIVITY

The townspeople took the idea and ran with it: one week later they staged the first gunbattle in Palisade's history. The good guy was played by Frank West, a tall, handsome cowhand from a nearby ranch; Alvin "Dandy" Kittleby, a popular, deeply religious man (who also happened to look like a villain), played the bad guy.

Just as the noon train pulled into town for a 10-minute stop, Kittleby began walking down Main Street toward the town saloon. West, who was standing near a corral about 60 feet away, stepped out into the street and shouted at the top of his lungs: "There ya are, ya low-down polecat. Ah bin waitin' fer ya. Ah'm goin' to kill ya b'cause of what ya did ta mah sister. Mah pore, pore little sister." Then he drew his revolver and fired it over Kittleby's head. Kittleby fell to the ground kicking and screaming as if he had been shot, and the passengers immediately dove for cover; several of the women fainted, and some of the men may have, too.

It takes 3,000 cows to supply the NFL with enough leather for a year's supply of footballs.

Ten minutes later, when the train pulled out of the station, nearly every passenger was still crouched on the floor of the passenger compartment.

A MILESTONE

That was probably the first faked gunfight in the history of the Wild West, but it wasn't the last. Over the next three years, the Palisadians staged more than 1,000 gunfights—sometimes several a day.

To keep the townspeople interested and the train passengers fooled, the town regularly changed the theme of the gunfight, sometimes staging a duel, sometimes an Indian raid (in which real Shoshone Indians on horseback "massacred" innocent women and children before being gunned down themselves), and bank robberies involving more than a dozen robbers and sheriff's deputies.

Those who didn't directly participate in the gun battles helped out by manufacturing blank cartridges by the thousands and collecting beef blood from the town slaughterhouse. Nearly everyone within a 100-mile radius was in on the joke—including railroad workers, who probably thought the battles sold train tickets and were good for business. Somehow they all managed to keep the secret; for over three years, nearly every passenger caught in the crossfire of a staged fight thought they were witnessing the real thing. The truth is, the town during those years was so safe that it didn't even have a sheriff.

NATIONAL OUTRAGE

One group of onlookers that weren't in on the joke were the metropolitan daily newspapers in towns like San Francisco, Chicago, and New York, which regularly reported the shocking news of the massacres on the front pages. Editorials were written by the dozens denouncing the senseless waste of human life and calling on local officials to get the situation under control. They even called on the U.S. Army to occupy the town and restore order...but since the Army itself was in on the joke, it never took action.

Over time, Palisade developed a reputation as one of the toughest towns in the history of the West—a reputation that it probably deserved more than any other town, since it worked so hard to earn it.

Thirty-five percent of the people who use personal ads for dating are already married.

"COME UP AND SEE ME..."

Comments from the outrageous film actress Mae West.

"Marriage is a great institution, but I'm not ready for an institution yet."

"It's hard to be funny when you have to be clean."

"She's the kind of girl who climbed the ladder of success, wrong by wrong."

Between two evils, I always pick the one I haven't tried before."

"I generally avoid temptation—unless I can't resist it."

"It's not the men in my life that counts—it's the life in my men."

"He who hesitates is last."

"When women go wrong, men go right after them."

"Too much of a good thing can be wonderful."

"I used to be Snow White ...but I drifted."

"I only like two kinds of men—domestic and foreign."

"Is that a gun in your pocket, or are you just glad to see me?"

"Give a man a free hand and he'll run it all over you."

"I've been in more laps than a napkin."

"A man in the house is worth two in the street."

"He's the kind of man a woman would have to marry to get rid of."

"Brains are an asset...if you hide them."

"I don't look down on men, but I certainly don't look up to them either. I never found a man I could love—or trust—the way I loved myself."

"When I'm good, I'm very good. But when I'm bad, I'm better."

"I always say, keep a diary and one day it will keep you."

"I've always had a weakness for foreign affairs."

The first novel ever written on a typewriter was *The Adventures of Tom Sawyer*.

TEST YOUR ELVIS MOVIE IQ

You probably know the King's biggest hits. But how much do you know about his 33 films? Take the Quiz below and find out. (Answers are at the end.)

1 **Which of the following best describes the storyline to the King's 1969 film *Change of Habit*?**

♦ **A)** Elvis, a hillbilly race car driver with a drinking problem, commits himself to a mental hospital in Puerto Rico to "dry out." With the help of Dr. Trisha Boyer (Tuesday Weld), he turns his life around.

B) Elvis is a physician working with a bunch of nuns in a ghetto health clinic. He and Sister Michelle (played by Mary Tyler Moore) fall in love; she spends the rest of the film trying to choose between the Prince of Peace and the King of Rock 'n' Roll.

C) Elvis quits his 9-to-5 job and joins the circus, bathing elephants and guessing people's weight. He teaches the clowns to sing and falls in love with Trixie the Bearded Lady (Angie Dickenson).

2. Elvis narrowly avoided serious physical injury—perhaps even death—while filming in 1960. What happened?

A) He was fooling around backstage with Frank Sinatra's girlfriend when Ol' Blue Eyes showed up on the set, walked into the King's dressing room, and caught them in the act.

B) After a long day of filming a difficult combat scene, the King and his entourage blew off steam by staging their own gun battles on the set, using rifles supplied by the prop department. It turned out one of the guns was loaded, and no one knew it.

C) He nearly choked to death wolfing down one of his fried peanut-butter-and-banana sandwiches.

3. What made Elvis's 1957 film *Loving You* different from all of his other films?

A) It was actually *praised* by movie critics.

B) His mother and father made cameo appearances in the film.

Stage fright: According to tradition, it's bad luck to say "MacBeth" in a theater.

C) The scene in which Elvis teaches Bobo the Orangutan to dance the Cha-Cha-Cha was suggested by the producer's 14-year-old nephew—a film prodigy named Steven Spielberg.

4. What makes Elvis's appearance unusual in *Charro*? (1969)

A) Elvis wore earrings and a necklace…but only after he protested that the jewelry made him look like "a damn sissy."

B) Elvis wore a beard throughout the entire film.

C) Elvis, playing a kindhearted longshoreman with a speech impediment, was heavily tattooed and completely bald.

5. Which of the following *isn't* the plot of an Elvis film?

A) Air Force officer Elvis has to talk a family of hillbillies into leasing their land to the military for use as a missile site.

B) Elvis, half Indian and half white, is forced to take sides when Mama's Indian relations declare war on Daddy's land-stealing frontier kin.

C) Elvis moves to Acapulco, works days as a lifeguard and nights as a nightclub singer, and falls in love with a women bullfighter named Dolores. A shoeshine boy helps him overcome his fear of heights, which he sustained after a terrible accident in his previous career as a trapeze artist.

D) Elvis, the leader of a rock band, is framed for the murder of his lead guitarist and sent to prison; he tunnels (and sings) his way to freedom using a guitar pick and a broken bottle.

E) Elvis and a gang of happy-go-lucky pickpockets save the king of Lunarkand after he is targeted for assassination by Middle Eastern extremists.

6. Which of the following lines *wasn't* spoken by Elvis in one of his films?

A) "Shucks, Ma'am, Ah just got into town and don't have no money to pay for supper. How's about Ah just sing to yore customers?"

B) "Last one out of the water is a papaya picker."

C) "I got plans for what I intend to do, and it's not stopping punches with my head."

D) "One of the bulls decided I was sitting on him too long, so he decided to sit on me."

The average caterpillar has 2,000 muscles in its body. The average human, less than 700.

7. What famous actress made her acting debut in the King's 1964 film *Roustabout?*

A) Raquel Welch

B) Goldie Hawn

C) Meryl Streep

D) Jane Fonda

ANSWERS

1. B) The movie was probably the most embarrassing of Mary Tyler Moore's career.

2. A) Juliet Prowse, Elvis's co-star in *G.I. Blues*, had been dating Sinatra, and Hollywood gossip columns were full of reports that the couple would marry.…But that didn't stop Elvis. He and Prowse spent all of their time between takes locked in the King's dressing room. Elvis's buddies used to play jokes on him by pounding on the door of the dressing room and shouting "Hey Elvis, quick, here comes Frank! He's on the set." Presley took the warnings seriously at first, but they happened so often that he finally just ignored them… until the day Sinatra really did show up on the set. "Hey, Elvis, here comes Frank! I mean it man, he's on the set!" Red West, one of Elvis's hangers-on shouted, but Elvis ignored him. Sinatra knocked on the door, Elvis opened it, and the two stepped inside for about 10 minutes. Then Sinatra left…and for whatever reason, the wedding with Prowse never materialized.

3. B) Gladys and Vernon Presley appeared in a scene as members of a TV studio audience: Gladys sat in the aisle seat in the fourth row; Vernon sat next to her.

4. B) Elvis played Jess Wade, a scruffy-faced reformed gunslinger who runs afowl of a gang of outlaws.

5. D) The other plots were for the following movies: A) *Kissin' Cousins* (1964); B) *Flaming Star* (1960); C) *Fun in Acapulco* (1963); and E) *Harum Scarum* (1965).

6. A)

7. A) Welch plays one of two college girls who go with their boyfriends to a place called Mother's Tea House. Her first line: "Uh, how come they call this place a tea house, dear?"

AROUND THE HOUSE

The origins of a few common items.

BAND-AIDS (1921)

In 1921, Earle Dickson, an employee of Johnson & Johnson, married a woman who kept injuring herself in the kitchen.

• As he repeatedly bandaged her cuts and burns with gauze and adhesive tape, he became frustrated; the clumsy bandages kept falling off. So he decided to create something "that would stay in place, be easily applied, and still retain its sterility." He stuck some gauze in the center of a piece of adhesive tape, and covered the whole thing with crinoline to keep it sterile. It worked.

• He made up a bunch for his wife and took a few in to show his co-workers. The company's owner, James Johnson, heard about it and asked for a demonstration—which convinced him to begin manufacturing the product.

• By the '80s, over 100 billion Band-Aids had been sold. Dickson, who became an exec at J & J, was amply rewarded for his efforts.

IVORY SOAP (1879)

Harley Procter and his cousin, chemist James Gamble, came up with a special new soap in 1878. It was smooth and fragrant and produced a consistent lather...but it wasn't Ivory—it was called White Soap—and it didn't float.

• One day in 1879, the man operating Proctor & Gamble's soap-mixing machine forgot to turn it off when he went to lunch. On returning, he discovered that so much air had been whipped into the soap that it actually floated.

• For some reason, the batch wasn't discarded—it was made into bars and shipped out with the other White Soap. Soon, to their surprise, P&G was getting letters demanding more of "that soap that floats." So they started putting extra air in every bar.

• Now that they had a unique product, they needed a unique name. And they found it in the Bible. Procter was reading the 45th Psalm—which says: "All thy garments smell of myrrh, and aloes, and cassia, out of the ivory palaces..." —when it hit him that *ivory* was just the word he was looking for.

• In October 1879, the first bar of Ivory Soap was sold.

Restroom tip: The first stall is usually the cleanest. Most people, seeking privacy, skip it.

VELCRO (1957)

A young Swiss inventor named George De Mestral went for a hike one day in 1948. When he returned, he was annoyed to find burrs stuck to his clothes. But his annoyance turned to fascination. Why, he wondered, wouldn't it be possible to create synthetic burrs that could be used as fasteners?

• Most people scoffed at the idea, but a French weaver took him seriously. Using a small loom, the weaver hand-wove two cotton strips that stuck together when they touched. The secret: one strip had hooks, the other had loops.

• But De Mestral had to figure out how to mass-produce it...and he needed tougher material than cotton, which quickly wore out.

• Years passed; De Mestral experimented constantly. Finally he found a suitable material—nylon, which, it turned out, became very hard when treated with infrared light.

• Now he knew how to make the *loops* by machine—but he still couldn't figure out how to mass-produce the *hooks*.

• Finally a solution hit him. He bought a pair of barber's clippers and took them to a weaver. With the clippers, he demonstrated his idea—a loom that snipped loops as it wove them, creating little nylon hooks. He worked on the project for a year—and when it was finally completed, Velcro ("Vel" for velvet, "cro" for crochet) was born. The product had taken a decade to perfect.

POP-UP ELECTRIC TOASTER (1919)

The first electric toasters, which appeared around 1900, were primitively constructed heating coils that were terrible fire hazards. However, they were a luxury—it was the first time in history that people didn't need to fire up a stove just to make a piece of toast.

• There was a built-in problem, though—the bread had to be constantly watched or it would burn to a crisp.

• In 1919, Charles Strite, a Minnesota factory worker, got sick of the burnt toast in the company cafeteria. So, in his spare time, he designed and patented the first pop-up toaster. Then he went into business manufacturing them. It took years to work out the bugs, but by 1926, Strite's "Toastmasters" were relatively foolproof.

• A few years later, a New York businessman purchased Strite's company and invested heavily in advertising—which proved to be the key ingredient in making the toaster a common household appliance. Every home "had to have one"...and now they do.

TOO DUMB FOR TELEVISON

If you thought "Gilligan's Island," "Alf," and "Dukes of Hazard" were goofy ideas for TV shows, you should see the stuff that doesn't make it on the air! Someone actually filmed pilot episodes of the following shows—and a few even made it onto the tube...briefly.

POOCHINSKI (NBC, 1990)

Peter Boyle plays a hard-nosed cop who is murdered in the line of duty and comes back as a wet-nosed, talking, flatulent dog who fights crime alongside his former partner. The show aired back-to-back with the TV adaptation of the film *Turner and Hootch*, a lineup that NBC promoted as "Two Dog Night." That turned out to be two dogs too many: TV critics and viewers hated both shows.

MR. AND MRS. DRACULA (ABC, 1980)

The peasants finally revolt and send the Dracula clan into permanent exile; the Draculas move to America and find an apartment in New York. Believe it or not, ABC tried and rejected this idea *twice*.

MARS: BASE ONE (CBS, 1988)

Created, produced, and written by Dan Aykroyd, "Mars: Base One" explores the adventures of a typical family living on Mars next door to a Soviet engineer and his American-stripper wife.

THE DECORATOR (ABC, 1965)

Bette Davis stars as an interior decorator who insists on living with her clients, so that she can fit her designs with their personalities. Each week she moves in with a different family and helps them solve their personal problems while helping them pick out drapes.

TAKE ME TO YOUR LEADER (ABC, 1964)

Two aliens from Venus land on Earth, meet up with a zany inventor, and go into business with him peddling interplanetary products to unsuspecting earthlings.

4) household chores; 5) car problems; 6) having sex.

WHERE'S EVERETT? (CBS, 1966)
Alan Alda plays family man Arnold Barker, who steps out of the house one morning to get the paper and discovers that an invisible alien baby has been left on his doorstep.

AFTER GEORGE (CBS, 1983)
Susan St. James, who plays the widow of a car accident victim, discovers that just before he died, her late husband programmed his personality into the computer that operates their futuristic house.

McGURK (NBC, 1979)
Another dog about dogs: Five actors dressed in dog suits play a family of dogs and bark one-liners about their human friends.

WHICH WAY TO THE MECCA, JACK? (Independent, 1965)
A Middle Eastern king comes to America in search of Yankee babes for his harem, which he bankrolls with the help of American foreign aid dollars. He butts heads with the U.S. emissary, a character akin to the "Beverly Hillbillies" Jane Hathaway, who controls the money.

WHO GOES THERE? (CBS, 1965)
A Southern California family living in a housing tract is haunted by the ghosts of General Custer and Chief Running Dog.

POOR DEVIL (NBC, 1973)
Sammy Davis, Jr. plays a disciple of Satan (Christopher Lee). Every week they try to win over someone's soul, but never quite make it. (The show didn't, either.)

WHERE'S MOMMA? (NBC, 1973)
A widowed real estate agent (Richard Mulligan) is having so much trouble raising his two kids that his wife returns from the grave to help.

MICKEY AND THE CONTESSA (CBS, 1963)
Eva Gabor stars as Contessa Czigonia, a down and out European noblewoman hired as a housekeeper by an uncouth American basketball coach with two children.

In their first year of life, puppies grow 10 times faster than human infants do.

ON THE BALLOT

*There's no easier way to get your name into print than
to run for office...unless you try to get a laugh at the
same time. Some notable politicians' names:*

SISTER BOOM-BOOM
A transvestite who dresses as a nun, he/she ran for mayor of
San Francisco in 1982...and received 23,121 votes.

JELLO BIAFRA
Lead singer of the Dead Kennedys, a San Francisco-based rock band.
Ran for mayor of San Francisco in 1982.

NONE OF THE ABOVE
Never actually made it to the ballot, but his heart was in the right
place. Luther Knox legally changed his name to "None of the
Above" in order to give Louisianans a chance "to say no" to mainstream candidates in their 1979 gubernatorial election.

BANANAS THE CLOWN
Another almost-made-it...onto the ballot, that is. When Lester
Johnson decided to run for a seat on the city council in Salt Lake
City, he submitted this name. He was rejected, although he accu-
rately protested that "it wouldn't be unprecedented for a clown to be
in city government."

LOUIS ABALOFIA
It's not a weird name, and we're not even sure it's the right spelling,
but he deserves some mention here. Running for president, he passed
out leaflets bearing his official campaign photo—a picture of himself
stark naked. His campaign slogan: "I have nothing to hide."

**TARQUIN FINTIMLINBINWHIMBINLIN BUS STOP-
F'TANG-F'TANG-OLE-BISCUIT BARREL**
In 1981, a new political party—the Raving Looney Society of Cambridge—nominated this candidate (a real person otherwise known as
John Lewis) for a seat in the British Parliament. The media referred
to him as "Mr. Tarquin Biscuit-Barrel," and more than 200 people
actually voted for him.

Placed end to end, the bad checks Americans write in one year would stretch 35,500 miles.

CUSTOM-MADE

You know these customs. Now, here's where they came from.

C LINKING GLASSES AFTER A TOAST
One explanation: Nobles and knights were sometimes assassinated by enemies who'd poisoned their wine. So when they got together socially, each poured a little of his own wine into everyone else's goblet, as a precaution. That way, if one man poisoned another, he poisoned everyone—including himself. Over the years, the tradition of exchanging wine has been simplified into this gesture of friendship.

BUTTONS ON COAT SLEEVES
Researchers credit this to Napoleon Bonaparte. Apparently, while inspecting some troops, he spotted a soldier wiping his nose on his jacket sleeve. Disgusted, Napoleon ordered new jackets for his army —this time with buttons on the sleeves, to prevent a recurrence.

WEARING BLACK FOR MOURNING
Until King Charles VIII died in the late 15th century, Europeans in mourning wore white (for hope or renewal). But when Anne Brittany, Charles's widow, went into mourning, she donned black. The result: a funeral fashion that continues today.

BUSINESS CARDS
Until the early part of the 20th century, "calling cards" were used by the upper class exclusively for social purposes. Presenting a calling card when you met or visited someone indicated that you didn't have to work for a living. But as the middle classes got into the act, the calling card became another means of making a business contact.

APRIL FOOLS' DAY
Until 1564, it was a tradition to begin the New Year with a weeklong celebration, ending with a big party. But the calendar was different then; the new year began on March 25—which meant the annual party was held on April 1. In 1564, a new calendar was instituted, making January 1 the New Year. People who forgot and still showed up to celebrate on April 1 were called "April fools."

BELIEVE IT OR NOT!

In his day, Robert LeRoy Ripley, creator of "Believe It or Not!," was as well known as P. T. Barnum or Walt Disney. In fact, according to the U.S. Postal Service, he received more mail than Santa Claus. Here's his story.

BACKGROUND

Robert Ripley grew up at the turn of the century in Santa Rosa, a small town in Northern California. A shy, athletic kid, he dropped out of high school partway through his senior year and signed on as a pitcher for a semi-pro baseball team. But Ripley also happened to be a good artist. One afternoon a journalist saw one of the posters he drew for his baseball team and was so impressed that he helped Ripley land a job as a sports cartoonist with the *San Francisco Bulletin*. From there, Ripley went to the *San Francisco Chronicle* and then to the New York *Globe*.

HARD TO BELIEVE

Ripley's job at the *Globe*, like the one he had at the *Bulletin*, was to draw cartoons depicting sporting events. One day in 1918, however, there wasn't anything to draw, so he drew a cartoon about sports oddities, including a man who hopped 100 yards in 11 seconds, one who held his breath underwater for 6 1/2 minutes, and another who jumped rope 11,800 times without stopping. Ripley gave the cartoon the title "Champs and Chumps" and submitted it to his editor.

The editor liked the idea, but not the title, because, he said, "These guys aren't really champs or chumps." Ripley changed it to "Believe It or Not!" The cartoon was printed on December 19, 1918, and was so popular that the editor asked Ripley to draw some more just like it.

Believe It or Not! started out as an occasional feature in Ripley's cartoon, but as it became increasingly popular, it became a weekly and then a daily feature, then branched out from sports trivia to include information on just about every subject. Over the years, there were over 340 different categories, including animals, architecture, records, occupations, religion, mineral and vegetable oddities,

If you pet your pig, it will have a larger litter. Pigs, like people, respond to kindness.

people who did weird things or had weird skills, puzzles, math, survival stories, coincidences, and, of course, sports.

By the mid-'20s, Ripley's column appeared in several dozen papers around the U.S. But his big break came in 1927. Shortly after Charles Lindbergh's famous solo flight across the Atlantic, Ripley wrote that Lindy was "the 67th man to make a nonstop flight over the Atlantic Ocean." The statement was true—Lindbergh was simply the first to make the trip *alone*—but it infuriated people. Ripley got 170,000 letters denouncing him for picking on America's #1 hero. The publicity made his new *Believe It or Not!* book a bestseller and Ripley a national celebrity.

In 1929, William Randolph Hearst signed him to a $100,000-a-year contract that included his newspaper column, a weekly radio show, and 26 film shorts. Within a couple of years, Ripley's name became a household word. His column appeared in 325 newspapers in 33 different countries, and that, combined with the profits from his numerous bestselling *Believe It or Not!* books, earned him as much as $1 million a year. He spent the money as fast as it came in, living in high style and making highly publicized trips all over the world in search of new oddities.

Ripley's success made him a record-holder in his own right: in his lifetime he would become the world's most highly paid journalist, the most traveled man on Earth, and the man who recieved more mail than any other human being in history. His celebrity and his globetrotting ways so impressed the Duke of Windsor that he reportedly dubbed Ripley "The Modern Marco Polo."

FROM THE MAILBAG

One of the ways Ripley popularized his column was through a series of locally run contests, which encouraged readers to send in their own *Believe It or Not!* experiences for possible use in his column. The contests generated an average of 3,500 letters a day (1 million a year) over Ripley's entire 30-year career. (One contest generated more than 250,000 letters in under *two weeks*.) Hundreds of the letters made it into his pages. "His fans specialized in creative correspondence," *Smithsonian* magazine wrote in 1995. "Letters were addressed in Morse code, sign language, and Confederate Civil War code. They were composed on tin, wood, turkey bones, and, in one case, on a grain of rice. Some were addressed to 'the biggest liar in the world,' while others bore a rippling line or were simply torn—ripped—to signify 'Ripley.' "

THE RIGHT MAN FOR THE JOB

In many ways, Ripley was as unusual as the people who appeared in his column. He dressed wildly and colorfully, preferring two-toned shoes, batwing ties, houndstooth jackets, and Chinese robes to ordinary clothing (one acquaintance from his baseball days described him as looking like "a paint factory that got hit by lightning"). He lived in three different residences—a 28-room Long Island mansion he named BION (short for Believe It or Not), a duplex in Manhattan's Central Park West, and a Florida estate—each of which was crammed so full of his oddities that a biographer accused him of "confusing tonnage with taste."

Ripley was selective about his excesses. He shunned gambling and smoking, but lived with groups of four or more women, rotating them in and out of his "harem" as his whim dictated. Friends credit the women with keeping him young, but blame alcohol and overwork for sending him to an early grave. Ripley died of a heart attack in 1949 at the age of 56. He was buried beside his parents in—appropriately enough—Santa's Rosa's Odd Fellows Cemetery. His books are still in print, and his column still appears in nearly 200 newspapers around the world.

BELIEVE IT OR NOT!

• According to Ripley Entertainment, Inc., Ripley drew his cartoons between the hours of 7 a.m. and 11 a.m.—and drew them all while hanging upside down.

• Ripley had a lasting impact on American culture. For example:

In 1920, he wrote that the United States still did not have an offical national anthem. More than 5 million shocked Americans signed petitions asking Congress to designate one, and in 1931 "The Star-Spangled Banner" was picked.

In 1933, Ripley reported that no one had yet been able to invent a machine that could twist pretzels into the curvy shape that bakers had been twisting them for centuries. A few months later, a Pennsylvania company called the Redding Pretzel Machine Corp. patented the world's first pretzel-twisting machine.

• In 1937, a 12-year-old boy sent in a drawing of his hunting dog,

---

Calorie counting? People who work at night tend to weigh more than people who don't.

which he said "eats pins, tacks, screws, and razorblades." The boy's name was Charles Schulz...and the dog he drew later became the inspiration for Snoopy, in the *Peanuts* comic strip.

• In 1940, Ripley broadcast a radio show while riding the rapids in the Grand Canyon. He was accompanied by a 31-year-old announcer for the Phoenix radio station that broadcast Ripley's show in Arizona. His name? Barry Goldwater—future U.S. senator.

• Ripley liked to boast that he never made any mistakes in his column, and for years he offered to prove the accuracy of any entry. Even so, he did make some errors. "There were...maybe one or two a year," says Edward Meyer, the president of Ripley Entertainment, Inc. "Ripley believed that if he had something in print it was gospel, and if he didn't have it in writing he tried to get a photograph. He could never substantiate his claim about the 254-year-old man (whose name, appropriately, was Li Yung). The note in the file says 'can't answer.' "

• In 1933, Ripley opened a museum of oddities, which he called an "Odditorium," as part of Chicago's Century of Progress World's Fair. The exhibit was packed with his drawings, thousands of unusual artifacts, and also had dozens of live performers. As Mark Sloan writes in *You'll Never Believe It,*

> More than two million people passed through the Odditorium doors in 1933. Inside they witnessed contortionists, fireproof people, razor-blade eaters, sword swallowers, eye poppers, and other live attractions....Viewers fainted by the dozens at the Chicago Odditorium, yet it was one of the most heavily visited of all the World's Fair attractions during the two-year run of the Century of Progress.

Ripley was so inspired by the success of the exhibit that he began opening museums all over the country. Today, there are 19 Ripley museums in eight different countries around the world.

• Ripley was particularly despised by Iowa Postmaster Wayne Harbour, who was so convinced that Ripley's columns were erroneous that he wrote an average of one letter a day for more than 26 years to people mentioned in the column—more than 22,700 letters in total. Of them, 10,363 wrote back...and not a single one contradicted the claims Ripley had made in his column.

A FAMILY AFFAIR

Did TV's "Brady Bunch" seem like a close family to you?
According to actor Barry Williams (Greg Brady) in his book
Growing Up Brady, *they were a lot closer than you think.*

"At some point throughout the five years of filming, every Brady (kid) paired up romantically with the opposite sex counterpart," Williams confesses, although as far as he knows, none of the encounters "went all the way." Still, here's the juicy details of some of the closer encounters of the Brady clan:

The Couple: Greg and Mrs. Brady (Williams and Florence Henderson)
The Place: The Coconut Grove Club in Los Angeles
Kiss and Tell: After sharing a dirty joke about lollipops with her on the set, "I got a case of the hots for my mom," Williams confesses, "I just couldn't control myself anymore and wound up asking her out. Amazingly, she accepted." Williams describes their first kiss: "No tongue, but nice."
Why It Ended: They just never hit it off. Henderson later told Williams: "You were really cute, and I was tempted a few times. I think we're lucky Carol never slept with Greg, but...uh...it coulda been."

The Couple: Greg and Marcia (Maureen McCormick and Barry Williams)
The Place: Waikiki beach, when the cast was in Hawaii filming the show's first Hawaiian special
Kiss and Tell: "I kissed her, and the floodgates opened; warm and hard and packed with the kind of osculatory excitement only teenagers can transmit....Years later, I'd find out that this had been Mo's first kiss."
Why It Ended: While on a cruise on the *Queen Elizabeth II*, Williams snuck into McCormick's bedroom, climbed into bed with her, and started caressing her. McCormick woke up and kicked him out of her room. According to Williams: "My desperate groping killed something between us that night."

The Couple: Jan and Peter (Eve Plumb and Christopher Knight)

The Place: Aboard the *Queen Elizabeth II*, and later in Knight's truck

Kiss and Tell: Unlike Williams, Knight didn't have to sneak into his female counterpart's stateroom in search of action—Plumb came to him. And Knight had better luck than Williams did: "Finally, as she nibbled on my ear, something clicked...I thought to myself, 'Oh, my God—now I understand what all the fuss is about!' I was 14."

A year after the show was canceled, Knight and Plumb had another encounter, an attempted "quickie" in Knight's truck. Says Knight: "*This* time, we quickly moved beyond the sensory pleasures of just making out."

Why It Ended: Before they could get very far, a police officer walked up to the truck and shined his flashlight in the window. The interruption killed the romance.

The Couple: Cindy and Bobby (Susan Olsen and Michael Lookinland)

The Place: Tiger's doghouse, Lookinland's dressing room

Kiss and Tell: "During our first season, Michael got the notion that he had a major crush on me. And he'd put his arm around me, and he'd kiss me, and...uh...I kinda liked it."

Why It Ended: "A couple years later...he seemed to have a kinda 'boob thing'...This is at like age 10 or 11....I of course had none, so he decided it was time to get rid of me and chase after Eve for a while. So we got a divorce."

• • •

WHAT ABOUT MR. BRADY?

According to *USA Today*, Robert Reed was "too busy firing off angry memos to the show's creators about how asinine the scripts were" to indulge in the pleasures of Brady flesh: "To blow off steam over crummy storylines, he sometimes went to a nearby bar and came back to work loaded." Alice the maid (Ann B. Davis), now a born-again Christian, also remained Brady-celibate. No word on Tiger the dog (who was run down by a florist's truck one day after he wandered off the set "looking for a place to relieve himself").

THE STORY OF LAYLA

*Several BRI members wrote and asked for the inside story
on this classic Eric Clapton tune—one of the most
popular rock songs of all time.*

E ric Clapton could play the blues as few other guitarists
could—a talent that both satisfied and tortured him. Unlike
some of his fellow British bluesmen, Clapton was keenly
aware that he was a white musician imitating an essentially black
art form. This created a terrible conflict; playing the blues was his
first love, but was he really entitled to practice his craft? In order to
reconcile his feelings, Clapton became a blues purist. He believed
that you had to suffer in order to be able to play the blues—so he
was miserable a lot of the time. He was particularly unhappy when
he wrote his most famous composition, "Layla."

THE BIRTH OF LAYLA

The real "Layla" was named Patti Boyd—or, more accurately, Patti
Boyd Harrison. She was the wife of Beatle George Harrison when
Eric Clapton began pursuing her.

• Harrison first met her on the set of *A Hard Day's Night* in 1964.
A stunning 19-year-old blonde model, she was only supposed to
make a brief appearance in the film and leave; instead, she and
George fell in love and eventually married.

• George and Eric were close friends. They'd known each other
since the days when the Beatles and the Yardbirds (Eric's group at
the time) were becoming popular. As they both became superstars,
they hung out together more and more. They even contributed to
each other's recordings. Eric played a magnificent solo on "While
My Guitar Gently Weeps"; George co-wrote and played on the
Cream's "Badge." George wrote "Here Comes the Sun" while sitting in Eric's garden; he wrote "Savoy Truffle" specifically for Eric,
who was having dental problems but still couldn't resist chocolates.

• George didn't realize, however, that over the years Eric had
quietly fallen in love with his wife. Eric told Patti (but not George)
about his feelings, but she wouldn't hear anything of it. She
remained dedicated to the man who had written "Something"
for her.

There are an average of 178 sesame seeds on a McDonald's Big Mac bun.

• Already a tortured soul, Clapton was plunged into despair. In an outburst of emotion, he wrote "Layla." Later, when people asked him who he was singing for, all he would say was, " 'Layla' was about a woman I felt really deeply about and who turned me down, and I had to pour if out in some way."

• You may be wondering how "Patti" became "Layla." The answer: Clapton lifted the name "Layla" from a Persian love story called "Layla and Mashoun." The tale had little similarity to the Eric-Patti-George love triangle. Clapton just liked the title. The song was recorded and released in 1970, but it flopped. The reason: The record was attributed to Derek and the Dominoes; no one knew it was Clapton, so it didn't get airplay.

• Clapton, who had poured his heart and soul into the record, threw in the towel. He gave up music and took up heroin. "I basically stayed in the house with my girlfriend for two and-a-half years," he told *Rolling Stone* magazine, "and we got very strung out. Dying from drugs didn't seem to me then to be a terrible thing."

• Ironically, during this low point in his life, "Layla" was rereleased and became one of the all-time FM favorites...then struck gold as a Top 10 single.

• In 1974, Clapton kicked the heroin habit and reemerged on the music scene with "I Shot the Sheriff," his first #1 song.

THE END OF LAYLA

• Patti eventually divorced George and, in a secret ceremony in Tucson, Arizona, in 1979, married Clapton. Ironically, Patti and Eric later joined George in a recording of the Everly Brothers' old hit, "Bye, Bye Love."

• Then in 1988, Patti and Eric's nine-year marriage ended. Patti was granted an uncontested divorce on the grounds of Clapton's adultery with Italian television personality Lory del Santo, with whom he had a baby boy.

• Though the marriage was over, the music lived on. In 1992, Clapton's acoustic version of "Layla" became a hit—introducing a whole new generation to the song.

FIRST FILMS

Stars like Madonna would probably just as soon you forgot about what they were doing before they hit it big. But Jami Bernard didn't. She wrote a book called First Films, *which we used as a reference to write this piece.*

TOM SELLECK
First Film: *Myra Breckinridge* (1970)
The Role: In his 17 seconds onscreen, Selleck plays an unnamed talent agent (listed as "The Stud" in the credits) opposite Mae West, the star of the film, who wants to help him find "a position." West discovered Selleck in a Pepsi commercial and had him cast in the bit part.

HARRISON FORD
First Film: *Dead Heat on a Merry-Go-Round* (1966)
The Role: 24-year-old Ford plays an unnamed bellhop who appears in only one scene, in which con man James Coburn gets some information from him and then refuses to give him a tip. The part is so small that Ford is not even listed in the credits.
Memorable Line: "Paging Mr. Ellis…"

MADONNA
First Film: *A Certain Sacrifice* (1979)
The Role: In this Super 8-mm student film, Madonna plays a minor character named Bruna, who shows her breasts, has "simulated" group sex, and gets smeared with a dead man's blood. The film is so bad that the home video version opens with a disclaimer warning the viewer of the film's "technical inconsistencies."
Memorable Line: "I'm a do-do girl, and I'm looking for my do-do boy."

JEFF GOLDBLUM
First Film: *Death Wish* (1974)
The Role: Goldblum plays Freak #1, one of three unnamed punks who break into Charles Bronson's house, kill his wife, and rape his daughter. Bronson spends the rest of the film (and three sequels)

When do shoplifters take the most stuff? Between 3 p.m. and 6 p.m. on Friday and Sunday.

gunning down punks on the streets of New York.

Memorable Line: "Don't jive, mother, you know what we want!"

KEVIN COSTNER

First Film: *Sizzle Beach, USA* (1974)

The Role: John Logan, a wealthy rancher. This film is about three big-breasted women who share a house in Malibu. The girls exercise and perform household chores while topless. One of them, Dit, falls in love with Costner's character (Costner also played a corpse in *The Big Chill*, but all of his scenes were cut out.)

Memorable Line: "L.A. women seem to be very impressed with money."

TOM CRUISE

First Film: *Endless Love* (1981)

The Role: Cruise plays Billy the teen arsonist, who gives the film's costar, Martin Hewitt, the idea of burning down Brooke Shields's house in order to act as a hero and win the respect of her parents.

Memorable Line: "When I was eight years old I was into arson."

SYLVESTER STALLONE

First Film: *A Party at Kitty and Stud's*, 1970 (later renamed *The Italian Stallion* to cash in on Stallone's fame)

The Role: In this pre-Rocky soft-core porno flick, Stallone plays Stud, a frisky playboy with big hair (and small muscles) who spends much of the film entirely nude except for a medallion around his neck and a wristwatch...though he never actually engages in intercourse.

Memorable Line: "Mmmmm."

�֍   �֍   ✶

Can't Get No Respect

Stallone never lived his blue movie down. According to *Esquire* magazine, "Even when *Rocky* won the Oscar for best picture of 1976...the [only] Stallone movie in demand for the private screening rooms of Bel Air and Beverly Hills was the soft-core porn film he'd made when it was the only work he could get."

Eagles see better than humans on clear days; humans see better than eagles on foggy days.

VICTIMS OF CIRCUMSTANCE

Sometimes it's impossible to win no matter how hard you try. Don't believe it? Take a look at the people and products listed below...

AYDS CANDY CUBES

Background: Ayds, an "appetite suppressant" candy, first went on the market in 1937. In 1981, 44 years later, it was still on the market...and Jeffrey Martin, Inc. decided to buy it. They put together a massive advertising campaign centered around the slogan, "Lose weight with Ayds." Within a year, Ayds became one of the best-known and strongest selling diet products in the country.

Unforeseen Circumstance: In July 1981, not long after Jeffrey Martin purchased Ayds, officials at the Centers for Disease Control met in New York to discuss a mysterious new disease known as "Kaposi's Sarcoma and Opportunistic Infections." At the meeting the CDC decided to rename it. They came up with "Acquired Immune Deficiency Syndrome," or AIDS for short.

Outcome: The company's "Lose weight with Ayds" commercials acquired a sinister new meaning. Sales plummeted, and in 1987 the company finally started looking for a new name. They settled on Aydslim—then found out that in many parts of Africa, AIDS is actually *known* as "slim" or "the slim disease" because of the emaciating effect it has on victims. Sales dropped further. So they tried renaming it again. This time they came up with Diet Ayds. Why keep "Ayds" in the name? "Kool-Aid and Band-Aid sales haven't dropped," explained the company chairman forlornly, "and if we change the name completely, we have nothing."

GHADA TURK

Background: In 1994, Ghada Turk, a 21-year-old philosophy major and recently crowned Miss Lebanon, traveled to South Africa to take part in the Miss World contest. At one point during the event, the contestants lined up alphabetically by country for a group photograph.

Unforeseen Circumstance: Miss Lebanon was standing between Miss Italy and Miss Malaysia. When Miss Italy stepped away for a minute, Turk was photographed standing alongside Miss Israel, Tamara Porat. "It was just a coincidence," Turk recalled later. "We were all just smiling and looking at the camera. I only found out what happened when I looked at the papers the next day."

Outcome: Israel and Lebanon were at war, so being photographed with Miss Israel was considered "collaboration with the enemy," punishable by 3 to 15 years in jail. The nationalist Lebanese press exploded with fury. "Couldn't she frown a little?" one magazine sneered. "Miss Lebanon looks very happy next to Miss Israel."

Turk was so afraid for her safety that she hid out in London for more than four months, waiting for the anger to die down before she returned home. When she finally did go back, she was interrogated for 2 1/2 hours by a military tribunal and officially charged with violating Lebanon's boycott of Israel. The judge let her off with a warning.

MARK LINDSAY

Background: Lindsay was an English bricklayer trying to break into acting. In 1984 his agent called him out of the blue and told him NBC wanted him to audition for a TV movie.

Unforeseen Circumstance: The film turned out to be *Imagine: The Story of John and Yoko*. Lindsay was asked to audition for the part of John Lennon...and to his astonishment, he got it. But in a bizarre coincidence, it turned out Lindsay's real name was Mark *Chapman*—the same name as the man who killed John Lennon.

Outcome: Lindsay had told the director about his real name before he auditioned for the part, but the director had shrugged it off. Yoko Ono, however, freaked and vetoed Lindsay. "It just seemed inappropriate to have an actor named Mark Chapman playing John Lennon," said executive producer John McMahon. "It would be like having an actor named Lee Harvey Oswald play John F. Kennedy."

The publicity generated by the hiring and firing actually helped Lindsay's career. Since then, he has landed a number of choice roles, including the lead in the 1995 Stephen King TV movie "The Langoliers."

PRIMETIME PROVERBS

TV comments about everyday life. From Prime Time Proverbs, by Jack Mingo and John Javna

ON AMBITION:
"I'm tired of being an object of ridicule. I wanna be a figure of fear, respect, and SEX!"
—Radar O'Reilly,
"M*A*S*H"

ON AMERICA:
George Jefferson: "It's the American dream come true. Ten years ago, I was this little guy with one store. And now look at me—"
Louise Jefferson: "Now you're the little guy with seven stores."
— "The Jeffersons"

ON THE ARTS:
"You know, if Michelangelo had used me as a model, there's no telling how far he could have gone."
—Herman Munster,
"The Munsters"

ON DATING:
"Randy, there are three reasons why I won't go out with you: one, you're obnoxious; two, you're repulsive; and three, you haven't asked me yet."
—Julianne,
"Van Dyke"

ON MEN:
"A good man doesn't happen. They have to be created by us women. A guy is a lump like a doughnut. So, first you gotta get rid of all the stuff his mom did to him. And then you gotta get rid of all that macho crap that they pick up from the beer commercials. And then there's my personal favorite, the male ego."
—Roseanne,
Roseanne

ON COURAGE:
"Wanna do something courageous? Come to my house and say to my mother-in-law, 'You're wrong, fatso!' "
—Buddy Sorrell,
The Dick Van Dyke Show

ON BANKERS:
"Why do they call them tellers? They never tell you anything. They just ask questions. And why do they call it interest? It's boring. And another thing—how come the Trust Department has all their pens chained to the table?"
—Coach Ernie Pantusso,
Cheers

Hoosier Pride: Kentucky Fried Chicken's Col. Sanders was actually born in Indiana.

GROUCHO SEZ...

A few choice words from the master.

"I must say I find television very educational. The minute somebody turns it on I go into the library and read a good book."

"Please accept my resignation. I don't want to belong to any club that will accept me as a member."

"I didn't like the play, but then I saw it under adverse conditions—the curtain was up."

"Dig trenches? With our men being killed off like flies? There isn't time to dig trenches. We'll have to buy them ready made."

"I've worked myself up from nothing to a state of extreme poverty."

Mrs. Teasdale: "He's had a change of heart."
Firefly [Groucho]: "A lot of good that'll do him. He's still got the same face."

"Do you suppose I could buy back my introduction to you?"

"Military intelligence is a contradiction in terms."

"Any man who says he can see through a woman is missing a lot."

"A man is as young as the woman he feels."

"She got her good looks from her father—he's a plastic surgeon."

"There's one way to find out if a man is honest—ask him. If he says 'Yes,' you know he is a crook."

[*Feeling patient's pulse*] "Either he's dead, or my watch has stopped."

"Age is not a particularly interesting subject. Anyone can get old. All you have to do is live long enough."

"Send two dozen roses to Room 424 and put 'Emily, I love you' on the back of the bill."

Hard to swallow: 9% of the world's ostriches suffer from eating disorders.

LIFE AFTER DEATH

Plenty has been written about people who nearly die, get a glimpse of the "other side," and then somehow make it back to the land of the living. Here are four examples of another kind of "rebirth": people who were declared dead, but were actually alive and well.

DECEASED: Ralph Neves, a famous jockey of the 1930s
NEWS OF HIS DEATH: On May 8, 1936, Neves was thrown from his horse during a race at the Bay Meadows Racetrack in San Mateo, California; then the horse fell on him. Two jockeys and a spectator pulled him out from under the horse, but doctors on the scene failed to find a heartbeat or a pulse, and pronounced him dead. His body was wrapped in a sheet and taken by ambulance to a nearby hospital, where it was placed in a cold-storage room to await pickup by a funeral director.
RESURRECTION: Thirty minutes later, Neves awoke naked in the dark room and had no idea where he was. So he grabbed a sheet, felt for the door, and ran out into the street…where he caught a cab back to the track.

He ran onto the track—where thousands of spectators were milling about, mourning his death—clad only in the sheet and his riding boots. Two jockeys recognized him and brought him to the same doctors who'd pronounced him dead an hour before. They now found he was suffering from only mild shock and some bruises. He returned to work the next day…and later won the season's award for riding the most winning horses.

DECEASED: Sipho Wiliam Mdletshe, a 24-year-old South African
NEWS OF HIS DEATH: Mdletshe was involved in a traffic accident in a small town south of Johannesburg. A medical examiner declared him dead and had his body taken to a morgue, where he was placed in a metal coffin.
RESURRECTION: Over the next 48 hours, Mdletshe slowly regained consciousness, realized he was trapped in the box, and screamed for the morgue attendants to let him out. They did.

The average bra is designed to last for only 180 days of use.

Mdletshe was happy to be alive...but sad at the way his fiancee responded to the incident. His "resurrection" convinced her that he was a zombie who had come back from the dead to haunt her, and she broke off their engagement.

DECEASED: Duncan Webb, a 23-year-old bakery truck driver from Oakland, California

NEWS OF HIS DEATH: Police reported that Duncan was killed in a high-speed chase with police when his car slammed into a telephone pole and exploded. The news came as a shock to Webb's friends and family...and especially to Webb himself, who learned of his death one morning when a co-worker called to offer her condolences to Webb's parents. "I heard you were dead!" the co-worker exclaimed. "I read it in the *San Francisco Examiner*."

RESURRECTION: Webb called the newspaper. "My name is Duncan Webb," he told the reporter, "and I'm not dead." It turned out the real dead man had robbed Webb earlier in the week. Police found papers with Webb's name on them in the car and Webb's credit card in the dead man's pocket, but no other ID. "Someone just assumed he was Webb," Oakland police explained to reporters.

DECEASED: Alan Abel, legendary hoaxer

NEWS OF HIS DEATH: Abel wanted to know what it would be like to read his obituary in *The New York Times*, so in 1979, he staged a "tragic accident" on the ski slopes of Sundance Ski Lodge. Then a fake funeral director from a fake funeral home turned up at the lodge to collect Alan's effects...and an actress posing as Alan's grieving widow called to inform the *Times*.

The *Times* called the ski lodge, the "funeral home" (Abel had intalled a phone line), and the church that had been booked for the funeral. Everything checked out, so the paper printed the obituary. It started: "Alan Abel, a writer...who specialized in satire and lampoons, died of a heart attack yesterday." Abel got 6 paragraphs; the inventor of the six-pack, who died the same day, only got 3.

RESURRECTION: Two days later, a tiny article appeared in the *Times* obituary section. It read: "An obituary in *The New York Times* Wednesday reported incorrectly that Mr. Alan Abel was dead. Mr. Abel held a news conference yesterday to announce that the obituary was the result of a hoax."

John Heisman (of trophy fame) also coined the word "hike" and split football games into 4 quarters.

TOY ORIGINS

You've loved them. You've played with them. You've lost parts of them. Now you can find out where they came from.

SCRABBLE

Created in 1931 by an out-of-work architect named Alfred Botts. He hoped he could support his family by inventing a successful word game, but before the game was refined, he had his job back. That was just as well; when he finally showed his handmade "Criss-Cross" to toy companies, they insisted it had no potential—it was too intellectual.

In 1948, Botts and a friend went into business manufacturing the game—now called Scrabble—in an old schoolhouse. It was an unsophisticated cottage industry that enabled the friend to barely eke out a living. But in the summer of 1952, for no apparent reason, Scrabble suddenly became a fad. In two years, the partners went from selling fewer than 10,000 games a year to selling more than 4 million. To meet the growing demand, the rights were sold to Selchow-Righter, and 30 years later, Scrabble ranks as the second bestselling game in history.

LINCOLN LOGS

In 1916, Frank Lloyd Wright went to Tokyo to supervise construction of the Imperial Palace Hotel, a magnificent building assembled with an inner frame of wood so it would withstand earthquakes better. Wright brought his son John with him, and as John watched workers move the huge timbers required for the structure, he came up with an idea for a wooden construction toy. When he returned to America, John created Lincoln Logs.

SILLY PUTTY

In 1945, an engineer at a General Electric laboratory in New Haven, Connecticut, was assigned the task of trying to create synthetic rubber. One day he combined boric acid with silicone oil. The result: a bizarre substance with a variety of fascinating properties (it bounced, stretched, and could be broken with a hammer), but no practical use. It became a New Haven conversation piece.

"Tug of war" was an Olympic event between 1900 and 1920.

Several years later, a marketing man named Peter Hodgson saw a group of adults playing with the stuff at a cocktail party. Hodgson was putting together a mail-order catalog for a toy store at the time, and decided to include this "nutty putty" in it.

The response was amazing. Even without a photo, the putty outsold everything in the catalog except crayons. Hodgson knew he had a winner—so he bought $147 worth of putty from G.E. and packaged it in little plastic eggs. In the first five years, over 32 million containers of the stuff were sold worldwide.

RUBIK'S CUBE

Devised by Hungarian mathematician Erno Rubik in 1974 as an aid for teaching math concepts to his students. Rubik realized the puzzle's possibilities as a toy and ended up selling 2 million of the cubes in Hungary alone—a total of one cube for every five Hungarians. In 1980, the Ideal Toy Corporation bought the rights, and the puzzle became a worldwide craze. Rubik reportedly became "the first self-made millionaire in a Communist country."

SLINKY

Richard James, a marine engineer, was trying to invent a spring that could be used to offset the effects of a boat's movement on sensitive navigational instruments. One day he knocked a sample spring off a high shelf—but instead of simply falling, it uncoiled like a snake and "crawled" down to the floor. James realized he had a toy product, gave it a name, and formed the James Toy Company to manufacture it.

TINKER TOYS

Charles Pajeau, an Evanston, Illinois, stoneworker, conceived of Tinker Toys in 1913 after observing some kids playing with "pencils, sticks, and empty spools of thread." He designed it in a garage in back of his house, and brought the finished toy—packed in its famous cannister—to the 1914 American Toy Fair. But the public wouldn't buy it. So Pajeau had to prove his marketing genius; at Christmastime, he dressed some midgets in elf costumes and had them play with Tinker Toys in the windows of New York's Grand Central Station and Chicago's Marshall Field's department store. The publicity this stunt attracted made all the difference—a year later, more than a million sets had been sold.

How many hairs on your head? If you're blonde, about 150,000; brunette, 100,000; redhead, 60,000.

WORD PLAY

We thought that while you're sitting there, you might like to improve your vocabulary a bit. So here are some obscure words and definitions to study.

Peccadillo: A slight or trifling sin; a fault

Sesamoid: Having the shape of a sesame seed

Anserine: Gooselike, as in goose bumps on skin

Wanion: Disaster or bad luck

Joad: A migratory worker

Pettifogger: An inferior lawyer

Feverwort: A weedy herb

Squamous: Covered with scales

Cachinnate: To laugh noisily

Erubescence: Process of turning red, blushing

Histoplasmosis: A respiratory illness caused by inhaling festered bat dung

Paraselene: A mock moon appearing on a lunar halo

Yerk: To tie with a jerk

Bilbo: A finely tempered Spanish sword

Verisimilitude: Appearance of truth

Salubrious: Wholesome

Fecund: Fruitful

Epistemology: A school of philosophy that includes the study of the nature of human knowledge

Yowie: A small ewe

Parsimony: Stinginess

Holm: An island in a river

Coriaceous: Tough, leathery texture

Mullion: A vertical dividing piece between window lights or panels

Sippet: A triangular piece of toasted or fried bread used to garnish a dish of hash

Infrangible: Not breakable

Sudorific: Causing perspiration

Cerulean: Sky blue

Pomology: The study of fruit

Rusticate: To send into the country

Agnomen: An added name due to some special achievement

Saponification: Process of making soap

Motet: A sacred musical composition for several voices

Lycanthropy: The power of turning a human being into a wolf by magic or witchcraft.

There are 10 doctors in the United States whose last name is "Nurse."

LEMONS

At one time or another, we've all had a car we thought was a lemon. But chances are, your worst car was nothing compared to these vehicles. Here are some of the strangest cars ever produced.

THE BURDICK SPRINGWOUND CAR (1895)

In the early days of the Automobile Age, no one knew that gasoline-powered cars would become the industry standard …so inventors tried to move horseless carriages with just about everything except horses. One example was the 1895 Burdick Springwound Car, powered by a spring, the same way old-fashioned watches ran off of a mainspring. Owners could "wind up" their car by hand, or by rolling it down a hill. Energy stored in the spring on the way down a hill was used to climb the next hill. It seemed that the car could run indefinitely.

Fatal Flaw: Unless the landscape was an endless series of small hills separated by short, flat valleys, the car quickly ran into problems: it overwound itself going down large hills, it could never climb a hill larger than the one it had just gone down, and it ran out of power on long flat stretches. All it took was one test drive for most people to give this car a pass.

THE BARSALEUX (1897)

Automakers of the 1890s faced major obstacles in winning public acceptance of their newfangled contraptions. People still trusted horsedrawn vehicles over the unreliable early autos, and because automobiles occasionally spooked the horses they passed on the road, many people considered cars a public nuisance.

In 1897, carmaker Joseph Barsaleux came up with a brilliant solution; he built a car that looked like a carriage, with a full-size replica of a horse in front. The horse camouflaged a fifth wheel that provided power and steering, literally pulling the rest of the vehicle along the road. The driver steered the vehicle using a brace and bit attached to the faux horse's mouth.

Fatal Flaw: Once the public got used to automobiles, there was no need for the Barsaleux and the horseless-carriage-with-a-horse was put out to pasture.

While performing her duties as queen, Cleopatra sometimes wore a fake beard.

THE OCTO-AUTO (1911)

Milton Reeves admired Pullman railway cars. Strangely, although Reeves was smart enough to invent his own automobile, he was also dumb enough to think that what gave Pullman cars their smooth ride was the fact that they had eight wheels, not four. He ignored completely the fact that trains rode on smooth rails and most cars still ran on bumpy dirt roads. So in 1911 he invented the Octo-Auto, which looked like a Model-T Ford except that it had extra sets of wheels in front and back.

Fatal Flaws: The extra wheels made the cars vibrate like jackhammers at high speeds and impossible to turn even at slow speeds. And they added so much weight that the only thing trainlike about the Octo-Auto was its sluggish acceleration—which reminded people of a train pulling out of a station. Besides, eight-wheeled cars were just plain goofy looking. Ultimately, Reeves realized that even if he worked out the technical glitches, the cars were so ugly that the public would never buy them. In 1912, he replaced the Octo-Auto with the Sexto-Auto, which had only six wheels. "Like its ill-fated predecessor," one observer wrote at the time, "the Sexto-Auto had more wheels than buyers."

THE HUNGERFORD ROCKET (1929)

In 1929, Daniel, Floyd, and William Hungerford, brothers from Elmira, New York, stripped a 1921 Chevrolet down to its frame and converted it into a "Hungerford," the world's first commercially made rocket car. The Hungerford was actually a hybrid: it kept the original Chevy engine for low-speed travel, but when the car hit 50 mph, the driver flipped a switch and the gasoline-powered, forced-air rocket engine roared to life. The Hungerford looked like a hot dog on wheels, except the rear end tapered to a point and had five rocket nozzles (four of which were fake). Safety was not an issue: the Hungerfords gave their cars sophisticated braking systems, and built the bodies out of linoleum and cardboard, so passengers could kick their way out of the wreckage in the event of an accident.

Fatal Flaws: The Hungerford Rocket was doomed from the start: it only got two miles per gallon, had a disappointing top speed of 70 mph, and left a 20-foot-long flame as it traveled, making it impossible to drive in traffic. The Hungerford brothers, never able to attract enough investors, went out of business in 1939.

Pound for pound, hamburgers cost more than new cars.

ROAD KILL

One of the stranger studies in human behavior we've ever heard
of was a recent experiment to find out how people react
to animals on the highway. Here are the results.

THE TEST

David Shepherd, a biology professor at Southeastern Louisiana University, put rubber reptiles "on or near roads" and watched how 22,000 motorists reacted to them. His conclusion: "There are apparently very few animals hit accidentally on the highway."

WHAT THEY DID

To find out how drivers would respond to reptiles on the road, Shepherd and his crew put fake snakes and turtles in places where drivers would hit them if they kept driving straight; they also put the rubber reptiles where drivers had to go way out of their way to hit them. Shepherd's comment: "We found that while eighty-seven percent of drivers tried to avoid the animals, six percent went out of their way to hit them—with snakes getting squashed twice as often as turtles."

WEIRD REACTIONS

Apparently, there's something about a reptile on the road that makes some drivers bloodthirsty. A few examples Shepherd witnessed:

• "A truck driver crossed the center line, went into the opposite lane of traffic, and drove onto the shoulder of the road to run over a 'turtle.' "

• A housewife who saw what she thought was a snake in the road swerved to kill it, "then turned around to run over it five more times."

• "A policeman crushed a 'snake' with his tires, then stopped and pulled his gun. I quickly jumped from some bushes and explained it was a fake."

CONCLUSION

"Some people just have a mean streak toward animals."

If you're a healthy, full-grown adult, your thigh bones are stronger than concrete.

HAPPY BIRTHDAY!

It may come as a surprise, but the fact is that celebrating birthdays is a relatively new tradition for anyone but kings and queens.

BIRTHDAY CELEBRATIONS. The first people known to celebrate birthdays were the ancient Egyptians—starting around 3000 B.C. But only the queen and male members of the royal family were honored. No one even bothered recording anyone else's birth dates.

• The ancient Greeks expanded the concept a little: they celebrated the birthdays of all adult males...and kept on celebrating, even after a man had died. Women's and children's birthdays were considered too unimportant to observe.

• The Greeks also introduced birthday cakes (which they got from the Persians) and birthday candles (which may have honored Artemis, goddess of the moon, because they symbolized moonlight).

• It wasn't until the Middle Ages that German peasants became the first to celebrate the birthdays of everyone in the family. Children's birthday celebrations were especially important. Called *Kinderfestes*, they were the forerunner to our toddler birthday parties.

THE BIRTHDAY SONG. Mildred and Patty Smith Hill, two sisters from Louisville, Kentucky, published a song called "Good Morning to All" in a kindergarten songbook in 1893. They wrote it as a "welcoming" song, to be sung to young students at the beginning of each school day.

In 1924, a songbook editor changed the lyrics to "Happy Birthday to You" and published it without the Hill sisters' permission. The new lyrics made it a popular tune, but the Hill family took no action...until the song appeared in a Broadway play in 1933. Then Jessica Hill (a third sister) sued for copyright infringement. She won, but most singers stopped using the song rather than pay the royalty fee. In one play called *Happy Birthday*, for example, actress Helen Hayes *spoke* the words to avoid paying it.

Today, whenever "Happy Birthday" is sung commercially, a royalty still must be paid to the Hills.

The U.S. government spent $277,000 on "pickle research" in 1993.

THEIR REAL NAMES

We know them as Doris Day, Woody Allen, etc. But that's not what their parents called them. Here are some celebs' real names...

Muddy Waters: McKinley Morganfield

Liberace: Wladziu Valentino Liberace

Wolfman Jack: Bob Smith

Stan Laurel: Arthur Stanley Jefferson

Dean Martin: Dino Crocetti

Twiggy: Leslie Hornby

Peter Lorre: Laszlo Lowenstein

Jerry Lewis: Joseph Levitch

Lauren Bacall: Betty Perski

James Stewart: Stewart Granger

Yves Montand: Ivo Livi

Shelley Winters: Shirley Schrift

Van Morrison: George Ivan

W. C. Fields: W. C. Dunkenfield

Roy Rogers: Leonard Slye

Charles Bronson: Charles Buchinsky

Irving Berlin: Israel Baline

Stevie Wonder: Steveland Judkins Morris

Doris Day: Doris Kappelhoff

Boris Karloff: William Henry Pratt

Natalie Wood: Natasha Gurdin

Tammy Wynette: Wynette Pugh

Kirk Douglas: Issur Danielovitch

Rock Hudson: Roy Fitzgerald

Sophia Loren: Sophia Scicolone

Tony Curtis: Bernie Schwartz

John Wayne: Marion Michael Morrison

David Bowie: David Jones

Greta Garbo: Greta Gustafsson

Woody Allen: Allen Konigsberg

Fred Astaire: Fred Austerlitz

Lucille Ball: Dianne Belmont

Anne Bancroft: Anne Italiano

Jack Benny: Joseph Kubelsky

Yul Brynner: Taidje Kahn, Jr.

George Burns: Nat Birnbaum

Michael Caine: Maurice Mickelwhite

Joan Crawford: Lucille Le Sueur

Rodney Dangerfield: John Cohen

John Denver: Henry John Deutschendorf, Jr.

Werner Erhard: Jack Rosenberg

Douglas Fairbanks: Julius Ullman

Redd Foxx: John Sanford

Mel Brooks: Mel Kaminsky

Thomas Edison invented wax paper.

THE ROCK 'N' ROLL RIOTS OF 1956

Were there really rowdy rockers in 1956 at Bill Haley and the Comets concerts? Did DJs really accuse Haley of being "a menace to life, limb, decency, and morals"? Believe it or not, they did. By the mid-'50s, parents were already sure rock 'n' roll had ruined their kids.

TEENS RIOT IN MASSACHUSETTS

Boston, Mass., March 26, 1956 (wire service report)

"Record hops by disc jockeys featuring 'rock and roll' tunes were banned in Boston today after a riot at Massachusetts Institute of Technology's annual charity carnival.

"The disturbance involved nearly 3,000 students. It began when hundreds of teenagers who paid the 99¢ admission fee to see WCOP disc jockey Bill Marlowe discovered the carnival wasn't a record hop, and they couldn't dance.

"More than 20 officers were summoned to the scene, but they were unable to cope with the surging mob of teenagers who overturned booths, smashed records, and battled M.I.T. students who tried to keep order.

" 'Some of that music is crazy,' commented Mary Driscoll of the Boston licensing board. 'Teenagers have no business listening to disc jockeys at 12:00 at night.

The way they're going, they'll have high blood pressure before they're 20.' "

WASHINGTON MELEE

Newsweek, June 18, 1956

"Even before the joint began to jump, there was trouble at the National Guard Armory in Washington, D.C. As 5,000 people, mostly teenagers, poured in for some rock 'n' roll, knives flashed and one young man was cut in the arm. Inside the auditorium, 25 officers waited tensely for Bill Haley and his Comets to swing into the 'big beat.'

"Haley gave the downbeat, the brasses blared, and kids leaped into the aisles to dance, only to be chased back to their seats by the cops. At 10:50, the Comets socked into their latest hit, 'Hot Dog, Buddy, Buddy!' and the crowd flipped.

"Some of the kids danced, some scuffled, fights broke out, a chair flew. William Warfield, 17, a high school junior, was hit. Suffering from a concussion and a severe cut over one eye, he was rushed to the hospital. 'Before I knew it, everybody was pounding everybody,' he said later.

"The fight overflowed into the street. A 19-year-old was struck over the head, and a 16-year-old was cut in the ear. Two cars were stoned and one exuberant teenager turned in a false alarm.

" 'It's the jungle strain that gets 'em all worked up,' said Armory manager Arthur (Dutch) Bergman, surveying the damage."

THEATER ATTACKED
Hartford, CT., March 28, 1956
"Hartford police have instituted action to revoke the license of the State Theater, as a result of a series of riots during rock 'n' roll shows. The latest took place this weekend during performances of an Alan Freed show.

"The 4,000-seat theater has had five police riot calls since last November. Over this past weekend alone, a total of 11 people were arrested. Practically all arrests have been teenagers."

ROCK, ROLL, AND RIOT
Time *magazine, June 18, 1956*
"In Hartford city officials held special meetings to discuss it....In Minneapolis a theater manager withdrew a film featuring the music after a gang of youngsters left the theater,

snake-danced around town and smashed windows....At a wild concert in Atlanta's baseball park one night, fists and beer bottles were thrown, and four youngsters were arrested.

"The object of all this attention is a musical style known as 'rock 'n' roll,' which has captivated U.S. adolescents.

"Characteristics: an unrelenting syncopation that sounds like a bullwhip; a choleric saxophone honking mating-call sounds; an electric guitar turned up so loud that its sound shatters and splits; a vocal group that shudders and exercises violently to the beat while roughly chanting either a near-nonsense phrase or a moronic lyric in hillbilly rhythm....

"Psychologists feel that rock 'n' roll's appeal is to teenagers' need to belong; [in concert], the results bear passing resemblance to Hitler mass meetings."

QUEEN SCREENS
Scholastic *magazine, Oct. 4, 1956*
"In England, over 100 youths were arrested in 'rock and roll' riots that broke out during showing of a 'rock and roll' film. Queen Elizabeth II, disturbed by the growing number of such arrests, has scheduled a private screening of the film at her palace for official study."

The 3 most valuable brand names on earth: Marlboro, Coca-Cola, and Budweiser, in that order.

THE NUMBERS GAME

You're in the supermarket checkout line and have a few dollars to spare. Should you buy some lottery tickets or a copy of the National Enquirer? *Here's some info to help you decide.*

THE EARLY DAYS

Lotteries in the United States may seem like a recent fad, but they date back at least as far as the 1700s. The original 13 colonies were financed with the help of lottery dollars, and the U.S. government used them to help pay for the Revolutionary and Civil Wars. Even the Ivy League universities—Harvard, Yale, and Princeton—used lotteries to get started.

State lotteries didn't begin until the 1960s. The first, a $100,000 sweepstakes tied to a horse race, was held in New Hampshire in 1964. Today, at least 30 states have lotteries, which generate $17 billion a year in revenues.

LOTTERY FACTS

• According to *Consumer's Research* magazine, lotteries have the worst odds of any form of legalized gambling. In terms of average payout, the highest percentage is craps (98%), followed by roulette (95%), slots (75%-95%), jai alai (85%-87%), and the race track (83%-87%); the lottery is last (49%). Only 0.000008% of the 97 million people who play the lottery annually win a million dollars.

• Lotteries with the best odds (1990 stats): Delaware, Maryland, Michigan, Pennsylvania, and Washington, D. C. The odds of winning their jackpots are 1 in 1,000. Worst odds: California and Florida. Their odds are 1 in 14 million.

WINNERS AND LOSERS

• In 1983, Joseph R. Wyatt, 29, of Union, New Jersey, ripped up his lottery ticket, which read "Void if torn or altered" on the back —before realizing it was worth $1.6 million. In tears, he taped his ticket back together and presented it to New Jersey lottery officials, begging them to overlook the rule. They did—he got his money.

• In 1983, Don Temple accidentally threw a lottery ticket worth $10,000 into a trash can outside a Seattle convenience store. When he realized his mistake, he talked the store into dumping that week's garbage onto the driveway of his father-in-law's home. Temple sifted through the trash for four days, but never found his ticket. The booby prize: he had to pay haulers $200 to take the garbage away.

• In 1985, Donna Lee Sobb won $100 in the California lottery, which qualified her for a $2 million jackpot. But when her photograph appeared in the paper, a local law officer recognized her—and arrested her on an eight-month-old shoplifting warrant.

• In 1986, California lottery winner Terry Garrett of San Diego was arrested only months after winning $1 million—for selling cocaine out of the sports car he had bought with his winnings.

• In 1988, Henry Rich, a computer expert from Harrisburg, Pennsylvania, used a computer at work to forge a winning ticket for a $15.2 million lottery prize that hadn't been claimed. He had a friend come forward with the fake ticket and explain that he had been using it as a bookmark without realizing that it was the winner. The scheme almost worked: the friend was actually issued a first installment check for $469,989. But lottery officials arrested Rich and his friend when they realized that the real ticket had been issued in another part of the state.

• In 1984, Hai Vo, a Vietnamese refugee, spent more than $200 of the spare change he had saved up from food stamp purchases to buy California lottery tickets. One ticket won him $2 million. A week later, a couple from Mill Valley, California, sued Vo to recover $616.26—the amount they paid in state income taxes that year—claiming Vo had used some of their earnings (in the form of state-subsidized food stamps) to buy the ticket. They lost; Vo kept his winnings.

THE SAD TRUTH

How much is a $1 million lottery prize *really* worth? The IRS deducts 20% automatically—and state and local taxes are also taken out, leaving about $560,000. The state pays the first $50,000 in cash, but pays the rest over 20 years, reducing the value by another $100,000. Conclusion: a $1 million prize is worth about $468,000.

When Heinz ketchup leaves the bottle, it travels at a rate of 25 miles per year.

THE MAGIC DRAGON

"Puff the Magic Dragon" is probably one of the best-known folk songs in the world. But is it really, as many people believe, about drugs? Here's the answer, from Behind the Hits.

L enny Lipton's first year of college wasn't easy. Not because he was homesick—he was glad to finally be out of Brooklyn—but because he was having a hard time getting used to being on his own. There were so many things to think about: girls, money, a career. Growing up obviously wasn't going to be easy. Lipton secretly began to miss his childhood.

The fall of 1958 and winter of 1959 passed. So did Lipton, who managed to survive at Cornell in spite of his emotional turmoil. And then one evening in the spring of 1959, a few days after his 19th birthday, Lipton made one of the most important decisions of his life. He decided to go to the library.

He was supposed to have dinner that night with a friend who lived off-campus, but it was still early. So Lipton wandered over to the library in the Cornell Student Union. He scanned the shelves until he found a volume of poems by Ogden Nash, then pulled it from the shelves and retired to a chair with it. Lenny was struck by a simple rhyme about the "Really-o Truly-o Dragon." In fact, he was inspired by it. "If Ogden Nash can write that kind of stuff, so can I," he thought.

Lipton returned the book, left the library, and headed for his friend's house. As he walked down the hill that led from Cornell into the town of Ithaca, he thought of Ogden Nash's dragon. And then he thought of his own dragon. As he approached his friend's house, Lipton incorporated his dragon into a little poem about a subject that was never far from his mind in those days—the end of childhood.

When Lipton got to 343 State Street, he knocked on the door. No answer. Apparently neither his friend nor his friend's roommate, Peter Yarrow, was home. But Lipton wanted to get this poem onto paper, so he went inside anyway. He headed straight for a typewriter—which happened be Yarrow's—sat down, and began typing as fast as he could. In three minutes, he typed out his poem—then he got up and left. He didn't bother taking "Puff the

---

Rule of thumb: Nearly all boys grow at least as tall as their mothers.

Magic Dragon" with him. He didn't care—he'd gotten it out of his system. He just left it sitting in the typewriter.

Folk music was popular at Cornell in the late '50s, and Peter Yarrow was a big man in the folk scene. Although he was still an undergraduate, he taught a class on folk music, performed, and often organized concerts. As Lipton tells it, Yarrow returned home that night, found the poem sitting in his typewriter, and wrote a melody for it. Eventually Yarrow became part of Peter, Paul, and Mary, and they included the song about "Puff" in their act.

Years went by, and Lipton forgot all about his three-minute poem until a friend from Cornell happened to mention that he'd seen Peter Yarrow perform "Puff" with his new group. Yarrow had told him that Lipton had written it. Was it true?

Suddenly, Lipton's little poem came back to him.

In the world of rock 'n' roll, one inevitably runs into stories about unscrupulous operators who've stolen songs from their rightful owners. So it's nice to be able to write about a case in which an honest man went out of his way to find a writer. That's what happened here. When it began to look as if "Puff" was really going to be worth something, Peter Yarrow tracked Lenny Lipton down to let him know about it. And he's always listed Lipton as co-writer—even when Lipton didn't remember having invented the world's most popular dragon.

For years, people have speculated about the meaning of "Puff," but Lenny is quite clear about what was on his mind when he wrote it: "Loss of innocence, and having to face an adult world," he says. "It's surely not about drugs. I can tell you that at Cornell in 1959, *no one* smoked grass." None of the "suggestive" names were thought out—they just popped into his head as he was walking along that night. "I find the fact that people interpret it as a drug song annoying," he says. "It would be insidious to propagandize about drugs in a song for little kids. I think it's a very sentimental tune."

"Puff the Magic Dragon" has had remarkable success for a poem that took three minutes to write. As a song, it reached #2 on the national charts in 1963, and in the '70s became the basis of a continuing series of children's cartoons.

UNCLE JOHN'S BATHROOM NEWS

Bits and pieces of bathroom trivia we've flushed out over the years.

THE BATHROOM POLL
Honest, we didn't make this up. In 1991, the Scott Paper Company did a survey to find out about people's bathroom habits. Here are a few of the highlights:

"You can gauge a person's education by whether they read in the bathroom. More than two-thirds of people with master's degrees and doctorates read in the stall, the survey shows. Only one in two high school grads read while in the bathroom, and 56 percent of those with college degrees do."

"Fifty-four percent of Americans fold their toilet tissue neatly while 35 percent wad it into a ball before using it."

"Seven percent of Americans steal rolls of toilet paper."

"More than 60 percent prefer that their toilet paper roll over the top, 29 percent from the bottom. The rest don't care."

LIFE-STALLS OF THE RICH AND FAMOUS

1. The urinal as art. Marcel Duchamp rocked the art world in 1917 when he made a urinal into sculpture by turning it upside down and signing it "R. Mutt." The piece, entitled "The Fountain," upset an art committee's dignified sensibilities—they refused to exhibit it. According to *The New York Times*, however, the work "is now considered a masterwork," although it exists only in a photograph taken by Alfred Stieglitz.

2. An historic site. On November 6, 1989, six feet under Ferry Street in Troy, New York, archaeologists discovered Uncle Sam's toilet. "The site is where 19th-century meatpacker Sam Wilson used to live," explained a news report. "During the War of 1812, Sam labeled his meat-crates 'U.S.,' which led American soldiers to joke that they were being fed by Uncle Sam....A developer is building a supermarket and a park on the site, but Uncle Sam's bathroom floor...will be preserved for visitors to view."

Charles Dickens always slept facing north. He thought it improved his writing.

3. Celebrity seat. In February 1979, Jacqueline Kennedy was on her way to her nephew's wedding in Gladwyne, Pennsylvania. She pulled into an Arco gas station to answer the call of nature. The owner of the gas station commemorated the event by mounting a plaque in the ladies room: "This room was honored by the presence of Jacqueline Bovier Kennedy Onassis on the occasion of the wedding of Joseph P. Kennedy II and Sheila B. Rauch, February 3, 1989."

THE HISTORY OF THE TOILET HANDLE

According to *Why Do Clocks Run Clockwise, and Other Imponderables*, here's why toilet flush handles are on the left side:

• "Most early flush toilets were operated by a chain above the tank that had to be pulled down by hand. Almost all of the chains were located on the left side of the toilet, for the user had more leverage when pulling with the right hand while seated.

"When the smaller handles near the top of the tank were popularized in the 1940s and 1950s, many were fitted onto existing toilets then equipped with pull-chains. Therefore, it was cheaper and more convenient to place the new handles where they fitted standard plumbing and fixtures."

STRONGER THAN DIRT

In his book *Bigger Secrets*, William Poundstone passed on this bit of bathroom science that we feel readers should know about.

• **"The combination of Sani-Flush and Comet cleansers can explode!** Comet (sodium hypochlorite and grit) is a common all-purpose abrasive, and Sani-Flush (a.k.a. sodium bisulfate) is designed to keep toilet bowls clean. Many think that the combination ought to work all the better.

"The Sani-Flush label warns consumers not to mix it with a chlorine-containing cleanser lest hazardous fumes be released. But few people know which other cleansers contain chlorine, and in any case the label says nothing about explosions. In 1985 Hilton Martin of Satellite Beach, Florida, cleaned the bowl of his toilet with Comet and then hung a Sani-Flush dispenser inside the tank. He noticed the water starting to bubble when the phone rang. While he was in another room on the phone, the toilet detonated. American Home Products has denied that Sani-Flush poses an explosion hazard."

FAMILIAR NAMES

Some people achieve immortality because their names are associated with an item or activity. You know the names—now here are the people.

R. J. Lechmere Guppy. A clergyman living in Trinidad. He sent several species of tropical fish to the British Museum, including a tiny specimen that now bears his name.

Dr. J. I. Guillotin. A French physician. Moved by mercy, he endorsed what he thought was a more humane method of execution than hanging. Ironically, the guillotine—which he did not invent—is now synonymous with needless and brutal slaughter.

Jules Leotard. A renowned French acrobat of the 19th century. Designed and introduced the tight-fitting outfit "that does not hide your best features."

Tom Collins. A 19th-century English bartender at Limmer's Old House in London.

Amelia Jenks Bloomer. An outspoken late-19th-century feminist. Did not invent bloomers, but advocated their use by women (instead of corsets and cumbersome hoopskirts).

Nicholas Chauvin. Fanatically loyal soldier in Napoleon's army. Inspired the word *chauvinism.*

Cesar Ritz. A Swiss hotelier. Founded a chain of fancy hotels, which he named after himself.

John Duns Scotus. A respected scholar and theologian of the 13th century. Two hundred years after his death in 1308, his followers were known as "Scotists," "Dunsmen," and "Dunses," and were reviled for their resistance to the new ideas of the Renaissance. More enlightened thinkers chided the Dunses for their ignorance. Eventually *Dunses* became *dunces.*

Jean Nicot. French ambassador to Portugal in the 1550s. First brought tobacco to France. When *nicotine* was found in tobacco leaves in 1818, it was named after him.

Henry Shrapnel. English artillery officer. Created the shell that helped beat Napoleon in 1815.

Helen Porter "Melba" Mitchell. A celebrated opera singer whose professional name, "Melba," was taken from her hometown of Melbourne, Australia. When she was dieting, she ate thin, crisp slices of bread now called Melba Toast. When she wasn't, she ate a dessert called Peach Melba.

Sylvester Graham. A food faddist of the early 1800s. Advocating vegetarianism and high fiber, he was called "the poet of bran meal and pumpkins" by Ralph Waldo Emerson. His followers were called *Grahamites*, and the food he recommended included *graham crackers* and *graham flour*.

Etienne de Silhouette. Louis XIV's unpopular controller-general in 1759. He made shadow portraits, "recommending them for their cheapness," and they were named after him.

Haile Selassie. The emperor of Ethiopia, known as "The Lion of Judah." His real name was "Ras Tafari"—which explains the origin of the term *Rastafarian*.

Charles Wenburg. A 19th-century shipping mogul. He discovered a new recipe for lobster and passed it on to Lorenzo Delmonico, who named it after him—Lobster Wenburg. Shortly after, Wenburg was ejected from Delmonico's Restaurant for fighting. His punishment: the first three letters of the dish were transposed; Lobster Wenburg became Lobster *New*burg.

Charles Cunningham Boycott. A tyrannical land agent for an absentee owner. The Englishman was overseer of the Earl of Erne's estate in Ireland. When, after two consecutive bad potato harvests, farmers demanded lower rents, Boycott tried to evict them. The result: The farmers banded together and harassed Boycott until he fled Ireland.

STAR TREK

*This is the show that started the cult TV boom. It has now spawned
an industry that includes movies, toys, videos, etc. Here are
some facts about it, from Cult TV, by John Javna.*

HOW "STAR TREK" BEGAN
Gene Roddenberry, the head writer for a popular Western called *Have Gun, Will Travel*, was also a science fiction buff. He saw a lot of similarities between space exploration
and the experiences of the American pioneers—so he conceived of
a TV space fantasy that would be similar to a Western series, complete with continuing characters (which hadn't ever been done).
He based his idea on a popular show named "Wagon Train." He
called his idea a "wagon train to the stars." A star trek.

In 1964, while producing an MGM series called "The Lieutenant," Roddenberry created a workable format for his space show.
MGM turned it down, but Desilu bought it and sold the idea to
NBC. The network financed the pilot, called "The Cage." This was
filmed in November and December. It cost $630,000—an outra-
geous amount for the time—and featured only two members of the
final cast—Majel Barret and Leonard Nimoy. The captain's name
wasn't Kirk—it was Pike. He was played by Jeffrey Hunter.

The pilot was submitted to NBC in February 1965. They rejected it. But the project wasn't canned; NBC still saw promise in the
series and authorized an unprecedented second pilot—including an
almost entirely new cast. The new pilot was entitled "Where No
Man Has Gone Before." It featured William Shatner as Kirk, Nimoy as Science Officer Spock, James Doohan as Scotty, and
George Takei as Physicist Sulu. For the record, the doctor's name
was Mark Piper. He was played by Paul Fix.

The second pilot was submitted in January 1966. A month later,
NBC accepted it for their coming fall schedule.

INSIDE FACTS
Easier Than Landing. The Enterprise's "transporter" was developed as a cost-cutting measure. It provided an inexpensive means
to transport characters from the ship to the next set (landings are

expensive). The "glittering" effect (as the transporter dissolved and relocated the passengers' atoms) was provided by aluminum dust.

The Starship Enterprise. Three models of the Enterprise were used in filming: a 4-inch miniature, a 3-foot model, and a 14-foot plastic model that now hangs in the Smithsonian.

Those Ears. Spock's pointed ears were originally included as a throw-in when Roddenberry contracted with a special effects house to produce three monster heads.

• The first pair were "gruesome," according to Nimoy. "They were rough and porous, like alligator skin." But two days before shooting, they were finally modified to everyone's satisfaction.

• Nimoy objected to wearing the ears, but Roddenberry offered a compromise—wear them for a while, and if they didn't work out, Spock could have "plastic surgery" and have them altered. Nimoy agreed.

• A pair of ears usually lasted from three to five days.

On the Air. Believe it or not, the highest that "Star Trek" ever ranked in a year's primetime rating was #52.

Logical Thinking. One of Leonard Nimoy's contributions to the show was the Vulcan nerve pinch. In one scene, he was supposed to sneak up behind a character and whack him on the head with a gun. But he objected that Vulcans wouldn't be so crude. As a substitute, he made up the legendary maneuver on the spot.

The Source. Incipient Trekkies who want a first-hand look at the inspiration for many of "Star Trek's" distinctive features should view the 1956 film *Forbidden Planet*, which starred Walter Pidgeon, Anne Francis, and Leslie Neilsen. Some of the "similarities" are amazing.

Fat City. Alert fans can tell in what part of the season an episode was filmed just by observing William Shatner's stomach. Always in top shape before shooting began, Shatner appeared trim and fit in early-season episodes. But as the season wore on, time to exercise became harder to find, and his waistline expanded.

STRANGE LAWSUITS

*These days, it seems people will sue each other over practically anything.
Here are a few bizarre real-life court cases, taken from news reports.*

THE PLAINTIFF: Randall Dale Adams
THE DEFENDANT: Filmmaker Errol Morris
THE LAWSUIT: Adams was convicted of murder in
1977. Ten years later, Morris made a film about the Adams case
and became convinced he was innocent. The movie, *The Thin Blue
Line*, presented the case for Adams's innocence so effectively that
he was released from prison. Morris's reward? When Adams got out
of jail, he sued the filmmaker for $60,000 for using his story.
THE VERDICT: Settled out of court. Adams dropped the suit,
and Morris agreed that Adams should receive full rights to any further commercial uses—notably films or books—of his life.

THE PLAINTIFF: 32-year-old Mary Sue Stowe
THE DEFENDANT: Junior Davis, her ex-husband
THE LAWSUIT: An unusual custody case: When they split up,
Mary wanted custody of seven frozen embryos that had been ferti-
lized by Junior's sperm. Junior wanted them brought back to room
temperature.
THE VERDICT: The case went all the way to the U.S. Supreme
Court—which sided with Junior. Mary Sue's lawyers said she was
"devastated" by the ruling—but nevertheless would try to "talk
one-on-one with her ex-husband" to get him to change his mind.

THE PLAINTIFF: J. R. Costigan
THE DEFENDANT: Bobby Mackey's Music World, a country
music bar in Wilder, Kentucky
THE LAWSUIT: Costigan claimed a ghost "punched and kicked
him" while he was using the bar's restroom one night in 1993. He
sued the bar, asking for $1,000 in damages and demanding that a
sign be put up in the restroom warning of the ghost's presence.
    The club's lawyer filed a motion to dismiss the case, citing the

difficulty of getting the ghost into court to testify for the defense.

THE VERDICT: Case dismissed.

THE PLAINTIFFS: The Cherry Sisters, an Iowa singing group
THE DEFENDANT: The Des Moines *Register*
THE LAWSUIT: A landmark libel case. At the turn of the century, the *Register* ran a scathing review of the Cherry Sisters' act. Their reporter wrote that "Their long, skinny arms, equipped with talons at the extremities...waved frantically at the suffering audience. The mouths of their rancid features opened like caverns, and sounds like the wailings of damned souls issued therefrom."

Outraged and humiliated, the singers sued for libel.

THE VERDICT: The judge asked the sisters to perform their act for him in court...and then ruled in favor of the newspaper.

THE PLAINTIFF: Andrea Pizzo, a 23-year-old former University of Maine student
THE DEFENDANT: The University of Maine
THE LAWSUIT: Apparently, Pizzo was taking a class in livestock management one afternoon in 1991, when a cow butted her. She sued, claiming the school "should have known that the heifer had a personality problem."

THE VERDICT: Verdict unknown. (Does any reader know? Write and tell us.)

THE PLAINTIFF: Robert Kropinski, a 36-year-old Philadelphia real estate manager
THE DEFENDANT: The Transcendental Meditation Society and the guru Maharishi Mahesh Yogi
THE LAWSUIT: Kropinski worked with TM groups for 11 years, but he finally sued them because "he was never able to achieve the 'perfect state of life' they promised, and suffered psychological disorders as a result. One broken agreement: he had been told he would be taught to 'fly' through self-levitation, but he learned only to 'hop with the legs folded in the lotus position.'"

THE VERDICT: A U.S. district court jury in Washington, D.C., awarded him nearly $138,000 in damages.

Musical note: A "Big Band" is any band with 10 or more musicians.

WILL POWER

A will is the last chance the deceased has to drive the living nuts.
Here are a few true-life examples of offbeat wills.

THE DECEASED: Ms. Eleanor Ritchey, unmarried granddaughter of Quaker State Oil founder Philip John Bayer

THE BEQUEST: Ritchey died in 1968, with an estate worth around $12 million. According to Scott Bieber in *Trusts and Estates* magazine: "Under her will, she left over 1,700 pairs of shoes and 1,200 boxes of stationery to the Salvation Army. The rest of her estate went to the dogs." Real dogs, he means—a pack of 150 strays that Ritchey had adopted as pets. The will set up a trust that permitted the mutts to live in the lap of luxury for up to 20 years. At the end of that period—or on the death of the last of the dogs, whichever came first—the remainder of the estate went to Auburn University.

WHAT HAPPENED: In 1984, Musketeer, the richest dog in America and the last of the original 150, went to that great kennel in the sky. Auburn got its money.

THE DECEASED: Patrick Henry, American patriot

THE BEQUEST: Everything he owned was left to his wife...as long as she never married again. If she did, she forfeited the whole thing. "It would make me unhappy," he explained, "to feel I have worked all my life only to support another man's wife!"

WHAT HAPPENED: She remarried anyway.

THE DECEASED: Charles Millar, famed Canadian lawyer

THE BEQUEST: According to Thomas Bedell in *Having the Last Word*, his will "consisted mainly of practical jokes. He willed shares in the Ontario Jockey Club to two crusaders against gambling. To three men who hated one another, he left equal shares of the same house. And part of his estate was promised to the Toronto mother giving birth to the largest number of children in the decade after his birth."

The #1 use of gold in the United States: class rings.

WHAT HAPPENED: The public either loved or hated it. Newspapers called it "the Stork Derby." Moralists tried to invalidate the will on the grounds that it promoted promiscuity. But in the end, half a million dollars was split between a quartet of women who had each had nine kids in the 10 ensuing years.

THE DECEASED: Robert Louis Stevenson, author of *Treasure Island, Dr. Jekyll and Mr. Hyde*, etc.

THE BEQUEST: In addition to his normal earthly goods, Stevenson tried to leave his birthday. He willed it to a good friend who'd complained that since she was born on Christmas, she never got to have a real birthday celebration.

THE DECEASED: An Australian named Francis R. Lord

THE BEQUEST: One shilling to his wife "for tram fare so she can go somewhere and drown herself."

WHAT HAPPENED: The inheritance was never claimed.

THE DECEASED: A rich, unmarried New Yorker who died in 1880

THE BEQUEST: He left everything to his nephews and nieces, with the exception of 71 pairs of pants. He wrote: "I enjoin my executors to hold a public sale at which these trousers shall be sold to the highest bidder, and the proceeds distributed to the poor. No one purchaser is to buy more than one pair."

WHAT HAPPENED: The auction took place. Each person who bought a pair of pants, upon examining their purchase, discovered "a $1,000 bill sewn into a pocket."

THE DECEASED: Sandra West, wealthy 37-year-old Beverly Hills socialite

THE BEQUEST: Her estate was worth about $3 million, most of which she left to her brother—provided he made sure she was buried "in my lace nightgown and my Ferrari, with the seat slanted comfortably."

WHAT HAPPENED: That's how they buried her, surrounding the Ferrari with concrete so no one would be tempted to dig it up and drive it away.

Chimpanzees lie a lot. How do scientists know? They taught them sign language.

THE BIRTH OF KLEENEX

Feel a sneeze coming on? If you're like most Americans, you reach for a Kleenex without even thinking about it. But that wasn't always true. In fact, not so long ago there was no such thing. Here's how they were invented.

MILITARY SUPPLIES

The Kimberly-Clark Corporation originally designed the product that evolved into Kleenex tissues for *military* use.

• It started in 1914. World War I was being fought in Europe, and the cotton soldiers needed for bandages was starting to run out.

• So Kimberly-Clark devised a product called Cellucotton—an absorbent, soft paper that could be used to dress wounds.

• It was so effective that the army looked for other uses. And they found one: They used it as an air filter for soldiers' gas masks.

PEACETIME PROBLEM

Kimberly-Clark got too enthusiastic about their new material and overproduced it. After the war, they had so much Cellucotton left over that they *had* to find a new way to sell the stuff.

• Their clever solution: They marketed it as a modern women's tool for cleaning off makeup and a "sanitary cold cream remover."

• Calling it Kleenex Kerchiefs, they hired movie stars to endorse it as a secret path to glamour. It was a big success.

SURPRISE SOLUTION

But Americans found another use for the product. Kimberly-Clark was inundated with letters that informed them the Kleenex Kerchiefs were great for nose-blowing.

• Men, in particular, wanted to know why Kleenex had to be a woman's product. And women griped that men were stealing their Kleenex to sneeze into.

• During the 1920s, Kimberly-Clark introduced a pop-up box that always left one tissue sticking out of the box, waiting to be used.

• But the question remained—were people buying Kleenex as a cold cream remover, or a nose-blower? A survey showed that 60 percent of the people used it as the latter. So that's what K-C emphasized, and that's how we think of it today.

If you're of average weight, multiply it by .02—that's how much your brain weighs.

FAMOUS LAST WORDS

When you gotta go, you gotta go. Here are some final quotes from people who really knew how to make an exit.

"I'll be in hell before you've finished breakfast, boys…let her rip!"
—**"Black Jack" Ketchum,** *murderer, before being hanged*

"The Countess Rouen sends her compliments but begs to be excused. She is engaged in dying."
—**The Countess Rouen,** *in a letter read by her attendant to her guests*

"Go away…I'm all right."
—**H. G. Wells,** *writer*

"God bless…God damn…"
—**James Thurber,** *writer*

"If this is dying, I don't think much of it."
—**Lytton Strachey,** *writer*

"Four o'clock. How strange. So that is the time. Strange. Enough."
—**Sir Henry Stanley,** *explorer*

"You sons of bitches. Give my love to mother."
—**"Two Gun" Crowley,** *sitting on the electric chair*

"Now comes the mystery."
—**Henry Ward Beecher,** *preacher*

"Oh God, here I go."
—**Max Baer,** *boxer*

"Friends applaud, the Comedy is over."
—**Ludwig van Beethoven**

"All my possessions for a moment of time."
—**Elizabeth I,** *queen of England*

"And now, in keeping with Channel 40's policy of always bringing you the latest in blood and guts, in living color, you're about to see another first—an attempted suicide."
—**Chris Hubbock,** *newscaster who shot herself during broadcast*

"Drink to me."
—**Pablo Picasso**

"Why yes—a bullet-proof vest."
—**James Rodgers,** *murderer, before the firing squad, when asked if he had a final request*

Bathroom fact: Armadillos can be housebroken.

THE ORIGIN OF SHERLOCK HOLMES

Sherlock Holmes is one of the most widely recognized characters in all of English literature. He isn't just a person, he's a cultural icon. His adventures are also some of our favorite bathroom reading. In his honor, we've done a little detective work and uncovered these facts.

THE DOCTOR IS IN

The year was 1877. Dr. Joseph Bell, a brilliant surgeon and lecturer at Scotland's prestigious Edinburgh University Medical School, was standing next to one of the hospital's patients. His students—including an 18-year-old named Arthur Conan Doyle—stood around him as he motioned to the patient and systematically ticked off his first observations about the case. "You'll notice, gentlemen," Dr. Bell began, "that the man is clearly a left-handed cobbler."

How could Dr. Bell tell a man's occupation—and the fact that he was left-handed—from a single glance at someone he had never met before? Doyle and the rest of the students were amazed. And this wasn't the first time, either. Bell made these amazing deductions every time he examined patients in front of the class.

Dr. Bell continued with his observations, this time pointing to the man's pants. "Notice the worn places in the corduroy breeches, where a cobbler rests his lapstone."

It was the pants! Dr. Bell read the man's life story from a patch of worn corduroy. It was amazing, and Arthur Conan Doyle would never forget it.

FROM BAD TO VERSE

Nine years later, in 1886, *Doctor* Arthur Conan Doyle—who had put himself through medical school largely through the sale of short stories—turned again to writing to try to save his failing medical practice. He decided to write a detective story using Dr. Bell as a model. "I thought of my old teacher," Doyle later recalled, "and his eerie tricks of spotting details. If he were a detective, he would surely reduce this fascinating but unorganized business to something nearer to an exact science. It was surely possible in real life, so why should I not make it plausible in fiction? It is all very well to say that a man is clever, but the reader wants to see examples of it—such examples as Bell gave us every day in the (hospital) wards. The idea amused me."

The Name Game

Originally, Doyle named his detective Sherrinford Holmes, after Oliver Wendell Holmes—and named Holmes's sidekick Ormand Sacker. But during the three weeks it took to write the story, Doyle renamed the characters: *Sherlock* Holmes, after a cricket player he had once played against, and Thomas Watson, after Patrick Watson, a colleague of Dr. Bell's.

Doyle sent the manuscript for *A Study in Scarlet* to a publisher…but it was returned unread. So he sent it to a second, a third, a fourth, and a fifth…and was rejected each time. Finally, Ward, Lock & Company agreed to publish it in a magazine called *Beeton's Christmas Annual*, where it was read by the English public and quickly forgotten.

BORN IN THE USA

Fortunately for Doyle, a pirated version of the story was printed in *Lippencott* magazine. "The wife of the editor of *Lippincott* liked *Study in Scarlet*," says Sherlock Holmes expert Ely Liebow, "and her husband arranged to dine with Doyle and a writer named Oscar Wilde" when he was visiting England. It was one of the most productive business meetings in the history of English literature, Liebow recounts. "At the end of the meal, the editor had commitments from Doyle for his second Holmes novel, *The Sign of the Four*, and from Wilde for *The Picture of Dorian Gray*."

But it wasn't until 1890 that Doyle made enough money from his writing to enable him to shut down his medical practice, and it wasn't until the story *Scandal in Bohemia* was published in *Strand* magazine in 1891 that he really made it big. "That story established his reputation," Liebow says. "Sherlock Holmes became very popular, and the money started pouring in."

THE PERFECT CRIME

Just as actors resent being typecast, so too did Doyle come to resent Sherlock Holmes. His interests turned to more "serious" works… but the public continued to clamor for Holmes tales. In 1893,

Doyle decided to kill Holmes off. He sent him over Switzerland's Reichenbach Falls wrestling with arch-villain Professor Moriarity. Called *The Final Problem*, the story killed both characters. The public was outraged—more than 20,000 people cancelled their subscriptions to the *Strand*—but Doyle still hoped it would be the end of Sherlock. "I am weary of his name," he sighed to a friend.

Beyond and Back

It wasn't the end. Public demand for Sherlock Holmes stories continued unabated. Doyle succumbed to the pressure in 1902 and published *The Hound of the Baskervilles*, in which Watson discovers a manuscript describing a previously unknown Holmes case.

But even this partial resurrection wasn't enough for Holmes fans, so in 1903 Doyle gave in and brought Holmes back to life in *The Adventure of the Empty House*. Why the change of heart? An American magazine offered him $5,000 per story, and a British publisher offered him almost $3,000 per story for the British rights, unheard-of sums in those days.

CASE CLOSED

Sir Arthur Conan Doyle would write a total 56 short stories and 4 novels featuring Sherlock Holmes, and, just as he feared, the general public came to associate him exclusively with that body of work. Still, his fate wasn't that terrible—his 1902 historical study of *The Great Boer War* won him great praise from historians and earned him a knighthood, and his 6-volume history of World War I is considered a masterpiece, even though it never won him the fame his novels did. Doyle became a very rich man—by the 1920s he was the highest-paid writer on Earth, and he left an estate so huge that his heirs were still suing each other over it well into the 1990s.

Note: How good a real-life sleuth was Dr. Joseph Bell? So good—at least according to legend—that he correctly identified "Jack the Ripper." "The story," says Dr. Ely Liebow, "is that Bell and his friend analyzed the Ripper killings and put the name of the killer in an envelope. They gave the envelope to the Edinburgh police, who sent it to London, where the crimes occurred. The contents of the envelope were never divulged, but there were no more murders after they named the killer."

Ten percent of the Russian government's income comes from the sale of vodka.

DEJA VOICE

Would you recognize your own voice if you heard it? After we ran across these two stories, we started thinking that it might be harder than it seems. So, for the truly paranoid, here's yet another thing to worry about.

DAFFY IDEA. Daffy Duck first appeared in the 1937 Warner Brothers cartoon, "Porky's Duck Hunt." But before animators could complete the cartoon, they needed a voice for the character. While they were brainstorming, someone did an impression of their boss, producer Leon Schlesinger, who had a heavy lisp, and the crew impulsively decided to use that voice.

In his book, *Chuck Amuck*, director Chuck Jones tells the story:

"Only when we were well into the production of the new film and incapable of retreat, did we realize the hideous, the lethal potential of the future: Leon Schlesinger was going to have to *see* this film and—more important to our future—to hear his very own voice emanating from that duck.

In order to save ourselves the embarrassment of being fired, all of us were careful to write out our resignations before that fateful day when Leon strode into our projection room and…the new Daffy Duck lit up the screen at Leon's command.…The cartoon played to the studio audience, accompanied mainly by prayer and silence. Then the lights went on and Leon leaped to his feet, glared around: "Jeethus Christh, that's a funny voithe! Where'd you get that voithe?"

PERFECTLY CLEAR. In 1970, Rich Little and other Hollywood stars were invited to a party at President Nixon's home. At one point in the evening, Debbie Reynolds got up and announced that Little would do his famous impression of the president. Little recalls:

"Mr. Nixon turned around and faced me. I finally wound up saying something inane like, 'Let me make this perfectly clear. I think this is a marvelous party. Make no mistake about that.' And I finished by giving the Nixon V-for-victory sign.

"There was dead silence when I finished. There was no laughing or clapping, just silence. Mr. Nixon simply stared at me. It became painfully obvious to me that he didn't know who I was or what I was doing.

"Then the president turned to Mrs. Nixon and whispered, 'Why is that man talking in that strange voice?' "

Hamsters get their name from *Hamstern*, a German word that means "to hoard."

START YOUR OWN COUNTRY

Ever wondered what it'd be like to be king or queen—or president—of your own country? Here are some people who found out.

ATLANTIS

Founding Father: J. L. Mott, a Danish sea captain

History: In 930 A.D., Leif Ericson, a Viking explorer, discovered some Caribbean islands he mistook for remnants of the lost continent of Atlantis. In 1934, claiming to be Ericson's descendant, Mott declared himself the rightful heir to the islands, which he could not locate but believed "were somewhere near Panama." He drafted a one-page constitution and began issuing passports and triangle-shaped postage stamps.

What Happened: The International Postal Union refused to recognize Mott's postage stamps. Then, in 1936, Mott was almost arrested for trying to enter the United States using an Atlantis passport. By 1954 the elusive country had been renamed the Empire of Atlantis and Lemuria. Despite the country's fancy new name, however, all attempts to actually *locate* it have failed.

GRANBIA

Founding Father: Andrew Richardson, a Liverpool postal worker

History: In the 1970s, Richardson declared his semidetached flat to be the independent nation of Granbia (the rest of the building remained a part of the United Kingdom).

What Happened: He lost interest, and the apartment reverted to England by default.

NEW ATLANTIS

Founding Father: Leicester Hemingway, little brother of author Ernest Hemingway

History: In 1964, he built an 8-by-30-foot floating bamboo platform 7 miles off the coast of Jamaica, anchoring it to the ocean floor with a Ford engine block. "I can stand on the platform, walk around on it, and salute the flag, all of which I do periodically,"

In 1900, the average American drank 12 sodas a year. Today it's 556.

Hemingway bragged to reporters. "There are no taxes here, because taxes are for people not smart enough to start their own countries."

What Happened: Part of the country was destroyed by fishermen in search of scrap wood; the rest sank in a storm.

THE HUTT RIVER PROVINCE PRINCIPALITY

Founding Father: "Prince" Leonard George Casely, an Australian wheat farmer

History: When the Western Australia Wheat Quota Board limited the amount of wheat he could grow in 1969, Casely and his 18,500 acre farm seceded from the union. He designed his own national flag and motto, printed his own money, and set up his own parliament.

What Happened: Australia refused to recognize his sovereignty, so in 1977 he declared war. Nothing came of it—he backed down two days later and reestablished diplomatic relations. Casely claims he pays no Australian taxes, but admits he makes payments to the Australian government as an "international courtesy."

ISLE OF THE ROSES

Founding Father: Giorgio Rosa, an Italian engineering professor

History: Rosa built a tower in the Adriatic Sea large enough to contain a bar, restaurant, and post office, and declared independence from Italy.

What Happened: The Italian government ignored him at first—but after a while they invaded the tower and blew it up.

THE SOLAR ATLANTIC EMPIRE

Founding Father: David Owen, a writer for *The Atlantic Monthly*.

History: Owen wanted to form his own country but couldn't find any available land. So the took possession of the sun, one of the last unclaimed territories in the solar system. He backed up his claim by writing a letter to the U.S. State Department asking for official recognition. "The sun should now be referred to as the Solar Atlantic Empire," he wrote, "and I, henceforth, will be known as Lord High Suzerain of Outer Space."

What Happened: The State Department wrote back saying that it was unable to consider his application.

Red-headed men are more likely to go bald than anyone else.

A FOOD IS BORN

These foods are common, but you probably don't know where they come from. If you want that info, keep reading.

KETCHUP. The Chinese invented *ke-tsiap*—a concoction of pickled fish and spices (but no tomatoes)—in the 1690s. By the early 1700s, its popularity had spread to Malaysia, where British explorers first encountered it...and by 1740 the sauce—renamed *ketchup*—was an English staple. However, it wasn't until the 1790s that New England colonists first mixed *tomatoes* into the sauce. The reason: Until then, it was widely believed that tomatoes (a close relative of the toxic belladonna and nightshade plants) were poisonous.

Making tomato ketchup at home is a tedious all-day project, and American housewives hated the process. So when Henry J. Heinz introduced bottled ketchup in 1875, he promoted it as a labor-saving device. His first slogan was: "Blessed relief for Mother and the other women of the household." By the 1980s, Heinz ketchup was in one of every two households in the U.S.

WHEATIES. Invented in 1921 by a Minneapolis health spa owner who fed his patients homemade bran gruel to keep them regular and help them lose weight. One day he spilled some on the stove, and it hardened into a crust. He was going to throw it out, but tasted it first. To his surprise, the flakes he scraped off the stove were better than the stuff in the pot. He made more and showed them to a friend at the Washburn Crosby Company (predecessor of General Mills). People at the company liked the flakes, too, but didn't like the way they crumbled. So they came up with a better flake—using wheat. Then they held a company-wide contest to name the product. Jane Bausman, the wife of a company executive, suggested *Wheaties*.

BUBBLE GUM. The first bubble gum was invented by Frank Fleer in 1906—but never made it to market. It was so sticky that the only way to remove it from skin was with vigorous scrubbing and turpentine. It took Fleer more than 20 years to fix the recipe. In 1928, the "new, improved" gum was introduced as Dubble

Bubble gum. Fleer made it pink because pink happened to be the only food coloring on the shelf the day the first commercial batch of Dubble Bubble was made. When his gum became the largest selling penny candy on the market, other manufacturers copied it... including the color. Now pink is the standard color for bubble gum.

GIRL SCOUT COOKIES. The Girl Scouts were founded in 1912. For 20 years they raised money by selling knitted clothes, baked goods, and chickens. Then, in 1934, a Philadelphia Girl Scout leader (who was also a press agent) came up with the idea of selling a vanilla cookie in the shape of the Girl Scout seal. She contracted with a local bakery to make them.

One day she heard that reporters would be interviewing actresses at a local flower show. Figuring her Girl Scout troop would get free publicity if they showed up selling cookies, she sent a contingent to the show. They were astounded by the response. The troop got so much publicity and sold so many cookies that Girl Scout troops all over the country began emulating them. Within three years, more than a hundred local councils were selling the same professionally baked cookies. It was the beginning of an American institution. In 1990 the Girl Scouts sold 130 million boxes of cookies—the equivalent of 13 cookies for every person in the United States.

PEPPERIDGE FARM PRODUCTS. One of Margaret Rudkin's sons suffered from severe asthma, a condition that became worse when he ate processed food. She couldn't find any bread that didn't make him ill, so in 1935 she started baking him stone-ground, whole-wheat bread. One day she brought a loaf to the boy's doctor; he liked it so much, he began recommending it to other patients. After building up a small mail-order business to local asthmatics and allergy-sufferers, she expanded her customer base to include people who weren't sick—and named her company after the family's 125-acre farm in Connecticut, *Pepperidge Farm*.

LIFESAVERS. In 1912, a Cleveland candy-maker named Clarence Crane decided to make a mint to sell in the summer. Until then, most mints were imported from Europe; Crane figured he could cut the price by making them in the U.S. He had the candy manufactured by a pill-maker—who discovered that his machinery would only work if it punched a hole in the middle of each candy. So Crane called the mints *Lifesavers*.

U.S. hens lay enough eggs in a year to circle the equator 100 times.

THE BIRDS

Some inside dope on one of Alfred Hitchcock's spookiest films.

A lfred Hitchcock's 1963 film *The Birds* was a milestone: no one had ever tried to work with so many animals at once; and no one has ever used live animals so effectively in a suspense film.

Much of the credit goes to Hollywood's #1 bird expert, Ray Berwick. He was familiar with the Daphne DuMaurier short story on which *The Birds* was based, but never imagined anyone would try to film it. Then, one morning at 6:30, he got a call telling him to be at Hitchcock's office in an hour. He walked in on a *Birds* production meeting, where he was told that $250,000 had already been spent on mechanical birds that didn't work. Could they use live birds? Not even Berwick was sure. But he agreed to try.

BERWICK'S APPROACH

• Although thousands of untrained birds—sparrows, finches, buntings, seagulls, and ravens—were ultimately used, Berwick only trained about 125 ravens, blackbirds, and seagulls for the film.

• Of the trained birds, only 25 to 30 were well trained; that's all they needed. Birds, says Berwick, have a tendency to follow leaders, so the well-trained birds led the others wherever the director wanted them to go.

• The small birds weren't trained—and they didn't have to be. In one convincing scene, for example, they were just "dumped down a chimney."

• According to Berwick: Once the wild birds were tamed, they lost their fear of humans and actually became "the birds," attacking members of the cast and crew.

• Hitchcock wanted to include an owl among his feathered fiends, but had to cut the owl's scene because it looked comical.

BEHIND THE SCENES

Years after the film was released, Berwick revealed the secret of making seagulls look as though they were attacking humans:

• He taught the birds to land on people's heads whenever people were standing still. And each time they performed that stunt successfully, they were fed.

• In the film, the audience sees what looks like people running down a street being chased by seagulls; in reality, the seagulls were flying along with the people, waiting for the people to stop moving so the birds could perform their trick.

• As soon as the director yelled "Cut!" the actors stopped running and the birds landed on their heads—and received their food rewards.

Postscript: After the film was completed, the seagulls that had been used were taken to the Pacific shore and set free. According to Berwick, trained seagulls will forget what they've been taught in about a week, if no one's working with them. But for the first week after the birds were released, there were strange reports of seagulls landing on people's heads at the beach. No one believed the reports, of course—except the people who'd worked on *The Birds*. And they weren't about to explain it to anyone.

ADVENTURES IN CINEMAGIC

In one carefully crafted scene, co-star Tippi Hedren was rowing across a lake when a seagull seemed to swipe her across the head—leaving her bloodied. Here's how Hitchcock's crew did it:

• They ran two tubes up Hedren's dress: one, which went to her forehead, spurted "blood"; the other, which went to the top of her head, was attached to an air compressor.

• Then they released the gull, which was one of the birds trained to land on people's heads.

• The gull started to land on Hedren's head. But at the moment it touched her, the air compressor was turned on. The burst of air scared the bird into flying away.

• At the same moment, the "blood" squirted through the other tube, making it seem as though the bird had attacked. A complicated stunt, but clever and effective.

AFTERMATH

Hitchcock and Berwick made a lot of enemies in pet shops with *The Birds*. After the film was released, sales of pet birds plummeted.

• Turnabout: Years later, Berwick was also responsible for a bird "boom" when he brought Fred the cockatoo to the screen in the TV show "Baretta."

Why is prostitution illegal in Reno and Las Vegas, but nowhere else in Nevada?

THE STORY OF ASTROTURF

*Provocative thought: Some people say that Astroturf is a symbol
of our culture. Do you agree? Here's a thumbnail
history of the stuff to help you decide.*

Most people assume (or have been told) that Astroturf was designed specifically for the Houston Astrodome. It wasn't; in fact, the Astrodome only turned to synthetic grass as a last resort. Actually, Astroturf was developed as part of an experiment in social engineering.

WAR BABY
During the Korean War (1950-1953), military medical records snowed that draftees from U.S. rural areas tended to be in better physical shape than draftees from large cities. Dr. Harold Gores studied the records and came to the conclusion that city kids were less healthy because they didn't get enough exercise. He blamed this on the lack of open space for them to play in.

Gores speculated that if a cheap, durable, artificial playing surface were developed, it could be used to convert vacant lots, alleyways, and even rooftops into playgrounds and athletic fields, which would help city kids to stay in shape. He took his idea to Monsanto, one of America's largest chemical companies, and together, a decade later, they came up with Chemstrand—a grass-like playing surface made up of nylon fibers woven into a polyester backing.

FIELD MANEUVERS
Ironically, the company didn't test it in the inner city. They took it to an exclusive Rhode Island prep school and installed it on an experimental field. The results: It worked. The field took more abuse and was easier to maintain than grass. Unfortunately, Chemstrand was prohibitively expensive. There was no way it could be used in blighted inner cities.

The synthetic grass would probably have died if it hadn't been for Judge Roy Hofheinz, the flamboyant Texas millionaire responsible for the Houston Astrodome. When he first proposed an indoor stadium in the '50s, most people thought he was nuts. They said a roof that big would collapse under its own weight.

Blinded By the Light

The Astrodome opened in 1965, and the roof didn't collapse. But the glare from the 4,796 transparent panels in the roof *did* make it impossible for fielders to see or catch fly balls. Hofheinz tried everything he could think of—including orange, polka-dot, and striped baseballs. But nothing helped; so he had the roof painted white.

But now he had a new problem: the painted roof didn't let in enough light to keep plants alive, and the grass on the field died. At first Hofheinz just had the dead grass spray-painted green. But he knew a permanent solution had to be found. "You'd better come up with something," the judge yelled to groundskeeper Lyndel Tutt, "because we *will* play ball in here!"

When Monsanto proposed using Chemstrand in the Astrodome, Tutt tested it by walking horses, mules, and finally elephants across it. The surface held up, so in 1966 Tutt had the infield torn out and replaced with Chemstrand (which Monsanto, sensing a public relations opportunity, quickly renamed *Astroturf*). He had the outfield resodded with natural grass, but when that died he had the whole Astrodome Astroturfed! They now had 14,000 square feet of plastic grass connected by three miles of zippers.

WAVE OF THE FUTURE

Astroturf attracted almost as much attention as the Astrodome itself, and orders poured into Monsanto. Just about every new domed stadium included plans to use it, and a host of companies jumped into the fray. They offered competing products such as Poly-Turf, Durra Turf, Tartan Turf, Poligras, ChemGrass, Wyco Turf, Desso Turf, SuperTurf, Omniturf, All-Pro Turf. Regular grass seemed doomed. "We believe," *The Sporting News* wrote in 1967, "that in the not too distant future, all stadiums will be covered with artificial sod that will react like grass, but will stand up better under the pressure of multi-sport use. The sooner, the better."

THE KILLING FIELDS

The fake-turfing of America continued well into the '80s, but over the years resistance to synthetic grass began to build. Professional athletes began to complain of Atroturf-related injuries, including "rug burn," "turf toe," and a number of foot, leg, and knee injuries—some career-ending—caused by the solid, unforgiving surface.

SPIT AND POLISH

Many stadiums found that the fake surface didn't live up to its low maintenance promises, either. The Kansas City Chiefs' groundskeeper, George Toma, told *Sports Illustrated* in 1985: "After just one game on the turf, we have to spend lots more time on it. Shoes leave shoe polish. There is tobacco juice on it, Gatorade, blood, gum, things like that. We have to use brushes and a special solution. It may take four or five guys two or three full days to get all that cleaned up. Right there, that's going to be at least 64 man-hours, minimum. If it was a hard-fought game there are more marks, and it can mean a whole extra day."

As if that weren't bad enough, the festering, rancid goo that collected on the surface—particularly the blood, sweat, and spit—increased players' staph infection rates dramatically. The problem was so bad that it became routine for players to scrub themselves down with iodine soap after playing or practicing on Astroturf.

GAME OVER

By the early '90s, Astroturf's image had evolved from that of a futuristic panacea into just another bad idea. The NFL Players Association lobbied for years to have the Consumer Product Safety Commission declare it hazardous product.

Finally, even Monsanto seemed to signal a lack of confidence in the product when it sold its Astroturf division to a German conglomerate in 1988 explaining that the product "just doesn't fit with the new Monsanto strategy for value-added businesses." (The German company, Balsam Sportstattenbau, was forced into bankruptcy in 1994. Astroturf then became the property of a Texas company.)

Some athletes are bitter about Astroturf.. Retired baseball player Andre Dawson, for example, blames it with worsening the arthritis that cut short his career. "Playing on the rock-hard artificial turf of Olympic Stadium of Montreal and in the cold, damp climate of eastern Canada was the worst thing possible for my knees," Dawson wrote in his autobiography. "Artificial turf was created for one purpose and one purpose only—to make more money for the owners."

On target: When a male camel spits at something, it aims for the eyes.

MYTH AMERICA

Here are a few more patriotic stories we all learned when we were young...all of which are 100% baloney.

THE MYTH: Nathan Hale, an American soldier during the Revolutionary War, was captured by the British and sentenced to hang. When the Redcoats asked if he had any last words, he replied defiantly: "I regret that I have but one life to lose for my country."

THE TRUTH: He never said that—or anything close to it. According to the diary of a British soldier who was there, Captain Frederick MacKenzie, Hale's last words were brave, but not very inspiring. They were: "It is the duty of every good officer to obey the orders given him by his commander-in-chief."

THE MYTH: Abraham Lincoln hurriedly composed his most famous speech—the Gettysburg Address—on the back of an envelope while riding on a train from Washington, D.C., to the site of the speech in Gettysburg.

BACKGROUND: The story apparently originated with Lincoln's son, Robert, who first created it in a letter he wrote after his father was assassinated.

THE TRUTH: Lincoln actually started writing the speech two weeks before the event, and wrote at least five drafts before even leaving Washington for Gettysburg. He wasn't particularly keen on speaking spontaneously—in fact, he refused to say anything to the crowd that met him at the Gettysburg train station because he was afraid he might say something foolish.

THE MYTH: The Liberty Bell was rung on July 4, 1776, to commemorate the colonists' declaration of independence.

BACKGROUND: This tale was invented by writer George Lippard in his 1847 book, *Legends of the American Revolution.*

THE TRUTH: The Liberty Bell was installed in Philadelphia in 1753—23 years before the colonists rebelled—and it has nothing whatever to do with the Revolution. Its nickname, "Liberty Bell," was coined by abolitionists in 1839. They were referring to the end of slavery in America, not to freedom from England.

The Pacific Ocean covers more of the Earth's surface than all the continents combined.

THE EVOLUTION OF SANTA CLAUS, PART I

Ever wonder how the Santa Claus of 20th-century Christmas lore came about? Here's the story of how an almost completely unknown bishop became the most recognized holiday character in Western civilization.

A MAN NAMED NICHOLAS

In the fourth Century A.D., a man named Nicholas became the bishop of a village called Myra in what is now Turkey.

That's about all we know about him.

Nevertheless, Bishop Nicholas of Myra was later canonized and went on to become the most popular saint in all of Christianity. He is the guardian saint of Russia, Austria, Belgium, France, Germany, Norway, and Greece. He is the patron saint of children, virgins, pawnbrokers, pirates, thieves, brewers, pilgrims, fishermen, barrel makers, dyers, butchers, meatpackers, and haberdashers. He has more churches named after him than any of the apostles. And he has evolved into one of the best-known characters in the world—the fat, jolly, red-suited Santa Claus who delivers presents on Christmas Eve, St. Nick.

How did that happen? It took centuries.

MAKING A SAINT

It's a pretty safe guess that the real Nicholas of Myra was a kind and generous man, because most of the legends attributed to him describe kind acts toward children. Here are two of the most famous:

1. The Three Daughters. Nicholas was walking past a house when he overheard a man telling his three daughters that he was selling them into prostitution because he didn't have enough money for the dowries that would make them desirable wives. Later that night, Nicholas snuck back to the house and threw a bag of gold through a window. He did the same thing the following night, and then again the third night, providing enough gold for all three daughters' dowries. (According to a later version of the story, one of the bags landed in a stocking that was hanging out to dry over the fireplace.)

Because of this, he became the patron saint of young brides and unmarried women. And because he delivered financial aid at a time when the girls needed it the most, *pawnbrokers* made him their patron saint. To this day, the symbol of the pawnbroker trade is three balls of gold—a spinoff of St. Nick's three *bags* of gold.

2. The Three Boys. For centuries, it was common to paint St. Nicholas holding his three bags of gold. But not every artist painted them well...and at some point during the Middle Ages, artists painting new pictures of the saint began mistaking the bags for three human heads. To explain this image, a second legend evolved. According to this tale, St. Nicholas checked into an inn during a terrible famine and was surprised when the innkeeper served him meat—which had been unobtainable for months—for dinner. Suspecting the worst, Nicholas snuck down into the cellar and found the pickled bodies of three murdered young boys floating in a barrel. He restored the boys to life and helped them escape.

ST. NICK AND KIDS

These tales helped make St. Nick the patron saint of children. And to honor him, Europeans began giving gifts to their children on the eve of the feast of St. Nicholas, which fell on December 6.

Nicholas was especially popular in Holland. The Dutch St. Nick was tall and gaunt, wore the traditional dress of a bishop, including the pointed bishop's hat (a *mitre*), and carried a large shepherd's staff. He also rode on a donkey, not in a sleigh. Later, it became a white horse. On St. Nicholas's Eve, children left shoes filled with straw for the donkey, and by morning the straw was gone and their shoes were filled with presents.

See page 201 for Part II of Santa's story.

★   ★   ★

"The way of the world is to praise dead saints and to persecute living ones." —*Nathaniel Howe*

A WILD & CRAZY GUY

Observations from Steve Martin, one of America's biggest hams:

"Sex is one of the most beautiful and natural things that money can buy."

"I gave my cat a bath the other day....He sat there, he enjoyed it, it was fun for me. The fur would stick to my tongue, but other than that..."

"What? You been keeping records on me? I wasn't so bad! How many times did I take the Lord's name in vain? One million and six? Jesus CH—!"

"A celebrity is any well-known TV or movie star who looks like he spends more than two hours working on his hair."

"In talking to girls I could never remember the right sequence of things to say. I'd meet a girl and say, 'Hi was it good for you too?' If a girl spent the night, I'd wake up in the morning and then try to get her drunk..."

"I learned about sex watching neighborhood dogs. The most important thing I learned was: Never let go of the girl's leg no matter how hard she tries to shake you off."

"Boy, those French, they have a different word for *everything*."

"I believe you should place a woman on a pedestal, high enough so you can look up her dress."

"I like a woman with a head on her shoulders. I hate necks."

"What is comedy? Comedy is the art of making people laugh without making them puke."

"There is something going on now in Mexico that I happen to think is cruelty to animals. What I'm talking about, of course, is cat juggling."

"I believe that Ronald Reagan can make this country what it once was—an arctic region covered with ice."

"I started a grease fire at McDonald's—threw a match in the cook's hair."

"I have a new book coming out. It's one of those self-help deals; it's called *How to Get Along with Everyone*. I wrote it with this other asshole."

Lingerie fact: According to a garment industry study, 75% of women wear the wrong size bra.

UNCLE JOHN'S BATHROOM LEADER

The Bathroom Reader Institute offers a special "Bowl Me Over" salute to Lyndon Baines Johnson—probably the only president who actually conducted affairs of state while seated on the pot.

GETTING IT BACKWARD

According to Doris Kearns Goodwin, in her biography *Lyndon Johnson and the American Dream*: "Few presidents have permitted the kind of intimacy between themselves and their staffs that Johnson encouraged. When he had to go to the bathroom in the middle of a conversation, it was not unusual for him to move the discussion there. Johnson seemed delighted as he told me of 'one of those delicate Kennedyites who came into the bathroom with me and then found it utterly impossible to look at me while I sat there on the toilet.'

" 'You'd think he had never seen those parts of the body before. For there he was, standing as far away from me as he possibly could, keeping his back toward me the whole time, trying to carry on a conversation. I could barely hear a word he said. I kept straining my ears and then finally I asked him to come a little closer to me. Then began the most ludicrous scene I had ever witnessed. Instead of simply turning around and walking over to me, he kept his face away from me and walked backward, one rickety step at a time. For a moment I thought he was going to run right into me. It certainly made me wonder how that man had made it so far in the world.' "

THE EARLY DAYS

LBJ's habit of making the most of his "down time" actually began in the 1930s—long before he was elected president. According to biographer Robert Caro, the 24-year-old Johnson, while secretary to a Texas congressman, bullied the other office workers while seated on the pot: "The toilet in the office was set in a short corridor between its two rooms. Johnson would sit down on it, and there would come a call: 'L. E.! [L. E. Jones, Johnson's assistant] L. E.!' L. E. would say, 'Oh, God,' because he hated this. At first, he attempted to stand away from the door, but Johnson insisted he come right into the doorway, so he would be standing over him, and L. E. would stand with his head and nose averted, and take dictation.... The tactic was, indeed, 'a method of control'...those who observed it, knew it was being done to humiliate [Jones], and to prove who was boss."

ONE-MAN SHOW

Though a big believer in bathroom business, Johnson would not tolerate it from his staff. According to Caro, he wouldn't allow them to go to the bathroom at all while they worked: "If he caught you reading a letter from your mother, or if you were taking a crap, he'd say, 'Son, can't you *please* try a little harder to learn to do that on your own time?' "

IN THE NEWS

People in Johnson's inner circle weren't his only victims—even members of the press got a taste of his bathroom manner. Steven Bates describes CBS reporter/White House correspondent Robert Pierpont's lunch with LBJ: "After they had eaten...the President told Pierpont to stay for coffee. By about 3:00 p.m. the conversation had become an LBJ monologue. Pierpont tried again to leave. Johnson stood up and said it was time to cross the hall.

"Pierpont followed Johnson into a bedroom. The President started undressing, handing each piece of his clothing to a valet. LBJ stripped naked, continuing his monologue the whole time. He put on a pajama top and walked into a bathroom, 'speaking loudly, over the sound of passing water.' Then LBJ put on the pajama bottoms and got into bed. He talked for another fifteen minutes, then said good-bye—three hours after the conversation had begun."

CONSTITUENT SERVICE

Even *voters* occasionally saw Johnson in the altogether. Caro describes a typical scene during LBJ's 1948 campaign for the U.S. Senate: "Rooms in many small-town hotels had only handbasins, with communal toilets at the end of the hall. These bathrooms were small and hot, and it was cooler if the door was left open, so often Johnson left it open. Not a few voters therefore saw the candidate for the U.S. Senate sitting on the toilet, and described that sight to relatives and friends."

One in three Taiwanese funeral processions includes a stripper.

COMIC BOOK HEROES

If you read comics as a kid, you probably remember that Spider-Man got his powers from a radioactive spider bite…but do you know how the character was invented in the first place? Let's take a look at the invention of Spidey and other comic heroes.

SUPERMAN (1938)

A direct result of writer and co-creator Jerry Siegel's inability to get girls when he was a young man. "As a high school student," he once explained, "I had crushes on several attractive girls who either didn't know I existed or didn't care I existed. It occurred to me: What if I was real terrific? What if I had something special going for me, like jumping over buildings or throwing cars around? Then maybe they would notice me."

Siegel and Joe Shuster, the other creator, named their character after movie actors *Clark* Gable and *Kent* Taylor, and named his hometown after the Fritz Lang science fiction movie *Metropolis*. Lois Lane was inspired by a woman named Lois Amster, whom Shuster had a crush on when he was in school.

Superman never married Lois Lane—but Shuster, who modeled Clark Kent after himself, eventually married Joanne Carter, the woman he had hired to model for Lois Lane.

SPIDER-MAN (1962)

In the early '60s, Marvel Comics published a comic book called *Amazing Fantasy*. "But after issue number ten," publisher Stan Lee recalls, "the sales began to soften and it seemed that [it was] running out of steam…so it was decided that the fifteenth issue… would be the final one."

This gave Lee the chance to experiment. "For quite a while," he writes, "I'd been toying with the idea of doing a strip that would violate all the conventions—break all the rules. A strip that would actually feature a teenager as the star, instead of making him an (ugh!) adult hero's sidekick. A strip in which the main character would lose out as often as he'd win—in fact, more often…"

"Yep, I knew what I wanted all right, but where would I get a chance to try it? Where—except in a magazine we were planning to kill anyway?"

Since Lee had a free hand to do what he wanted in the last issue of *Amazing Fantasy*, he used it to introduce his anti-superhero—Spider-Man. The web-slinger was based on *The Spider, Master of Men*, Lee's favorite pulp magazine character when he was a kid.

A few weeks after its publication, sales reports came back and showed that the issue had been a bestseller. It prompted a brand-new monthly comic called *The Adventures of Spider-Man*.

BATMAN (1939)

Bob Kane was a big fan of the 1926 movie *The Bat*—which featured a villain "who wore an awesome batlike costume." He also liked to read Sherlock Holmes mysteries. In 1939, he combined the two and came up with Batman.

Thirty-eight comic book episodes later, Kane decided to give Batman a sidekick—one that he conceived as "a laughing, fighting young daredevil who scoffs at danger like the legendary Robin Hood." Both the name and the costume were adaptations of the legendary English hero, but Kane modeled the *action* out of his own youthful fantasies: "In my subconscious mind I longed to be like Robin when I was his age, fighting alongside his idol Batman—or, in my case, Douglas Fairbanks, Sr. [who played Zorro]."

The Penguin was inspired by a Kool Cigarette ad, and Two-face was inspired by the 1932 film *Dr. Jekyll and Mr. Hyde*. Catwoman was based on screen siren Jean Harlow, and the Joker was inspired by a photograph of actor Conrad Veidt from a 1928 movie, *The Man Who Laughs*.

CAPTAIN AMERICA

In late 1940, as America's entry into World War II seemed more and more inevitable, Joe Simon, an artist with Marvel Comics, decided to create a superpatriotic comic character who could do battle with Hitler and the Nazis. He called his character Super American, but then decided that if the character was going to fight the German military, he should have a military rank. *Captain America* was born.

To popularize the new hero, Marvel Comics created a fan club called The Sentinels of Liberty. Kids paid 10¢ for a shield-shaped

---

U.S. women over 55 watch more TV than anyone else; men 18 to 24 watch the least.

badge and a membership card that read, "I solemnly pledge to up-hold the principles of the Sentinels of Liberty and assist Captain America in a war against spies in the USA." Some kids apparently took their oath a little *too* solemnly. According to Mike Benton in *Superhero Comics of the Golden Age*,

> The club quickly got out of hand and hundreds of young members started reporting suspicious neighbors as potential fifth columnists and traitors. The offices of Marvel Comics in New York City were threatened by German sympathizers. Eventually, Mayor Fiorello LaGuardia phoned editor Joe Simon to tell him not to worry—he was ordering extra police protection for the publishers of *Captain America*.

WONDER WOMAN

In 1915, a Harvard psychologist named William Moulton Marston discovered the systolic blood-pressure test, which resulted in the invention of the polygraph lie detector. Based on his polygraph experiments, Marston concluded that women were more hardworking and more honest than men, and became a champion of wom-ens' issues as the role of women in the workplace changed during World War II.

According to Ron Goulart in *Over Fifty Years of American Comic Books*, when comic publisher Max Gaines hired Marston as an edu-cational consultant, Marston "looked at Gaines's comic book titles, with the images of supermen like Flash and Green Lantern and wondered why he wasn't publishing any comics with women as the hero." At Gaines's urging, Marston then undertook to create a fe-male comic book hero, a *wonder woman*, "under the pen name of their combined middle names, Charles Moulton."

According to his wife, "Marston wrote every strip with the idea of making Wonder Woman 'a personal expression of the female character.' He wanted his creation, a comic book superheroine for children, to fill a void in a society whose mythology and culture were dominated by masculine images."

In 1943, Marston wrote: "Not even girls want to be girls, so long as our feminine archetype lacks force, strength and power....The obvious remedy is to create a feminine character with all the strength of a superman, plus all the allure of a good and beautiful woman." Wonder Woman was his answer.

FOUR FADS

"Fads," says one critic, "are characterized by an exhilarating absence of redeeming social value....Some make us laugh or smile, and others make us gag (like goldfish)." These days, they usually make (or lose) someone a ton of money, too. Here are four examples.

GOLDFISH SWALLOWING

Lothrop Withington, Jr., a freshman at Harvard University in 1939, ate a live fish on a dare. When word of the stunt got out, someone paid him $10 to do it again. He agreed....

But this time he did it in the packed dining hall of the Freshman Union. Word spread to other schools, and three weeks later Frank Hope, Jr., a student at Franklin and Marshall College in Pennsylvania, topped the record by swallowing three goldfish. The race was on: other students bested Hope's record—one student ate two dozen fish in one setting. By the end of the semester dozens of universities had entered the competition, pushing the record up to more than 300 live fish eaten in one sitting.

Note: The national craze was finally killed by a report from the U.S. Public Health Service. They warned that many goldfish contain tapeworms that can lodge in the intestines.

3-D MOVIES

Hollywood was in big trouble in the early 1950s...or at least people thought it was. Now that TVs were in American homes, why would people want to go to theaters and watch movies they had to *pay* for? To make the moviegoing experience as different from TV as possible, Hollywood introduced a number of technical "innovations" such as Cinerama, Glamarama, and Smell-O-Vision.

But the innovation given the greatest chance of success was "Natural Vision," what we know as 3-D film. The first 3-D movie was a low-budget gem called *Bwana Devil*, about a railroad construction crew in Africa that gets attacked by lions. It was panned by critics, but opened to sellout audiences in Los Angeles in November, 1952. The movie made $95,000 the opening weekend, a box office record, and went on to gross more than $5 million, a huge amount in the '50s. "By early 1953," Richard Johnson writes in his book *American Fads*, "most movie companies had at least one

---

The Statue of Liberty's mouth is only three feet wide.

3-D project in the works." Warner Brothers released *The House of Wax*, starring Vincent Price; it was the first big-budget 3-D film and was so successful that Warner announced that nearly all of its films would be released in 3-D. Before long, however, audiences tired of the novelty, and by 1954, 3-D films started losing money. Ironically, the only way to salvage them was to rerelease them as "regular" films. Some—including Alfred Hitchcock's *Dial M for Murder*—were *never* released in their original 3-D version; the studios just shelved them and released regular versions in their place.

HACKY SACK
Invented in the mid-1970s by 27-year-old R. John Stallberger, a former football player who had sewn one together and kicked it around to strengthen tendons he had torn in his knee playing football. Friends liked the little leather beanbag so much that Stallberger began manufacturing them for sale to sporting goods stores. He sold so many that Wham-O (makers of the Frisbee and Hula Hoop) bought him out for $1.5 million in 1983.

Wham-O promoted Hacky Sack the same way they'd marketed the Frisbee decades earlier—they created a "World Footbag Association" and used their promotional muscle to turn Hacky Sack into a "legitimate" sport, complete with sanctioned tournaments and televised championship events.

MONSTER TRUCKS
In 1974, Bob Chandler opened a four-wheel-drive parts and accessories store in Hazelwood, Missouri. Business was slow…so he put huge tires on his Ford pickup truck and parked it in front of the store, hoping it would attract attention. It did, so he put even larger tires on it, then even larger tires, then *even larger* tires. Soon he had 10-foot-high tires on his truck, making it ride so high that it hit low-hanging power lines and stoplights. One day in 1981, Chandler and his business partner "put two old cars out in a cornfield to see if we could just drive right over the top of them. It not only did that, I drove over them like they weren't even there!" Nine months later, a promoter hired them to wreck some cars at a tractor pull meet in Jefferson City, Missouri. "I could not believe the reaction of the crowd," Chandler recalls. "They went crazy. Kids, grandmothers, everybody loved it." Today an estimated 10 million Americans go to monster truck rallies every year.

A Dudley Do-Right lunch box and thermos sold at auction for $2,200 in 1992.

THE NAKED TRUTH

People get very strange in this country when they take their clothes off. Check out these excerpts from newspaper articles contributed by BRI correspondent Peter Wing.

A BIG SURPRISE

"A male motorist told authorities yesterday that a naked, red-haired woman—'the largest woman you ever saw'—jumped out of the woods and attacked his car on a dark country road in northern Michigan.

After briefly terrorizing the motorist, the woman disappeared into the woods."

—**United Press International**

AND WHAT ABOUT KETCHUP?

Lansing, Mich. — Oct. 16, 1981. "Two sisters who described their nude mustard-smeared joyride in a parcel delivery truck as a religious experience have been set free....A third sister was found mentally ill; sentencing in her case has been postponed.

"The three were arrested after driving off—nude except for their shoes and smeared with mustard—in a parked United Parcel Service truck. 'We were trying to find God,' one of the sisters explained."

—*San Francisco Chronicle*

THE CRISCO KID

"A Tifton, Georgia, man has been convicted of public indecency and placed on probation for slinging chunks of lard at women while driving a car in the nude."

—**Associated Press**

HOPPING AROUND THE NEIGHBORHOOD

Santa Cruz, Ca. — "A city police officer was investigating a complaint of a disturbance at a man's home when he spotted what looked like a tall, chocolate rabbit coming 'hippity hoppity' out of the yard. After a closer look, the officer discovered it was a 30-year-old female neighbor who had covered her nude body in chocolate glaze. She was disguised as the Easter bunny."

—**Associated Press**

America's first nudist organization was founded in 1929, by three men.

THE YEAR THEY STOLE THE PRESIDENCY, PART I

Here's an episode of American history we're rarely taught in school—a time when the democratic process didn't work ...and we narrowly averted a second Civil War.

CHANGING COURSE

Eighteen seventy-six was a watershed year in American political history. It was a "reunion" of sorts: The Civil War had been over for just 11 years, and citizens of the former Confederate states were going to be voting in the presidential election for the first time since then. Would the North and South—so recently bitter enemies—be able to pick a president without going to war? The future of American democracy depended on it.

THE CHOICES

Republican nominee: Ohio governor Rutherford B. Hayes, a "colorless" man who "fell like a wet blanket on the party." He was picked as a compromise candidate after President U.S. Grant withdrew from the race over corruption charges, and the party deadlocked on several more popular candidates at their convention.

Democratic nominee: New York governor Samuel J. Tilden—a crimefighting prosecutor famous for busting the Boss Tweed Ring and convicting its founder on charges of fraud, bribery, and graft. America desperately wanted clean government, and Tilden, who ran on the slogan "Tilden and Reform," promised to deliver it.

THE CAMPAIGN

Hayes and Tilden both ran extremely negative campaigns. "The campaign, focusing on personalities, became bitter and dirty," historian Norman J. Ornstein recounted in *Roll Call* magazine in 1992. "Each side hurled insults and lies at the other. Hayes was accused of stealing the pay of dead soldiers in the Civil War and shooting his mother in a fit of insanity, while Tilden, among other things, was called a drunkard, thief, syphilitic, liar, and swindler." The Republicans placed particular emphasis on reopening the wounds of the Civil War by painting the Democrats as the party of treason. And they weren't too subtle about it, either. "Every enemy this great republic has had for twenty years has been a Democrat," Union Colonel Robert B. Ingersoll proclaimed at one particularly nasty campaign stop.

> Every man that shot Union soldiers...was a Democrat. Every man that loved slavery better than liberty was a Democrat. The man that assassinated Abraham Lincoln was a Democrat....Every scar you have got on your heroic bodies was given to you by a Democrat.... Every arm that is lacking, every limb that is gone...is a souvenir of a Democrat!

Down to the Wire

The election had one of the highest turnouts in American history and one of the closest votes: Tilden won the popular vote by 51% to 47.9%, or by a margin of about 250,000 votes. When the nation went to bed on the night of the election, it seemed certain that by the end of the next day Tilden would be declared the first Democratic president in over 20 years.

STEALING THE ELECTION

...And that might well have happened, if John C. Reid, managing editor of the *New York Times* (then a pro-Republican paper), had not received a telegram from Democratic headquarters:

PLEASE GIVE YOUR ESTIMATE OF ELECTORAL VOTES FOR TILDEN. ANSWER AT ONCE.

The telegram also asked specifically for the returns from Florida, Louisiana, and South Carolina, the only three states in the South still ruled by the Republican "carpetbagger" governments imposed by the North following the Civil War. Preliminary returns showed that Tilden had carried all three states, giving him 204 electoral votes to Hayes's 165, making him the clear winner.

But the returns still had to be verified.

THE NUMBERS GAME

As Reid mulled over the surprisingly urgent tone of the telegram, he went over the electoral college votes in his head. Not counting the three states mentioned in the telegram, Tilden appeared to

---

Welcome to the U.S.: 90% of New York City cabbies are recently arrived immigrants.

have only 184 votes, 1 vote shy of the 185 he needed to win. Hayes had only 165 votes—but Florida, Louisiana, and South Carolina together made 19 votes, and Oregon had 1 contested vote that was up for grabs—so if all of these votes could be swung in Hayes's favor, he could still beat Tilden, 185 to 184.

But was such a maneuver even possible? Reid thought it was. The Oregon vote was a sure thing, since it was (illegally) held by a Republican appointee who stood to lose his job if the Democrats won. And because the governments of the three contested states were controlled by Republicans, if the vote tallies were contested, Republican-stacked certification boards would be called in to resolve the dispute. They had the power to disqualify "fraudulent" votes and adjust the official accounts accordingly, throwing the election to Hayes. The board members weren't exactly Puritans, either, as historian Roy Morris relates:

> South Carolina's board included three Republicans who were themselves candidates for office. Florida's board was Republican by a two-to-one margin, the swing vote in the hands of a former Confederate deserter. Louisiana's board consisted of an undertaker, a saloonkeeper, and two thoroughly disreputable carpetbaggers—all of whom would be indicted for fraud the following year.

GETTING THE WORD OUT

As soon as Reid realized the election was still up for grabs, he rushed over to the Republican headquarters at the Fifth Avenue Hotel, woke up several senior party officials, and explained the situation. Republican National Committee chair Zachariah Chandler reportedly told Reid to do "whatever he thought was best," and that's exactly what he did—he took a carriage down to the Western Union office and dashed off identical telegrams to Republican leaders in each of the three contested states:

> HAYES IS ELECTED IF WE HAVE CARRIED SOUTH CAROLINA, FLORIDA, AND LOUISIANA. CAN YOU HOLD YOUR STATE? ANSWER IMMEDIATELY.

When each state cabled back in the affirmative, Reid immediately dispatched "visiting statesmen" to the three contested states to make sure that the vote counting went according to plan.

What happened next? Part II is on page 410.

On average, 100 people choke to death on ballpoint pens every year.

DUMB SCIENCE

*Ever wonder what scientists do in their laboratories
all day? Here are a few real-life examples.*

EXPERIMENT: James McConnell, head of the University of Michigan's Planaria Research group, wanted to see if memory "can be eaten and reused." So he trained a batch of worms, ground them up, and fed them to a second group of untrained worms.

CONCLUSION: According to McConnell, it worked. The untrained worms demonstrated behavior he'd taught the ground-up worms. Minor problem: He never got the same results again.

EXPERIMENT: A scientist named Spalding brilliantly theorized that a baby chick's instinct to follow a mother hen originates in its brain. In an 1873 experiment, he removed the brains of baby chicks and placed the chicks a few yards from a mother hen.

CONCLUSION: Spalding's groundbreaking paper, "Instinct," tells us: "Decerebrated chicks will not move towards a clucking or retreating object."

EXPERIMENT: To test the rumor that Coca-Cola is an effective spermicide, Harvard University researchers added sperm samples to test tubes, each containing a different type of Coke.

CONCLUSION: A minor success. Diet Coke was the most effective, followed by Classic Coke, New Caffeine-Free, and in last place, New Coke. Researchers suggest that levels of acidic pH and perhaps some secret formula components were the determining factors. In any event, a Coca-Cola official was quoted to say: "We do not promote Coca-Cola for medical purposes. It is a soft drink."

EXPERIMENT: Are rats psychic? In 1974, two parapsychologists named Craig and Treuriniet decided to find out. They put rats in a lab maze with only two exits—one leading to freedom, the other to death. (They would kill the rats.)

CONCLUSION: Half chose the correct path; half didn't. Unsatisfied with the results, Craig and Treuriniet theorized a correlation between the rat's psychic powers and phases of the moon.

The world's first animated TV ad was created by Dr. Seuss in 1949, for the Ford Motor Co.

BEHIND THE STORY

It's fascinating (at least to us) to find out how classic children's books were created. There aren't necessarily magical stories behind them; some were conceived in bars or at business meetings, some were inspired by hated relatives, some just evolved out of other books. Still, it's interesting trivia. Here are some examples.

WHERE THE WILD THINGS ARE. In November 1955, Maurice Sendak, a young storybook artist, drew up a draft of a children's story he called *Where the Wild Horses Are*. The only problem: "I couldn't really draw horses," Sendak said, "and I didn't, for the longest time, know what to use for a substitute. I tried lots of animals in the title, but they just didn't sound right." In 1963, Sendak finally settled on *Things*, dumping the horses in favor of monsters that were based on the Brooklyn relatives he detested as a child. "I remember how inept they were at making small talk with children. There you'd be, totally helpless, while they cooed over you and pinched your cheeks. Or they'd lean way over with their bad teeth and hairy noses, and say something threatening like, 'You're so cute I could eat you up.' And I knew if my mother didn't hurry up with the cooking, they probably would."

CHARLOTTE'S WEB. E. B. White based the most famous of his three children's stories on his own experiences at his farm in Maine. "I like animals," he once explained, "and my barn is a very pleasant place to be....One day when I was on my way to feed the pig, I began feeling sorry for the pig because, like most pigs, he was doomed to die. This made me sad. So I started thinking of ways to save a pig's life. I had been watching a big, gray spider at her work and was impressed by how clever she was at weaving. Gradually I worked the spider into the story,...a story of friendship and salvation on the farm." (No word on whether he spared the *real* pig's life.)

CURIOUS GEORGE. When Hans Augusto Rey was growing up in Hamburg, Germany, he loved going to the zoo. Later, when he began writing children's stories, he filled his books with the exotic animals from his past. His first book, *Cicily G. and the Nine Monkeys*, was about a giraffe who befriends some monkeys. Rey gave

---

In a 1990 preschool poll, Mr. Rogers was first choice for president of the United States.

each of the monkeys personalities, including one named George, which he described as "clever and curious." He liked George so much that he wrote an entire story about him. *Curious George* was published in 1941.

Note: Curious George literally saved Rey's life. In 1940, Rey and his wife were in Paris when the Nazis invaded, and had to flee the country. While trying to escape on bicycles, they were arrested by police who thought they were spies. An officer searching their belonging came across the unpublished manuscript of *Curious George*, and released the Reys, saying that no spy could write such a wonderful story.

MADELINE. In 1939, Ludwig Bemelman wrote the first *Madeline* book in Pete's Tavern at 18th and Irving in New York City, using the backs of the tavern's menus as writing paper. The story was based on both his mother's life as a young girl in Bavaria, and his own recollections as the smallest boy in a boarding school. He named the main character after his wife Madeleine, a former nun (he changed the spelling so it would rhyme more easily).

THE LITTLE PRINCE. In 1941 Antoine-de Saint-Exupery, a famous French Air Force pilot, adventurer, and author, was having lunch with a publisher in New York. He happened to pick up a napkin and started doodling a picture of a little boy. "Who's that?" the publisher asked. "Oh," Saint-Exupery reportedly replied, "just a little fellow I carry around in my heart." The publisher suggested that Saint-Exupery write a book about the character. He agreed to give it a try, and *The Little Prince* was published in 1943.

WINNIE-THE-POOH. In 1921, essayist A. A. Milne gave his son Christopher Robin a stuffed bear for his first birthday. He named the bear "Winnie-the-Pooh" after Winnie, a real bear at the London Zoo. Milne entertained his son with stories about Pooh that were so charming, the editor of a children's magazine suggested he publish them. *When We Were Very Young*, a book of verse introducing Pooh, came out in 1924, and *Winnie-the-Pooh* was published in 1926.

Note: Christopher Milne was never comfortable with his fame. In his 1974 autobiography, he blamed his father for "getting where he was by climbing on my infant shoulders and filching my good name."

Most raindrops are round or doughnut shaped, not "raindrop shaped."

THEY WENT THAT-A-WAY

Malcolm Forbes wrote a fascinating book about the deaths of famous people. Here are a few of the unusual stories he found.

FRANCIS BACON

Claim to Fame: One of the great minds of the late 16th century. A statesman, philosopher, writer, and scientist. Some people believe he's the real author of Shakespeare's plays.

How He Died: Stuffing snow into a chicken.

Postmortem: One afternoon in 1625, Bacon was watching a snowstorm. He wondered if snow might be as good a meat preservative as salt...and decided to find out. With a friend, he rode through the storm to a nearby peasant's cottage, bought a chicken, and had it butchered. Then, standing outside in the cold, he stuffed the chicken with snow to freeze it. The chicken never froze, but Bacon did. He caught a serious chill and never recovered. He died from bronchitis a few weeks later.

AESCHYLUS

Claim to Fame: Greek playwright in 500 B.C. Many historians consider him the father of Greek tragedies.

How He Died: An eagle dropped a tortoise on his head.

Postmortem: According to legend, an eagle was trying to crack open a tortoise by dropping it on a hard rock. It mistook Aeschylus's head (he was bald) for a rock and dropped it on him instead.

TYCHO BRAHE

Claim to Fame: An important Danish astronomer of the 16th century. His groundbreaking research enabled Sir Isaac Newton to come up with the theory of gravity.

How He Died: Didn't get to the bathroom on time.

Postmortem: In the 16th century it was considered an insult to leave a banquet table before the meal was over. Brahe, known to drink excessively, had a bladder condition—but failed to relieve himself before the feast started. He made matters worse by drinking too much at dinner, and was too polite to ask to be excused. His bladder finally burst, killing him slowly and painfully over the next 11 days.

JEROME IRVING RODALE

Claim to Fame: Founding father of the organic food movement, creator of *Organic Farming and Gardening* magazine. Founded Rodale Press, a major publishing company.

How He Died: On the "Dick Cavett Show," while discussing the health benefits of organic food.

Postmortem: Rodale, who bragged "I'm going to live to 100 unless I'm run down by a sugar-crazed taxi-driver," was only 72 when he appeared on the "Dick Cavett Show" in January 1971. An eyewitness at the show recalls: "Rodale said that doctors had given him six months to live thirty years ago, but because of the food he ate he would live to be a hundred....A little later in the show he appeared to have fallen asleep, and Cavett and guest Pete Hamill chuckled about it—until they realized he was dead." Cause of death: a heart attack. The taped show was never aired.

JIM FIXX

Claim to Fame: The guru of jogging. Author of the bestselling *Complete Book of Running*, which started the jogging craze in the 1970s.

How He Died: A heart attack...while jogging.

Postmortem: Fixx was visiting Greensboro, Vermont. He walked out of his house and began to jog. He'd only gone a short distance when he collapsed and died, the victim of a massive coronary.

WILLIAM HENRY HARRISON

Claim to Fame: Ninth president of the U.S.; elected in 1841

How He Died: Pneumonia, contracted while giving his inaugural address.

Postmortem: The 67-year-old Harrison's advanced age had been an issue in his race against incumbent president Martin van Buren. Perhaps because of this—to demonstrate his strength—he rode on horseback in his inaugural parade without a hat, gloves, or overcoat. Then he stood outside in the snow and spoke for more than *one and a half hours*, delivering his inaugural address. Needless to say, this weakened him, and a few weeks later he caught pneumonia. Within a week he was delirious, and on April 4—one month after his inauguration—he died. He served long enough to keep just one campaign promise: not to run for a second term.

SUPERMARKET SECRETS

It may not seem like it when you're shopping, but supermarkets put a lot of thought into how products are organized on their shelves. Their goal: To make you spend more money.

WHAT'S IN STORE FOR YOU. The produce is over here, the dairy's over there. The soft drink specials are at the ends of the aisles, the candy's at the checkout. Always. A visit to your local supermarket isn't as haphazard as it seems. It's been laid out so that you spend as much as possible on what the store wants you buy. And that's often more than you came in for. Here's how a typical supermarket is designed to maximize sales.

ON THE EDGE. Why are the meat, poultry, and seafood displays almost always along the back of the supermarket? So that you'll see them every time you emerge from an aisle. Not a bad place to put the most profitable sections of the store.

• Why are the dairy products usually as far away from the entrance as possible? Most everybody buys milk when they shop. To reach it, you've got to walk through a good chunk of the supermarket, often along the perimeter. That's right where the store wants shoppers.

• The more time you spend shopping along the sides and back of the supermarket, the more money the store makes. About half its profits come from "perimeter" items like fruits and veggies, milk and cheese, and meat, poultry, and fish.

• Also, stores like to "anchor" a display by putting popular items at each end. That's why milk, for example, is often at one end of the dairy case and margarine and butter at the other. You've got to run the gauntlet of cheese, yogurt, chips, etc. to get what you came for.

SPACE EATERS. Some foods are so profitable that they command their own aisles. Breakfast cereals bring in more dollars per foot of shelf space than any other product in the interior of the store. So most supermarkets give cereals plenty of space. Soft drinks aren't so profitable...at least not on paper. But beverage manufacturers sweeten the pot with so much free merchandise and cash re-

---

Heavy thought: There are 6 pounds of pennies in the average American home.

bates that carbonated soft drinks end up being one of the biggest money-makers in a typical store.

PRODUCTIVE PRODUCE. Think it's a coincidence that you almost always have to walk through the produce department when you enter the supermarket? The look of those shiny, neatly stacked fruits and vegetables is *the* most important influence on where people decide to shop. It also doesn't hurt that produce is the second most profitable section. While it occupies a little over ten percent of the supermarket, it brings in close to 20 percent of the store's profits.

IN "PRISON." Some supermarket insiders call the aisles of the store the "prison." Once you're in one, you're stuck until you come out the other end. The "prison" is where most of the less-profitable (for the store) national and regional name brands are, so the more time you spend there, the less time you'll spend along the perimeter...buying higher-profit items.

THE SCAN SCAM. Checkout scanning errors may be beeping shoppers out of more than $1 billion a year. Last year, researchers in Southern California found that close to one out of every ten scans was wrong. Three out of four mistakes favored (surprise) the supermarkets. "It's a problem wherever we looked," says Ken Butcher, coordinator of weights and measures for the National Institute of Standards and Technology. What can you do? Watch the scanner display, for one thing. Pay particular attention to sale items. The lower price may not have been entered into the computer.

"Supermarket Secrets," Copyright 1994, CSPI. Reprinted from Nutrition Action Healthletter *(1875 Connecticut Ave., N.W., Suite 300, Washington, D.C. 20009-5728. $24.00 for 10 issues).*

★　　★　　★

"A 1990 survey by the Center for Science in the Public Interest found that high-sugar cereals were shelved at children's eye level, while the more nutritious brands were on higher shelves....And on the bottom shelf, at stooping level, are the staple cereals [like] Kellogg's Corn Flakes, and Post Toasties."

—Vince Staten,
Can You Trust a Tomato in January?

DOO-WOP SOUNDS

You've heard classic street-corner rock 'n' roll tunes like "Why do Fools Fall in Love" before...and you've probably noticed the crazy syllables the groups sing in the background. Ever wonder what they'd look like spelled out? Here are 20 classic examples, from The Doo-Wop Sing-Along Song Book.

1. **Hooodly-Papa-Kow, Papa-Kow, Papa-Kow (YEAH), Hooodly-Papa-Kow, Papa Kow, Papa Kow.** A gem from Frankie Lymon and the Teenagers.

2. **Pa-pa-pa-pa-pa-pa-pa-Oom-A-Mow-Mow, Papa-Oom Mow Mow.** One of the most famous rock syllable combos, from a group called the Rivingtons and their semi-doo-wop tune, "Papa Oom Mow Mow."

3. **Oop-Shoop, Shang-A-Lack-A-Cheek-A-Bock.** One of the all-time greats, a background section from the Earls' "Remember Then" (1961).

4. **Diddle-iddle-iddle-iddle-it (YEAH), Diddle-iddle-iddle-iddle-it.** Notable for its persistence, in a classic doo-wop tune by Herb Cox and the Cleftones, "Little Girl of Mine" (1956).

5. **Neh-neh-neh-neh, neh neh-neh-neh neh-neh-neh, Neh-neh-neh-neh-neh, neh-neh-neh-neh (repeat the whole thing two more times), Werp-A-Tul-Werp, Neh-Neh-Neh-Neh, Neh-Neh-Neh-Neh.** A perfect example of why you have to hear doo-wop to appreciate it. The opening of "The Closer You Are," by the Magnificent Four.

6. **I Su-mokem Boo-eye-ay, I sumokem boo.** Doo-wop's classic drug reference. From "Ling Ting Tong," by the Five Keys.

7. **(Bom-bom) Cheer-Up, (Bom-bom) Cheer-Up, (Bom-bom) Cheer-Up, (Bom-bom) Cheer-Up.** A favorite adaptation of a real word into a doo-wop. From the Pentagons' "To Be Loved."

8. **Rama Lama-Lama-Lama-Lama Ding Dong, Rama Lama-Lama-Lama-Lama-Lama Ding.** That's the Edsels playing homage to George Jones, Jr.'s girlfriend, "Rama Lama Ding Dong."

9. **Rang Tang Ding Dong, Rankety Sing.** Weird combination from the Cellos' "Ring Tang Ding Dong (I Am the Japanese Sandman)."

10. Ka-Ding-Dong, Ding-Dong, Ka-Ding-Dong, Ding-Dong, Ding. The singer's heartbeat in the G-Clefs' "Ka-Ding-Dong."

11. Yip, Yip, Yip, Yip Boom, Sha-Na-Na-Na, Sha-Na-Na-Na-Na. It's from "Get a Job," by the Silhouettes and it's not only a great doo-wop, it's the symbol of the '70s doo-wop revival.

12. Sho-Dot'n' Shoby-Doh, Sho-Dot'n' Shoby-Doh. From Fred Parris and the Five Satins' classic "In the Still of the Night."

13. Dom-Dooby-Dom Woh-oh, Dooby Dooby, Dom Dooby Dom, Woh-oh, Dooby Dooby, Dom Dooby Dom Woh-Oh, tonight I fell in love. Sort of a white-bread doo-wop, but kind of catchy. From the Tokens' "Tonight I Fell in Love."

14. Tuh-tuh-tuh-tuh-tuh-tuh-tuh-aaa-ooo-ooo-ooo-ooo-ooo. A super doo-wop. This is the end of a line in "Unchained Melody," by Vito and the Salutations. The one that starts "Oh my love, my darling, I hunger for your..." Originally, the next word was "touch." In doo-wop it became this 13-syllable creature.

15. A-Wop-bop-A-Loo-bop-A-Bop--Bam-Boom. For sentimental reasons. From Little Richard's "Tutti Frutti."

16. Iminni-ma-ma-ma-Iminni-ma-ma-ma-gin-A-tion. Iminni-ima-ima-ima-ma-gin-aaaa-tion. The doo-wop spelling for the word "imagination," as interpreted by the Quotations.

17. Shoh-Be-Doo-Wop-Wah-Da. The controversial last line in "What's Your Name," by Don and Juan. No one seems to agree on what they're saying. Here's our version.

18. Wah-Wah-OOO, Chop Chop Chop. An original from "Tell Me Why," by the Rob Roys.

19. Wop-wop-Doodly-wop - Wop-wop. Wop-wop, Doodly-wop - Wop-Wop. The El Doradoes' lead into the instrumental break in "At My Front Door."

20. Bomp-ba-ba-bomp, Ba-bom-ba-bom-bomp, Ba-ba-bomp-ba-ba-bomp, A-dang-a-dang-dang. A-ding-a-dong-ding, Bluuuue Moooon. From the Marcels' adaptation of the Rogers and Hart classic, "Blue Moon." (Written originally for Jean Harlow.)

Bowing to pressure from anti-smoking groups, Hasbro took away Mr. Potato Head's pipe in 1987.

PICASSO ORIGINALS

Pablo Picasso was known for his skill with lines.
Here are some you won't see in a museum.

"We know that art is not truth. Art is a lie that makes us realize truth."

"When I was a child my mother said to me, 'If you become a soldier you'll be a general. If you become a monk you'll become the pope.' Instead I became a painter and wound up as Picasso."

"I am only a public entertainer who has understood his time."

"There are only two kinds of women—goddesses and doormats."

"There are painters who transform the sun into a yellow spot, but there are others who, thanks to their art and intelligence, transform a yellow spot into the sun."

"One starts to get young at the age of sixty and then it is too late."

"There's nothing so similar to one poodle dog as another poodle dog, and that goes for women, too."

"You never see anything very great which is not, at the same time, horrible in some respect. The genius of Einstein leads to Hiroshima."

"God is really only another artist. He invented the giraffe, the elephant, and the cat. He has no real style, he just goes on trying other things."

"Ah, good taste! What a dreadful thing! Taste is the enemy of creativeness."

"An artist must know how to convince others of the truth of his lies."

"If only we could pull out our brains and use only our eyes."

"If I like it, I say it's mine. If I don't, I say it's a fake."

"Work is a necessity for man. Man invented the alarm clock."

"You invent something, and then someone comes along and does it pretty."

Q. Who founded the Kenwood stereo company?

MODERN MYTHOLOGY

These characters are as famous in our culture as Pegasus or Hercules were in Greek myths. Where did they come from?

THE PLAYBOY BUNNY. When Hugh Hefner was little, one of his prized possessions was "a blanket with bunnies all over it." Apparently, he never outgrew it—when he started *Playboy* magazine, he used the same bunny as his symbol.

THE JOLLY GREEN GIANT. In the early 1920s, the Minnesota Valley Canning Company introduced a large variety of peas to the American market. They called the peas "green giants," and—because the law required it to protect their trademark—they put a picture of a green giant on the label. Oddly enough, the original giant (lifted from a volume of Grimm's Fairy Tales) was white, not green; he looked like a dwarf, not a giant; and he wasn't jolly—he was scowling. His image eventually softened, and he became such a powerful symbol that the company changed its name to the Green Giant Co.

BETTY CROCKER. The Washburn Crosby Company, a Minneapolis flour maker, got so many letters asking for baking advice that, in 1921, they made up a character to write back to consumers. They picked "Betty" because it sounded "warm and friendly," and "Crocker" was picked to honor a former company director. To come up with a signature for Betty (so she could sign "her" letters), the company held a contest for its women employees. The winner—still used today—was submitted by a secretary.

ALFRED E. NEUMAN. *Mad* magazine artists adapted their mascot from a turn-of-the-century advertising postcard issued by "Painless Romaine," a dentist from Topeka, Kansas. Romaine, in turn, had lifted his drawing from an illustration in a medical textbook showing a boy with too much iodine in his system.

Mad first dubbed the boy "Melvin Koznowski." But he was eventually renamed Alfred E. Neuman, after a nerdy character on the "Henry Morgan Radio Show." *That* character had been named after a real-life Alfred Newman, the composer and arranger of more than 250 movie scores, including those for *The Hunchback of Notre Dame* and *The Grapes of Wrath*.

A. A guy named Ken Wood.

THE CAMPBELL'S SOUP KIDS. Grace Gebbie Wiederseim grew up in Philadelphia in the mid-1800s. One morning when she was a young girl, she stood in front of her parents' mirror and drew a picture of herself. She liked it so much that she saved it.

In 1904, Grace was a successful illustrator and the wife of a Campbell's Soup advertising executive. One afternoon he asked her to help create an advertising campaign for Campbell's. She pulled out her childhood self-portrait...and used it to create Dolly Drake and Bobby Blake—the Campbell's Soup Kids.

POPPIN' FRESH (THE PILLSBURY DOUGHBOY). In 1965, Rudy Pera was trying to design an advertising campaign for Pillsbury's new refrigerated dough product...but he couldn't think of anything that would make the brand stand out. One day he began playfully pounding on a container of the dough, hoping to drum up ideas. "I imagined what could pop out," he recalls. "A dough man? A dough baker? A *dough boy!*"

RONALD MCDONALD. Willard Scott, weatherman on NBC's "Today Show," was the first McClown. Here's the story he tells:

"The folks at the NBC television station in Washington— WRC-TV—had signed on a national kiddie show [called "Bozo the Clown"], and they tapped me to star in the thing....I did a lot of personal appearances as Bozo—at shopping malls, local fairs, that sort of thing. After a while a local McDonald's asked me to appear at an opening, and before too long my Bozo was a regular fixture at area franchises. When WRC dropped [the show], McDonald's didn't like the idea of having to drop a successful promotion. They were hooked on clowns....And so—you guessed it—Ronald McDonald was born....He was almost christened Donald McDonald, but Ronald sounded just a touch more natural, so we went with that."

THE QUAKER OATS MAN. In 1891, seven oatmeal millers combined to form the American Cereal Company. One of the seven was Quaker Mill of Ravenna, Ohio, which had trademarked the Quaker man 14 years earlier. In 1901 the American Cereal Company changed its name to Quaker Oats, and the Quaker man was revived as its symbol. The real Quakers weren't too happy about this. They tried unsuccessfully to get Congress to prohibit manufacturers from using religious names on products.

OTHER PRESIDENTIAL FIRSTS

We all know the first elected president (Washington), the first president to serve more than two terms (FDR), and so on. But who was the first to get stuck in a bathtub? Here's a list of unusual presidential firsts, with thanks to Bruce Fowler's book, One of a Kind.

THE PRESIDENT: Grover Cleveland (1885-89; 1893-97)
NOTABLE FIRST: First president to have hanged a man.
BACKGROUND: From 1871 to 1873, Cleveland was sheriff of Erie County, New York. When two men were sentenced to death, he put the hoods over their heads, tightened the noose, and sprung the trap door himself. He explained later that he couldn't ask his deputies to do it just because he didn't want to. The experience affected him so deeply that he didn't run for reelection.

THE PRESIDENT: James Garfield (1881)
NOTABLE FIRST: First president who could write in two languages at once.
BACKGROUND: Garfield was ambidextrous; he could write in Greek with one hand while writing in Latin with the other.

THE PRESIDENT: William Howard Taft (1909-1913)
NOTABLE FIRST: First president entrapped by a White House plumbing fixture.
BACKGROUND: Taft weighed in at between 300 and 350 pounds while he was president. He was so big that one morning he got stuck in the White House tub—and had to call his aides to help him get out. Taft subsequently ordered a tub large enough to hold four average-sized men. He never got stuck again.

THE PRESIDENT: James Madison (1809-1817)
NOTABLE FIRST: First president to weigh less than his IQ.
BACKGROUND: Madison, the unofficial "Father of the U.S. Constitution," was only five feet, four inches tall and never

---

In 10 minutes, a hurricane releases more energy than all the world's nuclear weapons combined.

weighed more than 98 pounds as president. One historian has called him "a dried-up, wizened little man"—and observed that when he went walking with his friend Thomas Jefferson, the two looked "as if they were on their way to a father-and-son banquet."

THE PRESIDENT: John Tyler (1841-1845)
NOTABLE FIRST: First president to elope while in office.
BACKGROUND: On June 26, 1844, the 54-year-old Tyler sneaked off to New York City with 24-year-old Julia Gardiner to tie the knot. They decided on a secret wedding because supporters were worried about the public's reaction to their 30-year age difference. It didn't matter—the press found out about it almost at once. Ironically, Julia turned out to be just about the most popular part of Tyler's presidency. (P.S.: They had seven kids—the last one when Tyler was 70.)

THE PRESIDENT: Herbert Hoover (1929-1933)
NOTABLE FIRST: First president to have an asteroid named after him.
BACKGROUND: No, it's not in honor of his presidency. In 1920, Austrian astronomer Johann Palisa discovered an asteroid and named it *Hooveria*, to honor Hoover's humanitarian work as chairman of the Interallied Food Council, which was helping to feed starving people in post-WWI Europe. Said Palisa: "It is a pity we have only a middle-magnitude asteroid to give to this great man. He is worthy of at least a planet."

THE PRESIDENT: Jimmy Carter (1977-1981)
NOTABLE FIRST: First president to see a UFO.
BACKGROUND: One evening in 1969, Carter and a few companions saw a "bluish...then reddish" saucer-shaped object moving across the sky. "It seemed to move toward us from a distance," Carter later told UFO researchers, "then it stopped and moved partially away. It returned and departed. It came close...maybe three hundred to one thousand yards away...moved away, came close, and then moved away." He added: "I don't laugh at people anymore when they say they've seen UFOs."

A monkey was once tried and convicted for smoking a cigarette in Indiana.

GIVE US A HAND

You probably can't put a finger on the origins of these common gestures, but here's some info you might find handy.

THE FINGER

It doesn't matter what you call it—"the bird," "the finger," or the "freeway salute"— the middle finger is among the most well-known symbols in America. Believe it or not, the gesture can be traced to the ancient Romans, who called it the "finger without shame," or *digitus impudicus*. Psychologists say it's a symbol of phallic aggressiveness.

THE RING FINGER

More than 2,000 years ago, Greek physicians believed that a special "vein of love" connected this finger to the heart. It logically became the finger to be "bound" by an affair of the heart.

CROSSING FINGERS

Ever cross your fingers for good luck? Historians suggest this popular gesture comes from the pre-Christian belief that a cross symbolizes perfect unity. The intersection point of the fingers was said to possess a mystical quality that would hold the wish until it was fulfilled.

THE SALUTE

The formal military salute seems to have started in medieval England, when soldiers were commonly clad in armor. Two possible explanations for its origin:

• At jousting tournaments, knights paraded past the queen with hands held over their eyes, a symbolic gesture suggesting that they were protecting themselves from her "blinding beauty."

• When two knights in armor met on the road, they raised their visors to show respect...and to demonstrate that they had no violent intentions. This position—one hand held at the forehead—became a formal military greeting. It outlasted the practice of wearing armor.

Check a map: Reno, Nevada, is west of Los Angeles, California.

THE SIMPUL SPELLING MOOVMENT

At the turn of the century, Andrew Carnegie spent more than $200,000 in an attempt to simplify spelling. Here are a few of the details of that forgotten episode in American history.

E -Z DUZ IT. In 1906, millionaire industrialist Andrew Carnegie was approached by Melvin Dewey, the head of the New York libraries, and Brander Matthews, a Columbia University professor, with a revolutionary plan to simplify spelling. Carnegie was enthusiastic. He believed that easier spelling could lead to world peace. Together, the threesome formed the Simplified Spelling Board; their expressed goal was to convince authorities to begin changing the spelling of 300 words.

Among the words targeted were though (tho), confessed (confest), dropped (dropt), through (thru), kissed (kist), fixed (fixt), enough (enuf), prologue (prolog), thoroughfare (thorofare) and depressed (deprest).

ENUF ALREDDEE. President Theodore Roosevelt was an instant convert to the plan. On August 29, 1906, he ordered the U.S. Printer to use the new spelling on all executive branch publications. For a moment, it looked as if simplified spelling would be instituted nationwide.

Roosevelt's plan made front-page news, both here and abroad. Unfortunately for TR, most of the publicity was unfavorable. U.S. newspapers mocked the idea, and the *London Times* ridiculed him with a headline reading "Roosevelt Spelling Makes Britons Laugh."

Congress was outraged by Roosevelt's decree, too. In late 1906, they started to debate the idea on the floor of the House. Sensing an embarrassing political defeat, Roosevelt quickly withdrew his support for the plan.

WEL, THATZ THAT. Carnegie was deeply disappointed. A practical man, he dropped his financial support for the Simplified Spelling Board, writing, "I think I have been patient long enuf...I have a much better use of $25,000 a year."

Four baseball promotions that ended in riots:

WEIRD PASTIMES

*When you ponder taking some time off from work and relaxing,
you probably think of activities like fishing, bike riding, and hiking.
But not everyone does. Here are a few of the more unusual
ways people around the world spend their leisure time:*

CHEESE ROLLING

An event that enthusiasts say got its start as a pre-Roman fertility rite. Every year the citizens of Cheltenham, England, get together on nearby Cooper's Hill to roll small wheels of Double Gloucester cheese down the hill. First prize: a *large* wheel of Double Gloucester cheese. But this is not as tame as it sounds. In 1995, 18 of the 20 contestants were injured—4 had to be hospitalized. By comparison, only 11 people were injured in the running of the bulls in Pamplona, Spain, that year.

FERRET-LEGGING

Ferrets are foot-long rodents with razor-sharp claws, piercing teeth, and a reputation for viciousness that has earned them the nicknames "shark-of-the-land," "piranhas with feet," and "fur-coated evil." In this "sport," practiced for centuries in Yorkshire, England, the participant's pant legs are tied shut at the ankles, a couple of ferrets are dropped down the trousers and then the waist is tied shut as well. First Prize goes to the person who can stand still longer than anyone else as the ferrets furiously claw and bite their way to freedom.

The sport dates back to the days when "ferreters," fur-trapping poachers who use ferrets as hunting animals, hid the creatures in their pants to avoid being caught by gamekeepers. Seventy-two-year-old Reg Mellor, the King of Ferret-Legging, explained the rules to *Outside* magazine in 1983. "No jockstraps allowed. No underpants—nothin' whatever. And it's no good with tight trousers, mind ye. Little bastards have to be able to move around inside there from ankle to ankle. And the ferrets must have a full mouth o' teeth. No filing of the teeth; no clipping. No dope for you or the ferrets. You must be sober, and the ferrets must be hungry—though any ferret'll eat yer eyes out even if he isn't hungry."

Beer Night, Scrap Metal Night, Wet T-Shirt Night, & Disco Demolition night.

In 1972, the world record for ferret-legging was 42 seconds: Today, thanks to the ever-increasing popularity of the sport, the record is 5 hours 26 minutes, although the *Guinness Book of World Records* refuses to recognize the achievement.

THROWING ORANGES

Every year in the tiny town of Ivrea, Italy, between 3,000 and 4,000 citizens celebrate the beginning of Lent by dividing into teams and throwing upward of 360 tons of unpeeled, overripe oranges at one another. The tradition, called "the Battle of Oranges," commemorates the local peasants' struggle against tyranny during the Middle Ages.

The *aranceri*—as the participants are called—battle each other either on foot or from horse-drawn carts in melees that last three days. Dozens of people were hospitalized with broken noses, fractures, bruises, and eye injuries during the 1995 battle, with a handful suffering permanent vision loss. "The carnival is first and foremost an entertainment and a holiday," says Dr. Biagio Spaziante, who runs Ivrea Hospital's emergency room. "Yet a lot of the accidents happen because people go beyond the dictates of common sense." Tourists who want to watch—but not participate—wear red hats sold in the village square. People wearing them are considered off-limits...most of the time.

WATCHING COWS FIGHT

Most countries that use cattle in sport prefer bullfights—but not the Swiss. They stage *cow* fights, pitting pregnant female cows against one another—in spite of the fact that the cows have no natural desire to fight one another...and can't even be *prodded* into fighting.

Actually, most of the time cows just moo, kick the earth, or push against one another as they engage in "shoving matches" to see who will lead the herd. But that doesn't stop the enthusiastic Swiss from putting on their annual cow fight each October in the tiny town of Martigny.

The *Wall Street Journal* provided this blow-by-blow account of one such contest:

A dozen pregnant cows enter the circular arena to duke it out. Cow No. 122 (Medallion) eats some grass. Five minutes pass. Cow No.

106 (Java) charges toward Cow No. 125 (Gitane), who drools and walks away. Cow No. 118 (Tigresse) strolls over to the sidelines to take some bread from her owner. The crowd of 6,000 is very quiet.... The cow fight nevertheless evokes strong passions among the Swiss, who, during fights, are considerably more animated than the animals.

The winner of the contest is named "Queen of the Alps," an honor that can actually be quite lucrative for the owner; calves of the winning cow sell for as much as $25,000, 10 times the price of an ordinary calf.

TOSSING TOMATOES

Tomatina is the legendary Spanish tomato-throwing festival. Each August, about 25,000 Spaniards in the village of Bunol hurl as many as 265,000 pounds of ripe tomatoes at each other for 45 minutes to an hour, after which a loud firecracker signals the end of the fight and everyone pitches in to clean up the mess. Unlike the Italian Battle of the Oranges, this tradition only dates back about 50 years, when locals got so fed up with the mayor and the town priest that they spontaneously began pelting them with tomatoes during the town's annual fiesta.

RAT RACING

There's a new form of entertainment in Russia. "Members of Grand Dynamo, a fancy private club in Moscow, have a new way of escaping the daily rat race," *The New York Times* reported on August 4, 1995. "At night, gamblers, with Scotch tumblers and scorecards in hand, place their bets ($10 minimum) on large trained rats that scurry through a neon-lit, glass-encased racecourse, prompted by a hand bell rung by a *dwarf dressed as an 18th-century page.* 'We've always had a lot of rats in Russia,' smirked the manager of the club, 'but this is the first time they've been organized.' "

HISTORIC PASTIME: Rat Baiting

Rat baiting was one of the most popular betting games of Eastern port cities in the 1800s. According to one account, "A promoter would hire youngsters to trap the biggest waterfront rats they could find. Each rat would be tagged; then the rats were put in cages and starved until they were ravenous. Then they were all put into a rat pit, and spectators bet on which one would last the longest."

Your tax dollars at work: According to one government study, pigs can become alcoholics.

JUNK FOOD CONTROVERSY

As junk food has become an integral part of American life, it has become the focal point in several issues unrelated to eating.

FRITOS CORN CHIPS
Background: Introduced in 1932 by Elmer Doolin. Doolin, a Texan, bought the recipe—and the whole concept of the corn chip—from a cook at a Mexican border cafe. (He paid $100 for it.) Then he began turning out the chips by hand in his mother's kitchen, 10 pounds an hour. When demand increased, Doolin invented a machine that would make the chips automatically. As the company grew, it moved into larger quarters in Dallas, Texas. In 1945, the Frito Company merged with H. W. Lay and Co., the Atlanta-based maker of Lay's potato chips, and got national distribution.

The Controversy: In the '60s, Frito-Lay was accused of anti-Mexican racism (an ironic assertion, considering the origin of the product). The reason: It introduced the Frito Bandito, a mustachioed cartoon character who showed up on TV in 1967, ready to steal your Fritos Corn Chips.

• In his prime, the Bandito devised some pretty sneaky ways of fleecing gringos. One commercial showed the Apollo astronauts landing on the moon. Who do you think they found there waiting for them? The Frito Bandito, standing next to a parking meter with his burro. "I ham the moon parking lot attendant," he announced. "Now if you will kindly deposit one bag of cronchy Fritos corn cheeps for the first hour..."

• But after Frito-Lay decided to use him in all its commercials, the Mexican-American Anti-Defamation Committee protested publicly that the Bandito was spreading the "racist message that Mexicans are sneaky thieves." Frito vehemently denied any hidden meaning or racist intent. But several California TV stations quickly banned the commercials, and the Anti-Defamation Committee announced its intention of asking the FCC for equal time.

There's a "Cinderella" story in Finnish folklore. But the girl's name isn't Cinderella. It's Tuna.

Although he was an effective TV salesman, the Frito Bandito was ultimately withdrawn from Frito commercials.

HOSTESS TWINKIES

Background: Invented in 1931 by James Dewar, manager of Continental Bakeries' Chicago factory. He envisioned the product as a way of using the company's thousands of shortcake pans (which were otherwise employed only during the strawberry season) full-time...and as a way of having a low-priced snack to sell during the Depression. The cakes were originally called Little Shortcake Fingers, but during a business trip Dewar and a friend noticed a shoe factory sign that read, "Home of Twinkle Toe Shoes." Dewar had been looking for a new name for his product; his friend suggested he call it "Twinkle Fingers," which was shortened to "Twinkies." The five-cent snack soon became one of Continental's bestselling items.

The Controversy: In 1979, a San Francisco employee named Dan White went on a rampage and killed two important politicians—Mayor George Moscone and Supervisor Harvey Milk—in City Hall. His case seemed indefensible...but in the ensuing trial White's attorney, Douglas Schmidt, did come up with a defense. He blamed his client's behavior on junk food—specifically Twinkies. Psychiatrist Martin Blinder testified that White had eaten too many Twinkies, and that their high sugar content had resulted in "diminished mental capacity." It sounded preposterous, but to the shock of the grieving city, the jury bought this explanation and convicted White of voluntary manslaughter instead of murder. In San Francisco, people still refer to it as the "Twinkie defense."

PRINGLE'S POTATO CHIPS

Background: The potato chip was invented in 1853 by a chef named George Crum in Saratoga Springs, New York. Apparently, a customer at the restaurant where Crum worked kept sending back french fries, complaining that they were too thick. Finally, the exasperated Crum cut the potatoes paper-thin...and the customer loved them. "Saratoga Chips" became the specialty of the house, and ultimately a national snack.

• For many years, large food companies avoided manufacturing potato chips, despite their popularity. The reasons: Potato chips were hard to transport long distances without heavy breakage, and they got stale too quickly.

• Then, in 1969, General Mills and Proctor & Gamble each introduced "newfangled" kinds of potato chips. General Mills called theirs "Chipos." P&G called theirs "Pringle's Potato Chips."

• This new product wasn't a sliced potato (as the traditional chip is), but a wafer made from reconstituted potato granules. Each chip was made from scratch, so each could be formed in exactly the same shape and size—which meant that the chips could now be designed to be stackable, and thus could be packaged in break-proof cannisters, complete with preservatives...a food conglomerate's dream.

The Controversy: Would this mean the end of the potato chip as we knew it? Potato chip manufacturers were afraid it would—so in 1970, the Potato Chip Institute (the trade organization for potato chip makers around the U.S.) went on the offensive and sued General Mills for calling their Chipos "new-fashioned potato chips." Chipos, the chipmakers asserted, were not authentic chips, and General Mills had no right to equate them with America's "classic snack." "We don't like synthetics riding on the potato chip's reputation," said Francis X. Rice, the president of the organization.

By the time the suit gathered steam, however, it was clear that the new chips would never be as popular as the old ones. So the suit was quietly dropped.

• Frito-Lay, the nation's largest potato chip manufacturer, straddled the issue. They joined as a party in the Potato Chip Institute's suit, but also came out with their own new-style chip—Munchos—just in case.

★   ★   ★

WORD ORIGINS

Potluck. In the Middle Ages, cooks threw all their leftovers into a pot of water that was kept boiling most of the time. This makeshift stew was eaten by the family or fed to strangers when no other food was available. Since food was thrown in at random, its quality and taste depended entirely on luck.

Jukebox. The term *juke* was originally a New Orleans slang expression meaning "to have sex." Juke boxes got their name because they were popular in houses of prostitution known as *juke joints*.

Tip: If you have to give your dog a pill, put it far back on its tongue, then blow in its nose.

RUMORS

Why do people believe wild, unsubstantiated stories? According to some psychologists, "rumors make things easier than they are." And besides, they're fun. Here are a few you might have heard.

RUMOR: Microsoft, Inc., the world's largest computer software company, has purchased the Roman Catholic Church for "an unspecified number" of shares of Microsoft stock.

HOW IT SPREAD: In December 1994, someone posted a fake Associated Press story on the Internet claiming that the Vatican had agreed to a "friendly takeover" by the software giant. The bogus story went on to say that senior Microsoft executives would be appointed to the College of Cardinals, that Pope John Paul II would be named the senior vice president of Microsoft's "religious software division," and that sacraments would be made available online for the first time in the Church's 2,000-year history.

WHAT HAPPENED: At first the story didn't attract much attention, but then Rush Limbaugh mentioned it on his show and Microsoft was swamped with letters and phone calls. They had to issue a press release stating that "the story has no truth and was not generated by the company." The company (which has also had to deny that it's going to buy the IRS) never found out who was behind the spoof.

RUMOR: "Buddy," a little boy living in Scotland, is dying of cancer. His last wish is that he be listed in the *Guinness Book of World Records* as having the world's largest postcard collection.

HOW IT SPREAD: First by chain letters in 1982, then by word of mouth, computer networks, and even CB radio. But there is no Buddy—the letters were a hoax.

WHAT HAPPENED: Since 1982, post offices in Glasgow, Aberdeen and Paisley have received more than 10 million postcards from well-wishers. Even Ronald Reagan was fooled; he wrote Buddy a get-well letter in 1983. In a futile attempt to stem the flow of mail, the Scottish postal authorities have run ads in stamp journals and CB radio magazines asking the public to ignore the story. They also put pressure on Guinness to eliminate the category from its record books. Guinness did, in 1989, but postcards continue to pour into Scotland from all over the world.

Average age of top GM executives in 1994: 49.8 years. Average age of the Rolling Stones: 50.6.

The "Buddy" letters hoax was so successful that at least two *real* cancer-stricken children in Great Britain made the same request and were similarly flooded with postcards. One boy, Mario Morby, received more than 2 million cards. "I thought I was only going to get 48,000," he told reporters in 1990, "but they kept coming."

RUMOR: Someone is circulating the secret recipe for Mrs. Field's chocolate cookies free of charge through the mail.

HOW IT SPREAD: Different versions of the story and recipe have been circulating since 1987. According to one version, a woman purchased the recipe from the Mrs. Fields company itself, for what she thought was $2.50. But the company billed her $250—and when it refused to let her off the hook, she retaliated by mailing copies of the recipe to dozens of her friends and relatives. They passed it on from there, until thousands of the recipes were floating around the country.

WHAT HAPPENED: The company posted a notice in each of its more than 400 franchises stating that the story was false. It didn't do any good—the fake recipes are still in circulation.

RUMOR: A baby was born at the Woodstock Music Festival in August 1969.

HOW IT SPREAD: No one knows. It's part of the mythology of the event.

WHAT HAPPENED: Joel Makower, author of *Woodstock: The Oral History*, says: "Over the years I've received countless calls from nearly every major news organization in the U.S., and some from abroad: ABC, CBS, CNN, and NBC; the Associated Press, UPI, and Reuters. NPR checked in, as did *Rolling Stone* and producers from "Oprah" and "Nightline." They all wanted to know the same thing: Where is the Woodstock baby? But there are no Woodstock babies. I know. I've searched everywhere—and talked to everyone else who's searched. I checked hospital records and birth certificates...I interviewed the festival's producers, stage hands, and the head of Woodstock security....I talked to doctors and nurses who were pressed into service at the festival and who worked at nearby hospitals...I've talked to *everyone*. Read my lips: There was no baby born at Woodstock."

MORE STRANGE LAWSUITS

Bizarre doings in the halls of justice, from news reports.

P LAINTIFF: Ronald Askew, a 50-year-old banker
DEFENDANT: His ex-wife, Bonnette
LAWSUIT: In 1991, after more than a decade of marriage, Bonnette admitted to her husband that although she loved him, she'd never really found him sexually attractive. He sued her for fraud.
THE VERDICT: Incredibly, he won. The jury awarded him $242,000 in damages. However, the award was overturned.

PLAINTIFF: John Moore
DEFENDANT: Regents of the University of California
LAWSUIT: Moore claimed one of his organs was pirated. In 1976, University of California-Los Angeles Medical Center doctors removed Moore's spleen in a successful effort to cure his cancer. Doctors later found that the spleen possessed unique cancer-fighting cells; experiments with the cells led to a new discovery worth an estimated $3 billion. Moore, who was never told that his ex-organ had commercial value, sued for part of the profits.
THE VERDICT: In 1990, 14 years after the operation, Moore lost the case.

PLAINTIFF: Carl Sagan, world-famous astronomer
DEFENDANT: Apple Computer, Inc.
LAWSUIT: Late in 1993, computer designers at Apple code-named a new computer model *Sagan*. Traditionally, this is an honor—"You pick a name of someone you respect," explained one employee. "And the code is only used while the computer is being developed. It never makes it out of the company." Nonetheless, Sagan's lawyers complained that the code was "an illegal usurption of his name for commercial purposes" and demanded that it be changed. So Apple designers changed it to BHA. When Sagan

The Neanderthal's brain was bigger than yours is.

heard that it stood for "Butt-Head Astronomer, " he sued, contending that "Butt-Head" is "defamatory on its face."
THE VERDICT: Apple won.

PLAINTIFF: The Karolinska Institute, Stockholm, Sweden
DEFENDANT: Olaf Olavson
LAWSUIT: In 1910, Olavson was desperate for cash, so he sold his body to the Karolinska Institute (to be used for medical research after he died). But in 1911 he unexpectedly inherited a fortune and decided to "buy himself back." To his surprise, the institute wouldn't cooperate.

When Olavson flatly refused to donate his body, the institute actually sued for breach of contract.
THE VERDICT: Not only did Olavson owe his body to the Institute...he actually owed them money as well. The judge decided that since he'd had two teeth removed without the Institute's permission, Olavson had illegally tampered with their property.

PLAINTIFF: A 40-year-old woman from Poughkeepsie, N.Y.
DEFENDANT: Her plastic surgeon
LAWSUIT: The woman had an operation to tighten her stomach in 1979. When it was over, she realized that her bellybutton was now two and a half inches off center. She sued for malpractice, claiming "the operation had left a large deformed hole in her stomach and had disrupted her business and her life."
THE VERDICT: She was awarded $854,000 by the New York State Supreme Court, and ultimately settled with the doctor for $200,000

PLAINTIFF: Relatives of a recently deceased man
DEFENDANT: A Vallejo, California, cemetary
LAWSUIT: At the end of a funeral, cemetary employees realized that the coffin they were about to lower into the ground was too wide for the hole. They tried turning the coffin on its side, but mourners stopped them. Then the employees tried breaking off the handles; it didn't work. Finally, "they tried to force it by jumping up and down on the lid." The coffin broke, and the funeral had to be stopped. Relatives sued for $500,000.
THE VERDICT: Settled out of court.

A TOY IS BORN

Here are more stories about the toys we all grew up with.

RAGGEDY ANN
In the early 1900s, a little girl named Marcella Gruelle found a handmade doll in the attic of her parents' Connecticut home. It was dusty and torn, but Marcella liked it so much that her father repaired it and gave it a name: Raggedy Ann (inspired by two poems by James Whitcomb Riley: "The Raggedy Man" and "Little Orphan Annie").

Marcella spent so much time with the doll that her father (Johnny Gruelle), a cartoonist, started writing and illustrating stories about it. His books—the original *Raggedy Ann* series—made Raggedy Ann one of the most popular dolls of the 20th century.

LEGOS
At a local toy fair in 1954, a shopkeeper complained to Danish toymaker Godtfred Kirk-Christiansen that most modern toys didn't challenge children to think. That night, Christiansen came up with an idea for an integrated system of building blocks that locked together, enabling children to use their imaginations and build interesting structures not possible with standard blocks. He called his creation *Legos*, from the Danish words *leg godt*, which means "play well." Today Legos are in 70% of American and 80% of European homes with children—more than any other toy.

LIONEL TRAINS
Joshua Lionel Cohen was an inventor in the late 1900s. His earliest creations included fuses for land mines, primitive versions of the electronic doorbell, and something he called a "flowerpot light," (a small, battery-operated lamp which was intended to illuminate plants in hotel lobbies). He also invented a tiny electric motor, but couldn't figure out what to do with it. He finally stuffed one into a model train, named it Lionel (after himself), and sold it with 30 feet of track to a novelty store. Within a day or two the store asked for more. Cohen went into train-making full-time. By 1903, his Lionel Train Company had an entire catalog of trains and accessories.

Half of all Americans live within 50 miles of where they grew up.

Note: Cohen's trains made him rich, but he never earned any money—or credit—for his most famous invention: the battery-operated flowerpot light. It was such a loser that he sold the design to his business partner. The partner started selling the lights *without* the flowerpots under a new name—*The Eveready Flashlight.*

CABBAGE PATCH KIDS

Xavier Roberts, a Georgia folk artist, was selling his soft sculpture dolls at a craft fair when a customer walked up and asked him how much the dolls cost. Roberts had a splitting headache. He snapped back: "They're not for sale"—but quickly recovered and said: "They're up for adoption." The idea behind Cabbage Patch Kids was born.

Roberts carried the concept to extremes. He converted an old medical clinic into Babyland General Hospital, where employees "delivered" his "babies" and gave them "birth certificates" with names like Bessie Sue and Billie Jo. His dolls were ugly, but they still became a national craze in 1983. Customers in one toy store rioted after waiting over eight hours to buy the dolls. One woman broke her leg—and the store owner had to protect himself with a baseball bat.

Note: In 1980, Martha Nelson, a craft artist Roberts had worked with in the past, sued him, claiming he had stolen some of her soft sculpture techniques. The court ruled that Roberts *had* used some of Nelson's ideas, but since she never copyrighted the design, she wasn't entitled to any of the profits.

ANT FARMS

It was July 4, 1956, when the idea struck. "It just came to me in a flash," says "Uncle" Milton Levine—then a 32-year-old entrepreneur looking for new products to help expand his mail-order business. "I was at a Fourth of July picnic at my sister's house…I saw a bunch of ants around the pool. I saw a bunch of kids interested in the ants…and it came to me."

Levine's first ant farms sold for $1.98. To attract customers, he bought a 2-inch ad in the *Los Angeles Times*, inviting the curious to "watch ants dig tunnels and build bridges." "I got so many orders, you wouldn't believe it," he says. By 1990, he'd sold more than 12 million ant farms, containing more than 360 million ants.

FUN WITH ELVIS

*Imagine what a kick it would have been to hang out with the
King at Graceland. Well, it's too late now—but here
are some of the exciting moments you missed.*

AT THE POOL

Want to go for a dip? According to David Adler in *The Life
and Cuisine of Elvis Presley*, "Elvis enjoyed sitting around the
pool eating watermelon hearts. For entertainment while he ate, he
would float flashbulbs in the pool. Then he would take out a .22 and
shoot at them. When they were hit, they would flash, and then sink
to the bottom."

ON THE 4TH OF JULY

Every Independence Day at Graceland, Elvis had a "fireworks display." His Memphis Mafia split into two teams, put on gloves and
football helmets, and shot fireworks at each other. "They would level
arsenals of rockets and Roman candles at each other and blast away
at point-blank range for hours," says Steve Dunleavy in *Elvis: What
Happened?*

It was all laughs: "I've backed into burning rockets and had my ass
burned half off," laughs Elvis aide Red West. "I've seen Elvis bending
over a giant rocket and watched the thing go off while he is leaning
over it, nearly blowing his fool head off. [My brother] Sonny carries a
scar on his chest to this day where one of us tried to blow a rocket
through him. Roman candles would blow up in our hands. The house
caught fire twice."

DEMOLITION DERBY

When the King was bored, you never knew what might happen.
There was a beautiful little cottage in the corner of the Graceland
property. One day, Elvis decided to demolish it...so he put on a football helmet and revved up his bulldozer. The only problem: his father,
Vernon Presley, was sitting on the cottage porch.

According to Red West, "[He yelled] 'You better move, Daddy.'
Vernon asks why and Elvis says, 'Because I'm gonna knock the god-
damn house down.' ...Vernon gives one of those looks like 'Oh, Lor-
die,' but he doesn't say anything...he just gets up and Elvis starts

roaring away." To make it more interesting, Elvis and Red set the house on fire while they battered it with heavy machinery.

AT THE MOVIES

The King couldn't just go out to the movies whenever he felt like it—he would have been mobbed. So he rented the whole theater instead. "Elvis had private midnight screenings at the Memphian Theater," writes David Adler. "They were attended by about a hundred of his friends. Admission was free, and so was the popcorn, but you had to watch the movie on Elvis's terms. Elvis made the projectionist repeat his favorite scenes. If the action got slow, such as during a love scene, the projectionist would have to skip to the next good part. Elvis once saw *Dr. Strangelove* three times straight, with a number of scenes repeated so he could figure out exactly what was going on.

"Elvis liked James Bond and *Patton*, and any movie with Peter Sellers. His favorite movie of all time was *The Party*."

WATCHING TV

And, of course, you could always stay home and spend a quiet evening watching TV…as long as Elvis liked the programs. If not, there was a good chance he'd pull out a gun and shoot out the screen. "Honestly," Red West says, "I can't tell you how many television sets went to their death at the hands of Elvis….He would shoot out television sets in hotel rooms and in any one of the houses he had. He shot out a great big one at Graceland, in Memphis, the one he had in his bedroom."

A classic example: One afternoon in 1974, the TV was blaring while Elvis was eating his breakfast. His least favorite singer, Robert Goulet, came on. As Red related: "Very slowly, Elvis finishes what he has in his mouth, puts down his knife and fork, picks up this big mother of a .22 and—boom—blasts old Robert clean off the screen and the television set to pieces….He then puts down the .22, picks up his knife and fork and says, 'That will be enough of that s---,' and then he goes on eating."

Elvis Trivia: On his way to meet Richard Nixon in 1970 (to pose for the famous photo), the King had a sudden craving. He insisted that his driver pull over to buy a dozen honey-glazed donuts; then he polished them off as they drove to the White House.

Lard has more calories—902 per 100 g—than any other food. Butter has 876 per 100 g.

THE KING OF FARTS

Just when you think you've heard it all...someone comes up with something like this. It's from a little book called It's a Gas, *by Eugene Silverman, M.D., and Eric Rabkin, Ph.D. It's required reading for BRI history buffs.*

In all fairness to the farters of the world, the greatest of them all was not by his passing of gas also passing a judgment. His completely conscious control of his abilities was confirmed by numerous chemical examinations, including two in published form. This man, a hero at bottom, was a gentle and loving father, a noble and steadfast friend, a successful and generous businessman, and a great stage entertainer. This unique individual, a phenomenon among phenomena, an explosive personality and credit to our subject, was christened Joseph Pujol, but invented for himself the name by which all history knows him: Le Petomane!

THE ART OF THE FART

Le Petomane could fart as often and as frequently as he wished. His farts were odorless. As other people use their mouths, Le Petomane had learned to use his anus. Furthermore, by constricting or loosening his anus he could vary the pitch of the air he expelled, and by controlling the force of abdominal contraction he could control its loudness. With these two fundamental tools, simple enough but rarely seen, Le Petomane contrived to imitate not only a variety of farts, but to make music.

He headlined at the Moulin Rouge in Paris, the most famous nightclub in the world at that time, and brought in box office receipts more than twice as high as those of the angelic Sarah Bernhardt. He was one of the greatest comedians of the turn of the century. The manager of the Moulin Rouge kept nurses in the theater to tend to female customers whose uncontrolled laughter in tight corsets often caused them to pass out as Le Petomane passed gas. Here was not a court fool at all, but the toast of civilized society.

DISCOVERING HIS GIFT

As a boy, Joseph had had a frightening experience in the sea. Holding his breath and ducking underwater, he suddenly felt a rush of cold water enter his bowels. He went to find his mother but was embarrassed to see water running out of himself. Although he recounted this in later years, apparently as a child he tried to keep his terrifying experience a secret.

Early in his married life he was called to military service and in the all-male atmosphere of the barracks he recounted for the first time his strange experience in the sea. When asked for a demonstration, he agreed to try again. On their next furlough, he and his unit went to the sea. He did succeed in taking water in and then letting it out. This might have been viewed as mere freakishness, but combined with Joseph's gentleness and good humor, it struck the soldiers as a delightful feat.

Pujol, using a basin, practiced this art in private with water and, once able to control the intake and outflow by combined exertions of his anal and abdominal muscles, he soon began to practice with air as well. This, of course, was only for his own amusement and the occasional amusement of his fellow soldiers.

A STAR IS BORN

When he returned home, he resumed his life as a baker and father but added to it his newfound love of entertainment. He began to work part-time in music halls as an ordinary singer, as a trombone player, and soon as a quick-change artist with a different costume for each song. He began to add comic routines of his own writing to his singing and playing acts, and was quite popular locally.

At the same time, he began to turn his special ability into an act, learning to give farts as imitations. Soon his friends urged him to add this to his act, but he was diffident about the propriety of such a thing. In order to give it a try, he rented a theater of his own. He was an almost instant success. He left the bakery in care of his family and went to a number of provincial capitals, at each stop playing to packed houses. Finally, in 1892, he blew into Paris.

HIS FART'S DESIRE

The Moulin Rouge was his aim—and he went right for it. The manager of the Moulin Rouge, one Oller, on hearing of Le Petomane's specialty, was astounded at Pujol's audacity but agreed to give him an audition. In Paris as in Marseille, the act was an instant success.

Ancient Egyptians shaved off their eyebrows when their cats died as a sign of mourning.

HIS ACT

Le Petomane would begin by walking out dressed quite elegantly in silks and starched white linen, a thorough swell.

After his opening monologue Le Petomane leaned forward, hands on knees, turned his back to the audience, and began his imitations. "This one is a little girl," he would say and emit a delicate, tiny fart. "This one is a mother-in-law," he'd say, and there would be a slide. "This is a bride on her wedding night," very demure indeed, "and this the morning after," a long, loud one. Then he would do a dressmaker tearing two yards of calico, letting out a cracking, staccato fart that lasted at least ten seconds, and then cannonfire, thunder, and so on. The public loved the act, and the Moulin Rouge gave him an immediate contract. In a short time, he was their headliner.

A PATRON OF THE FARTS

His act grew with his popularity. Among other feats he could mix into the performance were those dependent upon inserting a rubber tube in his rectum (very decorously passed through his pocket). With this tube he could amiably chat away while at the same time smoking a cigarette. Sometimes he would insert a six-stop flute into the tube and accompany his own singing. A few simple nursery tunes he could play without recourse to the tube at all. And finally, he would almost always end his acts by blowing out a few of the gas-fired footlights. All that was left, before rising and bowing out, was to invite the audience to join him—and they did with gusto, their own convulsed abdomens insuring that many of the patrons could indeed participate in the group farting at the appropriate moment.

SPECIAL PERFORMANCES

The management of the Moulin Rouge wanted Le Petomane to submit to a medical examination so that his authenticity would be even more accepted, and this he did. For similar reasons of believability, Oller allowed Pujol to give private performances for all-male audiences at which he could perform wearing pants with an appropriate cut-out.

Before these events, and before his regular performances as well,

Peanuts are one of the ingredients used to make dynamite.

he thoroughly washed himself by drawing water in and then shooting it out. In the smaller groups he would extinguish a candle at the distance of a foot and demonstrate his water jet over a range of four or five yards. These distances are also corroborated by medical observation.

FARTING IN EUROPE

The Moulin Rouge, acting as **Le Petomane's** agent, also encouraged him to travel abroad. In other European countries, and especially in Belgium, he was a star attraction. At his private performances in France, where no admission was charged, Pujol would finish by passing the hat. At one of these gatherings a man leaned forward and put a 20 louis gold piece in the hat and told him to keep it, that the show was worth it although he had had to travel from Brussels to see it. He had heard so much about Le Petomane but could not see him in his own country because his own movements were so closely watched there. So he had come to Paris that night incognito to see and hear the great Le Petomane. He was King Leopold II of Belgium.

FINAL PASSING

The Medical Faculty at the Sorbonne offered Pujol 25,000 francs for the right to examine his body after his death. He was a vigorous man, a proud patriarch, and, knowing what such a sum could mean to his children and grandchildren, he accepted. But, despite the fact that he had distinguished himself by publicly displaying himself for so many years, he was held in such regard by those around him that, on his peaceful demise in 1945 at the age of 88, the family refused the offer. And so, having made flatulence a subject not for aggression but for pleasantry, Joseph Pujol, the greatest farter in history, came to his proper end.

★ ★ ★

A PAUSE FOR POETRY

A profound poem by Sir John Suckling, 17th-century cavalier poet:
Love is the fart
    of every heart
        For when held in,
            doth pain the host,
                But when released,
                    Pains others most.

AT THE OSCARS

*Here are a few lesser-known stories about
the Academy Awards ceremonies.*

THAT LITTLE GOLD STATUE

• According to legend, the Oscar was named in 1931 when a secretary at the Academy saw the statuette and exclaimed, "Why, he reminds me of my Uncle Oscar!" A reporter overheard the remark and used it in a story, and the name stuck.

• In 1942, gold and bronze were being used in the war, so Oscars were made out of plaster. (Actor Barry Fitzgerald accidentally decapitated his plaster Oscar while practicing his golf swing indoors.)

• When Dustin Hoffman accepted his Oscar in 1979, he described the statuette for the audience: "He has no genitalia and he's holding a sword."

HOSTS WITH THE MOST (OR LEAST)

• At the 1947 Oscar ceremony, Ronald Reagan supplied live narration for "Parade of Stars," a silent compilation of Oscar-winning films. Oblivious to the fact that the film was running upside down, backward, and showing on the ceiling instead of on a screen, Reagan kept reading: "This picture embodies the glories of our past, the memories of our present, and the inspiration of our future."

• Comedian Jerry Lewis was the host in 1958, when the Oscar ceremony actually finished 20 minutes earlier than expected. No one realized the show was ending early until they were well into the closing number, "There's No Business Like Show Business." Lewis shouted "Twenty more times!" and tried to drag out the finale by grabbing a baton and conducting the orchestra. Actors onstage paired up and started dancing. Meanwhile, the audience started to get up and leave. Dean Martin danced by the podium and grabbed a leftover Oscar.

A few minutes later, Lewis picked up a trumpet and started trying to play it. That's when NBC turned its cameras off. Eventually, NBC had to plug the hole with a short film on pistol shooting.

If you're like most people, your fingernails grow 4 times as fast as your toenails.

NO-SHOWS

Not everyone shows up for Oscar night:

• Robert Rich won the Best Screenplay Oscar in 1956 for *The Brave One*, but never claimed his award. That's because there *was* no Robert Rich. The winner was actually Dalton Trumbo, one of the notorious Hollywood Ten, a group of writers who had been blacklisted for their left-wing views. Trumbo managed to sneak himself onto the nomination list by using "Robert Rich" as a pseudonym.

• In 1970, the Academy decided to give Orson Welles an honorary Oscar—presumably to make up for the fact that they'd snubbed him for *Citizen Kane* in 1941. When he didn't show up to accept it, the Academy announced that he was out of the country. Actually, he was just a few miles away, watching the Awards on television.

• That same year, George C. Scott refused a Best Actor Oscar for his title role in the movie *Patton*. Instead of attending the ceremony, he says he watched a hockey game on TV, then went to bed.

• In 1979, 79-year-old Melvyn Douglas was nominated as Best Supporting Actor for *Being There*. His chief competition was child star Justin Henry, who played the contested child in the divorce drama, *Kramer vs. Kramer*. Douglas didn't show up for Oscar night, and told reporters: "The whole thing is absurd, my competing with an 8-year-old." Although Henry did show up, Douglas still won.

AND THE WINNER IS...

• In 1984, F. Murray Abraham won the Oscar for Best Actor. (He played the jealous composer Antonio Salieri in the movie *Amadeus*.) Until then, Abraham's most prominent screen role had been as a leaf in a Fruit of the Loom underwear commercial.

• In 1946, *The Razor's Edge* failed to win the Oscar for Best Picture...but it *was* named the year's best by the National Association of Barbers.

• Humphrey Bogart wasn't thrilled at winning an Oscar for *African Queen*: "Hell," he remarked, "I hope I'm never nominated again. It's meat and potatoes roles for me from now on."

Five cows were killed in drive-by shootings in Clay County, Missouri, in 1992.

• Playwright George Bernard Shaw was livid about winning the Best Screenplay Oscar for *Pygmalion*. "It's an insult," he whined. "To offer me an award of this sort is an insult, as if they have never heard of me before…and it's very likely they never have."

• The nameplate on Spencer Tracy's first Oscar was mistakenly made out to *Dick* Tracy.

WINNERS, PART II

The ultimate Oscar winner-loser story involved a little-known Polish director named Zbignew Rybcyznski, who was nominated for Best Animated Short in 1983:

• Presenter Kristy McNichol tried to pronounce his name as a nominee, but giggled and gave up halfway through. When Rybcyznski won, McNichol tried again. This time she called him "Zbigniewski Sky."

• Rybcyznski made his acceptance speech through an interpreter, but they were cut off when the orchestra struck up the theme from "Loony Tunes."

• Co-presenter Matt Dillon tried to ease Rybcyznski off the stage, but the director held his ground by shaking Dillon's hand and kissing McNichol. He added some final words, but the interpreter lost them in the translation. They came out, "On the occasion of the film like *Gandhi*, which will portray Lech Walesa and Solidarity."

• Later in the evening, Rybcyznski stepped out for a cigarette. He tried to return to his seat, but a guard wouldn't let him back in. The guard didn't believe that Rybcyznski, who was dressed in a tuxedo and tennis shoes, was a guest. Rybcyznski got angry, kicked the guard, and wound up in jail.

• The director asked for attorney Marvin Mitchelson, who specializes in palimony cases, because he was the only Hollywood lawyer he could think of.

• Mitchelson took the case, but on the following conditions: "First, bring me an interpreter; and then tell me how to pronounce his name." The charges were dropped.

• Rybcyznski's conclusion: "Success and defeat are quite intertwined."

The Mirage Hotel in Las Vegas has 12 gardeners on its staff to care for artificial plants.

PRIMETIME PROVERBS

Here are some more TV quotes from the book
Primetime Proverbs, *by Jack Mingo and John Javna.*

ON POLITICS
"When I was in third grade, there was a kid running for office. His slogan was: 'Vote for me and I'll show you my wee-wee.' He won by a landslide."

> —Dorothy,
> **"The Golden Girls"**

ON "FREE LOVE"
"You American girls have such big breasts all the time...So please, give us the number of your apartment so we can go up there and have sex with you now!"

> —Dan Aykroyd
> **(The Wild and Crazy Guy),**
> **"Saturday Night Live"**

ON PETS
[*To his dog*] "You're glad to see me every minute of your life. I come home, you jump around and wag your tail. I go to the closet, I come out, you jump around and wag your tail. I turn my face away and turn it back, you wag your tail. Either you love me very much or your short-term memory is shot."

> **Dr. Harry Weston,**
> **—"Empty Nest"**

"The only good cat is a stir-fried cat."

> **—Alf, "ALF"**

COP TALK
Witness: [*refusing to testify because he doesn't want to "get involved"*] "Mr. Friday, if you were me, would you want to get involved?"
Sgt. Joe Friday: "Can I wait a while?"
Witness: "Huh?"
Friday: "Before I'm you."

> **—"Dragnet"**

Killer: "You made a mistake, and I'm not going to pay for it."
Sgt. Joe Friday: "You're going to use a credit card?"

> **—"Dragnet"**

ON LINGUISTICS
"Due to the shape of the North American elk's esophagus, even if it could speak, it could not pronounce the word *lasagna*."

> **—Cliff Clavin, "Cheers"**

"You must always keep abreast of other tongues."

> **—Batman, "Batman"**

The average yawn lasts 6 seconds.

GIVE 'EM HELL, HARRY

Here are a few words from President Harry Truman.

"I never did give anybody hell. I just told the truth, and they thought it was hell."

"The C students run the world."

"The only things worth learning are the things you learn after you know it all."

"You know what makes leadership? It is the ability to get men to do what they don't want to do, and like it."

"You want a friend in this life, get a dog."

"The best way to give advice to your children is to find out what they want and advise them to do it."

"Men don't change. The only thing new in the world is the history you don't know."

"It's a recession when your neighbor loses his job; it's a depression when you lose yours."

"If you can't convince them, confuse them."

"A politician is a man who understands government—and it takes a politician to run a government. A statesman is a politician who's been dead ten or fifteen years."

"Whenever you have an efficient government, you have a dictatorship."

"Whenever a fellow tells me he's bipartisan, I know he's going to vote against me."

"Polls are like sleeping pills designed to lull voters into sleeping on election day. You might call them 'sleeping polls.' "

"I think there is an immense shortage of Christian charity among so-called Christians."

"I look with commiseration over the great body of my fellow citizens who, reading newspapers, live and die in the belief they have known something of what has been passing in the world around them."

"Secrecy and a free, democratic government don't mix."

THE ROMAN GAMES

The Roman Colosseum is one of the most famous structures in the world. What went on there? You've probably seen a gladiator fight or two in films, but chances are it was tame compared to the real-life action. Here's the gruesome story, from the BRI's Ancient History Department.

HISTORY

The ancient Romans were afraid of ghosts and believed that restless spirits of the dead could be appeased through bloodshed. Thus, it was common that when a Roman noble died, his friends and loved ones would hire gladiators to fight to the death in a battle arranged especially for the funeral.

The first such battle was held in 264 B.C., and over the centuries they became so popular that people began to hold them whether or not there was a funeral, just for the thrill of watching people die.

As these spectacles grew in popularity, larger and larger staging areas were needed. In 69 A.D., the Roman Emperor Vespasian ordered the building of the Flavian Amphitheater, Rome's first permanent amphitheater. Today it's better known as the Colosseum.

Building the Colosseum allowed Vespasian to keep the more than one million citizens of Rome under control by quenching their thirst for blood in a way that did not threaten the Empire. Just as the earliest gladiator battles had soothed uneasy spirits, the games at the Colosseum soothed the restless population of Rome. And because most emperors were enthusiastic spectators at the games, it established a bond between emperors and the common person.

THE STRUCTURE

• The amphitheater was the largest building of its kind on Earth. More than 150 feet high, it measured 620 by 513 feet and enclosed an oval arena that was 287 feet long by 180 feet wide. It held 50,000 people.

• Seating was arranged according to class: the emperor, his Vestal Virgins, and other important officials sat in ringside boxes; behind them were tiers of marble seats divided into two areas: one for "distinguished private citizens"; and another for the members of the middle class. Behind the marble seats was a section for "slaves and

---

Elephants can't jump. Every other mammal can.

foreigners"; behind that was an enclosed gallery set aside for women and the poor, with wooden seats much like bleachers in today's baseball parks.

A TYPICAL DAY AT THE COLOSSEUM

• Festivities began at dawn and often lasted well into the night. "Second-rate" events were scheduled during mealtimes, however, so that spectators could return home for lunch without missing much. The feeding of Christians to the lions is believed by many historians to have been one of the mealtime events.

• On the mornings of the games, the gladiators rode by chariot from their barracks to the amphitheater and marched into the arena up to the Emperor's box, where they stuck their right arms straight out and chanted, "Hail, Caesar and emperor, those who are about to die salute you."

• The day often began with bloodless duels that mimicked the more violent events to come. Women, or sometimes dwarfs or cripples, battled one another using wooden swords that were made to look like metal.

• After this event ended, an attendant would blow the *tuba*, or war trumpet, to announce the beginning of the main event—most often a battle between gladiators.

The Gladiators

Finding enough gladiators to keep the bloodthirsty spectators happy was difficult. Most were recruited from the ranks of slaves, convicts, or prisoners of war. A handful were bankrupt nobles and freemen who needed money. Recruits signed contracts in which they agreed to be "burnt with fire, shackled with chains, whipped with rods, and killed with steel," and were trained in gladiator schools all over the empire.

• Each gladiator was trained to use a particular set of weapons. There were four main categories:

    1. The Samnite, who wore a helmet, a metal shin guard on the left leg, and a leather sleeve on the right arm; and carried a sword and shield;

    2. The Thracian, who wore no armor but carried a small sword and round shield;

    3. The Myrmillo, or Fishman, who wore a helmet and carried a small sword, shield, and a stick weighted with lead;

Taxpayers spent $57,000 on gold-embossed playing cards for Air Force One in 1992.

4. The Retiarii, who wore no armor and carried only a net, trident (three-pronged spear), and dagger.

• Gladiators sometimes fought either one-on-one or two-on-two. Other times, entire squads of gladiators battled it out. As many as 2,000 men might battle in a single day, with half of them getting killed in the process.

Begging for Mercy

Gladiators usually fought to the death, although the loser had a chance of escaping with his life (but not his dignity) intact. When it became clear to a gladiator that he was going to be defeated, he could cast away his shield and raise a finger on his left hand—this was the gesture used to throw oneself upon the mercy of the emperor.

• The emperor would then ask the crowd to help him decide the gladiator's fate. They would shout *Mitte!* ("Let him go free!") and give the emperor a thumbs-up, or *Iugula!* ("Pay the penalty!") and give the emperor a thumbs-down. The emperor would then give either a thumbs-up or a thumbs-down, and his orders would be carried out.

ANIMAL GAMES

The Romans also loved to watch professional *bestiarii* ("beast slayers," who weren't considered gladiators) kill fierce animals such as lions, tigers, bulls, or bears—or just about anything that could bleed to death. Many of the events involved the killing of ostriches, deer, and even giraffes.

• The Romans scoured the Empire and its provinces looking for things to kill; by the time the animal hunts were abolished in the sixth century A.D., several species of animals, including the elephants of North Africa, the hippopotami of Nubia, the lions of Mesopotamia, and the tigers of Hyrcania had all been driven to extinction.

• Some of the animal events involved audience participation. Spectators were invited to throw spears from their seats or to use bows and arrows; at other events, skilled hunters entered the arena and chased down the animals with hounds. At still other events, it was the wild animals who hunted *people*, when condemned criminals (or regular criminals, if condemned criminals were in short supply) would be thrown to them completely defenseless.

WATER SPORTS

For really special occasions, the heavy wooden planks that served as the floor of the arena would be removed and the stadium flooded with water so that mock sea battles could be staged. The Colosseum's opening day celebrations in 80 A.D. had just such a sea battle; it involved hundreds of boats, more than 3,000 participants, and was watched by an estimated 50,000 spectators. It was just as bloody as the regular gladiator fights; the only difference was that the gladiators were in boats. The sea battle was followed by an animal hunt, in which more than 5,000 animals were killed.

THE END

When Christianity became the official religion of the Roman Empire in 392, pressure began to build for the games to be abandoned. In 404, a Christian monk named Telemachus tried to break up a gladitorial duel by jumping into the ring and physically separating the combatants...and was stoned to death by the crowd for his efforts. The resulting scandal was so great that Emperor Honorius, who had previously been a fan of the games, abolished them later that year.

• Was it a mistake? As the Empire made a transition from paganism to Christianity, critics predicted that abandoning the old religion and ways—under which the Roman Empire had risen to unparalleled greatness—would cause Rome to collapse. The Colosseum closed amid dire predictions of doom. "If the Colosseum falls, Rome falls," the saying went. Sure enough, in 410 A.D., the Eternal City was sacked by the Visigoths.

Note: The Colosseum looks like it's been damaged by an earthquake, but actually most of the destruction has come at the hands of humans, who've plundered it for building materials over the centuries. (A lot of the stones were used to build St. Peter's Basilica.) The structure's pockmarked appearance is due to the fact that during the Middle Ages—when metal was particularly hard to come by—generations of Romans pried loose the metal fittings that held the stones together. Today gravity is the only thing that holds many of the stone blocks up; and thanks to the vibrations from auto traffic, the stones are slowly shifting and putting the entire Colosseum in danger of collapse.

Bloodhounds are the only animals whose evidence is admissible in U.S. courts.

THE SPACE RACE, PART I

It wasn't long ago that space travel was still just a dream. Then both the U.S. and Russia developed the technology to make it possible. Did we work together to benefit humankind? Don't be silly. We started a Space Race.

OCTOBER 4, 1957
Bulletin:

London—

Moscow radio said tonight that the Soviet Union has launched an Earth satellite.

The satellite, silver in color, weighs 184 pounds and is reported to be the size of a basketball.

Moscow radio said it is circling the globe every 96 minutes, reaching out as far out as 569 miles as it zips along at more than 17,000 miles per hour.

That was how the Associated Press reported the launching of *Sputnik*, the first shot fired by the Soviet Union in the Space Race. Within minutes, word of the launch spread around the globe.

Unspoken in the AP bulletin, but instinctively understood by every American who heard the news was the fact that America, the leader of the free world, was now in second place in the Space Race, trailing far behind a "backward" Communist country that couldn't even build decent refrigerators.

CAUGHT OFF GUARD

"The public outcry after Sputnik was ear-splitting," historian Walter McDougall writes in *The Heavens and the Earth*. "No event since Pearl Harbor set off such repercussions in public life." President Eisenhower dismissed *Sputnik* and promised that the U.S. was well ahead of the USSR in the ballistic missile race. But the public remained jittery and unconvinced. Alan Shepard writes in *Moon Shot*,

> The United States had been considered the world's unchallenged technological leader, with the Soviets trailing far behind. The satellite not only marked the emergence of the Soviet Union as a technologically accomplished society, but it demonstrated for the first time that the Russian military had the rocket power to deliver nu-

---

When Italy was founded in 1861, only 3% of Italians spoke Italian fluently.

clear weapons across continents and oceans. American skies had been violated. During World War II no Nazi or Japanese aircraft had penetrated U.S. air space. But here was Sputnik, made in Russia, passing overhead several times a day.

"People of the whole world are pointing to the satellite," Soviet Premier Nikita Khrushchev boasted to the Soviet media. "They are saying the United States has been beaten."

Sputnik II

Thirty days after the first launch, *Sputnik II* was sent into space carrying a live dog. *Sputnik II* did at least affirm America's sense of *moral* superiority to the Russians. "The fate of the space dog became a matter of sentimental concern," McDougall writes, "and Americans even hoped for days that the Soviets would return the pup safely to Earth. When it became clear that the dog would die in orbit, Communist 'beastliness' was confirmed."

THE U.S. RESPONDS

Shortly after *Sputnik II*, the Eisenhower administration announced that the U.S. would launch a satellite. The media buildup was enormous, and when the day came the eyes of the entire world were on the *Vanguard* rocket. Unfortunately, instead of soaring into space, it collapsed into flames on the launchpad, then exploded. Media reports called it "the most publicized failure in history," and even our Allies called it "flopnik," "Kaputnik," and "Stayputnik."

The U.S. finally succeeded in putting a satellite in orbit on February 1, 1958, but it was so small—12 pounds—compared to the *Sputnik* satellite that Khrushchev ridiculed it as an "orbiting grapefruit."

NASA IS BORN

Later in 1958, Congress created the National Aeronautics and Space Administration—NASA—to pursue the exploration of space. It was a statement to the world that regardless of what the Russians were doing, the U.S. would use space for peaceful purposes.

Selection of candidates for the space program began right away, even before NASA knew exactly what it wanted to do in space. President Eisenhower himself decided in late 1958 how the astronauts would be chosen. All would have to be military pilots, younger than 40, under 5'11" (a space capsule couldn't take anyone larger than that), in perfect physical shape, and an expert jet pilot with more than 1,500 hours of flying time.

NASA found 110 men who met these standards. Of these, 56 were picked to travel to Washington for interviews that would separate the "doubtfully motivated" from the genuinely qualified. ("We don't want any glory-seekers," one interviewer explained.) A sample question: "Give twenty answers to the question, 'Who am I?' " "The first few answers to that one were easy," astronaut John Glenn recalled years later. "I am a man, I am a Marine, I am a flier, I am a husband, I am an officer. When you got down to the end, it was not so easy to figure out just *who* you were." After intelligence and physical tests, the number of qualified candidates was reduced to seven. NASA was only looking for six, but they decided to take all seven anyway.

SPACE POLITICS

During the 1960 presidential campaign, space superiority became a volatile political issue. Senator John Kennedy cited the "space gap" as an example of America's lost international prestige and a threat to national security. "Control of space will be decided in the next decade," he said. "If the Soviets control space, they can control Earth, as in past centuries the nation that controlled the seas dominated the continents."

But when President Kennedy took office and discovered there wasn't really that much of a threat, he backed away from his campaign rhetoric. Approached for funds by his science advisor, he said: "Can't you fellows invent some other race that will do some good here on Earth?"

His attitude changed again in April when the Bay of Pigs fiasco made headlines just as Soviet cosmonaut Yuri Gagarin became the first human to orbit the Earth. Kennedy put the space program back on the front burner and called a meeting of America's space experts, demanding to know how they could overtake the Russians in space. "Nothing is more important," he told them.

See p. 383 for The Space Race, Part II.

Miller Brewing donated $150,000 to its Thurgood Marshall Scholarship Fund in 1993...

EVERYDAY ORIGINS

Some quick stories about the origins of everyday objects.

SCOTCH TAPE. Believe it or not, the sticky stuff gets its name from an ethnic slur. When two-toned paint jobs became popular in the 1920s, Detroit carmakers asked the 3-M Company for an alternative to masking tape that would provide a smooth, sharp edge where the two colors met. 3-M came up with two-inch wide cellophane tape, but auto companies said it was too expensive. So 3-M lowered the price by applying adhesive only along the sides of the strip. That caused a problem: the new tape didn't stick—and company painters complained to the 3-M sales reps, "Take this tape back to your stingy 'Scotch' bosses and tell them to put more adhesive on it!" The name—and the new tape—stuck.

BRASSIERES. Mary Phelps Jacob, a teenage debutante in 1913, wanted to wear a rose-garlanded dress to a party one evening. But as she later explained, her corset cover "kept peeping through the roses around my bosom." So she took it off, pinned two handkerchiefs together, and tied them behind her back with some ribbon. "The result was delicious," she later recalled. "I could move much more freely, a nearly naked feeling." The contraption eventually became known as a *brassiere*—French for "arm protector"—a name borrowed from the corset cover it replaced. (Jacob later became famous for riding naked through the streets of Paris on an elephant.)

DINNER KNIVES. Regular knives first had their points rounded and their sharp edges dulled for use at the dinner table in 1669. According to Margaret Visser, author of *The Rituals of Dinner*, this was done "apparently to prevent their use as 'toothpicks,' but probably also to discourage assassinations at meals."

WRISTWATCHES. Several Swiss watchmakers began attaching small watches to bracelets in 1790. Those early watches weren't considered serious timepieces and remained strictly a women's item until World War I, when armies recognized their usefulness in battle and began issuing them to servicemen instead of the traditional pocket watch.

FORKS. Before forks became popular, the difference between refined and common people was the number of fingers they ate with. The upper classes used three; everyone else used five. This began to change in the 11th century, when tiny, two-pronged forks became fashionable in Italian high society. But they didn't catch on; the Catholic Church opposed them as unnatural (it was an insult to imply that the fingers God gave us weren't good enough for food) and people who used them were ridiculed as effeminate or pretentious. Forks weren't generally considered polite until the 18th century—some 800 years after they were first introduced.

PULL-TOP BEER CANS. In 1959 a mechanical engineer named Ermal Cleon Fraze was at a picnic when he realized he'd forgotten a can opener. No one else had one either, so he had to use the bumper of his car to open a can of soda. It took half an hour, and he vowed he'd never get stuck like that again. He patented the world's first practical pull-top can later that year, and three years later, the Pittsburgh Brewing Company tried using it on its Iron City Beer. Now every beer company does.

REFRIGERATOR MAGNETS. Mass-produced magnets *designed* for refrigerators didn't appear until 1964. They were invented by John Arnasto (son of the guy who invented Eskimo Pies) and his wife, Arlene, who sold a line of decorative wall hooks. Arlene thought it would be cute to have a hook for refrigerator doors, so John made one with a magnet backing. The first one had a small bell and was shaped like a tea kettle; it sold well, so the Arnastos added dozens of other versions to their line. Believe it or not, some of the rare originals are now worth more than $100.

TOOTHPASTE TUBES. Toothpaste wasn't packaged in collapsible tubes until 1892, when Dr. Washington Wentworth Sheffield, a Connecticut dentist, copied the idea from a tube of oil-based paint. Increased interest in sanitation and hygiene made it more popular than jars of toothpaste, which mingled germs from different brushes. Toothpaste tubes became the standard almost overnight.

GONE, BUT NOT FORGOTTEN

You can see them in museums or in books—but you won't see them on the road, because no one makes them anymore. Here's some info about five automobile legends.

THE PIERCE-ARROW (1901-1938). One of the most prestigious cars of its day, the Pierce Arrow set the standards for luxury and performance. According to one auto critic, "Even a massive limousine could whisper along at 100-mph—uniformed chauffeur up front; tycoon, cigar, and *Wall St. Journal* in the rear. (Some cars had speedometers back there so the owner could keep an eye on the chauffer's lead-foot tendencies.)" Pierce Arrow was the car of choice for rumrunners—who liked its quiet engine and reliability—and presidents: Woodrow Wilson rode in a customized Pierce Arrow limousine; so did FDR and J. Edgar Hoover (theirs were bulletproof).

Fate: When the Depression hit, the company kept building expensive cars, thinking the business downturn was temporary. Sales dropped from a high of 10,000 cars in 1929 to only 167 in 1937. The company was sold at auction a year later.

THE REO (1905-1936). In 1904, Ransom Eli Olds left the Olds Motor Co. and began a new one. The Olds Motor Company wouldn't let him use his last name—but couldn't stop him from using his initials, so he called it the Reo Motor Car Co. By 1907 it had become the third largest auto manufacturer, after Ford and Buick. Five years later, Olds announced his retirement and introduced his last car, Reo the Fifth (the company's fifth model).

Fate: Olds retired from day-to-day operations but retained enough veto power to make himself a nuisance. As a result, Reo began to lag behind its competitors. Olds finally gave up control in 1934, but it was too late: two years later the company became yet another victim of the Great Depression.

THE STUTZ BEARCAT (1911-1935). Grandfather of the American muscle car, it was built for speed. According to legend,

---

There are 12 letters in the Hawaiian alphabet.

founder Harry Stutz designed his clutches with "springs so stiff that a woman couldn't operate them." It was a teenager's dream car in the 'teens and 'twenties because it won so many races. In 1912, it won 25 of the 30 national races it entered, and in 1915, Cannonball Baker drove a 4-cylinder Bearcat from San Diego to New York in less than 12 days, shattering the transcontinental record.

Fate: Another casualty of the Depression. Stutz couldn't slash costs and prices fast enough to stay competitive. In January 1935 it got out of the passenger-car business and went bankrupt 2 years later.

THE DUESENBERG (1920-1937). To the driver of the 1920s, the name Duesenberg meant the top of the line: "The Duesenberg was more than a status symbol; it was status pure and simple, whether the owner was a maharajah, movie star, politician, robber, baron, gangster or evangelist....'He drives a Duesenberg' was the only copy in many company advertisements." The first passenger cars rolled off the assembly line in 1920; for the next 17 years the phrase "It's a Duesy" meant the very best.

Fate: Duesenberg was the best carmaker of its day—but it was probably the worst run. The Duesenberg brothers were notoriously bad administrators. Chronic mismanagement, combined with the stock market crash of 1929, pushed the ailing company permanently into the red. It collapsed in 1937.

KAISER (1946-1955). When World War II ended in 1945, shipbuilding magnate Henry J. Kaiser decided to start his own car company. The U.S. government wasn't buying ships anymore, and the auto industry hadn't released any new models since the beginning of the war. Kaiser thought he could beat existing carmakers to market with flashy new models, and change the Big 3 to the Big 4.

Kaiser's 1946 models *did* make the Big 3's cars look dowdy and old-fashioned in comparison. The company's sales hit 70,000 in 1947—but it soon ran into trouble.

Fate: Ford, GM, and Chrysler shed their prewar image in 1947 and 1948, and began beating Kaiser on price. The situation became desperate: some years Kaiser's sales were so bad that rather than introduce a new model, the company just changed the serial numbers on unsold cars and introduced *them* as the new models. In 1954 the company merged with Willys-Overland (forerunner of the Jeep company); a year later the Kaiser line was discontinued.

Humans are the only animals that cry tears.

BASEBALL NAMES

If you're a baseball fan, you know these names by heart.
But we'll bet you don't know where they came from.
Here are the stories behind some team names.

Los Angeles Dodgers. Formed in Brooklyn, New York, in 1890. Brooklyn had hundreds of trolleys zigzagging through its streets, and pedestrians were constantly scurrying out of their way. That's why their baseball team was called the Brooklyn Trolley Dodgers (later shortened to Dodgers). The team moved to L.A. in 1958.

Houston Astros. Formed in 1961, they were originally called the Colt .45s, after the famous gun. But by 1965, when their new stadium opened, Houston had become famous as the home of NASA's Mission Control. Both the stadium (Astrodome) and the team were named in honor of America's astronauts.

Pittsburgh Pirates. In 1876, they were known as the Alleghenies (after the neighboring Allegheny River). But in the 1890s, they earned a new nickname—the Pirates—when they stole a few players from a rival Philadelphia baseball club.

San Francisco Giants. The New York Gothams baseball club was fighting for a National League championship in 1886. After one particularly stunning victory, their manager proudly addressed them as "my big fellows, my giants." The name stuck. The New York Giants moved to San Francisco in 1958.

Cleveland Indians. From 1869 to 1912, the Cleveland baseball team had five different names—including the Forest Citys, the Naps, and the Spiders. Then, in 1913, a popular player named Luis Francis Sockalexis died. He had been the first American Indian ever to play pro baseball, and the team was renamed in his honor.

Chicago Cubs. Apparently they had no official nickname at the turn of the century (although they were informally called both the

---

The real Daniel Boone detested coonskin caps.

Colts and the Orphans). Then, in 1902, a sportswriter dubbed them "the Cubs" because it was short enough to fit into a newspaper headline. The name caught on, and five years later the team officially adopted it.

Cincinnati Reds. Formed in 1869, the team was originally called the Red Stockings. Later, they were known as the Reds—until the early '50s, when McCarthyism was rampant. No one wanted to be called a "Red" then—it sounded too much like "Commie." So the team actually made an official name change, to the Redlegs. When the patriotic panic died down, they quietly switched back to Reds.

Detroit Tigers. Legend says that the Detroit Creams (the cream of the baseball crop) became the Tigers in 1896, when their manager decided their black and brown striped socks reminded him of tiger stripes.

Montreal Expos. The Canadian city was awarded a baseball franchise in 1968, partly because its 1967 World's Fair—called Expo '67—had been successful. The team was named in honor of the event.

New York Yankees. They were first called the Highlanders or Hilltoppers, because their ballfield was located at the highest point in the city. Again, sportswriters got fed up trying to fit the names into headlines. So in 1909, a newsman arbitrarily called them Yankees—patriotic slang for "Americans." After World War I, when jingoistic fervor was rampant ("The Yanks are coming"), the team officially became the Yankees.

Baltimore Orioles. Named for the Maryland state bird in the early 1900s.

Kansas City Royals, San Diego Padres, Seattle Mariners, Texas Rangers, Toronto Blue Jays. All five were expansion teams. All five got their names in public "name-our-new-team" contests. The Padres, although formed in 1969, got their name in 1935. The original contest was held to name a *minor league* team. Thirty-four years later, the new ballclub adopted the old name.

No kidding—the cigarette lighter was invented before the match.

LEFT-HANDED FACTS

We considered doing a piece about left-handedness for several years, but the question always came up—are there enough left-handed bathroom readers to make it worthwhile? After six years, we decided it didn't matter—we just wanted to use the info. So here's a section for you southpaws, from Vol. 6.

Are you left-handed? If so, you're not alone—but you're definitely outnumbered; lefties make up only 5% to 15% of the general population. If you're a female southpaw, you're even more unusual—there are roughly 50% more left-handed males than females. For centuries, scientists have tried to figure out what makes people left- or right-handed, and they still aren't sure why. (They're not even sure if all lefties are that way for the same reason.) Here are some theories:

WHAT MAKES A LEFTY?

✔ Scientists used to think that left- and right-handedness was purely a genetic trait, but now they have doubts. Reason: In 20% of all sets of identical twins, one sibling is left-handed, and the other is right-handed.

✔ Some scientists think the hand you prefer is determined by whether you're a "right-brained" person or a "left-brained" person. The right half of the brain controls the left side of the body, as well as spatial / musical / aesthetic judgment and perception; the left half controls the right side of the body, plus communication skills. Lefties are generally right-brained.

✔ Support for this theory: Most children begin demonstrating a preference for one hand over the other at the same time their central nervous system is growing and maturing. This leads some scientists to believe the two processes are linked.

✔ According to another theory, before birth all babies are right-handed—which means that the left side of their brain is dominant. But during a stressful or difficult birth, oxygen deficiency can cause damage to the left side of the brain, making it weaker and enabling the right side to compete against it for dominance. If the right side wins out, the baby will become left-handed.

Five Jell-O flavors that flopped: celery, coffee, cola, apple, and chocolate.

✔ This theory also explains, researchers claim, why twins, any child born to a smoker, or children born to a mother over 30 years old are more likely to be left-handed: they are more prone to stressful births. Children of stressful births are also more likely to stammer and suffer dyslexia, traits that are more common in lefties.

LEFT-HANDED HISTORY

No matter what makes southpaws what they are, they've been discriminated against for thousands of years—in nearly every culture on Earth. Some examples:

• The artwork found in ancient Egyptian tombs portrays most Egyptians as right-handed. But their enemies are portrayed as left-handers, a sign they saw left-handedness as an undesirable trait.

• Ancient Greeks never crossed their left leg over their right, and believed a person's sex was determined by their position in the womb—the female, or "lesser sex," sat on the left side of the womb.

• The Romans placed special significance on right-handedness as well. Custom dictated that they enter friends' homes "with the right foot forward"…and turn their heads to the right to sneeze. Their language showed the same bias: the Latin word for left was *sinister* (which also meant evil, or ominous), and the word for right was *dexter* (which came to mean skillful, or adroit). Even the word ambidextrous literally means "right-handed with both hands."

LEFT-HANDED MISCELLANY

• Lefties are more likely to be on the extreme ends of the intelligence scale than the general population: a higher proportion of mentally retarded people *and* people with IQs over 140 are lefties.

• Why are lefties called "southpaws"? In the late 1890s, most baseball parks were laid out with the pitcher facing west and the batter facing east (so the sun wouldn't be in his eyes). That meant left-handed pitchers threw with the arm that faced south. So Chicago sportswriter Charles Seymour began calling them "southpaws."

• What did traditional Christians believe was going to happen on Judgment Day? According to custom, God blesses the saved with His right hand—and casts sinners out of Heaven with His left.

• Why do we throw salt over our left shoulders for good luck? To throw it into the eyes of the Devil, who, of course, lurks behind us to our left.

Alexander Graham Bell insisted the best way to answer the phone was by saying "Ahoy!"

WHERE NO MAN HAS GONE BEFORE

How difficult is it to use the john in space? Tougher than you might think—one NASA engineer has described it as being "as difficult as using a toilet that's bolted to your ceiling." Here's a look at how the agency has conquered the astronauts' No. 1 (and No. 2) problems:

One of the questions people ask frequently about the space program is: "How do the astronauts go to the bathroom in space?" The answer has been an expensive and complicated problem for NASA scientists to solve.

THE MERCURY PROGRAM

America's very first attempt at a manned space flight was strictly no-frills. NASA had enough on its hands just figuring out how to get the astronauts into space, keep them alive, and bring them back without having to worry about how they would pee.

So they sidestepped the bathroom issue entirely. They gave the first astronauts no urination or defecation systems at all—a fact former President Harry Truman stumbled upon when shown one of the Mercury capsules in 1961. "How in the hell do these guys take a leak?" he asked the assembled NASA dignitaries. "There was a lot of foot shuffling," says Alan Shepard in his book *Moon Shot*. "Then someone finally responded, 'Uh, sir, they don't.' Truman walked away convinced that the country's space engineers were loonies."

Actually, the decision made sense. The early flights were so short—Alan Shepard's famous first-American-in-space flight in May 1961 was scheduled to last only 15 minutes—that the space agency figured if the astronauts *did* have to go, they could just hold it until they got home.

Payback Time

This strategy backfired right away, before Shepard even left Earth. On May 6, 1961, he was in the capsule waiting for his historic lift-off. Suddenly, 15 minutes before launch, the countdown was delayed. Shepard had to wait an hour and a half, and nature called. Finally, he couldn't wait anymore and demanded to be let out of the

In the Middle Ages, having ants in the house was a sign of good luck.

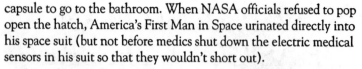

capsule to go to the bathroom. When NASA officials refused to pop open the hatch, America's First Man in Space urinated directly into his space suit (but not before medics shut down the electric medical sensors in his suit so that they wouldn't short out).

Shepard was lucky: Because he was sitting on his back in the capsule, the urine pooled in the small of his back, where the spacesuit's cotton undergarment quickly soaked it up, and where it was then quickly evaporated by the steady stream of pure oxygen blowing through the spacesuit.

Nip and Tuck

Astronaut Gus Grissom, scheduled to go into space two months later, was determined not to suffer the same fate. He demanded that Bill Douglas, the NASA flight surgeon assigned to his mission, find a solution to the problem.

Since there wasn't enough time to solve it from scratch, Douglas sent one of his nurses into town to find some kind of ready-made undergarment absorbent enough to do the job. She returned a couple of hours later with a women's panty girdle. So on July 21, 1961, Grissom became the first astronaut launched into space wearing women's lingerie.

On later Mercury flights, the astronauts were equipped with urination bags, but there were still no provisions for in-flight defecation. NASA officials chose instead to eliminate the problem at the source, by putting the astronauts on what they called a "low-residue" diet three days before every launch.

THE GEMINI AND APOLLO PROGRAMS

By the time the Gemini program got underway in the mid-'60s, astronauts had graduated to urine and fecal bags for use in flight, and special diapers to be used during spacewalks. But spaceflights were starting to get longer—some of the Apollo missions were scheduled to last up to two weeks—and nobody relished the idea of storing two weeks' worth of potentially leaky human waste containers in the cramped space capsules.

NASA solved the liquid waste problem by designing an overboard "dump valve." Urine was jettisoned outside the spacecraft, where it froze instantly and drifted alongside the spacecraft in a free-floating cloud that gradually dispersed over time. Believe it or not, the shiny gold crystalline clouds surrounding the spacecraft were actually quite pretty—some astronauts claimed they were among the most beautiful sights in space.

Solid waste was handled differently. "The spacesuit is taken off," *Reader's Digest* reported in 1969, "and the adhesive top of a plastic bag—equipped with toilet paper and a wet-wipe cleansing tissue—is affixed to the buttocks. When the operation is completed, a germicide is placed in the bag, the bag is sealed and then stored in a waste storage compartment."

On the Moon
That was how waste was handled on the way *to* and *from* the moon; *on* the lunar surface was a different story entirely. Though it wasn't widely reported at the time, Apollo 11 astronauts Armstrong and Aldrin planted more than just an American flag on the moon: "The lunar module has no overboard dump valve," *Reader's Digest* said, which meant that *all* of the astronauts' waste—solid and liquid— had to be stored in the waste bags. Furthermore, because the return trip to the command module was so risky, "Armstrong and Aldrin had to leave behind everything they could to lighten the lunar module for its blast-off from the moon—including the bags." They're still there today.

THE SPACE SHUTTLE
For the Space Shuttle Columbia, NASA developed a $3 million toilet officially known as a Waste Collection Facility, or WCF. Despite its fancy price tag, the unit was plagued with problems. In one 1990 mission, the shuttle had to return to Earth a day early when the thing malfunctioned, forcing the cancellation of several science experiments. "The plumbing is stopped up," chief flight director Randy Stone complained from space at the time, "And there's no Roto-Rooter."

Pay Toilet
In 1993, NASA dumped the WCF for the IWCF—*Improved* Waste Collection Facility—a more sophisticated toilet with a larger holding capacity for long flights. Projected to cost about $3.3 million, it ultimately cost taxpayers more than $30 million. The media had a field day when the financial figures were released—one newspaper headline snickered "GAO Sees Waste in Space Toilet"—but the space agency insisted that it was worth every penny.

According to the real estate industry, the average person looks at 8 houses before buying.

How It Works

This latest space toilet leaves nothing to chance: it has foot and thigh restraints to hold the user in place and an alarm that alerts Mission Control when the astronauts leave the seat up. About the only thing it doesn't have is water—liquids are too unpredictable in zero gravity. Instead, the toilet uses 12 high-pressure air jets under the seat to blast waste into the bowl.

Once the waste is in the bowl, astronauts "flush" the toilet by exposing the waste to space, freeze-drying it. The waste is then left to float in the bowl, but squeamish astronauts can use an elastic net to sweep old poop aside.

WASTE NOT, WANT NOT?

How will space waste be managed if astronauts are on the moon for extended periods or traveling to Mars? No one knows for sure, but Steven H. Schwartzkopf, Lockheed's chief scientist for life-support research, suggests sending astronauts into space with *tilapia*, a sewage-eating fish also known as "toilet trout." The fish would live in diluted wastewater and could also eat carrot tops, tomato stems, and other vegetable matter that the astronauts don't eat. The fish, in turn, would be eaten by the astronauts.

* * *

INTERSTELLAR GASSES

This exchange took place between Charles Duke and John Young during the Apollo 16 space mission in 1972. They didn't realize the press was listening.

Young: I got the farts again. I got 'em again, Charlie. I don't know what the hell gives 'em to me…I think it's the acid in the stomach, I really do.

Duke: It probably is.

Young: I mean, I haven't eaten this much citrus fruit in 20 years. But I'll tell you one thing—in another 12 f—— days, I ain't ever eating any more. And if they offer to serve me potassium with my breakfast, I'm going to throw up. I like an occasional orange, I really do. But I'll be damned if I'm going to be buried in oranges.

JUST PLANE WEIRD

If you bought this book in an airport, you might want to skip reading this page until your flight is over and you're safely back on the ground.

HAMMING IT UP. In April 1995, a South African Airways passenger flight carrying 72 prize stud pigs in the hold had to make an emergency landing in London. Apparently, their flatulence triggered the plane's fire alarms. As one airline spokesperson delicately put it, "the collective heat and methane that 72 pigs give off caused our alarms in the hold to activate."

AN EXPLOSIVE SITUATION. On January 4, 1993, a Trans Air flight was forced to return to Fort Lauderdale, Florida, when a German passenger told a flight attendant, "The roof will fly if I sit down." "I took this to mean that something would make the roof of the plane explode," the woman later testified. The man was arrested and hustled off the plane as soon as it landed. Then he was jailed and charged with making a bomb threat. It wasn't until the trial actually got underway that translators realized that "the roof will fly" is German slang for "my bladder is about to burst."

THEY JUST PLANE DIDN'T GET ALONG. In August 1994, a Korean Air jet skidded across a rain-soaked runway and rammed a safety barricade while landing in Cheju, Korea. All 160 passengers escaped safely…just moments before the plane exploded into flames. Cause of the accident: According to news reports, the pilot and co-pilot had gotten into a fist fight over who was in charge of the landing controls.

POWER TRIP. In 1989, USAir pilots mistook lights from a parking lot to be runway markers at the Kansas City airport. They pulled up after clipping high-voltage power lines, mistook the electrical flashes for lightning, and diverted to a nearby airport for safety. "All the while," *The New York Times* reported, "a Federal Aviation Administration inspector who was in the cockpit to check their performance did nothing." In his written report of the incident, the inspector did not even cite the pilots for mistaking the parking lot for a runway, "although he did fault them for striking the power lines."

SUPERSTITIONS

Many of us secretly believe that broken mirrors and black cats really do bring bad luck. It's amusing to discover the sources of our silliness.

LADDERS. The belief that walking under a ladder will bring bad luck comes from the early Christians. They held that a ladder propped up against a building formed a triangle, and that this symbol of the Holy Trinity shouldn't be violated by walking through it. People who did walk through it were considered in league with the Devil.

FRIDAY THE THIRTEENTH. Friday is generally considered an unlucky day. Adam and Eve were supposed to have been kicked out of the Garden of Eden on Friday; Noah's great flood started on Friday; and Christ was crucified on Friday. Couple this with the fact that 12 witches plus the Devil—totalling 13—are necessary for a Satanic meeting, and the combination of Friday plus 13 is a deadly one.

BREAKING A MIRROR. At one time in the ancient world, mirrors were used to tell fortunes. If a mirror was broken during the reading, it meant that the person was doomed. Later, a cracked image in a mirror meant illness. But the modern superstition that you get seven years of bad luck if you break a mirror originated in Europe in the 1400s and 1500s. It's a complete fake, created to scare servants into using extra care when polishing their masters' expensive mirrors. Nonetheless, the idea became ingrained in European culture.

BLACK CATS. "The origin of cat-power," writes Peter Lorie in *Superstitions*, "derives almost certainly from the original Egyptian worship of Bast," an ancient black cat-goddess. But by the Middle Ages, the black cat had become a symbol of black magic. European peasants, convinced that witches and evil demons lived among them, may have been suspicious of cats' silent, fluid movements, the way they stare, and their unworldly wailing. The fact that some of the women who cared for the cats were old and grizzled—i.e., witch material—probably added to the legend. "Today," says Lorie, "we fear the black cat that crosses our path. This represents most clearly the conflict that existed between the Church...and the pagan practices of witchcraft."

FOOD FIGHT!

This title probably conjures up visions of leftover vegetables being hurled across a school cafeteria. But in at least two instances, people actually used food as a weapon in real wars. Here are the stories.

TAKE THAT!

"The Uraguayan army once fought a sea battle using cheeses as cannonballs.

"It happened in the 1840s. The aggressive Argentine dictator Juan Manual de Rosas, in an attempt to annex Uraguay, ordered his navy to blockade Montevideo, the capital. The besieged Uraguayans held their own in battle until they ran out of conventional ammunition. In desperation, they raided the galleys of their ships and loaded their cannons with very old, hard Edam cheeses and fired them at the enemy.

"Contemporary chronicles record that the Uraguayans won the skirmish."

—From *Significa,* by Irving Wallace, David Wallechinsky, and Amy Wallace

YOU SAY POTATO...

"A World War II destroyer once defeated a submarine with the help of a seldom-used weapon of destruction: potatoes.

"The *USS O'Bannon* was on patrol off the Solomon Islands in April 1943 when it encountered a Japanese sub. The crew shot off the sub's conning tower, preventing it from diving, but the captain of the sub brought it so close to the destroyer that the *O'Bannon's* big guns couldn't be aimed at it....When the Japanese came topside, the gallant *O'Bannon* crewmen pelted them with potatoes. The Japanese thought they were being showered with grenades, threw their guns overboard, then panicked, submerged the sub and sank it.

"When the *O'Bannon* was decommissioned in the early 1970s, a plaque was made to commemorate the event, and donated to the ship, by the Maine potato growers."

—From *Beyond Belief!,* by Ron Lyon and Jenny Pacshall

Rough start: Baby giraffes drop 6 feet to the ground when they're born.

SIXTIES FASHION FADS

Here are four fashions that were hip for about 15 minutes in the 1960s.

POP-TOP CLOTHING

Remember the beer and soda can pull tabs that came off in your hand? They became a fashion statement in 1970 thanks to Gonzallo Chavez, a San Juan, Puerto Rico, man who didn't have anything to wear to a Tom Jones concert. He dug through some garbage cans, pulled out beer can pull tops, and connected more than 600 of them together to make a vest. The way Chavez remembers it, he got more attention at the concert than Tom Jones. "One poor lady who was leaning far out over a balcony to look at us lost her wig," he recalled in his 1975 book *Pop Topping!* "It fell to the tier below, but she didn't seem to notice. She kept right on staring at us."

Chavez was so impressed with the response that he changed his name to Pop-Top Terp and began making garbage fashions full-time, charging $60 for a vest and up to $350 for a full-length coat (made from 2,800 rings). Pop-topping blossomed into a cottage industry that cranked out hats, miniskirts, wall hangings, plant holders, napkin rings, and even dog clothing. But it all came to an end in the mid-'70s, when can manufacturers switched to nonremovable flip tabs.

NEHRU JACKETS

In 1966, Sammy Davis, Jr., bought a white, Indian-style jacket with a button front and a small, stand-up collar (similar to that worn by Indian prime minister Jawaharlal Nehru of India) at a pricy London boutique. He wore it to a party in Paris and caught the attention of designer Pierre Cardin, who decided to design a similar jacket and offer it in his 1967 collection.

Worn with turtleneck shirts and huge medallion necklaces, the jackets turned out to be just what fashion-conscious men of the late '60s were looking for. Sales surged as Joe Namath, the Smothers Brothers, and just about every other hip celebrity of the day were seen wearing them. The fashion *really* went mainstream when

Johnny Carson wore his on the "Tonight Show." Sears even featured a boy in a kid-sized Nehru jacket, "styled like big brother's," on the cover of its Spring 1969 catalog.

Ultimately, though, the Nehru jacket was a victim of its own simplicity. The jackets were so easy to design and tailor that cheap knockoffs hit the discount store shelves in record time, changing them from an upper-class status symbol to a "badge of squareness" overnight. Sales plummeted, leaving suppliers so overstocked that one company even tried sewing on new collars and reselling them as "slender-cut Edwardian topcoats." (It didn't work.)

GO-GO BOOTS

Introduced in February 1965 by French fashion designer André Courreges, who called them "kid boots" and saw them as an indispensable accessory to the *other* fashion focus that year, the miniskirt. "Without kid boots," he announced to the press, "short skirts look ridiculous." The skirts were an instant smash, but it wasn't until dancing girls—called "Go-Go girls"—at the hip Los Angeles nightclub Whiskey a Go-Go began wearing the boots that the fad really took off.

PAPER DRESSES

Invented in 1966 by the Scott Paper Company to promote its "Color Explosion" paper towels, napkins, and toilet paper. Scott probably never intended to take the dresses very seriously...but when they received more than 500,000 orders in six months, dressmaking companies got into the act. A full line of paper clothing, including $8 maternity dresses, $12 men's suits, and even $15 wedding gowns were available.

For a time, disposable paper vacation wear appeared to be the wave of the future; travelers wouldn't have to pack—they'd just pick up paper clothes when they arrived at their destination and throw away the garments at the end of the trip. The fad reached all the way to the top levels of society. The Duchess of Windsor, Joan Kennedy, and even the Beatles were spotted wearing paper clothing. "Paper clothing is here to stay," *Time* magazine announced in 1967...but it was wrong. Paper clothes ballooned out in unpredictable places, tore easily, and cost too much to replace constantly. The fad was completely dead by 1970.

P. J. Tierney, father of the modern diner, died of indigestion in 1917 after eating at a diner.

LIMERICKS

*Limericks have been around since the 1700s. The authors of these
silly ditties (except for the one by Edward Lear) are unknown.*

There was a young fellow
   named Clyde,
Who once at a funeral was
   spied.
When asked who was dead,
He smilingly said,
   "I don't know—I just came
   for the ride."

There was a young man of
   Calcutta
Who had a most terrible
   stutta,
He said: "Pass the h. . .ham,
And the j . . .j . . .j . . .jam,
And the b...b...b...b...b...
   b...butta."

There was a young man from
   Darjeeling,
Who got on a bus bound for
   Ealing;
It said at the door:
"Don't spit on the floor,"
So he carefully spat on the
   ceiling.

There was an old fellow named
   Cager
Who, as the result of a wager,
Offered to fart
The whole oboe part
Of Mozart's "Quartet in F
   Major."

There was a young fellow of
   Lyme
Who lived with three wives at
   one time.
When asked: "Why the third?"
He replied: "One's absurd,
   and bigamy, sir, is a crime."

There was a brave fellow
   named Gere,
Who hadn't an atom of fear.
He indulged a desire
To touch a live wire,
And any last line will do
   here.

An epicure, dining in Crewe,
Once found a large mouse in
   his stew.
Said the waiter: "Don't shout,
Or wave it about,
Or the rest will be wanting
   one, too."

A mouse in her room woke
   Miss Dowd,
Who was frightened and
   screamed very loud.
Then a happy thought hit
   her—
To scare off the critter,
She sat up in bed and
   meowed.

            —Edward Lear

MYTH AMERICA

*You've probably believed these stories since you were a kid.
Most Americans have, because they were taught to us
as sacred truths. Well, here's another look.*

BUNKER HILL
The Myth: The Battle of Bunker Hill—where the Americans first faced the Redcoats—was the colonists' initial triumph in the Revolutionary War.

The Truth: Not only did the British wallop the Americans in the encounter, the whole thing wasn't even fought on Bunker Hill. The American troops *had* actually been ordered to defend Bunker Hill, but there was an enormous foul-up and somehow they wound up trying to protect nearby Breed's Hill, which was more vulnerable to attack. They paid for it—when the fighting was over, the Americans had been chased away by the British troops. Casualties were heavy for both sides: about 450 Americans were killed, and a staggering 1,000 (out of 2,100) Redcoats bit the dust.

THE PILGRIMS
The Myth: The Pilgrims were headed for Massachusetts.

The Truth: They were headed for "Hudson's River." Because of poor navigation and unexpected winds, the first land they sighted was Cape Cod. They tried to sail south, but "dangerous shoales and roaring breakers" prevented it. So they reluctantly turned back. By this time, the crew of the *Mayflower* (no, the ship wasn't manned by Pilgrims) was sick of them and hustled them off the boat as fast as they could.

The Myth: The Pilgrims landed at Plymouth Rock.

Background: This tale originated in 1741, more than 100 years after the Pilgrims arrived. It has been attributed to a then-95-year-old man named Thomas Fraunce, who claimed his father had told him the story when he was a boy. However, his father didn't land with the pilgrims—he reached America three years after they did.

The Truth: The Pilgrims first landed in Provincetown, Massachusetts.

More than 2.2 million Americans play the accordion.

INDEPENDENCE DAY

The Myth: American independence was declared on July 4th.

Background: Because the Declaration of Independence is dated July 4, people associate that date with American independence. In fact, independence was declared first...and was confirmed with the document a few days later.

The Truth: The Continental Congress declared independence on July 2nd. One of the Founding Fathers, John Adams, is quoted as having written his wife on July 3rd: "The 2nd day of July, 1776, will be the most memorable...in the history of America. I am apt to believe it will be celebrated by succeeding generations, as the great anniversary Festival."

• **Note:** Actually, the first Independence Day celebration—by the Continental Congress—was on July 8, 1776.

DECLARATION OF INDEPENDENCE

The Myth: In a hushed hall in Philadelphia on July 4, 1776, each signer of the Declaration of Independence proudly and publicly took his turn affixing his signature to the document.

Background: This tale was apparently concocted by Thomas Jefferson and Benjamin Franklin, who wrote about it in letters after the event.

The Truth: Only two people—John Hancock and Charles Thomson—signed the Declaration of Independence on July 4. It wasn't until about a month later, on August 2nd, that the majority of the delegates signed it. And it wasn't until five years later, in 1781, that the last signature was finally added.

• How public was the signing? The Continental Congress would only admit that Hancock's and Thomson's names were on the document. Everyone else signed in secrecy. It wasn't until the following January that the signers' names were made public.

YANKEE DOODLE

The Myth: "Yankee Doodle" was originally a patriotic song.

The Truth: It was composed in England as an anti-American tune. The phrase "stuck a feather in his cap and called it macaroni" referred to a foppish English group called the Macaroni Club, whose members wore ludicrous "continental" fashions they mistakenly believed to be elegant. The British laughed at "Yankee Doodle dandies," bumpkins who didn't know how silly they really were.

FAMILIAR PHRASES

Here are the origins of some well-known phrases, taken from one of the Bathroom Readers' most popular features.

NOT UP TO SCRATCH
Meaning: Inadequate, subpar.
Origin: In the early days of boxing, there was no bell to signal the beginning of a round. Instead, the referee would *scratch* a line on the ground between fighters, and the round began when both men stepped over it. When a boxer couldn't cross the line to keep a match going, people said he was not "up to the scratch."

CAUGHT RED-HANDED
Meaning: Caught in the act.
Origin: For hundreds of years, stealing and butchering another person's livestock was a common crime. But it was hard to prove unless the thief was caught with a dead animal…and blood on his hands.

GIVE SOMEONE "THE BIRD"
Meaning: Make a nasty gesture at someone (usually with the middle finger uplifted).
Origin: There are many versions. The "cleanest": Originally "the bird" referred to the hissing sound that audiences made when they didn't like a performance. Hissing is the sound that a goose makes when it's threatened or angry.

LAY AN EGG
Meaning: Fail.
Origin: From the British sport of cricket. When you fail to score, you get a zero—which looks like an egg. The term is also taken from baseball, where a zero is a "goose egg."

BURY THE HATCHET
Meaning: Make peace with an enemy.
Origin: Some Native American tribes declared peace by literally burying a tomahawk in the ground.

Top 3 non-biters: Golden retrievers, Labrador retrievers, and Shetland sheepdogs.

CHEW THE FAT

Meaning: Chat; engage in idle conversation.

Origin: Originally a sailor's term. Before refrigeration, ships carried food that wouldn't spoil. One of them was salted pork skin, a practically inedible morsel that consisted largely of fat. Sailors would only eat it when all the other food was gone…and they often complained as they did. This (and other) idle chatter eventually became known as "chewing the fat."

TO THE BITTER END

Meaning: To the very end—often an unpleasant one.

Origin: Surprisingly, it has nothing to do with bitterness. It's a sailing term that refers to the end of a mooring line or anchor line that is attached to the *bitts*, sturdy wooden or metal posts that are mounted to the ship's deck.

HAVE A SCREW LOOSE

Meaning: Something is wrong with a person or mechanism.

Origin: The phrase comes from the cotton industry and dates back as far as the 1780s, when the industrial revolution made mass production of textiles possible for the first time. Huge mills sprang up to take advantage of the new technology (and the cheap labor), but it was difficult to keep all the machines running properly; any machine that broke down or produced defective cloth was said to have "a screw loose" somewhere.

SPEAK OF THE DEVIL

Meaning: Someone appears after you mention them.

Origin: People once believed that you could actually summon the Devil by saying his name.

BORN WITH A SILVER SPOON IN YOUR MOUTH

Meaning: Pampered; lucky; born into wealth or prosperous circumstances.

Origin: At one time, it was customary for godparents to give their godchild a silver spoon at the christening. These people were usually well-off so the spoon came to represent the child's good fortune.

CANDY BITS

A wise bathroom reader once wrote, "Reading about candy's origins is almost as fun as eating it." Here are a few candy pieces—short, but sweet.

POP ROCKS. In 1956, William Mitchell, a General Foods chemist, was looking for a way to make instant carbonated soda pop by trapping carbon dioxide in hard candy tablets. One afternoon he popped some nuggets he was experimenting with into his mouth…and felt them pop. No one at General Foods could think of a use for the substance, so it was shelved for almost 20 years. But in 1975 it was introduced as Pop Rocks—and became the hottest selling candy in history. Between 1975 and 1980, more than 500 million packets were sold.

PEZ. Invented in 1927 by Eduard Haas, an Austrian anti-smoking fanatic who marketed peppermint-flavored PEZ as a cigarette substitute. The candy gets its name from the German word for peppermint, *Pfefferminze*. Haas brought the candy to the U.S. in 1952. It bombed, so he reintroduced it as a children's toy, complete with cartoon heads and fruity flavors. (One of the most secretive companies in the U.S., PEZ won't even disclose who currently owns the company.)

CHARLESTON CHEW. Sometimes the names of candy bars come from the fads that are popular when they are introduced. The Charleston Chew was introduced during the roaring '20s, when the Charleston dance craze was in full swing.

M&Ms. In 1930, Frank Mars, a Chicago candy-maker, told his son Forrest to get out of the country and not come back. Forrest went to England with a few thousand dollars and the recipe for his father's Milky Ways. He set up shop and began selling his own versions of the candy bars. While in England, Forrest discovered Smarties, a candy-coated chocolate treat that was popular with the Brits. He bought the rights to market Smarties in America, where he went into partnership with a business associate named Bruce Murrie. The candies were called M&Ms, short for Mars and Murrie. In 1964, after much family bickering, the American and British Mars companies finally merged.

BLACK CROWS. The Mason Candy Company decided to introduce a new candy treat in 1890. The candy, a licorice-flavored gumdrop, was to be called Black Rose. But the printer misunderstood the instructions and printed the wrappers with the name "Black Crows." The printer refused to reprint the job, claiming it was Mason's mistake. Rather than pay to reprint the wrappers, the folks at Mason decided to change the name of the product. Today, 100 years later, Black Crows are still available by that name.

MEXICAN HATS. Heide's Mexican Hats candies were originally called "Wetem and Wearems." Kids were supposed to lick the candies and stick them to their foreheads. What possible reason for kids wanting to use the candies in this fashion is unknown.

HERSHEY'S. Milton Hershey, the inventor of the Hershey Bar, was an unusual man. As a child he was brought up in a strict Mennonite family. Unlike most entrepreneurs, he never sought the usual material wealth that accompanies success. In 1909, he took a large sum of the money he had earned making candy bars and opened the Milton Hershey School for orphaned boys. Nine years later he donated the candy company to a trust for the school. Today, the Milton Hershey School and School Trust still own 56% of the Hershey Company.

KRAFT CARAMELS. During the Depression, Joseph Kraft started making caramels. He didn't particularly like candy; he just needed another dairy product for cheese sales reps to carry on their routes. The product succeeded because grocers needed a summer substitute for chocolate, which melted in the heat.

THREE MUSKETEERS. Advertising in the '50s and '60s suggested that the Three Musketeers got its name because it was big enough for three people to share. The truth is, it was originally made of three separate nougat sections: vanilla, chocolate and strawberry. Eventually, the strawberry and vanilla nougat sections were eliminated, leaving only the chocolate nougat.

REAL-LIFE SONGS

What's the inspiration for a popular song? Often, an event in the life of the songwriter. Behind the Hits, by Bob Shannon and John Javna, offers good examples of the kinds of experiences that become hits.

THE DOCK OF THE BAY—Otis Redding. One warm morning in late 1967, Redding relaxed on a houseboat he'd rented in Sausalito, across the bay from the city of San Francisco. He was "just wastin' time"—and he could afford to. A few days earlier, he'd electrified the audience with his midnight show-closing performance at the Monterey Pop Festival. Then, he had headed north to the legendary Fillmore Auditorium in San Francisco and knocked out the audience there. He was definitely on his way to rock stardom. Satisfied, Redding kicked back in the sunshine, played a few chords on his guitar, and dreamed up a little tune: "Sittin' in the mornin' sun..."

When Redding got back to Memphis, he went into the studio and recorded his song. At the end he wasn't sure what to sing or say—so he just whistled, capturing the casual mood he'd been in on that houseboat in Sausalito.

For the Record: Three days later, Redding died in a plane crash near Madison, Wisconsin. "The Dock of the Bay" became the first posthumous #1 record in history—and Redding's only #1 pop hit.

ROXANNE—The Police. On October 20, 1977, the Police—a starving "art rock" band—were scheduled to be the opening act for a punk band in a Paris club. So they loaded up their car with equipment and drove to France. But when they arrived at the club, they found that there was no gig. They weren't opening for anybody, and no one had come to watch them. They played to an empty house anyway, and left disconsolate, because they could scarcely afford to have made a trip to Paris for nothing.

Things got worse: As they drove around the city right after the gig, their car broke down; it had to be towed back to London.

Their lead singer, Sting, decided that as long as he had to walk, he might as well take a stroll through Paris's famous red-light district. "It was the first time I'd seen prostitutes on the streets," Sting

---

Not one adult has ever appeared in a Peanuts cartoon strip.

recalls. "I imagined being in love with one of those girls. I mean, they do have fellas. How would I feel?" He translated the experience into a song called "Roxanne." Two years later it became the first big New Wave hit and established The Police.

For the Record: Where did he get the name? "It's a beautiful name, with such a rich history.…Roxanne was Alexander the Great's wife, and Cyrano de Bergerac's girlfriend."

THE SULTANS OF SWING—Dire Straits. The Sultans of Swing were a band that Mark Knopfler, the leader of Dire Straits, saw at a pub.

Knopfler: "'Sultans' was written quite a long time before we had the band.…My brother Dave was living somewhere in Greenwich and we went out to the pub—I think it was called the Swan …and we had a game of pool and a couple of pints. There was a jazz band playing and there was nobody in there except us and a couple of kids in the corner. They did a couple of requests. I asked them for 'Creole Love Call,' and it was great. There are loads of bands like that. They're postmen, accountants, milkmen, draftsmen, teachers. They just get together Sunday lunchtimes, nighttimes, and they play traditional jazz. It's funny, because they play this New Orleans music note-for-note…in Greenwich, England."

SOMEONE SAVED MY LIFE TONIGHT—Elton John. "She was six-foot tall and going out with a midget in Sheffield," Elton John told *Rolling Stone* about a woman he'd met in 1968. "He used to beat her up! I felt so sorry for her…I fell desperately in love." When they moved in together, "It was just like six months in hell. I tried to commit suicide. It was a very Woody Allen-type suicide. I turned on the gas and left all the windows open." Still, Elton planned to marry her. The night before the ceremony, his friend and manager, John Baldry, came over and convinced him to call it off. Some time later, Elton and Bernie Taupin wrote "Someone Saved My Life Tonight" about Baldry's 11th-hour wedding intervention.

For the Record: Elton didn't like the record. "I thought it was the worst vocal of all time." But it hit #4 on the charts and was nominated for a Grammy.

John Wilkes Booth's brother once saved the life of Abraham Lincoln's son.

THE ORIGIN OF FRANKENSTEIN

The original Frankenstein's monster wasn't Boris Karloff—it was
(believe it or not) a character created by a 19-year-old author
named Mary Shelley...more than 170 years ago.

BACKGROUND

In the summer of 1816, 19-year-old Mary Wollstonecraft Shelley and her 24-year-old husband, the poet Percy Bysshe Shelley, visited Switzerland. "It proved a wet, uncongenial summer," she wrote some 15 years later, "and incessant rain often confined us for days to the house."

To pass the time, the Shelleys and their neighbors—28-year-old Lord Byron, his 23-year-old personal physician, and his 18-year-old lover—read German ghost stories aloud. They enjoyed it so much that one day, Byron announced, "We will each write a ghost story." Everyone agreed, but apparently the poets, unaccustomed to prose writing, couldn't come up with anything very scary.

Mary was determined to do better. "I busied myself to think of a story," she recalled, "One which would speak to the mysterious fears of our nature and awaken thrilling horror." Yet she couldn't come up with anything. Every morning, her companions asked: "Have you thought of a story?" "And each morning," she wrote later, "I was forced to reply with a mortifying negative."

A FLASH OF INSPIRATION

One evening, Mary sat by the fireplace, listening to her husband and Byron discuss the possibility of reanimating a corpse with electricity, giving it what they called "vital warmth."

The discussion finally ended well after midnight, and Shelley retired. But Mary, "transfixed in speculation," couldn't sleep.

"When I placed my head on the pillow," she recalled, "I did not sleep, nor could I be said to think. My imagination, unbidden, possessed and guided me, gifting the successive images that arouse in my mind with a vividness far beyond the usual bounds of reverie. I saw—with shut eyes but acute mental vision—I saw the pale student of unhallowed arts kneeling beside the thing he had put together....I saw the hideous phantasm of a man stretched out, and then, on the working of some powerful engine, show signs of life and stir with an uneasy, half-vital motion.

"Frightful must it be; for supremely frightful would be the effect of any human endeavor to mock the stupendous mechanism of the Creator of the world. His success would terrify the artist; he would rush away from his odious handiwork, horror-stricken. He would hope that, left to itself, the slight spark of light which he had communicated would fade; that this thing would subside into dead matter; and he might sleep in the belief that the silence of the grave would quench forever the transient existence of the hideous corpse which he had looked upon as the cradle of life. He sleeps; but he is awakened; the horrid thing stands at his bedside, opening his curtains, and looking on him with yellow, watery eyes..."

THE PERFECT HORROR STORY
At this point, Mary opened her eyes in terror—so frightened that she needed reassurance it had all just been her imagination. She gazed around the room, but just couldn't shake the image of "my hideous phantom." Finally, to take her mind off the creature, she went back to the ghost story she'd been trying to compose all week. "If only I could contrive one," she thought, "that would frighten people as I myself had been frightened that night!" Then she realized that her vision was, in fact, the story she'd been reaching for.

As she recounted: "Swift as light and as cheering was the idea that broke in upon me. 'I have found it! What terrified me will terrify others; and I need only describe the spectre which had haunted my midnight pillow.' On the morrow I announced I had thought of a story. I began the day with the words, 'It was on a dreary night in November,' making only a transcript of the grim terrors of my waking dream."

THE NOVEL
The first version of Frankenstein was a short story. But Mary's husband encouraged her to develop it further, and she eventually turned it into a novel. It was published anonymously in 3 parts in 1818. "Mary," notes one critic, "did not think it important enough to sign her name to the book....And since her husband wrote the book's preface, people assumed he had written the rest of the book as well....It was not until a later edition of *Frankenstein* that the book was revealed as the work of a young girl."

It's elementary: 25% of Americans think Sherlock Holmes was a real person.

HONESTLY, ABE

Abraham Lincoln, our 16th president, was surprisingly quotable. Here are a few of his better-known sayings.

"The best way to destroy your enemy is to make him your friend."

"God must love the common man, He made so many of them."

"No man is good enough to govern another man without that other's consent."

"It's been my experience that people who have no vices have very few virtues."

"No matter how much cats fight, there always seems to be plenty of kittens."

"People who like this sort of thing will find this the sort of thing they like."

"Public opinion in this country is everything."

"Human action can be modified to some extent, but human nature cannot be changed."

"A man's legs must be long enough to reach the ground."

"Those who deny freedom for others deserve it not for themselves."

"My father taught me to work, but not to love it. I never did like to work, and I don't deny it. I'd rather read, tell stories, crack jokes, talk, laugh—anything but work."

"Tact is the ability to describe others as they see themselves."

"The things I want to know are in books; my best friend is the man who'll get me a book I ain't read."

"The man who is incapable of making a mistake is incapable of anything."

"The ballot is stronger than the bullet."

"As I would not be a slave, so I would not be a master. This expresses my idea of democracy."

"The best thing about the future is that it comes only one day at a time."

DIRTY TRICKS

*Why should politicians have all the fun? You can pull off some
dirty tricks, too. These five should inspire you to new lows.*

P OUND FOOLISH

Pay a visit to the local dog pound or SPCA, wearing a chef's
hat and an apron. Ask to see one of the kittens or puppies
that are available for adoption. Pick it up and act as if you're weighing it, then set it down and ask to see one that's "a little more
plump."

SOCK IT TO 'EM

Tired of looking for that one sock you lost in the laundry? Pass on
your anxieties: Stick the leftover sock in with someone else's washload. Let them look for the missing sock for a while.

SOMETHING FISHY

If you have a (clean) aquarium, toss some thin carrot slices into the
tank. Later when you have guests over, grab the slices out of the
tank and eat them quickly. If you do it quick enough, your victims
will assume you're eating a goldfish. (If you accidentally grab a *real*
goldfish, toss it back in, grab the carrot slice, and complain to your
victims that the first fish was "too small.")

LOST YOUR MARBLES?

Pry the hubcap off a friend's car, drop 2 or 3 steel ball bearings inside, and replace the hubcap. Then watch them drive off. The ball
bearings will make an enormous racket for a few seconds, until they
become held in place by centrifugal force. They'll stay silent until
the victim applies the brakes, then they'll shake loose again.

TV GUIDE

Got a friend who's a couch potato? Carefully remove the cover of
their *TV Guide* (or weekly newspaper TV schedule), then glue it to
an older schedule, so the TV listings are wrong. It'll drive a true
TV fanatic crazy.

THE THREE STOOGES

There's nothing like the sound of a good "Nyuk, nyuk, nyuk," to make a Three Stooges fan smile. And even if you don't like them, you have to be impressed by their enduring popularity.

HOW THEY STARTED
There are so many different stories about the Stooges' origin that it's hard to know which is correct. Probably none of them. Anyway, here's one that sounds good.

• There was a vaudevillian named Ted Healy, a boyhood friend of Moe and Shemp Horwitz. One night in 1922, some acrobats working for him walked out just before a show. Desperate, he asked Moe to fill in temporarily, as a favor.

• Moe, in turn, got his brother Shemp out of the audience, and the three of them did an impromptu routine that had the audience in stitches. Moe and Shemp loved the stage, so they changed their name from Horwitz to Howard and hit the road with their friend as "Ted Healy and the Gang" (or "Ted Healy and His Stooges," depending on who tells the story).

• In 1925, the trio was on the lookout for another member and spotted Larry Fine (real name: Louis Feinberg) playing violin with an act called the "Haney Sisters and Fine." Why they thought he'd be a good Stooge isn't clear, since he'd never done comedy before. But he joined as the third Stooge, anyway.

• They traveled the vaudeville circuit for years under a variety of names, including Ted Healy and His Racketeers...His Southern Gentlemen...His Stooges, etc. Then they wound up in a Broadway revue in 1929, which led to a movie contract.

• In 1931, Shemp quit and was replaced by his younger brother, Jerry. Jerry had a full head of hair and a handsome mustache—but Healy insisted he shave them both off...hence the name "Curly."

• Three years later, after a bitter dispute, the boys broke up with Healy. They quickly got a Columbia film contract on their own, and the Three Stooges were born.

• Over the next 23 years, they made 190 short films—but no features. For some reason, Harry Cohn, head of Columbia Pictures, wouldn't allow it (despite the Stooges' popularity and the fact that they were once nominated for an Oscar).

• From the '30s to the '50s, the Stooges had four personnel changes: In 1946, Curly suffered a stroke and retired; Shemp then returned to the Stooges until his death in 1955; he, in turn, was replaced by Joe Besser (Joe) and Joe DeRita (Curly Joe).

INSIDE FACTS

Two-Fingered Poker
One day backstage in the '30s, Larry, Shemp, and Moe were playing cards. Shemp accused Larry of cheating. After a heated argument, Shemp reached over and stuck his fingers in Larry's eyes. Moe, watching, thought it was hilarious…and that's how the famous poke-in-the-eyes routine was born.

Profitable Experience
By the mid-'50s, the average budget for a Three Stooges' episode—including the stars' salaries—was about $16,000. Depending on the time slot, Columbia Pictures can now earn more than that with one showing of the same film…in one city.

So What If He's Dead?
The last four Stooges episodes featuring Shemp were filmed after he died. The films' producer, Jules White, brought in a Shemp double who was only seen from behind.

The Stooges' Resurrection
By the mid-'50s the demand for short films had petered out. So, in 1957, Columbia unceremoniously announced they weren't renewing the Stooges' contracts. Moe and Larry were devastated. After 23 years, what else would they do? Moe was rich from real estate investments, but Larry was broke—which made it even harder. They decided to get a third Stooge (Curly and Shemp were dead) and go back on tour. Joe DeRita, "Curly Joe," was selected. They started making appearances in third-rate clubs, just to have work.

Meanwhile, Columbia, hoping to get a few bucks out of its old Stooge films, released them to TV at bargain prices. They had no expectations, so everyone (particularly Moe and Larry) was shocked when, in 1959, the Stooges emerged as the hottest kids' program in America. Suddenly the Stooges had offers to make big-time personal appearances and new films. And they've been American cult heroes ever since.

WORD ORIGINS

"One of the most intriguing things about language," says etymologist David Muschell, "is how words get passed on from generation to generation, from country to country, and how they change in the passing." Here are some examples of what he means.

PARAPHERNALIA. From the old Greek words *para,* "beside," and *pherne,* "dowery." Medieval Roman law stated that when a young woman married, her dowry became the legal property of her husband; the other stuff—the *paraphernalia* or "goods besides the dowry"—remained her own personal property.

ROSTRUM. As far back as 338 B.C., it was customary for the ships of the Roman empire to remove the prow, or *rostrum,* of an enemy ship, and return it to Rome after winning a battle at sea. A lot of these rostra were used to decorate the speaker's platform in the Roman Forum, and eventually the platform itself became known as a *rostrum.*

PEDIGREE. The term comes from the French words *pied de grue,* which mean "foot of a crane." French families of old kept family trees, but that's not what they called them. They thought the look of a genealogy chart—small at the top and branching out at the bottom—looked more like the webbed foot of a bird than the roots of a tree. Any Frenchman who came from a family prominent enough to have a family tree was said to have a *pied de grue.*

MALARIA. From *mala aria,* the Italian words for "bad air." Early sufferers assumed their illness was caused not by disease borne by mosquitos, but by the humid, strange-smelling air found in swamps.

SARCASM. From the Greek word *sarkazein,* which means "to tear the flesh."

GROTESQUE. Originally used to describe the artwork decorating the walls of ancient Roman *grottos,* which was characterized by lots of unusual and colorful animals, flowers, and fruits. Over time the *grotesque* art went out of style—and the word came to mean "ugly."

Wild West trivia: Billy the Kid was buried in a shirt five sizes too big.

STEEPLECHASE. The term dates back to the days when horseback riders, upon approaching a town, would point out a landmark—such as the *steeple* of a church—and race to see who could get there first.

MONSTER. The ancient Romans believed that when a deformed animal was born to a farmer's livestock, or even to a household pet, it was an omen of bad things to come. The word *monster* comes from *monstrum*, the Latin word for "warning."

EXPLODE. From the Latin roots *ex*, "out," and *plaudo*, "clap." As late as the 17th century the word *explode* meant literally to clap someone off the stage after a performance.

SALAD. A shortened version of the Latin words *herba salata*, which means "salted vegetables." The ancient Romans used saltwater as salad dressing.

AMAZON. The ancient Greeks had a legend about a tribe of warrior women who were so fierce that they cut off their right breasts in order to draw their bows more easily. The Greeks called these women *Amazons*—A, meaning "without," and *mazon*, meaning "breast."

OSTRICH. Comes from the Greek words *Megas strouthos*, which mean "great sparrow." The *Dictionary of Word Origins* calls the name "the understatement of the ancient world."

PROSTITUTE. From the Latin word *prostitutus*, which means "offered for sale."

BALLOT: From *ballota*, which means "little ball" in Greek. The ancient Greeks voted by dropping little balls into a particular candidate's container—a white ball was a vote in favor of a candidate, a *black ball* was a vote against.

TROPHY. From the old Greek word *trope*, which meant the turning point in a battle. The Greeks used to erect monuments at the exact spot on a battlefield where the tide had turned in their favor. Over the centuries the word evolved to represent *any* battle monument, whether or not it was on a battlefield...and even if it just commemorated a sporting victory.

Only 2% of Americans say they're in a good mood every day.

HULA HOOPS

The Hula Hoop was a pioneer, the first major fad created
and fueled by a new power in America—TV ads.

The Hula Hoop originated in Australia, where it was simply a bamboo exercise ring used in gym classes. In 1957, an Australian company began selling the ring in retail stores—which attracted the attention of a small California toy manufacturer named Wham-O.

Wham-O's owners made a few wooden rings for their kids ("They just wouldn't put the hoop down"), took them to cocktail parties ("Folks had to have a couple of drinks in them to take a whack at it")...and then decided they had a hot item on their hands. They began producing a plastic version, naming it a Hula Hoop after the motion it resembled—the Hawaiian hula dance.

A BIG HIT

Wham-O introduced the Hula Hoop to the American public in January 1958, and it quickly became the biggest toy craze in history (up to that time). During the year, more than 20 million— $30 million worth—were sold.

The Hula Hoop was the quintessential fad item, though; by November 1958, the *Wall Street Journal* was already announcing: "Hoops Have Had It." A brief comeback occurred in 1965, when Wham-O introduced the "Shoop-Shoop" Hula Hoop, with a ball bearing in it to make noise, but it just wasn't the same.

HOOP FACTS

• According to the *British Medical Journal*, the Hula Hoop was responsible for an increase in back, neck, and abdominal injuries.

• Indonesia banned Hula Hoops, because they "might stimulate passion." Japan forbade them on public streets.

• The official news agency in China called Hula Hoops "a nauseating craze." In the Soviet Union, the hoop was seen as a "symbol of the emptiness of American culture."

• Hula Hoop endurance records: longest whirl—four hours (more than 18,000 turns), by a 10-year-old Boston boy; most hoops twirled simultaneously—14, by an 11-year-old in Michigan.

Comic book fact: Superman is 6'2", but Clark Kent is only 5'11". (He slouches.)

FAMOUS FOR 15 MINUTES

*Here's another installment of our feature based on Andy
Warhol's comment that "in the future, everyone
will be famous for 15 minutes"*

THE STAR: Robert Opel, a 33-year-old unemployed actor

THE HEADLINE: *Streaker Steals Oscar Show*

WHAT HAPPENED: Near the end of the 1974 Academy
Awards ceremony, host David Niven was introducing the woman
who would present the Best Picture award—Elizabeth Taylor. "She
is," he was saying fondly, "a very important contributor to world
entertainment, and someone quite likely…"

Suddenly his speech was interrupted by screams and laughter as
a naked man streaked across the stage in back of him. Niven stut-
tered for a second, then recovered and commented, "Ladies and
gentlemen, that was bound to happen. Just think, the only laugh
that man will probably ever get is for stripping and showing off his
shortcomings." Then he gave the floor to Taylor, who quipped,
"That's a pretty tough act to follow."

Meanwhile, the streaker had been caught backstage and was produced by security, fully clothed, for the press. "I have no official
connection with the Academy," Robert Opel told reporters. Observers speculated that Oscar show producer, Jack Haley, Jr., had
created the whole incident as a publicity stunt. He denied it, de-
claring: "I would have used a pretty girl instead."

THE AFTERMATH: Opel made an appearance on "The Mike
Douglas Show," debuted as a stand-up comedian in Hollywood, and
was hired to streak at other Hollywood affairs (e.g., one honoring
Rudolf Nureyev). Then he disappeared from public view. Five years
later, he made the news again when he was brutally murdered at a
sex paraphernalia shop he owned in San Francisco.

THE STAR: Jimmy Nicol, a little-known English drummer

THE HEADLINE: *Ringo Heads to Hospital as Beatles Tour with
New Drummer*

WHAT HAPPENED: In June 1964, the Fab Four were in a

It's against the law to drink beer in Cedar City, Utah, if your shoelaces are untied.

photographer's studio when drummer Ringo Starr suddenly collapsed. He was rushed to a hospital, where he was diagnosed as having tonsillitis. This was a huge problem—the Beatles were about to leave for a world tour. Their solution: They hired a local session drummer named Jimmy Nicol to play with them while Ringo recovered. Overnight, the bewildered Nicol became a member of the world's most popular band.

Nicol played with the Beatles for two weeks, in Holland, Hong Kong, and Australia. Ringo finally recovered enough to join the band Down Under, and after one last performance—with Ringo watching—Jimmy reluctantly returned to England.

THE AFTERMATH: Inspired, Nicol started his own band, the Shubdubs. Unfortunately, they went nowhere.

THE STAR: Jackie Mitchell, 17-year-old left-handed pitcher for the Chattanooga Lookouts, a minor-league baseball team

THE HEADLINE: *Female Hurler Fans Ruth and Gehrig*

WHAT HAPPENED: It was April 2, 1931. The mighty New York Yankees were working their way north at the end of spring training, playing minor league teams along the way. On this day, they were in Chattanooga, Tennessee. When the first two Yankee batters got hits, the minor-league manager decided to make a pitching change. He brought in his latest acquisition, a local player who had never pitched in a pro game before—Jackie Mitchell. She was, in fact, the first woman *ever* to play in a pro game. And the first batter she had to face was Babe Ruth. A tough situation; but Mitchell was tough. She struck the Babe out in five pitches...then proceeded to strike out "Larrupin' Lou" Gehrig in three.

It was an impressive debut for a rookie pitcher, but it was a little suspect—Joe Engel, owner of the Lookouts, was known for publicity stunts, and this one had originally been planned for April 1 (the April Fools' Day game was rained out). Still, Mitchell insisted to her dying day that it was for real—and you can't argue with record books.

THE AFTERMATH: *The New York Times* praised Mitchell in an editorial, hailing her feat as a step forward for women's rights. She never made it as a pro—she played ball around Chattanooga for six more years, then quit to marry and take over the family business (optometry). She died in 1987.

Tony the Tiger turned 40 in 1995; the Jolly Green Giant turned 67.

THE STAR: Harold Russell, a disabled World War II veteran

THE HEADLINE: *Non-Actor Wins Oscar for First Film Role*

WHAT HAPPENED: In 1946, director William Wyler made a film called *The Best Years of Our Lives*, depicting the personal struggles of several returning World War II vets. It was a hot topic, and the movie attracted a first-class cast: Frederic March, Myrna Loy, Virginia Mayo, Dana Andrews…and Harold Russell.

Russell had lost both his hands in an explosion at a Georgia training camp during the war. The Army asked him to appear in a short film about disabled veterans, and Wyler spotted him in it.

The director essentially cast Russell as himself—a severely disabled man trying to readjust to everyday life. Wyler wouldn't let him take acting lessons, and Russell's performance was so powerful that it carried the film. *The Best Years of Our Lives* captured seven Oscars—including Best Picture, Best Actor (Frederic March), Best Director, Best Screenplay, and Best Supporting Actor—Russell.

THE AFTERMATH: Russell didn't appear in another film for 34 years. He can be seen in the 1980 feature, *Inside Moves*.

THE STAR: Valerie Solanas, founder of SCUM—Society for Cutting Up Men

THE HEADLINE: *Warhol Felled by SCUM*

WHAT HAPPENED: Valerie Solanas hung around Andy Warhol's studio in the '60s, even appearing in his movie *I, a Man*. So the artist whom friends called "the ultimate voyeur" was taken by surprise when Solanas pulled out a gun one day in June 1968 and shot him. It turned out she was irked that Warhol hadn't bothered commenting on the script of a play she'd left him.

Warhol was seriously wounded; doctors only gave him a 50-50 chance to survive. Meanwhile, Solanas turned herself in, telling the officer to whom she surrendered, "He had too much control over my life." She was immediately put under psychiatric observation, while she and her organization were splashed across the tabloid front pages.

THE AFTERMATH: Warhol lived, Solanas was imprisoned, and the whole incident stands as an ironic reminder that no one—not even the man who came up with the notion—is immune when someone's 15 minutes arrive.

Why did polyester blue jeans bomb in the '70s? They wouldn't fade.

THE EVOLUTION OF SANTA CLAUS, PART II

Here's the next installment of the Santa story (begins on page 103).

ST. NICK ARRIVES IN AMERICA

In 1664, the flourishing Dutch colony of New Amsterdam was taken over by the British forces—who renamed it "New York" after the Duke of York.

For the next 200 years or so, the Dutch citizens of the colony waged a losing battle to preserve what was left of their culture and traditions. One of the most active groups was an association of Dutch intellectuals who called themselves the "Knickerbockers."

FATHER KNICKERBOCKER

Writer Washington Irving was a member of the group, and in 1809 he published a satirical version of Dutch traditions in a book called *The Knickerbocker's History of New York*. It contained several dozen references to "Sinter Klaas" (an adaptation of "Sint Nikolass"), including a tale of how he flew across the sky in a wagon and dropped presents down chimneys for good little girls and boys—not just on Christmas, but on any day he felt like it.

Irving "created a new popularity for the bishop," Teresa Chris writes in *The Story of Santa Claus*. "He saw Saint Nicholas in America not in clerical robes, but as a jolly fellow, like the good Dutch burghers." And New Yorkers loved the image.

Irving's description of the saint rapidly became known to New Yorkers. The English settlers enthusiastically adopted the joyful Dutch celebrations of St. Nicholas' Day, but they gradually merged them with their own traditions of celebrating Christmas or the New Year. It is not hard to see how Sinter Klass became Santa Claus in the mouths of the English-speaking New Yorkers.

SANTA'S HELPER: CLEMENT CLARKE MOORE

The most important contributor to the modern image of Santa was a professor of divinity in New York—Dr. Clement Clarke Moore.

When Moore, a friend of Washington Irving, sat down to write his children a Christmas poem in 1822, he was heavily influenced by Irving's vision of Sinter Klaas and his flying wagon and gift-giving. But Moore made a few alterations to make the story more believable. For example, Chris writes, "The clogs that the Dutch children left in the chimney corner on December 6 became something all children could relate to in cold weather—stockings." And the wagon became a "miniature sleigh" pulled by "eight tiny reindeer."

> The sleigh and horse with its bells was a common means of transport in New England...And for it to be pulled by reindeer gave St. Nick an exotic link with the far North—a land of cold and snow where few, if any people traveled and hence was mysterious and remote.

Moore described Santa as a dwarfish "jolly old elf," dressed in furs, who goes down chimneys to give children their gifts. Moore even gave the reindeer names: Dasher, Dancer, Prancer, Vixen, Comet, Cupid, Donder, and Blitzen. Other Christmas stories had portrayed Saint Nicholas on a white horse, or with one or two reindeer—one version even had him in a cart pulled by a goat—but Moore's account was so vivid and compelling that it became the standard.

RELUCTANT HERO

Moore never intended for anyone other than his children to hear *A Visit from Saint Nicholas*—in fact, for more than 20 years he refused to admit he was the author (apparently because he was afraid it would damage his standing in the stuffy academic community of the 19th century). But his wife liked the story so much that she sent copies to her friends...and somehow the poem wound up printed anonymously in the Troy, New York, *Sentinel* on December 23, 1823. It eventually became known as *The Night Before Christmas*. It was so popular that within a decade it had become a central part of the Santa legend...as well as the best-known poem in American history.

Now Santa had a personality and a mission, and was permanently linked to Christmas. But what did he look like?

See page 341 for Part III of Santa's story.

FAMILIAR NAMES

Some people achieve immortality because their names are associated with common items or activities. You already know the names—now here are the people.

Antoine de la Mothe Cadillac. A French explorer, Cadillac founded Detroit in 1701.

Guy Fawkes. English political agitator who tried to blow up Parliament in 1605, but was caught and executed. The British began celebrating November 5 as Guy Fawkes Day, burning effigies of "the old Guy." Since the effigies were dressed in old clothes, the term *guy* came to mean "bum." In America during colonial times, its meaning was broadened to mean any male.

Captain William Lynch. A Virginia farmer during the Revolutionary War, Lynch organized bands of townspeople to dispense justice to outlaws and British collaborators. These bands became known as *Lynch* mobs, and hanging someone without a trial became known as *lynching*.

Henry Deringer. An American gunsmith of the 1840s, Deringer invented a tiny pistol that he named after himself. Imitators copied his guns—and misspelled his name. Today *derringer* is still spelled with two r's.

Thomas Derrick. A notorious hangman in England during the 17th century, Derrick designed a hoisting apparatus for the gallows—which he used to execute more than 3,000 people. The apparatus—and the crane that resembles it—are both called *derricks*.

Charles Henry Dow and Edward D. Jones. Journalists at the turn of the century, Dow and Jones created the first index of U.S. stock prices—the *Dow-Jones* Average. It later appeared in the newspaper they founded, the *Wall Street Journal*.

Captain Fudge. Though his first name has been forgotten, Captain Fudge is still known through his nickname. A captain in the

British Navy in the 1600s, he was called "Lying Fudge" because of his wild tales about his seafaring adventures. Sailors of the day referred to his story-telling as *fudging* it.

Dr. Thomas Lushington. Lushington was a heavy-drinking English chaplain in the 1600s. His reputation as a drunk was so great that the City of Lushington, a London drinking club, was named in his honor more than 200 years after his death. The club's inebriated clientele inspired the word *lush*.

Mr. Scheuster. Like Captain Fudge, Scheuster's first name has been forgotten. He was a crooked criminal lawyer in New York in the 1840s whose name inspired the term *shyster*.

E. A. Murphy, Jr. Murphy was not an optimist. An American engineer in the 1940s, he was the first to utter the words "Anything that can go wrong *will* go wrong"—*Murphy's Law*.

Alfredo di Lellio. A Roman restaurateur. His fettucine with butter, cream, and Parmesan cheese became famous in the '20s after Hollywood stars Mary Pickford and Douglas Fairbanks ate in his restaurant every day during their honeymoon.

Gabriel Daniel Fahrenheit. German scientist of the late 17th and early 18th centuries. Invented a new thermometer that used mercury instead of alcohol. Its new scale—which marks water's freezing point at 32° and its boiling point at 212°—was named *Fahrenheit* after him and became popular in English-speaking countries.

Josh Billings. A 19th-century humorist. He popularized a bantering comedy style that became known as *joshing*.

Charles Moncke. A British blacksmith. He is credited with inventing the *monkey* wrench (which the British call a "spanner").

Brandley, Voorhis, and Day. Owners of an underwear manufacturing company. Known by their initials: *BVDs*.

Lambert de Begue. A monk whose 12th-century followers were wandering mendicants. His name—pronounced *beg*—became synonymous with his followers' pleas for aid.

According to the book *The Intelligence of Dogs*, Border collies are the most

NO SWEAT, PART I

To tell the truth, we never expected to write so much on the subject of sweat. But the more we read about it, the more interesting it got. And what the heck, this is a bathroom reader—no one's going to be offended by the topic. So here it is: More than you ever wanted to know about your own perspiration, from the BRI's diligent Science Department.

Nobody knows why human beings ended up with stinky sweat. The fact is, most animals don't sweat at all. With the exception of horses, some apes, and a few types of cows, we are the only species of animal that uses perspiration to regulate body temperature. Jackrabbits, for example, cool down by flushing blood through their ears, and ostriches and emus chill out by urinating on their own legs. Just about every other warm-blooded animal cools off by panting.

The most plausible explanation for our body odor comes from anthropologist Louis S. B. Leakey, who believes the smell served as a defense mechanism, keeping predators at bay until we'd evolved enough to defend ourselves with weapons of our own construction.

COVERUP OF AN ANATOMY

Whatever the reason, as soon as people found new ways to protect themselves, they began looking for ways to quell the smell.

"The problem of body odor is ancient, as are man's attempt to solve it," Charles Panati writes in *Extraordinary Origins of Everyday Things*. "From the dawn of written history, 5,500 years ago in Sumer, every major civilization has left a record of its efforts to produce deodorants."

Considering how much time and effort have been spent on the struggle, it's surprising how little has been accomplished. For nearly 2,000 years the only ways people found to deal with B.O. was to bathe regularly and then cover up with sweeter smelling fragrances. The ancient Egyptians doused themselves with fragrant tree resin. The ancient Romans literally soaked themselves in perfume. They got so carried away with the practice, Diane Ackerman explains in *A Natural History of the Senses*, that "both men and women took baths in perfume, soaked their clothes in it, and perfumed their horses and household pets."

FOLLOW YOUR NOSE

One of the reasons it took so long to develop effective deodorants was that until the 19th century, people did not clearly understand the link between sweat and odor.

Galen, a second-century Greek physician, theorized that the skin releases liquids and gases into the air (in a process known as respiration) even when it isn't visibly releasing sweat. But his theory wasn't proven until the 1600s, when an Italian scientist named Santorio Santorio demonstrated that the body lost weight over time, as it gave off moisture. Santorio proved his theory by working and sleeping atop a massive scale that measured the weight his body lost as it perspired.

The next big advance came in the beginning of the 18th century, when the Dutch physician Hermann Boerhaave described sweat glands for the first time. Finally, in the mid-19th century, German anatomists put a corpse under a microscope and actually *counted* every single sweat gland on the cadaver's body, arriving at a final total of 2,381,248. Subsequent studies showed that human bodies actually contain anywhere from 2 million to 4 million sweat glands, which cover every square inch of the body except for the lips.

PARTNERS IN CRIME

By the late 19th century, scientists had a good understanding of how body odor is formed:

• The body has two different types of sweat glands: *eccrine* glands and *apocrine* glands.

• Technically speaking, neither kind *produces* body odor—the odor is produced by bacteria.

• The eccrine glands provide moisture which creates an environment in which bacteria thrive; the apocrine glands produce odorless, milky secretions that bacteria love to eat.

• It's the unending cycle of bacteria multiplying, dying, and decomposing that causes body odor to form.

THE SWEET SMELL OF SUCCESS

Once scientists understood the bacteria and moisture connection, they were finally able to move beyond soap and perfumes in the battle against body odor. They added anti-bacterial agents to perfumes to create the first truly effective deodorants and invented "anti-perspirants," products that use drying agents to block underarm moisture.

The world's first antiperspirant, a zinc-based cream called Mum, hit the market in 1888. It was followed in 1902 by Everdry, a product that used aluminum chloride as the drying agent. Few advances have been made since then: zinc- and aluminum-based compounds remain the most widely used ingredients in antiperspirants today.

NEW APPLICATIONS

About the only changes that have been made to deodorants and antiperspirants since their invention are improvements in the way they're applied to the body.

Both Mum and Everdry were creams applied by fingers or cotton swabs, which made them messy to use. Everdry was particularly bad—it was cold and sticky, took forever to dry, and was so acidic that it stung when applied and even burned holes in clothing.

The first (nonaerosol) spray deodorants were invented in the 1940s. They were popular, but they were cold, wet, and drippy. In the 1950s, Ban Roll-on—which used the same technology as the ballpoint pen—was introduced, and roll-ons took over the market. They, in turn, were outsold in the early 1960s by the new *aerosol* sprays, led by Gillette's Right Guard. But the aerosols used ozone-eating chemicals as propellants and lost popularity in the 1980s.

Today, Americans spend about $1.6 billion a year on deodorants. Nearly half of that goes for solid "stick" products; 24% is spent on ozone-friendly aerosols; and 22% is spent on roll-ons, which women prefer over all other forms. Least popular are creams, pump sprays, and deodorant pads, which make up 4% of the market.

Don't sweat—No Sweat, Part II is on page 423.

When he needed inspiration, Ludwig von Beethoven poured water on himself.

GOLDWYNISMS

*Samuel Goldwyn was one of Hollywood's great movie producers.
He was also famous for murdering the English language—sort of
the Yogi Berra of the film world. In Hollywood, his sayings were
called Goldwynisms. Here are some classic examples:*

"All this criticism—it's like ducks off my back."

"Too caustic? To hell with the cost—we'll make the movie anyway."

"We've all passed a lot of water since then."

Asked about the message of one of his films: "I'm not interested in messages. Messages are for Western Union."

"I'm willing to admit that I may not always be right...but I'm never wrong."

"Tell me, how did you love the picture?"

"I want a movie that starts with an earthquake and works up to a climax."

"I'll believe in color television when I see it in black and white."

"Don't let your opinions sway your judgment."

"Let's have some new clichés."

"These days, every director bites the hand that laid the golden egg."

"In two words: im possible."

"This music won't do. There's not enough sarcasm in it."

"Let's bring it up to date with some snappy nineteenth-century dialogue."

"If you can't give me your word of honor, will you give me your promise?"

"A verbal contract isn't worth the paper it's written on."

"Anyone who goes to see a psychiatrist ought to have his head examined."

"The most important thing in acting is honesty. Once you've learned to fake that, you're in."

"If I could drop dead right now, I'd be the happiest man."

Every 2.7 seconds, a Tupperware party begins somewhere in the world.

THE ORIGIN OF LEVI'S

Blue jeans are as American as apple pie and bathroom reading. In fact, you might have a pair around your ankles right now.

CANVASING THE CUSTOMERS

In 1850—during the California gold rush—a 17-year-old German-Jewish immigrant named Levi Strauss moved from New York City to San Francisco to sell dry goods to the miners.

• He tried to sell canvas to them for their tents, but found little interest in it. So he made pants out of the material instead.

• The miners loved them. Although the pants weren't particularly comfortable, they were the first ones durable enough to withstand the miners' rugged living conditions.

• People nicknamed the pants Levi's, after their creator.

A RIVETING EXPERIENCE

In the early 1860s, Levi Strauss began using denim in his pants. It was still tough, but it was softer and more comfortable than canvas.

• He also found that when the denim pants were dyed an indigo blue, they wouldn't show soil and stains as much. Miners appreciated this, and Levi's became even more popular.

• Meanwhile, miners found that carrying heavy tools in their pockets often ripped the pants at the seams.

• A Nevada tailor named Jacob Davis solved that problem for his customers by securing each pocket seam with a rivet. It worked so well, in fact, that Davis wrote to Levi Strauss offering to sell him the idea. Strauss took him up on it; copper rivets first appeared on Levi's in 1873. They became a hallmark of the company's product.

LEVI'S MIDDLE-AGE SPREAD

Levi's were working people's pants for their first 75 years. Then, in 1935, an advertisement featuring two high-society women wearing skintight jeans ran in *Vogue* magazine. The reaction was so great that jeans became the rage. Jitterbugging teenagers started wearing them with the cuffs rolled up, and they've been fashionable ever since.

• Meanwhile, the Levi Strauss Company branched out into manufacturing other items as well as blue jeans...and by 1970 it had become the largest clothing manufacturer in the world.

The average kid eats 15 pounds of cereal a year.

INSIDE MOTHER GOOSE

We've sung and recited these rhymes since we were kids. Little did we know that they weren't just nonsense. Here's the inside scoop about what they really mean.

Humpty Dumpty *sat on a wall, Humpty Dumpty had a great fall. All the king's horses and all the king's men, couldn't put Humpty together again.*

Background: According to Katherine Thomas in *The Real Personages of Mother Goose*, this rhyme is 500 years old and refers to King Richard III of England. In 1483, his reign ended when he fell from his mount during battle; he was slain as he stood shouting, "My kingdom for a horse!"

Originally the last line was "Could not set Humpty up again"—which can be interpreted as either putting him back on his horse, or back on the throne.

Old King Cole *was a merry old soul, a merry old soul was he. He called for his pipe and he called for his bowl, and he called for his fiddlers three.*

Background: There was actually a King Cole in Britain during the third century. No one knows much about him, but historians agree that he's the subject of the rhyme. Of interest: There's a Roman amphitheater in Colchester, England, that has been known as "King Cole's Kitchen" for centuries.

Little Jack Horner *sat in a corner, eating his Christmas pie. He stuck in his thumb and he pulled out a plum, and said "What a good boy am I."*

Background: In the mid-1500s, when King Henry VIII was confiscating lands belonging to the Catholic church, the Abbot of Glastonbury—the richest abbey in the British kingdom—tried to bribe the monarch by sending him a special Christmas pie. Inside the pie, the abbot had enclosed the deeds to 12 manor houses.

The courier who delivered the pie to the king was the abbot's aide, Thomas Horner. (The name "Jack" was contemporary slang for any male, particularly a "knave"). On his way, Horner stopped, stuck in his hand, and pulled out one of the deeds from the pie—a

---

Full-grown grizzly bears can bite through 1/2-inch steel.

plum called Mells Manor. Shortly after, Horner moved into Mells, and his family still lives there today (although they deny the story). Ironically, the abbot was later put on trial for his life—and Horner was one of the judges who condemned him to death.

Jack be nimble, Jack be quick, Jack jump over the candlestick.
Background: For centuries, jumping over a candlestick was a method of fortune-telling in England. According to *The Oxford Dictionary of Nursery Rhymes*: "A candlestick with a lighted candle was placed on the floor and if, when jumping over it, the light was not extinguished, good luck was supposed to follow during the coming year."

Ring around the rosy, a pocket full of posies. Ashes, ashes, we all fall down.
Background: According to James Leasor in *The Plague and the Fire*, this "had its origin in the [London Plague of 1664]. Rosy refers to the rosy rash of plague....The posies were herbs and spices carried to ward off the disease; sneezing was a common symptom of those close to death." In *The Annotated Mother Goose*, the authors note that the third line is often given as a sneezing noise ("At-choo, at-choo"), and that, " 'We all fall down' was, in a way, exactly what happened."

WHO WAS MOTHER GOOSE?
No one's quite sure. There are at least two possibilities, according to *The Annotated Mother Goose*:
• Charles Perrault, a French writer, "published a collection of fairy tales called *Tales of My Mother Goose* in 1697. The book contains eight stories [including]: 'Little Red Riding Hood,' 'Bluebeard,' [and] 'Puss In Boots,' " etc.
• But many scholars maintain that Mother Goose was actually Elizabeth Foster Goose, of Boston, Massachusetts. In 1692, when she was 27, Elizabeth married a widower named Isaac Goose and immediately inherited a family of 10 children. One of her stepdaughters married a printer several years later who enjoyed listening to "Mother Goose" recite old rhymes to the younger children. In 1719, he published a collection of them called *Songs for the Nursery, or Mother Goose's Melodies*.

Movie star Errol Flynn once worked on an Australian sheep ranch, castrating sheep with his teeth.

THE ORIGIN OF THE ATM

Originally denounced by bankers as an expensive gimmick, the automated teller machine has become an indispensable part of our lives. But the company that created it isn't around to cash in on the boom. Here's the story of how they turned a sure thing into a dramatic flop.

CASH COW

Do you remember where you were on June 27, 1967? That was the day Barclay's Bank installed the world's first "Barclaycash" cash dispensing machine in its Enfield, England, branch. It was a relatively unsophisticated machine; it could only handle withdrawals, and was intended mostly for use in emergencies when the bank was closed.

Yankee Ingenuity

An American business executive named B. J. "Jack" Meredith happened to see the machine during a trip to Europe and was impressed. But he was surprised the technology hadn't been used to build a machine that performed all of the basic banking transactions human tellers did.

"Here was something that would give customers 24-hour-a-day service," Meredith recalled years later, "and give banks a hell of a marketing tool." When he returned home, Meredith told people at his company, a maker of baggage handling equipment, what he had seen. He talked them into forming a new division to develop "automated teller machines"…but when they dragged their feet on the project, he decided to take it over himself.

GOING IT ALONE

B. J. suggested to his younger brother, Don Meredith, Dallas Cowboys quarterback and ABC Sports broadcaster, that they buy out his company's ATM division and form an independent company. His brother agreed. In 1969, with a handful of other investors, they founded Docutel, Inc., and in November 1971, they installed the world's first automated teller machine, a Docutel Total Teller (TT) 300, in the lobby of Atlanta's Citizens & Southern National Bank.

The word *noon* originally meant "3 p.m."

TOUGH SELL

Docutel actually had a difficult time interesting bankers in automated teller machines. Whenever banks installed them, it seemed that their customers either didn't know the machines existed or weren't sure what they did. "Banks were extremely slow to realize that customers would be hooked once they tried the machines," explains Linda Fenner Zimmer, a banking analyst. "The trick was getting them to try it. They should have painted them red, put plants around them, advertised, promoted, given them funny names, anything."

That's exactly what Docutel ended up doing. After more than four years of sluggish sales, it landed a client who was willing to promote the machines heavily. The customer, First National Bank of Atlanta, painted its machine bright red, called it "Tillie the All-Time Teller," and spent more than $500,000 on advertising and lobby demonstrations.

Taking Off

The bank's promotions made headlines all over the country, and the TT300 quickly came to be seen as the wave of the future. Within a week of the First National Bank's publicity blitz, major banks all over the country flooded Docutel with orders for ATM systems, creating a backlog of orders that was nearly a year long. "I looked like a damn genius," Meredith recalled years later. Seeing money to be made, other companies, including IBM and Diebold, a bank-vault manufacturer, jumped into the fray. Despite the intense competition, by the end of 1977 Docutel was a $31 million company commanding an 80 percent share of the market.

FUTURE SHOCK

Still, the technology was advancing so quickly—and Docutel's competitors were so well financed—that Meredith felt the company had to move to a new generation of machines to stay afloat. So Docutel rushed the new model, the TT2000, to market in September 1977 before it had been fully tested.

Unfortunately, the TT2000 was a dog. The buttons stuck, the machines ate ATM cards like they were candy, and the computer system overloaded after only a few hours of heavy use. Plus, the TT2000 was physically larger than the model it replaced, so banks had to knock bigger holes into their walls to accommodate it.

By changing the size of its machine, Docutel surrendered its competitive edge to any machine that could fit in the original hole. As *Forbes* magazine recounted in 1981:

> Rushing the TT2000 to market before it was thoroughly tested, sent Docutel from industry leader to industry joke. Its name became synonymous with unreliability—sure death in a service industry. In 1977 it lost $8 million on sales of $25 million, scared off potential customers and drove existing customers—its biggest asset— into the arms of the competition.

The TT2000 was eventually pulled from the market, but the damage was already done—Docutel's image as a supplier of high-quality equipment was ruined.

Sending the Wrong Signals

Docutel's share of the ATM market plunged from 80% to 27%, and the loss in income undermined the company's ability to research and develop new machines.

Desperate to stop the flow of red ink, Meredith slashed his sales force (most went to work for competitors), sold his ATM service and maintenance division and bought a highly profitable clothing company to generate cash for research and development.

The moves made good financial sense; they enabled Docutel to build an improved machine called the TT2300. Independent analysts ranked the machine as the most reliable on the market, but that did little to persuade banks to buy it. When they saw Docutel selling off its ATM businesses and buying non-ATM companies, they figured it was getting ready to pull out of the market entirely.

THE END

Docutel never did convince its customers that it was in the ATM business to stay. Ultimately, flagging sales forced the company to merge with Olivetti in 1982. It continued to take a beating from the competition, and B. J. Meredith resigned in 1984. Even the Italian giant's deep pockets weren't enough to keep the ATM divison afloat, though. Olivetti finally threw in the towel in October 1986. Docutel had changed the banking world forever, but it could not survive long enough to cash in on the world it had created.

Australian soldiers used "We're Off to See the Wizard" as a marching song during WWII.

BOX-OFFICE BLOOPERS

We all love bloopers. Here are a bunch of movie mistakes to look for in popular films. You can find more in a book called Film Flubs, *by Bill Givens.*

Movie: *The Wizard of Oz* (1939)
Scene: Dorothy, the Tin Woodsman, and the Scarecrow dance down the Yellow Brick Road singing, "We're Off to See the Wizard."
Blooper: A crew member can be seen in the background among the trees. (For years, rumors circulated in Hollywood that the crew member had committed suicide and hanged himself from one of the trees on the set. The rumors were false.)

Movie: *Spartacus* (1960)
Scene: Peter Ustinov gets off of his horse.
Blooper: His jockey shorts are visible under his tunic as he climbs down.

Movie: *The Alamo* (1960)
Scenes: The battle sequences.
Bloopers: Though the movie is a Western, you can see several mobile trailers in the distance. (And in another scene, you can see a stuntman falling into a mattress.)

Movie: *Children of a Lesser God* (1986)
Scenes: Several occasions in which Marlee Matlin (who is deaf and portrays a deaf character) and co-star William Hurt sign to each other during conversations in which Hurt is speaking.
Blooper: The sign language has nothing to do with the movie—it's about Matlin's and Hurt's private life. (At the time the movie was made, Matlin and Hurt were having an affair.)

Movie: *Ben Hur* (1959)
Scene: The chariot scene.
Blooper: A red sports car is driving by the Colosseum in the distance.

Movie: *Gandhi* (1982)
Scene: Crowd scene.
Blooper: One of the peasants is wearing Adidas tennis shoes.

Worldwide, there are 8,500 chapters of the Barbie Fan Club.

YOU'RE MY INSPIRATION

It's fascinating to see how many pop characters—fictional and real—are inspired by other characters. Here's a handful of examples.

TINKERBELL. Walt Disney's animators gave her Marilyn Monroe's measurements.

JAFAR, the Grand Vizier. The villain in the 1993 animated film *Aladdin*—described by the director as a "treacherous vizier...who seeks the power of the enchanted lamp to claim the throne for his own greedy purposes"—was inspired by Nancy Reagan. The Sultan, a doddering, kindly leader, was inspired by Nancy's husband.

THE EMPEROR in the *Star Wars* trilogy. In early drafts of the Star Wars scripts, George Lucas portrayed the emperor as "an elected official who is corrupted by power and subverts the democratic process." Lucas modeled him after Richard Nixon.

MICK JAGGER. Studied the way Marilyn Monroe moved and learned to mimic her onstage.

THE STATUE OF LIBERTY. The face of Miss Liberty, sculpted by Frederic-Auguste Bartholdi, was inspired by his mother. Although the statue has welcomed immigrants to New York City since 1886, Madame Bartholdi was reputedly "a domineering bigot."

DR. STRANGELOVE. Dr. Kissinger, I presume? According to Penny Stallings in *Flesh & Fantasy*, "[Director] Stanley Kubrick ...made a special trip to Harvard to meet Dr. Henry Kissinger while researching the title role for his screen adaptation of *Dr. Strangelove*."

DR. JEKYLL & MR. HYDE. Inspired by Dr. Horace Wells, celebrated inventor of modern anesthesia. He got hooked on ether and went mad; he was jailed for throwing acid in a woman's face while under its effects.

Weight-loss tip: Melting an ice cube in your mouth burns about 2.3 calories.

THE GREAT T.P. SHORTAGE

Back in the 1970s, there were shortages of things like gasoline and meat, and Americans were skittish about the issue. So in 1973, when Johnny Carson jokingly announced there was a toilet paper shortage, people took it seriously. Here's the story of America's first and only T.P. shortage, as TV Guide reported it in 1974. The article is by Ralph Schoenstein.

A t 11:35 on the night of December 19, 1973, Johnny Carson began his opening monologue.

Earlier in the day, his writers had heard that a Wisconsin congressman named Harold Froehlich had claimed the federal government was behind in getting bids to supply toilet tissue. "The United States may face a serious shortage of toilet tissue within a few months," the congressman had said.

It was a pretty funny concept, so they wrote it into the script. That night, Carson said to America, "You know what's disappearing from the supermarket shelves? Toilet paper. There's an acute shortage of toilet paper in the United States."

Then he swung at a phantom golf ball while 20 million people jumped out of bed and dashed to their shelves. These were people who recently had run out of gas, meat...onions too, so they were keenly "shortage conditioned." The next morning all of them rushed to their local supermarkets. By noon of December 20, some Americans owned enough T.P. to welcome the first man back from Mars.

"I never saw anything like it," said the manager of one New Jersey A&P.

"We tried to ration it," said the manager of an Acme Supermarket nearby. "Four single rolls to a customer or one four-roll pack, but we had no way to keep people from coming back again and again. I mean, there weren't any license plates we could check."

"I heard about it on TV," said Rosemary Wren, "so I bought an extra thirty rolls."

The only problem with such a passionate appreciation of the newest shortage was that everyone was going for the wrong toilet paper. Representative Froehlich had been talking only about government-issue tissue, not the soft kind.

Twenty percent of all publications sold in Japan are comic books.

By December 23, however, there was a shortage of good toilet paper, too, probably the first shortage in American history created entirely by consumers.

Carson tried to call off the hoarding hordes. "I'm in trouble again," he said. "I started talking about a toilet paper shortage. It's caused some problems. I'm sorry, I've done a lot of mean things in my life. I'd hate to think of people sitting...sitting around...just sitting. I don't want to be remembered as the man who took the toilet paper off the shelves. Anyway, there is no shortage."

But stampedes are easier to start than to stop. So Carson's retraction had little effect on the people who kept seeing empty shelves.

Many of the stores being hit by hoarders filled in with a coarser European toilet paper which people eagerly grabbed until they found that it was something that belonged on the Oregon Trail.

In a dramatic attempt to stop the panic, the Scott Paper Company allowed TV crews to film the tissue merrily rolling out in its Chester, Pennsylvania, plant, which was still turning out 18,000 cases of paper products every day.

Scott officials pleaded for sanity, an eccentric request in the U.S. today. "Stay calm," one official said. "There just isn't any shortage."

But no words from Carson or Scott or even Norman Vincent Peale could have stopped the stampeding hordes, because a panic feeds on itself. The sight of empty shelves in the markets was all the proof that people needed that there was no Scott Paper plant in Chester, Pennsylvania.

By the middle of January, after three weeks of hysteria, toilet paper was back in the stores and the panic disappeared.

"As soon as people saw that the shelves were full again the whole thing was over," the Jersey Acme manager said. "It's not quite *that* simple," said a Hudson Paper Co. official. "We're still trying to sort out all the canceled orders."

"It was a classic study in rumor," said Steurt Henderson Britt, a professor of marketing at Northwestern University. "It was the old did-you-hear-that syndrome. One person says there could be a problem, the next person says there probably is a problem, and the next person says there *definitely* is a problem. A rumor used to take a long time to spread, but now all it takes is one TV star to joke about it and the rumor is in all 50 states."

21% of U.S. children say that if they were president, they'd "eat ice-cream for every meal."

FOOTBALL NAMES

*Football fans know these names by heart—but not how the
teams got them. Here are the stories behind the
famous names, from* Name That Team!

St. Louis Rams. When they were founded in Cleveland in
1937, the team's owner resisted public pressure to call his
club the Indians, after the local baseball team. Instead, he
named them after a New York City college football team—the
Fordham Rams. In 1945, the Rams became the first NFL franchise
to switch cities when it moved to Los Angeles. In 1995 they moved
again, from L.A. to St. Louis.

Cleveland Browns. When the Rams left Cleveland, a new NFL
franchise took its place and a contest was held to pick a new name.
The winner was the "Panthers"…but the owners found out there
was already a semipro Ohio football team called the Panthers—and
they stunk. So another contest was held. This time the winner was
"Brown Bombers," inspired by boxing champion Joe Louis. The
name was then shortened to "Browns," probably because the
coach's name was Paul Brown.

Houston Oilers. The owner of the team made all his money in oil
and picked the name "for sentimental reasons."

Oakland Raiders. Originally called the "Metropolitan Oakland
Area Football Club." That was too unwieldy, so the Oakland
Chamber of Commerce held a contest to find a new one. The winner: "Oakland Senors." The team's reaction: "Forget it." The owners came up with "Raiders" on their own.

Green Bay Packers. The club was named for the Indian Packing
Company, which sponsored the team when it was formed in 1919.
Ironically, the company went out of business during the Packers'
first season. But the team was a success; they joined the NFL two
years later.

There's a town in Texas called "Ding Dong."

New Orleans Saints. The team was admitted to the NFL on November 1, 1966—which happens to be All Saints Day. But the team probably got its name from the classic New Orleans jazz tune, "When the Saints Go Marching In."

Philadelphia Eagles. When they first began playing, in 1924, they were a pathetic club called the Frankford Yellowjackets (Frankford was the section of Philly they played in). The team went belly-up during the Depression, and two local businessmen bought it for $2,500. FDR had just been elected president; his two major economic programs—the New Deal and the National Recovery Act—used an eagle as their symbol. The team's new owners adopted the New Deal eagle as their symbol, too.

Phoenix Cardinals. Originally the Chicago Cardinals. They got their name when the team's owner bought a batch of secondhand jerseys from the University of Chicago. Someone commented that they looked like the university's maroon shirts, and the owner replied defensively that they weren't maroon—they were "cardinal red." The name stuck.

Washington Redskins. They started out as the Duluth (Minnesota) Eskimos in 1928. In 1932, because they were having a tough time surviving, they moved to Boston. Their new home was the stadium owned by baseball's Boston Braves (now the Atlanta Braves), so they changed their name to the Boston Braves as well. But the arrangement didn't work out: the following season, the football team moved to Fenway Park, home of the Boston Red Sox. To avoid offending the Red Sox (by keeping the name of the local rivals), the football team changed its name from Braves to Redskins. In 1938, the Redskins moved to Washington.

New York Giants. When the team was formed in 1925, it played in the Polo Grounds—home of the New York Giants baseball team. Owner Timothy Mara was a Giants fan already, so he named his team after them.

Chicago Bears, Detroit Lions, and **New York Jets.** All derived their names from local baseball teams—the Chicago Cubs, Detroit Tigers, and New York Mets.

BEAGLE, SHYSTER, & BEAGLE

This script, from a radio show by the Marx Brothers, was recently re-discovered. So close your ears, listen with your eyes, and travel back in time to November 28, 1932, for the first episode of Five-Star Theater.

SCENE: *The offices of Beagle, Shyster, & Beagle, Attorneys at Law. Miss Dimple, the receptionist, is polishing her nails. Beagle (Groucho Marx) bursts in.*

MISS DIMPLE: Good morning, Mr. Beagle.

GROUCHO: Never mind that. Get President Hoover on the phone. There's a picture of me in the police station and it doesn't do me justice. It makes me look like my father. In fact, it *is* my father. Never mind calling the president. Just find out what the reward is.

MISS DIMPLE: Mr. Beagle, I've got some letters for you to sign.

GROUCHO: Not now, not now! I've had a big day in court.

MISS DIMPLE: What was the case?

GROUCHO: Disorderly conduct, but I think I'll get off. Why shouldn't I? She hit me first.

MISS DIMPLE: Mr. Beagle! You hit a woman?

GROUCHO: Well, she was my size. Even smaller. Besides, if it weren't for my own arrests, I'd never get a case. Any calls?

MISS DIMPLE: Yes, your creditors have been calling all morning. They said they're tired of phoning and that something will have to be done.

GROUCHO: All right. We'll do something. We'll have the phone taken out.

MISS DIMPLE: Okay.

GROUCHO: There's a good girl. Your salary is raised ten dollars.

MISS DIMPLE: Thank you, Mr. Beagle.

GROUCHO: It's nothing at all. Say, how about lending me that ten till payday?

MISS DIMPLE: But Mr. Beagle, I haven't been paid in weeks. Besides, you overlook the fact—

GROUCHO: I've overlooked plenty around here. A fine stenographer you are! What do you do with your time? The floors aren't washed, the windows aren't cleaned, and my pants aren't even pressed.

MISS DIMPLE: But Mr. Beagle—

GROUCHO: Enough of this small talk. Where's that ten dollars?

Ancient Roman banquet halls had "vomitoriums," so people could keep eating even when full.

Groucho retires to his office. Miss Dimple ushers in a client—a nervous, worried soul named Mr. Jones.

JONES: How do you do, Mr. Beagle. A friend of mine told me you were a good lawyer.

GROUCHO: You just *think* he's a friend of yours. Sit down. Have you got a couple of cigars?

JONES: Uh...no, I'm sorry.

GROUCHO: Well, why don't you send out for some? If you've got a quarter, I'll go myself.

JONES: Oh, no, no, Mr. Beagle.

GROUCHO: What's the matter? Don't you trust me?

JONES: Why—I'd like to talk to you. I'm having trouble with my wife.

GROUCHO: You are! Well, I'm having trouble with my wife, too, but I don't go around bragging about it. Hmm. You oughta be ashamed of yourself. Miss Dimple, show this gentleman the door. On second thought, never mind. He saw it when he came in.

JONES: But, Mr. Beagle—I came to you for advice. Let me tell you a story. My wife is in love with two men, and—

GROUCHO: Ha, ha, ha! Not a bad story. The boys are all repeating it around the club. Now let me tell you one. There were two traveling men named Pat and Mike—

JONES: No, no, Mr. Beagle. I came here with a problem. I'm looking for evidence against my wife.

GROUCHO: What you really want is someone to shadow your wife. I've got just the man for you—my new assistant, Emmanuel Ravelli. He looks like an idiot and talks like an idiot. But don't let that fool you. He really is an idiot. You and Ravelli will have a lot in common.

JONES: Mr. Beagle, my time is valuable. Let me give you the facts. I married my wife secretly.

GROUCHO: You married her secretly? You mean you haven't told her about it? No wonder she runs around with other men.

JONES: Mr. Beagle, we must get this divorce—I want your assistant, Mr. Ravelli, to follow my wife.

GROUCHO: One thing at a time. Let's get the divorce first and then we can all follow your wife.

CHICO: Here I am, boss. You callin' Ravelli?

GROUCHO: See here. I don't like your sleeping on the company's time.

CHICO: I don't like sleeping on it it, either. Why don't you buy me a bed?

JONES: Mr. Ravelli, I've just been telling Mr. Beagle that, much as I regret to say it, my wife is going around with other men.

The Pilgrims refused to eat lobsters. Reason: They thought they were really big insects.

CHICO: She's going around with other men? 'At'sa fine. Hey! You think she like me?

JONES: Well, Mr. Ravelli, as long as you're going to trail my wife, I think I ought to describe her to you. She's of medium height and...but never mind, I've got a photograph.

CHICO: Hey, 'at'sa fine. Awright. I'll take a dozen.

JONES: I'm not selling them.

CHICO: You mean, I get it for nothing?

JONES: Of course.

CHICO: Awright. Then I take two dozen.

JONES: One picture ought to be enough for the present. There's one man my wife has been paying particular attention to. I'm counting on you to find out who he is. Do you think you can do it?

CHICO: Sure, you leave 'im to me. I find out who the man was with your wife. And I find out quick.

JONES: Really? How you going to do it?

CHICO: Well, first I put on a disguise...

JONES: Yes?

CHICO: Then I get a bloodhound...

JONES: Yes??

CHICO: Then I go to your house...

JONES: Yes???

CHICO: Then I ask your wife.

(applause, commercial break)

Two weeks later at the offices of Beagle, Shyster, & Beagle.

MISS DIMPLE: Law offices of Beagle, Shyster, and Beagle...oh, hello, Mr. Jones. I didn't recognize your voice....Yes, Mr. Ravelli is still trailing your wife...but it hasn't been long...just two weeks. We expect Mr. Ravelli in the office this morning. He says he has some news....Okay, I'll tell Mr. Beagle you'll be in....Goodbye.

(Groucho comes in.)

MISS DIMPLE: Good morning, Mr. Beagle—

GROUCHO: Miss Dimple, before I forget—call Ravelli and tell him to be sure and oversleep.

MISS DIMPLE: But he phoned and said he was coming right in.

GROUCHO: In that case, I'm going right back to the poolroom (*he heads for the door*).

MISS DIMPLE: But Mr. Jones is on his way here to talk to you about his divorce.

GROUCHO: That's all he ever talks to me about. I'm getting pretty sick of it, too.

MISS DIMPLE: But Mr. Beagle, that's your business.

GROUCHO: Well, I wish he'd keep his nose out of my business.

(Door opens.)

There are 550 hairs in the average eyebrow.

MISS DIMPLE: Shh! Someone's coming in. I think it's Mr. Jones. How do you do, Mr. Jones?

JONES: How do you do, Miss Dimple? Morning, Mr. Beagle. About my divorce—

GROUCHO: Divorce! You going to start that again? Listen, Jones, can I sell you a ticket to the Firemen's Ball? It's a five-dollar ticket, and it's yours for a buck and a half.

JONES: Why, this is last year's ticket.

GROUCHO: I know it is, but they had a better show last year.

JONES: Mr. Beagle, when will I find out about my divorce case?

GROUCHO: See here, Jones, don't change the subject. What about that ticket?

JONES: I don't like to appear impatient, Mr. Beagle, but your assistant was supposed to bring in some evidence against my wife. Where is Mr. Ravelli?

CHICO: Hey! Who'sa calling Ravelli? Here I am.

JONES: Ah, Mr. Ravelli, I'd like to get the results of your investigation. Have you been trailing my wife?

CHICO: Sure, I shadow her all day.

JONES: What day was that?

CHICO: That was Shadowday. I went right to your house—

JONES: What did you find out?

CHICO: I find your wife out.

JONES: Then you wasted the entire two weeks?

CHICO: No. Monday, I shadow your wife. Tuesday, I go to the ball game—she don't show up. Wednesday, she go to the ball game—I don't show up. Thursday was a doubleheader. We both no show up. Friday it rain all day—there's a no ball game, so I go fishing.

JONES: Well, what's that got to do with my wife?

CHICO: Well, I no catcha no fish, but I catch your wife.

JONES: You caught my wife—with a man? Who was he?

CHICO: I don't wanna say.

JONES: I insist that you tell me the man's name.

CHICO: I don't wanna tell.

GROUCHO: Listen, Jones, my assistant isn't the type of fellow who'd bandy a man's good name in public—

JONES: For the last time, gentlemen—who was the man?

GROUCHO: Come clean, Ravelli, who was the man with his wife?

CHICO: Awright, awright. You maka me tell, I tell you. Mr. Jones, the man with your wife was my boss, Mr. Beagle.

JONES: This is an outrage. My attorney going out with my wife!

Believe it or not: Internationally, "Baywatch" is the most popular TV show in history.

GROUCHO: What do you mean, outrage? Don't you think I'm good enough for her?

JONES: I'm going to get a new attorney.

GROUCHO: Hmm! I suppose you think we can't get a new client?

JONES: Good day! (*He stomps out and slams the door.*)

GROUCHO: Ravelli, you did noble work. You can have the rest of the year off. And if you never come back, I'll give you a bonus.

CHICO: Well, boss, there's something I wanna tell you.

GROUCHO: Go right ahead. I'm not listening.

CHICO: You want I should never come back?

GROUCHO: In a word, yes.

CHICO: Awright, boss, I make you a proposition. If you want I should never come back, I gotta have more money.

GROUCHO: Ravelli, it's worth it. (*applause, theme music*)

ANNOUNCER: The crowd in the studio is giving the Marx Brothers a great ovation. We hope you in the radio audience enjoyed them as much as we did. They'll be back again next Monday at this same time.

✳   ✳   ✳

GROUCHO GOSSIP

• Julius Henry Marx (Groucho's real name) wasn't happy when his mother pushed him into becoming a vaudevillian. His dream was to become a doctor. But soon he, two brothers, and a friend were touring backwater theaters as the Four Nightingales. They were less than successful. During a performance in Texas, the entire audience left the theater to catch an escaped mule. When they returned, the angry brothers dropped their regular act and ad-libbed a routine mocking the patrons instead. They expected boos, but they got laughter. It changed the Marx brothers' act forever: they learned they could make fun of people and get away with it.

• Years later, another piece fell into place. Julius and his brothers were playing poker with a friend who was making fun of a popular comic character named "Knocko the Monk." The friend made up a similar name for each of them. Leo became Chicko because he chased women constantly. Adolph became Harpo (he played the harp). Milton became Gummo (because he liked to chew gum?). And Julius, who groused constantly, became Groucho.

BOW-WOW...OR WANG-WANG?

It's a truism we all learn as kids: A dog goes bow-wow...a cat goes meow...etc. A universal language, right? Nope. Believe it or not, animal sounds vary from language to language. Here are some examples.

PIGS
English: Oink Oink!
Russian: Kroo!
French: Groin Groin!
German: Grunz!

ROOSTERS
English: Cock-a-doodle-doo!
Arabic: Ku-ku-ku-ku!
Russian: Ku-ka-rzhi-ku!
Japanese: Ko-ki-koko!
Greek: Ki-ki-ri-koo!
Hebrew: Ku-ku-ri-ku!

DUCKS
English: Quack Quack!
Swedish: Kvack Kvack!
Arabic: Kack-kack-kack!
Chinese: Ga-ga!
French: Quahn Quahn!

FROGS
English: Croak!
Spanish: Croack!
German: Quak-quak!
Swedish: Kouack!
Russian: Kva-kva!

TWEETY-BIRDS
English: Tweet tweet!
French: Kwi-kwi!
Hebrew: Tsef Tsef!
Chinese: Chu-chu!
German: Tschiep Tschiep!

GEESE
English: Honk Honk!
Arabic: Wack Wack!
German: Schnatter-Schnatter!
Japanese: Boo Boo!

OWLS
English: Who-whoo!
Japanese: Ho-ho!
German: Koh-koh-a-oh!
Russian: Ookh!

CATS
English: Meow!
Hebrew: Miyau!
German: Miau!
French: Miaou!
Spanish (and Portuguese and German): Miau!

DOGS
English: Bow-wow!
Swedish: Voff Voff!
Hebrew: Hav Hav!
Chinese: Wang-wang!
Japanese: Won-won!
Swahili: Hu Hu Hu Huuu!

CHICKENS
English: Cluck-cluck!
French: Cot-cot-cot-codet!
German: Gak-gak!
Hebrew: Pak-pak-pak!
Arabic: Kakakakakakakakaka!

Sweet tooth: Americans consume more than 20 pounds of candy per person per year.

YOU CAN COLLECT TOILET PAPER!

According to Harry L. Rinker, "all toilet paper is not created equal." He should know; believe it or not, he collects TP. Here are excerpts from a column he wrote on the subject for Antiques and Collecting *magazine.*

If you have traveled abroad or used an outhouse, you are aware of one basic truth—all toilet paper is not created equal. What a perfect excuse to collect it.

On the surface, collecting toilet paper need not be an expensive hobby. Select pilfering from public restrooms and friends' bathrooms will provide enough examples to begin a collection. Of course, if you travel abroad to obtain examples, the costs increase considerably. However, I discovered that once my friends found out that I have a toilet paper collection...their personal contributions rolled in.

GETTING STARTED. I became aware of the collectible potential of toilet paper in the late 1970s when I learned about a woman appearing on the Women's Club lecture circuit, talking about the wide assortment of toilet paper that she encountered during her travels. She charged a fee for her presentation and did not seem to lack bookings. She was obviously cleaning up.

After resisting the urge to follow suit for almost a decade, I... gave up and began my own toilet paper collection. My initial [efforts] were modest. I wrote to several German friends and asked them to send some examples of German toilet paper. Udo, my friend in Hamburg, outdid himself. Among the examples he sent was toilet paper from the German railroad. A close examination of the light gray textured paper revealed that each sheet was stamped "Deutsche Bundesbahn." This says something about a nation's character. The German railroad administration is so concerned about a roll of toilet paper that they find it necessary to stamp their name on every sheet.

THE RULES. Since toilet paper collecting is in its infancy, now is an excellent time to create rules concerning how to validly accumulate this important new collectible. For example, how many

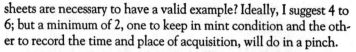

sheets are necessary to have a valid example? Ideally, I suggest 4 to 6; but a minimum of 2, one to keep in mint condition and the other to record the time and place of acquisition, will do in a pinch.

Do you collect single sheets or the entire roll? This is a tough one. I started out by collecting sheets. Then I began thinking about the potential value of wrappers and added them to my collection. Since I had gone that far, I figured why not save the entire roll. When I realized that same rolls were packaged in units of four to six, I was forced to save the entire package. My collection, which originally was meant to be confined to a shirt box, now occupies several large boxes.

CONVERSATION PIECES. Toilet paper collecting provides an engaging topic for cocktail parties and other social gatherings. Everyone has a toilet paper story to tell. I remember the time I had to use the facilities in the basement of the Moravian Archives in Herrnhut, East Germany. The nature of the call required my immediately locating a toilet with no regard to the toilet paper status. Later examination revealed no toilet paper, but rather an old railroad time schedule booklet with some of the pages torn out. As I tore a sheet loose, the ink on the paper came off on my fingers. You can imagine the rest. I should have saved an example, but I wasn't thinking of toilet paper collecting at the time....

As with all my collections, I have some favorite examples, among which are a half roll of toilet paper that a friend brought me from England that has a surface texture equivalent to wax paper and a German aluminum foil package that contains toilet paper moistened and perfumed to act and smell like a wash and dry. I have a special box in which I put translucent examples, those you can see through when held up to the light. Their use gives real meaning to the phrase "doubling up."

ROLL CALL. Thus far, I have been unsuccessful in locating other serious toilet paper collectors. They exist; there are collectors for everything. If I can locate them, I would be glad to discuss swapping duplicates. Meanwhile, you can help. The next time your travels in the USA or abroad bring you into contact with the unusual during a period of daily meditation, save a few examples and send them to me (care of *Rinker Enterprises*, 5093 Vera Cruz Rd., Erasmus, PA 18049). Is there the making of a future museum collection here? Time will tell.

Hair grows at a rate of .00000001 miles per hour.

CAFFEINE FACTS

What's America's favorite drug? You guessed it—caffeine. We use more caffeine than all other drugs—legal or illegal—combined. Want to know what the stuff is doing to you? Here's a quick overview.

BACKGROUND
If you start the day with a strong cup of coffee or tea, you're not alone. Americans ingest the caffeine equivalent of 530 million cups of coffee *every day*. Caffeine is the world's most popular mood-altering drug. It's also one of the oldest: according to archaeologists, people have been brewing beverages from caffeine-based plants since the Stone Age.

HOW IT PICKS YOU UP

Caffeine doesn't keep you awake by supplying extra energy; rather, it fools your body into thinking it isn't tired.

• When your brain is tired and wants to slow down, it releases a chemical called *adenosine*.

• Adenosine travels to special cells called *receptors*, where it goes to work counteracting the chemicals that stimulate your brain.

• Caffeine mimics adenosine; so it can "plug up" your receptors and prevent adenosine from getting through. Result: Your brain never gets the signal to slow down, and keeps building up stimulants.

JAVA JUNKIES

• After a while, your brain figures out what's going on and increases the number of receptor cells so it has enough for both caffeine *and* adenosine.

• When that happens, caffeine can't keep you awake anymore... unless you *increase* the amount you drink so it can "plug up" the new receptor cells as well.

• This whole process only takes about a week. In that time, you essentially become a caffeine addict. Your brain is literally restructuring itself to run on caffeine; take the caffeine away and your brain has too many receptor cells to operate properly.

Gone With the Wind is the only Civil War epic ever filmed without a single battle scene.

• If you quit caffeine cold turkey, your brain begins to reduce the number of receptors right away. But the process takes about two weeks, and during that time your body sends out mild "distress signals" in the form of headaches, lethargy, fatigue, muscle pain, nausea, and sometimes even stiffness and flu-like symptoms. As a result, most doctors recommend quitting caffeine gradually.

CAFFEINE'S EFFECTS

• **Good:** Caffeine has been scientifically proven to temporarily increase alertness, comprehension, memory, reflexes, and even the rate of learning. It also helps increase clarity of thought.

• **Bad:** Too much caffeine can cause hand tremors, loss of coordination or appetite, insomnia—and in extreme cases, trembling, nausea, heart palpitations, and diarrhea.

• Widely varying the amount of caffeine you ingest can put a strain on your liver, pancreas, heart, and nervous system. And if you're prone to ulcers, caffeine can make your situation worse.

• If you manage to consume the equivalent of 70 to 100 cups of coffee in one sitting, you'll experience convulsions, and may even die.

CAFFEINE FACTS

• The average American drinks 210 milligrams of caffeine a day. That's equal to 2 or 3 cups of coffee, depending on how strong it is.

• How you make your coffee has a lot to do with how much caffeine you get. Instant coffee contains 65 milligrams of caffeine per serving; coffee brewed in a percolator has 80 milligrams; and coffee made using the drip method has 155 milligrams.

• Top four sources of caffeine in the American diet: coffee, soft drinks, tea, and chocolate, in that order. The average American gets 75% of their caffeine from coffee. Other sources include over-the-counter pain killers, appetite suppressants, cold remedies—and some prescription drugs.

• What happens to the caffeine that's removed from decaf coffee? Most of it is sold to soda companies and put into soft drinks. (Cola contains some caffeine naturally, but they like to add even more.)

• Do you drink more caffeine than your kids do? If you correct for body weight, probably not. Pound for pound, kids often get as much caffeine from chocolate and soft drinks as their parents get from coffee, tea, and other sources.

Mussolini's favorite cartoon character was Donald Duck.

BE MY VALENTINE

Beginning in kindergarten, we exchange cards with classmates and friends on Valentine's Day. Later, we give flowers and presents to loved ones. Here's why we do it.

V ALENTINE'S DAY
   This "lover's holiday" is an anomaly. It was actually an effort by the Catholic Church to *keep* teenagers from becoming lovers.

Before Christ was born, it was a Roman tradition for teenage girls and boys to gather every February in the name of Lupercus, god of the flocks, to celebrate fertility and randomly choose a "mate" for the year. They were permitted to do anything they liked together (and what else would teenagers do?).

When Christians gained power in the Roman Empire, they wanted to bring this practice to an end. So they selected a substitute for Lupercus (to be the focus of a parallel holiday)—St. Valentine, a bishop who had reputedly been tortured and executed by Emperor Claudius II in 270 A.D. for performing marriages after Claudius had outlawed them. This symbol of more "wholesome" love was reluctantly accepted by the Romans. But just to be sure no one gave in to temptation, the Catholic Church made it a mortal sin to worship Lupercus. Eventually, Valentine's Day became a recognized holiday throughout Western Europe.

VALENTINE CARDS

If teens couldn't get together in February, what could they do? They could send each other respectful notes of affection. And they did, although it seems like a poor substitute. At any rate, sending lovers' greetings became a part of the Valentine's Day ritual, and when Christian influence grew, the practice of sending notes on February 14 spread with it.

The first greeting cards didn't appear until the 18th century. Printed cards were common in Germany by the 1780s; they were called *Freundschaftkarten*, or "friendship cards." The first American cards were manufactured in the 1870s, at an amazing cost of up to $35 apiece.

Film fact: Clint Eastwood was the #1 box office star in both the '70s *and* the '80s.

W. C. FIELDS SEZ

The original movie curmudgeon had a lot to say.

"Never give a sucker an even break."

"Women are like elephants to me. I like to look at 'em, but I wouldn't want to own one."

"Anyone who hates children and dogs can't be all bad."

"Reminds me of my safari in Africa. Somebody forgot the corkscrew and for several days we had to live on nothing but food and water."

"Never try to impress a woman because if you do, you'll have to keep up that standard the rest of your life."

"Show me a great actor and I'll show you a lousy husband; show me a great actress, and you've seen the devil."

"I've been asked if I ever get the DTs. I don't know. It's hard to tell where Hollywood ends and the DTs begin."

"I am free of all prejudices. I hate everyone equally."

"I never vote *for* anyone. I always vote against."

"Start every day off with a smile, and get it over with."

"A thing worth having is a thing worth cheating for."

"Twas a woman who drove me to drink....And I never had the courtesy to thank her for it."

"I always keep a supply of liquor handy in case I see a snake—which I also keep handy."

"All my available funds are completely tied up in ready cash."

"I have never struck a woman. Never! Not even my poor old mother."

"I like children. If they're properly cooked."

"If at first you don't succeed, try again. Then quit. No use being a damn fool about it."

Mahatma Gandhi is buried in California.

THE SOUND OF MUZAK

You hear it in the elevator, in your dentist's office, at the supermarket—even in the reptile house of the Bronx Zoo. Here's the inside story on the music you love to hate:

WAR BABY

During World War I, General George Squier, a pioneer in radio communications, figured out how to send several messages simultaneously over electric power lines—which proved quite useful on the battlefields. Squier believed that if his system could broadcast messages in times of war, it could broadcast music, news, and entertainment in times of peace. So after the war, he pitched his idea to a New York utility company as a way to make extra money off existing power lines. They liked the idea and founded Wired Radio, Inc. in 1922.

ROUGH START

Wired Radio began broadcasting from the balcony of a power plant to residential customers in the Lakeland area of Cleveland. For 11¢ a month, listeners could tune to 3 music channels and 1 all-news channel via a special receiver plugged into their electrical outlets.

This was moderately successful at first, but the company knew it couldn't last—why would anyone keep paying Wired Radio's monthly fee when they could listen to a regular radio for free?—so they began looking for a new way to make money from Squier's invention.

WORLD WAR II

In the 1930s, using the name Muzak (a takeoff on Kodak), Wired Radio decided to peddle background music for hotels, restaurants, and offices. They came up with a new sales pitch, too: listening to the music would actually make employees work harder. The claim seemed outlandish at the time, but Muzak backed it up with a 1937 British study called "Fatigue and Boredom in Repetitive Work," which concluded that people work harder when listening to the "proper" music.

Yum! Parrot tongue and ostrich brains were considered delicacies in the Roman Empire.

Once again, sales were slow...and might have stayed that way, if England hadn't been gearing up for World War II. The English government had also read "Fatigue and Boredom in Repetitive Work" and arranged for a special BBC music program to be piped into airplane, tank, and munitions factories to prevent fatigue.

When production in some factories increased as much as 6%, word quickly got back to Washington. The U.S. military hired Muzak to provide the same service to American defense plants...and *their* productivity went up 11%. Muzak had finally found a product that people wanted to buy.

Takeoff
After the war, Muzak expanded into bank lobbies, insurance companies, medical and dental offices, department stores...and, of course, elevators. Why play music in an elevator? In the '40s and '50s—when most office buildings phased out elevator operators—passengers were left alone for the first time. "People were nervous and tense," explains a Muzak franchiser, "because they no longer had anyone to talk to in the elevator." Muzak filled the void.

"STIMULUS PROGRESSION"
Over the years, Muzak programming became more scientific (or pseudoscientific, depending on whom you believe). The company calls it "Stimulus Progression." Here's how it works:

• Each song the company records is rated according to tempo, rhythm, instrumentation, and size of orchestra; then it's given an overall "stimulus value."

• Using a computer, Muzak programmers create a broadcast schedule divided into quarter-hour segments. The songs in each segment are always organized in *ascending* order of their stimulus value, "to provide people with a lift." Each 15-minute segment ends with 60 seconds of silence.

• Faster segments are played at 10:00-11:00 a.m. and 3:00-4:00 p.m., when employees are more likely to need a lift. Slow segments are played at 1:00-3:00 p.m. and after 6:00 p.m., when employees are thought to be the most energetic.

• The broadcasts that Muzak provides to supermarkets are *always* slow-paced—studies have shown that shoppers who listen to slow music *shop* slower and spend as much as 35% more money. Fast music has the opposite effect: shoppers are in and out of the store faster than if there had been no music playing at all.

SWAN SONG

In the '70s, Muzak faced a new problem. To save money, the company, which had been acquired by Westinghouse, stopped hiring unionized American musicians. Instead, they contracted with a non-union *Communist* orchestra—the Brno Radio Orchestra of Czechoslovakia—to record most of the songs in the company's music library. Few if any of the Eastern European musicians had ever heard songs like "Born Free" and "Raindrops Keep Falling on My Head." The result was a strange Muzak that even regular customers, people who *liked* Muzak, thought was terrible. By the early '80s, cancellation rates were so high that Westinghouse sold Muzak to department store heir and media mogul Marshall Field V.

The New Muzak

In 1987, Muzak did a major overhaul of its image. It banned Commie orchestras—as well as harmonicas, tubas, fluegelhorns, and "any instrument that would sound dated or hokey." Organs in particular had been a big problem—Jane Jarvis, a previous Muzak programming vice president, moonlighted as the organist at Shea Stadium, and it had shown in her work. They also added vocals, ending a 50-year tradition. Prior to the format change, human voices had only been heard on Muzak in 1981, when an announcer broke the news that American hostages had been released from Iran, and on Good Friday, 1985, when Muzak joined radio stations worldwide in a simultaneous broadcast of "We Are the World."

Today, Muzak broadcasts via satellite to 200,000 customers and more than 100 million "listeners" around the world. It is heard in just about every kind of workplace imaginable, including churches, prisons, mental institutions, the Pentagon, and at least one German whorehouse that the company knows of.

MUZAK FACTS

• According to one survey, more than 75% of Americans recognize the Muzak name, making the trademark as big a household word as Coke, Kleenex, and Xerox. The bad news: more than 50% of the respondents in the same survey said they don't like listening to it.

Something to look forward to: The average American develops their first phobia at age 13 1/2.

- Many songwriters, including Bruce Springsteen and Boz Scaggs, refuse to sell Muzak the rights to their songs. Not so with Paul Simon—"When I hear my song on an elevator," he says, "I know I've got a hit."

- President Dwight D. Eisenhower played Muzak in the White House—and Lyndon Johnson liked it so much he bought a local Texas franchise. He even had Muzak speakers installed in the trees of the LBJ ranch.

- Andy Warhol claimed Muzak was his favorite music.

- Neil Armstrong listened to Muzak during the Apollo XI voyage to the moon.

- During the fall of Saigon in 1975, State Department staffers evacuated the American embassy compound with Muzak playing in the background.

- Studies show that even cows and chickens increase productivity when "functional" music is played in the background.

- 7-Elevens in British Columbia, Canada, and Seattle, Washington, use Muzak to keep juveniles from loitering in front of the stores. The tactic has proven quite effective, but it drives Muzak nuts. "I'm opposed to a negative use of a positive thing in our lives," company official Tom Evans complains. "If they want to torture people, why don't they just blast air-raid sirens?"

*   *   *

A "Monday Night Football" Story

"The weirdest scene I ever witnessed in the broadcast booth happened in 1976," Frank Gifford remembers in his book *The Whole Ten Yards*. "The night before a game in Los Angeles, I ran into John Lennon at a cocktail party. On impulse, I invited him on the show. He liked the idea but warned me that he knew nothing about football. Meanwhile, I'd forgotten we had arranged for Ronald Reagan to come on the same show. Now it's just before halftime. I turned around and there's Reagan with his arm around Lennon, explaining what's going on down on the field. And John looked absolutely enthralled. Here were two of the most political, ideological, and cultural opposites on the entire planet standing in the 'Monday Night' booth—acting exactly like father and son!"

It takes seven standard shuffles to thoroughly mix a 52-card deck.

CRAZY NAMES

Believe it or not, these are actual names of real people.

A. Moron
Commissioner of Education in the Virgin Islands

Mrs. Belcher Wack Wack
Belcher was her maiden name. Her husband's name was Wack. When he died, she married his brother.

Buncha Love
Living in New York City

Cardinal Sin
Archbishop of Manila

Cumming & Gooing
Business in Louisiana

D. Schumuk
Political activist in Ukraine, USSR. He spent seven years in jail before the war for being a Communist. Then, after the war, he went back to jail for 30 years for being anti-Communist.

Hastie Love
Convicted rapist serving time in Tennessee

Halloween Buggage
Named for the day she was born. Her sister's name is Easter Buggage.

Hyman Pleasure
Assistant Commissioner, New York State Department of Hygiene.

Katz Meow
Living in Hoquiam, Washington

Lawless & Lynch
Law firm, Jamaica, New York

Mary Louise Pantzarooff
Living in Ohio

Moon Unit Zappa & Dweezle Zappa
Frank Zappa's kids

Original Bug
Living in Liverpool, England

Goody P. Creep
Runs a funeral home

Mrs. Screech
Teaches singing in British Columbia

Mrs. V. D. Whynot
Whereabouts unknown

Bambina Broccoli
Living in New York City

Caresse Pecor
Living in Burlington, Vermont

Major Minor
An officer in the U.S. Army

Luscious Pea
Born in New Orleans

Plummer & Leek
Plumbing firm, Norfolk, England

Suparporn Poopattana
Living in New York City

T. Hee
Works in a restaurant in New York City

Zezozose Zadfrack
Charles Manson's son

Dr. Zoltan Ovary
Gynecologist

Bela Lugosi was buried in the cape he wore as Dracula.

BIRTH OF THE BIKINI

*Conservatives have long pointed to the bikini as an example
of our moral decline; yet history shows that the bikini is
related to the A-bomb and war, not simply sex.*

The atomic bomb is responsible for many terrible things and at least one attractive thing—the bikini. In July 1946, the American government announced that it would be exploding an atomic bomb. It was just a test, but this was the first announced atomic bomb blast, and people's imaginations ran wild. Rumors spread that it was going to be a "super bomb" that could easily get out of control, start a massive chain reaction, and blow up the world.

PARTY TIME

These rumors were especially prevalent in Paris, which had recently suffered through the trauma of German occupation in World War II. Parisians simply couldn't take any more pressure....so instead of protesting the impending explosion, they celebrated. Hostesses used the bomb threat as an excuse to hold end-of-the-world parties; young men used it as an excuse to convince reluctant girlfriends to give in (if the world was going to end, why not break all the rules?). And when it was revealed that the test would take place in the then unheard-of Bikini Atoll, the parties became "Bikini" parties.

A PUBLICITY STUNT

Meanwhile, a fashion show was being planned for the Piscine Molitor in Paris on July 5, 1946 (note: *piscine* is French for "swimming pool"). Its promoters wanted to attract attention, and since people seemed to be throwing modesty to the wind, the promoters came up with the idea of a "Bikini" costume—one that would go as far as anyone dared go with a bathing suit. So in the middle of the fashion show, Paris model Micheline Bernardini suddenly stepped out before the audience wearing a scanty two-piece bathing suit—the world's first "bikini." Of course, the scandalous suit got international publicity...and a new style was born.

Nothing New Under the Sun. Archaeologists have found evidence that bikinis were worn in Sicily as early as 2000 B.C.

See for yourself: TV sitcom characters rarely say goodbye when they hang up the phone.

MYTH AMERICA

You may have believed these myths all your life; after all, they were taught to us as sacred truths. But here's another look...

REMEMBER THE ALAMO
The Myth: The defenders of the Alamo fought for justice, political freedom, and independence.

The Truth: It was as much an issue of slavery as it was independence. In the 1820s, Texas was a part of Mexico, and much of its land was being settled by slave-owning farmers and ranchers from the South. But in 1830, the Mexican government passed a law outlawing slavery. Soon after, American settlers revolted, and the Alamo was defended—at least in part because American settlers wanted to keep their slaves.

CHARGE!
The Myth: Teddy Roosevelt commanded his hardy band of Rough Riders on their charge up Cuba's San Juan Hill in the Spanish-American War.

The Truth: Contrary to the popular image of the courageous cavalry charge on horseback, the cavalry unit was on foot; their horses had accidentally been left in Florida. And Roosevelt wasn't even on San Juan Hill. He did take part in the charge on nearby Kettle Hill, but only watched from there as Colonel C. Wood led the Rough Riders up San Juan Hill.

ASLEEP AT THE WHEEL
The Myth: John F. Kennedy was a hero in World War II; when his tiny PT-109 patrol boat was rammed and sunk by a destroyer, he singlehandedly saved three members of his crew.

Background: In his (ghostwritten) book *PT-109*, Kennedy presented this version of the events that night. Yet, while he apparently showed great endurance and courage after his boat sank, there's some question as to whether the incident might have been avoidable in the first place.

The Truth: At least one Kennedy biographer argues that Kennedy's own negligence may have doomed his boat. According to a

---

What do raccoons, slugs, and ants have in common? They all like to get drunk.

number of the ship's crew members, Kennedy and most of the crew were sleeping when PT-109 was rammed—not attacking the destroyer as Kennedy later claimed. Naval experts point out that it is unlikely for a ship as small and quick as a PT-109 to be outmaneuvered by a ship as large as a destroyer, unless the crew is caught off guard.

SO HIGH, SOLO

The Myth: Charles Lindbergh was the first person to fly nonstop across the Atlantic Ocean.

The Truth: He was the 67*th* person to fly nonstop across the Atlantic. The first nonstop flight was made by William Alcock and Arthur Brown in 1919, eight years before Lindbergh's flight. Lindbergh was famous because he did it *alone*.

THE FATHER OF OUR COUNTRY

The Myth: George Washington was the first president of the U.S.

The Truth: Washington was the first to serve as America's president under the Constitution of 1789, but the United States was a sovereign nation 13 years before the Constitution was written. In 1777, the Congress adopted the Articles of Confederation, which were ratified by the states in 1781. Later in 1781, this new legislative body convened and elected John Hanson as "President of the United States in Congress assembled." Hanson had been a member of the Maryland assembly and the Continental Congress, where he played a key role in convincing Maryland, the only state against the Articles of Confederation, to ratify them. Washington himself sent Hanson a letter of congratulations on his "appointment to fill the most important seat in the United States." However, Hanson and the *seven* other presidents who served before George Washington have been forgotten.

SWAN SONG

The Myth: General Douglas MacArthur coined the saying "Old soldiers never die; they just fade away."

The Truth: He was just quoting a British Army song from World War I.

INCOMPETENT CRIMINALS

A lot of Americans are worried about the growing threat of crime. Well, the good news is that there are plenty of crooks who are their own worst enemies. Here are a few true-life examples.

ARE WE HIGH YET?

When Nathan Radlich's house was burgled on June 4, 1993, thieves left his TV, his VCR, and even his watch. All they took was a "generic white cardboard box" of grayish white powder. A police spokesman said it looked similar to cocaine. "They probably thought they scored big," he mused.

The powder was actually the cremated remains of Radlich's sister, Gertrude, who had died three years earlier.

—From the *Fort Lauderdale Sun-Sentinel*

POOR PENMANSHIP

In 1992, 79-year-old Albert Goldsband walked into a San Bernardino, California, bank and handed the teller a note demanding money. When she couldn't read the note, he pulled out a toy gun. But the teller had already taken the note to her supervisor for help deciphering it.

Goldsband panicked and fled...to a nearby restaurant that was frequented by police officers. He was arrested immediately.

—From the *San Francisco Chronicle*

STUCK ON GLUE

Rio de Janeiro — Nov. 5, 1993. "A thief was found stuck to the floor of a factory Thursday after trying to steal glue in Belo Horizonte, 280 miles north of Rio, newspapers reported.

"Edilber Guimaeares, 19, stopped to sniff some of the glue he was stealing when two large cans fell to the floor, spilling over.

"When police were called Thursday morning, Guimaeares was glued to the floor, asleep."

—From the *San Francisco Examiner*

Elvis's favorite amusement park ride was the bumper cars.

MISTAKEN IDENTITY

"Warren Gillen, 26, was arrested for trying to rob a bank in Glasgow. Police put him in a lineup, but no one identified him. He was booked anyway after calling out from the lineup, 'Hey, don't you recognize me?' "

—From *More News of the Weird*

A CASE OF NERVES?

Lee W. Womble, 28, was spotted and picked up a few minutes after robbing the Lafayette Bank in Bridgeport, Connecticut.

Police said that even if they hadn't seen him, he would have been easy to identify; he had written his name on the note he handed to the teller demanding money.

"He wrote his name on it twice—once on top of the other," said police. "He could have been trying to kill time. He could have been nervous or something. Who knows?"

—From the *Oakland Tribune*

WRONG TURN

"An alleged drunk driver who led police on a wild, midnight chase landed in jail even before his arrest. His car crashed into the jail building.

"He didn't have too far to go from there,' said Police Capt. Mike Lanam. 'It was like a drive-up window.' "

—From the *Chicago Tribune*

EMPLOYMENT OPPORTUNITY

"A man accused of stealing a car was easy to track, police said, especially after they found his resume under one of the seats.

"Police discovered the handwritten resume when they looked through the stolen 1985 Chevrolet Celebrity they had recovered.

"Police then telephoned an employer listed on the resume for a different sort of reference."

—From the Associated Press

THE DUSTBIN OF HISTORY

They were VIPs in their time...but they're forgotten now.
They've been swept into the Dustbin of History.

FORGOTTEN FIGURE: Lord Cornbury (Edward Hyde), colonial governor of New York from 1702 to 1708

CLAIM TO FAME: Hyde, a cousin of Queen Anne, was appointed governor of New York in 1702. When colonists went to welcome him, they found him rocking on his porch, knitting a doily and wearing one of his wife's dresses.

Things got weirder when he threw his first dress ball. Not only was he decked out in a formal gown, he also charged an admission fee and insisted that his guests all feel his wife's ears...which he had described in a long poem as "conch shells."

For many years, he was the talk of New York—especially when it turned out he had taken the governorship to escape creditors in England. Then, in 1708, he was caught embezzling public funds.

INTO THE DUSTBIN: Cornbury was confined to debtor's prison until his father died, when he inherited a title and returned to England. No monuments to his rule were built, but he did leave his family name on land along the Hudson: Hyde Park.

FORGOTTEN FIGURE: Lucy Page Gaston, 1860-1924, American anti-tobacco reformer

CLAIM TO FAME: After legendary prohibitionist Carrie Nation, she was the most famous American female reformer of her time. In 1899 she founded the Chicago Anti-Cigarette League, which became the National Anti-Cigarette League two years later. For a while the movement she inspired was a real threat to the tobacco industry, as cigarette sales dipped by 25 percent.

By 1920 she was so well-known that she became a candidate in the Republican presidential race, vowing to "emancipate" the country from smoking. But she won few votes, and Warren Harding, a smoker, was nominated.

INTO THE DUSTBIN: In June 1924, Gaston was hit by a trolley while crossing the street. She was taken to a hospital, but did not respond well to treatment. That's when doctors discovered she was terminally ill. She died two months later—of throat cancer.

FORGOTTEN FIGURE: Louise Rainer, a film star of the '30s

CLAIM TO FAME: She was the first person ever to win two consecutive Academy Awards—for Best Actress in 1936 (for *The Great Ziegfield*) and in 1937 (for *The Good Earth*).

In 1936, nominations were still carefully controlled by movie studios. Rainer's first nomination was engineered by MGM to help develop her career. (It was only her second film, and it was a relatively small part.) No one thought she would actually *win* the Oscar. That's why everyone voted for her.

The following year, voting was opened up for the first time to thousands of actors, writers, etc. Rainer, who was well-liked for not acting like a "star," beat out Greta Garbo and Barbara Stanwyck.

INTO THE DUSTBIN: For some reason, MGM forced Rainer into a quick series of throwaway roles; two years and five insignificant pictures later, she was a has-been. Her downfall led gossip columnist Louella Parsons to coin the term "Oscar jinx."

FORGOTTEN FIGURE: Smedley Butler, America's most famous soldier—a U.S. Marine and two-time Medal of Honor winner, nicknamed "Old Gimlet Eye"

CLAIM TO FAME: Once called "the finest fighting man in the armed forces" by Teddy Roosevelt, Butler was renowned for personal bravery, tactical brilliance, and the ability to inspire his fellow soldiers. He joined a Marine force in China during the Boxer rebellion and helped carry a wounded comrade 17 miles through enemy fire back to their camp. He was promoted to captain—at age 18. He later served in Cuba, Nicaragua, Panama, Honduras, and Haiti.

Butler served in France during World War I—not at the front, but as commander of a troop depot, Camp Pontanezen. Ironically, his greatest fame came from this post. The camp was practically buried in mud; and the troops were short of food and blankets. But somehow, Butler scrounged a huge supply of slats used for trench floors and created walkways and tent floors to keep the troops out of the mud.

The grateful soldiers never forgot him; as one said, "I'd cross hell on a slat if Butler gave the word."

After the war, Butler was regarded as presidential material (he didn't run). He was also a popular figure on the lecture circuit.

In the early '30s, he was approached by men claiming to be associated with the American Legion. They wanted him to organize a fighting force to overthrow Franklin Roosevelt—and said there was $300 million available to fund the insurrection. Butler played along and eventually learned he was being courted by the American fascist movement. He divulged the plot before the Un-American Activities Committee in 1934, but nothing much came of it; the story was hushed up because several prominent figures were involved.

INTO THE DUSTBIN: Butler retired from the Corps in 1931, but continued to speak out on military and foreign-policy issues. He died in 1940.

FORGOTTEN FIGURE: William Walker, American journalist, physician, lawyer, and soldier of fortune

CLAIM TO FAME: Walker is the only native-born American ever to become president of a foreign nation. From July 1856 to May 1857, he was self-appointed dictator of Nicaragua, a nation he took over with a hand-picked force of mercenaries who called themselves "The Immortals."

Walker's success made him a hero throughout the U.S., where the notion of "manifest destiny" was gaining wide acceptance. Crowds cheered his exploits, newspapers hailed his triumphs. But a coalition of Central American nations, financed in part by Cornelius Vanderbilt, overthrew Walker. On May 1, 1857, he and his troops fled back to the United States.

Walker made three more attempts to win control in Central America. Finally, in the fall of 1859, he and his men attacked Honduras and were captured by British and Honduran troops.

INTO THE DUSTBIN: Walker surrendered to the British, expecting he would again be returned to the States. But he was turned over to the Hondurans instead, and was executed by a firing squad on September 12, 1860.

He was so hated by Nicaraguans that he became a symbol of "Yankee Imperialism." He is still remembered there.

Cracker Jack is the world's largest purchaser of popcorn.

HOLY PUNCTUATION

What's the difference between good and evil? Maybe just a little grammar. The following are excerpts from real church bulletins, collected by the BRI's Les Boies.

"This afternoon there will be a meeting in the south and north ends of the church. Children will be baptized at both ends."

"Tuesday, at 4 p.m., there will be an ice cream social. All ladies giving milk, come early."

"Wednesday, the Ladies Liturgy Society will meet. Mrs. Johnson will sing, 'Put Me in My Little Bed,' accompanied by the Pastor."

"Altar flowers are given to the glory of God in memory of her mother."

"This being Easter Sunday, we will ask Mrs. Johnson to come forward and lay an egg on the altar."

"The service will close with 'Little Drops of Water.' One of the rest of the congregation will join in."

"Thursday, at 5 p.m., there will be a meeting of the Little Mothers Club. All those wishing to become little mothers, please meet the pastor in his study."

"On Sunday, a special collection will be taken to defray the expense of the new carpet. All those wishing to do something on the new carpet, come forward and get a piece of paper."

"The ladies of the church have cast-off clothing of every kind and they may be seen in the basement on Friday afternoon."

"A bean supper will be held Saturday evening in the church basement. Music will follow."

"The rosebud on the altar this morning is to announce the birth of David Alan Belser, the sin of Rev. and Mrs. Julius Belser."

FIRST HITS

Here are the inside stories of the first hit records for three of the most successful music acts in history—the Beatles, Elvis, and Simon and Garfunkel—from Behind the Hits, *by Bob Shannon and John Javna.*

THE BEATLES

First Hit: "Love Me Do," 1962

Background: The tune was written by Paul McCartney, who called it "our greatest philosophical song." He skipped school and wrote it when he was 16 years old.

By the time the Beatles went to London in 1962 to try to get a recording contract, it was one of their best numbers.

They played it at their audition...but the record executive assigned to work with them, George Martin, wasn't particularly impressed. Still, he agreed to give them a contract—and even make "Love Me Do" their first single—provided they got a new drummer.

The Session: The recording session took place on September 11, 1962, at Abbey Road Studios. The Beatles arrived with a new drummer, Ringo Starr...but Martin didn't trust him and brought his own session drummer, Andy White, to make the record. Ringo was despondent, so Martin took pity on him; he recorded several versions with Ringo, and several with White. (In fact, Ringo played on the English version, and White was the drummer on the single released in America.) It took 17 takes to get the song right. By the time they were done, John Lennon's lips were numb from playing the harmonica so much.

It's a Hit. On October 4, 1962, "Love Me Do" was released in England on Parlophone Records. It surged into the Top 20 and established the Beatles as a viable commercial group. But behind the scenes was manager Brian Epstein, making sure that the Beatles succeeded. He bought 10,000 copies himself, knowing that was the minimum amount their record company had to sell to make it a bestseller. Epstein's gimmick worked. The record company was impressed and got behind the Beatles' next single, "Please Please Me," which reached #1 in Britain and started a chain of events that revolutionized popular music.

Thanks, Dad: Calvin Coolidge was sworn in as U.S. president by his father.

In America in 1962, no one wanted any part of the silly "Love Me Do." Capitol Records, which owned the rights to the song, practically gave it to Vee Jay Records, which later issued it on an album called "Introducing the Beatles."

On May 2, 1964, about a year and a half after it was first released, "Love Me Do" became the Beatles' fourth American #1 record.

ELVIS PRESLEY

First Hit: "Heartbreak Hotel," 1956

Background: The headline on the front page of the *Miami Herald* read, "Do You Know This Man?" Below it was a photograph of a suicide victim. Who was he? The story explained that he'd left no clue about his identity behind—only a pathetic handwritten message that read, "I walk a lonely street." The *Herald* asked the family—or anyone who recognized the photo—to get in touch with the police.

The Song: In Gainesville, Florida, a songwriter named Tommy Durden read the paper and was struck by the suicide note. Now *that* was a great line for a blues tune, he mused. The more he thought about it, the more he liked it...so he hopped in his car and drove over to Mae Axton's house to work on it. Axton was Durden's collaborator in songwriting; she was also a local TV and radio personality. When Elvis Presley had come to town earlier in the year, she'd befriended the young singer and reportedly assured him that she'd be the one to write his first million-seller.

Axton agreed that the suicide line might make a good song, but couldn't stop thinking about how the guy's family would suffer when they found out about him. He might have walked a lonely street, but at the end of it there was surely going to be heartbreak for the people who loved him. So Axton decided there should be a "heartbreak hotel" at the end of "lonely street." From there it took 15 minutes to write the whole song.

It's a Hit: A friend of Axton's named Glen Reeves dropped by her house and agreed to tape a version of the song in a pseudo-Elvis style—so Elvis would be able to imagine how he'd sound on the tune. Then Axton, demo in hand, drove up to Tennessee to play it for Elvis. "Hot dog, Mae!" Presley is said to have exclaimed, "Play it again!" Legend has it that when he recorded the song, Presley copied Reeves's version note for note.

The ballpoint pen was patented in 1938.

In exchange for agreeing to make it his first RCA record, Elvis got an equal share of the writer's credit. "Heartbreak Hotel" went to the top of the charts, establishing Elvis as the most popular new singer in America.

SIMON & GARFUNKEL

First Hit: "Hey Schoolgirl," 1957

Background: Paul Simon got to know Artie Garfunkel in P.S. 164 in Queens when they both appeared in their sixth-grade graduation play, *Alice in Wonderland*. Paul was the White Rabbit, Artie the Cheshire Cat. Because of their mutual interest in music, they became close friends, and when they were 14, they began writing songs together.

The Singers: According to Paul Simon: "We were fifteen years old when we signed a contract with Big Records as Tom and Jerry. 'Hey Schoolgirl' was the first song we recorded. To go along with the Tom and Jerry thing, I took on the stage name of Tom Landis and Artie took Jerry Graph. I picked Landis because I was going out with a girl named Sue Landis at the time and Artie picked Graph because he used to [keep track] of all the current hit records on big sheets of graph paper. 'Hey Schoolgirl' was sold in both 45 and 78 rpm; on the 45 it says 'by Landis-Graph', but on the 78 it's got 'P. Simon and A. Garfunkel.' "

It's a Hit: The song was released in 1957 and sold 120,000 copies, peaking at #54 after being on *Billboard*'s Top 100 for nine weeks. "You can't imagine," says Simon, "what it was like having a hit record behind you at the age of sixteen. One month Artie and I were watching 'American Bandstand' on television and the next month we were on the show." They had to follow Jerry Lee Lewis playing "Great Balls of Fire." It's one of the few "Bandstand" shows not preserved on tape.

"Hey Schoolgirl" was "Tom and Jerry's" only hit. Simon says he bought a red Impala convertible with the royalties.

* * *

IF THE SHOE FITS...
In ancient Inca weddings, the bride and groom weren't considered "officially" married until they had taken off their sandals and traded them with one another.

OTHER
PRESIDENTIAL FIRSTS

Who was the first president to throw out the first ball of the baseball season? Why did he do it? The story is interesting…but it almost always gets left out of the history books. But we've got it. Here's another B.R.I. look at forgotten moments in U.S. history.

THE PRESIDENT: Harry S Truman

NOTABLE FIRST: First president to buzz the White House in an airplane.

BACKGROUND: On May 19, 1946, President Truman climbed aboard his presidential aircraft, the *Sacred Cow*, for a flight to Independence, Missouri. Shortly after takeoff, he asked his pilot to fly the plane into restricted airspace above the White House, where First Lady Bess Truman, daughter Margaret, and several other guests were waiting on the roof.

As the *Sacred Cow* approached the executive mansion, Truman asked Myers to dive bomb the White House. "I've always wanted to try something like that," the president explained. The pilot sent the *Sacred Cow* into a dive, taking it from 3,000 feet to 500 feet in a matter of seconds. "At 500 feet, I had the *Cow* leveled and we roared over the White House roof. Everyone there was frozen with fear. We climbed to 3,000 feet again, swooped, circled, and fell into another dive. But this time Margaret and her mother were jumping and waving. We shot past them, at a little below 500 feet and roared back upstairs once more." From there the plane proceeded directly to Independence, where the president visited his mother.

THE PRESIDENTS: Thomas Jefferson and James Madison

NOTABLE FIRSTS: The only presidents to be arrested together.

BACKGROUND: One afternoon in the spring of 1791, future presidents Jefferson and Madison were riding a carriage through the Virginia countryside when a rural sheriff pulled them over and arrested them on the spot. Their crime: riding in a carriage on Sunday.

Tweety Pie won an Oscar in 1940.

THE PRESIDENT: Theodore Roosevelt

NOTABLE FIRST: First and last (that *we* know of) president to wear another president's body part during his inauguration.

BACKGROUND: The night before he was sworn into office in 1901, was given an unusual gift—a ring containing strands of hair that had been cut from President Abraham Lincoln's head the night he was assassinated. Roosevelt wore the ring to his inauguration the next day.

THE PRESIDENT: William Howard Taft

NOTABLE FIRST: First president to throw out the first pitch of the baseball season.

BACKGROUND: Weighing in at over 330 pounds, Taft was our fattest president. His handlers feared his girth might make him seem weak when he ran for office again. So, in 1910, one of them suggested to the president that he begin playing a sport to prove that he still had his youthful vigor. When Taft vetoed the idea, his aide suggested that he at least make a *ceremonial* appearance at a sporting event—say, to throw out the first ball of the baseball season. Taft agreed, and on April 14, 1910, he waddled out to the pitcher's mound at Griffith Stadium in Washington, D.C., and pitched a ball to home plate. (It went wild.)

Note: Continuing the tradition started by Taft, subsequent presidents' pitches were just as wild. By 1929, rather than actually *pitch* the ball, most presidents just threw it onto the field from their seat in the stands.

THE PRESIDENT: Warren G. Harding

NOTABLE FIRST: First president to bet (and lose) White House china in poker games.

BACKGROUND: Harding was an enthusiastic poker player; unfortunately, he wasn't very good at it and was often short of cash. End result: when he was low on cash during poker games with his buddies, he used individual pieces of fine White House china for poker chips. It is not known how many pieces of the china were lost in this way.

ABOUT JAMES DEAN

What was "the rebel without a cause" really like?

Dean was fascinated with death. He wrote poems about dying and often drew pictures of himself hanging by a noose from the ceiling of his apartment. During one trip to his home town, he had a local funeral parlor photograph him lying in a casket.

★

His main body of work consisted of several TV appearances and only three motion pictures—*East of Eden*, *Rebel Without a Cause*, and *Giant*.

★

While filming *Giant*, Dean annoyed his coworkers by walking around with unfurled pastries hanging out of each nostril.

★

Once on the set he even urinated in full view of the public. His explanation: "I figured if I could piss in front of those 2,000 people, man, and I could be cool....I could get in front of the camera and do just anything, anything at all."

★

Dean didn't have any front teeth; he had to wear a special bridge to fill in the gap. He liked to startle people by smiling at them with his teeth out.

★

Dean had several gay roommates while living in Hollywood. When asked whether he was bisexual, he reportedly responded: "Well, I'm certainly not going through life with one hand tied behind my back!" He also avoided the military draft by registering as a homosexual.

★

In late 1955, Dean filmed a TV commercial on auto safety for teenagers. One of his lines: "Drive safely, the life you save may be mine." A few weeks later, he was killed in a car wreck.

★

Dean's last words before he slammed into Donald Gene Turnupseed's 1950 Ford Tudor near Cholame, on California Highway 466: "That guy up there has to stop, he's seen us."

★

Dean really did say, "Live fast, die young and leave a good-looking corpse."

In some parts of Africa, ostriches are used to herd sheep.

LOST IN SPACE

This show still has a cult following. Why? Don't ask us. We've never even been able to figure out why the Robinsons didn't just push that whining S.O.B. Dr. Smith out the airlock and forget him.

HOW IT STARTED

After producing everything from documentaries to comedies in the '50s, filmmaker Irwin Allen discovered kids' science fiction/adventure films in the '60s. He made *The Lost World* (1960), *Voyage to the Bottom of the Sea* (1961), and Jules Verne's *Five Weeks in a Balloon* (1963), all successful. But special-effects films are hard to finance, so Allen decided to move to TV.

His first effort was a popular 1964 adaptation of *Voyage to the Bottom of the Sea*. His second was to be a live-action version of a comic book called *Space Family Robinson* (Swiss Family Robinson in space). But while Allen was still making the two-hour pilot in 1964, Walt Disney, who owned the rights to the name, decided that Allen couldn't use it. So Allen changed it to "Lost in Space."

It was supposed to be a serious space adventure show, like "Star Trek" (no kidding), but when Allen showed it to CBS executives for the first time, he got a rude shock. One of the men who was there that day recalls: "Irwin, who has absolutely no sense of humor, thought he was making a very serious program. But in the viewing room, the network executives who were watching the pilot were absolutely hysterical, laughing...Irwin got furious and wanted to stop the showing...But his assistant kicked him under the table and whispered, 'Never mind. They love it.'" And they did. CBS bought the show and ran it for three years, from 1965 to 1968. Allen went on to make films like *The Poseidon Adventure* and *Towering Inferno*, for which he is known as "The Master of Disaster."

INSIDE FACTS

You Bet Your Life

The man who financed "Lost in Space" was "the one, the only... Groucho!" Marx and Allen were good friends. Groucho included a photo of himself and Allen in his book, *The Groucho-Phile*. The caption: "I taught him everything he knows about 'disaster' pictures. This picture was taken either at his wedding or mine."

What are *eructations*, *stenutations*, and *pandiculations*? Burps, sneezes, and yawns, in that order.

Saved by the Mail
Dr. Smith (Jonathan Harris) was originally supposed to be killed off after six weeks. In fact, he was such a "minor" character that his contract stated he couldn't be billed higher than seventh in the credits! But fan mail was overwhelmingly in favor of keeping him.

Adventures of Zorro
Harris's popularity was particularly frustrating to Guy Williams (John Robinson), who—guaranteed top billing—assumed he'd be the star. Instead, he rarely got *any* important dialogue. "I must be getting paid more per word than Lawrence Olivier," he groused.

Special Effects
Irwin Allen was notoriously cheap. For example, the dome on the frog alien's spaceship in the episode "The Golden Man" was actually a giant champagne glass from a Marilyn Monroe film, salvaged by the director from the 20th Century Fox junkpile. Originally the space ship in the episode was budgeted at $10,000. But when Allen was told the cost, he hit the roof. "Let the frog walk," he screamed. So the director had to scrounge and get it for free.

TV Robotics
• The Robot (no name) bore a striking resemblance to Robby, the famous robot from the film *Forbidden Planet* (1956). No coincidence. He was created by Bob Kinoshita, Robby's co-designer.
• Lights flashed on the robot in synchronization with his voice. An electronic innovation? No. A little actor was inside, pressing a telegraph key in the left claw as he spoke.
• The actor in the robot saw out via the robot's plastic collar. Viewers couldn't see him in the shell, because he was in blackface.

Phony Numbers
The Robinsons traveled on planet surfaces in a vehicle with the official-looking call numbers "277-2211 IA" painted on it. Actually, the seven digits are 20th Century Fox's phone number. And the IA is producer Irwin Allen's initials.

Surprise!
Every member of the cast learned that the show had been cancelled by reading about it in the newspapers.

FROM THE PORCELAIN FILE

Over the years, the Bathroom Readers' Institute has built up a large collection of bathroom-related news clippings from around the world. Here are some of the more unusual items.

TOILETS IN THE AIR

• In April 1988, a toilet on an Eastern Airlines flight from Colombia to the U.S. clogged and began leaking. When the flight crew examined it to see what was wrong, they found more than $1 million worth of uncut cocaine. Officials speculated that it had been jammed into the toilet before takeoff by Colombian ground crew members with drug cartel connections.

• In July 1989, hundreds of travelers were stranded for more than an hour at Boston's Logan International Airport after a flooding toilet shorted out the control tower radar system. Airport officials launched an immediate investigation. Their findings: "Somebody plugged it up or something."

• In January 1990, a Northwest Airlines 727 flying to Minneapolis had to make an emergency landing in Tampa, Florida, after one of its engines fell off during the flight. No one was hurt. Cause of the problem: a leaky toilet. Fluid from the in-flight john had leaked out onto the fuselage, where it froze into "blue ice" and was sucked into the engine.

LAST STOPS

• In December 1986, Nathan Hicks, of St. Louis, Missouri, shot his brother Herbert with a .22-caliber rifle. Why? According to news reports, Hicks "was angry that Herbert had used up a new 8-roll pack of toilet paper."

• In December 1993, a real estate agent in Merriam, Kansas, discovered the body of a man in one of the bathrooms of a house as she showed it to prospective buyers. The body had been there for at least three days while she was showing the house. According to news reports: "Apparently neither the agent nor prospective buyers had been interested in looking inside that particular bathroom."

GOING AT SCHOOL
• In September 1988, South Carolina's Socastee High School launched a crackdown on students who go to the bathroom too much during class. Their solution: charging students $2.25 per bathroom visit during class. "Unless you've got diarrhea or food poisoning," Superintendent John Dawsey explained, "your system is such that you can go two hours without using the bathroom." The policy was later abandoned.

YOUR TAX DOLLARS AT WORK
• In July 1990, the U.S. Air Force admitted that it paid $1,868.15 for a "toilet cover assembly"—a toilet *cover*, not a toilet—for a C-5B transport plane. It claimed the cost was "reasonable," but Congressional staffers investigating Pentagon waste found a similar toilet cover available commercially for $182.

• In January 1990, California state officials approved the purchase of a $38,000 floating restroom for Santa Barbara's Lake Cachuma, a popular spot for area boaters. Reason: dropping water levels, caused by a six-year drought, "had put too much terrain between boaters and shoreside privies when nature called....Too many buckets were being filled and dumped into the lake when nobody was watching."

TOILET TALES FROM SANTA ROSA, CA
• In September 1993, Betty Crawford was using the restroom at her new office in Santa Rosa, California, when an 8-inch-long rat jumped out of the toilet and into her lap. "I just yelled and jumped up," Crawford told reporters, and the rat fled. Santa Rosa city officials said they get about 12 calls a year from citizens complaining about rats...but only rarely about rats in toilets. "You see it in movies about things coming up through the sewer system," one utility official told reporters, "but you only half-believe it."

• Opposite problem: On January 19, 1994, a Santa Rosa woman was giving "Tiny," her 6-foot python, a bath when her phone rang. She stepped out of the bathroom to answer it, and when she returned 20 minutes later, Tiny was gone. Suspecting the snake had crawled into the toilet and down the sewer pipes, she called the utility company. They spent three hours searching the pipes with a camera...and found nothing. Police and utility workers warned neighbors to be on the lookout, as Tiny might crawl up *their* toilets.

The average American consumes 87 hot dogs a year.

ORDER IN THE COURT!

Disorderly Conduct and Disorder in the Court are two books featuring amusing selections from court transcripts. They make great bathroom reading material—especially for lawyers. These quotes are taken directly from actual court records.

BORED IN COURT

Defendant: Judge, I want you to appoint me another lawyer.

Judge: And why is that?

Defendant: Because the public defender isn't interested in my case.

Judge (to public defender): Do you have any comments on your defendant's motion?

Public defender: I'm sorry, Your Honor, I wasn't listening.

JUDGE AND JURY

Judge: Is there any reason you could not serve as a juror in this case?

Potential juror: I don't want to be away from my job for that long.

Judge: Can't they do without you at work?

Potential juror: Yes, but I don't want them to know it.

Judge to defendant: You have a right to a trial by jury, but you may waive that right. What do you wish to do?

Defendant: (*Hesitates.*)

Lawyer to defendant: Waive.

Defendant: (*Waves at the judge.*)

OPEN AND SHUT CASE

Lawyer: Were you leaning up against the shut door or open door?

Witness: A shut door. How can you lean against an open door? There's a hole there. You'd fall through the hole.

UNTIL PROVEN GUILTY

Lawyer: Have you ever been convicted of a felony?

Ringo Starr was born during a World War II air raid.

Defendant: Yes
Lawyer: How many?
Defendant: One, so far.

Judge: The charge here is theft of frozen chickens. Are you the defendant, sir?
Defendant: No, sir, I'm the guy who stole the chickens.

Defense Attorney: Are you sure you did not enter the Seven-Eleven on Fortieth and Northeast Broadway and hold up the cashier on June seventeen of this year?
Defendant: I'm pretty sure.

Judge: Mr. E., you're charged here with driving a motor vehicle under the influence of alcohol. How do you plead, guilty or not guilty?
Defendant: I'm guilty as hell.
Judge: Let the record reflect the defendant is guilty as hell.

ALICE IN LAWYERLAND

Lawyer: Could you briefly describe the type of construction equipment used in your business?
Witness: Four tractors.
Lawyer: What kind of tractors are they?
Witness: Fords.
Lawyer: Did you say 'four?'
Witness: Ford. Ford. Like the Ford. It is a Ford tractor.
Lawyer: You didn't say 'four,' you just said 'Ford?'
Witness: Yes, Ford. That is what you asked me, what kind of tractors.
Lawyer: Are there four Ford tractors? Is that what there is?
Witness: No, no. You asked me what kind of a tractor it was and I said *Ford* tractors.
Lawyer: "How many tractors are there?
Witness: Four.

Only 4% of Americans can say they didn't eat at McDonald's last year.

ZAP!

Frank Zappa was one of the first rock musicians to admit publicly that he could think. Here are a few of his thoughts.

"In the fight between you and the world, back the world."

"One of my favorite philosophical tenets is that people will agree with you only if they already agree with you. You do not change people's minds."

"Without deviation, progress is not possible."

"In the old days your old man would say 'Be home by midnight' and you'd be home by midnight. Today parents daren't tell you what time to be in. They're frightened you won't come back."

"Most rock journalism is people who can't write interviewing people who can't talk for people who can't read."

"Everyone has the right to be comfortable on his own terms."

"Most people wouldn't know good music if it came up and bit them in the ass."

"Pop is the new politics. There is more truth in pop music than in most political statements rendered by our leaders, even when you get down to the level of really simplified pop records. What I'm saying is that's how bad politics is."

"If your children ever found out how lame you are, they'd kill you in your sleep."

"Politics is a valid concept but what we do is not really politics...it's a popularity contest. It has nothing to do with politics. What it is, is mass merchandising."

"I can't understand why anybody would want to devote their life to a cause like dope. It's the most boring pastime I can think of. It ranks a close second to television."

"I think cynicism is a positive value. You have to be cynical. You can't not be cynical. The more people that I have encouraged to be cynical, the better job I've done."

World's first copyrighted motion picture: *Record of a Sneeze,* by Thomas Edison.

FINAL THOUGHTS

When you gotta go, you gotta go. Here are some "last words" from some people who really knew how to make an exit.

"No. I came here to die. Not make a speech."
—**Cherokee Bill,** *outlaw, when asked "if he had anything to say"*

"So little done, so much to do."
—**Alexander Graham Bell**

"I hope that the edge of your guillotine is sharper than your scissors."
—**Jean-Francois Ducos,** *to the executioner, who was cutting off his hair*

"Ah…you might make that a double."
—**Neville Heath,** *murderer, asking for a last whiskey*

"It is a reproach to the faculty that they cannot cure the hiccup."
—**James Hogg,** *poet, …who died from hiccups*

"I've never felt better."
—**Douglas Fairbanks, Sr.**

"I have only two regrets—that I have not shot Henry Clay or hanged John C. Calhoun."
—**President Andrew Jackson**

"Are you sure it's safe?"
—**William Palmer,** *murderer, stepping onto the gallows*

"Go on, get out! Last words are for fools who haven't said enough."
—**Karl Marx,** *communist*

"I am dying like a poisoned rat in a hole. I am what I am! I am what I am!
—**Jonathan Swift**

"I shall hear in heaven!"
—**Ludwig van Beethoven**

"At least one knows that death will be easy. A slight knock at the window pane, then…"
—**Bertolt Brecht,** *playwright*

"Get my swan costume ready."
—**Anna Pavlova,** *Russian ballerina*

The Bible is the most shoplifted book in the United States.

A TOY IS BORN

*You've bought them. You've played with them. You've wondered where
they came from and who created them. Now the BRI offers
these bits of useless information to satisfy your curiosity.*

WIFFLE BALLS

In 1953 David Mullaney noticed that his son and a friend were playing stickball in the small backyard of their Fairfield, Connecticut, home...but they were using one of Mullaney's plastic golf balls instead of a rubber ball. It seemed like a good idea; that way the ball couldn't be hit or thrown too far.

Mullaney cut holes in some of his plastic golf balls with a razor blade and discovered that, with the right configuration, players using a lightweight plastic ball could even throw curves and sliders. In 1955, he began manufacturing his new creation, marketing it as a Wiffle Ball—a name he adapted from the baseball term "to whiff," or strike out.

SUPERBALLS

In the early '60s a chemist named Norman Stingley was experimenting with high-resiliency synthetics for the U.S. government when he discovered a compound he dubbed *Zectron*. He was intrigued; when the material was fashioned into a ball, he found it retained almost 100% of its bounce...which meant it had six times the bounce of regular rubber balls. And a Zectron ball kept bouncing—about 10 times longer than a tennis ball.

Stingley presented the discovery to his employer, the Bettis Rubber Company, but the firm had no use for it. So, in 1965, Stingley took his Zectron ball to Wham-O, the toy company that had created Hula Hoops and Frisbees. It was a profitable trip. Wham-O snapped up Stingley's invention, called it a "Superball," and sold 7 million of them in the next six months.

TROLL DOLLS

In the early '50s a Danish woodcarver named Thomas Dam made a wooden doll as a birthday gift for his teenage daughter. The doll, Dam's interpretation of "the mythical Scandanavian elves visible only to children and childlike grown-ups," was so popular with local kids that a Danish toy store owner insisted he make more of them. Eventually, to keep up with European demand, Dam began mass-producing them out of plastic.

In the early '60s they were exported to the U.S. as Dammit Dolls...and quickly became a teenage fad, adapted to everything from key chains to sentimental "message" dolls. But since Dam had no legal protection for the design, dozens of manufacturers jumped on the troll-wagon with knockoffs called Wish Niks, Dam Things, Norfins, etc.

The original Dammit Dolls are now collectors' items.

TWISTER

The first game in the history of the American toy industry "to turn the human body into a vital component of play" enjoyed instant popularity when Milton Bradley introduced it in 1966. Why? TV and sex.

When it first came out, Bradley's PR firm brought Twister to the "Tonight Show" and showed it to Johnny Carson's writers. They thought it was hilarious and promised to get it on the show right away.

They were true to their word. Carson's guest that night was Eva Gabor, and when millions of viewers saw the two glamorous celebrities climbing all over each other as they played the game on national television, they understood exactly what Twister was really about—SEX. The next day, toy stores were flooded with demands for the game.

That year, over 3 million games were sold—more than 10 times the amount that Milton Bradley had anticipated. It became the most popular new game of the '60s.

BINGO

In 1929, a tired, depressed toy salesman named Edwin Lowe set out on a night-time drive from Atlanta, Georgia, to Jacksonville, Florida. On the way, he noticed the bright lights of a carnival; he decided to stop to investigate. Lowe found only one concession open—a tent full of people seated at tables, each with a hand-stamped, numbered card and a pile of beans. As the emcee called out numbers, players put beans on the corresponding squares on their cards. If they got five beans in a row, they won a Kewpie doll. The concessionaire called his game Beano. Lowe was so impressed that he tried it at his own home, where one young winner became so excited that she stammered out "B-b-bingo!" instead of "Beano." So that's what Lowe called it.

Hard to imagine: In 1910, Georgia Tech's football team beat Cumberland University 222 to 0.

A MATTER OF LIFE AND DEATH

What would happen if you suddenly decided (or announced, anyway) that you had to do something...or you'd die? Here are three case histories.

THE WINCHESTER CURSE

Background: In 1858, Sarah Pardee married William Winchester, heir to the Winchester rifle fortune. When her husband and infant daughter died a few years later, she became convinced that she was haunted by the ghosts of people killed with Winchester rifles—especially Indians.

Voices from Beyond: Sarah consulted a medium in Boston, who said that she could only escape the spirits if she built a home for them. Not only that, but construction on the house had to go on day and night, forever. If construction ever ceased, Sarah would die.

Life-Saver: Sarah, who had a $20 million fortune, bought an 8-room farmhouse in California and started work on it. "It grew to 20 rooms," says one report, "then 40, then 60. A hundred rooms, and still it grew. It spread over the flats like a Victorian gingerbread version of the Blob."

For 38 years a crew of 20 carpenters worked day and night on the house. It eventually rose to a height of seven stories and covered six acres. Servants needed maps to find their way around the 160-room structure, with its 2,000 doors, 10,000 windows, 40 staircases, and 6 kitchens. Construction was still going strong when Sarah died in 1923, at age 81. Today, the house is a tourist attraction.

STUCK IN AN IVORY TOWER

Background: Oral Roberts, a successful TV preacher with a "$500 million evangelical empire," built a medical center called City of Faith in 1982. It was a financial disaster. In its first five years of operation, only two months were profitable. By 1987 it was, as *U.S. News & World Report* said, "Beginning to erode the rest of Roberts's empire." The Bible-thumper needed a lot of cash to keep it afloat. That's when he heard from God.

Big day: Louis XIV bathed once a year.

Voices from Beyond: Apparently, Roberts received an ultimatum from the Supreme Being at the beginning of January: either come up with $8 million by the end of March, or die. Roberts put it this way: "The Lord told me, 'I'll call you home.'"

Life-Savers: Roberts's followers responded to his story—and by March 19, they had coughed up more than $6.3 million. That was a lot of money, Roberts admitted, but not enough for the Lord. Roberts beseeched his followers for even more, and they responded...but they still couldn't reach the goal. Roberts's case seemed desperate until Jerry Collins, Florida millionaire and dog track mogul, agreed to contribute the remaining $1.3 million. He also contributed some free advice: "I think Roberts needs psychiatric treatment."

GERM WARFARE

Background: Howard Hughes, movie mogul and founder of Hughes Aircraft Corp., was one of the wealthiest men in America in the 1960s, and, according to some accounts, one of the craziest. Haunted by the early deaths of both parents, he became obsessed with his own mortality.

Voices from Beyond: Something told Hughes that the only way to protect himself was to keep away from germs. "Everybody carries germs around," he once told a reporter. "I want to live longer than my parents, so I avoid germs."

Life-Saver: He wrapped his hands in Kleenex before touching anything. When he married actress Jean Peters in 1957, he insisted on separate *kitchens*, so that his wife would be unable to touch his food.

After the marriage failed, he moved to a bungalow in the desert to escape invisible contamination; people who came to visit him had to stand in a chalk square drawn on the driveway while aides inspected them for germs before they could approach the front door. Hughes wouldn't even allow his personal physician to touch him; during infrequent visits to the bungalow, the physician was only allowed to examine Hughes from across the room.

Eventually, Hughes became convinced that even the bungalow was infested with germs. He spent the rest of his life moving from one hotel to another. Each time he moved into a hotel, he took an entire floor. All the windows were covered and sealed, and all the furniture was removed except for a single bed, a chair...and a big box of Kleenex.

PIRATE LEGENDS

*We've all got an idea of what it was like to be a pirate in the 1700s—but
a lot of it is pure Hollywood hooey. Here are a few of our most common
misconceptions about pirates…and the truth about them.*

NICKNAMES

Why did so many pirates have colorful nicknames like
"Blackbeard" and "Half Bottom"? The main reason was to
prevent government officials from identifying and persecuting their
relatives back home. (How did "Half Bottom" get his nickname? A
cannonball shot half his bottom off.)

WALKING THE PLANK

Few (if any) pirate ships ever used "the plank." When pirates took
over a ship, they usually let the captured crewmembers choose between joining the pirate crew or jumping overboard. Why go to all
the trouble of setting up a plank to walk off ? As historian Hugh
Rankin put it: "The formality of a plank seems a bit absurd when it
was so much easier just to toss a prisoner overboard."

BURIED TREASURE

Another myth. No pirate would have trusted his captain to bury
treasure for him. According to pirate expert Robert Ritchie, "The
men who turned to piracy did so because they wanted money. As
soon as possible after capturing a prize they insisted on dividing the
loot, which they could then gamble with or carry home. The idea
of burying booty on a tropical island would have struck them as
insane."

BOARDING A SHIP BY FORCE

It's a scene from the movies: A pirate ship pulls up alongside another ship, and then the pirates swing across on ropes and storm
the ship. But how realisitic is this scene? Not very, experts say.
Most ship captains owned their cargos, which were usually fully
insured. They preferred to surrender the minute they were approached by a pirate ship, seeing piracy as one of the costs of
doing business.

Liechtenstein, the world's smallest country, is also the world's largest manufacturer of false teeth.

THE JOLLY ROGER (SKULL AND CROSSBONES)

Pirates used a variety of flags to communicate. The Jolly Roger was used to coerce nearby ships into allowing the pirates to board. But it wasn't the only flag used—some pirate ships preferred flags with hourglasses on them (to let would-be victims know that time was running out); others used black or red flags. How did the Jolly Roger get its name? Nobody knows for sure—although some historians believe it comes from the English pronunciation of *Ali Raja*, Arabic for "King of the Sea."

PIRATE SHIPS

In the movies they're huge—but in real life they were much smaller. "Real Pirates," one expert writes, "relied on small, swift vessels and hit-and-run attacks.

ROWDINESS

Not all pirate ships were rough-and-tumble. Pirates often operated under a document that had some similarity to a constitution. Here are a few of the articles from an agreement drawn up by the crew of Captain John Phillips in 1723.

1. Every man shall obey civil Command; the Captain shall have one full Share and a half in all prizes; the Master, Carpenter, Boatswain, and Gunner shall have one share and a quarter.

2. If any man shall offer to run away, or keep any Secret from the Company, he shall be maroon'd with one Bottle of Powder, one Bottle of Water, one small Arm, and Shot.

3. If any Man shall steal any Thing in the Company, or game, to the Value of a Piece of Eight, he shall be maroon'd or shot.

4. That Man that shall strike another whilst those Articles are in force, shall receive Moses's Law (that is 40 stripes lacking one) on the bare Back.

5. That Man that shall not keep his Arms clean, fit for an Engagement, or neglect his Business, shall be cut off from his Share, and suffer such other Punishment as the Captain and the Company shall think fit.

6. If any Man shall lose a Joint in time of an Engagement, shall have 400 Pieces of Eight; if a limb 800.

7. If at any time you meet with a prudent Woman, that Man that offers to meddle with her, without her Consent, shall suffer Death.

CAR NAMES

They're a part of your life; you know them as well as you know your own name. But do you know where they come from?

SOME REAL PEOPLE

Chevrolet. Louis Chevrolet, a race-car driver and designer who co-founded the company that later merged with GM.

Oldsmobile. Ransom Eli Olds, an auto pioneer who started the Olds Motor Vehicle company in 1897.

Rolls-Royce. Sir Henry Royce founded the company in 1903; Charles Rolls promoted the car.

Mercedes-Benz. Carl Benz is believed by many to have invented the automobile in 1879. Mercedes Jellinek was a young girl; her father was a German diplomat and an investor in Benz's company.

Buick. David Dunbar Buick, a Scotsman, sold his failing Buick Motor Car Company to William Durant in 1908. Durant used it as the cornerstone of the General Motors empire. Buick died broke; he was "so poor he could afford neither a telephone nor a Buick."

SOME "INSTANT WORDS"

Nissan Sentra. According to one of the men who named it: "It's the company's mainstream, or central, car. The word *Sentra* sounds likes *central*, as well as *sentry*, which evoke images of safety."

Volvo. Means "I roll" in Latin.

Camaro. According to GM in 1967, it meant "pal" in French, because "the real mission of our automobile is to be a close companion to its owner." A French auto executive corrected them: "It doesn't mean anything in English, and doesn't mean anything in French, either."

A NEAR DISASTER

Pontiac Firebird. Originally called the *Banshee*. The press releases were out, the announcement had been made, and then someone at GM discovered that in Irish folklore, a banshee is "a supernatural being whose wailing foretells death." That would have been a public relations disaster—like calling a car the "Grim Reaper." Who'd dare buy it? So they quickly changed it to *Firebird*, a creature of American Indian legends.

Good news? Americans smoked 485 billion cigarettes in 1993—down from 594 billion in 1985.

MORE STRANGE LAWSUITS

More bizarre doings in the halls of justice,
from contemporary news reports.

THE PLAINTIFF: James Hooper
THE DEFENDANT: The Pizza Shuttle
THE LAWSUIT: Hooper, a 25-year-old Oklahoma State University student, ordered an "extra cheese, pepperoni, sausage, black olive, and mushroom pizza" from the Pizza Shuttle. He sued for $7 in damages because he got "a pizza with something green on it" instead.
THE VERDICT: The court found in favor of the Pizza Shuttle—and ordered Hooper to pay $57 in court costs.

THE PLAINTIFF: Frank Zaffere, a 44-year-old Chicago lawyer
THE DEFENDANT: Maria Dillon, his 21-year-old ex-fiance
THE LAWSUIT: When Dillon broke off their engagement in June 1992, Zaffere sued her for $40,310.48 to cover his "lost courting expenses." In a letter sent to Dillon, he wrote, "I am still willing to marry you on the conditions herein below set forth: 1) We proceed with our marriage within 45 days of the date of this letter; 2) You confirm [that you]...will forever be faithful to me; 3) You promise...that you will never lie to me again about anything." He closed with: "Please feel free to call me if you have any questions or would like to discuss any of the matters discussed herein. Sincerely, Frank."
THE VERDICT: The case was dismissed. So was the wedding. "I can't imagine telling my children as a bedtime story that Mommy and Daddy got married because of a lawsuit," Dillon said.

THE PLAINTIFF: Tomontra Mangrum, a 15-year-old West Palm Beach girl
THE DEFENDANT: Marlon Shadd, her 17-year-old prom date
THE LAWSUIT: Mangrum claimed Shadd stood her up on prom night. "I talked to him a few days before, and he said he already

had his tux and the tickets," she told reporters. "I was very upset when he didn't show up." Shadd, on the other hand, insisted he'd called off the date a week before the prom. "I told her I fractured my ankle," he said. Tomontra's mother filed suit, seeking $49.53 for the cost of the shoes, flowers, and hairdo her daughter had gotten for the prom.

THE VERDICT: We don't know—if *you* do, write and tell us.

THE PLAINTIFF: Elizabeth M., a nurse from Irvine, California
THE DEFENDANT: Her ex-husband
THE LAWSUIT: In 1991, Mr. M. became a monk. He filed court papers to have his alimony payment of $739 a month eliminated, since he was no longer earning anything. Ms. M. argued that her ex-husband's situation was "no different than if he had simply decided to stop all work and spend the rest of his life surfing."
VERDICT: The ex-husband won the case.

THE PLAINTIFF: Frederick Newhall Woods IV, serving a life sentence for the infamous Chowchilla schoolbus kidnapping
THE DEFENDANT: The American Broadcasting Company
THE LAWSUIT: In 1976, Woods and two accomplices kidnapped a bus driver and 26 elementary school students and buried them underground. When ABC aired a TV movie docudrama about the kidnapping in 1994, Woods was offended. He sued the network, claiming that the show "portrayed (him) as being callous, vicious, hardened, wild-eyed, diabolical, and uncaring."
THE VERDICT: Case dismissed.

THE PLAINTIFF: John M., a 50-year-old Philadelphia teacher
THE DEFENDANT: His ex-wife, Maryann, a 46-year-old receptionist
THE LAWSUIT: One day after her divorce from John became final, Maryann turned in a lottery ticket that was about to expire and won $10.2 million. Her lawyer claimed that "Lady Luck" led her to find the ticket and turn it in two weeks before it expired. Her husband said she deliberately waited until after the divorce was final to turn it in. He sued to get his share.
THE VERDICT: Unknown—but we'd like to find out.

The Hundred Years War lasted for 116 years.

PRIMETIME PROVERBS

TV comments about everyday life. From Primetime
Proverbs, *by Jack Mingo and John Javna*

ON RAISING KIDS:

Fred Sanford: "Didn't you learn anything being my son? Who do you think I'm doing this all for?"
Lamont Sanford: "Yourself."
Fred: "Yeah, you learned something."
—Sanford and Son

Sophia: "She's always tellin' me what to do!"
Rocco: "Don't worry. My daughter treats me the same way."
Sophia: "Kids. Once they're over fifty, they think they know everything."
—The Golden Girls

ON PETS:

"He who lies down with dogs gets up with fleas."
*—Herman Munster,
The Munsters*

Morticia Addams: "Now Pugsley darling, who could be closer than a boy and his mother?"
Pugsley Addams: "A boy and his octopus?"
Morticia[smiling]: "Hmmm... Perhaps."
—The Addams Family

ON MAKEUP:

"City women is spoiled rotten. All they think about is smearin' themselves with beauty grease. Fancy smellin' renderin's. Why, if you was to hug one of 'em, she'd squirt out of yore arms like a prune pit!"
*—Granny,
The Beverly Hillbillies*

"I haven't worn makeup in years. It takes away that unnatural look that we girls like."
*—Lily Munster,
The Munsters*

ON SCIENCE:

"The roots of physical aggression found in the male species are in the DNA molecule itself. In fact, the very letters, dna are an acronym for 'Dames Are Not Agressors.'"
*—Cliff Claven,
Cheers*

Aesop, Jr.: "There's no fuel like an old fuel!"
Aesop, Sr.: "Hmmm...I *gas* you're right."
—The Bullwinkle Show

64% of Americans say they have confidence in the U.S. military;

MONSTER MOVIES

The inside dope on a few of the all-time great horror flicks.

FRANKENSTEIN (1931). The role that made Boris Karloff a star was originally offered to both Bela Lugosi and John Carradine; both turned it down. Two of the factors: the monster costume weighed 62 pounds, and the makeup took four hours to apply every day.

• Karloff had to wear 22-pound, size-24 boots. He also donned two pairs of pants with steel struts shoved in them and a double-thickness quilted suit.

• His facial makeup was one-sixteenth of an inch thick, and the bolts on the side of his neck left long-term scars.

• The famous scene in which the monster carries Dr. Frankenstein was memorable for Karloff, too—he strained his back and ultimately had to have an operation to fix it.

• Bette Davis wanted the part of Mrs. Frankenstein, but was turned down because she was "too aggressive."

DRACULA (1931). Bela Lugosi became the first great monster of the talkie era with his role in this film. He had been playing Count Dracula on Broadway since 1927, so he already knew the part. Unfortunately, he was only paid $500 for this classic film performance.

• Among the film's lighting tricks: "Twin pencil-spotlights" were shined in Lugosi's eyes to give Count Dracula his legendary hypnotic stare.

• The Castle Dracula and Carfax Abbey sets were so expensive to build that Universal Pictures kept and reused them. You can spot them in numerous Universal films of the '30s.

• The enormous spider web on Dracula's staircase was actually a string of rubber cement. And the mountains shown in the first scenes were really the Rockies—not the Alps or Carpathians.

THE MUMMY (1932). Boris Karloff's second big monster flick was inspired by the discovery of King Tut's tomb in 1922...and the widespread belief—because several men on the Tut expedition had died mysteriously—that there was a real-life curse connected to it.

• Karloff was wrapped every day in linen and gauze, then was covered with mud.

19% say the same thing about the Congress.

• He had become so famous as Frankenstein's monster the previous year that he was billed simply as "Karloff." Only Greta Garbo could match that.

THE WOLF MAN (1941). Lon Chaney, Jr. starred; it was his favorite role. Based on a popular 1935 English film, *Werewolf of London*, it was a surprise hit. Universal released it two days after Pearl Harbor and expected low box-office receipts. But instead of being distracted *by* the news, Americans wanted to be distracted *from* it.
• Chaney's werewolf makeup took five hours to apply every day.
• The same makeup man who created the Mummy and Frankenstein's monster for Boris Karloff created Chaney's werewolf.
• The werewolf costume was actually made of yak hair.

THE THING (1951). Director Howard Hawks's flick about an alien discovered near an Arctic research station is notable for two reasons: first, it kicked off the whole "it came from outer space" genre in the '50s; second, the actor who played the monster was James Arness—"Gunsmoke"'s Matt Dillon. Already six feet five inches tall, Arness wore four-inch lifts. He was onscreen about three minutes.

THEM! (1954). Another B-film breakthrough—the first of the "giant mutated insects" genre. In this one, huge killer ants were found in the desert. But again, it was one of the actors who made the film memorable—Fess Parker. In 1954, Walt Disney, planning a feature about Davy Crockett, couldn't find the right man to play the lead...until he saw *Them!* He immediately hired Parker, who became one of America's hottest actors as the King of the Wild Frontier—and later, as Dan'l Boone. Also featured in the film: Arness, who was a year away from TV stardom, and Leonard Nimoy.

THE CREATURE FROM THE BLACK LAGOON (1954). The star of this 3-D epic, the scaly creature who's become the symbol of all '50s cheapo monsters, was actually modeled after the Oscar statue given at the Academy Awards.
• Two different actors appeared inside the latex costume. On land, it was a big fellow named Ben Chapman. In water, it was champion swimmer Ricou Browning, whose main claim to fame was that a decade later, he created TV's most famous aquatic hero—Flipper.

Denver, Colorado, consumes less prune juice per capita than any other city in the U.S.

THE MYSTERY OF OAK ISLAND

The romance of searching for pirate treasure has been celebrated in dozens of stories since Robert Louis Stevenson's Treasure Island. *But is there really any buried treasure to be found? Maybe so…on Oak Island.*

TREASURE ISLAND

In 1795, a teenager named Daniel McGuinnis discovered an unusual, saucer-shaped depression on Oak Island, a tiny island off the coast of Nova Scotia. Next to the hole was an ancient oak tree with sawed-off limbs. And, according to legend, a ship's tackle hung from the tree directly over the depression—as if it had been used to lower something very heavy into the hole.

McGuinnis was certain he had found buried pirate treasure, and with the help of two friends he began digging for it. Within minutes they hit rock—which turned out to be a flagstone buried two feet below the surface. They hit another barrier made of oak logs at 10 feet deep; another at 20 feet, and a third at 30 feet. McGuinnis and his friends kept digging—but they never found any treasure and eventually gave up. Still, word of their discovery spread.

SECOND TRY

In 1803, a wealthy man named Simeon Lynds took up the search. The diggers he hired found another platform at 40 feet, and found several more deeper down. Finally, at 90 feet, the workers found a large stone with strange symbols carved into it. No one could decipher what the stone said, but the workers were convinced they were close to treasure and kept digging. (The stone was later stolen.) At 98 feet deep, their shovels struck what felt like a wooden chest. But the sun was going down, so they stopped for the night.

By the time the workers got back the next morning, the hole had flooded to the top with seawater. And it somehow kept refilling, even as the workers tried to bail it out. They never were able to drain the pit enough to finish digging.

Like McGuinnis, Lynds had hit a dead end.

There are 364 gifts in "The Twelve Days of Christmas."

AMAZING DISCOVERIES

Lynds wasn't the last person to dig for treasure on Oak Island. In fact, so many excavations have been attempted that the precise location of the original hole—known as the "Money Pit" because so much money has been spent trying to solve its mysteries—has been forgotten because so many other holes have been dug nearby. Even young Franklin D. Roosevelt supervised a dig in 1909 (he followed Oak Island's progress even as president). And the search continues today. Some findings:

• There's at least *some* gold down there. In 1849, treasure hunters sank a drill to the 98 foot level. Like Lynds, they hit what felt like a wooden chest. They dug through the top into what felt like "22 inches of metal in pieces (possibly gold coins)," through more wood, and into another 22 inches of metal. When they pulled the drill back up to the surface, three links of a gold chain were stuck to it. In nearly 200 years of digging, that's all the treasure that's been found.

• In 1897, another group of drillers dug down to 155 feet. They pulled up a half-inch-square piece of parchment—but that was all. They also hit what they thought was a heavy iron plate at 126 feet, but couldn't pull it up.

• In 1987, an IBM cryptologist finally deciphered an engraving of Lynds's lost stone. The message read: "Forty feet below, two million pounds are buried."

HIGH SECURITY

• Whoever dug the original pit went to a great deal of trouble to do it. In 1850, explorers resting on a nearby beach noticed that the beach "gulched forth water like a sponge being squeezed." So they dug it up—and discovered it was a *fake*. The beach was actually a manmade network of stone drains that filtered seawater and fed it into the Money Pit. The drains—designed to flood the pit whenever treasure hunters got close to the treasure—had been buried in sand to avoid detection.

• The Money Pit may even be protected by poison gas. On August 17, 1965, treasure hunter Bob Restall blacked out and fell into the pit he had dug. His son and four others tried to rescue him, but they also blacked out and fell in. Restall, his son, and two of the workers were killed. The autopsy finding: death by "marsh-gas poisoning and/or drowning."

TODAY

In 1977, the Montreal-based Triton Alliance Ltd., a consortium of 49 investors headed by David Tobias, bought the 128-acre Oak Island for $125,000. They have spent more than $3 million digging for treasure.

• During one drill, Triton's workers found bits of china, glass, wood, charcoal—even cement. But no treasure.

• Perhaps the strangest incident associated with Oak Island occurred in 1971 when Tobias's partner Dan Blankenship lowered an underwater video camera into a water-filled cavity at the bottom of a shaft. On the monitor, Blankenship suddenly saw what looked like a human hand. Horrified, he called over three crew members, who later verified his story. Asked by *Smithsonian* magazine about the legitimacy of his hand-sighting, he answered, "There's no question about it."

WHAT'S DOWN THERE?

Oak Island's "treasure," if there is one, could be worth over $100 million. Among the many theories of what the Money Pit could be hiding:

1. The missing crown jewels of France. The Nova Scotia area was frequented by pirates in the 16th and 17th centuries—when the jewels were stolen. The local Mahone Bay takes its name from the French word *mahonne*, a craft used by Mediterranean pirates.

2. Inca gold plundered by Spanish galleons and later pirated by Sir Francis Drake. A carbon analysis of wood samples recovered from the area dated them back to 1575, around the time of Drake's explorations. However, there is no record of Drake ever having been to Nova Scotia.

3. Captain Kidd's buried treasure. Some believe Kidd buried his treasure there before being extradited and later hanged by the British. Before Kidd was executed in 1701, he offered a deal: "He would lead a fleet to the spot where he had hidden his East Indian treasure, if the authorities would put off his execution. The deal

---

It takes about 3 1/2 hours for sound waves to travel from San Francisco to New York

was refused—and Kidd's treasure has never been found." There is, however, no evidence that Kidd was ever near Oak Island.

Others have their doubts. Some feel that the Money Pit is merely an elaborate decoy and that the treasure is actually buried in a nearby swamp. Others think it is just a sinkhole. Many doubt whether pirates had the resources and engineering know-how to construct such an elaborate trap.

POSTSCRIPT

Similar Money Pits are rumored to have been found in Haiti and Madagascar, although these discoveries have not been confirmed by archaeologists.

• • •

...And Now a Little Mood Reading

Here's a brief quote from Treasure Island, *by Robert Louis Stevenson. Appropriately, it's the part when they find the spot where the treasure should be...and see that it's already been dug up.*

"We were now at the margin of the thicket.

" 'Huzza, mates, altogether?' shouted Merry; and the foremost broke into a run.

"And suddenly, not ten yards further, we beheld them stop. A low cry arose. Long John Silver doubled his pace, digging away with the foot of his crutch like one possessed; and next moment he and I had come also to a dead halt.

"Before us was a great excavation, not very recent, for the sides had fallen in and grass had sprouted on the bottom. In this were the shaft of a pick broken in two and the boards of several packing-cases strewn around. On one of these boards I saw, branded with a hot iron, the name *Walrus*—the name of Flint's ship.

"All was clear to probation. The *cache* had been found and rifled: the seven hundred thousand pounds were gone!"

If you're into classic books and buried treasure, Treasure Island *is a good bathroom reader. The chapters are all about six pages long, and a new copy doesn't cost more than $5.*

Tennessee got its name in 1796; before that it was known as "Franklin."

THE NAME IS FAMILIAR

*Some people have achieved immortality because their
names became identified with products. You already
know the names—now here are the people.*

King C. Gillette.
William Painter—the man who invented the bottle cap—
suggested that Gillette, a traveling salesman, invent something that people could use a few times and throw away. In 1895, while cursing his dull razor, Gillette realized that disposable razors would be a perfect invention. Devising a thin enough blade was the problem: Gillette tinkered with 700 blades and 51 razors before getting it right in 1903. Within three years, he was selling more than 500,000 blades annually.

Sir Joseph Lister.
Even before the mouthwash that bears his name was invented, Lister fought germs: he campaigned against filthy hospitals and against doctors who performed surgery in their street clothes. When St. Louis chemist Joseph Lawrence invented the famous mouthwash, he named it "Listerine" both to honor and to take advantage of Lister's well-known obsession with cleanliness.

Clarence Birdseye.
Brooklyn-born "Bob" Birdseye was the first person to figure out how to freeze fresh food and still preserve its taste and nutrition. Birdseye's insight came from an Arctic expedition; he observed that caribou meat, quickly frozen in the sub-zero temperatures, retained its flavor when cooked months later. He returned to America and worked for years to develop a quick-freezing process. When he succeeded in 1929, he sold his invention for the then-enormous sum of $22 million; Birdseye foods still bears his name.

Charles Fleischmann.
An Austrian native who first visited the United States during the Civil War, he found our bread almost as appalling as our political situation. At the time, bread was mostly home-baked, using yeast made from potato peelings, and its taste was unpredictable. The

---

It takes about four hours to hard-boil an ostrich egg.

next time he came to America, Fleischmann brought along samples of the yeast used to make Viennese bread. In 1868, he began to sell his yeast in compressed cakes of uniform size that removed the guesswork from baking. In 1937, yeast sales reached $20 million a year. After Prohibition ended, Fleischmann and his brother Maximillian found another use for their yeast—to make Fleischmann's distilled gin.

William and Andrew Smith.

The makers of the Smith Brothers Cough Drops were the sons of Poughkeepsie, New York, restaurateur and candymaker James Smith. In 1870, one of Smith's customers gave him a recipe for a "cough candy." Smith made a batch and quickly sold it all. People in the windswept Hudson Valley—plagued by constant colds during the long winters—clamored for more…so the Smith family became America's cough drop kings. When copycat "Smith" cough drops appeared, the bearded brothers introduced the famous box that bears their pictures, as a means of guaranteeing authenticity.

John B. Stetson.

While traveling out West in the 1850s, Stetson became adept at trapping animals and sewing the skins together, to make hats for sun protection. When he returned to Philadelphia, he started a hat business with $100; his mainstay, "The Boss of the Plains" hat, became the classic symbol of the Wild West.

William Scholl.

As an apprentice to the local shoemaker, "Billy" Scholl's work led him to two conclusions: feet were abused, and nobody cared. So, in a burst of idealism, Scholl appointed himself the future foot doctor to the world. Strangely enough, it actually happened. By the time he became a doctor at 22, Scholl had invented and patented his first arch support; in fact, he held more than 300 patents for foot treatments and machines for making foot comfort aids. And his customers seemed to appreciate it—a widow once wrote him that she buried her husband with his "Foot-Eazers" so he would be as comfortable as he was in life. Until he died, in his 80s, Dr. Scholl devoted himself to saving the world's feet, adhering always to his credo: "Early to bed, early to rise, work like hell, and advertise."

Science fact: Pure alcohol freezes at –125°F.

DUMB PREDICTIONS

*Elsewhere in the book, we've included amazingly accurate predictions.
Here are some amazingly dumb ones.*

The abolishment of pain in surgery is a chimera. It is absurd to go on seeking it today. Knife and pain are two words in surgery that must forever be associated in the consciousness of the patient. To this compulsory combination we shall have to adjust ourselves."

**—Dr. Alfred Velpeau, 1839
(anesthesia was introduced seven years later)**

"While theoretically and technically television may be feasible, commercially and financially I consider it an impossibility, a development of which we need waste little time dreaming."

**—Lee DeForest,
"Father of the Radio," 1926**

"At present, few scientists foresee any serious or practical use for atomic energy. They regard the atom-splitting experiments as useful steps in the attempt to describe the atom more accurately, not as the key to the unlocking of any new power."

—*Fortune* magazine, 1938

"What can be more palpably absurd than the prospect held out of locomotives traveling twice as fast as stagecoaches?"

—The *Quarterly Review*, 1825

"The ordinary 'horseless carriage' is at present a luxury for the wealthy; and although its price will probably fall in the future, it will never, of course, come into as common use as the bicycle."

—*The Literary Digest*, 1889

"The energy necessary to propel the ship would be many times greater than that required to drive a train of cars at the same speed; hence as a means of rapid transit, aerial navigation could not begin to compete with the railroad."

—*Popular Science* magazine, 1897

Heavy thought: The hippo weighs about 100 pounds at birth.

FAMOUS FOR 15 MINUTES

*We'd like you to meet a few more members of our
Andy Warhol Memorial Hall of Fame.*

THE HEADLINE: *Stripper Sinks Political Career*

THE STAR: Annabella Battistella, a.k.a. Fanne Foxe, "The Argentine Firecracker," a voluptuous Latin "exotic dancer"

WHAT HAPPENED: Late one night in October 1972, a Washington, D.C., cop pulled over an erratically moving vehicle. The inebriated driver turned out to be Representative Wilbur Mills of Arkansas, a 36-year veteran of the House and chair of its powerful Ways and Means Committee. In the car with him were his next-door neighbor, 38-year-old Annabella Battistella (a stripper known onstage as Fanne Foxe), and some friends—all headed home after a night of carousing. At some point during the confrontation—no one is sure exactly why—Battistella suddenly ran screaming from the car and jumped or slipped into the Tidal Basin, a shallow section of the Potomac River. The event became front-page news, and it was revealed that the staid Mills—happily married for 40 years—had been having an affair with her.

Foxe cashed in immediately, booking a tour of East Coast strip joints as the "Washington Tidal Basin Girl." ("You've read about her, now see her in person!") She claimed to be making $3,000 a week, and that a "big toy company" was planning a Fanne doll. She even got the Harvard Republican Club *Newcomer of the Year* award.

THE AFTERMATH: Two months later, Mills suddenly appeared onstage in a seedy Boston strip joint and gave Foxe a kiss. That was the end of his political career. "I'm a sick man," he told colleagues. Mills was hospitalized, and Foxe continued to take it off, but faded into obscurity.

THE HEADLINE: *No Nudes Is Good Nudes? Naked Guy Nixed*

THE STAR: Andrew Martinez, a University of California, Berkeley, college sophomore

WHAT HAPPENED: In September 1992, Martinez began attending classes completely in the buff, calling his nudity a "form of free speech." The university did nothing until it received numerous complaints from students and school employees.

There weren't any university regulations banning public nudity, so the school updated its student-conduct regulations to forbid indecent exposure, public nakedness, and "sexually offensive conduct." Martinez was then suspended for two weeks when he gave a nude interview to a (clothed) reporter. When he showed up nude at an administrative hearing to protest the charges, he was permanently expelled from school for failing to wear "proper attire."

"I didn't think this was so controversial," Martinez told the *San Francisco Chronicle*. "I was surprised they gave me the boot."

THE AFTERMATH: Martinez became a mini-celebrity, featured in magazine and newspaper stories all over the world and appearing on several TV talk shows. His expulsion didn't stop him from waging his lone crusade. In March 1993, he was arrested near the campus for distributing free beer to the homeless while shouting the slogan, "Drink for the Revolution." He was, of course, nude.

THE HEADLINE: *Brando Refuses Oscar, Sends Surrogate in Protest Over Indian Rights*

THE STAR: Sacheen Littlefeather, a Native American political activist and Oscar stand-in for Marlon Brando

WHAT HAPPENED: In 1972, Marlon Brando was nominated for a Best Actor Oscar for his role in *The Godfather*. Brando was becoming increasingly political and at the time, the plight of the American Indians was his primary interest. So he arranged to have a young activist named Sacheen Littlefeather accept the award (if he won) in his place, and gave her a three-page speech to read. When the time came, Littlefeather, dressed in full Indian regalia, shocked the audience and TV network—and Roger Moore, the man trying to present it—by refusing the award for Brando and reading a short speech (the Academy refused to allow the long one) which decried the treatment of Indians in Hollywood films.

THE AFTERMATH: Littlefeather had regularly gotten bit parts in films, but for years after the incident, found herself blacklisted. She was also harassed by the FBI and other unknown individuals. She's still an activist, but says she feels bitter about the experience.

Nine most-used words in the English language: and, be, it, of, the, will, I, have, you.

THE HEADLINE: *Frisco Cabbie Nabs Runaway Crook*

THE STAR: Holden Hollom

WHAT HAPPENED: On a June night in 1989, Hollom, a 51-year-old San Francisco cabbie (and former stunt driver) was driving a fare up Market Street when he saw someone knock down a woman and steal her purse. He gave chase, yelling to his surprised passenger, "You're riding for free!" He cornered the purse snatcher (a 212-pound ex-convict) in an alley. To keep him from running away, Hollom pinned him to the wall with his cab bumper. Newspapers all over the country reported the citizen's arrest as an example of what's *right* about America, and lauded Hollom for getting involved. He appeared on "Larry King" and "Donahue."

THE AFTERMATH: The crook had to undergo three operations on his legs, and in 1992 sued Hollom for "using excessive force." When he won, and was awarded $24,500 by a jury, the verdict got as much attention as the original incident. It generated over $100,000 from outraged sympathizers who felt the cabbie had been shafted. (The verdict was later overturned.) Hollom later ran for the S.F. Board of Supervisors, but came in 19th in a field of 26 candidates. In 1995, he was in the news again—for nabbing another thief who had assaulted a tourist.

THE HEADLINE: *Blonde Bimbo's Billboards Bring Big Bonus*

THE STAR: Angelyne (she won't reveal her real name)

WHAT HAPPENED: In 1981, Angelyne began posting billboards of herself all over L.A. (they simply said *Angelyne* and listed a phone number) and distributing hot-pink press releases describing her as "a living icon, Hollywood billboard queen, the new Love Goddess of the Future!" from her pink Corvette. Later, she had an 85-foot-high likeness of herself painted on the side of a building at Hollywood and Vine.

THE AFTERMATH: Angelyne made more than 250 media appearances, including bit parts in films like *Earth Girls Are Easy* and *L.A. Story*. She came to represent, as one writer put it, "raw fame, unsullied by any known talent, charm, or accomplishments." But Angelyne doesn't mind. "I'm the first person in the history of Hollywood to be famous for doing nothing," she says. "I really don't want to be famous for being an actress. I just want to be famous for the magic I possess."

Shrimp can only swim backward.

MONEY TALK

What do you really know about your money?

THE GREENBACK DOLLAR

The federal government didn't start printing paper money until 1861.

• When the Civil War broke out, people began hoarding coins—and soon there was virtually no U.S. money in circulation. So Congress was forced to authorize the Treasury Department to create paper currency.

• These bills were nicknamed "greenbacks" after the color of ink used on one side. Lincoln, then president, was pictured on them.

• Congress stipulated that paper money had to be signed either by the Treasurer of the United States or people designated by him. Today the signature is printed on the bills, but in 1862 money had to be signed by hand. So six people—two men and four women—worked in the attic of the Treasury building every day, signing, sorting, and sealing our first $1 and $2 bills.

THE BUCK STOPS HERE

Today, paper money worth over $12 billion is printed every year—an average of more than $10 million a day.

• About two-thirds of the paper money printed is $1 bills.

• A $1 bill lasts for about one and a half years in circulation.

• The average bill is exchanged 400 times in its lifetime.

• It costs the government about 2.5¢ to print a bill.

• Modern U.S. currency is printed on special paper, a blend of rag bond, cotton, and linen, supplied by a single manufacturer, Crane and Company of Massachusetts.

• U.S. paper money is printed three separate times—once each for front and back, and then it's reprinted with an overlay of green ink.

• The current U.S. dollar is a third smaller than it was in 1929.

VITAL STATS

Size of a bill: 2.61 inches by 6.14 inches
Thickness: .0043 inches (233 bills make a stack 1 inch high)
Weight: 490 bills weigh 1 pound. A million bills weigh approximately 1 ton.

Colonial Governor John Winthrop introduced the table fork to America in 1620.

THE BIG BUCKS

• There are officially 12 different denominations of U.S. paper money, ranging from $1 to $100,000.

• The highest denomination printed in the last 45 years is $100. In fact, everything over $100 has been officially retired from circulation for 30 years.

• The $100,000 bill has never been available to the public. It's only for transactions between the Treasury Department and the Federal Reserve.

• The $2 bill was resurrected in 1976—the only piece of new engraved currency in 60 years. It was a flop; the mint had to get rid of the bills by burning them.

• Who's on what? $50—Ulysses S. Grant; $100—Benjamin Franklin; $500—William McKinley; $1,000—Grover Cleveland; $5,000—James Madison; $10,000—Salmon P. Chase; $100,000—Woodrow Wilson.

COIN COMMENTS

• The first U.S. coin to bear the words, "United States of America," was a penny piece made in 1727. It was also inscribed with the plain-spoken motto: "Mind Your Own Business."

• All American coins struck since 1792, when the first United States mint was established in Philadelphia, have been stamped with the word "Liberty."

• The average coin circulates for a minimum of 15 years.

• Originally, the dime, quarter, and half dollar were 90% silver, 10% copper. But in the early '60s, the price of silver began to climb, and government officials worried that people would melt coins down for the precious metals. The result: Congress passed the 1965 Coinage Act, eliminating all silver from the three coins. Instead, the composition was changed to "clad" metal—a combination of three strips of metal. The faces are made of 75% copper and 25% nickel; the core is pure copper, which you can see on the side.

• In 1965, anticipating the disappearance of old quarters due to the value of the silver, the government issued almost 2 billion new ones (compared to an average annual production of 225 million). That's why there are so many 1965 quarters in circulation.

• Nickels are now made of 75% copper, 25% nickel.

• Pennies are now bronze. They contain 95% copper, 5% zinc.

WHY YOUR FEET SMELL

This is dedicated to our good friend Pete McCracken. It originally appeared as an article in Health *magazine. It's written by Teo Furtado.*

Like lots of other people I've always been self-conscious about the bouquet of my feet. No wonder books on hygiene refer to smelly feet—*bromidrosis*, in medical jargon—as "the social disease" or "the unmentionable." Funny, when I was growing up, no one in my family ever had trouble mentioning it.

My brothers and I were in a no-win situation. While watching TV, we weren't allowed to put our feet up on the cocktail table with our shoes on. But taking our shoes off raised a loud...protest from my sisters. As they pinched their noses and gagged dramatically, they wiggled their toes in smug, odorless condescension.

IT'S THE SHOES!

Fortunately, we can take some comfort in the knowledge that the source of all this social angst isn't our feet; it's the shoes we wear. "There's no such thing as foot odor," says William Rossi, a podiatrist who's written extensively on foot problems. "There's only *shoe* odor. Just look at societies in which people go unshod. You never hear of foot odor problems."

Yes, it's civilization that's to blame—never mind the fact that there are more than a quarter of a million sweat glands in a pair of feet. That's more than in any other part of the human body, including the underarms.

The glands release about one gallon of moisture every week, but there's no problem so long as you're roaming around barefoot, says Rossi: Most of the sweat simply evaporates when your feet go through the world au naturel.

IF THE SHOE FITS...

All that changes when you confine a foot in a shoe. The buildup of sweat creates a nearly unlimited food supply for hungry bacteria, with salt, vitamins, glucose, fatty acids and lactic acid—nutritious stuff for the nearly six trillion bacteria that thrive on our feet.

With so much food and housing available, the organisms are fruitful and multiply. The food is digested; what's not used is broken down and excreted.

"You mean that the smell is bacterial poop?" I asked Rossi.

"Something like that," he responded.

THE CULPRITS

Researchers recently discovered that the main culprits in shoe odor are *micrococci*, bacteria that break sweat down into sulfur compounds that smell like rotten eggs or Limburger cheese.

How to attack them?

ODOR EATERS

There are plenty of over-the-counter remedies, but University of Pennsylvania microbiologist Ken McGinley advises some skepticism. It's true that foot powders absorb sweat and antiperspirant sprays cut down on its production. But, says McGinley…neither product adequately reduces the offending microbe's numbers because micrococci don't need as much moisture as other bacteria to survive.

Before you make that trip to the drugstore, there are some simpler—and usually more effective—solutions to try. First, the Imelda Marcos approach.

"Avoid wearing the same shoes over and over again," Rossi says.

Even if you don't have a roomful of shoes to choose from, rotate the ones you do wear. Each pair should air out for at least twenty-four hours between uses, says Rossi.

That advice, I figure, partly explains why my sisters didn't have bromidrosis: they simply changed shoes more often to match different outfits. The boys wore the same clodhoppers over and over again. Yet researchers say it's particularly important for men to rotate their shoes, because—silly as it sounds—they have larger toes that often stick together, making it harder for sweat to evaporate.

PLAYING HARDBALL

If a favorite pair of shoes is excessively odoriferous, Rossi offers a tip to try before you toss them out: sterilization. Roll some blotting paper into a cylinder to make a wick, and insert it partway into a small jar of formaldehyde (available at any pharmacy). Then place the jar and the shoes inside a cardboard box, tape the box shut, and put it into a closet or garage for a day or two. After taking the shoes out, be sure to let them dry overnight before you wear them again.

The word "sermon" does not appear in the Bible.

SHAKESPEARE SAYETH...

Here's the high-culture section of the Bathroom Reader.

"The first thing we do, let's kill all the lawyers."

"Neither a borrower, nor a lender be; For oft loses both itself and friend."

"He is well paid that is well satisfied."

"What's in a name? That which we call a rose / By any other name would smell as sweet."

"Some are born great, some achieve greatness, and some have greatness thrust upon them."

"Though this be madness, yet there is method in it."

"When Fortune means to men most good, she looks upon them with a threatening eye."

"Remuneration! O! That's the Latin word for three farthings."

"Words pay no debts."

"You taught me language; and my profit on't is, I know how to curse."

"Talkers are not good doers."

"The saying is true, the empty vessel makes the loudest sound."

"My words fly up, my thoughts remain below: Words without thoughts never to heaven go."

"If all the year were playing holidays / To sport would be as tedious as to work."

"The fault, dear Brutus, is not in our stars / But in ourselves."

"A politician...One that would circumvent God."

"When my love swears that she is made of truth / I do believe her, though I know she lies."

"Let me have no lying; it becomes none but tradesmen."

"If it be a sin to covet honor, I am the most offending soul."

"One may smile, and smile, and be a villain."

"Time is come 'round, and where I did begin, there shall I end "

A cubic yard of air weighs about two pounds.

CUSTOMS

Where do customs come from? Some random examples:

TIPPING

Some think it began in the 17th century, when restaurants had boxes labeled T.I.P.—To Insure Promptness—on the wall beside their entrances. Patrons who wanted their food in a hurry deposited a few coins in the box before they sat down.

AN APPLE FOR THE TEACHER

Now an outmoded custom, it stems from the days when public schoolteachers were paid with whatever the community could afford. Often they were given food or goods in lieu of cash.

THE TOOTH FAIRY

In Germany, where the idea apparently originated, the tooth was not placed under a pillow. Instead, it was put in a rat hole, because it was thought that the new tooth growing in would take on the "dental quality" of the animal who found it.

STRIPED BARBER POLES

Barbers were once a lot more versatile than they are today. They not only cut hair, they performed surgery as well. When the barbers finished, the towels used to soak up excess blood were hung outside to dry on a pole. As the wind dried them they wrapped around the pole, making a design, so to speak, of red and white stripes.

COVERING A YAWN

People once thought that their souls—or perhaps even their life forces—could escape during a yawn. They covered their mouths to prevent this and, since yawns can be contagious, to try to keep people around them from "catching" the yawn. The apology after a yawn originated as an expression of regret for having exposed people to mortal danger.

Q. What is the moon's astronomical name?

CELEBRITY IMPOSTORS

A lot of people don't know it, but Uncle John got his start in show business providing the voice for TV's Mr. Ed. Okay, okay...we made that up. Here's a look at some other celebrity impostors.

The Impostor: Norman Shelley, an English actor
Posing As: British Prime Minister Winston Churchill
Background: On June 4, 1940, about a week after the evacuation of Dunkirk, Prime Minister Churchill rallied the downcast nation with what would become one of the most famous speeches of his career. Over the radio, he told the embattled British:

> We shall fight in France, we shall fight on the seas and oceans, we shall fight with growing confidence and growing strength in the air, we shall defend our island, whatever the cost may be, we shall fight on the beaches, we shall fight on the landing grounds, we shall fight in the fields and in the streets, we shall fight in the hills; we shall never surrender.

But it wasn't Churchill speaking. The Prime Minister had asked Norman Shelley, who could do an almost perfect Churchill impersonation, to give the speech for him. Listeners were completely fooled; even Churchill himself was impressed. "Very nice," he told friends after the speech, "He's even got my teeth right."

The Impostor: Elizabeth Bigley, a convicted forger living in Cleveland, Ohio, in the 1890s
Posing As: Andrew Carnegie's illegitimate daughter
Background: In 1893, Bigley met a banker friend from Cleveland while visting New York City. She asked him for a ride to Andrew Carnegie's home, and he waited outside while she ran inside for a few minutes. Bigley had only gone in to ask for directions, but when she returned, she fooled her friend into thinking she was Carnegie's daughter—and would inherit a large portion of the steel baron's estate. The man decided to take advantage of the future heiress by lending her money against her inheritance at exorbitant rates of interest. Other Cleveland bankers learned of the story, and over the next 9 years, lent her millions of dollars on the assumption

that they'd clean her out when Carnegie died.

The party ended in 1904, when the *Cleveland Press* exposed Bigley as a fraud, causing several Ohio banks to collapse overnight. She was tried and convicted, and sentenced to 10 years in the Ohio State Penitentiary, where she died before completing her sentence.

The Impostors: Seven people...who happened to have the same names as New York's leading theater critics

Posing As: New York City's seven leading theater critics

Background: When Broadway producer David Merrick's play *Subways Are for Sleeping* opened in 1962, he didn't want to risk being panned by the critics, so he came up with a plan to blunt their attacks. As Candace Fuhrman describes in her book *Publicity Stunts,*

> In the New York phone directories, he found seven names identical to those of the leading critics. Merrick called these men and invited them to see the show as his guest. Afterwards he treated them to a lavish meal and party. In exchange, he asked to use their names and photographs in an upcoming promotion. All agreed, and Merrick and his press agents then produced an ad with this headline:
> SEVEN OUT OF SEVEN ARE ECSTATICALLY UNANIMOUS ABOUT *SUBWAYS ARE FOR SLEEPING.*
> The ad featured photos of Merrick's seven citizens and their enthusiastic comments about the play.

Merrick tried to run the ad in all seven of the newspapers that the critics worked for. Six of them caught on and refused to print it. The *New York Herald Tribune* accepted it at first, but pulled it after the first edition. Still, the controversy surrounding the ad was a news story in its own right, and all seven newspapers reported it, which in turn generated even more publicity for the play.

The Impostor: David Hampton, a 19-year-old from Buffalo, New York

Posing As: Sidney Poitier's son

Background: Working from an address book stolen from a college student, Hampton went through the list and contacted wealthy New York families, most of whom had children attending Harvard, Yale, and other prestigious schools. He passed himself off as a friend of the family. According to one newspaper account,

> Mr. Hampton telephoned two families—on successive nights—and told them that his name was David Poitier and that he was a college

friend of their children. He said he had been mugged, that his money and thesis—on the criminal justice system—had been taken, and that he needed a place to stay until his father arrived in town at the Pierre Hotel the next day. Both couples invited him to their homes, where he dined with them, borrowed money and spent the night.

One of Hampton's victims, Osborne Elliott, dean of the Columbia School of Journalism, became suspicious of Hampton, and called around to verify his identity. He found out Hampton was a fake, and had him arrested. Hampton eventually served 21 months in prison for the scam.

The incident inspired a hit play (and film) called *Six Degrees of Separation*. Hampton sued the playwright for a share of the royalties, saying the work was about him. The court ruled against him.

The Impostor: Unknown
Posing As: "Joe Louis, Jr.," son of the famous boxer
Background: In 1992, someone began running up huge bills claiming he was Joe Louis, Jr., the president of the Joe Boxer Company, a leading maker of boxer shorts. Nicholas Graham, the *real* president of Joe Boxer—and *not* Joe Louis's son—was not amused. A newspaper described the scam:

> The impostor has managed to do things like run up a hefty $17,000 bill for Joe Boxer at the Peninsula Hotel in New York and get access to the entertainment department at Time/Warner....The company hopes anyone who is approached by Joe Louis, Jr., will contact Joe Boxer immediately.

"Joe Louis, Jr." was never caught.

The Impostor: Bill English, grocery bagger for Smitty's Supermarket in Tempe, Arizona
Posing As: Bill Thomas, Buckwheat of the Little Rascals
Background: On October, 5, 1990, the ABC news program "20/20" ran a segment featuring an interview with Thomas, called "Whatever Happened to Buckwheat?" Former Little Rascal George "Spanky" McFarland happened to see it...and called to tell ABC that Thomas had died 10 years earlier. The producer responsible for the segment resigned a few days later.

Fish with forked tails swim faster than fish with straight tails.

NO NUKES
IS GOOD NUKES

*We don't want to make you paranoid, but
all of these incidents really happened.*

1. In July 1956, a B-47 aircraft plowed into a storage igloo 20 miles outside of Cambridge, England. The plane's jet fuel burst into flames almost immediately, but for some reason didn't ignite the contents of the igloo. A lucky thing, too—it contained three Mark 6 nuclear bombs.

2. In 1958, a B-47E accidentally dropped a nuclear bomb into a Mars Bluff, South Carolina, family's vegetable garden. The bomb didn't explode, but the impact damaged five houses and a church. Air Force officials "apologized."

3. In 1961, a B-52 dropped two 24-megaton bombs on a North Carolina farm. According to one physicist: "Only a single switch prevented the bombs from detonating."

4. In 1966, another B-52 carrying four 20-megaton bombs crashed in Palomares, Spain—with one of the bombs splashing into the Mediterranean Sea. It took the U.S. 6th fleet—using 33 ships and 3,000 men—several weeks to find the missing bomb.

5. In 1980, a repairman working on a Titan II missile in Arkansas dropped a wrench—which bounced off the floor, punctured the missile, and set off an explosion that blew the top off the silo and threw the warhead 600 feet into the air.

6. Did June 3, 1980, seem tense to you? It did to the Strategic Air Command in Omaha, Nebraska. Their computers detected a Soviet submarine missile attack in progress. Within minutes, more than 100 B-52s were in the air, but the SAC soon called off the counterattack—the computers had made a mistake. The culprit: a 46¢ computer chip. Three days later the same mistake happened again.

90% of Americans aren't aware that being overweight increases the risk of strokes.

THE NEW YORK TIMES CROSSWORD PUZZLE

Today The New York Times crossword puzzle is considered the puzzle of choice for hardcore addicts, but that hasn't always been true. Believe it or not, the Times resisted crosswords for more than two decades. Here's the story of how the newspaper changed its mind.

HARD TIMES

By the late 1930s, the crossword puzzle boom that started in 1924 (see page 30) had begun to fizzle—largely because the crossword puzzles in most newspapers had become predictable. They constantly repeated boring clues like "Headgear" (hat), "Writing instrument" (pen) and "Woody plant" (tree).

But readers of *The New York Times* never got bored with *their* crossword puzzle...because the *Times* didn't have one. Then, as now, the *Times* considered itself America's "newspaper of record" and the guardian of journalistic standards. It scoffed at crossword puzzles as "a primitive form of mental exercise" in a 1924 editorial, and refused to print them.

Eighteen years later, it was one of the last puzzle holdouts among America's major newspapers.

ALL THIS AND WORLD WAR II

Still, the *Times* had crossword puzzle fans on its staff. Publisher Arthur Hays Sulzburger is said to have loved crosswords almost as much as he hated having to buy copies of the rival *New York Herald Tribune* in order to get them. And as America teetered on the brink of war in the early 1940s, the mood at the paper began to change.

Less than two weeks after the bombing of Pearl Harbor in December 1941, Lester Markel, the *Times*'s Sunday editor, dashed off a memo to his superiors suggesting that they consider adding a puzzle to the Sunday paper. The pressures and demands of the war played heavily on his mind. "We ought to proceed with the puzzle," he wrote, "especially in view of the fact that it is possible that there

---

Take it easy: 28% of household injuries in the summer are caused by yardwork.

will now be bleak blackout hours—or if not that, then certainly a need for relaxation of some kind or other....We ought not to try to do anything essentially different from what is now being done—except to do it better."

Markel had met with Margaret Petherbridge Farrar, senior crossword puzzle editor at Simon & Schuster, and he attached a memo from her:

> The *Herald Tribune* runs the best puzzle page in existence so far, but they have gotten into a bit of a rut. Their big puzzle never ventures even one imaginative definition, and lacks the quality that I believe can be achieved and maintained. We could, I dare to predict, get the edge on them.
>
> I don't think I have to sell you on the increased demand for this kind of pastime in an increasingly worried world. You can't think of your troubles while solving a crossword...

Getting Started

The argument worked. The *Times* hired Farrar away from Simon & Schuster and made her its crossword editor, a position she held until she retired in 1969. The first puzzle appeared on February 15, 1942, in the Sunday magazine section. (Weekday puzzles weren't added until September 1950.) "The puzzle," writes *Times* reporter Richard Shepard, "was an instant success."

Under Margaret Farrar's direction, the crossword "constructors" (freelance puzzle makers) developed a clever and elaborate style. Instead of giving clues like "Stinging insect" (bee) and "Bird's home" (nest), they phrased them as "Nectar inspector" and "Nutcracker's suite." The *Times*'s clever, whimsical style almost single-handedly ushered in a crossword renaissance, as newspapers all over the U.S. followed its lead.

Today, more than 90 percent of newspapers around the world have crossword puzzles, and, according to a study by the U.S. Newspaper Advertising Bureau, 26 percent of people who read newspapers regularly attempt to solve them.

SETTING THE PACE

The New York Times crossword puzzle sets the standard that other puzzles follow. Here are just some of the informal (but strictly followed) "rules" that were established by the *Times*'s example:

✓ There can be no "unkeyed" letters—letters that appear in only one word of the puzzle. Every single letter of the puzzle must be part of both a horizontal and a vertical word.

✓ The black and white pattern must be "diagonally symmetrical."

✓ The black squares should not take up more than one-sixth of the total design.

✓ The puzzle shouldn't have "dirty double-crossers"—that is, obscure words should not intersect one another.

PUZZLING FACTS

• The *Times* estimates that it takes the average puzzler half an hour to solve the 15-square-by-15-square daily puzzle, and two hours to solve the much larger Sunday puzzle.

• The *Times* daily puzzles are designed to get progressively harder from Monday through Saturday. The Saturday puzzle is nearly impossible for anyone but experts to solve. The Sunday puzzle is even worse. The paper figures that the weekend puzzles should be the hardest, because that's when people have the most time to work on them.

• Constructing the crossword puzzles takes a lot more time than solving them. "It takes me four days to make a *Times* Sunday puzzle," says Maura B. Jacobson, one of the *Times'* constructors. "I spend at least 10 or 12 hours making definitions. My research takes a day, then a day to get the words into the diagram to make them cross. But the hardest is making the definitions."

• Making a puzzle that lives up to *New York Times* standards isn't easy—Eugene Maleska, the paper's crossword editor in 1992, estimates that there aren't more than 600 people in the entire country skilled enough to do it. And the puzzles have to be thoroughly edited before they go to press. "I and all editors change about a third of the definitions," Maleska told reporters in 1992. "I have a notebook filled with definitions so that I don't repeat them."

• *The New York Times* goes to great lengths not to offend anyone with its puzzles. Words as innocuous as "bra" are forbidden, as are the names of illegal drugs. Words such as "ale" and "rum" are considered to be at the extreme limit of good taste—they are permitted but aren't used often.

MUSTANG: CAR OF THE '60s

The original Ford Mustang, a sporty car for "everyman" introduced in 1964, is now a symbol of the entire decade. Here's a bit of its history.

The Mustang was the most successful new car ever introduced by the American auto industry. But in terms of the '60s, it was more than a car. Its popularity was an expression of the simple truth of the decade—that everyone wanted to look, feel, and act young.

ORIGIN OF THE CAR

• The Mustang was the pet project of Ford General Manager Lee Iacocca who kept notes on new car ideas in a little black book. Because Ford kept getting letters from car buffs who wanted a car like the 1955 T-Bird, Iacocca felt there was a market for a new "personal sports car" waiting to be developed. Research also showed that the population was getting younger and that young people bought more cars per capita than any other segment of the population.

• Based on these findings—and Iacocca's instinct—Ford decided to create a car that was sporty yet low-priced, so young people and middle-income groups could afford it. But it also had to be capable of taking enough options to make it a luxury car.

• The new project was dubbed "T-5." Ford engineers and designers worked under maximum security in a windowless room, known as "The Tomb"; even the wastepaper had to be burned under supervision.

• Over a three-year period they came up with many two-seat prototypes—XT-Bird, Median, Mina, Allegro, Aventura, and Mustang I (loved by car enthusiasts but considered too sporty by Iacocca)—but all were scrapped in favor of a four-seat model with a large trunk. It was completed in spring 1963.

• The Mustang was designed to be versatile. The buyer had options: two different engines, air conditioning, whitewalls, power disc brakes, racing hubcaps, sports console, and so on. As Dr. Seymour Marshak, Ford's market research manager, said admiringly, "This flexibility makes this car the greatest thing since the Erector set."

• Since Ford figured the T-5's market was the young sports car buyer, the name "Torino" was chosen because it sounded like an Italian sports car. The projected ad campaign called it "the new import…from Detroit."

• But last-minute market research showed that the car could appeal to all buyers, so a new name had to be chosen. Colt, Bronco, and Maverick (all used for later cars) were considered. But "Mustang" seemed best for T-5, bringing to mind cowboys, adventure, and the Wild West. As one Ford man put it, "It had the excitement of the wide-open spaces, and it was American as all hell."

• The Mustang was introduced on April 17, 1964. On that day, more than 4 million people visited the 6,500 Ford dealers across the country to get a look at it…and they bought 22,542 of them.

• In the first three months of production, a record 100,000 Mustangs were sold. It was an instant status symbol, with people vying for the limited supply as though it were contraband.

MUSTANG FEVER

The introduction of the Mustang was a big event. Here are five of the bizarre things that happened that day.

1. A Mustang was the pace car for a stock car race in Huntsville, Alabama. When it drove onto the track, thousands of people scaled the retaining wall to get a better look at it. The race was delayed for over an hour.

2. A cement truck crashed through the plate-glass window of a Seattle Ford dealer when the driver lost control of his vehicle. The reason: He was staring at the new Mustangs on display there. They looked "like some of them expensive Italian racers," he explained.

3. A Chicago Ford dealer was forced to lock the doors of his showroom models because too many people were trying to get into them at the same time.

4. A Texas dealer put a new Mustang on a lift to show a prospective customer the underside of the vehicle. By the time his demonstration was over, the showroom was filled with people, and he had to leave the Mustang up in the air for the rest of the day.

5. A New Jersey Ford dealer had only one Mustang but fifteen eager buyers, so he auctioned it off. The winner of the auction insisted on sleeping in the car to be sure the dealer didn't sell it to someone else before his check cleared.

Seventy percent of the world's oxygen supply is produced by marine plants.

FABULOUS FLOPS

These products cost millions to invent.
Their legacy is a few bathroom laughs.

Studebaker Dictator. Not exactly "the heartbeat of America" when it was introduced in 1934. According to one auto industry analyst, "after Hitler and Mussolini came to power, a name like Dictator was downright un-American." Yet incredibly, the nation's #5 automaker stuck with it for three years.

Bic Perfume. The snazzy $5 perfume that looked like a cigarette lighter. Why wasn't it a hit with women? According to one industry expert, "It looked like a cigarette lighter." Bic lost $11 million.

Chilly Bang! Bang! Juice. The kiddie drink in a pistol-shaped package. Kids drank it by putting the barrel in their mouths and squeezing the trigger. Outraged parents—and complaints from officials in at least two states—got it yanked from the shelves.

Hop 'N' Gator. The inventor of Gatorade sold his original drink to a major corporation in 1966. Then, in 1969, he used the money to create another can't-miss product: a mixture of beer and Gatorade. The Pittsburgh Brewing Company tried it out for a couple of years. Unfortunately for them, people didn't want Gatorade in their beer.

Zartan the Enemy Action Figures. Hasbro promoted the soldier doll as a "paranoid schizophrenic" that becomes violent under pressure. They pulled the product after mental health organizations complained.

Pepsi A.M. Why not get your morning caffeine from cola instead of coffee? The world's first breakfast soft drink didn't get far. Pepsi found out that most consumers didn't *want* a breakfast soft drink—and people who *did* "still preferred the taste of plain old Pepsi."

Hands Up! Kids' soap in an aerosol can, introduced in 1962. Instead of a nozzle, there was a plastic gun mounted on top. Kids got soap out of the can by pointing the gun at each other—or themselves—and squeezing the trigger. The Hands-Up slogan: "Gets kids clean and makes them like it."

THE MONSTER MASH

This Halloween classic swept across America in 1962—
and 1973—like a bat out of... Here's the inside story,
from Behind the Hits, *by Bob Shannon and John Javna.*

BACKGROUND
In the late '50s, Universal Studios syndicated a package of its greatest monster movies—including *Dracula, The Mummy,* and *Frankenstein,* featuring Boris Karloff—to television stations around the country. That's how baby boom kids got their first look at classic horror films. It was love at first sight; by the early '60s, a monster craze was under way. There were monster models, monster trading cards, monster wallets, monster posters...and a monster song: "The Monster Mash," by Bobby "Boris" Pickett.

KARLOFF DOO-WOP
Pickett was an aspiring actor who made his living singing with a Hollywood rock 'n' roll group called the Cordials at night, while he went on casting calls during the day. He'd always done impressions, and Karloff was one of his best. So one night just for the hell of it, while the Cordials doo-wopped their way through a classic tune called "Little Darlin'," Bobby did a monologue in the middle with a Karloff voice. The crowd loved it. A member of the band suggested that Bobby do more with the Karloff imitation—write an original song, perhaps.

Pickett resisted for a while, but finally he and a friend wrote a monster take-off of Dee Dee Sharp's hit, "Mashed Potato Time." They recorded it at a studio on Hollywood Boulevard for Gary Paxton's Garpax Records.

SOUND EFFECTS
Paxton, who'd had his own hit with "Alley Oop" a few years earlier, came up with some clever low-budget techniques to produce the background noises that made the rock 'n' roll's ultimate Halloween party so effective.

The Dodgers' original name was the Bridegrooms. Reason: Lots of newlyweds on the team.

For example:

• "The sound of the coffin opening was actually a rusty nail being drawn out of a two-by-four."

• The cauldron bubbling was really water being bubbled through a straw.

• The chains rattling was just the sound of chains being dropped on a tile floor.

Pickett thought of "Monster Mash" as a cute novelty tune and didn't understand the power of the monster mania that was sweeping America. The song sold a million copies and became a #1 hit in October 1962—just in time for Halloween. One of its fans, who received free copies from Pickett, was Boris Karloff.

RETURN FROM THE DEAD

Pickett followed "Monster Mash" with "Monster's Holiday" and with an album of monster rock 'n' roll. But he had no more monster hits until 1970, when "Monster Mash" was re-released. It was released again in 1973 and really hit it big, reaching the Top 10. Pickett, by then a cabdriver in New York City, attributed its 1973 success, in part, to Nixon's Watergate scandal. "At this point in time, with what's coming down with Watergate, people need some relief from the tension that's building up," he explained.

ROCKIN' MONSTERS

Before "Monster Mash," the most popular monster tune in rock history was "Purple People Eater," recorded in 1958 by Sheb Wooley. Here's how Wooley came up with it:

• A friend of Wooley's told him a riddle he'd heard from his kid: "What flies, has one horn, has one eye, is purple, and eats people?" The answer: "A one-eyed, one-horned, flying purple people eater." Wooley thought it was amusing and wrote a song based on it.

• A short time later, Wooley met with the president of MGM Records to decide on his next single. Wooley played every song he'd written, but still couldn't come up with one the guy liked. "You got anything else?" the president asked. "Well, yeah, one more thing, but it's nothing you'd wanna hear." "Let's hear it."

• It was "Purple People Eater." Wooley recorded it, and three weeks later it was the #1 single in the United States.

The gorilla's scientific name is "Gorilla, gorilla, gorilla."

CAMPAIGN SMEARS

Campaign smears are ugly, but they're a part of American politics and have been since the first elections. A few notable examples:

THE PRESIDENTIAL CAMPAIGN OF 1828
During his second try for the presidency, Andrew Jackson was subjected to vicious slander by incumbent John Quincy Adams.

Jackson was termed "a blood-thirsty wild man, the son of a black and a prostitute and a murderer who had put to death soldiers who offended him." And he was accused of being an adulterer. This hit home. Unfortunately, Jackson's wife, Rachel, had married him unaware that she was still legally married to someone else; her previous marriage hadn't been officially dissolved.

It was merely a technicality, but Adams's supporters relentlessly pursued it, dragging Rachel's name through the mud throughout the country. By the time the matter was straightened out, Jackson had won the election...but he went to the White House alone. Rachel Jackson had died of a heart attack; Jackson and his supporters attributed it to the brutal attacks during the campaign.

THE PRESIDENTIAL CAMPAIGN OF 1864

Anticipating the next election, Abraham Lincoln's enemies tried to undermine his presidency. A whispering campaign in Washington suggested that Lincoln's wife, Mary Todd, was secretly aiding the Confederates. It was a spurious charge, but it gained enough credibility to force the president to appear before a secret congressional committee investigating the matter. His prestige was slightly tarnished, but Lincoln was still reelected.

THE 1884 PRESIDENTIAL CAMPAIGN

In 1884, the governor of New York, Grover Cleveland, was closing in on the Democratic nomination for president when a Buffalo newspaper accused him of fathering an illegitimate boy 10 years earlier.

Over 28 million copies of Jacqueline Susann's, *Valley of the Dolls* have been sold.

Had he? Cleveland, a bachelor at the time, had indeed dated the woman. And he had contributed to the support of a child. But Cleveland was never proved to be the child's father; in fact, the woman admitted it could have been any one of a number of men. Nonetheless, when the presidential campaign began, the child was a part of it. Cleveland had to live with the chant: "Ma, Ma, Where's my Pa? Gone to the White House, ha! ha! ha!"

Interestingly, Cleveland's opponent, James G. Blaine, had his own problems—political scandals in his home state of Maine, and anti-Catholic prejudice—and wasn't able to capitalize on Cleveland's vulnerable position. Cleveland won.

THE FLORIDA SENATORIAL CAMPAIGN OF 1950

This is a textbook case of a politician using rhetoric to pander to the fears of less-educated people. Congressman George Smathers was challenging incumbent Senator Claude Pepper in Florida's Democratic senatorial primary in 1950. Smathers, the underdog, circulated printed material in the rural towns of central and northern Florida accusing Pepper of the following "indecencies":

• That his brother was a "practicing Homosapien."

• That he had a sister in New York who was a "thespian."

• And that Pepper himself had "matriculated" with young women. To top it off, Smathers jumped on the early McCarthy bandwagon and saddled Claude with the nickname "Red" Pepper. Smathers won.

* * *

Origin of the Tuxedo

Pierre Lorillard IV, scion of the tobacco company, lived in Tuxedo Park, New York. In 1886, sick of the formalwear of the day, he had his tailor make suits without tails—a daring move for a Victorian high-society gent. He planned to wear one of these scandalous suits to the annual Autumn Ball, but chickened out at the last minute. Instead, his son and his friends wore the suits. No scandal, though —since the Lorillards were rich, everyone copied them. The outrageous suit became a fashion and was named for its birthplace. The tux industry now grosses half a billion dollars a year.

On a clear day, you can see five different states from the top of the World Trade Center.

MYTH AMERICA

Some of the stories we now recognize as American myths were taught as history for many years. Here are a few that might surprise you.

MANHATTAN ISLAND
The Myth: In 1626, Peter Minuit bought Manhattan Island from the Canarsee Indians for $24 worth of beads and other trinkets.

The Truth: Minuit did give 60 guilders (roughly $24) worth of beads, knives, axes, clothes, and rum to Chief Seyseys of the Canarsee tribe "to let us live amongst them" on Manhattan Island—but the Canarsee actually got the best of the deal...because they didn't own the island in the first place. They lived on the other side of the East River in *Brooklyn*, and only visited the southern tip of Manhattan to fish and hunt. The Weckquaesgeeks tribe, which lived on the upper three-fourths of the island, had a much stronger claim to it and were furious when they learned they'd been left out of the deal. They fought with the Dutch settlers for years until the Dutch finally paid them, too.

THE LIBERTY BELL
The Myth: The Liberty Bell has always been a precious symbol of our nation's heritage.

The Truth: The bell, installed in the Pennsylvania State House in Philadelphia in 1753, was almost bartered off as scrap metal in 1828 when the building was being refurbished. According to one account, "The Philadelphia city fathers...contracted John Wilbank, a bell maker from Germantown, Pennsylvania, to cast a replacement for the Liberty Bell. He agreed to knock $400 off his bill in exchange for the 2,000-pound relic. When Wilbank went to collect it, however, he decided it wasn't worth the trouble. 'Drayage costs more than the bell's worth,' he said." The city of Philadelphia actually sued to force him to take it. But Wilbank just gave it back to them as a gift, "unaware that he'd just bartered away what would become the most venerated symbol of American independence."

A black widow spider's venom is more potent than a rattlesnake's.

TICK, TICK, TICK...

*When you think about it, that ticking stopwatch on "60 Minutes"
is as familiar a cultural icon as a Coke bottle or McDonald's
golden arches. Here's how the show got started.*

MINUTE MAN

Don Hewitt was a pioneer of TV journalism. He started
work at CBS television in 1948, as studio director for Edward R. Murrow's "See It Now"; he was the director of the famous
Nixon-Kennedy debates in 1960; and he was the first executive
producer of "CBS Evening News with Walter Cronkite."

But even though Hewitt was an industry legend, he became a
victim of corporate politics in 1965, and was demoted. He ended
up in CBS's documentary division, where he spent more than four
years making hour-long "prestige" programs (Hewitt called them
"snoozers") that CBS liked to brag about, but that nobody watched.
"I sure as hell didn't want to do documentaries for the rest of my
life," he wrote in his book *Minute by Minute.*

> I began to think there had to be a way to make information more
> palatable....Sometime in 1967 it dawned on me that [we could] split
> those public affairs hours into three parts to deal with the viewers'
> short attention spans....So I made a proposal to Richard S. Salant,
> president of CBS News. "Why don't we try to package sixty minutes
> of reality as attractively as Hollywood packages sixty minutes of
> make-believe?"

GETTING STARTED

One evening, Hewitt asked veteran CBS reporter Harry Reasoner
and two film editors to stay after work for a couple of hours to help
him put together a pilot episode to show CBS top brass. Reasoner
agreed, explaining "I owed him a wasted evening." But it wasn't a
waste—network executives were impressed and asked for more
information.

Hewitt proposed filming almost everything in the field, as if the
correspondent were taking viewers along with him to do the story.
He also wanted to focus the segments on *people*, not on issues.
"To me," Hewitt explained to *TV Guide* in 1993, "Noah will always
be a more interesting subject than flood control."

Eighty percent of Americans will be fired from a job at least once in their lives.

MULTIPLE PERSONALITIES

CBS executives liked all of Hewitt's ideas except one: Harry Reasoner; he was so casual that he came off as boring. So the executives suggested pairing him up with someone a little bit more hard-edged. Hewitt picked Mike Wallace, the most hard-edged person on television at the time. Wallace was qualified—he'd already established a reputation as a pit-bull interviewer—but he considered the show a dumb idea. "I thought Hewitt was off on a pipe dream," he recalled years later. Nonetheless, he agreed to do it.

ON THE AIR

The first episode of "60 Minutes" aired Tuesday September 24, 1969, at 10 p.m. The first segment, reported by Mike Wallace, dealt with police-citizen relationships; the second segment covered that summer's presidential conventions; and the third segment was an Art Buchwald piece called "Why Man Creates."

High-Brow. The pilot was well received, but only by TV *critics*. The show came in 72nd out of the 72 primetime shows that week, and was slaughtered alongside the new drama show "Marcus Welby, M.D." Today a show with ratings that low would probably be cancelled, but "60 Minutes" was lucky. In 1969, CBS News had a huge budget and lots of prestige, thanks to attacks on Walter Cronkite's integrity by Vice President Spiro Agnew. Besides, in those days, news shows were *supposed* to lose money. News shows were *prestige* shows: they supposedly made the networks and their other shows look better.

Slow Going. 60 *Minutes* continued to be a critical success, but nobody at CBS knew where to put it on the broadcast schedule or believed it would *ever* get good ratings. As a result, it became the putty that CBS used to fill the holes in its weekly lineup: first on Tuesday at 10:00 p.m.; then Sunday at 6:00; then Friday at 8:00; then back to Sunday at 6:00; then to Sunday at 9:30; then *back* to Sunday at 6:00; *then* back to Sunday at 9:30. Finally, in December 1975, the show was moved to its Sunday at 7:00 p.m. spot, which meant that during football season it had a huge lead-in audience and played opposite "World of Disney" and "The Hardy Boys"—giving viewers no other choice but CBS if they wanted to watch a show for grownups.

OFF THE CHARTS

"That's when we took off," Hewitt writes, "That's when our percentage of the audience, which had been creeping up, began to impress the network brass." The show earned its first #1 rating, though only for a week, in 1979; came in first place for the year in 1981; and has been at or near the top ever since. "60 Minutes" passed another milestone in April 1991, when it became the only TV show to rank #1 in three different decades. It's the longest-running show in television history and has been on the air longer than "The Cosby Show," the "Mary Tyler Moore Show," and "I Love Lucy" combined.

60 MINUTIAE

• One of the things that kept "60 Minutes" afloat was its penchant for reporting stories no one else would touch. In a January 1974 segment called "Press Junkets," the show even took on CBS itself, reporting that the network forbade the news division from accepting free trips from anyone, while the entertainment division doled out the same kinds of trips to other news organizations to promote its shows. The segment identified the Ford Motor company, the sole sponsor of "60 Minutes" at the time, as another organizer of such trips, and even identified Walter Cronkite as a recipient of free trips. These and other risky topics—including an interview with Black Panther leader Eldridge Cleaver while he was on the lam from the feds in Algeria—made "60 Minutes" a news item in its own right.

• In the summer of 1978, the show ran a piece on the Ford Pinto—whose poor design allowed gas tanks to explode in rear-end collisions. Ford was a major sponsor of "60 Minutes" at the time and was so outraged that it pulled all of its commercials...for a week. The show was so popular that Ford feared losing sales from the ad cancellations, so it chickened out and put the ads back on.

• Which segment has generated the most mail? The one in 1975 in which First Lady Betty Ford told Morley Safer she wouldn't be surprised if her children smoked pot or if her daughter had an affair.

• Despite all the controversy it has generated over the years, "60 Minutes" has never lost a lawsuit, and has settled out of court only once—for $5,000.

STENGEL-ESE

Legendary New York Yankees and Mets manager Casey Stengel offers a few confusing words of wisdom.

To a hitter with the bases loaded: "Let him hit 'ya; I'll get you a new neck."

"There are three things you can do in a baseball game. You can win, or you can lose, or it can rain."

"Now all you fellers line up alphabetically by height."

"You have to have a catcher, because if you don't, the pitch will roll all the way back to the screen."

"They say you can't do it, but sometimes it doesn't always work."

"Look at that guy. Can't run, can't hit, can't catch. Of course, that's why they gave him to us."

On two 20-year-old players: "In ten years, Ed Kranepool has a chance to be a star. In ten years, Greg Goosen has a chance to be thirty."

"We're in such a slump that even the ones that are drinkin' aren't hittin'."

"Good pitching will always stop good hitting, and vice versa."

"I love signing autographs. I'll sign anything but veal cutlets. My ballpoint pen slips on veal cutlets."

"The secret of managing a club is to keep the five guys who hate you away from the five who are undecided."

"The Mets have come along slow, but fast!"

"Being with a woman all night never hurt no professional ballplayer. It's staying up all night looking for a woman that does him in."

"I'll never make the mistake again of being seventy years old."

"They say some of my stars drink whiskey, but I have found that the ones who drink milkshakes don't win many ball games."

"Most ball games are lost, not won."

On average, American males spend 11.4 minutes taking a shower. Females take 13 minutes.

THE LAST WORD

*Some unusual epitaphs and tombstone rhymes sent in
by our wandering BRI tombstone-ologists.*

Seen in Enosburg, Vermont:
In memory of Anna
Here lies the body of our
Anna,
Done to death by a banana.
It wasn't the fruit that laid her
low,
But the skin of the thing that
made her go.

Seen in Burlington, Mass.:
Anthony Drake
Sacred to the memory of
Anthonly Drake,
Who died for peace and
quietness sake.
His wife was constantly
scoldin' and scoffin',
So he sought for repose in a
$12 coffin.

Seen in Winslow, Maine:
Beza Wood, 1792-1837
Here lies one Wood
enclosed in wood,
One within the other.
The outer wood is very good.
We cannot praise the other.

*Seen in Boot Hill Cemetery,
Dodge City, Kansas:*
He played five Aces.
Now he's playing the harp.

Seen in the English countryside:
Mary Ford, 1790
Here lieth Mary—the wife of
John Ford.
We hope her soul is gone to
the Lord.
But if for Hell she has changed
this life,
She would rather be there
than be John Ford's wife.

Seen in Canaan, N.H.:
Sarah Shute, 1803-1840
Here lies, cut down like unripe
fruit,
The wife of Deacon Amos
Shute.
She died of drinking too much
coffee,
Anno Domini eighteen forty.

Seen in Burlington, N.J.:
Mary Ann Lowder, 1798
Here lies the body of Mary
Ann Lowder,
Who burst while drinking a
Seidlitz powder.
Called from this world to her
Heavenly Rest
She should have waited till it
effervesced.

ELVIS'S TOOTHBRUSH

A bizarre-but-true tale of fan weirdness, from the book How to Meet
the Stars, *by Missy Laws. (Ross Books, Berkeley, CA)*

THE SCENARIO: *A rabid Elvis fan called "Sir Mordrid" and
two women were visiting Las Vegas. A celebrity they met in a
casino invited them to "meet my good friend Elvis."*

"The four of them went to the Hilton Hotel, where Elvis was performing two shows nightly. They entered the backstage area and
confronted a mob. Sir Mordrid could feel the pounding of his heart
as he grew nearer to the superstar's private dressing room.

"Because he had an enormous collection of Elvis memorabilia
and had attended a vast quantity of his concerts, Sir Mordrid considered himself to be the number one fan of the legendary performer.

"Upon seeing Elvis, Sir Mordrid began to feel dizzy and got
sweaty palms. In order to hide his nervous behavior, he headed for
a table of food in the corner. Nonstop, he crammed lobster, finger
sandwiches and strawberries into his mouth. Between bites, he
could see across the room where [the celebrity] was introducing the
two girls to Elvis.

" 'Where's Sir Mordrid?' [the celebrity] questioned. But upon noticing him hunched over the snack table, he continued, 'Sir Mordrid, come on over. I want to introduce you to Elvis.'

"Panic struck Sir Mordrid as he almost choked on an entire
sandwich. Hesitantly he walked over to his idol.

"Sir Mordrid meekly said, 'Hi,' but then, without giving Elvis a
chance to speak, he chattered on, attempting to cover his anxiety.
The only thing he could think of to say was a joke that he had
learned the previous day. Elvis quietly listened, certain that there
must be some significance to the joke if this guy insisted on telling
it at what seemed to be such an inappropriate time.

[Sir Mordrid told the joke and, staring at Elvis, asked him if
he knew what the punchline was.]

"Smiling, the singer answered, 'What?'

"Suddenly, Sir Mordrid was so absorbed in his own feelings of
anxiety that he couldn't remember the punchline. He panicked.
He could feel the lobster, finger sandwiches and strawberries
threatening to come up.

In 1948, four men tried to take a cow to the top of the Matterhorn. They all froze to death.

"He broke away from the singer and muttered, 'Excuse me.' He sprinted toward a gentleman standing near the doorway. He pleaded, 'Do you know where the rest room is? I feel really sick!'

"The man pointed to Elvis's private bathroom and said, 'I think it's in there.' Although it was obvious that this was designated as an exclusive chamber for only Elvis, Sir Mordrid ignored this minor detail as he hurled himself inside, slamming and locking the door.

"While Sir Mordrid expelled every bit of food from his stomach, there was a knock. A voice firmly called, 'I'm sorry, but you're not allowed in there.'

"Sir Mordrid ignored this remark. After several minutes of screaming and banging on the door, the man stopped trying to get Sir Mordrid out of the restroom.

"Sir Mordrid stood in silence and noticed a disgusting taste in his mouth. Glancing at the sink, he saw a clear, oblong box engraved with the initials 'E.P.' Inside was a toothbrush. A tube of toothpaste rested behind it.

"After checking to make sure the door was indeed locked, he brushed his teeth with his idol's personal toothbrush. Afterward, he dried it off and replaced it exactly as he had found it. He returned to the party, but kept his distance from Elvis for the rest of the evening."

∞   ∞   ∞

Elvis Facts

• For one stretch of two years, the singer reportedly ate nothing but meatloaf, mashed potatoes, and tomatoes.

• His idol was General Douglas MacArthur.

• He memorized every line of dialogue from the George C. Scott film, *Patton.*

• In his youth, Elvis tried out for his high school glee club...and didn't make it. Reason: "He couldn't sing well enough."

• In his lifetime, Elvis bought more than 100 Cadillacs...and gave more than 80 of them away. His first Caddy: a pink one that he gave to his mom.

• Elvis put lifts in the shoes he wore during performances...and also put them in his bedroom slippers.

King George I of England couldn't speak a word of English. (He spoke German.)

FAMILIAR PHRASES

Here are more origins of common phrases.

TO CLOSE RANKS

Meaning: To present a united front.

Origin: "In the old-time European armies, the soldiers were aligned side by side, in neat rows, or ranks, on the battlefield. When the enemy attacked, officers would order the troops to close ranks; that is, to move the rows close together, so that the enemy faced a seemingly impregnable mass of men." (From *Fighting Words*, by Christine Ammer)

FOR THE BIRDS

Meaning: Worthless.

Origin: According to Robert Claiborne in *Loose Cannons and Red Herrings*, it refers to city streets as they were before cars. "When I was a youngster on the streets of New York, one could both see and smell the emissions of horse-drawn wagons. Since there was no way of controlling these emissions, they, or the undigested oats in them, served to nourish a large population of English sparrows. If you say something's for the birds, you're politely saying that it's horseshit."

BEYOND THE PALE

Meaning: Socially unacceptable.

Origin: "The pale in this expression has nothing to do with the whitish color, but comes originally from Latin *palus*, meaning a pole, or stake. Since stakes are used to mark boundaries, a *pale* was a particular area within certain limits." The *pale* that inspired this expression was the area around Dublin in Ireland. Until the 1500s, that area was subject to British law. "Those who lived beyond the pale were outside English jurisdiction and were thought to be uncivilized." (From *Getting to the Roots*, by Martin Manser)

I'VE GOT A FROG IN MY THROAT

Meaning: I'm hoarse from a cold.

Origin: Surprisingly, this wasn't inspired by the croaking sound of a cold-sufferer's voice, but by a weird medical practice. "In the Middle Ages," says Christine Ammer in *It's Raining Cats and Dogs*, in-

---

fections such as thrush were sometimes treated by putting a live frog head first into the patient's mouth; by inhaling, the frog was believed to draw out the patient's infection into its own body. The treatment is happily obsolete, but its memory survives in the 19th-century term *frog in one's throat*."

SOMETHING FITS TO A "T"

Meaning: It fits perfectly.

Origin: Commonly thought of as a reference to the T-square, which is used to draw parallel lines and angles. But this phrase was used in the 1600s, before anyone called it a T-square. "A more likely explanation is that the expression was originally 'to a tittle.' A tittle was the dot over the "i," so the phrase meant 'to a dot' or 'fine point.' "(From *Why Do We Say It*, by Nigel Rees)

X X X

Meaning: A kiss, at the end of a letter.

Origin: In medieval times, when most people were illiterate, "contracts were not considered legal until each signer included St. Andrew's cross after their name." (Or instead of a signature, if the signer couldn't write.) To prove their sincerity, signers were then required to kiss the X. "Through the centuries this custom faded out, but the letter X [became associated] with a kiss." This is also probably where the phrase "sealed with a kiss" comes from. (From *I've Got Goose Pimples*, by Martin Vanoni)

READ BETWEEN THE LINES

Meaning: To perceive or understand a hidden meaning.

Origin: In the 16th century it became common for politicians, soldiers, and businesspeople to write in code. To ordinary folks, this writing was unintelligible. They concluded that the meaning was not in the lines of gibberish, but in the space between them.

YOU'RE NO SPRING CHICKEN

Meaning: You're not young anymore; you're past your prime.

Origin: Until recent generations, there were no incubators and few warm hen houses. That meant chicks couldn't be raised during winter. New England growers found that those born in the spring brought premium prices in the summer market places. When these Yankee traders tried to pass off old birds as part of the spring crop, smart buyers would protest that the bird was "no spring chicken."

Handy facts: 8% of Americans twiddle their thumbs; 15% bite their fingernails.

STAR WARS

"There's a whole generation growing up without any kind of fairy tales. And kids need fairy tales—it's an important thing for society to have for kids." —George Lucas

BACKGROUND. In July 1973, George Lucas was an unknown director working on a low-budget 1950s nostalgia film called *American Graffiti*. He approached Universal Studios to see if they were interested in a film idea he called *Star Wars*. Universal turned him down.

It was the biggest mistake the studio ever made.

Six months later, Lucas was the hottest director in Hollywood. *American Graffiti*, which cost $750,000 to make, was a smash. It went on to earn more than $117 million, making it the most profitable film in Hollywood history—even today.

While Universal was stonewalling Lucas, an executive at 20th Century Fox, Alan Ladd, Jr., watched a smuggled print of *American Graffiti* before it premiered and loved it. He was so determined to work with Lucas that he agreed to finance the director's new science fiction film.

Star Wars opened on May 25, 1977, and by the end of August it had grossed $100 million—faster than any other film in history. By 1983 the film had made over $524 million in ticket sales worldwide—making it one of the 10 highest grossing films in history.

MAKING THE FILM

• It took Lucas over two years to write the script. He spent 40 hours a week writing and devoted much of his free time to reading comic books and watching old "Buck Rogers" episodes and other serials looking for film ideas.

• Lucas insisted on casting unknown actors and actresses in all the important parts of the film—which made the studio uneasy. Mark Hamill had made more than 100 TV appearances, and Carrie Fisher had studied acting, but neither had had much experience in films. Harrison Ford's biggest role had been as the drag racer in *American Graffiti*, and when he read for the part of Han Solo he was working as a carpenter.

The U.S. bought Alaska from Russia in 1867 for 2¢ an acre.

THE CHARACTERS

Luke Skywalker. At first Lucas planned to portray him as an elderly general, but decided that making him a teenager gave him more potential for character development. Lucas originally named the character Luke Starkiller, but on the first day of shooting he changed it to the less violent Skywalker.

Obi-Wan Kenobi. Lucas got his idea for Obi-Wan Kenobi and "the Force" after reading Carlos Castaneda's *Tales of Power*, an account of Don Juan, a Mexican-Indian sorcerer and his experiences with what he calls "the life force."

Darth Vader. David Prowse, a six-foot, seven-inch Welsh weightlifter, played the part of Darth Vader. But Lucas didn't want his villain to have a Welsh accent, so he dubbed James Earl Jones's voice over Prowse's. Still, Prowse loved the part. "He took the whole thing very seriously," Lucas remembers. "He began to believe he really was Darth Vader."

Han Solo. In the early stages of development, Han Solo was a green-skinned, gilled monster with a girlfriend named Boma who was a cross between a guinea pig and a brown bear. Solo was supposed to make only a few appearances in the film, but Lucas later made him into a swashbuckling, reckless human (allegedly modeled after film director Francis Ford Coppola).

Chewbacca. Lucas got the idea for Chewbacca one morning in the early 1970s while watching his wife Marcia drive off in her car. She had their Alaskan malamute, Indiana (the namesake for Indiana Jones in *Raiders of the Lost Ark*), and Lucas liked the way the large shaggy dog looked in the passenger seat. So he decided to create a character in the film that was a cross between Indiana, a bear, and a monkey.

Princess Leia. Carrie Fisher was a beautiful 19-year-old actress when she was cast to play Princess Leia, but Lucas did everything he could to tone down her femininity. At one point, he even ordered that her breasts be strapped to her chest with electrical tape. "There's no jiggling in the Empire," Fisher later joked.

R2-D2. Lucas got the name R2-D2 while filming *American Graffiti*. During a sound-mixing session for the film, editor Walter Murch asked him for R2, D2 (Reel 2, Dialogue 2) of the film. Lucas liked the name so much that he made a note of it, and eventually found the right character for it.

C-3P0. Inspired by a robot character in Alex Raymond's science fiction novel, *Iron Men of Mongo*. Raymond's robot was a copper-colored, polite robot who was shaped like a man and who worked as a servant. Lucas intended that C-3P0 and R2-D2 be a space-age Laurel and Hardy team.

SPECIAL EFFECTS

• The spaceship battles were inspired by World War II films. Before filming of the special effects began, Lucas watched dozens of war movies like *Battle of Britain* and *The Bridges of Toko-Ri*, taping his favorite air battle scenes as he went along. Later he edited them down to a 10-minute black-and-white film, and gave it to the special effects team—which reshot the scenes using X-wing and T.I.E. fighter models.

• None of the spaceship models ever moved an inch during the filming of the flight sequences. The motion was an optical illusion created by moving the cameras around motionless models. The models were so detailed that one of them even had Playboy pinups in its cockpit.

MISCELLANEOUS FACTS

• The executives at 20th Century Fox hated the film the first time they saw it. Some of the company's board of directors fell asleep during the first screening; others didn't understand the film at all. One executive's wife even suggested that C-3PO be given a moving mouth, because no one would understand how he could talk without moving his lips.

• The underwater monster in the trash compactor was one of Lucas's biggest disappointments in the film. He had planned to have an elaborate "alien jellyfish" in the scene, but the monster created by the special effects department was so poorly constructed that it reminded him of "a big, wide, brown turd." Result: The monster was filmed underwater during most of the scene—so that moviegoers wouldn't see it.

Male seals don't eat during mating season. (Too many other things on their mind.)

WHAT'S IN A NAME?

You know these corporate and product names, but not where they come from. Well, the BRI will fix that. Here's a little trivia you can use to entertain store clerks the next time you're shopping.

Kodak. No meaning. George Eastman, founder of the company, wanted a name that began and ended in the letter K. "The letter K has been a favorite with me," he explained. "It seems a strong, incisive sort of letter."

Chanel No. 5 Perfume. Coco Chanel considered five her lucky number. She introduced the perfume on the fifth day of the fifth month of 1921.

Lucky Strikes. Dr. R. A. Patterson, a Virginia doctor, used the name to sell tobacco to miners during the California Gold Rush in 1856.

Ex-Lax. Short for Excellent Laxative.

Reebok. An African gazelle, "whose spirit, speed, and grace the [company] wanted to capture in their shoes."

Avon Products. Named for Stratford-on-Avon, William Shakespeare's birthplace.

Random House. America's biggest publisher started out in the 1920s, offering cheap editions of classic books. But founder Bennett Cerf decided to expand the line by publishing luxury editions of books selected "at random."

Kent Cigarettes. Herbert A. Kent, a Lorillard Tobacco Company executive, was so popular at the office that the company named a cigarette after him in 1952.

Toyota. Sakichi Toyoda made the first Japanese power loom. His son Kiichiro expanded into the automobile business.

Xerox. The Haloid Company originally called its copiers "electrophotography" machines. In the 1940s, they hired a Greek scholar at Ohio State University to think up a new name. He came up with *xerography* for the process (after the Greek words for "dry" and "writing") and called the copier itself a *Xerox* machine.

Medical fact: 95% of food-poisoning cases are never reported.

MTV FACTS

These pages were contributed by Larry Kelp, whose picture has been on the back cover since the first Bathroom Reader. He's a music writer in the San Francisco Bay Area, as well as Uncle John's neighbor.

I WANT MY MTV!

In 1981, Robert Pittman, a 27-year-old vice president in charge of new programming at Warner-Amex, came up with an idea for "Music Television," an all-music channel that would play almost nothing but rock videos. The gimmick: free programming—the videos would be supplied by record companies at no charge. "The explicit aim," explains one critic, "was to deliver the notoriously difficult-to-reach fourteen to thirty-four demographic segment to the record companies, beer manufacturers, and pimple cream makers."

Based on that appeal, Pittman talked Warner into investing $30 million in the idea. Four years later, Warner-Amex sold MTV to Viacom for $550 million. In 1992 its estimated worth was $2 billion. Today it broadcasts in more than 50 different countries.

GETTING STARTED

• Pittman planned to call the channel "TV-1," but immediately ran into a problem: "Our legal department found another business with that name. The best we could get was TV-M...and TV-M it was, until our head of music programming said, "Don't you think MTV sounds a little better than TV-M?"

• The design for the logo was another fluke. "Originally," Pittman recalls, "We thought MTV would be three equal-size letters like ABC, NBC, and CBS. But...three 'kids' in a loft downtown, Manhattan Design, came up with the idea for a big M, with TV spray-painted over it. We just cut the paint drips off the TV, and that's the logo. We paid about a thousand dollars for one of the decade's best-known logos."

• MTV originally planned to use Astronaut Neil Armstrong's words, "One small step for man, one giant leap for mankind," with its now-famous "Moon Man" station identification. "But a few days before we launched," Pittman says, "an executive came flying into my office. We had just received a letter from Armstrong's lawyer threatening to sue us if we used his client's voice. We had no time and, worse, no money to redo this on-air ID. So we took his voice off and used the ID with just music. Not at all what we had envisioned, yet, fortunately, it worked fine."

MTV DATA

• MTV went on air at midnight, August 1, 1981. Its first video was The Buggles' prophetic "Video Killed the Radio Star."

• The average MTV viewer tunes in for 16 minutes at a time.

• MTV's VJs have a short shelf life. Once they start looking old, they're retired.

• Not all of the music channel's fans are teenagers. One unusual audience: medical offices. *Prevention* magazine says MTV in the doctor's office helps relieve tension before medical exams.

• MTV reaches 75% of households inhabited by people 18 to 34 years old and 85% of the households with one teenager.

• While many countries served by MTV Europe have local programming with their own VJs, most are in English, the official global language of rock. In Holland, a Flemish language show was dropped because viewers complained that it wasn't in English.

YO, MTV!

It took constant badgering by 25-year-old former intern Ted Demme (nephew of film director Jonathan) to get MTV to air a rap show, "Yo! MTV Raps," in 1989. He argued that white suburban kids wanted rap. The execs gave him one shot at it. "Yo!" was aired on a Saturday. By Monday, the ratings and calls were so impressive that "Yo!" got a daily slot and quickly became MTV's top-rated show.

UNPLUGGED

In 1990, MTV first aired "Unplugged," which went against everything music videos had stood for. Instead of stars lip-synching to prerecorded tracks, "Unplugged" taped them live in front of a studio audience and forced them to use acoustic instruments, making music and talent the focus. What could have been a gimmick turned into a trend when Paul McCartney released his "Unplugged" appearance as an album, and it became one of his bestselling albums. Two years later, Eric Clapton did the same with his MTV performance, which made "Layla" a hit song all over again and earned him Grammy Awards as well as a platinum record. (See page 53, "The Story of Layla.")

King Henry VI banned kissing in England in 1439. Reason: He thought it spread disease.

BONEHEAD ADS

*Businesses spend billions of bucks on ads every year—
but some of them backfire. A few amusing examples:*

SAY WHAT?
Translating U.S. advertising slogans into other languages doesn't always work.

• In China, a Coca-Cola ad used Chinese symbols to sound out "Coca-Cola" phonetically. The soda company withdrew the ad after learning the symbols "Co" "Ca" "Co" " La" meant "Bite the wax tadpole."

• In Brazil, an American airline advertised that its planes had "rendezvous" lounges, not realizing that in Portuguese "rendezvous" means a place to have sex.

• "In Taiwan," according to a book called *The Want Makers*, "Pepsi's 'Come Alive with the Pepsi Generation' was reportedly translated on billboards as 'Pepsi brings your ancestors back from the dead.' "

• "In French Canada, Hunt-Wesson attempted to use its 'Big John' brand name by translating it into French as 'Gros Jos,' a colloquial French phrase that denotes a woman with huge breasts."

• When the gringos at General Motors introduced the Chevrolet *Nova* in Latin America, it was obvious they didn't know their Spanish. Ads all across Latin America heralded the arrival of the new, reliable *Nova*, which in Spanish means "Doesn't go."

SMELL IT LIKE IT IS
Two of the most ludicrous Scratch'n'Sniff ads ever:

• In June 1977, the Rolls-Royce Motor Car Company introduced a campaign entitled "This, in Essence, Is Rolls Royce." Apparently, the company's executives hired scientists to analyze the smell inside a Rolls. They came up with a scent strip that was supposed to smell like leather upholstery.

• In 1989, BEI Defense Systems ran a Scratch'n'Sniff ad for its Hydra 70 weapons system in *The Armed Forces Journal*. It pictured two battling helicopters; when scratched, it gave off the smell of cordite, the odor left in the air after a rocket explosion.

CARTOON NAMES

How did our favorite cartoon characters get their unusual names? Here are a few answers.

Bugs Bunny: In 1940, cartoonist Bugs Hardaway submitted preliminary sketches for "a tall, lanky, mean rabbit" for a cartoon called "Hare-um Scare-um"—and someone labeled the drawings "Bugs's Bunny." Hardaway's mean rabbit was never used—but the name was given to the bunny in the cartoon, "A Wild Hare."

Casper the Friendly Ghost: Cartoonist Joe Oriolo's daughter was afraid of ghosts—so he invented one that wouldn't scare her. "We were looking for a name that didn't sound threatening," he says.

Chip 'n' Dale: Disney animator Jack Hannah was meeting with colleagues to pick names for his two new chipmunk characters. His assistant director happened to mention Thomas Chippendale, the famous furniture designer. "Immediately," Hannah remembers, "I said 'That's it! That's their names!'"

Mickey Mouse: Walt Disney wanted to name the character *Mortimer* Mouse—but his wife hated the name. "Mother couldn't explain why the name grated; it just did," Disney's daughter Diane remembers. Disney wanted the character's name to begin with the letter M (to go with Mouse)—and eventually decided on Mickey.

Porky Pig: According to creator Bob Clampett: "Someone thought of two puppies named Ham and Ex, and that started me thinking. So after dinner one night, I came up with Porky and Beans. I made a drawing of this fat little pig, which I named Porky, and a little black cat named Beans."

Rocky and Bullwinkle: Rocky was picked because it was "just a square-sounding kid's name;" Bullwinkle was named after Clarence Bulwinkel, a Berkeley, California, used-car dealer.

Elmer Fudd: Inspired by a line in a 1920s song called "Mississippi Mud." The line: "It's a treat to meet you on the Mississippi Mud—Uncle Fudd."

Foghorn Leghorn: Modeled after Senator Claghorn, a fictional politician in comedian Fred Allen's radio show.

IT'S A MIRACLE!

The tabloids are full of stories about people who see Jesus in everything from a lima bean to a smudge on a car window. Could they be true? Here are the details of five sightings. Judge for yourself.

The Sighting: Jesus in a forkful of spaghetti, Stone Mountain, Georgia

Revelation: Joyce Simpson, an Atlanta fashion designer, was pulling out of a gas station in Stone Mountain when she saw the face of Jesus in a forkful of spaghetti on a billboard advertising Pizza Hut's pasta menu. Simpson says at the time she was trying to decide whether to stay in the church choir or quit and sing professionally. (She decided to stick with the choir.)

Impact: Since the sighting, dozens of other people called Pizza Hut to say that they, too, had seen someone in the spaghetti. But not all the callers agreed that the man in the spaghetti was Jesus; some saw Doors singer Jim Morrison; others saw country star Willie Nelson.

The Sighting: Jesus in a tortilla, Lake Arthur, New Mexico

Revelation: On October 5, 1977, Maria Rubio was making burritos for her husband when she noticed a 3-by-3-inch face of Jesus burned into the tortilla she was cooking. Local priests argued that the image was only a coincidence, but the Rubio family's faith was unshaken. They saved the tortilla, framed it, and built a shrine for it in their living room.

Impact: To date more than 11,000 people have visited it.

The Sighting: Jesus on a soybean oil tank, Fostoria, Ohio

Revelation: Rita Rachen was driving home from work along Ohio Route 12 one night in 1986 when she saw the image of Jesus with a small child on the side of an Archer Daniels Midland Company oil tank containing soybean oil. She screamed, "Oh, my Lord, my God!" and nearly drove off the side of the road, but recovered enough to continue driving.

A. It doesn't have any nostrils.

Impact: She spread the word to other faithful, and the soybean tank became a popular pilgrimage site. (Since then, however, the oil tank has been repainted. Jesus is no longer visible.)

The Sighting: Jesus on the side of a refrigerator, Estill Springs, Tennessee

Revelation: When Arlene Gardner bought a new refrigerator, she had the old one dragged out onto her front porch. A few nights later, she noticed that several of her neighbors were standing around staring at the old fridge. They told her that the reflection from a neighbor's porch light had created an image of Jesus on the side of the refrigerator. Gardner took a look and agreed.

Impact: Soon thousands of faithful were making pilgrimages to the site—so many, in fact, that Gardner's neighbors had their porch light disconnected, so Jesus could be seen no more. (*Note:* Not everyone agreed that Jesus had really made an appearance; as one local skeptic explained to a reporter, "When the good Lord comes, He won't come on a major appliance.")

The Sighting: A 900-foot Jesus at the City of Faith, Tulsa, Oklahoma

Revelation: This vision—one of the most publicized Jesus sightings ever—came to famed televangelist Oral Roberts on May 25, 1980 …but he inexplicably kept it secret for over five months. Then one day he shared his vision and explained what he'd seen to reporters: "He reached down, put His hand under the City of Faith (a city Roberts had built), lifted it, and said to me, 'See how easy it is for me to lift it?'"

On January 4, 1987, Roberts told his followers that God had appeared again, this time demanding $8 million. Roberts warned that if the money wasn't sent in by March 31, "God would call me home."

Impact: Roberts's followers coughed up $9.1 million.

★ ★ ★ ★

Royal Gossip
Queen Elizabeth likes to do crossword puzzles. She also likes to read mysteries by Dick Francis and play parlor games like charades.

Geography lesson: Roughly one-third of Americans live within five miles of a lake.

THE MINISKIRT SAGA

Today, when practically anything goes in fashion, people have forgotten how revolutionary the miniskirt was in its day. In the mid-'60s, when it caught on, it was more than a fashion—it was a philosophy, a political statement, a news event. Here are some facts to remind you.

HISTORY

The miniskirt was created by an English seamstress named Mary Quant. As a girl, Quant hated the straightlaced clothes grown-ups wore, so when she got older, she made unconventional clothes for herself.

In 1955, she opened the world's first clothing boutique in London, selling "wild and kinky" handmade clothes like the ones she wore. She used bright colors and lots of plastic, and kept hemlines shorter than normal (though they weren't minis yet). Her fashions caught on with hip Londoners. They became known as "mod" (for modern) clothes, and Mary became a local celebrity.

In 1965, young girls in London were beginning to wear their dresses shorter than ever. Taking a cue from them, Quant began manufacturing skirts that were outrageously short for the time. She called them "mini-skirts." They took off like wildfire.

Later that year, respected French designer Andre Courreges brought the miniskirt and go-go boots (his own creation) to the world of high fashion. This made the mini a "style" instead of a "fad" and inspired influential women—movie stars, models, heiresses—to shorten their skirts. But the largest American clothing manufacturers weren't sure whether to hop on the mini bandwagon until the day that Jackie Kennedy appeared in public with a shortened hemline. After that, it was full speed ahead.

The mini fad lasted for less than a decade, but it permanently altered the concept of what was acceptable in women's attire and helped break down traditional barriers for women in other areas of society.

The Meaning of the Miniskirt, Part I
In 1965, Quant was asked to reveal the meaning of the miniskirt. Her reply: "Sex."

The Meaning of the Miniskirt, Part II
"Without a doubt, the pill bred the mini, just as it bred the topless bathing suit by Rudi Gernreich in 1964. They were intended to prove that women were in control of their destiny and could choose whom they wished to mate with."
—*In Fashion*, by Prudence Glynn

THE MINISKIRT—INTERNATIONAL CONTROVERSY
Today, the miniskirt is a fashion, not a political issue, but in the '60s, it was a major controversy. Here's how some people reacted:

• **In the Vatican:** Women in miniskirts were not allowed to enter Vatican City.

• **In the Malagasy Republic:** An antiminiskirt law went into effect in 1967. Violators were subject to 10 days in jail.

• **In the Congo:** In 1967, police arrested 300 women wearing miniskirts, which were banned.

• **In Venezuela:** Churches in Caracas put up signs telling people to give up their minis or "be condemned to hell."

• **In Egypt:** Women in minis were subject to a charge of indecent behavior. This law was passed because two women wearing miniskirts in the center of the city caused a two-hour traffic jam.

• **In Zambia:** Gangs of youths roamed the streets assaulting girls in miniskirts and forcibly lowering their hemlines. After a week, the war against miniskirts was declared officially over when women went on television and said they "realized their mistake."

• **In Greece:** Anyone wearing a miniskirt was jailed.

• **In the Philippines:** A congressman proposed that miniskirts be banned. But the proposal was withdrawn when a congresswoman threatened to retaliate by outlawing elevator shoes.

• **In Rio de Janeiro:** In 1966, a 63-year-old man on a bus was overcome when a young woman wearing a miniskirt crossed her legs in the seat next to him. He bit her on the thigh and was sentenced to three days in jail.

• **In the United States:** Disneyland outlawed miniskirts—the gate-keepers measured the distance from the woman's knee to her hemline and restricted her entrance until she ripped out the hem.

In most schools during the '60s, if the hem of a dress didn't touch the floor when a girl was kneeling, it was considered a mini, and the guilty party was sent home. "And don't come back until you look respectable, young lady."

Do it again: 75% of divorced women will eventually remarry.

LEGENDARY SCAMS

You've probably heard the expression, "If you believe that, I've got a bridge I'd like to sell you"—but do you know the story behind it? The BRI looks at some classic ripoffs.

FOR SALE: The Brooklyn Bridge

BACKGROUND: Not long after the Brooklyn Bridge was completed in 1883, a shifty 20-year-old named George C. Parker decided on a whim to see if he could "sell" it to an unsuspecting tourist. He did. In fact, it was so easy that he tried it on someone else a few days later and pulled it off again. He dropped his other cons and went into Brooklyn Bridge sales full-time.

THE SCAM: His usual approach was to walk up to a "mark," introduce himself as the owner, and offer a job as tolltaker in the tollbooth he was about to build. Parker would then gently guide the conversation to the point where the mark would offer to buy the bridge, set up his own tollbooth, and keep all the toll money for himself. Parker, "more a bridge builder than a toll taker," was happy to have the bridge taken off of his hands in exchange for anywhere from $50 to $50,000, depending on how wealthy the tourist looked. And he accepted payments in installments when a sucker didn't have enough cash to buy the bridge outright. Some of his victims paid him regularly for months before they realized they'd been had; and more than once, police had to be called to the bridge to prevent its latest "owner" from erecting a toll barrier.

WHAT HAPPENED: Parker specialized in selling the Brooklyn Bridge, but also sold other prominent New York landmarks on the side, including Madison Square Garden, the Metropolitan Museum of Art, Grant's Tomb, and even the Statue of Liberty. Amazingly, he remained in business from 1883 to 1928, when he was finally arrested on a swindling charge and sentenced to life in prison. He died in Sing Sing prison—where the other con men treated him like a king—in 1937.

FOR RENT: The information booth in New York's Grand Central Station.

BACKGROUND: In 1929, a well-dressed man claiming to be

"T. Remington Grenfall," vice president of a company called the "Grand Central Holding Corporation," walked into the Fortunato Fruit company and told the owners, Tony and Nick Fortunato, about a unique real estate opportunity. The man told them that the operators of Grand Central Station had decided to shut down the information booth and refer all inquiries to the ticket sellers. Since the information booth was no longer needed, the station had decided to rent the space out to merchants—fruit merchants.

THE SCAM: The Fortunatos were at the top of the list. All they had to do was come up with the first year's rent in cash: $2,000 a week for 50 weeks, or $100,000. It seemed like a great opportunity, so the next morning the brothers showed up at the Grand Central Holding Corporation—in a building next door to the train station—and gave the "president" of the company, a man calling himself Wilson A. Blodgett, a cashier's check for $100,000 in exchange for a contract saying they could take over the booth beginning on April 1 (April Fools' Day).

On April 1, the brothers—accompanied by several workers and a huge supply of lumber—went to Grand Central Station to take possession of the booth and begin renovations. The only problem: the information booth employees were still in the booth and refused to leave. Grand Central officials refused to honor the contract and had the Fortunato brothers kicked out of the station.

WHAT HAPPENED: Grenfall and Blodgett were never caught, and the Fortunato brothers never got their money back or took possession of the information booth. They did, however, become a semi-regular tourist attraction. For years afterward they returned periodically to the train station to yell at officials and intimidate the clerks in the information booths. New Yorkers began taking out-of-town guests to the station in hopes of witnessing the spectacle.

FOR SALE: The Eiffel Tower
BACKGROUND: In 1925, a Czech con artist named Victor Lustig read in the newspaper that the Eiffel Tower needed major repairs. The article gave him an idea for a scam, and he set sail for Paris. Posing as "Deputy Director-General of the Ministry of Mail and Telegraphs," he contacted six of the country's largest scrap metal dealers and brought them together for a face-to-face meeting.

Like cats, Brahma bulls purr when they're happy.

THE SCAM: At the meeting, Lustig told the dealers that the French government had decided the repairs on the Eiffel Tower were too expensive and had also decided to tear the landmark down. Fearing that the public would be furious when it learned of the decision, he told them, the government wanted the story kept a secret until the demolition actually began. After asking the dealers to submit bids for the contract, Lustig pulled one of the men aside and told him that for a $100,000 bribe, he would award him the contract. The dealer went back to his office, got the money and gave it to Lustig, who caught the next train to Vienna.

WHAT HAPPENED: The scrap dealer never reported the scam to the police, so Lustig returned to France and conned a *second* scrap dealer out of $100,000. This time, the dealer went to the police. But it was too late. Lustig had already fled to the United States, where he resumed his career as a con artist.

FOR SALE: Big Ben

BACKGROUND: In a 1920 play, Scottish actor Arthur Ferguson played a gullible American tourist who is swindled by a con man. When the play closed, Ferguson decided to find out if real American tourists were as dumb as the one he'd played.

THE SCAM: World War I had just ended; England's finances were strained to the breaking point. But Ferguson "confided" to American tourists that the fiscal situation was even worse than the British government was letting on, and he had been hired by the Prime Minister to quietly sell off some of London's most famous landmarks to raise cash. Ferguson "sold" just about every London landmark several times over, usually charging $5,000 for Big Ben, $30,000 for Nelson's column in Trafalgar Square, and $10,000 as a down payment for Buckingham Palace.

WHAT HAPPENED: The scam was successful for many years. Finally, so many Americans complained to the U.S. Embassy that Ferguson decided it was time to leave the country. He moved to *America*, where he set up shop selling U.S. landmarks—including the White House, which he rented out for $10,000 a year—to wealthy *English* tourists.

Ferguson was finally arrested for trying to sell the Statue of Liberty to an Australian for $100,000. He spent five years in prison for the crime.

QUOTES FROM JFK

Some better-known remarks made by our 35th president.

"There is no city in the United States in which I get a warmer welcome and less votes than Columbus, Ohio."

[*To his brother in 1960, before the election*] "Do you realize the responsibility I carry? I'm the only person standing between Nixon and the White House."

"When we got into office, the thing that surprised me most was to find that things were just as bad as we'd been saying they were."

[*At a press conference prior to the 1960 election*] "I have just received the following telegram from my generous Daddy. It says, 'Dear Jack: Don't buy a single more vote than is necessary. I'll be damned if I'm going to pay for a landslide.'"

"When power corrupts, poetry cleanses."

"When written in Chinese, the word "crisis" is composed of two characters: one represents danger, the other represents opportunity."

Question: "The Republican National Committee recently adopted a resolution saying you were pretty much of a failure. How do you feel about that?"
President Kennedy: "I assume it passed unanimously."

"In a free society, art is not a weapon."

"Failure has no friends."

"Conformity is the jailer of freedom and the enemy of growth."

"Let us never negotiate out of fear. But let us never fear to negotiate."

"We must use time as a tool, not as a couch."

"The war against hunger is truly mankind's war of liberation."

"The blessings of liberty have too often stood for privilege, materialism and a life of ease."

Cleopatra tested the potency of her poisons by feeding them to her slaves.

CLOUDMASTER ELVIS

We try to include at least one Elvis story in every Bathroom Reader.
Here are a few bizarre tales from B.R. volumes 6 and 7.

CONTROLLING THE CLOUDS

As Elvis got more famous, he came to believe that he was no ordinary human being. For one thing, he believed he could move clouds.

"I remember one day in Palm Springs," says former aide Dave Hebler. "It was hotter than hell, over a hundred degrees, and Elvis wanted to go shopping. So we all jam into this car....Elvis was talking about the power of metaphysics, although I'm not quite sure he knew the real definition of the word.

The sky in the desert was cloudless, except for one small, far-off cloud. "Suddenly Elvis yells out, 'Stop the car. I want to show you want I mean, Dave. Now see that cloud? I will show you what my powers really are. Now I want you all to watch. All of you, look at that cloud.'

"Well, we all look at the damn little cloud up there like a bunch of goats. Elvis is staring a hole through the damn thing. Well, the perspiration is dripping off us. Not a sound in the car, just a whole bunch of dummies dying of heat stroke looking up at the cloud....

"After about ten minutes, thank God, the damn thing dissipated a little. I saved the day by noticing it first....I said, 'Gee, Elvis, you're right. Look it's moving away.' [He] gave me one of those sly little smiles that told me he had done it again. 'I know, I moved it,' he says. Then we drive off."

SHOT OFF THE CAN

You never knew when Elvis might get the urge to engage in a little shooting practice, so it paid to be on guard at *all* times.

On one memorable night, Elvis and some friends were relaxing in the Imperial Suite on the 30th floor of the Las Vegas Hilton after his show. "The very elegant Linda Thompson [Elvis's girl-friend] was sitting in the well-appointed and luxurious bathroom," writes Steve Dunleavy in *Elvis: What Happened?*, "when her reverie was rudely interrupted by a resounding blast. At the same time, a tiny rip appeared in the toilet paper on her right side [and] the mirror on the closet door splintered into shards of glass."

"I think Elvis was trying to hit a light holder on the opposite wall," explains Sonny West, Elvis's bodyguard. "Well, he's a lousy shot and he missed. The damn bullet went straight through the wall and missed Linda by inches. If she had been standing up next to the toilet paper holder, it would have gone right through her leg. If it had changed course or bounced off something, it could have killed her, man."

PLAYING IT SAFE

Elvis had hundreds of guns, and he liked to keep them loaded at all times. But he always left the first bullet chamber empty. "It is a habit he got from me," says Sonny West. "I had a friend who dropped his gun. It landed on the hammer…fired and hit him right through the heart, killing him instantly."

But Elvis had another reason. "Elvis knew what a real bad temper he had," says Sonny. "When he flashed, anything could happen. If he pulled the trigger in a rage, it would come up blank and give him just enough time to realize what on earth he was doing."

It paid off. One evening when the Elvis entourage was at the movies (Elvis rented the entire movie theater and brought his friends with him), Elvis went to the men's room and stayed there for a while. One of the group—a visitor who wasn't part of the regular "Memphis Mafia"—started joking around, pounding on the bathroom door. West recalls:

"Elvis yells back, 'Okay, man, okay.'

"But this guy just kept banging on the door….Apparently Elvis flashed. 'Goddammit!' he yelled as he charged out the door. Then he screamed, 'Who do you think you are, you m-----f----r?,' whipped out his gun, pointed it right at the guy and pulled the trigger. Jesus, thank God, he didn't have a bullet in that chamber; otherwise, he would have blown the man's head clean off his shoulders."

COMMUNING WITH THE DEAD

One of Elvis's favorite late-night haunts was the Memphis funeral home where his mother's body had originally been laid out.

There are an estimated three hundred $10,000 bills in circulation in the U.S.

A FOOD IS BORN

Somehow, it seems like poetic justice to be reading about where foods come from...while you're in the bathroom.

DUNCAN HINES. Duncan Hines was a traveling restaurant critic in the 1930s. His book *Adventures in Good Eating*—a guide to restaurants along major highways—was so popular that his name became a household word. Hines's notoriety attracted the attention of Roy Park, a New York businessman who was looking for a way to promote his new line of baked goods. He asked Hines to become a partner in the company, and Hines agreed. Together they formed Hines-Park Foods, Inc. in 1948. Their line of cake mixes captured 48% of the American cake mix market in less than *three weeks.*

MCDONALD'S FILET-O-FISH SANDWICH. The first successful non-burger "entree" in McDonald's history was a concession to organized religion. In the early '60s, the McDonald's in Cincinnati lost sales every Friday because the large Catholic population couldn't eat meat—and McDonald's had nothing else to offer. The owner asked chairman Ray Kroc for permission to expand the menu. Kroc resisted at first ("Let 'em eat burgers, like everyone else!"), but ultimately supported research into selling a fish sandwich. McDonald's researchers decided to use codfish, but didn't call it that for two reasons: one, they were legally allowed to call it the much classier "North Atlantic Whitefish," and two, Kroc's childhood memories of cod liver oil were too unpleasant. After successful test-marketing, the fish sandwich went on the McDonald's menu permanently in 1963.

MACARONI AND CHEESE. During the Depression, the Kraft Company tried to market a low-priced cheddar cheese powder—but the public wouldn't buy it. One St. Louis sales rep, looking for a way to unload his allotment of the stuff, tied individual packages of the cheese to macaroni boxes and talked grocers on his route into selling them as one item, which he called "Kraft Dinners." When the company found out how well they were selling, it made the Dinners an official part of its product line.

There are an estimated 10 trillion cells in your body.

CELESTIAL SEASONINGS. In the 1960s, four hippies spent their time roaming the Rocky Mountains gathering herbs for their own homemade tea. They got so good at it that they decided to sell herbs to local health-food stores. They bankrolled the operation by selling an old Volkswagon and named the company after one of the women, whose "cosmic" '60s name was *Celestial*. Today, Celestial Seasonings is the largest herbal tea company on Earth.

CAESAR SALAD. The name of this unique salad doesn't refer to the Roman conqueror, but to the man who created it—a Tijuana restaurateur named Caesar Cardini. Here's one account of its origin: "Cardini started several restaurants in Tijuana, Mexico, in the early '20s. He devised the salad in 1924 during the Fourth of July weekend at Caesar's Place. He served it as finger food, arranging the garlic-scented lettuce leaves on platters. Later, he shredded the leaves into bite-sized pieces. The salad became a hit with the Hollywood movie stars who visited Tijuana, and soon was a specialty of such prestigious restaurants as Chasen's and Romanoff's."

MAXWELL HOUSE COFFEE. In the 1880s, a young Tennessee-an named Joel Cheek became obsessed with the idea of roasting the perfect blend of coffee. After years of experiments, he came up with a blend he liked. Then, in 1892, he persuaded the owners of Nashville's ritzy Maxwell House Hotel to serve it exclusively. Cheek was so encouraged by the clientele's enthusiastic response to his coffee that he named it after the hotel.

BISQUICK. In 1930, a General Mills executive traveling by train ordered some biscuits in the dining car. He expected them to be cold and stale, since it was long past the usual dinner hour. But instead, they were hot and fresh—and they arrived almost instantly. He inquired how this was possible, and was told that the bread dough had been mixed in advance and stored in the refrigerator. The executive thought it was a great idea. He worked with General Mills chemists and created a similar product—but one that could be kept in a box, unrefrigerated. It was so popular when it was introduced in the '30s that it revolutionized American baking habits.

AT THE DRIVE-IN

*In this chapter, the BRI revisits a beloved-but-endangered
American institution: the drive-in movie theater.*

IN THE HEAT OF THE NIGHT

It was a summer evening in the late 1920s. Richard M. Hollingshead was trying to show friends some home movies in his living room, but the stifling heat was making them uncomfortable. On an impulse, he took his projector outside, set it on the hood of his Model A Ford, and showed the films on a sheet draped across the garage door instead. The guests loved it. In fact, they were so enthusiastic about watching movies outdoors that it gave Hollingshead a business idea: why not show short movies at gas stations to keep patrons entertained while they're filling up their tanks?

OUT OF GAS

That idea went nowhere, because gas station owners weren't willing to pay for it. But it evolved into a new scheme. Hollingshead decided to show full-length films outdoors to paying customers—who would watch the movies from their automobiles. To make it possible, he created a system of ramps that tilted cars up so people could see over the vehicles in front of them. He even watched films with his lawn sprinkler going to see if it was possible to see a movie during a rainstorm.

Hollingshead patented his designs, and on June 6, 1933, he opened the world's first drive-in theater in Camden, New Jersey. More than 600 people showed up for the premier, paying 25 cents per car plus 25 cents per occupant ($1 tops) to see *Wife Beware*, a second-run film starring Adolphe Menjou.

A SLOW START

Soon, drive-ins were popping up all over the country. But they faced some formidable opposition. In those days, the studios that made movies also owned nearly all of the movie theaters in the country. They saw the drive-in as a threat to their indoor theater profits, and retaliated by charging exorbitantly high rental prices and withholding their best first-run films. Business was so slow that Hollingshead got out of the drive-in business in 1935.

Pogo sticks were first used by sacrificial dancers in Borneo.

THE FABULOUS FIFTIES

Everything changed after World War II. Americans had money, cars, kids, and homes in the suburbs—and drive-ins were the perfect family outing. People could dress casually, bring their own food, smoke, talk, and entertain the kids without paying for a sitter. For teens, roomy back seats provided a private place to go on a weekend night. The marriage of car and movie seemed perfect, and drive-ins opened up all over the country: by 1957, considered the peak year, there were approximately 4,100 drive-ins from coast to coast, accounting for 31% of all movie business in the U.S.

FROM BOOM TO BUST

By the '60s, however, rising land costs, shrinking cars, the declining quality of drive-in film fare, and the improving quality of TV all combined to put the drive-in on the endangered list. Loosening sexual mores were another problem. As casual sex became more commonplace and acceptable, drive-ins lost much of their allure. They began disappearing from across the landscape, and by the '80s the industry was in freefall. More than 1,000 drive-ins bit the dust in 1988 alone, and fewer than 870 remain today. A fur store is now on the site of Hollingshead's original drive-in.

DRIVE-IN-NOVATION

At least one company, American International Pictures, sprang up to make movies just for drive-ins. Over 25 years, AIP cranked out more than 500 low-budget films with titles like *I Was a Teenage Werewolf*, *The Brain Eaters*, and *A Bucket of Blood*. While other Hollywood studios made a film and then advertised it, AIP came up with a film title they thought would sell first, then drew up movie posters and sent them to theater owners to see if they were interested. "If it passed all those things," producer Samuel Z. Arkoff explains, "*then* we'd get a script and a director. We made $100,000 pictures with million-dollar titles. We *owned* the drive-ins."

IT CAME FROM THE DRIVE-IN

Several drive-ins offered church services on Sunday mornings. By 1967, *Time* reported, there were more than 70 in operation around the country. The services were popular with churchgoers: they didn't have to get dressed up to attend, and they could say Amen, as one pastor described it, with "a gentle, dignified horn toot."

Heavy thought: The average American eats 21.4 pounds of snack foods each year.

MYTH AMERICA

You may have believed these stories since you were a kid—
after all, they were taught as sacred truths.
Well, it's time to take another look...

FOR WHOM THE BELL TOLLS

The Myth: Alexander Graham Bell invented the telephone.

Background: About 15 years before Bell uttered the famous words, "Mr. Watson, come here; I want you," German scientist Johann Philipp Reis had developed a crude working telephone. And about five years before Bell's historic race to the patent office, an Italian scientist named Antonio Meucci offered the patent office a rough description of a telephone's structure and principles. But nothing ever came of it.

The Truth: Bell wasn't the first to develop the device—but he was the first to patent it...barely. Many scientists were working on a telephone at the same time; one of them—Elisha Gray—arrived at the U.S. Patent Office with a model telephone just *two hours* after Bell. In fact, some say Gray's telephone was better than Bell's and more like the one we use today. By the time Bell received his patent, so many people had claimed the telephone as their own invention that Bell had to defend his patent in court. In fact, the case went to the U.S. Supreme Court. The verdict: The high court was divided in his favor, allowing him the rights to the telephone.

FULTON'S FOLLY

The Myth: Robert Fulton invented the steamboat.

The Truth: Twenty years before Fulton built his first steamboat, *Fulton's Folly*, in 1807, James Rumsey had a steamboat chugging up the Potomac and John Fitch had one traveling the Delaware. In some states, Fitch even secured exclusive rights to run passenger and freight steamboat trips. So why does Fulton get the credit for the invention 20 years later? Rumsey and Fitch died broke, while Fulton had a knack for promotion and fund-raising. But Fulton did fail to make one key sale—to Napoleon Bonaparte, who thought the idea of steamships impractical. Some historians say the little conqueror's bad decision might have saved the English.

It takes about 12 ears of corn to produce a single tablespoon of corn oil.

REPUTATION ON THE LINE

The Myth: Henry Ford invented the auto assembly line.

The Truth: No, chalk this one up to Ransom E. Olds, creator of the Oldsmobile. Olds introduced the moving assembly line in the early 1900s and boosted car production by 500%. The previous year, the Olds Motor Vehicle Company had turned out 425 cars. The year after, they made more than 2,500 of them. Ford improved Olds's system by introducing the conveyor belt, which moved both the cars *and* needed parts along the production line. The belt cut Ford's production time from a day to about two hours. A significant contribution, but not the original.

TORY, TORY, TORY

The Myth: The vast majority of American colonists supported the rebellion during the Revolutionary War.

The Truth: According to President John Adams, at the beginning of the war only about a third of the people were on the side of the revolution. Another third were on the side of the British, and the rest didn't care either way. After a while, the ratio changed as British supporters were terrorized, publicly humiliated, and finally attacked. Many fled to Canada.

IN THE GROOVE

The Myth: Thomas Edison invented the phonograph to bring music to the masses.

Background: When Edison first played "Mary Had a Little Lamb" on his crude recording device, he knew he was onto something commercially significant. But he didn't have a clue as to what it was.

The Truth: He was actually trying to create the first telephone answering machine. The problem he saw with the telephone was that, unlike the telegraph, you couldn't leave messages for people. Edison came up with an idea and—to his shock—it worked the first time he tried it. Still, it became clear that his machine wasn't suited for telephones. So Edison began marketing the phonograph to businesses, believing that it was suitable only as a dictating machine. It took 15 years and the successes of other manufacturers for him to be convinced that people would buy phonographs to play music at home.

One billion seconds is about 31.7 years.

SESAME STREET

"Sesame Street" is the most popular kid's show in television history. Did you grow up with it? Here's a little info on how it got into your life.

IN THE BEGINNING

In 1966, Joan Ganz Cooney was the publicity director of a New Jersey television station. One evening, she and a psychologist friend were sitting around in her apartment after dinner, discussing TV. A recent report had showed that preschool children watched an average of 27 hours of television a week; Cooney and her friend agreed that if toddlers were going to spend so much time in front of the tube, it made sense to try to educate them while they were there. But how?

Shortly afterward, Cooney took a leave of absence from her job to found the Children's Television Workshop. She began researching the idea of an entertaining, fast-paced educational show for preschoolers—modeled after beer commercials and the hit show "Laugh-In." "We decided to co-opt what we called 'the Devil's tunes,'" Cooney remembers. "Back then, kids were singing beer commercials. We decided to use the idea of commercials to teach."

A ROUGH START

Building a kid's show around teaching numbers and letters may not seem like such a big deal today, but back hardly anyone believed it would work. "The teaching profession assumed preschoolers weren't ready to read," remembers Caroll Spinney, who plays Big Bird on the show, "so we seemed crazy, proposing to sell kids the ABCs, like other shows hustled sugar-coated breakfast cereals."

NBC, CBS, and ABC thought the show was too risky—particularly when Cooney told them it would cost $8 million a year—making it the most expensive (and most heavily researched) show on television. So Cooney turned to other sources for money. She was in luck: the federal government saw the show as a valuable addition to its Headstart program and chipped in $4 million. Once the government was committed, Cooney raised the rest from the Corporation for Public Broadcasting, The Carnegie Foundation, and the Ford Foundation.

Got a sick fish? Japan has at least one "fish hospital" that can treat it.

STREET TALK

Cooney and producer Jon Stone knew that they wanted a set that would seem familiar to their target audience: middle- and lower-income children ages one to five. "We wanted it to be more than just another escapist show set in a tree house or a badger den," Stone remembers, "but the only models we had were educational TV's desks and blackboards and the fairy castles of children's shows. Yet the consensus was that kids learn best in a setting similar to their daily lives." No one had any idea how to translate that idea into a set for the show...until Stone saw a commercial recruiting college students to work at an inner-city tutoring project. The TV ad, filmed on a city street with brownstones and front stoops in the background, was the direct inspiration for the urban residential setting of "Sesame Street."

NAMING THE SHOW

Finding a *name* for the set's street proved a much more daunting task. Various staff writers suggested "104th Street," "Columbus Avenue," and several other names . . . including "Sesame Street," but Stone hated them all—especially Sesame Street, which reminded him of the corny "Open sesame!" expression used by the third-rate magicians of his childhood. ("Besides," he argued at one meeting, "Sesame Street will be too hard for little kids to pronounce.") The decision dragged out until literally one-half hour before the national press announcement for the show. When Cooney finally showed up at the meeting and asked the writers what name they had come up with, they hadn't come up with any. "I guess we'll have to go with Sesame Street," Stone sighed. "Ironically," he recalls, "Virginia Schone, the writer who suggested the name, left the show soon afterward, and we haven't heard from her in twenty years. Yet she named the landscape of a whole generation's fantasy life."

ENTER THE MUPPETS

Perhaps Cooney's most important stroke was hiring Jim Henson, a brilliant young puppeteer whose "muppets" (part marionette, part puppet) starred in a Washington, D.C., TV show called "Sam and Friends," had appeared in commercials, and had made several appearances on "The Tonight Show," "The Ed Sullivan Show," and "The Jimmy Dean Show."

It takes seven to eight tons of sugarcane to produce one ton of sugar.

CRITICISM

"Sesame Street" hit the airwaves on November 9, 1969, earning mixed reviews from both parents and the media. Critics complained that the show's fast pace would make kids skittish and give them short attention spans. But studies showed that preschool kids who watched "Sesame Street" were better prepared to make the transition from home to classroom than kids who didn't. Within a year, "Sesame Street" had more than 7 million regular viewers.

CHARACTER ORIGINS

Kermit the Frog. The very first muppet, Kermit was created in 1956 when Henson, a college freshman studying art at the University of Maryland, cut up his mother's old green coat, sewed it into a puppet and added the halves of a Ping-Pong ball for eyes.

Cookie Monster. Cookie was just another anonymous monster when he ate the letter W in a 1969 sketch with Kermit the Frog. . . but that changed a few episodes later, when he appeared in a game show sketch in which he had to choose between a trip to Hawaii and some cookies. He took the cookies. In 1992, his trademark "Me want cookie!" made it into *Bartlett's Familiar Quotations*.

Big Bird. Because all of the muppets were smaller than the humans on the show, Jim Henson suggested adding a larger-than-life character, "say a big bird for example." But nobody had any idea what kind of personality an eight-foot-tall yellow canary creature should have...until Caroll Spinney, who plays Big Bird, saw a youngster having a temper tantrum. "I thought, 'I bet other kids can relate to that.' So when the script called for Big Bird to not get his way, I acted just like that child and threw an all-out screaming fit. It clicked and thus immediately fixed the character: an 8-foot bird with the emotional responses of a wide-eyed 4-year-old."

Oscar the Grouch. Caroll Spinney also plays Oscar, who was one of the most difficult characters to develop. Making him grouchy and putting him in a trash can were easy...but no one could figure out what he should sound like. Then, one day, as Spinney got into a cab, the driver asked him in a thick New York accent, "Where to, Mac?" Oscar's voice was born.

SESAME FACTS

• Today "Sesame Street" is a worldwide phenomenon. The English language version airs in more than 80 countries, and there are more

A swarm of 50,000 bees weighs about 10 pounds.

than a dozen international coproductions. German kids watch "Sesamstrasse," Tunisian kids watch "Iftah Ya SimSim," Israeli kids watch "Rechov SumSum," and Latin American kids watch "Plaza Sesamo."

• However, the international reaction to "Sesame Street" wasn't always positive. In 1973, for example, the BBC snubbed it as "authoritarian." And a few months later, a Russian youth publication attacked it as "cultural imperialism." Their complaint: it spread "American concepts of private enterprise and the importance of money."

• Are the kid actors thrown off when they see the muppets being operated by the "muppeteers?" Not really. "It's great to see kids who are in the studio," one staffer says. "The man who's playing the part is right there wearing the puppet on his arm, but the child completely disregards the person and talks to that puppet." That isn't always the case: One child was stunned when he saw Caroll climbing out of the Big Bird costume. "Mom," the stunned toddler yelled, "Do you think Big Bird knows he has a *man* inside of him?"

• How do Big Bird, Snuffleupagus, and the other giant-sized muppets move about so realistically when the operators inside can barely see out? By watching themselves on miniature TVs mounted *inside the costumes*, an innovation Henson himself cooked up in 1969.

• "Sesame Street" was one of the first shows on television to feature an ethnically diverse cast. Segregationists pressured a Mississippi TV station to cancel the show in 1969, but a local parents group led a successful campaign to get it back on the air. A year later, the cast (protected by police wearing riot gear) visited Jackson, Mississippi, to promote the show. "Little white kids would reach out to kiss me or 'Gordon,' the other black character," Loretta Long, the black actress who plays Susan, remembers. "You could see their mothers were uneasy. But they'd loosen up, because how can you hate someone who makes your child so happy?"

• Fresh from the success of "Sesame Street," Henson, in the mid-'70s, tried to interest the TV networks in a muppet-based variety show for adults. But they wouldn't buy it, so Henson sold it to an English company. "The Muppet Show," which ran from 1976 to 1981, quickly became the most widely viewed television in the world, with 235 million viewers in more than 100 different countries.

Horses can only breathe through their nostrils.

THE EVOLUTION OF SANTA CLAUS, PART III

Here's the next installment of the Santa story that begins on page 103.

SANTA'S HELPER: THOMAS NAST

In the mid-1800s, it was popular to draw St. Nick either in his bishop's robes or as a man with a pointed hat, a long coat, and straight beard. Sometimes he even had black hair.

This changed in 1863, when *Harper's Weekly* hired 21-year-old Thomas Nast to draw a picture of Santa Claus bringing gifts to Union troops fighting the Civil War. The Santa that Nast drew combined Clement Moore's description of St. Nicholas in his poem, "Twas the Night Before Christmas" with, believe it or not …Uncle Sam. Nast's Santa was a jolly, roly-poly old man who wore a star-spangled jacket, striped pants, and a cap.

"The drawing boosted the spirits of soldiers and civilians alike because it showed that the spirit of Christmas had come to the Civil War," says historian James I. Robertson. It was so popular that every year, for 40 years, when the magazine asked Nast to draw Santas, he stuck to the same concept—although he did drop the stars and stripes in favor of a plain wool suit. "Hence," Robinson says, "the American Santa Claus took shape by repetition. We just became accustomed to this same figure."

A GROWING IMAGE

Nast added new little details every Christmas: one year he showed Santa pouring over a list of naughty and nice children; another year showed him in a toy workshop in the North Pole.

Nast also went on to become the most famous *political* cartoonist of the 19th century—he's responsible for giving the Democratic Party its donkey and the Republican Party its elephant—but his Santa drawings are his best remembered works.

In fact, Nast almost singlehandedly established the Santa "image" as it is today…except in one major area: the color of his suit. That was a product of Coca-Cola.

You'd have to walk five miles to burn off the calories of a single hot fudge sundae.

SANTA'S HELPER: HADDON SUNDBLOM

In 1931, the Coca-Cola company hired an artist named Haddon Sundblom to create the artwork for a massive Christmas advertising campaign they were preparing.

Until then, the soda was primarily a summer drink, with sales dropping off sharply in the cooler winter months. Coke hoped to reverse this trend by somehow linking the drink to the winter holidays...and they decided the most effective way to do that would be to make Santa a Coke drinker. Sundblom was told to create a painting of Mr. Claus that the company could use in magazine advertisements.

Sundblom's first brainstorm was to dump Nast's black-and-white Santa suit in favor of one in Coca-Cola red and white. Then he managed to find a real-life retired Coca-Cola sales rep named Lou Prentice who looked so much like Santa that he could be used as a model. "Prior to the Sundblom illustrations," Mark Pendergrast writes in *For God, Country and Coca-Cola*, "the Christmas saint had been variously illustrated wearing blue, yellow, green, or red.... After the soft drink ads, Santa would forever more be a huge, fat, relentlessly happy man with broad belt and black hip boots—and he would wear Coca-Cola red....While Coca-Cola has had a subtle, pervasive influence on our culture, it has directly shaped the way we think of Santa."

SANTA'S HELPER: ROBERT MAY

More commercial influence: In 1939, Montgomery Ward hired ad man Robert May to write a Christmas poem that their department store Santas could give away during the holiday season.

He came up with one he called "Rollo the Red-Nosed Reindeer." Executives of the company accepted it, but didn't like the name Rollo. So May renamed the reindeer Reginald—the only name he could think of that preserved the poem's rhythm. Montgomery Ward rejected that name, too. Try as he might, May couldn't come up with another name that fit—until his four year-old daughter suggested *Rudolph*. The rest is history. When the poem was put to music and recorded by singing cowboy Gene Autry, it became the second-bestselling single in history.

What's happening with Santa today? Check out Part IV, p. 475.

15% of U.S. women say they send flowers to themselves on Valentine's Day.

RUMORS

Rumors are a special kind of gossip—outrageous stories that, one expert explains, "reveal the desires, fears, and obsessions of a society." They're also a lot of fun. Did you hear the one about...

THE RUMOR: Dr. Pepper's secret ingredient is prune juice.

HOW IT STARTED: Unknown, but it's been whispered for about 40 years. The company speculates that the combination of Dr. Pepper's unidentifiable "fruity taste" and the company's penchant for secrecy about the formula stimulates kids' imaginations.

WHAT HAPPENED: The company prepared a pamphlet, which they send out to people who ask about the ingredients. It says: "There are 23 flavors and other ingredients (none of which are prunes) that produce the inimitable taste of Dr. Pepper."

THE RUMOR: Mama Cass of the group The Mamas and the Papas, died by choking on a ham sandwich.

HOW IT STARTED: When the 220-pound Mama died suddenly in 1974, her doctor issued a quick statement speculating that "she probably choked on a sandwich."

WHAT HAPPENED: The bizarre report was picked up by the media, including *The New York Times*, and by *Rolling Stone* magazine, and was presented as fact. Actually, when the coroner's report was issued a week later, it gave the cause of death as a heart attack "brought on by obesity." Too late—the rumor was already circulating.

THE RUMOR: In the mid-'80s, three Midwestern women, visiting New York City for the first time, were on an elevator in their hotel. A large man with a big dog got on and hissed, "Sit, Lady." The terrified women immediately slid to the floor—whereupon the man informed them he was actually talking to his dog, Lady. The embarrassed women got up and contritely began asking about restaurants. They got the gentleman's recommendation for a good one, went, and enjoyed it. And when it came time to pay the bill, they were informed it had already been taken care of...by Reggie Jackson, the man they'd "met" in the elevator.

Henry Ford was the first billionaire in America.

HOW IT STARTED: Unknown, but the story was reported as fact all over the country, by newspapers in New York, L.A., Detroit, and Salt Lake City.

WHAT HAPPENED: A New York reporter finally called Jackson and asked him to confirm it. Jackson's reply: "I've heard that story a million times, and it's not true. I would never own a dog in New York. It would be cruel."

THE RUMOR: When Army brass was planning its 1983 invasion of Grenada, they decided they needed someone who could speak Spanish, to communicate with the Grenadian citizens. So they convinced a Spanish-speaking supply sergeant named Ontiveros to land with the first paratroopers. He jumped, came under fire, and spent the entire invasion morning shouting *'Qué pasa?'* at uncomprehending Grenadians. Finally, Sergeant Ontiveros realized that English—not Spanish—is the language spoken in Grenada.

HOW IT STARTED: It circulated extensively in the armed forces, "reflecting the feelings of enlisted soldiers toward the officers who had planned the invasion."

WHAT HAPPENED: A reporter checked the names listed on the invasion force and found there was no one named Ontiveros in it. An Army press officer added: "I don't doubt the story for a minute.…Except that it's not true."

THE RUMOR: "Sesame Street" is planning to "kill off" Ernie, the famous muppet of "Bert and Ernie" fame.

HOW IT STARTED: The Children's Television Workshop believes the rumor started somewhere in New England after the 1990 death of muppet creator Jim Henson—who was Ernie's voice. CTW denied the rumor, but it quickly gained strength; according to Ellen Morgenstern, CTW's spokeswoman, "We've also heard that Ernie was going to die of AIDS, leukemia, a car crash.… Someone in New Hampshire even started a letter-writing campaign to save him."

WHAT HAPPENED: "Sesame Street," the Children's Television Workshop, and PBS have repeatedly denied the story. As Morgenstern puts it, "Ernie's not dying of AIDS, he's not dying of leukemia. Ernie is a puppet."

It's estimated that you'll spend a year of your life looking for misplaced objects.

DINER LORE

As Richard Gutman said in American Diner: *"One nice thing about a diner is that anyone who shares American values and American ways of doing things...can function here."*

O RIGIN OF THE LUNCHWAGON
The year was 1872.
The city was Providence, Rhode Island.
Thousands of late-night factory workers had a problem—every restaurant in town closed promptly at 8:00 p.m., so they couldn't get anything to eat when their shifts let out.

The solution was provided by an enterprising pushcart peddler named Walter Scott. He outfitted a horse-drawn wagon with a stove and storage space and drove around the streets selling sandwiches, boiled eggs, and coffee for a nickel. The wagon only provided shelter for Scott—his customers had to stand out on the street. But it was a welcome service and an instant success. Before long, "after-hours lunchwagons" were operating all over town.

INDOOR SEATING

Fifteen years later, an enterprising worker named Sam Jones introduced the first custom-made walk-in lunchwagon, complete with a kitchen, a counter, and stools. It seated four to five people, and it was immediately successful. Walk-in lunchwagons became popular all over the Northeast; soon they were being made in factories.

THE DINER EVOLVES

By 1910 dozens of lunchwagons—many of them decrepit eyesores—were rumbling around the streets of most New England cities. Although city ordinances permitted them to operate only between dusk and dawn, many were staying on the streets until noon—which outraged many "respectable" citizens. Cities began cracking down on them, forcing the wagons off the streets by 10:00 a.m.

Lunchcart owners didn't like the idea of closing up when there was plenty of business around, so they came up with a way to skirt the rules—they simply picked good sites where they could set up

Some material brought back from the moon is 4.72 billion years old.

their lunchcarts permanently. Then they took off the wheels; hooked up to power, water, and gas lines; and expanded their kitchens. Now they were officially called "street cafes" and could operate all day and night. These were the original 24-hour diners.

DINER FACTS

• The term *diner* originated with manufacturer Patrick J. Tierney, who called his pre-fab early-1900s restaurants "dining cars." Salesmen shortened them to "diners."

• Tierney was proud that, in 1911, his company built the first diner with an indoor toilet.

• Contrary to popular belief, diners were never converted from railroad dining cars. Rather, in the late '30s, manufacturers were so impressed by the streamlined look of modern locomotives that they imitated the style. They called these diners "streamliners."

• Diners reflected technological advances. When, in the late '30s, materials like stainless steel, Naugahyde, and Formica became available, diner makers put them to use. So, what we call a "classic" diner was actually state of the art in its time.

• At their peak in the late '40s, there were some 7,000 diners. Today there are approximately 2,000.

DINER DIALOGUE (from the film *Five Easy Pieces*)

Jack Nicholson: I'd like a plain omelette—no potatoes on the plate—a cup of coffee, and a side order of wheat toast.

Waitress: I'm sorry, we don't have any side orders here.

Nicholson: No side orders? You've got bread...and a toaster of some kind?

Waitress: I don't make the rules.

Nicholson: Okay, I'll make it as easy for you as I can. I'd like an omelette—plain—a chicken salad sandwich on wheat toast—no mayonnaise, no butter, no lettuce, and a cup of coffee.

Waitress: A Number Two, chicken salad sandwich—no butter, no mayo, no lettuce, and a cup of coffee. Anything else?

Nicholson: Yeah. Now all you have to do is hold the chicken, bring me the toast, give me a check for the chicken salad sandwich, and you haven't broken any rules.

Waitress: You want me to hold the chicken, huh?

Nicholson: I want you to hold it between your knees.

DINER LINGO

Diner waitresses and short-order cooks have a language all their own—a sort of restaurant jazz, with clever variations on standard menu themes. Here's a little collection of some of the best.

Burn the British: Gimme an English muffin

Draw one in the Dark: A black coffee

Balloon juice: Seltzer

An M.D.: A Dr. Pepper

Hold the hail: No ice

Wreck 'em: Scrambled eggs

Sweep the kitchen: A plate of hash

Adam and Eve on a raft: Two poached eggs on toast

A spot with a twist: A cup of tea with lemon

Bossy in a bowl: Beef stew

A blonde with sand: Coffee with cream and sugar

Break it and Shake it: Add an egg to a drink

A stack of Vermont: Pancakes with maple syrup

Million on a platter: A plate of baked beans

A white cow: A vanilla milkshake

Let it walk: It's to go

Noah's boy on bread: A ham sandwich

A Murphy: A potato

Nervous pudding: Jello

Paint a bow-wow red: Gimme a hot dog with ketchup

Eve with a lid: A piece of apple pie

Burn one, take it through the garden, and pin a rose on it: Gimme a burger with lettuce and onion

Mike and Ike: Salt and pepper shakers

Angels on horseback: Oysters rolled in bacon and placed on toast

Cow paste: Butter

Lighthouse: Bottle of ketchup

Hounds on an island: Franks and beans

Frog sticks: French fries

Houseboat: A banana split

Wax: American cheese

Fry two, let the sun shine: Two fried eggs with unbroken yolks

Throw it in the mud: Add chocolate syrup

Hug one: Squeeze a glass of orange juice

Life preservers: Doughnuts

Put out the lights and cry: An order of liver and onions

One from the Alps: A Swiss cheese sandwich

Put a hat on it: Add ice cream

Splash of Red Noise: Bowl of tomato soup

Haircut hint: Thursday is the least busy day for barbershops.

THE "10 MOST WANTED"

*For a lot of folks, sneaking a peek at the posters of the FBI's
10 Most Wanted is as important a part of going to the post office
as buying stamps. If you're one of them, this chapter is for you.*

A SHOT IN THE DARK

In June 1932, the FBI moved in on John Dillinger and his gang—then the most notorious bank robbers in the country. Dillinger had broken out of prison and escaped in a stolen police car on March 3, 1934; three months later the FBI received a tip that he and his gang were hiding out in a lodge in Little Bohemia, Wisconsin. G-Men surrounded the lodge, and when three men came out of the building FBI agents opened fire. They killed one of the men and seriously injured the other two.

Unfortunately, the men the FBI shot weren't criminals—they were innocent bystanders, locals who had stopped by the lodge for a drink. Meanwhile, when Dillinger and his gang heard the shots, they escaped out the back window.

Public Error #1. The blunder created the biggest public relations disaster in FBI history. Because FBI director J. Edgar Hoover had alerted newspapers all over the country to Dillinger's "capture" in advance, they had plenty of room on their front pages for the story. They made the FBI look like idiots and murderers, a point that was driven home in most cases with banner headlines and photographs of the three innocent victims.

Eager to blunt criticism and put his own spin on the story, Hoover doubled the number of agents tracking Dillinger, increased the reward for his capture to $10,000, and, in a Bureau first, gave John Dillinger the title "Public Enemy Number One." The tactics paid off, and a month later the FBI redeemed itself when agents caught up with Dillinger and gunned him down.

AMERICA'S MOST WANTED

No one would have guessed it at the time, but in years to come, about the only thing people would remember of the debacle at Little Bohemia was the Public Enemy Number One label that

---

Sound travels five times faster under water than in air.

Hoover gave Dillinger. The FBI director didn't even invent the term; it had been circulating in newspaper circles for two years. According to Michael and Judy Ann Newton in their book *The FBI Most Wanted: An Encyclopedia*: "Throughout the 1930s, public enemies were named and numbered by the press, contenders moving up the ladder as their predecessors were consigned to the prison or the grave. With notoriety came nicknames—Scarface, Mad Dog, Pretty Boy—designed to make the headlines sing, surrounding thieves and killers with an air of romance and adventure."

The List Is Born. Hoover continued to use the term "Public Enemy," but he only applied it to one person at a time. Then, in 1949, a reporter for International News Service asked the Bureau for the names and descriptions of the "toughest guys" the bureau would like to capture. The FBI provided the information, and the news report generated so much positive press for the Bureau that Hoover turned it into an official and permanent list. On March 14, 1950, FBI's "10 Most Wanted Fugitives" list was born. First on the list: Thomas James Holden, a bank and train robber wanted for murdering his wife and her two brothers. He was arrested in June 1951 and died in prison two years later.

MAKING THE GRADE

The FBI uses two criteria to determine which federal criminals belong on its 10 Most Wanted Fugitives list:

1. The candidate has to be a "particularly dangerous menace to society." He (or she) has to have a long history of run-ins with the law. First-time offenders have to pose a special threat to public safety.

2. The FBI must be convinced that national publicity will help the case. If the fugitive's already well-known (like Patty Hearst or O. J. Simpson), or if the hunt is being conducted only in a particular part of the country, there's not much point in putting the person on the list, since national publicity either exists already or isn't needed.

FBI STATS

• According to the FBI, the average "10 Most Wanted" fugitive is a 36-year-old male who is 5'9" and weights 167 pounds. He will have traveled an average of 969 miles in his attempts to evade capture, and will be caught 157 days after his name is added to the Most Wanted list.

Note: Does that last statistic sound a little *too* impressive? Critics charge that during his tenure, J. Edgar Hoover "cooked the books" by only adding people whose capture the Bureau believed was imminent.

• What kind of criminals end up on the list? In the '50s, bank robbers, burglars, and—believe it or not—car thieves dominated the list; in the '60s it was antigovernment and anti-Vietnam radicals; and in the '70s it was terrorists and organized crime members. Since the early '80s the emphasis has been on serial murderers and other violent criminals.

• Until 1961, there were never more than 10 people on the list at any given time. Since then, however, the number has occasionally risen above 10 when circumstances warrant "special postings." The number peaked at 16 in October 1970, when radicals connected to university bombings and bank robberies were added to the list.

• *Where* a person is placed on the list is based strictly on seniority—you have to start at the bottom and work your way to the top. The only way to become *the* most wanted person in America is to evade capture longer than everyone else on the list. "Top Tenners," as the FBI calls them, have spent as little as 2 hours on the Most Wanted List before capture, and as long as 18 years, 4 months, and 9 days. That record goes to Charles Lee Herron, who was finally arrested in 1986 for the January 1968 murder of two police officers.

• The 10 Most Wanted List was an exclusively all-male club until 1968, when kidnapper Ruth Eisemann-Schier was added. She was caught two months later. Since then, fewer than 10 other women have been placed on the list.

• About a third of all Top Tenners are captured through tips from the public, which learns of the cases from the media and from FBI notices in post offices. According to Special Agent Jim Price, "We've had people turn *themselves* in because they kept seeing their picture everywhere."

Heavy fact: There are an estimated 5 1/2 million billion tons of air in the atmosphere.

FAMOUS (ANIMALS) FOR 15 MINUTES

When Andy Warhol said "In the future, everyone will be famous for 15 minutes," he obviously didn't have animals in mind. Yet, even they haven't been able to escape the relentless publicity machine that keeps cranking out instant celebrities. Luckily, it makes for entertaining bathroom reading.

THE HEADLINE: *Lost Cat Logs 30,000 Miles, but Denied Frequent Flyer Miles*

THE STAR: Tabitha, a cat owned by aspiring actress Carol Ann Timmel, 26, of Westchester County, New York

WHAT HAPPENED: In June 1994, Timmel checked two of her cats in as baggage for a Tower Air flight from New York to Los Angeles. But when she got off the plane in LA., there was only one cat left in the cage. The other one, a three-year-old named Tabitha, had escaped into the bowels of the plane during the flight.

Tower Air refused to ground the plane long enough for a thorough search—instead, it kept the plane in operation and had ground crews search the cargo hold at every stop. The plane logged more than 30,000 miles traveling between New York, Los Angeles, Miami, and San Juan, Puerto Rico, while Timmel sued to take the plane out of commission. Twelve days later she prevailed; the plane was grounded in New York for 24 hours while more than 100 Tower employees—aided by one psychic—scoured the plane looking for the cat. Timmel herself found the cat after she called out to it and it returned her calls. "The cat didn't look out of whack," one Tower employee told reporters. "It just looked like it needed a good dinner."

THE AFTERMATH: Timmell sold Tabitha's life story to a TV producer for $30,000...but her own acting career did not take off. At last report, she was working in a Los Angeles gardening store.

THE HEADLINE: *Mayor's Office Goes to the Dogs*

THE STAR: Bosco Ramos, a part Labrador-part Rottweiler living in Sunol, California

---

Snakes are immune to their own poison.

WHAT HAPPENED: The town of Sunol never had a city council or mayor…until 1980, when Tom Stillman overheard two town blowhards debating which of them could win an election for mayor. "He had about all he could stand of it," said town resident Kathy Anderson, "and one night he jumped up and said, 'My dog could beat you guys!' They campaigned for a month—Bosco ran under the slogan 'A bone in every dish, a cat in every tree, and a fireplug at every corner'—and when the dust settled, the dog had won. It wasn't even close."

Bosco was the first dog ever elected mayor of an American city.

THE AFTERMATH: Bosco was international news. In the People's Republic of China, for example, the *People's Daily* newspaper condemned him as a symbol of Capitalist decadence. It wrote:

> Western "democracy" has reached such a peak of perfection that not only can one talk of "democracy" between people, but "democracy" between dogs and people. There is no distinction between people and dogs.…Dressed in a shirt, trousers and tie, the dog goes to work every day.…When it opens its mouth it barks only "wong, wong." How can it deliberate at meetings of the mayor and decide big administrative strategies? No wonder some people prostrate themselves in worship of Western democracy.

Bosco ignored the criticism. He resigned from office in 1991, when his master moved to another town.

THE HEADLINE: *Give This Cat Some Credit—but Not That Much Credit*

THE STAR: Theo Theoklitos, a six-year-old black cat

WHAT HAPPENED: In October 1992, Theo's owner, Helen Krikris, sent in an application for a rebate on cat food. Somehow Theo ended up on a bunch of mailing lists and since then, he's received as much mail as his owner, including video club offers, credit card applications, and discount magazine subscriptions. (One flyer read, "So you think you're smarter than your cat?") He's even become a finalist in Ed McMahon's $10 million sweepstakes.

THE AFTERMATH: Newspapers all over the country picked up the tale of junk mail gone crazy. Meanwhile, Krikris decided she knew why Theo's so popular. "You know," Helen says, "these people who send him all this mail probably think he's a wealthy Greek shipping magnate because of his name."

FAMILIAR NAMES

Some people become famous because their names are
commonly associated with an item or activity. You
know the names—now here are the people.

Patrick Hooligan. A notorious hoodlum in mid-1800s London. His name became a generic term for "troublemaker."

Charles Mason and Jeremiah Dixon. English surveyors. In the 1760s, they were called in to settle a boundary dispute between two prominent colonial families—the Penns of Pennsylvania, and the Calverts of Maryland. A hundred years later, the line they laid out became the North/South border—the Mason-Dixon line.

Arnold Reuben. New York deli owner in the '40s and '50s. Put corned beef, sauerkraut, and Russian dressing on a piece of rye bread and named the whole thing after himself—the Reuben sandwich.

Alexander Graham Bell. Inventor of the telephone (1876). The standard measurement of sound intensity, the *decibel*, was named in his honor.

Sir Benjamin Hall. The "chief commissioner of works" for the British government in the 1850s, when the tower clock on the Houses of Parliament got its largest bell. Newspapers of the time dubbed it "Big Ben," after Hall.

Samuel A. Maverick. Texas cattle baron in the mid-1800s. Had so many unbranded stray calves they became known as *mavericks*. The term came to include independent-minded people as well.

Franz Anton Mesmer. An Austrian physician. Popularized outrageous medical theories on animal magnetism in Paris in the 1780s. He *mesmerized* the public.

Mr. Doily (or Doyley). A 17th-century London merchant whose first name has been forgotten. "He became prosperous," says *Webster's Dictionary*, "by selling various summer fabrics trimmed with embroidery or crochet work. Being a good businessman, he used up the remnants by making ornamental mats for tables, called *doilies*."

The state capital of Texas has been moved 15 times.

Madame de Pompadour. Mistress of King Louis XV of France in the mid-1700s. Popularized the hairstyle that reappeared, in modified form, on the heads of Elvis and James Dean.

William Beukel. A 14th-century Dutchman. Invented the process "by which we shrink and sour cucumbers." The result was originally called a *beckel* or *pekel*, after him. It eventually became known as a *pickle*.

Colonel E. G. Booz (or Booze). An 18th-century Philadelphia distiller who sold his Booz Whiskey in log cabin-shaped bottles. His product helped make the Old English term *booze* (from *bouse*, "to drink") slang for alcohol.

Archibald Campbell, Duke of Argyll. Powerful Scottish noble in the early 1700s. Had the Campbell clan tartan woven into his *argyle* socks.

Count Paul Stroganoff. A 19th-century Russian diplomat. He funded archaeological expeditions, supervised a Russian educational district, and ate huge amounts of the beef dish now named after him.

Adolphe Sax. A Belgian musical-instrument maker. In the early 1840s, he turned the music world on its ear with his invention, the *saxophone*.

Mr. and Mrs. Legrand Benedict. After complaining that there was nothing new being served by New York restaurants, this high-society couple cooked up the idea of *eggs benedict*.

John Montague. The fourth Earl of *Sandwich*. A compulsive gambler who would not leave any game to dine, he had his valet serve him a piece of cold meat placed between two slices of bread.

Captain Bo. A legendary English fighter. His exploits inspired other combatants, who used a variation of his name, *boo*, as a blood-curdling war cry.

James Thomas Brudenell. The seventh Earl of *Cardigan*. The button-up sweater is named after him.

Sam Ellis: A tavern keeper on what was later called Ellis Island.

The average drinking glass holds 50 teaspoons of water.

FABULOUS FLOPS

Next time you see the hype for some amazing "can't-miss" phenomenon, hold on to a healthy sense of skepticism by remembering these duds.

ESPERANTO

Glorious Prediction: "Where will Esperanto be tomorrow as a world language? (1) Everyone will *learn* Esperanto; (2) Everyone will *use* Esperanto; (3) It will be the international *neutral* language; and (4) It will be a major step toward *world peace and prosperity.*"

Background: Esperanto was created in 1887 by Lazarus Ludwig Zamenhof, an idealistic 28-year-old Polish ophthalmologist. According to one account, "Zamenhof's neighbors—Poles, Russians, Estonians, Latvians, and Germans, profoundly misunderstood and mistrusted each other in a multitude of tongues. It was his dream to fashion a new language they could share, and through which they could learn to coexist." Drawing on nearly all the romance languages, Zamenhof created a simplified, hybrid version with only 16 rules of grammar, no irregular verbs (English has 728), and words that could be changed from nouns to adjectives, adverbs, or verbs by changing the vowel at the end of the word. He published his language under the pseudonym Dr. Esperanto, which means "one who hopes."

What Happened: Despite more than 100 years of lobbying by Esperanto devotees, the language has never taken hold. Still, today there are thousands of Esperanto devotees organized into clubs in 100 countries around the world—including special-interest chapters for vegetarians and nudists.

THE COMET KAHOUTEK

Glorious Prediction: "Kahoutek will be the greatest sky show of the century, with a brilliance 50 times that of Halley's comet and a tail extending across a sixth of the sky." One Harvard astronomer even predicted that the comet's tail length "might reach 36 times the apparent diameter of the full moon."

Background: The comet, "a grimy lump of chemical ice some three

---

Toads don't have teeth. Frogs do.

miles in diameter" was discovered by German astronomer Lubos Kahoutek in 1973.

What Happened: Nothing. On January 15, 1974, the comet came as close to the earth as it would get in 80,000 years—and no one on Earth could see it. One astronomer described the spectacle as "a thrown egg, that missed." Where was Dr. Kahoutek? He and 1,692 other passengers were on the Queen Elizabeth 2, which had been specially chartered for the event. As *Newsweek* magazine put it, "The weather turned out rough and overcast, and Dr. Kahoutek spent much of the voyage too seasick to leave his cabin." Two weeks later the comet did emit a burst of explosive color—but by then it was so close to the sun that only three people saw it—the astronauts aboard Skylab.

THE WORLD FOOTBALL LEAGUE

Glorious Prediction: The WFL would become a successful alternative to the NFL by 1978. "The National Football League has grown arrogant and complacent," announced the WFL's founder in 1973. "The doors are open to a rival....The war is on!"

Background: In October 1973, Gary Davidson, a Newport Beach lawyer, announced he had formed the World Football League. The league started with 12 domestic teams but predicted that it would become the first international football league, with franchises in Tokyo, Madrid, London, Paris, and other cities within five years.

What Happened: The WFL went broke in its first season and collapsed 12 weeks into its second season more than $20 million in debt. Nearly all the teams in the league went bankrupt. The Florida franchise was so broke that the coach had to pay for the team's toilet paper out of his own pocket, and the Philadelphia team had to fire its cheerleaders because it couldn't come up with enough cash to pay them their $10-per-game salary.

But perhaps the worst embarrassment came after the 1974 championship "World Bowl" game between the Birmingham Americans and the Florida Blazers. Americans owner Bill Putnam owed the IRS money, and, according to *Sports Illustrated*, "After the game, sheriff's deputies moved right into the locker room to repossess the uniforms as soon as the champions took them off."

THE LONG & SHORT OF THINGS

Believe it or not, most of our traditional measurements have been more or less unchanged since the days of the Anglo-Saxons, who invaded England in the 5th and 6th centuries. The earliest form of the yard, for example, is only about 1/100 of an inch different from today's version. Here are some origins of our modern measurements.

The Inch. In its earliest form, the inch was the width of a grown man's thumb. In the 14th century, King Edward II of England decreed that "the length of an inch shall be equal to three grains of barley, dry and round, placed end to end lengthwise." This evolved into today's standard measurement.

The Foot. Originally the length of a person's foot (obviously), the foot was later standardized in English-speaking countries to be 12 inches long. In other parts of the world, however, it could be anywhere from 11 to 14 inches in length.

The Yard. Originally the standard length of the belt that Anglo-Saxons wore. In the early 1100s, King Henry I of England decreed that a yard would be the distance from his nose to the thumb of his outstretched arm, which came to about 36 inches.

The Mile. A descendant of the ancient Roman measure called the *mille passuum*, which meant "a thousand paces." Each pace was the equivalent of 5 Roman feet, which meant there were 5,000 feet to the mile. Today there are 5,280 feet to the mile. Why the extra feet? Because when the English incorporated the mile into their system of measurement, they wanted it to be equal to 8 *furlongs*. A furlong—originally defined as the distance a horse could pull a plow without resting—was exactly 660 feet long, so the English multiplied 660 by 8 to get 5,280. (Why didn't they just knock some feet off the furlong and keep the mile a tidy 5,000 feet long? Because property was measured in furlongs—and changing the furlong would have screwed up every property holding in the kingdom.)

The Ton. No one knows for sure where the ton comes from. One

Singer Wayne Newton is a descendant of Pocahontas.

theory: It is descended from the *tun*, a large cask that was used to hold wine. (What's half a ton called? A *kip*, short for *kilo pound*—one thousand pounds.)

The Gallon. Comes from the ancient Gallic word for "bowl."

The Quart. Short for "quarter gallon."

THE METRIC SYSTEM

In the years following the French Revolution of 1789, the French Republic tried to make a clean break from the past by inventing a new form of government, new names for the seasons, a new calendar with new names for all of the days and months, and other such innovations. Over the next 30 years most of these reforms fell by the wayside, but one of them didn't—the metric system.

Unlike traditional systems of measurement, the metric system actually made *sense*—it was a decimal system and so used multiples of ten, and there were direct relationships between the units of length, weight, and capacity.

The Meter. Originally intended to be exactly one ten-millionth the length of the distance between the North Pole and the equator. The only problem: measuring instruments weren't precise enough to measure such a vast distance accurately, so the length that was chosen for the meter turned out to be the wrong one. By the time scientists discovered this, however, the meter's length—39.37 inches—was so widely accepted that they decided not to change it.

Liters, Kilograms and Grams. Once the scientists designing the metric system settled on the length of the meter, they used it to create measurements for mass and volume. They designed a cube with each side exactly one-tenth of a meter (a *decimeter*) long, and filled it with water. The space that the water filled was designated as a *liter*, and the amount the water weighed was called a *kilogram*, which was then subdivided into 1,000 units called *grams*.

NOTE: One reason the metric system caught on with scientists was that in the traditional measurement system, there were no standard units smaller than an inch or larger than a mile, which made it tough to measure extremely large and extremely small distances. With the metric system, it was much easier to invent new measurements when they became necessary.

THE JEEP STORY

Are you a four-wheel-drive fanatic? Here's a story you'll like. It's about the vehicle that General George Marshall called "this country's most important contribution to World War II."

BACKGROUND
The U.S. Army of 1939 wasn't much like the one that won World War II six years later. Convinced that World War I had been "the war to end all wars," the U.S. government had cut military spending to the bone during the '30s. The Army wasn't even *close* to bringing American troops into the automobile age at that time. In fact, there weren't enough vehicles to transport troops to the front lines. If the United States had gotten involved in a military action, most soldiers would have gone into battle either on foot or on *horseback*.

The problem drove officers nuts, particularly as another war in Europe began to look inevitable. "The humblest citizen rides proudly and swiftly to his work in his Model T or his shivering Chevrolet," one colonel complained to his superiors in 1940. "The infantryman alone, sole contemporary of the sodden coolie or the plodding Hindu, carries the supplies and implements of his trade upon his stooping back or loads them upon two-wheeled carts drawn by himself or by a harassed and hesitating mule."

THE CAR WARS
The Army finally began to address the problem in 1940, when it drew up specifications for a zippy, four-wheel-drive "low-silhouette scout car" large enough to carry four men and low enough to dodge enemy fire. It sent the specs to 135 different manufacturers, insisting that the vehicle weigh no more than 1,300 pounds and stand no taller than three feet high with its windshield folded down over the hood. Only two companies expressed interest: American Bantam of Butler, Pennsylvania, and Willys-Overland of Toledo, Ohio. Only American Bantam submitted a prototype to the military for testing.

The Army liked the American Bantam model, but worried that the company, which had only 15 employees and no assembly plant, was too small to manufacture the hundreds of thousands of vehicles that would be needed. So it scheduled a special "field test" of the American Bantam prototype, invited engineers from Willys-Overland and Ford Motor Company to stop by as "observers"... and passed out the vehicle's blueprints to everyone who attended. The competition took the hint, and a few months later Ford and Willys-Overland delivered "remarkably similar" vehicles of their own. Willys-Overland won the contract. Later, when production demands outstripped even Willys-Overland's production capacity, Ford agreed to build the vehicle in its own factories. American Bantam spent the rest of the war building truck trailers and torpedo motors.

THE NAME GAME

When the first jeeps rolled off the assembly lines in 1941, they were known as "G.P.s," short for "general purpose." But they came to be known by other nicknames, including beetle bug, blitz buggy, Leaping Lena, beep, peep, and puddle jumper. Jeep was the one that stuck, not only because of the vehicle's initials but because of the 1930s *Popeye* cartoon character Jeep, who was "neither fowl nor beast, but knew all the answers and could do most anything."

The new vehicle was a hit, because *it* could do almost anything, too. As *Smithsonian* magazine put it, "Mounted with a machine gun, it became not just a means of transport, but a combat vehicle....They plowed snow and delivered mail to foxholes at the front. Their engines powered searchlights, their wheels agitated washtubs....With a special waterproofing kit, jeeps crawled through water up to their hoods....The Army ordered an amphibious jeep (the seep) and a lightweight jeep for air drops (the fleep)."

COMING HOME

The jeep was so popular that when the war ended, Willys-Overland trademarked the jeep as a Jeep (after a lengthy court battle with Ford) and began manufacturing models for the domestic market. But in the 1940s and 1950s, the public wanted big, luxurious cars. Jeep sales stayed sluggish until the 1970s. Then, for some reason, they began to pick up—and have kept growing. In fact, in the '80s, Chrysler bought American Motors just to get the Jeep line.

In the 1993-1994 model year, Americans bought over 1.4 million jeep-type vehicles—more than twice as many as were built during *all* of World War II.

M*A*S*H

*"M*A*S*H" was the first comedy on television to deal directly with the ugly facts of war, as well as the funny ones. The American public responded by making it one of the most popular programs in the history of the medium.*

HOW IT STARTED

When Richard Hornberger (pen name: Richard Hooker) completed the memoirs of his days with the 8055th MASH unit in Korea, he hardly expected he'd have a bestseller on his hands. And for the next eight years, his expectations were borne out—by rejection slips. He couldn't even get it published.

Finally, in 1968, after securing a partner to polish up the manuscript, M*A*S*H was published by William Morrow and Co. Initially the book was a flop. But it caught the eye of Ingo Preminger (Otto's brother), who bought the movie rights and commissioned a screenplay (adapted by Ring Lardner, Jr.). Directed by Robert Altman and starring Eliot Gould and Donald Sutherland, M*A*S*H was a phenomenal success—which caused M*A*S*H (the book) to become a surprise bestseller. 20th Century Fox elected to further capitalize on the movie by creating a low-budget television pilot using sets and props from the film.

When CBS decided to give the series a shot (or at least finance a pilot), nothing had been written yet. So producer Gene Reynolds called his friend Larry Gelbart in England and asked for a script. Gelbart whipped one out in two days.

"M*A*S*H" (the TV show) premiered in September 1972 to low ratings and poor reviews. But CBS didn't lose faith. It allowed the show to struggle through its first season and, in an unusual act of foresight, kept it going into the next season—when it became a hit.

INSIDE FACTS

Just the Facts. More than half of the "M*A*S*H" storylines were the product of painstaking research. Larry Gelbart worked with photocopies of '50s issues of *Time* magazine and kept a master list of Korean names, a map of Korea, and an Army handbook on his desk.

Ladies' Man. Alan Alda's support of the feminist movement is a tribute to Sister Elizabeth Kenney, whose cure for infantile paralysis (discovered during World War I) wasn't recognized by the male-dominated medical profession for nearly 20 years. The application of her theories cured Alda's childhood case of polio.

The Real Thing. The model for the "M*A*S*H" 4077th was the 8055th. In real life, the 8055th had a staff of 10 doctors and 12 nurses, and treated roughly 200 patients at a time.

Star Trouble. Wayne Rogers signed on as "Trapper " John McIntyre, after being promised he would costar equally with Alan Alda. But when his role was downplayed in favor of Alda's Hawkeye Pierce, he quit. McLean Stevenson, who played Lt. Col. Henry Blake from 1972 to 1975, left after 3 years because he was annoyed by the primitive facilities at the show's outdoor set. The producers got their revenge; they made sure he could never return to the show by having Blake's plane crash as he headed back to the U.S.

Funnier Than Fiction. Many of the episodes were based on stories purchased from Korean War MASH unit veterans.

Right Flank. Richard Hornberger (author of the book *M*A*S*H*) is actually a conservative Republican who fashioned Hawkeye after himself (real hometown: Crabapple Cove, Maine)—and didn't like the way Alda portrayed him at all. In fact, he was offended by the anti-war message of the show.

Korea or Vietnam? Make no mistake—the apparent anti-Vietnam bent of the early "M*A*S*H" wasn't coincidental. It was specifically written that way. Reynolds and Gelbart managed to air a weekly vilification of U.S. involvement in Southeast Asia by pre-dating it 20 years. Neat trick.

The Set. "M*A*S*H" outdoor scenes were shot at the 20th Century Fox Ranch (now Malibu Canyon State Park). But most of the footage was shot at Fox Studios, where the "M*A*S*H" compound measured only 45 by 90 feet, and came complete with a Korean landscape backdrop and a *rubber* floor!

The elephant is the only animal with four knees.

MORE VICTIMS OF CIRCUMSTANCE

*More examples of how it's sometimes impossible
to win—no matter how hard you try.*

THE FORD AEROSTAR

Background: In August 1985, the Ford Motor Company launched the Ford Aerostar minivan with a multimillion-dollar advertising campaign comparing it to the Space Shuttle. TV commercials showed the Shuttle swooping down and dissolving into an Aerostar; print ads showed the Shuttle and the Aerostar sitting side by side on a runway. Ford faced tough competition from Chrysler's popular minivans. Everything was riding on the Space Shuttle ads.

Unforeseen Circumstance: On January 28, 1986, the Space Shuttle Challenger exploded, killing everyone on board. It was the worst accident in NASA history; the entire nation was rocked.

Outcome: Within 24 hours, Ford decided to abandon the entire ad campaign. The van's most distinguishing feature, its resemblance to the Space Shuttle, was quietly ignored and never used in advertising again, and the vans never sold as well as Chrysler's.

GLENYS MORGAN and GEORGE PEARSON

Background: Morgan and Pearson were teachers at Oakwood Park Grammar School in Maidstone, England. In 1995, Pearson told some students to take an instructional videotape from a cupboard and view it in the next room. The boys inadvertently took one from a pile of blank tapes instead.

Unforeseen Circumstance: The tape wasn't blank. When the students popped the cassette into the VCR, they were astonished to see that it was a film of Mr. Pearson and Ms. Morgan engaging in "extracurricular activities." The English tabloid *The Daily Mirror* described the scene:

> The students watched amazed as naked physics teacher Glenys Morgan stood lashed to wall bars by two purple and blue school ties. Chemistry master and fifth form head George Pearson is heard to say on the tape: "This has always been a fantasy of mine." Later in

---

Before 1850, most golf balls were stuffed with feathers.

the film, Mr. Pearson strips off down to his T-shirt and the couple make passionate love on a gym bench.

Morgan and Pearson apparently didn't even know the tape existed. The school's principal explained: "The two had been bringing equipment back to school during the holiday after doing some filming of a mountaineering trip. I think the video camera was accidentally left running, and they didn't realize it when the situation became rather intimate....Subsequently the tape ended up back in the cupboard with all the blank videotapes, and lay there in the dust for eight years."

Outcome: The two teachers were suspended from their positions. And the school got a number of requests for a copy of the tape.

ARTHUR DOLLISON

Background: Arthur Dollison graduated from college in 1929, just as the Stock Market crashed and the Great Depression began. Work was scarce, so he took the only job he could find—as a guard in the federal prison system.

He worked his way up, and in 1961 he was promoted to the prestigious position of associate warden of Alcatraz. Eighteen months later, Warden Olin Blackwell decided to take a brief vacation and Dollison became "acting" warden of Alcatraz.

Unforeseen Circumstance: For months, three convicts had been digging out of their cells, using spoons they'd stolen from the cafeteria. They finally broke open a vent duct leading to the roof on June 10, 1962—the day Warden Blackwell went on vacation. And in the early morning hours of June 11—just as Dollison took over as warden—they escaped. Guards didn't realize they were missing until 7:20 the next morning, which gave them a 10-hour lead.

Outcome: The breakout, the largest (and most embarrassing) in Alcatraz's history, completely destroyed the prison's "escape-proof" reputation. And the subsequent FBI manhunt, the largest since the Lindbergh baby kidnapping, turned up nothing.

An official investigation cleared Dollison of any blame, but he never lived down his record as the "One-Day Warden" of Alcatraz. He was transferred to the minimum security prison at Seagoville, Texas, in what has been called "an unofficial way to show disfavor," and spent the rest of his career there.

UNCLE JOHN'S "CREATIVE TEACHING AWARDS"

At the BRI, we think it's important to salute teachers who are willing to take a creative approach to education. That's why we're happy to announce our first annual Creative Teaching Awards.

SUBJECT: Athletics
WINNER: Dale Christensen, coach of the Libertyville High School football team in Libertyville, Illinois
APPROACH: In 1994, Christensen had two students stage a fake fight at a pep talk before a game against the rival Libertyville Wildcats. Then he pretended to intervene, and during the scuffle secretly pulled out a starter's pistol, shot himself with a blank round... then fell to the ground as if he'd been hit by real bullets.

A few minutes later he got up—his chest drenched with the fake blood he'd hidden under his shirt—and announced that the whole thing had been a "motivational skit" to get the team ready for the game. Unfortunately, someone had already fled the room and called the police. Three cruisers were speeding to the scene.

REACTION: "Most of us were scared out of our minds," one team member told reporters. Christensen, mystified by the controversy his actions generated, resigned a few days later. As the school superintendent put it, "Mr. Christensen believes people outside the football team don't understand what he was trying to accomplish."

SUBJECT: Language
WINNER: Richard Ehret, Latin instructor in two Toledo, Ohio junior high schools in the early '90s
APPROACH: Trying to put some life into a dead language, Ehret taught his seventh-graders unconventional Latin phrases such as "Your fly is open," and "I'd like to by some condoms."
REACTION: Parents weren't amused. When confronted, Ehret explained that when he was hired, school officials encouraged him to use "outside materials" and that he had taken the phrases from a book he'd bought. Ehret was suspended for 10 days without pay.

The hippopotamus has skin that's two inches thick in some places.

SUBJECT: Mathematics

WINNER: Charles Routen, a math teacher at the inner-city May Elementary School in Chicago

APPROACH: In May 1994, a colleague showed Routon a mock math quiz that had been circulating around the country for months.

The questions involved drug dealing, prostitution, and car theft. For example:

> Johnny can get $150 for a stolen Chevrolet, $250 for a stolen Jeep, and $600 for a stolen BMW. How many Jeeps will Johnny have to steal to pay for a $1,200 packet of uncut cocaine?

and

> If Benny's AK-47 uses 20-round clips, how many times will he have to reload to pump 150 rounds into a gang rival?

Routen was inspired. He made copies of the quiz, passed it out to his class of 11 to 13-year-olds, and had them answer it.

REACTION: Routen was temporarily suspended and then transferred to a desk job "away from children." He later resigned.

SUBJECT: History

WINNER: Sharon Naugler, teacher at Riverport District Elementary School in Nova Scotia, Canada

APPROACH: In November 1994, Naugler decided to teach a lesson about the Holocaust by having her five-year-old students act it out. Dark-haired children were assigned the part of the Jews; fair-haired children played Nazis. "The scenario," said one news report, "called for the Nazis to send the Jews to the gas chamber and burn their bodies afterward."

REACTION: Parents complained that "it was a bit much for five-year-olds to handle." Naugler, who had been teaching young children for more than 20 years, was suspended without pay for four days.

SUBJECT: Sex Education

WINNERS: Chris Derham and Susan Hogan of the Holly Lodge High School near Birmingham, England

APPROACH: In July 1994, some Holly Lodge students were wandering the school grounds near the faculty offices when they heard

---

The telephone was invented in 1876; the telephone *booth* was patented in 1883.

some strange noises coming from one of the rooms. So they peeked through a gap in the window curtains and saw Mr. Derham and Ms. Hogan—both of whom were marred to other people—making passionate love on the floor. Word quickly spread, and more than 30 students witnessed the spectacle. "The two teachers had locked themselves in and were completely naked," one 15-year-old giggled to reporters. "They thought no one could see them, but some third- and fourth-year students peeked in and caught them hard at it."

REACTION: Hogan resigned some two weeks after the incident; Derham quit a few days after that. "The school has lost two staff who have given very good service," schoolmaster John Caine said of their departures.

SUBJECT: Citizenship

WINNERS: Florence Gilliam, a teacher at Winchester Elementary School near Memphis, Tennessee; and LaGretta Walker, a counselor at the same school

APPROACH: Gilliam and Walker were supervising a special dance rewarding students for good behavior when they started arguing about how to dismiss the event. Walker wanted students to stop and gather at the back door; Gilliam told her students to keep walking. The two teachers worked their differences out by "pushing, pulling, and hitting" each other. A third teacher stepped in to break up the fight as other faculty members led the astonished students out of the building.

REACTION: Gilliam was suspended without pay for six months for "conduct unbecoming a teacher," and Walker "exercised her option to retire," school officials said. "It's pretty obvious to everybody that's not the kind of message we want to send to children."

Runner-Up: Reverend Kenneth Humphreys, a minister and music teacher at Henry County High School in Paris, Tennessee

In 1994, while planning the school's annual Christmas pageant, Humphreys got into an argument about the music selection with band director Martin Paschall. Displaying true Christmas spirit, he threw a chair at Paschall and hit him in the face and chest—breaking a rib, severely injuring his lip, and knocking out several teeth. Humphreys was suspended without pay for two months and later pled guilty to assault charges. The Christmas pageant was cancelled.

The American robin isn't a robin. It's a thrush.

LILY TOMLIN SAYS...

Comments from a great comedienne.

"No matter how cynical you get, it's impossible to keep up."

"There will be sex after death; we just won't be able to feel it."

"The trouble with the rat race is that even if you win, you're still a rat."

"For fast-acting relief, try slowing down."

"If truth is beauty, how come no one has their hair done in the library?"

"Why is it when we talk to God, we're said to be praying— but when God talks to us, we're schizophrenic?"

"If you read a lot of books, you're considered well-read. But if you watch a lot of TV, you're not considered well-viewed."

"The best mind-altering drug is truth."

"If something's true, you don't have to believe in it."

"You are what you think.... Geez, that's frightening."

"Sometimes I worry about being a success in a mediocre world."

"I had a friend who was getting married. I gave her a subscription to *Modern Bride*. The subscription lasted longer than the marriage."

"If love is the answer, could you rephrase the question?"

"What most distinguishes us humans from lower animals is our desire to take drugs."

"Sometimes I feel like a figment of my own imagination."

"We're all in this alone."

What goes up must come down...but don't expect it to land where you can find it— Murphy's Law applied to Newton's.

"Our ability to delude ourselves may be an important survival tool."

THE MONOPOLY STORY

*If there was ever a way to introduce kids to capitalism, Monopoly is it.
It's the bestselling board game in history—and has been published
in 28 countries and 19 different languages. But who invented it?
No one is sure. The answer you get depends on whom you ask.*

OFFICIAL ORIGIN

According to Parker Brothers, Monopoly was invented by a man named Charles Darrow in the 1920s. Darrow—an engineer by trade—created the game after the stock market crash of 1929, when he found himself unemployed and short of cash, like the rest of the country. To kill time (and keep his spirits up), he devised a game involving "plenty of money for the player to invest or speculate with." Because he was interested in real estate, he made buying land the primary focus...and because he personally didn't believe in credit or borrowing money, he made the whole thing a cash proposition.

Takin' It to the Streets

Darrow had visited Atlantic City shortly before the stock market crashed, so he transferred his fond memories of the town to the board. That's why the Boardwalk, railroad lines, and streets of the New Jersey resort are represented there.

Passing Go

The original version of the game was crudely painted on a piece of linoleum. But that didn't stop family and friends from getting hooked on it—and demanding their own sets. "I hadn't anything better to do, so I began to make more of the games," Darrow explained. "I charged people $4 a copy." Although Darrow did no advertising, he soon began to receive orders from all over the country. He was shocked but excited. Looking for more distribution, he took the game to Parker Brothers...and was turned down cold. Says one historian: "George and Charles Parker thought Monopoly took much too long to play, the rules were hopelessly complicated, and there were at least 52 other weak points they believed ruled the game out. Darrow was upset by the decision, but decided to distribute Monopoly on his own. He took it to two major retailers—Wanamaker's in Philadelphia, and FAO Schwartz, New York's most prestigious toy store—and convinced them to stock his game. When both stores quickly sold their entire stock, the Parker brothers reconsidered. They purchased the rights to Monopoly...and watched, astounded, as it sold as fast as they could make it. Ironically, Monopoly actually kept their toy company—which was on the edge of insolvency—from going bankrupt.

By mid-February 1935, Parker Brothers was selling more than 20,000 sets of Monopoly a week. Darrow, as one would imagine, was financially set for life. And the reluctant toy company had its hands on the most lucrative game in the history of the toy industry.

THE REAL STORY?

Did Darrow really invent the game that he sold to Parker Brothers? Possibly not. In recent years, the Monopoly "legend" has been discredited during a long, bitter legal fight between Parker Brothers and Ralph Anspach, maker of a game called "Anti-Monopoly." Take these facts, for example:

• In 1904—roughly 15 years before Darrow "invented" his game— a Chicago woman named Elizabeth Magie-Phillips patented "The Landlord's Game," a board game that included the purchasing of property, utilities and a "public park" space.

• She wasn't alone—there were at least eight different groups that played Monopoly-like games before Darrow, including one at Harvard Law School and another at a utopian community in Arden, Delaware.

• There's evidence that Darrow may have learned his version of the game from a group of Quakers in Atlantic City, possibly adding only Chance cards and the Railroads as original contributions.

• What was the *real* reason Parker Brothers rejected Darrow's game in the 1920s? One theory: There were so many versions of Monopoly floating around that the company knew it could not legally claim ownership of a game that was already in the "public domain."

• But Darrow's game sold so well, the theory goes, that the Parker brothers changed their minds, bought the rights to his version—as well as to all other known versions of the game—and then spread the story of Darrow's "invention" of the game in order to claim exclusive rights to it. It's a great conspiracy story, but we'll probably never know if it's true.

Walter Cronkite is a college dropout; Peter Jennings is a high school dropout.

Q & A:
ASK THE EXPERTS

Everyone's got a question or two they want answered—basic stuff like "Why is the sky blue?" Here are a few of those questions, with answers from books by some top trivia experts.

NAVEL ENCOUNTER

Q: *Where does belly button lint come from?*

A: "Your navel is one of the few places on your body where perspiration has a chance to accumulate before evaporating. Lint from your clothing, cottons especially, adheres to the wet area and remains after the moisture departs." (From *The Straight Dope*, by Cecil Adams)

INFLATED WITH PRIDE

Q: *Why is Chicago called the windy city?*

A: Chicago is pretty windy (with a 10.3-mph wind average), but that's not where the nickname comes from. It comes from the 1893 Chicago World's Columbia Exposition—which was supposed to commemorate the 400th anniversary of Columbus's "discovery" of the New World, but ended up being used by city politicos to hype Chicago. "So boastful and overblown were the local politicians' claims about the exposition and the city that a New York City newspaper editor, Charles A. Dana, nicknamed Chicago 'the windy city.' " (From *The Book of Totally Useless Information*, by Don Voorhees)

CIRCULAR LOGIC

Q: *Why do clocks run clockwise?*

A: No one knows for sure, but here's one answer: "Before the advent of clocks, we used sundials. In the Northern Hemisphere, the shadows rotated in the direction we now call 'clockwise.' The clock hands were built to mimic the natural movements of the sun. If clocks had been invented in the Southern Hemisphere, [perhaps] 'clockwise' would be in the opposite direction." (From *Why Do Clocks Run Clockwise, and Other Imponderables*, by David Feldman)

Top 5 new car colors in 1994: White, green, red, black, and teal.

ON THE SPOT

Q: *What causes freckles?*

A: "Except in the case of albinos, every person's skin has cells called *melanocytes*, which produce a certain amount of *melanin*, a dark pigment that absorbs ultraviolet light. These cells produce melanin at increasing rates when the skin is exposed to sunlight—hence the sunbather's tan. Some melanocytes are more active than others. Thus when groups of active melanocytes are surrounded by groups of less active melanocytes, the results are islands of pigment known as freckles." (From *Do Elephants Swim?*, by Robert M. Jones)

STAYING COOL

Q: *Does iced tea or iced coffee really cool you off?*

A: "Contrary to popular belief, neither iced tea nor iced coffee will really cool you off much because they contain caffeine, which constricts the blood vessels. Because of this effect, coffee or tea, either iced or hot, can cause you to become overheated...so it's best to avoid these drinks on hot days. But don't substitute a cola drink for them; colas also contain caffeine. Instead, drink water or juice." (From *FYI, For Your Information*, by Hal Linden)

GONE TO THE DOGS

Q: *Is a dog year really the equivalent of seven human years?*

A: "No—it is actually five to six years. The average life expectancy of a dog is 12-14 years. However, most dogs mature sexually within six to nine months, so in a sense there is no strict correspondence to human years." (From *The Book of Answers*, by Barbara Berliner)

TO PEE OR NOT TO PEE?

Q: *Why does people's pee smell funny after they eat asparagus?*

A: "The odor is caused by an acid present in the vegetable, and it doesn't happen to everybody. Whether you produce the odor or not is determined genetically." In a British study using 800 volunteers, only 43% of the people "had the characteristic ability to excrete the 6 sulfur alkyl compounds that combine to produce the odor in urine. This inherited ability is a dominant trait. If one of your parents had it, so will you." (From *Why Do Men Have Nipples?*, by Katherine Dunn)

What is the richest country on the planet? Lichtenstein.

THE LATEST THING

Nothing is sacred in the bathroom—go ahead and admit that you owned a pet rock or a mood ring (we understand...confession is good for the soul). And while you're pondering your follies, we'll tell you where they came from.

PAC-MAN. A Japanese import that hit American shores in late 1980, Pac-Man got its name from the word *paku*, which means "eat" in Japanese. The video game was so popular that Pac-Man was named *Time* magazine's "man" of the year in 1982. That year, Americans pumped $6 *billion* worth of quarters into Pac-Man's mouth, more than they spent in Las Vegas casinos and movie theatres combined.

MOOD RINGS. The temperature-sensitive jewelry that supposedly read your emotions, Mood Rings were the brainchild of Joshua Reynolds, a New Age heir to the R. J. Reynolds tobacco fortune. Reynolds envisioned them as "portable biofeedback aids" and managed to sell $1 million worth of them in a three-month period in 1975. Even so, the company went bankrupt—but not before it inspired a hoard of imitators, including "mood panties" (underwear studded with temperature-sensitive plastic hearts).

PET ROCKS. One night in 1975, an out-of-work advertising executive named Gary Dahl was hanging out in a bar listening to his friends complain about their pets. It gave him an idea for the perfect "pet": a rock. He spent the next two weeks writing the *Pet Rock Training Manual*, which included instructions for housetraining the rock. ("Place it on some old newspapers. The rock will know what the paper is for and will require no further instructions.") He had a friend design a box shaped like a pet carrying case—complete with air holes and a bed of straw—and then filled them with rocks he bought from a builder's supply store for a penny apiece. The Pet Rock debuted in August 1975, selling for $3.95; by the end of October, Dahl was shipping 10,000 a day. The fad encouraged a host of imitations as well as an entire Pet Rock service industry, including dude ranches, hair-care products, and burials-at-sea. The fad died the following year.

Coca-Cola was originally green.

EARTH SHOES. Earth Shoes were one of the bestselling shoes of the 1970s. Invented by a Danish shoe designer named Anne Kalsø, they were brought to the United States in 1969 by a woman who discovered them on a trip to Europe. She claimed they cured her back pains, but foot experts argued that the shoes—which forced wearers to walk on the backs of their feet—were actually pretty bad for you. One study found that most wearers suffered "severe pain and cramping for the first two weeks of wear"; another expert predicted that the shoes would "cripple everyone who wears them." Still, they were a counterculture hit, and thousands of pairs a year were sold in their peak. The original Earth Shoes company went bankrupt in 1977, a victim of cheap knockoffs and changing times.

COATS OF ARMS. In the '60s, anyone with $20 could send away for a crest corresponding to their last name. At the fad's peak in 1969, status-seeking Americans spent $5 million a year displaying their "crests" on sport coats, ashtrays, bank checks, etc. Elitists were outraged. "People of good taste," one blue-blood sniffed, "don't use a coat of arms they're not entitled to." But by the early 1970s, just about everyone had a crest—which defeated the purpose of having one in the first place. The fad died soon afterward.

SMILEY FACES. Introduced in 1969 by N. G. Slater, a New York button manufacturer. At first, sales were slow, but by the spring of 1971 more than 20 million buttons had been sold—enough for one in every ten Americans—making it a craze as popular as the Hula Hoop of the 1950s. Pop-culture pundits called it the "peace symbol of the seventies," and presidential candidate George McGovern adopted it as his campaign logo. The fad died out after about a year, but in the mid-'70s made a comeback—this time colored yellow and bearing the cheerful message, "Have a Happy Day!" By the late 1970s, however, Americans were completely sick of it.

Smiley Face Update

"Attorneys for a convicted killer asked yesterday that his death sentence be overturned because a judge signed the July 15, 1993, execution order with a 'happy face' sketch....The judge has said that he always signs his name that way as a symbol of his faith in God and that he does not plan to change it."

—The Associated Press

There are roughly 50 female professional boxers in the United States.

VONNEGUT SAYS...

*A few thoughts from Uncle John's favorite
writer, novelist Kurt Vonnegut, Jr.*

"What passes for culture in my head is really a bunch of commercials."

"Laughing or crying is what a human being does when there's nothing else he can do."

"It strikes me as gruesome and comical that in our culture we have an expectation that a man can always solve his problems. This is so untrue that it makes me want to laugh—or cry."

"People don't come to church for preachments, of course, but to daydream about God."

"The canary bird in the coal mine theory of the arts: artists should be treasured as alarm systems."

"People need good lies. There are too many bad ones."

"Thinking doesn't seem to help very much. The human brain is too high-powered to have many practical uses in this particular universe."

"We are healthy only to the extent that our ideas are humane."

"Beware of the man who works hard to learn something, learns it, then finds himself no wiser than before."

"Any reviewer who expresses rage and loathing for a novel is preposterous. He or she is like a person who has put on full armor and attacked a hot fudge sundae."

"I can think of no more stirring symbol of man's humanity to man than a fire engine."

"There is no reason why good cannot triumph as often as evil. The triumph of anything is a matter of organization. If there are such things as angels, I hope they are organized along the lines of the Mafia."

"Say what you will about the sweet miracle of unquestioning faith. I consider a capacity for it terrifying."

"We are what we pretend to be."

HOW PANTYHOSE HATCHED

Today, you can find pantyhose in every supermarket, clothes store, department store, and drugstore. Surprisingly, they've only been around since the mid-'60s.

In the early '60s, women were still wearing traditional stockings with garter belts, as they had since 1939, when DuPont introduced nylons.

But as the miniskirt caught on, stockings became impossible to wear. Whenever a woman sat down, the tops of her stockings showed. It was embarrassing. But what could she do instead?

Hosiery manufacturers looked desperately for a solution to the problem. They tried all kinds of bizarre things—stocking glue (roll it onto the top of your leg, and the stocking will stick there—no garters needed), decorating the tops of the stockings (so it looked like they were meant to be seen), even girdles with stockings already attached. The only alternative that really made sense was a new kind of sheer tights called pantyhose. But they were much more expensive than stockings. Would women pay for them?

Enter Mary Quant, the creator of the miniskirt. She added patterns to tights and—accompanied by a huge publicity campaign—introduced them as an integral part of the miniskirt outfit. It was not only the solution to embarrassing stocking problems, she said, but an essential element of the "mini-look." Since it was in fashion, woman gladly paid the price.

Once the market for pantyhose was established, manufacturers developed ways to cut prices. Soon, undecorated pantyhose were cheaper than traditional stockings, and—since they were more convenient—they quickly replaced the old-fashioned kind. By the early '70s, 95 percent of all women's hosiery sold was pantyhose.

FASHION FLOP. In the mid-'60s, Coty tried cashing in on the colored pantyhose craze by offering "Body Paint." Why bother wearing expensive pantyhose, they asked, when you can color your legs? The "mini, kicky, bare-as-you-dare fashion" was packaged in a paint can and came complete with a roller and paint tray. There were four colors: blue, green, mauve, and "flesh." It bombed.

Ashes to ashes: 20% of Americans are cremated when they die.

LAST WISHES

You've got plenty of time in the bathroom for thinking. So here's something to ponder: What's the one special thing you'd want to be sure took place after you died? To give you ideas, we've provided a few well-known people's last requests.

Eleanor Roosevelt: Fearful of being buried alive, the former first lady requested that her major veins be severed to eliminate the possibility of regaining consciousness after burial.

Harry Houdini: The famous escape artist asked to be buried in the "trick" coffin he used in his magic act—with letters from his mother tucked beneath his head.

William Shakespeare: Wanted his oldest daughter, Susanna, to inherit his favorite bed. He left his wife "my second best bed."

President Andrew Johnson: The president who came closest to impeachment asked to be wrapped in an American flag, with a copy of the U.S. Constitution placed beneath his head.

J. Paul Getty: Requested a burial on the property of the Getty Museum in Malibu. However, his lawyers never applied for burial permits, so his remains had to be refrigerated and stored in a nearby mausoleum for *three years* until the necessary paperwork was completed. (Getty left his son J. Paul, Jr. "the sum of $500, and nothing else.")

W. C. Fields: Wanted a portion of his estate to be used for a "W. C. Fields College for orphan *white* boys and girls." (The request was never honored.)

P. T. Barnum: Wanted to keep the Barnum name from dying with him…so he left his grandson, Clinton Seeley, $25,000—on the condition that he change his middle name to Barnum. Seeley did.

Janis Joplin: Asked friends to have a farewell party for her at her favorite pub, the Lion's Share, in California—and left $2,500 in her will to finance it.

Albert Einstein: No one knows what his last wishes were. On his deathbed, he said something in German to his nurse—but she didn't speak German.

THE BASEBALL MYTH

According to traditional baseball lore, our national pastime was invented by Abner Doubleday, in Cooperstown, New York. Was it? Not even close. Here's the story.

THE MISSION

At the turn of the century, baseball was becoming a popular pastime...and a booming business. Albert G. Spalding, a wealthy sporting goods dealer, realized that the American public would be more loyal to a sport that had its origins in the U.S. than one with roots in Europe. So it became his mission to sell baseball to Americans as an entirely American game.

THE COMMISSION

In 1905, Spalding created the Special Baseball Commission to establish the origin of baseball "in some comprehensive and authoritative way, *for all time*." He appointed six cronies to serve on it: Alfred J. Reach, head of another sporting goods company; A. G. Mills, the third president of the National League; Morgan G. Bulkeley, first president of the National League; George Wright, a businessman; and Arthur P. Gorman, a senator who died before the study was completed. James Sullivan, president of an amateur athletic union, functioned as secretary for the commission.

In 1907, the commission issued its report, which it called "The Official Baseball Guide of 1906-1907." One member, A. G. Mills, declared confidently that it "should forever set at rest the question as to the origin of baseball." But the truth was, they had done almost no research. Their files contained just three letters—one from Henry Chadwick, an Englishman who had helped popularize baseball; one from Spalding himself; and one from James Ward, a friend and supporter of Spalding.

THE "ROUNDERS CONTINGENT"

In his letter, Chadwick pointed out the obvious similarities between baseball and a game called "rounders," a popular sport in England as well as colonial America. Rounders was played on a diamond with a base on each corner. A "striker" with a bat would stand beside the fourth base and try to hit balls thrown by a "pecker." If he hit the ball fair, the striker could earn a run by "rounding" the bases. If the striker missed the ball three times, or if his hit was caught before touching the ground, he was "out." After a certain number of outs, the offensive and defensive teams switched. Ring a bell? It didn't with Spalding and his men. The commission, which selected Chadwick's letter to represent the "rounder's contingent," quickly dismissed it, because Chadwick was born in England.

THE "AMERICAN CONTINGENT"

In deference to Spalding, James Ward supported the theory of American origin, though his letter stated that "all exact information upon the origin of Base-Ball must, in the very nature of things, be unobtainable." His testimony amounted to no more than a friendly opinion.

In his own letter, Spalding argued vehemently that baseball had been created by Abner Doubleday in 1839 in Cooperstown, New York. "The game of Base-Ball," he said, "is entirely of American origin, and has no relation to, or connection with, any game of any other country." On what evidence did he base this argument? On the letter of a mystery man named Abner Graves, a mining engineer from Denver, who, Spalding said, recalled Doubleday inventing the game 68 years earlier (Graves was over 80 years old when he gave his account).

CREATING HISTORY

In his report, Spalding stated that Graves "was present when Doubleday first outlined with a stick in the dirt the present diamond-shaped field Base-Ball field, including the location of the players on the field, and afterward saw him make a diagram of the field, with a crude pencil on paper, memorandum of the rules of his new game, which he named 'Base Ball.' "

However, none of this romantic imagery was actually in the Graves letter—no stick and no "crude pencil diagram of the rules." Spalding made the whole thing up. Nor was Graves present at the first game, as Spalding claimed. Graves stated in his letter, "I do not know, nor is it possible to know, on what spot the first game was played according to Doubleday's plan." Graves's letter simply recounted the rules of the game and how he thought Doubleday "improved" an *already existing game* called "Town Ball." Spalding cleverly embellished and promoted the old miner's tale to make it the stuff of legends.

Heavy thought: The Great Pyramid in Egypt weighs an estimated 6.6 million tons.

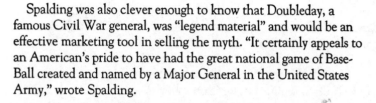

Spalding was also clever enough to know that Doubleday, a famous Civil War general, was "legend material" and would be an effective marketing tool in selling the myth. "It certainly appeals to an American's pride to have had the great national game of Base-Ball created and named by a Major General in the United States Army," wrote Spalding.

DOUBLEDAY AND BASEBALL

The fact is, no record anywhere associated Doubleday with baseball before 1905. Circumstantial evidence indicates that the Baseball Hall of Fame in Cooperstown should probably be somewhere else.

✓ Doubleday entered West Point on September 1, 1838, and was never in Cooperstown in 1839.

✓ Doubleday's obituary in *The New York Times* on January 28, 1893, didn't mention a thing about baseball.

✓ Doubleday was a writer, but never wrote about the sport he supposedly invented. In a letter about his sporting life, Doubleday reminisced, "In my outdoor sports, I was addicted to topographical work, and even as a boy amused myself by making maps of the country." No mention of baseball.

★ ★ ★

Just Say "No-Hit"

From 1968 to 1979, Dock Ellis pitched for the Pittsburgh Pirates, New York Yankees, Oakland Athletics, Texas Rangers, and New York Mets. He won 138 games and played in two World Series, but his biggest achievement was the no-hitter he pitched as a Pittsburgh Pirate on June 12, 1970. Fourteen years later, Ellis revealed that he'd accomplished this feat while under the influence of LSD.

Apparently, Ellis took the dose at noon—then realized he had to pitch at 6:05 p.m. that night. "I thought it was an off-day," Ellis explained to the *Pittsburgh Press* in 1984. Despite the powerful effects of the LSD, Ellis pitched brilliantly for nine innings. "I can only remember bits and pieces of the game," Ellis later recounted. "I was psyched. I had a feeling of euphoria." According to one source, Ellis believed the ball was talking to him, telling him what pitches to throw. Ellis didn't dare admit what he'd done, and never pitched on psychedelics again. Years later, he was treated for drug dependency and became the coordinator of an antidrug program in L.A.

THE GUMBY STORY

He's the "Clayboy of the Western World," an American icon.
But what does he stand for, and where did he come from?

A STAR IS BORN. Gumby was created in the mid-'50s by Art Clokey, a filmmaker who had learned stop-motion animation (film is shot one frame at a time, and the inanimate subject is moved between shots) at the University of Southern California, working with a world-famous expert.

• After graduating, Clokey experimented with his stop-motion techniques in an art film he called *Gumbasia*. The stars of the film were geometric clay forms ("It was cheaper than getting actors") that metamorphized to the rhythm of a jazz soundtrack.

• Clokey took *Gumbasia* to a Hollywood producer, hoping to make feature films. Instead, the producer decided Clokey ought to make a kids' television show. He put up the money for a pilot, and Clokey created the star—a clay character named Gumby. NBC then commissioned several six-minute films.

• Gumby made his first appearance on "The Howdy Doody Show" in 1956. In March 1957 he got his own NBC program.

• Beginning in 1958, "The Adventures of Gumby" was offered as a syndicated show. By the mid-'60s, Gumby was everywhere.

GUMBY: PERSONAL DATA

• His name comes from a type of sticky clay soil found in Michigan, known as "gumbo."

• The shape of his head was inspired by a photo of Clokey's father. In it, the senior Clokey had a cowlick that looked to his son like "the bump of wisdom that Buddhists have." So Clokey passed it on to Gumby.

• According to Clokey: "His green color represents the chlorophyll found in plants, while his bluish tint reflects the sky. He's got his feet on the ground and his head in the sky."

• His pal, Pokey, is orange because, says Clokey, "Pokey represents the critical, doubting, more earthy side of life."

• His television voice was supplied by Dick Beals. Pokey's voice was supplied by Clokey himself.

In 1913, the income tax on $4,000 was 1¢.

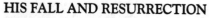

HIS FALL AND RESURRECTION

Gumby's popularity lasted through the '60s and into the early '70s. But by the late '70s, he was washed up; TV stations had dropped the show, and toymakers had stopped manufacturing Gumby toys.

• Art Clokey was nearly broke. His house was about to be foreclosed on, and the new toy product in which he had invested heavily—something called Moody Rudy—was proving to be a bomb. Worse, his daughter had recently been killed in a car accident. Life was not going his way.

• In 1979, Clokey went to Hong Kong to take a look at the Moody Rudy manufacturing facilities. While he was there, he decided to visit Satya Sai Baba, an Indian holy man he'd once seen in a film.

• As one writer describes it: "On that day in 1979, Clokey and his wife, Gloria, were among the faithful hundreds sitting outside Bab's ashram, awaiting a glimpse of the Master. Once or twice a day Baba would make the rounds, pouring ash from his hand onto objects that the devout held up to be blessed: books, photographs, religious statues. That afternoon, Sai Baba found Clokey in the lotus position, holding a small likeness of Gumby. Ash poured forth from his hand onto Gumby's sloping head, and the master moved on. 'Then I went home,' says Clokey, 'and things began happening.' "

THE GUMBY REVIVAL

• It started at the Pasadena Art Center, where Clokey gave a talk on animation. The Gumbyphiles who attended enjoyed it so much that they set up some screenings of Gumby films (remember, it was pre-video, and they hadn't been on television for years) in the auditorium of the Beverly Hills Library.

• The screenings were sold out for two weeks—which prompted the owners of a chain of movie theaters to send Clokey around the country, appearing with his Gumby films. He was a hit everywhere.

• Inspired by the Gumby revival, a couple of cadets painted a Gumby sign and flew it during the 1980 Army-Navy football game. This, in turn, was spotted by the producer of "Saturday Night Live," who decided it would be a kick to dress Eddie Murphy in a Gumby suit. Suddenly Gumby was a star again.

• Clokey is clear about who's responsible for his turn in fortunes—Satya Sai Baba. "He's the epitome of cosmic creation in human form," he explains. "He taught me that Gumby is me, and since we're all alike, Gumby is everyone."

So far, 11 presidents have been military generals.

THE SPACE RACE, PART II

Here are more details about how Neil Armstrong (and others) got to the moon. Part I is on page 160.

TO THE MOON

The decision to put a man on the moon was as much a product of superpower rivalry as was the space program itself. The largest concept in NASA's plan was a circumlunar flight, but scientists could not guarantee that the U.S. could beat the Russians to it. Their technology was too advanced. But a manned lunar landing would be an equal challenge to both nations. America had a long way to go—up to that point, the entire U.S. manned space program had consisted of a single 15-minute flight into space by Alan Shepard.

President Kennedy accepted the challenge and on May 25, 1961, announced to a joint session of Congress, "This nation should commit itself to achieving the goal, before this decade is out, of landing a man on the moon and returning him safely to the Earth."

ORGANIZING THE EFFORT

The American space effort was divided into three programs:

• **The Mercury Program (1961-1963),** which would put a man in orbit around the Earth to find out whether humans could survive in space (many scientists believed that people could not live long in weightlessness), and if returning space capsules could be recovered.

• **The Gemini Program (1963-1966),** two-man missions that included practice space walks, space docking maneuvers, and other activities that would be needed in a trip to the moon.

• **The Apollo Program (1966-1972),** the big enchilada—putting a man on the moon and bringing him safely back home.

THE APOLLO FLIGHTS

The first manned flight of the Apollo program, Apollo 7, was launched on October 11, 1968. The Apollo 7 astronauts spent 11

The housefly's tastebuds are in its feet.

days orbiting the Earth to make sure that the ship could handle the rigors of space travel. The next four missions moved progressively closer to the ultimate goal: Apollo 8 orbited the moon without landing; Apollo 9 tested the Lunar Module (LM) in Earth orbit; and Apollo 10 tested the LM in lunar orbit.

The Landing
On July 16, 1969, Apollo 11 blasted off from Cape Kennedy and headed toward the moon, arriving four days later on July 20. While Michael Collins orbited the moon in the Command Module (CM) *Columbia,* astronauts Neil Armstrong and Buzz Aldrin climbed into the Lunar Module *Eagle* for the trip to the lunar surface. They landed on the moon at 4:17 p.m. Eastern daylight time. At 10:56 p.m., Neil Armstrong took his historic first steps.

Buzz Aldrin followed a few minutes later, and together the astronauts unfurled the American flag. They erected scientific equipment, took photographs and soil samples, and spent a total of 2 hours, 13 minutes outside the Lunar Module. Then they climbed back in the module, returned to *Columbia,* and headed back to Earth, splashing down on July 24, 1969.

FALLING TO EARTH

With the moon landing, the United States was clearly the winner of the Space Race and interest in the space effort began to wane. Continued spending on the space program seemed almost frivolous when we were fighting poverty and crime in the streets—not to mention the Vietnam War—here on Earth.

As public support declined, so did political support: Congress scrubbed Apollos 18, 19, and 20 following the near-fatal disaster of Apollo 13, when an oxygen tank overheated and exploded on the way to the moon. Apollos 14, 15, and 16 went off as scheduled, as did Apollo 17, the last trip to the moon, which took place in December 1972. It was followed in July 1975 by the Apollo-Soyuz Project, in which U.S. and Soviet space capsules docked in Earth orbit. After that, NASA turned its attention to unmanned space probes and the Space Shuttle, which made its first flight in 1981. The first golden era of the U.S. space program had drawn to a close.

Identical twins always have the same blood type.

STAR BUCKS

• The U.S. space program was one of the most expensive public works projects ever undertaken. It cost an estimated $30 *billion* 1969 dollars to pay for the Mercury, Gemini, and Apollo space programs. At its peak, space was Florida's third largest industry after tourism and citrus fruit.

• The astronauts actually took a pay *cut* when they traveled in space. Neil Armstrong, for example, saw his pay reduced from $16 a day to $4 a day during the Apollo 11 flight. Reason: While in space he was considered to have been "housed and fed at government expense."

THE SPACE SUITS

• The Mercury space suits were little more than cotton underwear covered by a plastic suit, which was itself covered by an outer suit made of aluminized nylon, and leather gloves and boots. Each Mercury suit cost about $4,000.

• The Apollo space suits were much more complicated. Designers added 18 layers to the original suit—17 for strength and insulation to protect against the sun's heat, and a layer of felt to absorb the impact of micrometeoroids. Each Apollo suit was made of 1,050 individual components, weighed 60 pounds (the life-support system the astronauts carried on their backs weighed an additional 100 pounds), and cost about $100,000 in 1968 dollars. The suits were heavy, but that didn't matter—they would be completely weightless in space and would weigh only about 27 pounds on the moon.

THE ROCKETS

• The Saturn V rocket that put men on the moon was a marvel in its own right: it stood 36 stories tall, had 91 different engines and 8 million moving parts, and weighed as much as a Navy destroyer.

• With its engines roaring at full blast during the 2 minutes and 40 seconds of liftoff, the Saturn V consumed 559,218 gallons of liquid oxygen and kerosene—roughly 3,500 gallons a *second*.

• Building the Saturn V was no piece of cake: an estimated 300,000 workers and 20,000 companies worked on the rockets, which cost as much $355 million (in 1969 dollars) apiece. The rockets were so complicated—and the risk of problems during flight so great—that all suppliers to the Apollo program (numbering 40,000 people) were kept on call during the Apollo flights.

• On January 13, 1920, *The New York Times* criticized Professor Robert Goddard, considered the father of space exploration, for theorizing that a rocket could function in the vacuum of outer space. "He seems only to lack the knowledge ladled out daily in high schools," it said at the time.

The paper changed its position as Apollo 11 headed toward the moon in 1969: "It is now definitely established that a rocket can function in a vacuum. The *Times* regrets the error."

BITS AND PIECES

• Astronaut Alan Shepard was asked what thoughts ran through his mind as he waited for the countdown that would send him into space. "I just kept looking around me, remembering that everything in the capsule was supplied by the lowest bidder," he replied.

• Dr. Sidney Schwartz, a scientist with the Grumman Corp., thought he had a viable alternative to stocking backup food supplies on a space mission: making the space capsules edible. He baked a mixture of flour, corn starch, powdered milk, banana flakes, and hominy grits in a hydraulic press at 400°F under 3,000 pounds of pressure. The result was a slab as hard as tempered masonite. He figured the stuff could be used to build shelves and cabinets aboard space capsules, so that astronauts could eat their way out of crisis if necessary. NASA didn't bite.

• Spacecraft names were chosen by the astronauts. Alan Shepard's *Freedom 7* capsule started the tradition of giving all of the Mercury rockets a "7" in honor of the 7 Mercury astronauts. John Glenn's two children picked the name *Friendship 7*. The Apollo 10 mission called its lunar and command modules the *Charlie Brown* and the *Snoopy*, which did not impress NASA officials. They strongly suggested to Neil Armstrong that he pick something more dignified for the Apollo 11 modules, so he chose the *Columbia* and the *Eagle*.

• Since the U.S. is the only country ever to land on the moon, why isn't the moon considered U.S. territory? Because the U.S. waived any claim to the moon when it signed the Treaty on Exploration and Use of Outer Space in 1967. The treaty established the lunar surface as the property of all humankind.

COLD FOODS

*This title doesn't really mean anything. We had a bunch of stories
about food we wanted to use, and "cold" was the only thing
we could think of that these foods have in common.*

SWANSON TV DINNERS. When Carl Swanson stepped off
the boat from Sweden in 1896, the only thing he owned was
the sign around his neck, which read, "Carl Swanson, Swedish. Send me to Omaha. I speak no English." Someone sent him to
Omaha, where he started a grocery wholesale business that grew
into the largest turkey processor in the United States. When his
sons took over the company after his death, they began expanding
their product line beyond turkeys. One of their first additions: frozen turkey and fried-chicken meals they called "TV dinners," packaged in wood-grain boxes that looked like televisions. (Swanson
never intended that the meals be eaten while watching TV—it just
wanted customers to associate its "heat-and-eat miracle" with the
magic of television.)

Swanson's first TV dinners bombed. The sweet potatoes in the
turkey dinner were too watery, and customers complained that
the fried chicken tasted like bananas—a problem caused by slow-drying, banana-scented yellow die that leached from the cardboard
box onto the chicken. Swanson fixed the first problem by switching to regular potatoes; it solved the chicken problem by giving the
boxes a longer time to dry. (What did it do with the chicken that
had already been contaminated? It sold it to a Florida food chain
that said its customers preferred the "new" banana taste.)

ESKIMO PIES. Christian Nelson owned a candy and ice cream
store in Onawa, Iowa. One day in 1920, a kid came into the store
and ordered a candy bar…and then changed his mind and asked for
an ice-cream sandwich…and then changed his mind again and
asked for a marshmallow nut bar. Nelson wondered for a minute
why there wasn't any one candy-and-ice cream bar to satisfy all of
the kid's cravings—and then decided to make one himself: a vanilla bar coated with a chocolate shell. Once he figured out how to
make the chocolate stick to the ice cream, he had to think of a
name for his product. At a dinner party, someone suggested

In Kentucky, it's illegal to marry your wife's grandmother.

"Eskimo," because it sounded cold. But other people thought it sounded too exotic—so Nelson added the word "pie."

MINUTE MAID ORANGE JUICE. In 1942, the U.S. Army announced it would award a $750,000 contract to any company that could produce an orange juice "powder" cheap enough to send to troops overseas. After three years of intense research, the National Research Corporation (NRC) developed a way to concentrate and freeze orange juice powder, and was working out the bugs in the drying process. It won the contract—but just as it was lining up the financing for an orange juice plant, the U.S. dropped the A-bomb on Hiroshima, and World War II came to an end.

Convinced that powdered orange juice had a future, the NRC decided to forge ahead with its efforts to perfect the drying process. To raise money for the research, the company decided to unload some of its backlog of frozen concentrated orange juice. Marketed under the name Minute Maid, the stuff sold so well that NRC went into the frozen orange juice business instead.

ICE CREAM MISCELLANY

Ice Cream Sodas. In 1874, soda-fountain operator Robert M. Green sold a drink he made out of sweet cream, syrup, and carbonated soda water. One day he ran out of cream…so he used vanilla ice cream instead.

Ice Cream Sundaes. It seems ridiculous now, but in the 1890s, many religious leaders objected to people drinking ice cream sodas on Sunday. It was too frivolous. When "blue laws" were passed prohibiting the sale of the sodas, ice-cream parlor owners fought back—they created the "Sunday," which was only sold on the Sabbath; it contained all of the ingredients of a soda *except* the soda water. A few years later the dish was being sold all week, so the name was changed to *sundae*.

Baskin-Robbins 31 Flavors. After World War II, Irvine Robbins and Burton Baskin built a chain of ice cream stores in Southern California. One day in 1953, Robbins says, "we told our advertising agency about our great variety of flavors and we said, almost in jest, that we had a flavor for every day of the month—thirty-one. They hit the table and said that was it, the thirty-one. So we changed the name of the company to Baskin Robbins 31. Like Heinz 57."

A camel can drink 25 gallons of water in half an hour.

INNOVATIONS
IN YOUR HOME

*You probably have some of these products around
the house. Here's how they were created.*

COPPERTONE SUNTAN LOTION
Background: In the early part of the 20th century, suntans were the mark of the lower classes—only laborers who worked in the sun, like field hands, had them. But as beaches became more popular and bathing suits began revealing more skin, styles changed. Suntans became a status symbol that subtly demonstrated that a person was part of the leisure class.

Innovation: The first suntan lotion was invented in the 1940s by Dr. Benjamin Green, a physician who'd helped develop a petroleum-based sunblock for the military to protect soldiers from the sun. After the war, Green became convinced that civilians would buy a milder version of his product—one that protected them from the sun while letting them tan. He called his lotion Coppertone, because it produced a copper-colored tan on the people who used it.

RUNNING SHOES WITH "WAFFLE" SOLES
Background: In the late 1950s, Phil Knight was a track star at the University of Oregon. His coach, Bill Bowerman, was obsessed with designing lightweight shoes for his runners. "He figured carrying one extra ounce for a mile," Knight recalls, "was equivalent to carrying an extra thousand pounds in the last fifty yards."

When Knight began his graduate work at the Stanford Business School, he wrote a research paper arguing that lightweight running shoes could be manufactured cheaply in Japan and sold at a low price in the United States. Then he actually went to Japan and signed a distribution deal with a Japanese shoe company called Tiger. He and Bowerman each invested $500 to buy merchandise, and the Blue Ribbon Sports Company (later Nike) was founded.

Innovation: Bowerman developed Nike shoes to meet runners' needs. *Swoosh: The Story of Nike* describes the origin of the celebrated "waffle" shoe: "It occurred to Bowerman to make spikes out of

It would take 7 billion particles of fog to fill a teaspoon.

rubber....One morning while his wife was at church, Bowerman sat at the kitchen table staring at an open waffle iron he had seen hundreds of times. But now, for some reason, what he saw in the familiar pattern was square spikes. Square spikes could give traction to cross-country runners sliding down wet, muddy hills.

"Excited, Bowerman took out a mixture of liquid urethane... poured it into about every other hole of the waffle iron in...just the right pattern, and closed the lid to let it cook. Legend had it that he opened the waffle iron and there was the waffle sole that became Nike's first signature shoe. But what really happened that morning is that when he went to open the smelly mess, the waffle iron was bonded shut....[He] switched to a plaster mold after that."

THERMOS JUGS

Background: In the 1890s, British physicist Sir James Dewar invented a glass, vacuum-walled flask that kept liquids hot longer than any other container in existence. Dewar never patented his invention, however; he considered it his gift to the scientific world.

Innovation: Reinhold Burger, a German glass blower whose company manufactured the flasks, saw their potential as a consumer product. Dewar's creations were too fragile for home use, so Burger built a sturdier version, with a shock-resistant metal exterior. He patented his design in 1903 and held a contest to find a name for the product. The contest was more of a publicity stunt than anything else, but Burger liked one entry so much that he used it: "Thermos," after the Greek word for heat.

S.O.S. SOAP PADS

Background: In 1917, Edwin W. Cox was peddling aluminum cookware door to door in San Francisco. He wasn't making many sales, though; aluminum cookware was a new invention, and few housewives would even look at it.

Innovation: In desperation, Cox began offering a free gift to any housewife who'd listen to his presentation—a steel-wool soap pad he made in his own kitchen by repeatedly soaking plain steel-wool pads in soapy water. (His wife used them in their own kitchen and loved them; she called them "S.O.S." pads, meaning Save Our Saucepans.) The gimmick worked—sort of. Housewives still weren't interested in the cookware, but they loved the soap pads. Eventually he dropped pots and pans and began selling soap pads full-time.

FAMILIAR PHRASES

We use these phrases all the time, but most of us have no idea where they come from. Well, don't worry—the BRI has the answers.

STEAL SOMEONE'S THUNDER
Meaning: To preempt; to draw attention away from someone else's achievements in favor of your own.
Origin: English dramatist John Dennis invented a gadget for imitating the sound of thunder and introduced it in a play in the early 1700s. The play flopped. Soon after, Dennis noted that another play in the same theater was using his sound-effects device. He angrily exclaimed, "That is my thunder, by God; the villains will play my thunder, but not my play." The story got around London, and the phrase grew out of it.

PAY THROUGH THE NOSE
Meaning: To pay a high price; to pay dearly.
Origin: Comes from ninth-century Ireland. When the Danes conquered the Irish, they imposed an exorbitant Nose Tax on the island's inhabitants. They took a census (by counting noses) and levied oppressive sums on their victims, forcing them to pay by threatening to have their noses actually slit. Paying the tax was "paying through the nose."

HAPPY AS A CLAM
Meaning: Blissfully happy; perfectly content.
Origin: The original phrase was, "happy as a clam at high tide." Why at high tide? Because people can't dig clams then. They're "safe and happy" until low tide, when their breeding grounds are exposed. The saying was shortened through use.

CHARLEY HORSE
Meaning: A muscle cramp.
Origin: In 1640, Charles I of England expanded the London police force. The new recruits were nicknamed "Charleys." There wasn't enough money to provide the new police with horses, so they patrolled on foot. They joked that their sore feet and legs came from riding "Charley's horse."

Reindeer milk has five times as much fat as cow milk.

PRIMETIME PROVERBS

TV comments about everyday life. From Primetime
Proverbs, *by Jack Mingo and John Javna.*

ON DOCTORS:

Henry Blake: "I was never very good with my hands."

Radar O'Reilly: "Guess that's why you became a surgeon, huh, Sir?"

—*M*A*S*H*

Sophia: "How come so many doctors are Jewish?"

Jewish Doctor: "Because their mothers are."

—*The Golden Girls*

ON GOD:

"It's funny the way some people's name just suits the business they're in. Like God's name is just *perfect* for God."

—Edith Bunker,
All in the Family

ON FRIENDS:

"I've never felt closer to a group of people. Not even in the portable johns of Woodstock."

—Reverend Jim Ignatowski,
Taxi

"A friend, I am told, is worth more than pure gold."

—*Popeye*

ON GREED:

"Oh, yes indeed, it doesn't pay to be greedy."

—Popeye,
The Popeye Cartoon Show

Robin [*anguished*]: "The Batdiamond!"

Batman: "What about it, Robin?"

Robin: "To think it's the cause of all this trouble!"

Batman: "People call it many things, old chum: passion, lust, desire, avarice....But the simplest and most understandable word is greed."

—*Batman*

ON SEX:

Sam Malone: "I thought you weren't going to call me stupid now that we're being intimate."

Diane Chambers: "No, I said I wasn't going to call you stupid *while* we were being intimate."

—*Cheers*

ON DEATH:

"Death is just nature's way of telling you, 'Hey, you're not alive anymore.' "

—Bull,
Night Court

Alvin the Chipmunk's favorite food was "Jello with a hot dog in it."

THE LEGEND OF BIGFOOT

Ever been to Humbolt County, California? It's considered the marijuana
capital of the state, as well as the birthplace of the Bigfoot legend.
(Who knows, maybe these two facts are somehow related...)

BIGFOOT
One afternoon in October 1958, a logger named Jerry Crew was bulldozing a logging road in the woods of Humbolt County, California...when he discovered what he claimed was a set of enormous, humanlike footprints in the mud. Crew and his team later said they'd seen similar tracks for a number of weeks—but for some reason, this time they decided to make a plaster cast of one of the prints. Not knowing what kind of animal could have made it, Crew nicknamed the animal "Bigfoot."

It was an historic moment. A new creature was about to take its place alongside the Loch Ness monster and aliens from outer space in the pantheon of tabloid mythology.

HISTORY

Actually, legends of Bigfoot-like creatures have been a part of Native American tradition for centuries. In fact, they're a part of native folklore all over the world. The Yeti, or Abominable Snowman, which supposedly lives in the Himalayas, is the most famous example, but there are numerous others, including the Orang-Dalam of Malaysia, the Agogues of East Africa, the Duendi of the Colombian Andes, and the Almasty of the Caucasus in the former Soviet Union. But it wasn't until Crew emerged from the forests of California with his plaster footprint that America began taking the legends seriously.

Crew's "sighting" was reported in newspapers around the country...and was followed by dozens of other sightings. It became such a phenomenon that the local chamber of commerce started selling plaster replicas of Bigfoot footprints. Indeed, Humbolt County turned itself into the self-described "Bigfoot Capital of the World," complete with annual Bigfoot parades, Bigfoot softball tournaments, Bigfoot barbecues, a Bride of Bigfoot beauty contest, and a statue of Bigfoot located downtown in Bigfoot Square. Bigfoot believers complain that all the hoopla is undermining the serious side of the Bigfoot experience. "People come in here and tell the most ridiculous stories," says Al Hodgson, a Humbolt County variety store owner and discoverer of a set of Bigfoot tracks in 1963. "One woman insisted she went up there and fed him grapes."

"THE FILM"

If it had had to survive on footprints alone, the Bigfoot legend might have died out. But in 1967, Bigfoot enthusiast Roger Patterson came forward with a remarkable story: While searching on horseback for Bigfoot in Bluff Creek Valley in Northern California, he had stumbled onto a female Bigfoot near a dried streambed. Patterson had a movie camera with him at the time, he said, and he had filmed the entire encounter.

What the film purports to show is astonishing: it appears to be a female Bigfoot walking in the distance. Suddenly the creature turns toward the camera, sees it, then turns away and strides into the forest at an unhurried pace. In his book *Bigfoot: The Yeti and Sasquatch in Myth and Reality*, anthropologist John Napier describes its appearance:

> Physically the creature was heavily built, particularly around the chest and shoulders; the trunk was chunky with hardly a change in width from shoulders to hips. The whole body was covered in short, dark reddish-brown hair. The top of the head was somewhat conical and flowed into the trunk without the interruption of a neck. The face was bare and, as far as far as could be seen, dark in color.

"The Film," as serious enthusiasts call it, quickly became the backbone of the Bigfoot movement, a real piece of physical evidence. Even so, Napier and others suspect that it was faked. Reason: The size and depth of the footprints taken at the site are huge—the kind an animal about eight feet tall would make—but the distance *between* the individual prints is, on average, only 41 inches, easily within the stride of a man of average height, provided that he "strode out" or exaggerated his steps to make them as far apart as possible.

THE BOTTOM LINE

Is there really a Bigfoot? Just about every unbiased observer says no, pointing to the fact that not a single shred of verifiable physical evidence—not a single live or dead specimen, not even a piece of bone or hair or skin, or even a mound of dung—has ever been found.

Bigfoot enthusiasts, of course, pooh-pooh the total-lack-of-physical-evidence argument: they counter that it took decades after the first sightings for Westerners to bring such "legendary" creatures as the giant panda, the pygmy chimpanzee, and the Komodo lizard out of the wild; so, they reason, a creature as large and intelligent as Bigfoot could easily have remained in hiding this long.

ENDNOTE

As with the Loch Ness monster and the Shroud of Turin, the enthusiasm surrounding Bigfoot will probably never die, even if it is proved conclusively that it doesn't exist. "We're all enthusiasts," says Jess Garst, editor of the weekly *Kourier* newspaper in Humbolt County. I won't tell you whether I'm a believer, but I'm an enthusiast. Whether you believe in it or not, it's something that seems to keep hanging on."

★　　★　　★

BIGFOOT HIGHLIGHTS

1982: "Self-proclaimed Bigfoot atheist Paul Freeman becomes, in one horrifying moment, a believer. Freeman, a U.S. Forest Service patrolman, sees a brown-haired giant step toward him in Oregon's Blue Mountains. He says, 'The hair on its neck and head just went forward like the hair on a wild dog's back,' and he will not recant his story. In 1983, after being constantly ridiculed, Freeman resigns from the Forest Service. 'I know what I saw,' he explains, 'and I'm not going to change my mind on it.' "

1992: "The legend continues as a Seattle secretary, Katie Martin, tells a tabloid, the *Weekly World News*, that Bigfoot sired her 4-year-old, furry-faced son. The couple communicated 'through some sort of telepathic link,' Martin claimed. Bigfoot brought her flowers, berries, and fresh fish while she camped. And then? 'I really don't want to get into that,' Martin said."

—*Chicago Tribune*, July 2, 1995

Bathroom fact: The average baby spends 27.5 months in diapers.

GREAT AMERICAN QUACKS

Americans are suckers for "sure-fire" medical cures. And there's never a shortage of "doctors" willing to provide them...for a fee. Here are some of the most outrageous (and successful) medical fakes in U.S. history.

THE QUACK: Dr. Elisha Perkins

Specialty: A contraption called "the Tractor," patented in 1796

Treatment: The Tractor, which was made up of two rods—one copper, zinc, and gold, and one silver, platinum, and iron—was passed over the sick person. Perkins preached that it literally pulled diseases out of the body; patients like George Washington and Chief Justice Oliver Ellsworth of the U.S. Supreme Court believed him.

Final Diagnosis: Medical experts of the day knew Perkins was a fake, but Perkins may have managed to fool himself. Armed with his magic rods, he traveled to New York in 1799 to treat the victims of a yellow fever epidemic that was sweeping the city. He didn't cure a single person and, a few weeks later, succumbed to the disease himself.

THE QUACK: Dr. Albert Abrams, "dean of 20th-century charlatans"

Specialty: Hermetically sealed machines called "dynamizers" and "oscilloclasts"

Treatment: Dynamizers supposedly identified the individual "signature vibrations" that illnesses give off inside the body. And oscilloclasts supposedly bombarded the body with the same vibrations, curing the disease by cancelling out the original vibrations.

Final Diagnosis: Abrams claimed that his machines could diagnose and treat illnesses over the telephone, but would not work when "skeptics" were in the room. He leased them to other doctors, who paid a $250 deposit and took $200 worth of classes. Then they could charge $200 per patient for the worthless treatments.

Only 33% of patients admitted to emergency rooms for heart attacks have actually had one.

Abrams made more than $2 million between 1909 and 1923, and won the hearts (and wallets) of Upton Sinclair and other gullible celebrities of the day.

Final Diagnosis: Abrams was exposed in 1923, when the American Medical Association sent him some blood for analysis. His diagnosis included acute cases of cancer, diabetes, malaria, and venereal disease, but the blood actually came from a perfectly healthy *rooster*. Abrams's career ground to an immediate halt, and he died a year later. Cause of death: pneumonia, one of the diseases his contraptions were supposed to cure.

THE QUACK: Gaylord Wilshire, celebrated magazine publisher, health enthusiast, and inventor

Specialty: The "I-ON-A-CO Electric Belt"

Treatment: In 1925, Wilshire announced that his new I-ON-A-CO belts cured heart disease, cancer, diabetes, prostate problems, and other illnesses by magnetizing iron in the blood and giving the body's cells a mild jolt of electricity. "All you have to do," one of his advertisements read, "is to place over your shoulders the Wilshire Ring or I-ON-A-CO. That's all. You may then light a cigarette and read your newspaper for 10 or 15 minutes....Often patients at the first treatment, like Lazarus, arise well and whole."

Final Diagnosis: Wilshire's wild claims quickly attracted the attention of the American Medical Association, the Public Health League, the Better Business Bureau, and other organizations. After a scientific study, the AMA announced that the I-ON-A-CO was about as helpful in curing illness as "the left hind foot of a rabbit caught in a churchyard in the dark of the moon." Exposed as a fraud, Wilshire moved to New York, where he died in 1927.

Note: Wilshire is best remembered for the road he cut through a barley field in 1896 in what is now downtown Los Angeles— *Wilshire Boulevard.*

THE QUACK: Dr. John "Goat Gland" Brinkley, M.D., Ph.D., M.C., LL.D., D.P.H., Sc.D., etc., a meatpacker-turned-surgeon who parlayed his diploma-mill medical degrees into one of the nation's largest medical practices of the '20s and '30s

Specialty: Transplanting goat testicles into the scrotums of male patients

There are at least 10 towns named Hollywood in the United States.

Treatment: Brinkley claimed the procedure would restore impotent patients to full sexual health. Actually, the human body rejects animal tissue automatically, so the treatment was completely useless. Even so, the *placebo* effect of the operation was phenomenal in hundreds of cases, and Brinkley used testimonials from these satisfied customers to increase sales.

Brinkley's outrageous hard-sell advertising was world-famous. One advertisement read, "Friends, don't let the roaring twenties roar by you. A man is only as old as his glands. Just let me get your goat and you'll be a Mr. Ram-What-Am with every lamb!"

At his peak in the 1930s, Brinkley and his associates transplanted 500 pairs of goat glands a day, earning him more than $1 million a year in profits. He used the money to buy mansions, yachts, radio stations, airplanes, Cadillacs, a flock of penguins, and other expensive toys.

"Goat Gland" Brinkley was so popular that he was almost elected governor of Kansas. In 1930 he ran as a write-in candidate under the slogan, "Let's pasture the goats on the Statehouse lawn." He lost—but only after 50,000 of his votes were disqualified. In 1934 he ran again, and lost by a similar margin—although he did carry four counties in Oklahoma, where he wasn't even a candidate.

Final Diagnosis: Hounded by state governments and the American Medical Association in the '30s, Goat Gland Brinkley moved his operations from Kansas to Texas to Arkansas and, finally, to Mexico, where he bought the most powerful radio transmitter on the North American continent. He died of a heart attack in 1942, not long after the Mexican government—fed up with him as well— tore down his radio transmitter.

THE QUACK: Edward Hayes, a turn-of-the-century con man
Specialty: "Man Medicine," an over-the-counter laxative
Treatment: Hayes passed his laxative off as an anti-impotence cure-all, claiming that users would be filled "once more with gusto, the joyful satisfaction, the pulse and throb of physical pleasure, the keen sense of man sensation."
Final Diagnosis: Man Medicine made Hayes a millionaire, but in 1914 he was convicted of fraud and fined $5,000. He pulled his laxative from the shelves and remarketed it as a treatment for obesity.

THE PATENTED CAR

This is a bit of lost history. We take it for granted that anyone who wants to can build a car. Few people realize that that right was won in court at the beginning of this century, by Henry Ford.

CASHING IN

In the late 1870s, George Selden, a lawyer/inventor specializing in patents, heard about the development of the automobile in Europe. He realized that it was a product of the future, and "set his mind to working out the precise legal definition and wording of a patent that would give him the sole right to license and charge royalties on future automobile development in America." Some 20 years later, with the auto industry beginning to show signs of life, he set up a partnership with a few wealthy Wall Street sharks and began asserting his "rights" with automakers. To his surprise, even the five biggest car manufacturers agreed to pay him royalties rather than go to court.

THE CARMAKERS' CARTEL

By 1903, this royalty-paying alliance of carmakers had officially become the Association of Licensed Automobile Manufacturers (ALAM). Henry Ford, then a fledgling automaker, applied for membership...and was refused. His reaction: "Let them try to put me out of business!" He took out ads telling his dealers that "the Selden patent does not cover any practicable machine," and dared Selden's group to take him to court. They did.

BATTLING IN COURT

Ford and the ALAM battled it out for six years. Then, in 1909, a federal judge determined that Selden's patent was valid; Selden and his allies legally owned all rights to car manufacturing. Immediately, carmakers that had held off on joining the ALAM—including the newly formed General Motors—fell in line to pay royalties.

The ALAM magnanimously offered to settle cheaply with Ford, but Henry fought on. "There will be no let up in this legal fight," he announced angrily. Finally, on January 9, 1911, a federal court of appeals ruled in Ford's favor. Selden and his cronies were forced to give up; the ALAM was never heard from again.

The jugular vein is an artery, not a vein.

MYTH AMERICA

A few things you probably didn't know about the founding fathers who wrote the U.S. Constitution.

THE MYTH: The men who attended the Constitutional Convention in 1787 were a sober, well-behaved group. They showed up on time, stuck it out 'til the end, and were all business when it came to the important task at hand.

THE TRUTH: Not quite. According to historical documents found by researchers at the National Constitution Center in 1992:

• Nineteen of the 74 people chosen to attend the convention never even showed up. (At least one of them had a good excuse, though—William Blount of New York refused to make the horseback ride to Philadelphia because of hemorrhoids.)

• Of the 55 who *did* show up, only 39 signed the document. Twelve people left early, and 4 others refused to sign. "A lot of them ran out of money and had to leave because they were doing a lot of price gouging here," observes researcher Terry Brent. Besides, he adds, the hot weather and high humidity must have been murder on the delegates, who wore wool breeches and coats. "They must have felt like dying. Independence Hall must have smelled like a cattle barn."

• And how did the Founding Fathers unwind during this pivotal moment in our nation's history? By getting drunk as skunks. One document that survived is the booze bill for a celebration party thrown two days before the Constitution was signed on September 17, 1787. According to the bill, the 55 people at the party drank 54 bottles of Madeira, 60 bottles of claret, 8 bottles of whiskey, 22 bottles of port, 8 bottles of cider, 12 bottles of beer, and 7 large bowls of alcoholic punch. "These were really huge punch bowls that ducks could swim in," Brent reports. "The partiers were also serenaded by 16 musicians. They had to be royally drunk—they signed the Constitution on the 17th. On the 16th, they were probably lying somewhere in the streets of Philadelphia."

Study results: Termites eat wood twice as fast when listening to heavy metal music.

OTHER PRESIDENTIAL FIRSTS

We all know the first president to resign (Nixon), the first Catholic president (Kennedy), and so on. But who was the first to be interviewed in the nude? Here's the BRI's list of other presidential firsts.

THE PRESIDENT: Theodore Roosevelt (1901-1909)
NOTABLE FIRST: First president to coin an advertising slogan.
BACKGROUND: While he was visiting Andrew Jackson's home in Nashville, Tennessee, Roosevelt was offered a cup of the coffee sold at the nearby Maxwell House hotel. When someone asked if he'd like another cup, Roosevelt replied: "Will I have another cup? Delighted! *It's good to the last drop!*" His words were eventually used by Maxwell House in their ad campaigns.
Note: Teddy was also the first president to be blinded while in office. He liked to box, and during one White House bout was hit so hard he became permanently blind in one eye.

THE PRESIDENT: James Madison (1809-1817)
NOTABLE FIRST: First commander-in-chief to actually command a military unit while in office.
BACKGROUND: When the British attacked Washington, D.C., during the War of 1812, President Madison personally took charge of an artillery battery. But that didn't last long; when the Americans started to lose, Madison fled the city.

THE PRESIDENT: Benjamin Harrison (1889-1893)
NOTABLE FIRST: First president with a fear of electricity.
BACKGROUND: President Harrison knew two things about electricity: The White House had just been wired for it, and it could kill people (the electric chair was becoming a common form of execution). That was all he needed to know—he didn't want anything more to do with it. Throughout his entire term, he and his wife refused to turn the lights on and off themselves. They either had the servants do it or left the lights off or on all night.

Medical note: Mental patients suffer from far fewer headaches than the general public.

THE PRESIDENT: Andrew Jackson (1828-1837)

NOTABLE FIRST: First president to be born in more than one place.

BACKGROUND: The following places claim themselves as Andrew Jackson's birthplace: Union County, North Carolina; Berkeley County, West Virginia; Augusta County, West Virginia; York County, Pennsylvania; as well as England, Ireland, and the Atlantic Ocean (he may have been born at sea). His "official" birthplace: Waxhaw, South Carolina.

THE PRESIDENT: John Quincy Adams (1825-1829)

NOTABLE FIRST: First president interviewed in the nude.

BACKGROUND: President Adams loved to skinny-dip. In hot weather he'd sneak out for a swim in the Potomac. One morning Anne Royall—a reporter who had been trying to interview him for months—sneaked up while he was swimming, sat on his clothes, and refused to leave until he granted her an interview. He did.

THE PRESIDENT: Martin Van Buren (1837-1841)

NOTABLE FIRST: First president to forget about his wife.

BACKGROUND: In his autobiography, Van Buren did not mention his wife, Hannah, once.

THE PRESIDENT: Warren G. Harding (1921-1923)

NOTABLE FIRST: First president to pardon a dog.

BACKGROUND: One morning Harding read a newspaper article about a Pennsylvania dog that had been ordered destroyed because it had been brought into the country illegally. Harding—who loved animals—wrote a letter to the governor of Pennsylvania. The governor saw to it that the dog's life was spared.

THE PRESIDENT: David Rice Atchison (1849-1849)

NOTABLE FIRST: First president to serve for one day.

BACKGROUND: Zachary Taylor was so religious that he refused to take the oath of office on a Sunday. So Atchison, President Pro Tempore of the U.S. Senate, stood in for him until he could be sworn in the next day.

THE TWILIGHT ZONE

Picture, if you will, a five-foot, five-inch ex-boxer who produced, created, and often wrote what may be the best television program in history. (From Cult TV, *by John Javna.)*

Y ou're traveling through another dimension, a dimension not only of sight and sound, but of mind; a journey into a wondrous land whose boundaries are that of the imagination. That's the signpost up ahead! Your next stop...the Twilight Zone!"

HOW IT STARTED

In the mid-'50s, Rod Serling was an award-winning writer for the celebrated TV anthology series, "Playhouse 90." However, he became frustrated with the inane changes sponsors insisted on making to his scripts. One sponsor (an automaker) demanded that the Chrysler building be painted out of a scene. Another (a tobacco company) deleted the word "lucky" from a script because Lucky Strikes weren't their brand. And when an insurance company refused to allow a central character to commit suicide, Serling quit. People were shocked that the outspoken playwright would leave a cushy job with one of the most prestigious programs to write and produce his own "fantasy" show. But Serling knew exactly what he was doing. By operating under the cover of fantasy, Serling could get his message across without getting it censored.

In 1957, he reworked a script that had aired years before on a local Cincinnati station and presented it to CBS as the "Twilight Zone" pilot. CBS wasn't interested, but Desilu Productions aired it as an episode of "Desilu Playhouse." It generated more viewer response than any other show that season, so CBS decided to take another look. They requested a second script from Serling ("The Happy Place"), which was deemed too depressing. So he wrote a third, this time keeping the concept simple and straightforward. In February 1959, "Where Is Everybody," was accepted by CBS as a pilot; in March, General Foods bought it; and on October 2, 1959, living rooms across America entered "The Twilight Zone."

INSIDE FACTS

The Amazing Serling: In real life, Rod Serling was a nervous wreck in front of the camera. It was his idea to introduce and close the episodes himself, but he remained an uneasy, sweating mess right through the last show. "Only my laundress really knows how frightened I am," he said of his appearances.

He was incredibly productive. He worked 18-hour days and could turn out a completed "Twilight Zone" script in around 35 hours—much of it dictated into a tape recorder while he sat by the swimming pool of his Los Angeles home. In the first season, he wrote a phenomenal 80 percent of the scripts; by the fifth season, he was still producing about 50 percent of them.

Sadly, Serling died during open-heart surgery in 1975. He was 50 years old.

Calling All Writers. One of Serling's biggest complaints about network procedure was that new talent was constantly being smothered by the system. So he invited amateur writers to send in their manuscripts if they thought they were good enough. It was an interesting lesson—he received 14,000 scripts in five days. Of the 500 that Serling and his staff got around to reading, only 2 were of "professional quality." Did he use those 2? He couldn't—they "didn't fit the show."

Name Game. Fans think that Rod Serling invented the term "twilight zone." So did Serling. He'd never heard anyone use it before, so he assumed he'd created it. He was in for a surprise: after the show debuted, he was informed that Air Force pilots used the phrase to describe "a moment when a plane is coming down on approach and it cannot see the horizon."

Belated Thanks. Although it was considered a "prestige" show, "The Twilight Zone" never had good enough ratings to excite advertisers. Sometimes, in fact, sponsors didn't even understand what the show was about. In the first season, one of the sponsors called CBS every Monday to demand an explanation of Friday's show. "And then," said Serling, "he demanded an explanation of the explanation."

THE SINGING NUN

She's mostly forgotten now, but the "Singing Nun" was one of the most famous nuns in modern history. Here's a look at her unusual career.

POP NUN

Remember the *Ed Sullivan Show*? If you had tuned in to watch it one particular evening in 1963, you would have seen a peculiar sight: a Belgian nun in full habit, playing a guitar and singing a song called "Dominique." The nun's name was Sister Luc-Gabrielle, but she was better known as Soeur Sourire ("Sister Smile")—and her song was fast becoming a pop-music hit all over the world.

Hardly anyone who tuned in that night had any idea what Soeur Sourire was singing—"Dominique's" lyrics were entirely in French. But the tune's light melody was so catchy that the song went all the way to #1 on U.S. pop-music charts and ultimately sold more than 1.5 million copies.

The song was a critical success as well, winning the 1963 Grammy for the best religious song and numerous other awards. Soeur Sourire became a star in her own right. In 1966, Debbie Reynolds portrayed her in the film *The Singing Nun*.

IN THE BEGINNING

Soeur Sourire got her start singing songs during religious retreats. As one nun told *Time* magazine in 1963, "We have these retreats for young girls at our Fichermont monastery, and in the evenings we sing songs composed by Sister Luc-Gabrielle. The songs are such a hit with our girls that they asked us to transcribe them." One of the catchiest tunes was "Dominique," a song that honors St. Dominic Guzman, founder of Soeur Sourire's Dominican order (and the man credited with introducing rosary beads to the Roman Catholic faith).

In 1961, the nuns decided to record some of Soeur Sourire's songs and give them away during the retreats...but they couldn't afford to rent a recording studio or manufacture their own records, so they asked the Philips record company to lend them one of its

---

Arachibutyrophobia: The fear of having peanut butter stuck to the roof of your mouth.

studios. After a few months of prodding, the company agreed. Philips initially planned to issue a few dozen pressings of the album and donate them to the nuns for their own use, but company executives liked the album so much they contracted with the convent to sell it all over Europe.

Philips issued Sister Luc-Gabrielle's album in Europe under the name *Soeur Sourire*, and it took the continent by storm. But when it was released in the United States a few months later under the name *The Singing Nun*, no one bought it. So Philips issued "Dominique" as a 45-rpm single and sold more than 400,000 copies in three weeks.

GETTING OUT OF THE HABIT

Soeur Sourire seemed to adjust quite well to her celebrity status at first…but it didn't last long: she left her convent in 1966 before taking her final vows, telling the press that she wanted to continue her missionary work while pursuing a recording career. (She did, however, turn all of her song royalties over to her religious order before she left.)

For her next single, she chose a song called "Glory Be to God for the Golden Pill," a tribute to artificial birth control. It didn't have quite the same ring to it that "Dominique" had. Nobody bought it, nor did they buy the updated synthesizer version of "Dominique" that she issued in 1983.

A Sad Note: Soeur Sourire lived to regret her decision to give up all of her royalties. The Belgian government hounded her for $63,000 in back taxes for the next 20 years, and in 1983 the center for autistic children that she and a friend (also an ex-nun) founded closed its doors due to lack of funds. Her life ended tragically in 1985 when she and the friend were found dead in their apartment, the victims of an apparent double suicide brought on by their financial problems. She was 51.

• • •

Q: How do fabric brighteners make clothes white?

A: "By reflecting blue light. The blue light combines with the yellow discoloration in a fabric to produce white light that makes fabric seem brighter."

—*The Book of Answers*

Medical note: Pigs can catch swine flu from humans.

AGATHA CHRISTIE'S REAL-LIFE MYSTERY

What would happen if a mystery writer who spent all her time concocting "perfect" crimes for her books actually tried to pull one off? It might result in a situation like this. From BRI contributor Jack Mingo.

Agatha Christie started writing detective stories to show up her sister, Madge. They were discussing Sherlock Holmes one day, when Agatha said she'd like to try her hand at writing one. "I don't think you could do it," said Madge. "They are very difficult to do. I've thought about it."

Since then, Christie has become one of the most popular detective fiction writers of all time, selling over 2 billion copies of her books in 104 languages.

Still, one of the most sensational and mysterious events in her life was her own 11-day disappearance in December 1926. Although her defenders believe Agatha was suffering from some kind of amnesia, all available evidence suggests that she used her expertise as a mystery writer to set up her husband as the prime suspect in a murder case—with herself as the supposed victim.

Here's What Happened: On a chilly December night, Agatha's car was found at the bottom of a chalk pit some distance from her home. Although it was cold, her fur coat was still in the car. There was no driver in sight, and the car was turned off—indicating that someone had pushed it into the pit. Police suspected foul play.

THE SUSPECT

Agatha's husband, Colonel Archibald Christie, was immediately questioned by the police. Where had he been that night? At a dinner party. What was the occasion? The Colonel, abashed, admitted that it was a party to announce his engagement to his new love, Nancy Neele. Had he and Agatha been getting along? No. In fact, he had recently told her he was having an affair and wanted a divorce. They'd even had a screaming battle about his infidelity the morning before she disappeared.

The questions took a harder edge. Was he at the party all evening? No, he admitted. While at the party, he had received a call from his wife, who'd threatened to come and make a scene. He drove home to try to placate her, but when he arrived, no one was there. So he went back to the party. The detectives let the Colonel go, but told him not to leave town.

FINDING AGATHA

A massive search began for the missing celebrity. Two thousand volunteers searched 40 square miles of countryside, while the police dragged nearby rivers and lakes looking for her body.

But Agatha was still alive. She had fled to the far side of England and checked into a hotel in Harrogate under the name Mrs. Neele (the name of her husband's true love). And after 11 days of intense publicity, hotel employees (who had seen a reward offered in the paper) recognized her and called the police. They informed the Colonel, and he rushed to Harrogate to be with his wife. The next day, the Christies sneaked out the hotel's back door to escape the press.

A CASE OF AMNESIA?

Two physicians were called in to examine Agatha, and shortly afterward, Archibald Christie announced to the press that his wife had amnesia and remembered nothing of the previous 11 days. She had no idea why her car was miles away from her home, how it got into the pit, how she got from one end of England to the other, or where she got the large sum of money she used to rent her hotel room...and buy an expensive new wardrobe.

Skeptical, the press accused Agatha of playing an elaborate hoax —a hoax that cost taxpayers thousands of dollars, and police and volunteers hours of needless labor. The novelist's extreme dislike of publicity throughout her life can perhaps be traced back not just to her natural shyness, but to the overdose of attention she received at that time.

Aftermath. Agatha claimed that her very unusual case of "amnesia" obscured the complete truth from her for the rest of her life. According to her authorized biography, under psychotherapy, she regained *some* of her memories of staying in the hotel. But she never discussed the incident publicly, even in an autobiography that she wrote for publication after her death.

Oink! The average American eats the equivalent of 28 pigs in their lifetime.

NIXON SEZ

It's probably been a while since you've thought about Tricky Dick. Just in case you're beginning to wonder why you didn't trust him in the first place, here's a refresher.

"I'll speak for the man, or against him, whichever will do him most good."

"We cannot judge it before it is concluded, and we cannot judge it even after it has been concluded."

"I rate myself a deeply committed pacifist."

"You won't have Nixon to kick around anymore, gentlemen. This is my last press conference."

"Let us begin by committing ourselves to the truth, to see it like it is and to tell it like it is, to find the truth, to speak the truth and live with the truth. That's what we'll do."

"You can say that this administration will have the first complete, far-reaching attack on the problem of hunger in history. Use all the rhetoric, so long as it doesn't cost money."

"I never made the [football] team…I was not heavy enough to play the line, not fast enough to play halfback and not smart enough to be a quarterback."

"When the president does it, that means it is not illegal."

"I like the job I have now, but, if I had my life to live over again, I'd like to have ended up as a sports writer."

"I would have made a good pope."

"I hear that whenever anyone in the White House tells a lie, Nixon gets a royalty."

"I'm not a lovable man."

"Call it paranoia, but paranoia for peace isn't that bad."

"Once you get into this great stream of history, you can't get out."

THE YEAR THEY STOLE THE PRESIDENCY, PART II

*Here's the rest of the story about the presidential
election of 1876 (started on page 114).*

E LECTION SURPRISE
On the afternoon of November 8, 1876, Republican Party
chairman Zachariah Chandler announced to the press that
Rutherford B. Hayes had received the 185 votes needed to win the
election. The shocking announcement sent the country into an up-
roar. Riots broke out, and President Grant had to dispatch federal
troops to maintain order.

Sure enough, the Republican-controlled election committees
had "reviewed" the unofficial totals and "corrected" them in favor
of Hayes, making him the new winner of the election.

FIGHTING BACK

The Democrats, however, refused to concede the 20 disputed electoral votes. New Democratic governors had just been elected to replace the outgoing "carpetbagger" governments in all three contested states, and though they would not take office for several weeks,
they protested the final returns and submitted their own versions to
the Electoral College showing Tilden as the winner. Confronted
with multiple sets of returns, the College was unable to declare a
victor.

A CONSTITUTIONAL CRISIS

Some vague wording in the U.S. Constitution made the situation
even worse. William McFeely writes in his biography of Ulysses S.
Grant,

> The Constitution calls for the electoral votes to be opened in the
> presence of both houses of Congress, but it does not say *who* should do
> the counting. If the Republican Senate majority decided the count
> went one way, the Democratic majority of the House of Representa-
> tives might decide it went the other. Another possibility was a Sen-
> ate filibuster, begun before the count could be made, that might

extend past Grant's last day in office, leaving the United States without a president.

CIVIL WAR II?

As the stalemate dragged into December, the mood in the country turned increasingly hostile. Rumors circulated that Tilden sympathizers were preparing to install him as president by force, and "Tilden Minutemen" militia groups sprang up in a number of states. Even the Democratic sergeant-at-arms of the House was causing trouble, threatening to deputize 100,000 men and use them to guarantee Tilden's election. Violence actually did erupt in a few instances in Louisiana, where the Republican candidate for governor was shot and wounded by an outraged Democrat, and in Ohio someone fired a shot through the window of the Hayes family home while they were sitting down for dinner.

President Grant took these threats seriously—he ordered several artillery companies into the capital and he issued a statement warning the public that "any demonstrations or warlike concentration of men threatening the peace of the city or endangering the security of public property would be summarily dealt with by a declaration of martial law." Tilden urged his supporters to remain calm. "It will not do to fight," he told his allies. "We have just emerged from one civil war, and it will never do to engage another."

A COMPROMISE

Finally, in January 1877, both houses of Congress agreed to appoint an independent electoral commission, composed of five senators, five congressional representatives, and five Supreme Court justices, to decide the election. It was hoped the commission would be impartial. Seven of the members would be Democrats, seven would be Republicans, and the 15th and tie-breaking member would be Supreme Court Justice David Davis of Illinois, whom both sides considered to be independent.

At the last minute, however, the Republican-controlled Illinois legislature elected Justice Davis to the U.S. Senate, which disqualified him from serving on the committee. This turned out to be a master stroke. He was replaced by Justice Joseph P. Bradley, a Republican considered the least partisan of the remaining Supreme Court Justices.

Camel's hair brushes are made from squirrel hair.

THE END OF THE LINE

On February 1, 1877, both houses of Congress met to count the electoral votes. When the role call got to "Florida," the 15-man electoral commission paused for nine days' worth of hearings to decide who would get Florida's votes. In the end, Justice Bradley voted with his fellow Republicans to award Florida's four electoral votes to Hayes. When he did it again with Louisiana's votes, Tilden and the Democrats knew the game was up.

Meanwhile, Southern Democrats—who didn't particularly like Tilden to begin with—had been in secret talks with Hayes's people for weeks—and on February 26 they cut a deal: in exchange for not protesting Hayes's election, Hayes agreed to appoint a Southerner to his cabinet and speed Southern "home rule" by removing all federal troops from the three remaining "carpetbagger" states.

LAST GASP

But that didn't stop Tilden's allies from fighting to the bitter end. "The House session on March 1 was one of the stormiest in history," Roy Morris writes,

> Members roared with disapproval as House Speaker Samuel Randall, a former Tilden supporter, stymied all efforts to stop the vote. Some congressmen waved pistols, one climbed atop his desk, screaming with anger....Oaths and insults filled the air. Finally, after 18 tumultuous hours, the session ended with a telegram from Tilden graciously requesting that the vote be completed. He knew he must accept the electoral commission's results or risk the nation erupting into civil war.

The inevitable became official just after four in the morning on March 2, 1877, as the final votes were counted. Governor Hayes got 185 votes, Governor Tilden got 184. Hayes, denounced as "His Fraudulency" and "Rutherfraud" B. Hayes, became the 19th president of the United States.

★　★　★　★

Banana Facts

"The banana does not grow on a tree. Although the plant may look like a tree, it is actually considered a very large herb."

—*Myth Information*, by J. Allen Barasdi

In the '40s, the Bich pen was changed to Bic; the company thought Americans would call it *bitch*.

THE KING AND I

You may have already seen the famous photos of Elvis Presley and Richard Nixon in the Oval Office. Here's the inside story behind that meeting—taken directly from the memos of the White House staff.

Even Elvis was starstruck. He thought J. Edgar Hoover was "the greatest living American"...and that Nixon "wasn't far behind." On December 21, 1970, Elvis dropped by the White House unannounced, asking to see the president. He brought this letter with him:

DEAR MR. PRESIDENT:

First, I would like to introduce myself. I am Elvis Presley and admire you and have great respect for your office. I talked to Vice President Agnew in Palm Springs three weeks ago and expressed my concern for our country. The drug culture, the hippie elements, the SDS, Black Panthers, etc. do not consider me as their enemy or as they call it, the establishment. I call it America and I love it. Sir, I can and will be of any service that I can to help the country out. I have no concerns or motives other than helping the country out. So I wish not to be given a title or an appointed position. I can and will do more good if I were made a Federal Agent at Large and I will help out by doing it my way through my communications with people of all ages. First and foremost, I am an entertainer, but all I need is the Federal credentials. I am on this plane with Senator George Murphy and we have been discussing the problems that our country is faced with.

Sir, I am staying at the Washington Hotel, Rooms 505-506-507. I have two men who work with me by the names of Jerry Schilling and Sonny West. I am registered under the name of Jon Burrows. I will be here for as long as it takes to get the credentials of a Federal Agent. I have done an in-depth study of drug abuse and Communist brainwashing techniques and I am right in the middle of the whole thing where I can and will do the most good.

I am glad to help just so long as it is kept very private. You can have your staff or whomever call me anytime today, tonight, or

---

Myth-understood: Ostriches do *not* bury their heads in the sand.

tomorrow. I was nominated this coming year one of America's Ten Most Outstanding Young Men. That will be in January 18 in my home town of Memphis, Tennessee. I am sending you the short autobiography about myself so you can better understand this approach. I would love to meet you just to say hello if you're not too busy.

> Respectfully,
>
> Elvis Presley

P.S. I believe that you, Sir, were one of the Top Ten Outstanding Men of America also. I have a personal gift for you which I would like to present to you and you can accept it or I will keep it for you until you can take it.

Dwight Chapin, the White House appointments secretary, met with Elvis. He wasn't sure what to do—did Nixon want to speak with the King? Was he a Presley fan? Did he even know who the singer was? Chapin passed the buck and wrote a memo to H. R. Haldeman, White House chief of staff:

DEAR H.R.:

Attached you will find a letter to the President from Elvis Presley. As you are aware, Presley showed up here this morning and has requested an appointment with the President. He states that he knows the President is very busy, but he would just like to say hello...I think that it would be wrong to push Presley off on the Vice President since it will take very little of the President's time and it can be extremely beneficial for the President to build some rapport with Presley.

Haldeman approached Nixon about meeting with Elvis, and Nixon agreed. Here are the official White House notes describing the meeting:

DECEMBER 21, 1970

The meeting opened with pictures taken of the President and Elvis Presley. Presley immediately began showing the President his law enforcement paraphernalia including badges from police departments in California, Colorado, and Tennessee. Presley indicated that he had been playing Las Vegas and the President indicated that he was aware of how difficult it is to perform in Las Vegas.

The President mentioned that he thought Presley could reach young people, and that it was important for Presley to retain his credibility. Presley responded that he did his thing by "just singing." He said that he could not get to the kids if he made a speech on the stage, that he had to reach them in his own way. The President nodded in agreement.

Presley indicated that he thought the Beatles had been a real force for anti-American spirit. He said that the Beatles came to this country, made their money, and then returned to England where they promoted an anti-American theme. The President nodded in agreement and expressed some surprise. The President then indicated that those who use drugs are also those in the vanguard of anti-American protest. "Violence, drug usage, dissent, protest all seem to merge in generally the same group of young people."

Presley indicated to the President in a very emotional manner that he was "on your side." Presley kept repeating that he wanted to be helpful, that he wanted to restore some respect for the flag which was being lost. He mentioned that he was just a poor boy from Tennessee who had gotten a lot from his country, which in some way he wanted to repay. He also mentioned that he is studying Communist brainwashing and the drug culture for over ten years. He mentioned that he knew a lot about this and was accepted by the hippies. He said he could go right into a group of young people or hippies and be accepted which he felt could be helpful to him in his drug drive. The President indicated again his concern that Presley retain his credibility.

At the conclusion of the meeting, Presley again told the President how much he supported him, and then, in a surprising, spontaneous gesture, put his left arm around the President and hugged him.

* * *

During a 1958 visit to Venezuela, Vice President Richard Nixon was spit upon by a protester. After Secret Service agents grabbed the man, Nixon kicked him in the shins. He admitted in his book *Six Crises* that "nothing I did all day made me feel better."

Public trust: 32% of all land in the U.S. is owned by the federal government.

NAME THAT FOOD

Here's where these household product names originated.

Aunt Jemima: Charles Rutt invented America's first pancake mix, but it bombed without a catchy name. One night in 1889, he saw a blackface vaudeville show featuring a tune called "Aunt Jemima"—which was sung by an actor in drag. Somehow, that inspired the image of Southern hospitality Rutt was looking for.

Spam Luncheon Meat: Combines the SP from spice and the AM from ham.

Tootsie Roll: Leo Hirschfield, an Austrian immigrant, originally hand-rolled the candies for his daughter, Tootsie.

Chef Boy-ar-dee Spaghetti & Meatballs: Boy-ar-dee is a phonetic spelling of the inventor's name—Hector Boiardi. An Italian immigrant and restaurateur, Boiardi devised the recipe in a small room above his Cleveland restaurant in 1929. His picture still appears on the label.

Oreo Cookies: *Oreo* means "hill" in Greek. The original version of the cookie was mound-shaped, not flat.

Fig Newtons: In 1895, a new machine was installed at a Massachusetts cookie company called the Kennedy Biscuit Works. Among the machine's capabilities: it could wrap cookie dough around jam. The first jam the company tried it with just happened to be made from figs. Their policy was to temporarily name products after neighboring towns (until they came up with something better). Newton, Massachusetts, was honored in the title...and the name stuck.

Coca Cola: Named for two of its original ingredients—coca leaves (yes, the ones that give us cocaine) and Kola nuts.

Budweiser Beer: In the 1870s, German-born Adolphus Busch and his partner produced a light-colored beer, inspired by a beer they'd seen brewed in Budweis, Czechoslovakia.

Q: Who nicknamed New York the "Empire State?"   A. George Washington.

MYTH CONCEPTIONS

At the BRI, we love "facts" that aren't true.
Here's some info that may surprise you.

Myth: The Great Wall of China is visible from the moon.
Truth: No manmade objects are visible from that far out in space. According to astronomers, it's about as visible from the moon as a popsicle stick would be from 240 miles away.

Myth: Alligator shirts have alligators on them.
Truth: They're crocodiles—René Lacoste, a French tennis star known as *Le Crocodile*, invented them in the 1920s.

Myth: The sardine is a species of fish.
Truth: The word "sardine" actually refers to any breed of small fish—including herring and pilchard—that's been stuffed into a sardine can.

Myth: S.O.S. stands for "Save Our Ship."
Truth: It doesn't stand for anything—it was selected as a distress signal because it's easy to transmit in Morse code: 3 dots, 3 dashes, 3 dots.

Myth: Your ears are the things you see on the side of your head.
Truth: Technically, the human ear is located inside the skull, and stops at the end of the ear canal. The parts you can see are called the *pinnas*.

Myth: Fortune cookies were invented in China.
Truth: They were invented in the United States in 1918 by Charles Jung, a Chinese restaurant owner, to amuse customers while they waited for their food. Only later were they served *after* the meal.

Myth: The French poodle originated in France.
Truth: The breed was created in Germany around the 16th century.

In Switzerland, it's against the law to slam your car door.

Called *Pudel*, or "splash," dogs, they were bred to retrieve ducks. They didn't become popular in France until years later.

Myth: According to the Bible, angels have wings.
Truth: Nowhere in the Bible does it say that angels have wings. The idea didn't become popular until painters and sculptors began adding them.

Myth: The Romans used chariots in battle.
Truth: Chariots weren't effective on the battlefield—soldiers couldn't fight while holding onto the reins. The Romans used them only in sports and as transportation.

Myth: Dogs sweat through their tongues.
Truth: Dogs cool off by breathing rapidly; not by sticking their tongues out. Their tongues don't have sweat glands—and the only large sweat glands they have are in their feet.

Myth: The song "Chopsticks" was named after the Chinese eating utensils with the same name.
Truth: The song was written by Euphemia Allen, a 16-year-old British girl in 1877. She advised pianists to play it with their hands turned sideways, using chopping motions.

Myth: If too many pores in your skin clog up, you can get sick—even die.
Truth: The pores in your skin don't breathe—and you don't need to keep them "open." It is possible to clog all the pores in your body for an extended period of time without suffering any ill effects.

Myth: Cold-blooded animals have cold blood.
Truth: A "cold-blooded" animal's body temperature changes with the surrounding air temperature. Many cold-blooded animals have body temperatures that are higher than "warm-blooded" animals.

Myth: I.O.U. stands for "I owe you."
Truth: Originally the borrower wrote "I Owe Unto," followed by the lender's name.

The world's longest Monopoly game, played in 1981, lasted more than 660 hours.

FABULOUS FOOD FLOPS

Americans will consume almost anything. We eat billions
of Twinkies, drink oceans of Kool-Aid, devour millions of
pounds of processed cheese spread. But even we have
our limits—some food products are so outrageous that
no one will touch them. Like these.

CORNFLAKES WITH FREEZE-DRIED FRUIT
In 1964, the lure of space-age food technology was too seductive for cereal giants Kellogg and Post to resist.
Freeze-drying had been "perfected" by NASA, so Post decided to put freeze-dried strawberries in with its cornflakes. Just add milk, they told wide-eyed consumers, and these dried-out berries will miraculously turn back into real fruit.

Cornflakes with Strawberries took off like a rocket; supermarkets couldn't keep the product on their shelves. Exulting, Post built a multimillion-dollar plant to produce the cereal and added two new varieties to the line: Cornflakes with Blueberries and Cornflakes with Peaches.

Meanwhile, Kellogg's was test-marketing its own version of high-tech fruit 'n' cereal: Cornflakes with Instant Bananas. The Battle Creek cereal giant bought the rights to the song, "Yes, We Have No Bananas," and hired Jimmy Durante to croak new lyrics at a piano: "Yes, we now have bananas..." But the prognosis wasn't good. One Kellogg's sales rep described the product as "cardboard discs in a box."

It turned out that freeze-dried fruit gets soft on the outside when soaked in milk, but stays crunchy on the inside. What's worse: by the time the fruit is soft enough to eat, the cereal will be soggy. Millions of families bought Cornflakes with Strawberries once, but never came back for a second helping—leaving both cereal giants stuck with a bountiful harvest of unwanted pseudo-fruit.

Other Freeze-dried Flops
Freeze-dried mushrooms in a box, from Armour foods; and freeze-dried cottage cheese ("with cultured sour cream dressing"), from Holland Dairies.

The full-grown porcupine has as many as 35,000 quills on its body.

WEIRD BEER

Here are three beer ideas that America refused to swallow:

• **Flavored beer.** Introduced by the Lone Star Brewing Company in 1970. It was available in three exciting tastes: cola, grapefruit, and lemon-lime. But of course, it wasn't available too long. Cola-flavored beer?

• **Billy Beer.** First marketed in 1977 by the Falls City Brewing Company of Kentucky in partnership with Jimmy Carter's "good-ol'-boy" brother Billy. The beer looked like it would be a strong seller…but it went belly up about a year later. Why? Two reasons: 1) People who tried it said it tasted like it had already passed through Billy himself; and 2) Billy Carter checked into an alcoholism treatment center about a year later, which took all the fun out of having a laugh at his expense. Unlike most beer failures, Billy Beer flopped twice: once with drinkers…and then again with collectors, who'd bought so much of the stuff thinking it would be collectable some day that it's now just about worthless. Some beer can conventions even give them away free at the door.

• **Dry beer.** In 1990 three major brewers introduced "dry" beers to the public: Coors Dry, Bud Dry, and Michelob Dry. They spent more than $40 million on advertising…and nothing happened. What went wrong? As one beer industry analyst put it, "Nobody can figure out what the hell dry beer is. The opposite of wet beer?"

McDONALD'S MISTAKE

In the '60s, Catholics still weren't permitted to eat meat on Friday—a problem for McDonald's. Since the fast food giant only had hamburgers on its menu, sales slumped every week in Catholic areas. McDonald's needed a creative alternative…and Ray Kroc, chairman of the board, had one. Putting his marketing genius to work, he came up with the Hula Burger. Picture a toasted bun, covered with a piece of melted American cheese, mustard, ketchup, a pickle…and a slice of grilled pineapple. Sound appetizing?

The Hula Burger had no meat, so it was perfect for Fridays. But it had another problem—no one would buy it. Customers all said, "I love the Hula, but where's the burger?" McDonald's vegetarian experiment was abandoned after a few months. It wasn't until 1962 that the religious crisis was solved with the Filet-O-Fish sandwich (see page 331).

A QUICK ONE

In the mid-'60s, Hires developed a brand-new product and rushed it out to supermarkets...where it went sour. The product: root beer-flavored milk.

GIMME A LIGHT

Believe it or not, "light" beer—a huge success today—was a dud in 1967. Two light beers were introduced that year.

The first was Gablinger's—also which became known as "the Edsel of Beers." Brewed on the East Coast by Reingold, it was named after the Swiss chemist who'd formulated it—Hersch Gablinger. Reingold put his picture on the cans, trying to make him a celebrity, but it was no use. The "no-carbohydrate" beer was so watery it wouldn't even hold a head. And the slogan, "It doesn't fill you up," didn't mean anything to beer drinkers in 1967.

If that wasn't enough, the federal government seized a shipment of Gablinger's because of "misleading" statements on the label, and a Reingold competitor filed a lawsuit, charging that the product was falsely promoted. Reingold made all the necessary changes, but by that time Gablinger's was a lost cause.

The other "light" beer was called...Lite Beer. That's right—the same one that over-the-hill athletes have promoted on television for the last decade. In 1967, it was marketed by a Cincinnati brewery named Meister Brau. They called it "low-calorie beer," and their ads featured "Miss Lite," a 21-year-old California blonde in a leotard. But Lite was ahead of its time, and people who were into low-cal foods weren't into drinking beer. It lasted for about a year, then disappeared (for a while).

It ain't over til it's over

In the late '70s, the Miller Brewing Company purchased Meister Brau and its various assets—including the trade name Lite. Styles had changed in a decade, and the time was right for diet beer. So, in 1979, Miller launched its "new" beer with a memorable ad campaign featuring aging macho men fighting over whether Lite was more attractive because it tasted good or because it didn't make them feel full. The result: The beer that flopped in 1967 was the second-leading beer in America (behind Bud) 20 years later.

The Atlantic Ocean is saltier than the Pacific Ocean.

OH NO, IT'S MR. BILL

*Comments from William F. Buckley, one of
America's best-known conservatives:*

"I get satisfaction of three kinds. One is creating something, one is being paid for it, and one is the feeling that I haven't just been sitting on my ass all afternoon."

"I would like to take you seriously, but to do so would affront your intelligence."

"Idealism is fine, but as it approaches reality the cost becomes prohibitive."

"I'd rather entrust the government of the United States to the first four hundred people listed in the Boston telephone directory than to the faculty of Harvard University."

"Life can't be all bad when for ten dollars you can buy all the Beethoven sonatas and listen to them for ten years."

"I, for one, yearn for the days of the Cold War."

"One must bear in mind that the expansion of federal activity is a form of eating for politicians."

"Kennedy, after all, has lots of glamour. Gregory Peck with an atom bomb in his holster."

"Any sign of weakness by the Free World increases the appetite of the enemy for more war and more conquest as surely as the progressive revelations of the stripteaser increase the appetite of the lecher."

"All civilized men want peace. And all truly civilized men must despise pacifism."

"In the wake of yet another disappearance of a teenager into the mortal coils of the flower world in Greenwich Village, where love is exercised through rape made tolerable by drugs and abstract declarations of fellowship with the North Vietnamese, one wonders anew about the pretensions of progress."

"What has détente done for us except provide a backdrop for the exchange of toasts between American presidents and Communist tyrants?"

Say Ah-h-h: The most sensitive part of your tongue is in the back.

NO SWEAT, PART II

*Here's even more info on a topic near and dear to you—
your sweat.(Check out Part I on page 205.)*

MAKES SCENTS
"For many years," writes Charles Panati in *Extraordinary Origins*, "Americans remained so sensitive to the issue of antiperspirants that they asked for them in drugstores with the same hushed confidentiality with which they requested prophylactics."

That began to change when a deodorant called Odor-Ro-No hit store shelves in 1914. Unlike its predecessors, Odor-Ro-No made its debut with a nationwide magazine advertising campaign that was as high-profile as the product name itself. Still, the campaign did manage to tiptoe around the issue: Odor-Ro-No promised to keep women "clean and dainty"—but didn't mention exactly *how*. It wasn't until 1919 that the Odor-Ro-No ads mentioned "body odor" directly, and even then, rather than spell the offending words out, they pioneered the expression "B.O."

IF YOU THINK YOUR JOB STINKS...

• Ever wonder how deodorant companies test the effectiveness of their products? They actually hire people, known in the industry as "odor judges," to smell other people's armpits. At the Gillette Odor Clinic in Boston, Massachusetts, human guinea pigs apply the product to be tested and sweat it out in a "human incubation chamber," heated to 100°F. Then the odor judges come in and check to see how the product is working.

• The job isn't so bad...most of the time. "You might hear an occasional 'Whoa!' " admits Brian Rogers, who works in the company's Toiletries Technology Lab. "We try to let the odor judges take a few breaths in between, but if the product isn't effective or there's a lot of odor, they may need longer to clear their sinuses." Even the most squeamish judges get used to the job after a while, Rogers says. "They can do the tests and go eat a doughnut afterward." And besides, most of them prefer the assignment to testing, say, mouthwash or disposable diapers.

President Andrew Jackson wasn't sure whether the Earth was round or flat.

SWEAT FACTS

• In an average day, Americans sweat enough moisture to provide the city of Pittsburgh, PA, with a 24-hour supply of water.

• For some reason, many Asian people have fewer apocrine glands than most Westerners. Result: Their sweat doesn't smell as bad. A Japanese clothing and cosmetics company named Kanebo has actually tried to make up for this by inventing underwear drenched with artificial sweat—intended to increase the user's sex appeal. The boxer shorts contain millions of microscopic capsules containing a synthesized pheromone found in male underarm sweat. Friction causes the capsules to break, releasing the scent. The pheromones are supposed to last through at least 10 washings.

• When you exercise strenuously in hot weather, you can sweat away as much as two quarts of water in an hour, enough to actually cause your weight to drop during the workout. But this weight loss is only temporary. Since the weight you lose is all water, you gain it back as soon as you drink liquids and your fluid levels return to normal. *Note:* Many serious athletes measure their weight immediately before and after their workouts to determine how much water they need to drink to "rehydrate" themselves: about one pint per pound of weight loss.

• Do men sweat more than women? On average, women can tolerate a body temperature of 1°F. higher than men before they break into a sweat. But once they start to perspire, women produce just as much sweat as men do.

• Where on your body you sweat the most depends on the reason why you're sweating: are you hot…or nervous? *Cooling* sweat shows up most on your forehead, upper lip, neck, and chest; *nervous* sweat appears most in your palms, feet, and armpits.

• What is it like to sweat in the weightlessness of space? It's pretty gross…at least according to Rhea Seddon, a NASA doctor and astronaut who has flown on the Space Shuttle Columbia. "It pools on your skin and balls up into large, *fist-size* globules of sweat that sort of land on you. It's kind of yucky."

CAN'T TAKE THE HEAT

• What happens when it's so hot outside that your body can't

There are eight "1"s and seven "one"s on a $1 bill (not counting the serial numbers).

sweat fast enough and cool down enough to maintain a constant body temperature of 98.6°F? You may actually stop sweating entirely, which causes your internal temperature to soar to 105°F or higher—which, in turn, causes your pulse and respiration rate to double. These are the first signs of heatstroke—and if you don't seek medical attention or take steps to cool down immediately, you can experience delirium, slip into a coma, and even die. Left untreated, heatstroke is *always* fatal.

SWEATING AND HISTORY

• B.O. may have been a critical factor in keeping Napoleon Bonaparte's marriage to Josephine alive. Apparently he really liked the way she smelled. How historians know this: Napoleon often referred to her smell in his love letters from afar. "Will be home in three days," he wrote to her after the Battle of Marengo, "...don't wash."

• Excessive sweat may have even cost Vice President Richard Nixon the presidency in 1960. Remember his famous TV debate against John F. Kennedy? Nixon, a relatively inexperienced television performer, refused to wear any makeup except for a light dusting of a stubble-hiding powder called Lazy Shave. His decision came back to haunt him when he began sweating profusely under the hot studio lights, causing a mini-mudslide on his face. "Probably no picture in American politics," Theodore White wrote in *The Making of the President 1960*, "tells a better story of crisis and episode than that famous shot of the camera on the vice-president as he half slouched, his Lazy Shave powder faintly streaked with sweat, his eyes exaggerated hollows of blackness, his jaw, jowls, and face drooping with strain." Rumor has it that the future president learned his lesson well—from that moment on, insiders say, Nixon smeared his face with antiperspirant whenever he went on TV.

YOU CAN TELL BY THE SMELL...

Before advances in medicine made it easier to diagnose illness, it was common for doctors to smell patients' sweaty skin to figure out what was wrong with them. A lot of illnesses had surprisingly familiar smells. Some examples: the smell of "freshly baked brown bread" indicated typhoid; the smell of "stale beer" usually meant tuberculosis; and the smell of a "butcher shop" meant yellow fever.

The bones of a pigeon weigh less than its feathers.

MYTH AMERICA

Most of what we "know" about Christopher Columbus is a myth.
Here are a few tall tales that used to be taught in school.

THE MYTH: Columbus proved the Earth was round.

THE TRUTH: The ancient Greeks knew the world wasn't flat 2000 years before Columbus was born. Pythagoras came up with the theory in the sixth century B.C., and Ptolemy proved it in the second century A.D. Before Columbus even left on his first voyage to the New World, he studied globes and maps depicting a round planet. He had a hard time finding funding for his voyage, not because his contemporaries thought he would sail off the Earth's edge, but because they thought the Orient was too far to reach by sailing west.

THE MYTH: Columbus was the first European to discover North America.

THE TRUTH: Columbus never even set foot on the North American continent. The closest he ever came was the islands of the Caribbean and South America. The America whose "discovery" we celebrate is actually a tiny island near San Salvador, which was already inhabited, anyway. Even Columbus wouldn't take credit for discovering a new continent—he died thinking he had reached India. Actually, the Vikings were the first Europeans to reach North America, around 1000 A.D.

THE MYTH: Columbus was a friend to the American Indians.

THE TRUTH: Sad to say, that's not even close. Take his Haitian exploits for example—according to historian Howard Zinn, Arawak Indians who didn't honor Columbus and his crew with regular contributions of gold "had their hands cut off and bled to death." After two years, half of Haiti's 250,000 inhabitants were dead "through murder, mutilation, or suicide." Many of the native Indians who survived were enslaved and brought back to Spain. "Let us in the name of the Holy Trinity, go on sending all the slaves that can be sold," Columbus wrote.

Thunder is caused when air rushes into the vacuum created by a bolt of lightning.

FAMILY HOLIDAYS

Every year, Americans celebrate holidays honoring their mothers and fathers. Whose idea were these events? Here's the story.

MOTHER'S DAY (Second Sunday in May). Anna Jarvis, a West Virginia schoolteacher, mounted a one-woman crusade to create this holiday in 1908—three years after her own mother died. She persuaded pastors in nearby Grafton, West Virginia, and Philadelphia, Pennsylvania, to hold special services in their churches on May 10. (They handed out carnations, Jarvis's mother's favorite flower.) From there she launched a letter-writing campaign to U.S. governors, congressmen, clergy, media, etc. Congress endorsed the idea, and on May 9, 1914, President Wilson issued a proclamation establishing the holiday.

But Jarvis—who never had children—grew to hate the holiday and was sorry she'd created it. She railed against the commercialism surrounding it and especially loathed Mother's Day cards. "Any mother would rather have a line of the worst scribble from her son or daughter," she complained, "than any fancy greeting card."

FATHER'S DAY (Third Sunday in June). Jarvis unintentionally inspired other Americans to work for a Father's Day. First among them was Sonora Smart Dodd, a Spokane, Washington, housewife whose father had raised six children by himself. Dodd proposed making Father's Day the first Sunday in June (the month of her father's birthday), but local religious leaders preferred the third Sunday. Father's Day was first celebrated in Spokane on June 19, 1910. The all-male U.S. Congress didn't immediately acknowledge the day; they feared voters would think it was too self-serving. In fact, it wasn't until 1972 that Father's Day was proclaimed a federal holiday by President Nixon.

Although she turned down offers to endorse products, Dodd had nothing against giving gifts on Father's Day. "After all," she said, "why should the greatest giver of gifts not be on the receiving end at least once a year?" She'd probably be delighted to know that more than a million electric shavers are bought for Father's Day every year...and Americans annually spend some $20 million on Father's Day ties.

TGIF? Nearly 50% of all bank robberies take place on Friday.

FAMILIAR PHRASES

Here are some more origins of common phrases.

SON OF A GUN
Meaning: An epithet.
Origin: In the 1800s, British sailors took women along on extended voyages. When babies were born at sea, the mothers delivered them in a partitioned section of the gundeck. Because no one could be sure who the *true* fathers were, each of these "gunnery" babies was jokingly called a "son of a gun."

PUT UP YOUR DUKES
Meaning: Raise your fists and get ready to fight.
Origin: In the early 1800s, the Duke of York, Frederick Augustus, shocked English society by taking up boxing. He gained such admiration from boxers that many started referring to their fists as the "Dukes of York," and later, "dukes."

HAVE AN AXE TO GRIND
Meaning: Have a hidden agenda.
Origin: The expression comes from a story told by Benjamin Franklin. A man once praised Franklin's father's grindstone and asked young Benjamin to demonstrate how the grindstone worked. As Franklin complied, the stranger placed his own axe upon the grindstone, praising the young boy for his cleverness and vigor. When the axe was sharpened, the man laughed at Franklin and walked away, giving the boy a valuable lesson about people with "an axe to grind."

UPPER CRUST
Meaning: Elite.
Origin: In the Middle Ages, the highest-level nobility and royalty were served the choice part of a loaf of bread, the "upper crust," before it was offered to other diners.

MEET A DEADLINE
Meaning: Finish a project by an appointed time.
Origin: The phrase was born in prisoner-of-war camps during the Civil War. Because resources were scarce, the prison camps were

---

The worst nightclubs were traditionally located in basements—hence the name "dives."

sometimes nothing more than a plot of land surrounded by a marked line. If a prisoner tried to cross the line, he would be shot. So it became known as the "deadline."

TOE THE LINE

Meaning: Behave or act in accordance with the rules.

Origin: In the early days of the British Parliament, members wore swords in the House of Commons. To keep the members from fighting during heated debates, the Speaker of the House of Commons forced the Government and Opposition parties to sit on opposite sides of the chamber. Lines, two sword-lengths plus one foot apart, were drawn in the carpet. Members were required to stand behind the lines when the House was in session. To this day, when a member steps over the line during a debate, the speaker yells: "Toe the line!"

SECOND STRING

Meaning: Replacement or backup.

Origin: You might have caught William Tell without an apple, but not without a second string. In medieval times, an archer always carried a second string in case the one on his bow broke.

IN THE LIMELIGHT

Meaning: At the center of attention.

Origin: In 1826, Thomas Drummond invented the limelight, an amazingly bright white light, by running an intense oxygen-hydrogen flame through a lime cylinder. At first, the bright light was used in lighthouses to direct ships. Later, theaters began using the limelight like a spotlight—to direct the audience's attention to a certain actor. If an actor was to be the focal point of a particular scene, he was thrust "into the limelight."

FLASH IN THE PAN

Meaning: Short-lived success.

Origin: In the 1700s, the *pan* of a flintlock musket was the part that held the gunpowder. If all went well, sparks from the flint would ignite the charge, which would then propel the bullet out of the barrel. However, sometimes the gun powder would burn without igniting a main charge. The flash would burn brightly but only briefly, with no lasting effect.

Before 1863, mail service in the U.S. was free.

THE BIRTH OF THE BUG

*The Volkswagen beetle is one of the most unusual-looking cars on
the road, and it has one of the most interesting histories as well.
BRI contributor Jack Mingo tells the story.*

BACKGROUND

Although the VW bug was designed by Ferdinand Porsche
before Adolf Hitler came to power in the '30s, the Führer was
the guy—like it or not—who made the car possible. When German
automakers balked at his plans for manufacturing affordable cars,
Hitler founded the Society for the Development of the German
People's Car. This precursor to the Volkswagen company was
owned and operated by the Nazi regime and was one of Hitler's pet
projects; he even presided over the groundbreaking ceremonies at
the ultramodern Volkswagenwerk factory.

But by 1945, only 210 of the goofy-looking "people's cars" (*Volks
Wagens*) had ever been built...and that was *before* the war. Since
then, the Volkswagen factory had been cranking out vehicles for
the war effort. Now it didn't look like any more of the cars would
ever be built. The plant was so damaged by bombs that Allied
occupation forces planned to dismantle it.

A CLOSE CALL

However, a few of the former car workers, while waiting for the
building to be torn down, cleaned up what was left of the assembly
line and dug up some old parts that had been lying around. Then
they cobbled together a handful of Volkswagens to barter with the
Allied troops for food and other necessities.

The little cars proved popular with the occupying British forces,
especially since the soldiers were short of vehicles. Besides, the
Volkswagen plant had the potential to provide jobs to the restless
and hungry townspeople. So the British changed their plans and
approved of the car-building efforts. They allowed the VW workers
to scrounge the occupied zones for raw materials...and by the end
of 1945, 6,000 people worked at the plant—half building cars, the
other half repairing roofs, walls, and machinery. On their own,

the impoverished, unmanaged workers produced 1,785 cars. The following year, they pumped out 10,020.

WORKING THE BUGS OUT

However, despite its success, it was clear that the VW factory couldn't go on forever building cars out of scrounged materials. The British occupiers tried to get British carmakers to take over Volkswagen production, but none were interested. In 1948, the plant was offered *for free* to Henry Ford II. He turned down the offer on the recommendation of his chief executive officer, Ernest Breech, who told him, "Mr. Ford, I don't think that what we are being offered here is worth a damn!"

The Soviet government, noting that the zone they controlled started less than five miles east of the factory, offered to readjust borders westward and take the VW plant off the hands of the Allies. The Allies refused. There were no other takers.

COMING TO AMERICA

In 1947, Heinrich Nordhoff, a former Opel executive, literally moved his family into the factory and started running it. He improved productivity and quality, and plowed earnings back into the business. Soon it was a profitable enterprise. But the struggling company needed a more lucrative market than postwar Germany, so Nordhoff decided to invade America.

VW's international distributor took a VW Beetle to the United States to open the market. However, newspapers kept referring to the Bug as "Hitler's car" and U.S. auto dealers refused to take it seriously. Finally, the distributor gave up; he sold his single model to a dealer for $800 to pay for his hotel room and return ticket, and went back to Europe defeated.

HOME-GROWN SALES

Although the Volkswagen company couldn't sell VWs to the American public, the little cars could sell themselves. American vets stationed in Europe discovered how good VW Bugs were and began bringing them back to the United States. Word-of-mouth praise began stimulating demand, and a small network of dealerships started to develop. In 1950, 330 VWs were sold in America;

in 1955, 30,000 were sold; and in 1957, the figure more than doubled, to 79,000.

IF IT AIN'T BROKE...

In the meantime, Nordhoff firmly turned aside the suggestion that the ugly little car should be restyled. "The only decision I am really proud of," he once said, "is that I refused to change [the] design." Instead, he concentrated on improving the car's engineering and on creating a reliable service network. Since VW models went through so few changes from year to year, keeping up an inventory of their parts was simple compared with other cars.

Everything about the VW Bug was in marked contrast with American cars. This was, after all, the era of planned obsolescence, of "fins and chrome," of "bigger is better." Detroit didn't know what to make of VW's success, since it was the opposite of what they believed consumers wanted, and cost only $1,280. Henry Ford II called it "a little shitbox."

But VW sales kept climbing. And American executives were shaken when surveys revealed that people buying the Bugs could generally afford better cars...but liked the VW's no-frills design and good engineering. "The Volkswagen sells because it is, more than anything else, an honest car," explained Arthur Railton in a 1956 issue of *Popular Mechanics*. "It doesn't pretend to be anything it is not. Being an honest piece of machinery, it is one the owner can be proud of. Wherever he looks, he sees honest design and workmanship. There are no places where parts don't fit, where paint is thin, where the trim is shoddy. There are no body rattles, no water leaks....There is nothing about the car that is not sincere."

RECORD-BREAKER

In the '30s, Ferdinand Porsche had traveled to the United States to meet Henry Ford and tour his factories. He told Ford about his plans for the Volkswagen and asked him if he minded a little competition. "No," Ford replied, "If somebody can build a car better or cheaper than I can, that serves me right."

On February 15, 1972, the 15,007,034th Beetle rolled off the Volkswagen assembly line, breaking the Ford Model T's record as the most produced automobile in history.

Is a cigar just a cigar? Sigmund Freud smoked 20 of them a day.

IF HEARTACHES WERE WINE

*Are you a fan of country-western music? Here are some toe-tappin'
titles picked by the* Pittsburgh Post-Gazette *for their "Annual All Time
Best of the Worst Country Song Titles." (Dedicated to BRI veteran and
country music fanatic, Melissa Schwarz.)*

"Get Your Tongue Outta My Mouth 'Cause I'm Kissing You Goodbye"

"You're a Cross I Can't Bear"

"Mama Get the Hammer (There's a Fly on Papa's Head)"

"She Made Toothpicks Out of the Timber of My Heart"

"You're the Reason Our Kids Are So Ugly"

"If Fingerprints Showed Up on Skin, Wonder Whose I'd Find on You"

"It Ain't Love, but It Ain't Bad"

"I've Been Flushed from the Bathroom of Your Heart"

"I'm the Only Hell Mama Ever Raised"

"I Got in at 2 with a 10 and Woke Up at 10 with a 2"

"I Don't Know Whether to Come Home or Go Crazy " (*Not to be confused with* "I Don't Know Whether to Kill Myself or Go Bowling")

"If You See Me Gettin' Smaller, It's Cause I'm Leavin' You."

"If Heartaches Were Wine (I'd Be Drunk All the Time)"

"If You Can't Feel It (It Ain't There)"

"Touch Me with More Than Your Hands"

"I've Got the Hungries for Your Love and I'm Waiting in Your Welfare Line"

"The Last Word in Lonesome Is 'Me' "

"I'll Marry You Tomorrow but Let's Honeymoon Tonite"

"When We Get Back to the Farm (That's When We Really Go to Town)"

"You Stuck My Heart in an Old Tin Can and Shot It Off a Log"

"Why Do You Believe Me When I Tell You That I Love You, When You Know I've Been a Liar All My Life?"

"He's Been Drunk Since His Wife's Gone Punk"

"Wild Bill" Hickock had a brother. His nickname was "Tame Bill."

LET *ME* WRITE SIGN— I SPEAK ENGLISH GOOD

When signs in a foreign country are written in English, any combination of words is possible. Here are some real-life examples.

"It is forbidden to steal hotel towels please. If you are not person to do such thing is please not to read notis."

—*Japanese hotel*

"You are invited to take advantage of the chambermaid."

—*Japanese hotel*

"Do not enter the lift backwards, and only when lit up."

—*Leipzig hotel elevator*

"To move the cabin, push button for wishing floor. If the cabin should enter more persons, each one should press a number of wishing floor. Driving is then going alphabetically by national order."

—*Belgrade hotel elevator*

"Please leave your values at the front desk."

—*Paris hotel elevator*

"Our wines leave you nothing to hope for."

—*Swiss restaurant menu*

"Visitors are expected to complain at the office between the hours of 9 and 11 a.m. daily."

—*Athens hotel*

"The flattening of underwear with pleasure is the job of the chambermaid."

—*Yugoslavia hotel*

"The lift is being fixed for the next day. During that time we regret that you will be unbearable."

—*Bucharest hotel lobby*

"Not to perambulate corridors in the hours of repose in the boots of ascension."

—*Austrian hotel for skiers*

"Salad a firm's own make; limpid red beet soup with cheesy dumplings in the form of a finger; roasted duck let loose; beef rashers beaten up in the country people's fashion."

—*Menu at a Polish hotel*

THE "LOUIE, LOUIE" STORY

*"Louie, Louie" is arguably the most recorded rock 'n' roll song of
all time. The following history is from* Behind the Hits, *by Bob
Shannon and John Javna. The authors credit "extensive liner
notes" written by Doc Pelzell for Rhino Records' "Louie, Louie"
album—consisting completely of different versions of the song.*

B esides groupies and recording contracts, what do Frank Zappa, Julie London, Iggy Pop, Barry White, Tom Petty and the
Heartbreakers, Blondie, the Beach Boys, David McCallum,
Toots and the Maytals, and the Kinks have in common? They—
and thousands of other artists—have all performed versions of the
most easily recognizable rock 'n' roll song ever—"Louie, Louie."
This three-chord wonder has been singled out by many critics as *the*
definitive rock 'n' roll song. Yet it wasn't until seven or eight years
after it was originally recorded that most American teens heard it
for the first time.

WRITING IT
In 1955, Richard Berry, a young black musician, was playing in
Los Angeles with a Mexican group called Ricky Rivera and the
Rhythm Rockers. One of the band's songs, "El Loco Cha Cha
Cha," had a contagious rhythm in it that Berry just couldn't get out
of his mind. And while he was waiting backstage to perform at the
Harmony Club Ballroom one night, the words "Louie, Louie"
popped into his head and superimposed themselves around the per-
sistent riff; "the rest just fell into place." His main lyrical influence:
a composition called "One for My Baby," which was sung from the
viewpoint of a customer who was speaking to a bartender named
Joe. In it, the singer said: "One for my baby / One for the road / Set
'em up Joe." In Berry's composition, the bartender became Louie,
and the customer was telling Louie how he intended to sail to
Jamaica to find his true love. The speech patterns and the use of
Jamaica in the song were inspired by Berry's exposure to Latin
music and by Chuck (no relation) Berry's "Havana Moon," a similarly styled song that was popular at the time.

RECORDING IT
When Berry wrote "Louie, Louie," he was under contract to

The words "assassination" and "bump" were invented by Shakespeare.

Modern Records. But because of a dispute over the royalties for the 60-plus songs he had written for the label, he saved the tune until his contract expired and he could record it for Flip Records. Flip released it in 1956, and it became a respectable R&B hit, selling (according to Berry) around 130,000 copies. A year later, however, sales had tapered off, and Berry needed some money for his upcoming wedding. So he sold the record sales publishing rights to "Louie Louie," retaining only the radio and television performance rights. He philosophically chalks this sale up to experience. After all, who could have predicted the bizarre set of circumstances that would, a few years later, turn this song into a monster hit?

DISCOVERING IT

About five years later in Seattle, Washington, an obscure singer by the name of Rockin' Robin Roberts discovered Berry's recording of "Louie, Louie" while browsing through the bargain bin of a local record store. It soon became Robert's signature song and he took it with him through a succession of local bands. Finally, he joined one of the area's more popular groups, the Wailers (no relation to Bob Marley's group), and they decided to cut the song for their own Etiquette Records label. It was a regional hit in the Northwest, but when Liberty Records released it nationally, it flopped.

COPYING IT

Kids in most of America still didn't know the song, but in Portland, Oregon, "Louie, Louie" was hot. One night, a Portland Top 40 band called the Kingsmen were playing a local dance with friendly rivals Paul Revere and the Raiders. During one of their breaks, they happened to notice that a lot of their audience had gathered around a jukebox and were dancing enthusiastically to the Wailers' record. Since this reaction was exactly what the Kingsmen were looking for in their own performances, they decided to include the song in their act; each member agreed to learn the song by their next rehearsal. But the only one to follow through on the pact was lead singer Jack Ely. Consequently, he had to teach it to the rest of the group; when he remembered it incorrectly, no one knew it. He taught the band a 1-2-3, 1-2, 1-2-3, 1-2 version, rather than the Wailers 1-2-3-4, 1-2, 1-2-3-4, 1-2 rendition. The result: He made the tune faster. It's interesting to speculate: would the song have been as successful if Ely hadn't accidentally altered it?

Anyway, the group got the response it was looking for. They were asked to play it as much as eight or nine times a night. One Friday in May 1963, the band decided, just for kicks, to do a marathon version of the song to see who could last longer, the dancers or the band. Even bass player Bob Norby, who didn't sing, warbled a few verses to keep the song going for approximately 45 minutes. Audience response was so positive that arrangements were made that night to record "Louie, Louie" the next day.

RECORDING IT AGAIN

Actually, the Kingsmen had been wanting to get into the studio for some time. Their reason: a summer job. "That's really what 'Louie, Louie' was intended for," members of the band admit now, "an audition tape for a job on a steamship line for the summer. To Australia. We never got there, though. We had this hit record instead and had to go play the White House. And Wyoming. And Iowa." After pooling their money to come up with the $50 they needed for the two-hour session, the group went to the only recording studio in Portland and made their demo. Facilities were, at best, primitive. Microphones were placed next to amps that had been muffled with coats and blankets. Jack Ely's lead vocal was yelled up to a mike that was suspended near the studio's 15-foot ceiling—which explains the garbled lyrics that ultimately helped make the Kingsmen's record so successful. Strange twist: The very next day, Paul Revere and the Raiders, with Mark Lindsay on sax, went into the same studio to record *their* version of "Louie, Louie."

Both the Kingsmen's and Paul Revere's versions got local airplay, and Revere's actually did much better at the outset.

BROADCASTING IT

The Kingsmen recall: "Radio stations in those days used to promote their own shows—dances, record hops, local supermarket openings...and we were the house band for a station called KISN—y'know, we'd go out and do all the shows with all the jocks. And so, as soon as we recorded 'Louie, Louie,' of course, they put it on the air...Paul Revere's version got instant play all up and down the West Coast as soon as it was released; ours was only played in the Portland area, basically. But after a few months, toward the end of '63, a copy of two of our records got back to Boston. A disc jockey named Early Bird on an FM R&B station started playing it, thinking that we were an East Coast rhythm and blues group or something. There was no precedent for this type of sound east of the Rockies. Eventually, Arnie 'Woo-Woo' Ginsberg on WBZ started blasting it all over the Northeast. Then it spread out all over the East Coast, into New York City. And then it became a national hit."

LISTENING TO IT

Going back a few months: After "Louie, Louie" began getting airplay in Boston, it was picked up for pressing and distribution by Wand Records. It fared well; by September, the record had reached #94 on the *Billboard* charts and was climbing fast. But the final shot in the arm that boosted the record to the top of the charts for four months caught even the Kingsmen off-guard; someone, somewhere, decided that the words were "dirty." Without warning, rumors spread that Ely's slurred vocals were laced with obscenities, and soon every teenager in America was buying the record, trying to figure out what he was "really" saying. They even did it at the band's live performances.

REMEMBERING IT

The Kingsmen recall: "It was kind of disheartening at first. Before we knew that there was this 'dirty lyrics' controversy, we thought something was wrong with the band because we'd be playing all night long and when we'd hit our closer, which was 'Louie, Louie'— at the time our only hit—everyone would stop watching us. No one would pay attention any longer; they'd all pull these pieces of paper out of their pockets and start reading along...and singing. And they're going, 'Y'know, which version is right?' It was weird, having all these people come up to you like that."

INVESTIGATING IT

J. Edgar Hoover certainly wasn't going to stand for obscenity on the airwaves. The FBI and FCC launched a "Louie, Louie" investigation, playing the record at every speed from 16 to 78 rpm. They called in both Jack Ely and Richard Berry to testify about the lyrics. And in the end, the FCC concluded that the record was "unintelligible at any speed we played it." They hadn't found what they were looking for, but their efforts weren't entirely fruitless—they helped create a rock 'n' roll classic. With all that "negative" publicity, the record took off. It sold over 8 million copies. "Well, you know," the Kingsmen laugh today, "when the FBI and Lyndon Baines Johnson say, 'You can't do this,' that really does wonders for record sales."

In France, it was once considered bad luck to cut your fingernails on a Friday.

RUMORS

Here are some more classic rumors.

THE RUMOR: The spark from Wint-O-Green Lifesavers can cause explosions.

HOW IT STARTED: In 1968, Dr. Howard Edward and Dr. Donald Edward wrote a letter to the *New England Journal of Medicine* warning that the eerie green sparks given off when you chomp on the Lifesavers could, under certain conditions (like if you ate them in an oxygen tent or a space capsule) start a fire.

WHAT HAPPENED: The letter inspired a number of researchers to experiment with Wint-O-Green Lifesavers. Their findings: The sparks are caused by *methyl salicylate*, a synthetic crystalline substance that's used for flavoring instead of real wintergreen oil. The sparking effect is known scientifically as *triboluminescence*, which is what happens when a crystalline substance is crushed. And since the spark is a "cold luminescence" and not a real spark, it can't cause an explosion.

THE RUMOR: While President Richard Nixon was visiting China, he tried to steal a priceless Chinese teacup by slipping it into his briefcase. The Chinese spotted him. But instead of confronting Nixon directly, they entertained him with a magician who—while performing—surreptitiously retrieved the cup and substituted a worthless replica. Nixon didn't realize it until he got back to the United States.

HOW IT STARTED: The official Chinese news agency released the story.

WHAT HAPPENED: The American government ignored it. Experts explained that the Chinese used it as propaganda to reinforce their self-image: "It symbolized the victory of the resourceful Chinese over the crafty foreigner, and the ability of the Chinese to know how to act without having anyone lose face."

THE RUMOR: Silent screen starlet Clara Bow slept with the entire starting lineup of the 1927 USC football team.

HOW IT STARTED: The story was started by Bow's private secretary, Daisy DeVoe, whom Bow had fired after DeVoe tried to blackmail her. DeVoe got back at her by selling an "inside story" account of Bow's private life to *Graphic*, a notorious New York tabloid. The USC rumor was only part of the story; DeVoe also claimed that Bow had had affairs with Eddie Cantor, Gary Cooper, Bela Lugosi, and other celebrities.

WHAT HAPPENED: The surviving members of the 1927 team deny the story. Author David Stenn tracked them down while researching his biography *Clara Bow Runnin' Wild*. They admit that Bow often invited them to her parties, but they were entirely innocent—Bow didn't even serve alcohol. Even so, the tabloid story destroyed her career: Paramont Studios refused to renew her contract, and Bow "spent the greater part of the rest of her life suffering a series of nervous breakdowns in sanitariums."

THE RUMOR: In the early 1930s, a leper was working at the Chesterfield cigarette factory in Richmond, Virginia.

HOW IT STARTED: Unknown, but executives of the Liggett & Meyers Tobacco Co. believed a competitor was responsible.

WHAT HAPPENED: The "Chesterfield Leper" story spread across the United States in the fall of 1934, costing Chesterfield a big chunk of its business as panicky puffers, fearful of catching leprosy themselves, switched brands overnight. The company fought the rumor hard—it invited government officials to visit the plant and offered $1,000 for information on who had started the rumor. But they never found out.

Interestingly, the rumor didn't disappear—it merely switched brands. In the 1940s, it surfaced as "inside information" about Spud Cigarettes, the first king-size menthol-filter brand. Spud was gone six months later.

THE RUMOR: Mikey, the cute kid in the Life cereal commercials, died in the late '70s when the combination of Pop Rocks candy, and soda pop he'd ingested exploded in his stomach.

HOW IT STARTED: Unknown.

WHAT HAPPENED: The rumor was so prevalent that Pop Rocks were eventually taken off the market, and Life redesigned their cereal boxes to include a photo of Mikey, now grown up…to show that he hadn't exploded, after all.

What do Shakespeare, Louis Armstrong, and Telly Savalas have in common?

THE DUSTBIN
OF HISTORY

*People say fame is fleeting. Here's proof. They were well-known
in their own time...but they're forgotten now.*

JOHN BANVARD

Claim to Fame: One of America's most famous 19th century painters.

Story: In the 1830s, Banvard traveled down the Mississippi River on a raft. Then, using sketches he'd made along the way, he created the largest painting in history—a 12-foot-high, 3-mile-long depiction of more than 1,200 miles of the Mississippi's shoreline. In 1845, he took the painting on the road, charging 25 cents to view the entire work—which took more than two hours as his two assistants rolled it off of one spindle and onto another.

The painting—called "Panorama"—was considered one of the wonders of the day. Throngs of viewers flocked to see it wherever it was displayed, including President Polk and England's Queen Victoria—both of whom sat through the entire viewing. Banvard made more than $200,000 from it.

Into the Dustbin: Not long after Banvard died in 1891, "Panorama" was cut up into hundreds of smaller paintings, most of which were quickly discarded or lost. None survive today.

"DADDY" AND "PEACHES" BROWNING

Claim to Fame: Edward W. "Daddy" Browning was the Donald Trump of his day. He started out as an office boy, but by 1915 he had become a multimillionaire thanks to shrewd investments in New York real estate. Like Trump in the 1980s, he dressed loudly, hobnobbed with celebrities, and craved the spotlight.

Story: It wasn't his money or his wardrobe that made "Daddy" famous, it was his love of adolescent girls. Not long after his wife ran off with the family dentist in 1924, Browning made national headlines when he placed an ad in the New York *Herald Tribune* offer-

They all died on their birthdays.

ing to adopt an impoverished young girl, "about fourteen years old," and raise her as his daughter in wealth and splendor. Scores of mothers responded to the classified ad, and "Daddy" interviewed more than 12,000 teens before settling on "16-year-old" Mary Spaas. But the adoption fell through when reporters discovered that Spaas wasn't 16, she was 21-year-old with a fiance, whom she had dumped in order answer Daddy's newspaper ad. Surprisingly, the publicity made Browning *more* popular with the public, which now saw him as a harmless old fool who had been taken in by a gold-digging young hussie.

Trying Again: Deeply embarrassed by the scandal but still attracted to young girls, Daddy abandoned adoption in favor of sponsoring sorority dances—which he, of course, attended. At one of these he met Frances Belle Heenan, a 15-year-old flapper and high school dropout. For Daddy it was love at first sight. "You look like peaches and cream to me," he told her moments after laying eyes on her. "I'm going to call you 'Peaches.'"

When Daddy married Peaches in 1926, he again made national news…but it was nothing compared to the headlines he got when he divorced her six months later. Trying to win punitive damages in the divorce settlement, Peaches went public with their sex life. "He made me run up and down in front of him naked, while he lay in bed," she told the packed courtroom. "If I refused he became very angry and raved. . . . He tried to make me a pervert on five different occasions." For his part, Daddy denied sleeping with Peaches at all, claiming he was more a father figure than a true husband. "Yes, I anointed her back with oils, but her mother was always there. Never has Peaches gone to sleep in my arms or in my bed." The trial was one of the most closely watched of the 1920s.

Into the Dustbin: Divorce was granted at the end of a five-day trial, but Peaches was awarded only $350 a week in alimony—and that was cut off as soon as the divorce became final. Peaches was hardly destitute, however: she went on to earn more than $8,000 a week on the vaudeville circuit, telling her story to packed auditoriums around the country, and later married (and divorced) three more times. Browning died in 1934; Peaches died in 1956, after falling in the tub. "You know why I married that old bozo," she told a friend after her divorce, "I married him for his jack [money]."

There are more than 500 words for "macaroni" in Italian.

I LOVE LUCY

*"I Love Lucy" ran from 1951 to 1957. It was the
#1 show in America for four of those six years.*

HOW IT STARTED

In 1948, Lucille Ball became a radio star in the CBS series, "My Favorite Husband." It co-starred Richard Denning as her spouse, a Midwestern bank president.

Two years later, CBS decided to move the show to TV, with Denning continuing as Ball's husband. But to their surprise, Ball refused. She insisted that the only way she'd do a TV series was if her real-life husband—Desi Arnaz—was her co-star. CBS balked. "Who," they asked, "would believe that a red-headed movie star and a Cuban bandleader were married?" But Lucy was determined; she thought it was the only way to save her marriage.

To prove to CBS that the public would accept them together, Lucy and Desi put together a vaudeville act and went on the road, performing live. They were billed as *Desi Arnaz and Band with Lucille Ball.* They got rave reviews in New York and Chicago—and interest from NBC.

CBS didn't want to let Lucy get away, so they capitulated and half-heartedly authorized a pilot. At first, they couldn't find a sponsor for it and had practically given up on the project when Phillip Morris cigarettes finally agreed to back it.

But there was still a problem. The sponsors wanted the show done live in New York (where the biggest audience was), but Ball and Arnaz refused to leave Hollywood. They came up with a unique (for the time) compromise: each program was filmed in front of a live audience in California, then edited and transported to the East Coast for a "live" broadcast. This made it the first TV series ever filmed, and gave us "I Love Lucy" reruns.

INSIDE FACTS

Sorry About That, Chief

On January 20, 1953, two important events were televised: Lucy's giving birth to Little Ricky in the "Lucy Goes to the Hospital" episode, and Dwight D. Eisenhower's inauguration. Lucy outdrew Ike by 15 million viewers—44 million to 29 million.

Five other names considered for the 7 Dwarfs: Snoopy, Dippy, Blabby, Woeful, and Flabby.

Good Timing
When "I Love Lucy" premiered, Lucy was 40, Desi was 35, Vivian Vance was 39, and William Frawley was 64.

Out of Sight
After the success of "I Love Lucy," Desi changed hats again, this time from actor to producer. One of his productions, "The Untouchables," put mobster Al Capone in such a bad light that the Mafia reportedly put out a contract on Arnaz's life. After selling his share of Desilu to Lucy for more than $2.5 million in 1962 (she sold it for $17 million just five years later), Desi retired to a ranch east of Los Angeles to raise thoroughbred horses. He died in 1986.

Name Game
Coming up with a name for the program was a struggle. Sponsors wanted to call it "The Lucille Ball Show," but Lucy wanted Desi's name on it, too. They finally agreed that "I Love Lucy" was acceptable, since the "I" referred to Desi, and it came first in the title. Clever solution to a potentially volatile problem.

Paley's Folly
Bill Paley, president of CBS, thought there was absolutely no hope for a series about a dingbat redhead and her Cuban bandleader husband. So he cheerfully handed over all future rights for "I Love Lucy" to Desilu Productions.

Star Wars
While all appeared calm to viewers at home, squabbles on the set were common. Lucy and Desi's tiffs were the stuff of legend, while William Frawley and Vivian Vance really couldn't stand each other. Vance couldn't see why anyone would believe she was married to "that old man;" Frawley often referred to Vance as "that sack of doorknobs."

Red-dy or Not
During the McCarthy "Red scare" in the early '50s, Ball was accused of being a Communist by columnist Walter Winchell, who discovered that she had once joined a leftist organization in the '30s. Amazingly, this actually threatened her career. Desi went to her defense: "The only thing red about Lucy," he responded, "is her hair. And that's not even real." She was exonerated by the House Un-American Activities Committee.

ELVIS LIVES

Who really believes Elvis is still alive? Plenty of people do. As RCA Records used to ask: Can millions of Elvis fans be wrong? BRI member John Dollison wrote this piece so you can judge for yourself.

Early in the morning on August 16, 1977, Elvis Presley and his girlfriend, Ginger Alden, returned to Graceland from a late-night dentist appointment. The two stayed up until about 7:00 a.m. Then Alden went to bed. But, according to one source, "because he had taken some 'uppers,' Elvis was still not sleepy."

So the King retired to his bathroom to read a book. (Sound familiar?) That was the last time anyone ever saw him alive.

THE OFFICIAL STORY

• When Alden woke up at 2:00 in the afternoon, she noticed that Elvis was still in his bathroom. So she decided to check up on him.

• When she opened the door, she saw Elvis sprawled face forward on the floor. "I thought at first he might have hit his head because he had fallen," she recalls, "and his face was buried in the carpet. I slapped him a few times and it was like he breathed once when I turned his head. I lifted one eyelid and it was just blood red. But I couldn't move him." The King was dead.

• Elvis was rushed to Baptist Memorial Hospital in Memphis, but doctors could not revive him. He was pronounced dead at 3:00 p.m. The official cause of death: cardiac arrhythmia brought on by "straining at stool." (The actual cause of death: most likely a massive overdose of prescription drugs.)

That is what is supposed to have happened. Nevertheless, Elvis aficionados across the country see a host of mysterious circumstances that suggest that the King may still be alive.

SUSPICIOUS FACTS

• The medical examiner's report stated that Elvis's body was found in the bathroom in a rigor-mortised state. But the homicide report said that Elvis was found unconscious in the bedroom. In *The Elvis Files*, Gail Brewer-Giorgio notes: "Unconsciousness and rigor mor-

---

tis are at opposite ends of the physical spectrum: rigor mortis is a stiffening condition that occurs after death; unconsciousness, a state in which a living body loses awareness. Bedroom and bathroom are two different places."

• The medical examiner's report lists Elvis's weight at the time of death as 170 pounds; he actually weighed about 250 pounds.

• Elvis's relatives can't agree on how Elvis died. His stepbrother Rick claims Elvis suffocated on the shag carpet; his stepbrother David thinks Elvis committed suicide. Larry Geller, Elvis's hairdresser and spiritual adviser, claims that Elvis's doctors told Vernon Presley (Elvis's father) that the King had leukemia, which may have contributed to his death. Some theorists charge that the confusion surrounding Elvis's death proves that the star faked his death—if the King is really dead, why can't his loved ones get their stories straight?

UNANSWERED QUESTIONS

Elvis's fans want the answers to the following mysteries:

Did Elvis Foresee—or Fake—His Death?

• Elvis didn't order any new jumpsuits—his trademark outfit—in all of 1977. Why not? Did he know he wasn't going to need any?

• On his last concert tour, Elvis was overheard saying, "I may not look good tonight, but I'll look good in my coffin."

• Was Elvis imitating his manager, Colonel Tom Parker? As a young man, Parker also faked his death. An illegal immigrant from Holland whose real name was Andreas Van Kujik, Parker left Holland without telling his relatives; they thought he was dead.

Was the Corpse in Elvis's Coffin Really Elvis's?

• Country singer Tanya Tucker's sister LaCosta was at the King's funeral, and she was shocked at the body's appearance: "We went right up to his casket and stood there, and God, I couldn't believe it. He looked just like a piece of plastic laying there. He didn't look like him at all…he looked more like a dummy than a real person. You know a lot of people think it was a dummy. They don't think he was dead."

• Some observers said they thought the corpse's nose looked too "pugged" to be the King's. They speculated that even if the King had fallen forward and smashed his nose at the time of his death, it would have naturally returned to its original shape, or would at least have been fixed by the undertaker—if the body was really Elvis's. (*The Elvis Files*)

Was the Corpse in Elvis's Coffin a Wax Dummy?

• Some theorists believe that Elvis's coffin weighed more than it was supposed to. Brewer-Giorgio reports receiving a letter from an Elvis fan who claimed to have "personally" known the man who made the King's coffin. The coffin maker revealed that the casket was a "rush" order—and that "there was no way" the coffin could have weighed 900 pounds, as the press reported—even with the King in it. So what was in the coffin with Elvis that made it so heavy?

• According to Brewer-Giorgio, the discrepancy between the coffin's actual weight with Elvis in it and its weight at the funeral is about 250 to 275 pounds, "the weight of a small air-conditioner." "Was there an air-conditioner in the coffin?" Brewer-Giorgio asks, "Wax dummy? Something cool to keep the wax from beading up?"

• To many witnesses, Elvis's corpse appeared to be "sweating" at the funeral. Brewer-Giorgio says she asked Joe Esposito, Elvis's road manager, about TV reports that there were "beads of sweat" on Elvis's body. "He said that was true, that everyone was sweating because the air-conditioner had broken down. Except that dead bodies do not sweat." *But wax melts.*

Why Were the Mourners Acting So Strange at the Funeral?

• Parker wore a loud Hawaiian shirt and a baseball cap to Elvis's funeral and never once approached the casket to say farewell to the King. Elvis's fans argue that if Elvis were *really* dead, Parker would probably have shown a little more respect.

• Elvis's hairdresser claims that he saw Esposito remove Elvis's TCB (Takin' Care of Business) ring from the corpse's finger during the funeral services. Why would he remove one of Elvis's favorite pieces of jewelry—Elvis would surely have wanted to have been buried with it—unless the corpse being buried wasn't the King's?

Is Elvis in the Federal Witness Protection Program?

• In 1970, Presley—a law enforcement buff—was made an honorary Agent-at-Large of the Drug Enforcement Administration by President Nixon after a visit to the White House. According to some theorists, Presley became more than just an honorary agent—he actually got involved in undercover narcotics work.

• In addition to his DEA work, Elvis may have been an FBI agent. During the same trip to Washington D.C., Elvis also wrote a letter to J. Edgar Hoover volunteering his confidential services to the FBI. Hoover wrote back thanking Elvis for his offer, but there is no record of him ever taking it up. Still, Brewer-Giorgio and other theorists argue, the government may have been keeping the King's government service a secret.

• According to Brewer-Giorgio, Elvis was also "a bonded deputy with the Memphis Police and was known to don disguises and go out on narc busts."

• Elvis took his law enforcement role seriously. More than one biography details the time that the King ran out onto the runway of the Las Vegas airport, flagged down a taxiing commercial airliner, and searched it for a man whom he believed had stolen something from him. Elvis looked around, realized his quarry wasn't aboard, and gave the pilot permission to take off.

• Some theorists believe that Elvis's extensive work in law enforcement made him a target for drug dealers and the Mob—and that he entered the Federal Witness Protection Program out of fear for his life. According to Brewer-Giorgio, when Elvis supplied the information that sent a major drug dealer to prison, the King and his family received death threats.

Could Elvis Be in Hiding?
Hundreds of Elvis's loyal fans think they have spotted the King since his "death." He's been sighted at a Rolling Stones concert, working at a Burger King in Kalamazoo, buying gas in Tennessee, and shopping for old Monkees records in Michigan. One woman even claims that Elvis gave her a bologna sandwich and a bag of Cheetos during a 1987 visit to the Air Force Museum in Dayton, Ohio. Could so many people be lying or mistaken?

OTHER MYSTERIES COLLECTED BY ELVIS FANS
• Vernon Presley never went to the hospital the night Elvis "died." If Elvis were really dead, some theorists speculate, he probably would have.

Mary Stuart became Queen of Scotland when she was only six days old.

- According to some reports, within hours of Presley's death, souvenir shops near Graceland began selling commemorative T-shirts of his death. How could they have made so many T-shirts in so little time—unless Graceland had let them know about the "death" in advance?

- Elvis's middle name, Aron, is misspelled "Aaron" on his tombstone. If he's really dead, why don't his relatives correct the mistake?

- Elvis is not buried next to his mother as he requested. Says Brewer-Giorgio: " 'Elvis loved his mother very much and always said he would be buried beside her,' many fans have noted. 'So why is he buried between his father and grandmother?' they ask."

- On a number of occasions after the King's death, Priscilla Presley referred to Elvis as a *living* legend—strange words for a woman who supposedly believes that Elvis is dead.

- Before he died, Elvis took out a multimillion-dollar life insurance policy. To date, no one in his family has tried to claim it. If Elvis is really dead, why haven't they cashed in the policy?

PASSING ON

- The people who were in Elvis's home when he died insist that he really *did* die. Joe Esposito, Elvis's road manager for 17 years, was one of the first people to see the body. "Believe me, the man that I tried to revive was Elvis."

- Elvis may even have committed suicide. According to his stepbrother David Stanley, "Elvis was too intelligent to overdose [accidentally]. He knew the *Physician's Desk Reference* inside and out." Why would Elvis take his own life? He was getting old, and the strain of his stagnating career may have become too much to bear. The pressure showed: in the last years of his life, Elvis's weight ballooned to more than 250 pounds, and his addiction to prescription drugs had gotten out of control.

- The impending publication of a book chronicling the King's vices may have been the final straw. In August 1977, the month of his death, two of his former aides were about to publish a book revealing much of his bizarre personal life to the public for the first time. He was already depressed, and the imminent public exposure of his drug habit may have pushed him over the edge.

NASA invented the "Dust-Buster."

MARK TWAIN SAYS...

No one in the history of American literature has combined sardonic wit, warmth, and intelligence as Mark Twain did in his writings.

"Adam and Eve had many advantages, but the principal one was that they escaped teething."

"Reader, suppose you were an idiot. And suppose you were a member of Congress. But I repeat myself."

"Get your facts first, and then you can distort them as much as you please."

"It is better to keep your mouth shut and appear stupid than to open it and remove all doubt."

"It is by the goodness of God that we have in our country three unspeakably precious things: freedom of speech, freedom of conscience, and the prudence never to practice either."

"Truth is the most valuable thing we have. Let us economize it."

"There are three kinds of lies—lies, damned lies, and statistics."

"Be good, and you will be lonesome."

"A man pretty much always refuses another man's first offer, no matter what it is."

"Noise proves nothing. Often a hen who has merely laid an egg cackles as if she has laid an asteroid."

"The principle difference between a cat and a lie is that a cat only has nine lives."

"Man is the only animal that blushes. Or needs to."

"I believe that our Heavenly Father invented man because he was disappointed in the monkey."

"War talk by men who have been in a war is always interesting, whereas moon talk by a poet who has not been in the moon is likely to be dull."

"The difference between the right word and the almost-right word is the difference between 'lightning' and 'lightning bug.'"

Three Mile Island is two and a half miles long.

OXYMORONS

*Here's a list of oxymorons sent to us by BRI member Peter McCracken.
Peter writes: "I've been collecting these for a while...and sometimes spend
valuable throne time trying to come up with new ones. In case you
don't know, an oxymoron is a common phrase made of two
words that appear to be contradictory."*

Military Intelligence
Light Heavyweight
Jumbo Shrimp
Painless Dentistry
Drag Race
Friendly Fire
Criminal Justice
Permanent Temporary
Amtrack Schedule
Genuine Imitation
Mandatory Option
Protective Custody
Limited Nuclear War
Dear Occupant
Standard Deviation
Freezer Burn
Pretty Ugly
Industrial Park
Loyal Opposition
Eternal Life
Natural Additives
Student Teacher
Educational Television
Nonworking Mother
Active Reserves
Full-Price Discount
Limited Immunity

Death Benefits
Upside Down
Original Copy
Random Order
Irrational Logic
Business Ethics
Slightly Pregnant
Holy Wars
Half Dead
Supreme Court
Even Odds
Baby Grand
Inside Out
Fresh Frozen
Moral Majority
Truth in Advertising
Friendly Takeover
Good Grief
United Nations
Baked Alaska
Plastic Glasses
Peacekeeping Missiles
Somewhat Addictive
Science Fiction
Open Secret
Unofficial Record
Tax Return

Vanilla is used to make chocolate.

APRIL FOOLS!

Why is April 1 a "fools' day"? The most plausible explanation is one we wrote in the first Bathroom Reader, *and reprinted on page 46 in this volume. "These days, most of the memorable April Fools' jokes are played by radio and TV stations. Here are a few recent classics.*

PASTA FARMING

On April 1, 1966, the BBC broadcast a TV documentary on spaghetti-growing in Italy. Among the film's highlights: footage of Italian farmers picking market-ready spaghetti from "spaghetti plants." To the BBC's astonishment, British viewers accepted the news that Italy's "pasta farmers" had been able to fight off the "spaghetti weevil, which has been especially destructive recently."

HE'S BA-A-ACK

In 1992, National Public Radio's "Talk of the Nation" news show announced on April 1 that Richard Nixon had entered the race for president. They actually interviewed the "former president" (played by impressionist Rich Little) on the air. "I never did anything wrong," he announced, "and I won't ever do it again." Listeners actually called the show to comment. "Nixon is more trustworthy than Clinton," one remarked. "Nixon never screwed around with anyone's wife except his own. And according to some accounts, not even with her."

GRAVITATIONAL PULL

On April 1, 1976, a famous British astronomer told BBC radio audiences that since the planet Pluto would be passing close to Jupiter on April 1, the Earth's gravitational pull would decrease slightly for about 24 hours. He explained that listeners would feel the effect most if they jumped into the air at precisely 9:47 a.m. that morning. The BBC switchboard was jammed with listeners calling to say that the experiment had worked.

COLORFUL BROADCAST

In the '70s, Britain's Radio Norwich announced on April 1st that it

---

In 1789, there were 840 men in the U.S. Army.

was experimenting with "color radio," and that the tests would affect the brilliance of tuning lights on radios at home. Some listeners actually reported seeing results: one complained that the experiment had affected the traffic lights in his area; another asked the station managers how much longer the bright colors he saw would be streaming out of his radio.

ANIMAL BEHAVIOR
On April 1, 1992, TV's Discovery Channel ran a "nature documentary" called "Pet Hates," actually a spoof of nature films by a British humorist posing as an animal expert. In the show, the humorist criticized the animals for their "sexual excesses, appalling sense of hygiene, and all-around stupidity"—and denounced them as "sex-crazed, bug-awful, foul-breathed, all-fornicating, all-urinating, disease-ridden, half-wit, furry, four-legged perverts."

DRIVING PRANK
One year, a Paris radio station announced that from April 1 on, all Europe would begin driving on the left. Some drivers actually started driving on the left side of the road. A number of accidents resulted (no fatalities, though).

NEEDLING PEOPLE
In 1989, a Seattle TV station interrupted its regular April 1 broadcast with a report that the city's famous Space Needle had collapsed, destroying nearby buildings in the fall. The report included fake eyewitness accounts from the scene, which were punctuated with bogus updates from the studio newsroom. The "live" footage was so realistic that viewers jammed 911 lines trying to find out if their loved ones were safe. The station later apologized.

THE JOKE IS RED
Even the Russian media celebrates April Fools' Day. In 1992, the Moscow press printed stories claiming that gay rights activists had crossed the Atlantic Ocean in condoms, and that the Moscow City Council was planning a second subway system "in the interest of competition."

There are 33 vampire fan clubs in the United States.

MEET DR. SEUSS

Say hello to Dr. Seuss. A master of nonsense, he was the creator of The Cat in the Hat *and* Green Eggs and Ham *and is one of the most popular kids' authors ever.*

VITAL STATS
Born: March 2, 1904
Died: Sept 25, 1991, age 87

• Although married twice, he never had any children. His slogan: "You have 'em, I'll amuse 'em."

Real Name: Theodor Seuss Geisel

• He adopted "Seuss" as his writing name during Prohibition, while attending Dartmouth College. The reason: He was caught with a half-pint of gin in his room and was told to resign as editor of the college humor magazine as punishment. Instead, he just stopped using Geisel as a byline.

• Years later, he added "Dr." to his name "to sound more sci-entific." He didn't officially become a doctor until 1956, when Dartmouth gave him an honorary doctorate.

CAREER STATS
Accomplishments: He wrote 48 books, selling more than 100 million copies in 20 languages. (Including four of the top 10 bestselling hardcover children's books of all time: *The Cat in the Hat, Green Eggs and Ham, Hop on Pop*, and *One Fish, Two Fish, Red Fish, Blue Fish.*)

• As a filmmaker, he won three Oscars—two for documentaries made in the 1940s ("Hitler Lives," about Americans troops, and "Design for Death," about Japanese warlords), and one in 1951 for animation ("Gerald McBoing-Boing"). By that time he had written four kids' books and turned down Hollywood screenplay offers in order to keep writing them.

• In 1984, he won the Pulitzer Prize for his contribution to children's literature.

Flops: Only one—a novel called *The Seven Lady Godivas*, an "utterly ridiculous retelling of the story of Lady Godiva" first

---

The word *walrus* comes from the Dutch term that means "horse whale."

published in 1937 and republished 40 years later…but the book bombed in 1977, too.

How He Got Started: He was working as a cartoonist in the late '20s for *Judge* magazine. One of his cartoons "showed a knight using Flit insecticide to kill dragons." Someone associated with Flit's ad agency (McCann-Erikson) saw the cartoon and hired Geisel. For the next 10 years he created ads for Flit and other Standard Oil products. His greatest claim to fame at the time: the well-known ad phrase: "Quick Henry, the Flit!"

His contract with McCann-Erikson allowed him to write and publish books for kids, so he wrote *To Think That I Saw It on Mulberry Street.* It was turned down by 27 publishers. Said Seuss: "The excuse I got for all those rejections was that there was nothing on the market quite like it, so they didn't know whether it would sell." Vanguard Press finally picked it up in 1937, and it was an immediate success. So he quit the ad agency and began writing kids' books full-time.

HOW HE GOT HIS IDEAS
"The most asked question of any successful author," Seuss said in 1989, "is 'How do you get your ideas for books?'" Over the years he did reveal a number of his inspirations. For example:

Horton Hatches the Egg
• "Sometimes you have luck when you are doodling. I did one day when I was drawing some trees. Then I began drawing elephants. I had a window that was open, and the wind blew the elephant on top of the tree; I looked at it and said, 'What do you suppose that elephant is doing there?' The answer was: 'He is hatching an egg.' Then all I had to do was write a book about it. I've left that window open ever since, but it's never happened again."

Green Eggs and Ham
• Bennett Cerf, the founder and publisher of Random House, bet Geisel $50 that he couldn't write a book using just 50 words.
• Geisel won the bet. "It's the only book I ever wrote that still makes me laugh," he said 25 years later. He added: "Bennett never paid!"

Mark Twain coined the term "gossip column" in 1893.

Yertle the Turtle
• "Yertle the turtle is Adolf Hitler."

Marvin K. Mooney, Will You Please Go Now?
• "The puppylike creature constantly asked to 'go' is ex-President Richard M. Nixon."

The Lorax
• Dr. Seuss's favorite book, he said, "is about people who raise hell in the environment and leave nothing behind." He wrote the story on a laundry list as he sat by a hotel pool in Kenya watching a herd of elephants. "I wrote it as a piece of propaganda and disguised the fact," he told a reporter. "I was on the soapbox. I wasn't afraid of preaching—but I was afraid of being dull."

The 500 Hats of Bartholomew Cubbins
• In 1937, Geisel was on a commuter train in Connecticut. "There was a very stiff broker sitting in front of me. I wondered what his reaction would be if I took his hat off and threw it out the window. I decided that he was so stuffy he would grow a new one."

The Cat in the Hat
• In the early 1950s, novelist John Hersey was on a panel that analyzed how reading was taught in a Connecticut school system. In May 1954, *Life* magazine published excerpts of the panel's report (called "Why Do Students Bog Down on the First R?"). In it, Hersey wrote that one of the major impediments to learning was the dull "Dick and Jane" material students were given—especially the illustrations. Kids, he said, should be inspired with "drawings like those wonderfully imaginative geniuses among children's illustrators, Tenniel, Howard Pyle, Dr. Seuss."

• A textbook publisher read the article and agreed. He contacted Dr. Seuss and asked him to create a reading book. The publisher sent Seuss a list of 400 words and told him to pick 220 to use in the book. The reason: People felt this was the maximum that "kids could absorb at one time."

• "Geisel went through the list once, twice and got nowhere," reports *Parents* magazine. "He decided to give it one more shot; if he could find two words that rhymed, they'd form the title and theme of the book. Within moments, *cat* and *hat* leaped off the page. But then it took him nine months to write the entire book."

Literally translated, the word *carnival* means "flesh, farewell."

ALLENISMS

Some of Woody Allen's best lines.

"Thought: Why does man kill? He kills for food. And not only food: frequently there must be a beverage."

"Showing up is 80 percent of life."

"Is sex dirty? Only if it's done right."

"If only God would give me some clear sign! Like making a large deposit in my name at a Swiss bank."

"I'm a practicing heterosexual...but bisexuality immediately doubles your chances for a date on Saturday night."

"My brain: it's my second favorite organ."

"I don't want to achieve immortality through my work...I want to achieve it through not dying."

"Not only is there no God, but try getting a plumber on weekends."

Q. "Have you ever taken a serious political stand on anything?"
A. "Yes, for twenty-four hours I refused to eat grapes."

"Eternal nothingness is OK if you're dressed for it."

"I'm not afraid to die. I just don't want to be there when it happens."

"Money is better than poverty, if only for financial reasons."

"I want to tell you a terrific story about oral contraception. I asked this girl to sleep with me and she said 'no.' "

"My one regret in life is that I'm not someone else."

"I asked the girl if she could bring a sister for me. She did. Sister Maria Teresa. It was a very slow evening. We discussed the New Testament. We agreed that He was very well adjusted for an only child."

FAMOUS FOR 15 MINUTES

Here are some more folks who lived up to Andy Warhol's prediction that "in the future, everyone will be famous for 15 minutes."

THE HEADLINE: *Man Boldly Goes Where No Man Has Gone Before…In a Lawn Chair*

THE STAR: Larry Walters, self-proclaimed "settled-down dude"

WHAT HAPPENED: On July 2, 1982, Walters strapped 42 helium-filled weather balloons to his $109 aluminum Sears lawn chair and took off from the backyard of his girlfriend's San Pedro, California, home.

Walters planned to travel more than 300 miles across the desert, but shot straight up instead, flying so high that he turned numb and lost his breath. He began to panic. He tried shooting out some of the weather balloons with the pellet gun he'd brought with him, but accidentally dropped the gun after hitting only seven of them. He then began calling for help on his CB radio.

Walters drifted eight miles downwind into Long Beach Municipal Airport airspace, where a Delta pilot saw the wingless craft and reported it to federal authorities. A police helicopter followed Walters until he flew into some power lines (blacking-out one Long Beach neighborhood for 20 minutes) then crashed onto the driveway of a private home.

THE AFTERMATH: Walters's flight broke the world altitude record for clustered balloon flight, but because it was unlicensed and unsanctioned, the record is not official. Even worse, the FAA fined him $1,500. Still, not all the news was bad: he got to appear on "The Tonight Show," "Late Night with David Letterman," and other TV shows. "I had to do it," he told reporters, "If I hadn't done it, I'd have ended up in the funny farm!"

In October 1993, Walters shot himself to death. He did not leave a suicide note.

There was so little dialogue in the original "Mission Impossible" TV show that

THE HEADLINE: *Man Floats Like Butterfly into Boxing Ring… Gets Stung Like a Bee*

THE STAR: James Miller, Las Vegas resident and self-proclaimed "fan man"

WHAT HAPPENED: Professional boxers Riddick Bowe and Evander Holyfield were in the middle of their heavyweight title fight on November 6, 1993, when the TV blimp noticed a man with a paraglider (a small parachute-glider) flying about 800 feet over the Caesar's Palace outdoor pavilion. The man circled for about 20 minutes, then suddenly plunged into the ring, stopping the fight.

The fight was delayed for 21 minutes while security officials tackled the man and carried him away on a hospital gurney as he shouted repeatedly, "I'm the fan man, the man with the fan." The Reverend Jesse Jackson and Louis Farrakhan of the Nation of Islam were sitting so close to the spot he landed that they became entangled in the parachute lines and might have been killed had they not gotten out of the way in time.

THE AFTERMATH: Miller was arrested again on January 9, 1994, after he circled the Los Angeles Coliseum during a Raiders-Broncos play-off game…and was arrested a *third* time on February 5, 1994, when he paraglided onto the roof of Buckingham Palace, stripped off his flight suit, and taunted police in the nude as they scrambled to arrest him.

THE HEADLINE: *Boy Wins Pardon After Telling Lie*

THE STAR: Cody McGannon, a 10-year-old from Gladstone, Montana

WHAT HAPPENED: One afternoon in January 1995, Cody McGannon told his parents he hadn't opened his bedroom window, even though he actually had. When his mother caught him in the lie, they grounded him for a week: no allowance, no TV, no bike riding, and no visiting with friends. His stepfather told him that if he didn't like his punishment, he should ask the governor for a pardon. And to his parents' surprise, Cody wrote a two-paragraph letter to Missouri governor Mel Carnahan. "I hope you will grant me amnesty on Saturday, January 21, 1995," it read. "Love, Cody."

Peter Graves, the star, once fell asleep in the middle of a scene…and no one noticed.

Impressed with Cody's initiative, his mom faxed the letter to the governor's office and, amazingly, the governor granted the pardon that same day. "I hope the authorities (your parents) are not too upset with me, and that they decide to accept my act of clemency in the same spirit of goodwill in which it was given," Governor Carnahan wrote.

THE AFTERMATH: The media got wind of the story, and it made headlines all over the country. "Can you believe this? I know I can't." McGannon's mom told reporters, " 'Donahue' wants to fly Cody and me out to New York City, and Jay Leno's office called last night. It has been a tremendous boost to Cody's self-esteem."

THE HEADLINE: *Spurned by TV's Greg Brady, Office Worker Finds Fame as "The Snapple Lady"*

THE STAR: Wendy Kaufman, an administrator in the orders department of the Snapple Beverage Corporation

WHAT HAPPENED: In the early 1970s, young Wendy Kaufman fell in love with teen actor Barry Williams, who played Greg Brady on "The Brady Bunch." She wrote to him, "but he never answered," she says…and she never forgot.

That's why, years later, when she got a job at Snapple in 1991, she took it upon herself to answer consumers' letters to the company. "The letters started coming in," she says. "People were sharing the most unbelievable stories. There were car fires that people put out with a quart of Snapple, people meeting who they would marry because of Snapple."

The unusual letters caught the eye of Snapple's advertising agency in 1992. They decided to build an advertising campaign around them…and around Kaufman, figuring that someone so unaffected would make an ideal spokesperson for a drink that's supposedly "made from the best stuff on Earth."

THE AFTERMATH: The ads worked—sales of Snapple went from $200 million in 1992 to almost $700 million in 1994, making the "Snapple Lady" a star. "It's too hilarious," Kaufman says. "Who would ever have expected this?" She has appeared in nearly 40 commercials, but remains in charge of answering Snapple's mail—about 2,000 letters a week.

THE HEADLINE: *Dowdy Housewife Who Can't Carry a Tune Makes It Big...as a Rock Star*

THE STAR: Mrs. Elva Miller, a 59-year-old Los Angeles housewife

WHAT HAPPENED: In the early '60s, Mrs. Miller tried out for the First Presbyterian Church choir in Los Angeles. Her voice was so bad, they kicked her out on the spot. "Among the hundred other voices," she explained, "mine stuck out like a sore thumb." So Mrs. Miller decided to indulge her passion for music by making private recordings. They were so awful that they were funny.

When someone gave a copy to an L.A. disk jockey, he played it on the air. The song quickly became one of the station's most-requested songs and Capitol Records rushed to sign Mrs. Miller to a record contract. Capitol executives told her she was part of an "experiment," an "operatic type of voice doing rock 'n' roll." But what they really wanted was a *bad* voice doing rock 'n' roll. Mrs. Miller didn't catch on at first, but the executives deliberately sabotaged the session in order to get the "sound" they were looking for. *Life* magazine described the scene in 1967:

> First the light signal from the control room went on ahead of time. Then behind time. "I just couldn't follow along," recalls Mrs. Miller. Her performance went from bad to worse—which of course was just what was wanted. Conducted a half-beat ahead of the orchestra and choral group, she slowed down, whereupon the accompaniment was deliberately accelerated. When she caught up, the director again dropped a half beat behind. Another time, after six or eight tries at "The Shadow of Your Smile," the version farthest off-key was chosen. At last the light came to Mrs. Miller. "They considered me very naive, I guess. When we did that off-meter part, I suspected. And when they printed the worst 'The Shadow of Your Smile,' I knew it was a gag."

THE AFTERMATH: Mrs. Miller laughed with them—all the way to the bank. Her first record, *Mrs. Miller's Greatest Hits*, sold 200,000 copies, spawned two other successful albums, and propelled her into the limelight. Stories about her appeared in *Time, Life, Newsweek,* etc. She appeared on "The Ed Sullivan Show," toured Vietnam with the USO, and earned well over $100,000—a substantial sum in the late 1960s.

BASKETBALL NAMES

Here's what we dug up about origins of pro basketball names.

Seattle Supersonics. Named after a supersonic jet proposed by Seattle-based Boeing in the late '60s. (The jet was never built.)

Washington Bullets. Originally the Baltimore Bullets, they were named in honor of a nearby ammunition factory that supplied American troops during World War II.

Los Angeles Lakers. There are no lakes in L.A. The team was originally the Minneapolis Lakers; Minnesota is the "Land of 1,000 Lakes."

Detroit Pistons. Not named for the auto industry. The team's founder, Fred Zollner, owned a piston factory in Fort Wayne, Indiana. In 1957, the Zollner Pistons moved to Detroit.

New Jersey Nets. Originally called the New York Nets to rhyme with New York Mets (baseball) and New York Jets (football).

Houston Rockets. Ironically, it has nothing to do with NASA. They began as the San Diego Rockets—a name inspired by the theme of a "city in motion" and its "space-age industries."

Orlando Magic. Inspired by Disney's Magic Kingdom.

New York Knicks. Short for knickerbockers, the pants that Dutch settlers in New York wore in the 1600s.

Indiana Pacers. Owners wanted to "set the pace" in the NBA.

Los Angeles Clippers. Started out in San Diego, where great sailing boats known as clipper ships used to dock a hundred years ago.

Sacramento Kings. The Cincinnati Royals moved to Kansas City in 1972. The city already had a Royals baseball team, so they became the Kansas City Kings, then the Sacramento Kings.

Atlanta Hawks. Started in 1948 as the Tri-Cities Blackhawks (Moline and Rock Island, Illinois, and Davenport, Iowa)How much does teh . They were named after Sauk Indian chief Black Hawk, who fought settlers of the area in the 1831 Black Hawk Wars. In 1951, the team moved to Milwaukee and shortened its name to Hawks.

FABULOUS FLOPS

*Next time you read about some amazing overnight success,
remember these equally fabulous stinkers.*

THE GTO SHOE

In the '60s, Thom McAn Shoes cashed in on every fad.
They had Beatle Boots, Monkee Boots, Chubby Checker
Twister boots, and even Ravi Shankar "Bombay Buckles." But they
lost their magic touch when they tried to ride the hot car fad of the
mid-'60s with GTO shoes, "the world's first high-performance
shoe." Promoted in conjunction with Pontiac's celebrated GTO,
the footwear came equipped with "pointed toes, beveled accelera-
tor heels, and double-beam eyelets."

The Pontiac GTO was a huge success, but most of Thom
McAn's GTO shoes wound up being donated to charity.

INSTANT FISH

In the early '60s, one of the owners of the Wham-O Mfg. Co.—
makers of Hula Hoops and Frisbees—was on vacation in Africa.
One evening, he camped beside a dry lakebed; during the night it
rained, and the lake filled up. The next day he noticed there were
fish in the lake. "How could that be?" he thought. "Fish don't grow
overnight."

When he got back to California, he asked a biologist friend what
had happened and was told that there is indeed a fish in that part
of the world whose eggs lay dormant until they are exposed to water. Then the eggs hatch and the fish emerge.

It sounded like an incredible idea for a product—"Instant Fish."
Wham-O hurriedly built huge fish tanks in their factory and imported thousands of fish so they could start collecting the eggs.

Meanwhile, the annual New York Toy Fair, where toy store
owners from all over the U.S. buy merchandise, was taking place...
and "Instant Fish" was the smash of the show. In a week, Wham-O
took orders for $10 million worth of fish (an incredible amount in
the mid-'60s). Even when the company refused to take any more
orders, people sneaked to Wham-O's hotel rooms and slipped orders under the door. "Instant Fish" was a gold mine.

Except that nobody told the fish. They just couldn't lay eggs fast enough to supply all the excited toy store owners. Desperate, Wham-O tried everything they could think of: They tried covering the windows to darken the inside of their plant; they tried warmer room temperatures and cooler ones; they even tried piping romantic music into the tanks. But nothing worked. Wham-O finally had to admit that "Instant Fish" had laid its own enormous egg. After shipping only a fraction of the fish, they cancelled all orders.

"TURN ON"

In 1968 and 1969, "Laugh-In" was TV's #1 show. Hoping to buy themselves a copycat hit, ABC hired "Laugh-In" executive producer George Schlatter to create an identical series. And by mid-1969, he'd put together "Turn-On," which ABC promoted as "the second coming of 'Laugh-In,'" a "visual, comedic, sensory assault." "Turn-On" premiered on February 5, 1969. It was so bad that the next day phone calls poured in from ABC affiliates all over the United States to say that they refused to carry the show. Embarrassed, the network cancelled it immediately, making it the shortest-lived nighttime series in television history.

THE ANIMAL-OF-THE-MONTH CLUB

In the '50s and '60s, mail-order "thing-of-the-month" clubs were big business—worth close to a billion dollars a year. Americans were buying Fruit-of-the-Month, Candy-of-the-Month, House-of-the-Month (architectural plans), Cheese-of-the-Month, Flowers-of-the-Month, and so on. How far could the fad go? Creative Playthings took it to the limit when it introduced the "Animal-of-the-Month Club" in the late '60s. Every month, the company promised, an exotic "pet"—such as an Argentine toad snail, a musk turtle, a newt, a Mongolian gerbil, or something else—would arrive through the mail at subscribers' houses.

But shipping exotic pets turned out to be a crazy—and cruel—idea. In 1968, for example, Creative Playthings had orders for 4,000 Argentine toads but couldn't find enough of them in the Argentine swamps to supply the demand. But that wasn't the worst of their problems. Ever try bulk-mailing animals? The creatures-of-the-month arrived dead, squashed, or dehydrated. Mercifully, Creative Playthings took its losses and gave up.

BANNED BOOKS

It can't happen here? Guess again. Each year, the American Booksellers Association holds a "Banned Books Week" to call attention to the issues surrounding censorship. Here are some books that were banned, or nearly banned, during the 1980s.

The **Diary of Anne Frank**, by Anne Frank. In 1983, members of the Alabama State Textbook Committee wanted the book rejected because it was "a real downer."

Lord of the Flies, by William Golding. In 1981, the book was challenged by a high school in Owen, North Carolina, because it was "demoralizing inasmuch as it implies that man is little more than an animal."

Biology, by Karen Arms and Pamela S. Camp. In 1985, the Garland, Texas, textbook selection committee complained of "overly explicit diagrams of sexual organs."

The American Pageant: A History of the Republic, by Thomas A. Bailey and David M. Kennedy. In 1984, officials in the Racine, Wisconsin, School District complained that the book contained "a lot of funny pictures of Republicans and nicer pictures of Democrats."

Zen Buddhism: Selected Writings, by D. T. Suzuki. In 1987, the school system of Canton, Michigan, was informed that "this book details the teaching of the religion of Buddhism in such a way that the reader could very likely embrace its teachings and choose this as his religion."

1984, by George Orwell. In 1981, the book was challenged in Jackson County, Florida, because it was "pro-communist and contained explicit sexual matter."

Slugs, by David Greenburg. In 1985, an elementary school in Escondido, California, banned the book for describing "slugs being dissected with scissors."

A Light in the Attic, by Shel Silverstein. In 1986, the popular children's book was challenged at an elementary school in Mukwonago, Wisconsin, because it "gloried Satan, suicide and cannibalism, and also encouraged children to be disobedient."

The Crucible, by Arthur Miller. In 1982, citizens of Harrisburg, Pennsylvania, complained about staging a play with "sick words from the mouths of demon-possessed people. It should be wiped out of the schools or the school board should use them to fuel the fire of hell."

Slaughterhouse Five, by Kurt Vonnegut. In 1985, complaints were made in an Owensboro, Kentucky, high school library because the book had "foul language, a section depicting a picture of an act of bestiality, a reference to 'Magic Fingers' attached to the protagonist's bed to help him sleep, and the sentence: 'The gun made a ripping sound like the opening of the fly of God Almighty.' "

Meet the Werewolf, by Georgess McHargue. In 1983, the school district of Vancouver, Oregon, claimed that the book was "full of comments about becoming a werewolf, use of opium, and pacts with the devil."

Album Cover Album, by Roger Dean. (A book of album covers.) In 1987, the Vancouver, Washington, school district objected to a photo of the "Statue of Liberty with bare breasts as exemplary of several photos that were pretty raw toward women."

The Amazing Bone, by William Steig. In 1986, a parent in Lambertville, New Jersey, complained to the local school library about "the use of tobacco by the animals" in this fantasy.

The Haunting of America, by Jean Anderson. In 1985, an elementary school in Lakeland, Florida, claimed it "would lead children to believe in demons without realizing it."

Note: Lewis Caroll's **Alice's Adventures in Wonderland** was banned in China in 1931. Authorities objected that "animals should not use human language, and that it was disastrous to put animals and human beings on the same level."

The word *Mafia* comes from an Old Arabic word that means "sanctuary."

WHO'S ON FIRST?

The Abbott and Costello baseball routine "Who's on First?" is considered a landmark in the history of comedy.

Abbott and Costello's recording of "Who's on First?" became the first gold record placed in the Baseball Hall of Fame in Cooperstown, New York.

• "The Baseball Scene," as it was known before it was given the title "Who's on First?" was a burlesque standard long before Abbott and Costello popularized it. In fact, Abbott and Costello each performed it with other vaudeville partners before teaming up in 1936.

• When the duo first performed the routine on radio's "The Kate Smith Hour," they were forced to change the ending from "I don't give a damn!" / "Oh, that's our shortstop" to "I don't care" / "Oh, that's our shortstop." President Roosevelt was listening; he enjoyed it so much that he called them personally to offer congratulations after the show.

HERE'S THE ROUTINE

BUD: You know, strange as it may seem, they give baseball players peculiar names nowadays. On the St. Louis team Who's on first, What's on second, I Don't Know is on third.

LOU: That's what I want to find out. I want you to tell me the names of the fellows on the St. Louis team.

BUD: I'm telling you. Who's on first, What's on second, I Don't Know is on third.

LOU: You know the fellows' names?

BUD: Yes.

LOU: Well, then, who's playin' first?

BUD: Yes.

LOU: I mean the fellow's name on first base.

BUD: Who.

LOU: The fellow's name on first base for St. Louis.

BUD: Who.

LOU: The guy on first base.

BUD: Who.

LOU: Well, what are you askin' me for?

BUD: I'm not asking you. I'm telling you. Who is on first.

LOU: I'm askin' you, who is on first?

BUD: That's the man's name.

LOU: That's whose name?

BUD: Yes.

The yolk's on you: If you're an average American, you'll eat 5,666 fried eggs in your lifetime.

LOU: Well, go ahead and tell me.

BUD: Who?

LOU: The guy on first.

BUD: Who.

LOU: The first baseman.

BUD: Who is on first.

LOU: (*trying to stay calm*) Have you got a first baseman on first?

BUD: Certainly.

LOU: Well, all I'm trying to find out is what's the guy's name on first base.

BUD: Oh, no, no. What is on *second* base.

LOU: I'm not askin' you who's on second.

BUD: Who's on first.

LOU: That's what I'm tryin' to find out.

BUD: Well, don't change the players around.

LOU: (*starting to get angry*) I'm not changin' anybody.

BUD: Now take it easy.

LOU: What's the guy's name on first base?

BUD: What's the guy's name on *second* base.

LOU: I'm not askin' you who's on second.

BUD: Who's on first.

LOU: I don't know.

BUD: He's on third. We're not talking about him.

LOU: (*begging*) How could I get on third base?

BUD: You mentioned his name.

LOU: If I mentioned the third baseman's name, who did I say is playing third?

BUD: (*starting all over again*) No, Who's playing first.

LOU: Stay offa first, will ya?

BUD: Please, now what is it you'd like to know?

LOU: What is the fellow's name on third base?

BUD: What is the fellow's name on second base.

LOU: I'm not askin' ya who's on second.

BUD: Who's on first.

LOU: I don't know.

BUD & LOU: (*together*) Third base!

LOU: (*tries again*) You got an outfield?

BUD: Certainly.

LOU: St. Louis got a good outfield?

BUD: Oh, absolutely.

LOU: The left fielder's name.

BUD: Why.

LOU: I don't know. I just thought I'd ask.

BUD: Well, I just thought I'd tell you.

LOU: Then tell me who's playing left field.

BUD: Who's playing first.

LOU: Stay outa the infield!

BUD: Don't mention any names there.

LOU: (*firmly*) I wanta know

what's the fellow's name in left field.

BUD: What is on second.

LOU: I'm not askin' you who's on second.

BUD: Who is on first.

LOU: I don't know!

BUD & LOU: (*together*) Third base! (*Lou makes funny noises*)

BUD: Now take it easy, man.

LOU: And the left fielder's name?

BUD: Why?

LOU: Because.

BUD: Oh, he's center field.

LOU: Wait a minute. You got a pitcher on the team?

BUD: Wouldn't this be a fine team without a pitcher?

LOU: I dunno. Tell me the pitcher's name.

BUD: Tomorrow.

LOU: You don't want to tell me today?

BUD: I'm telling you, man.

LOU: Then go ahead.

BUD: Tomorrow.

LOU: What time?

BUD: What time what?

LOU: What time tomorrow are you gonna tell me who's pitching?

BUD: Now listen, who is not pitching. Who is on—

LOU: (*excited*) I'll break your arm if you say who is on first.

BUD: Then why come up here and ask?

LOU: I want to know what's the pitcher's name!

BUD: What's on second.

LOU: (*sighs*) I don't know.

BUD & LOU: (*together*) Third base!

LOU: You gotta catcher?

BUD: Yes.

LOU: The catcher's name.

BUD: Today.

LOU: Today. And Tomorrow's pitching.

BUD: Now you've got it.

LOU: That's all. St. Louis got a couple of days on their team. That's all.

BUD: Well, I can't help that. What do you want me to do?

LOU: Gotta catcher?

BUD: Yes.

LOU: I'm a good catcher, too, you know.

BUD: I know that.

LOU: I would like to play for St. Louis.

BUD: Well, I might arrange that.

LOU: I would like to catch. Now Tomorrow's pitching on the team and I'm catching.

BUD: Yes.

LOU: Tomorrow throws the ball and the guy up bunts the ball.

BUD: Yes.

LOU: So when he bunts the ball, me, bein' a good catcher, I want to throw the guy out at first base. So I pick up the ball and I throw it to who?

BUD: Now that's the first thing you've said right!

LOU: *I don't even know what I'm talkin' about!*

BUD: Well, that's all you have to do.

LOU: I throw it to first base.

BUD: Yes.

LOU: Now who's got it?

BUD: Naturally.

LOU: Naturally.

BUD: Naturally.

LOU: I throw the ball to naturally.

BUD: You throw it to Who.

LOU: Naturally.

BUD: Naturally, well, say it that way.

LOU: That's what I'm saying!

BUD: Now don't get excited, don't get excited.

LOU: I throw the ball to first base.

BUD: Then Who gets it.

LOU: He'd better get it.

BUD: That's it. All right now, don't get excited. Take it easy.

LOU: (*beside himself*) Now I throw the ball to first base, whoever it is grabs the ball, so the guy runs to second.

BUD: Uh-huh.

LOU: Who picks up the ball and throws it to What. What throws it to I Don't Know. I Don't Know throws it back to Tomorrow. A triple play!

BUD: Yeah, could be.

LOU: Another guy goes up and it's a long fly ball to center. Why? I don't know. And I don't give a damn!

BUD: What was that?

LOU: I said, I don't give a damn!

BUD: Oh, that's our shortstop.

★ ★ ★ ★

BASEBALL'S UNOFFICIAL ANTHEM

In the summer of 1908, a vaudevillian named Jack Norworth was riding the New York City subway when he noticed an ad that read "Baseball Today—Polo Grounds." He'd never been to a baseball game, but knew the sport was popular…and it hit him that a baseball song might fit into his act. He jotted down some lyrics and took them to a friend named Albert von Tilzer—who'd never seen a baseball game either. Von Tilzer set the words to music.

Norworth turned the song into a "Nickelodeon slide show"—a sort of turn-of-the-century MTV. (Slide shows featuring sing-along lyrics were shown at movie theaters between films.) Audiences followed the bouncing ball and made "Take Me Out to the Ballgame" a hit. Ironically, it wasn't until *after* the tune was popular that Norworth finally did get out to see an "old ballgame."

FAMILIAR PHRASES

What do these familiar phrases really mean? Here are some more explanations, researched by BRI etymologists.

HAM ACTOR (HAM)

Meaning: Someone who enjoys putting on a show, or who plays rather obviously to an audience (though not necessarily on stage).

Origin: An American phrase originating in the 1880s. Minstrel shows, the mass entertainment of the time, often featured less-than-talented performers who overacted. They frequently appeared in blackface, and used ham fat to remove their makeup. Thus, they were referred to as "ham-fat men," later shortened to "hams."

WHIPPING BOY

Meaning: A scapegoat, or someone who is habitually picked on.

Origin: Hundreds of years ago, it was normal practice for a European prince to be raised with a commoner of the same age. Since princes couldn't be disciplined like ordinary kids, the commoner would be beaten whenever the prince did something wrong. The commoner was called the prince's "whipping boy."

GO BERSERK

Meaning: Go crazy or to act with reckless abandon.

Origin: Viking warriors were incredibly wild and ferocious in battle, probably because they ate hallucinogenic mushrooms in prebattle ceremonies. They charged their enemies recklessly, wearing nothing more than bearskin, which in Old Norse was pronounced "*berserkr*" or "*bear-sark*."

PULL SOMEONE'S LEG

Meaning: Fool someone.

Origin: Years ago back-alley thieves worked in pairs. One thief, known as a "tripper up," would use a cane, rope, or piece of wire to trip a pedestrian, knocking them to the ground. While the victim was down, the second thief would rob them. *Pulling your leg* originally referred to the way the "tripper up" tried to make someone stumble. Today it only refers to tripping up someone figuratively.

RAINING CATS AND DOGS

Meaning: Torrential rain.

Origin: In the days before garbage collection, people tossed their trash in the gutter—including deceased housepets—and it just lay there. When it rained really hard, the garbage, including the bodies of dead cats and dogs, went floating down the street.

PIE IN THE SKY

Meaning: An illusion, a dream, a fantasy, an unrealistic goal.

Origin: Joe Hill, a famous labor organizer of the early 20th century, wrote a tune called "The Preacher and the Slave," in which he accused the clergy of promising a better life in Heaven while people starved on Earth. A few of the lines: "Work and pray, live on hay, you'll get pie in the sky when you die (That's a lie!)."

HACK WRITER

Meaning: Writer who churns out words for money.

Origin: In Victorian England, a hackney, or "hack," was a carriage for hire. (The term is still used in reference to taxi drivers, who need their "hack's licenses" to work.) Hack became a description of anyone who plies their trade strictly for cash.

LONG IN THE TOOTH

Meaning: Old.

Origin: Originally used to describe old horses. As horses age, their gums recede, giving the impression that their teeth are growing. The longer the teeth look, the older the horse.

STOOL PIGEON

Meaning: Informer, traitor.

Origin: To catch passenger pigeons (now extinct), hunters would nail a pigeon to a stool. Its alarmed cries would attract other birds, and the hunters would shoot them by the thousand. The poor creature that played the traitor was called a "stool pigeon."

BEAT AROUND THE BUSH

Meaning: Go about things in a circuitous manner, go around an issue rather than deal with it directly.

Origin: In the Middle Ages, people caught birds by dropping a net over a bush and clubbing the ground around it to scare the birds into flying into the net. Once a bird was caught, you could stop beating around the bush and start eating.

Hotel industry study: 70% of people who lock themselves out of their rooms are women.

BUT THEY'D NEVER BEEN THERE

*Songs about places can be so convincing that it's hard to believe
the people who wrote them haven't been there themselves.
But that's often the case. Three prime examples:*

TAKE ME HOME, COUNTRY ROADS; JOHN DENVER

John Denver sounds so sincere singing this song that it's
hard to believe he wasn't born and raised in West Virginia. But
he wasn't. Denver didn't even write it; two musicians named Bill
Danoff and Taffy Nivert did.

And they didn't grow up in West Virginia, either. In fact, they'd
never even been there when the song was composed.

It was actually written while they were on their way to a Nivert
family reunion in *Maryland*. As they drove through the countryside, along the winding, tree-lined roads, Bill passed the time by
writing a little tune about their rural surroundings. Gradually, it became "Take Me Home, Country Roads."

How did West Virginia get into the song? A friend of Bill's kept
sending him picture postcards from the Mountain State with notes
like, "West Virginia's almost heaven." Bill was so impressed by the
postcards that he incorporated them into the lyrics of the song.

John Denver discovered the tune in 1970, while he was performing at a Washington, D.C., folk club. Danoff and Nivert were
also performing there, and one evening they played Denver their
half-finished "Country Roads." The three of them stayed up all
night finishing it. Denver put it on his next RCA album; it made
him a star, and made Danoff and Nivert some hefty royalties.
Presumably, they've been to West Virginia by now.

WOODSTOCK; CROSBY, STILLS, NASH, AND YOUNG

The most famous tribute to the most famous musical event in rock
history was written by Joni Mitchell. Millions of young Americans
have listened to the hit versions by Crosby, Stills, Nash, and Young
and by Matthews' Southern Comfort (as well as an album cut

Say "3,000 puppies." In the time it took to say it, about 3,000 puppies were born in the U.S.

featuring Joni herself) and imagined enviously what it was like to be at Woodstock.

But what they don't know is that Joni *wasn't at the festival.* She was watching it on TV, like most of America.

She'd been traveling with Crosby, Stills, and Nash (who played one of their first gigs ever at the mammoth rock concert), and they were all staying in New York City before heading up to the festival. But Mitchell's managers, David Geffen and Elliot Roberts, decided she wouldn't be able to make her scheduled appearance on "The Dick Cavett Show" if she went to Woodstock—so they cancelled her appearance there; Joni was left behind in New York.

Mitchell says: "The deprivation of not being able to go provided me with an intense angle on Woodstock. I was one of the fans."

But in the song, she sounds like one of the eyewitnesses.

PROUD MARY;
CREEDENCE CLEARWATER REVIVAL

This million-selling single about an old Mississippi paddlewheeler established Creedence Clearwater Revival as America's chief exponent of "swamp rock," and they were quickly recognized as the most promising artists to emerge from New Orleans since Fats Domino.

There was only one catch: Creedence Clearwater Revival wasn't from New Orleans. They were from El Cerrito, California. And they had never even been to New Orleans. In fact, the farthest east that songwriter John Fogarty had ever gotten was Montana. And the closest thing to a bayou that he'd ever seen was the swampland around Winters, California.

Actually, Proud Mary wasn't originally going to be a Mississippi riverboat at all. Fogarty initially envisioned her as a "washer woman." But the first few chords he played reminded him of a paddlewheel going around. That brought him to thoughts of the Mississippi River, and Mary became a boat.

How did Fogarty manage to pull it off so well? The best explanation he can come up with for his "authentic" sound is that he'd listened to a lot of New Orleans music (like Fats Domino) when he was young.

IRRELEVANT NOTE: Not even one of the 13 actors who played Charlie Chan in movies, radio, Broadway, or TV were Chinese or of Chinese ancestry.

THE EVOLUTION OF SANTA CLAUS, PART IV

Here's the final installment of the Santa story (begins on page 103).

S ANTA IN AMERICA
Santa is now such an integral part of American culture that news reports like these appear regularly...and no one is surprised.

JACKSONVILLE, Fla. — It was more "Bah, humbug," than "Ho, ho, ho," when a surly Santa Claus told a six-year-old boy he wasn't getting any presents and challenged the kid's dad to a fight.

"Santa Claus doesn't like Gator fans," Santa told the boy, according to his father, Chip Crabtree. "Santa Claus wishes that Florida State would beat the Gators in the Sugar Bowl."

The Seminole fan in Santa apparently came out when he spotted the Gators sweatshirt Crabtree's wife, Lori, was wearing when the couple brought their boys—ages 2, 4, and 6—to the mall Friday.

When Crabtree and his wife said he was being rude, the less-than-cheerful old soul got rid of the kid on his lap and stood up to poke his white-gloved finger into Crabtree's chest.

"You want to do something about it, right now, pal? Right here on stage?" Santa said, according to Crabtree.

Crabtree said he didn't.

Then mall security jumped in, Crabtree said "I'm out of here," and Santa walked off the job, stunning the other children in line.

Mall officials apologized for the clash, and said they didn't know the grumpy Santa's real name.

Crabtree later told his boys that wasn't the *real* Santa at the mall. His six-year-old already knew: "There wasn't any magic in his eyes."

PAINESVILLE, Ohio — A woman who took her grandchildren to see the movie "The Santa Clause" was out for some good family fun. The fun ended when the children called an 800 number mentioned in the movie and were connected to a sex line.

"I don't think children need to be exposed to that," said Shirley

---

Dearth of Concord Township, about 25 miles east of Cleveland.

Dearth took her seven-year-old granddaughter and nine-year-old grandson on Monday to see the PG-rated Walt Disney film starring Tim Allen. In the movie, Allen's ex-wife wants to give him her phone number. He quips, "What is it? 1-800-SPANK ME?"

When Dearth's grandchildren wanted to call the toll-free number, she let them, thinking it probably didn't exist. The children put it on the phone's speaker so she could hear.

"Hi, sexy! You've just connected to the hottest phone line in America, brought to you by American TelNet," said a recording of a sultry woman's voice. "Our one-of-a-kind service lets you choose your own phone fantasy."

Said Disney spokesman Howard Green, "I can't imagine that people would call that number....If it exists, it's a coincidence."

Insurance Clauses a Catch for High-Flying Santa

MILWAUKEE —Santa Claus would have to pay premium prices for life insurance because of his weight and aerial deliveries, an insurance company said.

But unlike cigarette smokers, he would not be penalized for pipe smoking, Northwestern Mutual Life Insurance Co. said.

While pilots are acceptable risks, "Santa might pay a hefty extra premium for those rooftop drops," the company said. It also said there would be a "further modest premium" for his "chubby and plump" girth. Exactly what his premium would be could not be calculated since costs are based on age and Santa "after all, is ageless."

GLASGOW, Scotland — Chinese-made Santa Claus dolls on sale in Scotland play music, light up—and may explode, Scottish safety officers warned.

The "Christmas in Motion Musical Santa with Lite-up Candle" is battery-operated but comes with an electronic transformer that experts say is easily overloaded.

"Once the transformer was switched on, according to one consumer who bought the musical Santa, it exploded and sprayed him with the contents of the batteries," said trading standards director Bruce Collier. The man was not seriously hurt.

Police responsible for enforcing trading standards urged buyers Tuesday to return the Chinese-made Santas to shops for a refund.

If a family had 2 servants or less in 1900, census takers recorded it as "lower middle-class."

MONDAY NIGHT FOOTBALL

Here's an instant replay of the show that almost single-handedly converted sports broadcasting from a sleepy, weekends-only affair into one of the biggest money-makers in TV history.

FALSE START

In 1964, a hot young marketing executive with the Ford Motor Company made an unprecedented proposal to the National Football League and the ABC network: if the league and the network would broadcast a pro football game one evening a week during the football season, Ford would sponsor every broadcast by itself.

Until this point, sports had not been primetime TV fare. "Sports had neither the prestige of news nor the glamour of entertainment," Marc Gunther and Bill Carter explain in *Monday Night Mayhem*, "and besides, sports programs were messy; they could run long and play havoc with the broadcast schedule....The sports establishment [didn't] welcome the networks, either. The conventional wisdom was that television exposure could ruin a sport. The prevailing attitude was summed up by baseball commissioner Ford Frick. 'The view a fan gets at home,' Frick once said, 'should not be any better than that of the fan in the worst seat of the baseball park.' "

Nevertheless, ABC agreed to give it a try. Weekday games were out of the question—they disrupted football training schedules—and Saturday night was too important for ABC to push aside entertainment shows. That left only Friday night—which was fine with Ford. However, Friday night was also traditionally the time high schools played football; when hardcore fans realized that the show would pose a threat to high school game attendance, they mounted an intense letter-writing campaign opposing it. Neither Ford nor ABC wanted that kind of publicity, so the idea was scrapped. "Friday Night Football" died before a single game had been broadcast.

Trying to save the deal with Ford, NFL commissioner Pete Rozelle suggested scheduling the games on Monday night instead. But

---

Police report: When burglars break into a home, they usually go straight for the master bedroom.

ABC rejected the idea—"Ben Casey," the network's most popular show, aired on Monday night, and the network didn't want to tamper with it. Primetime football was quietly shelved.

PASS COMPLETED

Four years later, billionaire Howard Hughes revived the idea of Monday night football and approached the NFL with an offer to buy the broadcasting rights. He had just purchased a TV production company, and he wanted to make his mark by selling football programming to local TV stations around the country.

Rather than cut a deal on the spot, Pete Rozelle pitched the idea to the Big Three networks to see if he could get a better offer. CBS said no—its Monday night lineup was too strong. NBC refused after "Tonight Show" host Johnny Carson balked at being preempted by football games. ABC also said no, but changed its mind when Roone Arledge, president of the sports division, warned that as many as 100 affiliates would dump ABC's Monday night programming to air the football game if Hughes got it. A deal was struck, and "Monday Night Football" was born.

THE TEAM

Arledge knew that "Monday Night Football" would have to be more than a run-of-the-mill sports broadcast to compete against sitcoms, dramas, and other popular evening fare. It had to have something extra: controversy. So he hired "Wide World of Sports" announcer Howard Cosell, who was already famous for sticking up for Muhammad Ali when Ali refused to be inducted into the Army.

Arledge figured Cosell could just be himself in the broadcasting booth; Don Meredith, a former Dallas Cowboys quarterback, would provide color; and Keith Jackson, another ABC sports announcer, would handle the play-by-play. Frank Gifford, a former New York Giants halfback, replaced Jackson the following year. "Roone put that show together like a Hollywood casting director," Gifford recalls in his book *The Whole Ten Yards.* "Howard was the elitist New York know-it-all, the bombastic lawyer that Middle America loved to hate. Don Meredith was the good ole country boy who put Howard in his place. As for me, I was cast as the nice guy, the one who got the numbers down and the names out."

Good buy: NASA spent $200,000 on a "sanitary-napkin disposal unit" for female astronauts in 1992.

A ROUGH START

"Monday Night Football" set out to be provocative. Unlike most broadcasters, "MNF" announcers—Cosell in particular—actually expressed their *opinions*, praising some teams and players and attacking others. TV and sports critics were almost unanimously negative toward the show. One newspaper said Cosell's "retching prattle took the fun out of a really good football game"; another said he displayed a "towering ignorance of football."

Even Ford Company chairman and principal sponsor Henry Ford II hated it. After the first game, he called ABC chairman Leonard Goldenson to complain. "I listened to that gab between Don Meredith and Howard Cosell last night, and I couldn't concentrate on the game. Take that guy Cosell off." But the network talked Ford into withholding judgment for four weeks. That was all it took—once people adjusted to Cosell, they began to warm up to him. The reviews improved, the ratings soared, and Ford called back two weeks later to apologize for attacking Cosell.

TOUCHDOWN

Within weeks, "Monday Night Football" became a cult phenomenon: a man in California added a $3,000 den to his house so he could watch the games without being interrupted by his family; restaurants all over the country began investing in TV sets to recapture customers who were staying home on Monday nights; and according to one report, a Seattle hospital tried to ban baby deliveries between 7:00 and 10:00 p.m. on Monday nights. By the end of the first season, 31 percent of TV viewers in the U.S.—many of whom weren't football fans—were watching football on Monday night, making what critics dubbed "The Howard Cosell Show" the third most popular show, after "The Mary Tyler Moore Show" and "The Flip Wilson Show."

END OF AN ERA

The show had its ups and downs over the next several years: Don Meredith left in 1974 and was replaced by Fred Williamson and then Alex Karras, but returned in 1977 after Karras didn't work out. Cosell left the show after the 1983 season, and Don Meredith left for good a year later, leaving Frank Gifford, who was still working on the show in 1995." Monday Night Football" filled the line-

In 1992, 2,421 people checked into U.S. emergency rooms with injuries involving house plants.

up with a variety of personalities, including Joe Namath, Jim Lampley, O. J. Simpson, Dan Dierdorf, and Al Michaels.

Somehow, though, everything was different without Cosell and Meredith. Although the ratings were consistently high, and "MNF" became the second-longest running show in TV history (second only to "60 Minutes"), the show never reached the heights it had in the early and mid-'70s. As Gunther and Carter put it in *Monday Night Mayhem*, "Same night, same network, same name. But it was not "Monday Night Football" anymore. It was football on Monday nights."

BEHIND THE SCENES
• Early in the first season, Cosell and Company went to Philadelphia to broadcast a game between the Eagles and the New York Giants. During the broadcast, Eagles owner Leonard Tose sent up a "generous jug of vodka martinis," which Cosell—who was freezing in the open-air broadcast booth—drank to keep warm. He apparently drank too much—his words began to slur, to the point where he was pronouncing Philadelphia as "Full-a-dull-fa."

Suddenly at the end of the second quarter, Cosell pitched forward and vomited. "Cosell got sick in the booth, all over his mike, his clothes, and my boots," Meredith recalls. The incident may have actually boosted the fledgling show's ratings: "The next day, rumors ran wild," *TV Guide* reported in 1974. Tales of Cosell getting bombed circulated, and the reputation of "Monday Night Football" as a madcap adventure began to spread.

• At a game in Dallas, Cosell dropped a cigarette butt into what he thought was a trash can under the announcer's table. The butt landed on a pile of debris, setting it on fire and igniting play-by-play announcer Keith Jackson's pants. Jackson actually announced an entire series of plays with his pants on fire before he was able to put it out.

• Frank Gifford had a reputation for stumbling over one name or fact every broadcast. For example, during just about every Atlanta Falcons game, he mispronounced coach Leeman Bennet's name as "Leeman Beeman." The problem was so bad that production assistants set up a betting pool to guess the time and the quarter that he would make the mistake. Gifford even began one broadcast by saying, "Hi Frank, I'm everybody."

WHAT A DOLL!

Here are the stories of the two most popular
dolls in U.S. history—Barbie and G.I. Joe.

THE BARBIE DOLL

Children have been playing with dolls for thousands of years, but the most popular doll in the history of the world has only been in existence since 1959. Since Mattel's buxom fashion plate was first introduced, more than 500 million Barbie dolls have been sold, and the number grows every day.

Barbie's Roots. The real Barbie (yes, there was one) was the daughter of Ruth and Eliot Handler, who founded Mattel after World War II. The idea for the teenage fashion doll came to Ruth when she noticed that Barbie preferred playing with shapely paper dolls to playing with baby dolls. The Handlers gambled that other modern girls would feel the same way. (The Handlers had a son, too, named Ken.)

Barbie (the doll) was originally called a "three-dimensional fashion drawing." Said Ruth Handler, "Barbie was originally created to project every little girl's dream of the future," and, to a little girl, the future means having breasts, clothes, a car, and a boyfriend. It was no accident that a lingerie line was one of the first sets of Barbie clothes available.

Barbie's Body. Collectors have revealed that Barbie's design was copied from a German doll name "Lilli"—which was, in turn, based on a cartoon character created for the newspaper *BildZeitung*. Ironically, the German Lilli was not a wholesome teenager, but a winsome, sexually loose gold-digger.

The rest of her appearance was based on the prevailing standards of beauty in 1959—Brigitte Bardot's perky ponytail and knock-out figure, and Grace Kelly's patrician blondness.

Her Debut. Barbie was introduced at the New York Toy Fair in February 1959. She was an instant hit. The first Barbie doll cost $3; today, in mint condition, they're worth over $1,500, and the value keeps rising.

Number one dispenser of college scholarships for women in the U.S.: the Miss America pageant.

G.I. JOE

By 1963, Mattel's Barbie doll was so popular that Don Levine, creative director of the Hasbro Toy Co., suggested manufacturing a boys' version. "But instead of fashion," he explained, "we'll make it a soldier, and we'll sell extra uniforms and weapons."

But would boys buy dolls? Hedging its bets, Hasbro decided never to call it a "doll"—only an "action soldier." And they decided to give it a scarred face to make it seem more masculine.

His Name and Body. Hasbro planned to make different sets of uniforms for each branch of the service (Army, Navy, Air Force, Marines) and give each a different name—Salty the Sailor, Rocky the Marine, etc. But the marketing department insisted on one name. One night, Levine happened to see the 1945 film *The Story of G.I. Joe* on television, and realized that "G.I. Joe" was perfect.

Unlike Barbie, the boy doll had to be fully movable. But Hasbro wasn't sure if it could be done. One day Levine was walking past an art-supply store when he noticed a display of the small wooden, jointed models that artists use to draw different body positions. He bought a dozen, and Hasbro copied the construction.

His Debut. Joe was introduced at the New York Toy Fair in February 1964. But unlike Barbie, he was not an immediate success. At first, toy store owners avoided him, sure that American parents wouldn't buy their sons dolls. Frustrated, Hasbro managed to get a few stores to carry the doll; when G.I. Joe sold out, other retailers bought it. By the end of the first year, over $30 million worth of G.I. Joe and accessories had been sold—including 2 million dolls.

Joe's Problems. In the late 1960s, with the increasing unpopularity of the war in Vietnam, parents began to reject war toys. Joe's sales plummeted to less than a third of their previous level. He was almost wiped out, but Hasbro saved the day by transforming him from a soldier to an adventurer. Then in the late 1970s, tastes changed again. Exotic Star Wars "action figures" were hot, and no one wanted simple G.I. Joe dolls anymore. Sales were so poor that Hasbro dropped him from their line.

But the political climate changed again in the '80s. Sales of toy guns shot up...and G. I. Joe was resurrected. In 1982, he stormed the toy market with his "G.I. Joe Team" and became the #1 seller again. From 1982 to 1995, he racked up $600 million in sales.

CARY GRANT, ACID-HEAD

*We think of Timothy Leary, Jimi Hendrix, etc., as the
quintessential LSD freaks. But Cary Grant, of all people,
was into acid before those guys ever heard of it.*

Before Timothy Leary and the counterculture discovered
LSD—before it was even illegal—the unflappable, ultimately
dignified Cary Grant was tripping out every Saturday. It was
1957. Grant's wife, Betsy Drake, had been going to the Psychiatric
Institute of Beverly Hills to undergo an unusual form of chemical
therapy. The Institute's directors believed that the little-known
drug LSD "acted as a psychic energizer, emptying the subconscious
mind and intensifying emotions a hundred times." Drake had been
taking it regularly, and it had done wonders for her. So when she
realized that Grant was on the verge of a nervous breakdown, she
convinced him to try it, too.

MEDICAL TRIP

Working with Dr. Mortimer Hartman, whom the actor referred to
as "my wise Mahatma," Cary began the sessions under strict medical supervision. First he was given a dose of LSD in the therapist's
offices; he spent several hours in treatment. Then he was given a
depressant to calm him down. Finally, he was driven home to rest
and recover for a day. Grant found the effects of the drug astound-
ing. "The first thing that happens to you," he told friends, "is you
don't want to look at who you are. Then the light breaks through;
to use the cliché, you are enlightened." Hallucinating under the
drug gave the otherwise staid Briton a new freedom. Once, he admitted, "I imagined myself as a giant penis launching off from Earth
like a spaceship."

GOOD TRIP

Grant continued this treatment for two years; he took hundreds of
acid trips. Previously he had been reluctant to talk about his personal life. (An instructive anecdote: a reporter once cabled this
question to him: "How old Cary Grant?" Grant's evasive reply:

Q. In which continent do college graduates outnumber high school grads?   A. Antarctica.

"Old Cary Grant fine.") Now at age 55, thrilled by the new outlook on life that the drug gave him, he spoke to friends, the media, college students—anyone who would listen—about the benefits of LSD therapy.

"I have been born again," he declared. I have been through a psychiatric experience which has completely changed me. It was horrendous. I had to face things about myself which I never admitted, which I didn't know were there. Now I know I hurt every woman I ever loved. I was an utter fake, a self-opinionated bore, a know-all who knew very little."

A SAMPLING OF GRANT'S "ACID REVELATIONS"

• "Respect women because they are wiser than men....(they) have an innate wisdom we men try to dispoil from the time we're sixteen years old."

• "The only way to remain happy is to know nothing or everything. Unfortunately, it is impossible to know nothing for very long."

• "A man owes it to me—if I have to look at him—to keep his hair combed and his teeth cleaned."

• "Deplore your mistakes. Regret them as much as you like. But don't really expect to learn by them."

• "Don't expect to be rewarded if you...tell the truth. Hypocrisy no longer has any power to shock us. We encounter it every day. But we encounter the truth so seldom that it shocks and embarrasses us, and we run from it."

BAD TRIP

Unfortunately, Grant's acid-inspired statement that "my next marriage will be complete" wasn't accurate—although he did have the child he said he was now ready to "beget." When he and actress Dyan Cannon (who swore she had only taken acid once before their marriage—and never during) decided to divorce, it turned ugly. She accused him of being an "apostle of LSD," "an unfit father," and said he insisted that she trip out. "He told me the new me would be created through LSD," she declared in court.

In later years, Grant refused to discuss the remarkable drug. "My intention in taking LSD," he finally told a reporter, "was to make myself happy. A man would have to be a fool to take something that *didn't* make him happy."

DOROTHY PARKER SEZ...

Wisecracks from one of America's sharpest wits:

"Hollywood money isn't money. It's congealed snow: melts in your hand, and there you are."

"You can lead a horticulture ...but you can't make her think."

"If all the girls who attended the Yale prom were laid end to end—I wouldn't be a bit surprised."

"Wit has truth in it. Wise-cracking is simply calisthenics with words."

"The only *ism* Hollywood believes in is plagiarism."

"The two most beautiful words in the English language are 'check enclosed.' "

"That would be a good thing for them to cut on my tombstone: 'Wherever she went, including here, it was against her better judgment.' "

"This is not a novel to be tossed aside lightly; it should be thrown with great force."

"Most good women are hidden treasures who are safe because nobody looks for them."

"I misremember who first was cruel enough to nurture the cocktail party into life. But perhaps it would be not too much to say, in fact it would be not enough to say, that it was not worth the trouble."

"Excuse me, everybody, I have to go to the bathroom. I really have to telephone, but I'm too embarrassed to say so."

"One more drink and I'd have been under the host."

"You can't teach an old dogma new tricks."

"The best way to keep children at home is to make the home atmosphere pleasant and let the air out of the tires."

"His voice was as intimate as the rustle of sheets."

"These young writers...are worth watching. Not reading; just watching."

In 1992, 5,840 people checked into U.S. emergency rooms with "pillow-related injuries."

HERE'S LOOKING AT YOU, KID

Humphrey Bogart is one of the most popular movie stars of all time. Here are some inside facts about two of his most popular films.

THE MALTESE FALCON (1941)

The film that made Bogart a star was adapted from a 1929 novel by Dashiell Hammett (who also wrote *The Thin Man*). Warner Brothers bought the screen rights in 1930 and milked the story for all it was worth; they made three different versions of *Falcon* in 10 years.

• Bogart's film, the third version, was regarded as a minor picture by Warner Brothers...so they let a screenwriter named John Huston make his directing debut with it.

Bogart vs. Raft

• George Raft, a popular personality who played slick gangsters, was Warners' first choice for Sam Spade. He turned it down because he didn't like the idea of working for a first-time director. "I feel strongly that *The Maltese Falcon* is not an important picture," he explained.

• It was the fifth time in five years that Bogart (a minor star who specialized in tough gangster roles) was forced to take a part Raft didn't want. Earlier in 1941, Raft even refused to appear in a film if Bogart was cast in a supporting role. He once protested to Jack Warner: "You told me I would never have to play a Humphrey Bogart part." After *Falcon*, he never had the chance again.

Supporting Cast

• Sydney Greenstreet, "the Fatman," had never acted in a movie before *Falcon*. He was an English stage actor who specialized in comedy. He earned an Oscar nomination for his movie debut... and was typecast as a film heavy.

• Mary Astor prepared for her scenes as conniving, unstable Brigid Wonderly, by hyperventilating almost to the point of dizziness. "It gives me the heady feeling of thinking at cross purposes," she said.

Bad year: NASA "blew up or lost" $567 million worth of equipment in 1993.

Life Imitates Art
• In 1975, one of the seven falcons used in the movie was stolen from its exhibit in a Los Angeles art museum.

CASABLANCA (1943)
The Oscar winner for Best Film in 1943 started out as an unproduced play called *Everybody Comes to Rick's.*

• It was written by a New York City schoolteacher whose inspiration was a visit to a nightclub in southern France in 1938. The club's mix of refugees, Nazis, and French made it, he remarked to his wife, "a marvelous setting for a play."

• The rights to the play were purchased by Warner Brothers the day after Pearl Harbor was attacked.

Bogart vs. Raft II
• Legend has it that George Raft was offered the leading role of Rick and, as usual, turned it down. Actually, Raft *wanted* the part...but by this time Bogart was a bigger star and got first choice.

• It's also been said that Ronald Reagan was one of the actors initially considered for Rick.

• *Casablanca*'s famous theme, "As Time Goes By," was included in the original play because the author had been fond of it in college. It first appeared in a 1931 Broadway show called *Everybody's Welcome.*

As Time Goes By
• Believe it or not, that classic song was nearly cut out of the movie. After *Casablanca* had been shot, the composer who'd scored it decided to write his own tune, because theme songs are worth a lot of money in royalties. But that would have meant reshooting several scenes—and Ingrid Bergman had already cut her hair for her next role (in *For Whom the Bell Tolls*). So reshooting was impossible and the song was left in.

• Dooley Wilson (Sam) didn't really know how to play the piano. He just pretended to finger the keys as he sang, while a studio musician did the playing offstage.

The Script

• *Casablanca* won an Oscar for best screenplay, yet the actors never had the luxury of a complete script. In fact, Bogart and Bergman were sometimes handed their lines just before a scene was to be shot. Other times Bogart and the screenwriters would sit around with a bottle of whiskey and argue what should happen next. Ingrid Bergman didn't even know which of the story's main characters she was supposed to love more. She found out when everyone else did—in the final scene.

Bogart and Bergman

• Humphrey Bogart's agents took out a $100,000 insurance policy on the actor (a huge amount in those days) during the filming. Bogart's wife was convinced that Bogie was having an affair with Ingrid Bergman and had threatened to kill him if she found them together. The agents decided they'd better not take any chances.

Casablanca and the War

• Good timing may have been what turned *Casablanca* into a hit. In November 1942, Allied forces launched a successful assault on occupied cities in North Africa, including Casablanca. Less than three weeks later the movie premiered in New York. It opened throughout the rest of the country in January 1943, just as Franklin Roosevelt, Josef Stalin, and Winston Churchill were holding a secret conference—in Casablanca.

• The Germans considered *Casablanca* a propaganda film, and banned it. Even after the war, only a censored version was allowed to be shown; all references to Nazis were cut out.

Miscellaneous Bogart

• After the success of *Casablanca*, Bogart signed a contract that made him the world's highest-paid actor.

• Bogart got his distinctive lisp as the result of a childhood accident. A tiny piece of wood lodged in his lip, and the operation to remove it was botched. It left him with a partially paralyzed lip and a permanent speech impediment.

Casablanca on TV

• *Casablanca* was turned into an ABC-TV series in 1955. It flopped, and was cancelled after only a few months.

MORE LEMONS

Here are some more of the worst cars ever manufactured.

THE BMW ISETTA (1950s)

In the 1950s, BMW introduced a sub-subcompact car called the Isetta, a tiny little auto that made the Volkswagen Beetle look like a Lincoln. The car was little more than an enclosed lawn chair: the entire front pulled open for driver and passenger to get in and out—and that was the only door on the whole car. The steering wheel was on a hinge and pulled to the side when the door opened, and, unlike most cars, the rear wheels did the steering.

What Happened: Called a "little deathtrap" by one critic, the Isetta had a poorly thought-out design and flimsy construction. In the event of a front-end collision, the door almost invariably became disabled, trapping the passengers inside. But in an accident that serious, the occupants would probably be dead already, since the car didn't have any seatbelts and crumpled like aluminum foil on impact. As if this weren't enough to scare away customers, in the late 1950s BMW replaced the two rear wheels with a single rear wheel. Demand for the car, already sluggish, dried up completely. BMW pulled it off the market.

THE TRABANT (1957)

In 1957, not long after the Soviet Union launched *Sputnik*, the world's first orbiting satellite, East Germany commemorated the event with a new automobile called "Trabant" (the German word for "satellite"). The car was technologically backward even then. Unlike the cars of the West, where four-stroke engines had been standard for decades, Trabants had lawnmower-like two-stroke engines that belched so much bluish smoke the cars were nicknamed "Little Stinkers." But East German auto factories were still coughing them up when the East German government collapsed in 1989.

What Happened: Millions of East Germans spent years on waiting lists hoping for a chance to buy a Trabant; even so, when the Berlin Wall came down, they literally walked away from their cars. By 1992 there were an estimated 3 million abandoned Trabants in Germany.

Your mouth produces a quart of saliva every day.

THE MOHS SAFARIKAR (1972)

In 1967, the troubled Mohs Seaplane Corporation of Madison, Wisconsin, diversified by creating an automobile division. But the only thing the company proved was that while previously it had only failed in one business, now it could fail in two. Mohs autos were ugly, expensive gas-guzzlers. The company's first car, the Ostentatienne Opera Sedan, weighed almost three tons, cost about $20,000, and had only one huge door. Almost nobody bought it. In 1972, Mohs introduced the SafariKar, a two-door convertible with a retractable metal top. The strangest feature of all was the car's upholstery, most of which was on the *outside* of the car. Not content with covering the *seats* with foam-padded black Naugahyde, Mohs gave the same treatment to the hood, the trunk, the fenders, and the rest of the body, creating a visual impression that only Elvis could have loved.

What Happened: The "overpriced, overweight, overupholstered, and over-ugly" look never caught on with the public, and Mohs pulled out of the car business completely in 1975.

THE CONVAIRCAR (1946)

Daimler, Benz, and Ford each spent millions of dollars and countless years researching the concept of a flying car, but ultimately all came to the same conclusion: a vehicle that could both drive on the ground and fly would do each so poorly that no one would buy it. Then, in 1945, an aircraft engineer named Theodore Hall designed a regular car so small and light that you could attach an airplane engine, wing, and tail unit to the roof...and make it fly. Hall planned to make the airplane units available at every airport in the country, where Flying Car owners could rent them for a small fee. He sold his idea to the airplane manufacturer Convair, which marketed it in 1946 under the name ConvAirCar.

What Happened: The ConvAirCar might well have changed the face of the automobile industry forever. Unfortunately, in 1947 a Convair pilot miscalculated the amount of fuel he needed and was forced to crash-land his ConvAirCar on a dirt road, shearing off the plane's wings in some trees. The adverse publicity doomed the project. Convair folded after building only a few vehicles.

HOT DOG!

A brief history of an American favorite.

Sausage: Ancient History. The ancient Babylonians came up with the concept of sausages over 3,500 years ago when they stuffed spiced meat into animal intestines. Other civilizations adopted and modified the food. The Greeks called it *orya*. The Romans called it *salsus*—from which we get the word *sausage*.

The Weiner. By the Middle Ages, sausages began to take on regional characteristics. Their shape and size varied from country to country, and local creations were named for the towns in which they originated. Austria gave birth to the "Vienna sausage," or *Wienerwurst*, from which the term *weiner* derived.

The Frankfurter. The modern hot dog—the frankfurter—is descended from a spiced, smoked, slightly curved thin sausage developed in Frankfurt, Germany. According to German lore, the shape of this *Frankfurter* was a tribute to a local butcher's pet dachshund. The result: By the 1850s, it was commonly called a "dachshund sausage" and it was customarily eaten with sauerkraut and mustard. In the 1890s, a German immigrant named Charles Feltman began selling "dachshund sausages" on the street in Coney Island. He was so successful that he opened the first "frankfurter" restaurant in the U.S.

The Bun. In 1904, at the St. Louis Exposition, another Frankfurt native was selling dachshund sausages. Gloves were customarily supplied for customers to wear while eating the frankfurters, but so many people walked away still wearing them that the vendor ran out of spare gloves. In desperation, he convinced a nearby baker to make frank-shaped rolls as a substitute. The rolls actually worked better than gloves, and a new tradition was born.

The Hot Dog. The name *hot dog* was coined in 1906. A syndicated cartoonist named Tad Dorgan was enjoying a baseball game at New York's Polo Grounds. Inspired by the vendors' call of "Get your red hot dachshund dogs!" he went back to his office and sketched a cartoon of a real dachshund in a bun, covered with mustard. When he couldn't come up with the correct spelling of dachshund, he just settled for "hot dog." Unfortunately, the original cartoon has never been found.

AMERICA'S NOSTRADAMUS

If you read the National Enquirer *at the checkout counter of your local supermarket, you've seen that people like Jeanne Dixon are always trying to predict the future. They rarely get it right, of course. But in 1900, John Watkins did. In an article written for the* Ladies' Home Journal, *he looked a century into the future and foresaw subways, air-conditioning, satellite TV, and lots more. No one has ever come close to this feat— except maybe Nostradamus. Here's a small excerpt.*

BACKGROUND. John Elspeth Watkins was a Philadelphia newspaperman whose predictions were recently rediscovered by two Indiana professors. They call him "The Seer of the Century" and note that he was lucky enough to see many of his predictions come true before dying in the '40s.

What's amazing about these predictions? Remember what was going on in 1900: Production on primitive autos had just begun; they were still just a novelty. People lived in squalor and ill health and died young. There was no such thing as an airplane. There was no radio; the first feature movie hadn't yet been made; the telephone had been invented a scant 25 years earlier. It was a whole different world—yet somehow, Watkins described ours in detail.

"These prophecies," he wrote in his introduction, "will seem strange, almost impossible."

It's a fascinating measure of how things have changed to realize that our way of life seemed like science fiction to the average American of 1900.

EXCERPTS FROM WATKINS'S PREDICTIONS

"**Man will see around the world.** Persons and things of all kinds will be brought within focus of cameras connected electrically with screens at opposite ends of circuits, thousands of miles at a span. American audiences in their theatres will view upon huge curtains before them the coronations of kings in Europe or the progress of battles in the Orient. The instrument bringing these distant scenes to the very doors of people will be connected with a giant telephone apparatus transmitting each incidental sound into its appropriate place. Thus the guns of a distant battle will be heard to

---

Q: Where is Mozart buried?   A: Nobody knows.

boom when seen to blaze, and thus the lips of a remote actor or singer will be heard to utter words or music when seen to move."

"The American will be taller by from one to two inches. His increase in stature will result from better health, due to vast reforms in medicine, sanitation, food and athletics. He will live fifty years instead of thirty-five as at present—for he will reside in the suburbs."

"Hot and cold air from spigots. Hot or cold air will be turned on from spigots to regulate the temperature of a house as we now turn on hot or cold water from spigots to regulate the temperature of the bath....Rising early to build the furnace fire will be a task of the olden times. Homes will have no chimneys, because no smoke will be created within their walls."

"No mosquitoes nor flies. Boards of health will have destroyed all mosquito haunts and breeding grounds, drained all stagnant pools, filled in all swamp-lands, and chemically treated all still-water streams. The extermination of the horse and its stable will reduce the house-fly."

"Ready-cooked meals will be bought from establishments similar to our bakeries of today. Such wholesale cookery will be done in electric laboratories...equipped with electric stoves, and all sorts of electric devices, such as coffee-grinders, egg-beaters, stirrers, shakers, parers, meat-choppers, meat-saws, potato-mashers, lemon-squeezers, dishwashers, dish-dryers and the like. All such utensils will be washed in chemicals fatal to disease microbes."

"There will be no street cars in our large cities. All traffic will be below or high above ground when brought within city limits. In most cities it will be confined to broad subways or tunnels, well lighted and well ventilated, or to high trestles with "moving-sidewalk" stairways leading to the top. These underground or over-head streets will teem with automobile passenger coaches and freight wagons, with cushioned wheels. Subways or trestles will be reserved for express trains. Cities, therefore, will be free from all noises." [Ed. note: Not quite.]

Eighteen U.S. amateur soccer players have been killed by falling goalposts since 1979.

"Photographs will be telegraphed from any distance. If there be a battle in China a hundred years hence snapshots of its most striking events will be published in the newspapers an hour later. Even today photographs are being telegraphed over short distances. Photographs will reproduce all of Nature's colors."

"Automobiles will be cheaper than horses are today. Farmers will own automobile hay-wagons, plows, harrows and hay-rakes. A one-pound motor in one of these vehicles will do the work of a pair of horses or more....Automobiles will have been substituted for every horse vehicle now known....The horse in harness will be as scarce, if, indeed, not scarcer, then as the yoked ox is today."

"Everybody will walk ten miles. Gymnastics will begin in the nursery, where toys and games will be designed to strengthen the muscles. Exercise will be compulsory in the schools. Every school, college and community will have a complete gymnasium....A man or woman unable to walk ten miles at a stretch will be regarded as a weakling."

"There will be no wild animals except in menageries. Rats and mice will have been exterminated. The horse will have become practically extinct....The automobile will have driven out the horse. Cattle and sheep will have no horns. They will be unable to run faster than the fattened hog of to-day. Food animals will be bred to expend practically all of their life energy in producing meat, milk, wool and other by-products. Horns, bones, muscles and lungs will have been neglected."

"Submarine boats submerged for days will be capable of wiping a whole navy off the face of the deep."

"To England in two days. Fast electric ships, crossing the ocean at more than a mile a minute, will go from New York to Liverpool in two days. The bodies of these ships will be built above the waves. They will be supported upon runners, somewhat like those of the sleigh. These runners will be very buoyant. Upon their undersides will be apertures expelling jets of air. In this way a film of air will be kept between them and the water's surface. This film, together

---

On average, men are 40% muscle and 15% fat...and women are 23% muscle and 25% fat.

with the small surface of the runners, will reduce friction against the waves to the smallest possible degree." [Ed. note: Wow! He's predicting hydrofoils.]

"Telephones around the world. Wireless telephone and telegraph circuits will span the world. A husband in the middle of the Atlantic will be able to converse with his wife sitting in her boudoir in Chicago. We will be able to telephone to China quite as readily as we now talk from New York to Brooklyn. By an automatic signal they will connect with any circuit in their locality without the intervention of a 'hello girl.'"

"Automatic instruments reproducing original airs exactly will bring the best music to the families of the untalented. In great cities there will be public opera-houses whose singers and musicians are paid from funds endowed by philanthropists and by the government. The piano will be capable of changing its tone from cheerful to sad. Many devices will add to the emotional effect of music."

"How children will be taught. A university education will be free to every man and woman. Several great national universities will have been established. Children will study a simple English grammar adapted to simplified English, and not copied after the Latin. Time will be saved by grouping like studies....Medical inspectors regularly visiting the public schools will furnish poor children free eyeglasses, free dentistry and free medical attention of every kind. The very poor will, when necessary, get free rides to and from school and free lunches between sessions." [Ed. note: An incredible, revolutionary concept in 1900.]

"Oranges...in Philadelphia. Fast-flying refrigerators on land and sea will bring delicious fruits from the tropics and southern temperate zone within a few days. The farmer of South America, South Africa, Australia and the South Sea Islands, whose seasons are directly opposite to ours, will thus supply us in winter with fresh summer foods which cannot be grown here. Scientists will have discovered how to raise here many fruits now confined to much hotter or colder climates."

Since 1876, 69 pro baseball players have hit a home run their first time at bat. 11 never hit another.

YOGI SEZ

*Gems from Yogi Berra, Hall of Famer and
catcher for the New York Yankees.*

"It's deja vu all over again."

[*Explaining a loss*]
"We made too many wrong mistakes."

"The game's not over 'til it's over."

"You give 100% in the first half of the game, and if that isn't enough, in the second half you give what's left."

[*On quotes like these*]
"I really didn't say everything I said."

[*On being asked why he hadn't been to a favorite restaurant lately*]
"It's so crowded, nobody goes there anymore."

"If people don't want to come out to the ballpark, nobody's going to stop them."

[*On being honored with a "Yogi Berra Night"*]
"I want to thank all you people for making this night necessary."

[*On being asked during spring training what his hat size was.*]
"I don't know. I'm not in shape yet."

"You've got to be careful if you don't know where you're going, because you might not get there."

"We have deep depth."

[*On seeing a Steve McQueen movie*]
"He must have made that before he died."

"I never blame myself when I'm not hitting. I just blame the bat and if it keeps up, I change bats....After all, if I know it isn't my fault that I'm not hitting, how can I get mad at myself?"

[*On meeting King George IV*]
"Nice to meet you, King."

"Baseball is ninety percent mental. The other half is physical."

"It gets late early out there."

THE DEATH OF MARILYN

Ever wondered what really happened to Marilyn Monroe? You're not alone. Here's a version that appeared in It's a Conspiracy!, *by The National Insecurity Council. It's great bathroom reading; be sure to pick up a copy for yourself.*

A t 4:25 a.m. on August 5, 1962, Sergeant Jack Clemmons of the West Los Angeles Police Department received a call from Dr. Hyman Engelberg. "I am calling from the house of Marilyn Monroe," he said. "She is dead."

When Clemmons arrived at 12305 Helena Drive, he found the body lying face down on the bed. The coroner investigating the case ruled that Monroe, 36, had died from "acute barbiturate poisoning due to ingestion of overdose...a probable suicide."

THE OFFICIAL STORY

• The night before, Monroe had gone to bed at about 8:00 p.m., too tired to attend a dinner party at actor Peter Lawford's beach house. A few hours later, Monroe's housekeeper, Eunice Murray, knocked on the star's bedroom door when she noticed a light was on inside, but got no response. Assuming that Monroe had fallen asleep, Murray turned in.

• When Murray awoke at about 3:30 a.m. and noticed the light still on in Monroe's room, she went outside to peek into the window. She saw Monroe lying nude on the bed in an "unnatural" position. Alarmed, Murray called Dr. Ralph Greenson, Monroe's psychiatrist, who came over immediately and broke into the bedroom. She also called Dr. Engelberg, Monroe's personal physician. After Engelberg pronounced her dead, they called the police.

SUSPICIOUS FACTS

From the start, there were conflicting versions of what had happened.

When Did Monroe Die?

Although Murray told the police she'd found the body after 3:30 a.m., there's evidence that Monroe died much earlier.

• Murray first told the police that she'd called Dr. Greenson 3:30 a.m. Sgt. Clemmons claims that when he first arrived on the scene, Engelberg and Greenson agreed that Murray had called them at about midnight. But in their official police statements, the doctors said they were called at 3:30 a.m.

• According to Anthony Summers in his book *Goddess*, Monroe's press agent, Arthur Jacobs, may have been notified of Monroe's death as early as 11:00 p.m., when he and his wife were at a Hollywood Bowl concert. According to Jacob's wife, Natalie, "We got the news long before it broke. We left the concert at once."

• In 1982, Peter Lawford admitted in a sworn statement that he learned of Monroe's death at 1:30 a.m., when her lawyer, Milton Rudin, called from the house to tell him about it.

• The ambulance crew summoned by the police noticed that Monroe's body was in "advanced rigor mortis," suggesting that she had been dead for four to six hours. That would mean she died about midnight.

Where Did Monroe Die?

Monroe supposedly died in her bedroom. But did she?

• Monroe's body was stretched out flat on the bed, with the legs straight—not typical for a person who had overdosed on barbiturates. According to Sgt. Clemmons, barbiturate overdoses often cause a body to go into convulsions, leaving it contorted: "You never see a body with the legs straight. And I've seen hundreds of suicides by drug overdose." He speculated that she had been moved.

• William Shaefer, president of the Shaefer Ambulance Service, insists that "in the very early morning hours"—well before 3:00 a.m.—one of his ambulances was called to Monroe's house. She was comatose; the ambulance took her to Santa Monica Hospital, where she died. "She passed away at the hospital. She did not die at home." And he was certain it was Monroe: "We'd hauled her before because of [earlier overdoses of] barbiturates. We'd hauled her when she was comatose."

How Did Monroe Die?

• Though Deputy Medical Examiner Thomas Noguchi speculated that Monroe had swallowed roughly 50 Nembutal pills, a common barbiturate, he found "no visual evidence of pills in the stomach or the small intestine. No residue. No refractile crystals." Yet, as

Noguchi recounted in his book *Coroner*, toxicological reports of Monroe's blood confirmed his suspicions of an overdose.

• Why was there no pill residue in Monroe's body? Noguchi said that some "murder theorists" have suggested that an injection of barbiturates would have killed her without leaving pill residue. Other theorists have suggested that a suppository with a fatal dose of barbiturates would also have left no residue in her stomach. Or, at some point after her death, her stomach may have been pumped.

MISSING EVIDENCE

Why has so much evidence pertaining to Marilyn Monroe's case disappeared or been destroyed?

Phone Records

• Did Monroe try to call anyone the night she died? When a reporter for the *Los Angeles Herald Tribune* tried to get her phone records and find out, a phone company contact told him, "All hell is breaking loose down here! Apparently you're not the only one interested in Marilyn's calls. But the tape [of her calls] has disappeared. I'm told it was impounded by the Secret Service....Obviously somebody high up ordered it."

• In 1985, a former FBI agent claimed: "The FBI did remove certain Monroe records. I was on a visit to California when Monroe died, and became aware of the removal of the records from my Los Angeles colleagues. I knew there were some people there, Bureau personnel, who normally wouldn't have been there—agents from out of town. They were there on the scene immediately, as soon as she died, before anyone realized what had happened. It had to be on the instruction of somebody high up, higher even than Hoover...either the Attorney General or the President."

Monroe's Diary

• Monroe supposedly kept a detailed diary. According to Robert Slatzer, a longtime friend of the actress, "For years, Marilyn kept scribbled notes of conversations to help her remember things." What things? Slatzer said the diary included her intimate discussions with people like Robert Kennedy. Monroe supposedly told Slatzer, "Bobby liked to talk about political things. He got mad at me one day because he said I didn't remember the things he told me."

• After Monroe's death, Coroner's Aide Lionel Grandison claimed that the diary "came into my office with the rest of Miss Monroe's personal effects" during the investigation. But by the next day the diary had vanished—and, according to Grandison, someone had removed it from the list of items brought in for investigation.

The Original Police Files

• In 1974, Captain Kenneth McCauley of the Los Angeles Police Department contacted the Homicide Department about the files. The department responded that it had no crime reports in its files pertaining to Monroe's death. Even the death report had vanished.

• The files on Monroe may have disappeared as early as 1966. That year, Los Angeles Mayor Sam Yorty requested a copy of the files from the police department. The police declined, saying that the file "isn't here."

• What happened to the files? Lieutenant Marion Phillips of the Los Angeles Police Department claimed that he was told in 1962 that a high-ranking police official "had taken the file to show someone in Washington. That was the last we heard of it."

MONROE AND THE KENNEDYS

• As part of his research for *Goddess*, the most authoritative book on Marilyn Monroe, Anthony Summers interviewed more than 600 people linked to her. He quotes friends, acquaintances, reporters, and politicians who confirm what many Americans already suspected—that Monroe had had affairs with both John and Robert Kennedy.

• Apparently, John Kennedy met her through his brother-in-law, Peter Lawford. According to Lawford's third wife, Deborah Gould, "Peter told me that Jack…had always wanted to meet Marilyn Monroe; it was one of his fantasies." Quoting Lawford, Gould says "Monroe's affair with John Kennedy began before he became president and continued for several years."

• According to Gould, JFK decided to end his affair with Monroe early in 1962. He sent his brother Robert to California to give her the news. "Marilyn took it quite badly," says Gould, "and Bobby went away with a feeling of wanting to get to know her better. At the beginning it was just to help and console, but then it led into an affair between Marilyn and Bobby."

Top 3 most hated foods in the U.S.: tofu, liver, and yogurt.

• It didn't last long. By the summer of 1962, RFK began having second thoughts and decided to break off the affair. Monroe, already severely depressed, began acting erratically after being dumped by Bobby. She began calling him at home; when he changed his unlisted phone number to avoid her, she began calling him at the Justice Department, the White House, and even at the Kennedy compound in Hyannisport. When Bobby still refused to take her calls, Monroe threatened to go public with both affairs.

WAS IT A CONSPIRACY?

THEORY #1: Monroe was distraught about her affairs and committed suicide. To protect the Kennedys from scandal, someone tried to cover up the suicide and cleaned up Monroe's house.

• Monroe may have become frantic when Robert Kennedy cut her off, perhaps—as some theorists guess—because she was pregnant.

• Fred Otash, a Hollywood private detective, claimed that a "police source" told him that weeks before her death Monroe had gone to Mexico to have an abortion. According to Otash, "an American doctor went down to Tijuana to do it, which made Monroe safe medically, and made the doctor safe from U.S. law," since at that time abortion was illegal in the U.S. But author Summers disagrees, noting: "There was no medical evidence to support the theory that Monroe had been pregnant."

• In any event, if Monroe was threatening to embarrass the Kennedys by going public about their affairs, it was cause for alarm. According to several reports, Robert Kennedy—who was vacationing with his family near San Francisco—flew to Los Angeles on August 4 to meet with Monroe and try to calm her down. It didn't work.

• Terribly depressed, Monroe took a massive dose of sleeping pills, but not before calling Peter Lawford and saying, in a slurred voice, "Say goodbye to Pat [Lawford's wife], say goodbye to Jack [JFK], and say goodbye to yourself, because you're such a nice guy."

• The call may have frightened Lawford so badly that he—and perhaps RFK—drove to Monroe's home. There he may have found her comatose and called an ambulance. (This would explain the Shaefer Ambulance claim of having taken Monroe to the hospital that night.) If Monroe had been taken to a hospital emergency room because of an overdose, her stomach would almost certainly have been pumped—which would account for the coroner's finding no "pill residue" in her stomach. When even the hospital's best attempts could not save Monroe, perhaps her body was returned to her bedroom in an effort to avoid controversy.

The Cleanup

• No suicide note was ever found, nor was Monroe's personal phone book. Someone had probably "sanitized" her bedroom before the police came. Most likely person: Peter Lawford. His ex-wife Deborah Gould claimed, "He went there and tidied up the place, and did what he could, before the police and the press arrived." She also claimed Lawford had found and destroyed a suicide note.

• Lawford may also have hired detective Fred Otash to finish the cleanup. According to a security consultant who worked with Otash, Lawford hired him on the night of the death to "check her house, especially for papers or letters, that might give away her affairs with the Kennedys."

THEORY #2: The Mob killed Monroe to embarrass—or even frame—Attorney General Robert Kennedy.

• The Mob almost certainly knew of Monroe's affairs with the Kennedys: in fact, several reputable accounts claim that the star's house had been bugged by the Mob. By recording intimate moments between Monroe and Robert Kennedy, the syndicate may have hoped to blackmail the attorney general and thus end his prosecution of Teamster boss Jimmy Hoffa and other gangsters.

• In their book *Double Cross*, Chuck and Sam Giancana—the brother and godson of Mob godfather Sam "Mooney" Giancana— allege that the Mafia eventually decided to kill Monroe and make it look like a suicide. Once the press learned of her recent affair with RFK, they figured, the public would decide that Monroe had killed herself over him. They figured a sex and suicide scandal would force him to resign. So, the Mob waited for Kennedy to visit Monroe, in response to her desperate phone calls.

• Finally, Kennedy took the bait. According to the authors of *Double Cross*, when Sam Giancana learned that Bobby would be in California the weekend of August 4, he arranged the hit on Monroe. The authors allege he chose Needles Gianola, an experienced killer, for the mission. Needles selected three men of his own to

---

The odds are good that the Empire State Building will be struck by lightning twice this month.

help him. Together they traveled to California "under Mooney's orders, to murder Marilyn Monroe."

• According to *Double Cross*, the mob had already bugged Monroe home, and the hit men were waiting at their secret listening post nearby when Kennedy arrived late Saturday night. They heard Bobby and another man enter the home and begin talking to Monroe, who was extremely upset. Monroe, the authors report, "became agitated—hysterical, in fact—and in response, they heard Kennedy instruct the man with him, evidently a doctor, to give her a shot to 'calm her down.' Shortly afterward, RFK and the doctor left."

• *Double Cross* claims that the four killers waited until nightfall, then sneaked into Monroe's home to make the hit. Monroe resisted, but was easily subdued because of the sedatives: "Calmly, and with all the efficiency of a team of surgeons, they taped her mouth shut and proceeded to insert a specially 'doctored' Nembutal suppository into her anus." According to the authors, the killers waited for the lethal combination of barbiturates and chloral hydrate to take effect. Once she was totally unconscious, the men carefully removed the tape, wiped her mouth clean, and placed her across the bed. Their job completed, they left as quietly as they had come.

• Unfortunately for the conspirators, however, Kennedy's close friends and the FBI so thoroughly cleaned up Monroe's house and commandeered her phone records that any proof of the romance was eliminated. The Giancanas say that J. Edgar Hoover protected the Kennedys because, after keeping their secrets, he knew that they'd never fire him. *Double Cross* also alleges that the CIA was also in on the hit, but its reasoning is not convincing.

FOOTNOTE

In 1982, after reinvestigating Marilyn Monroe's death, the Los Angeles District Attorney's Office released the following statement: "Marilyn Monroe's murder would have required a massive, in-place conspiracy covering all of the principals at the death scene on August 4 and 5, 1962; the actual killer or killers; the Chief Medical Examiner-Coroner; the autopsy surgeon to whom the case was fortuitously assigned; and almost all of the police officers assigned to the case, as well as their superiors in the LAPD...our inquiries and document examination uncovered no credible evidence supporting a murder theory."

There is no rice in rice paper.

THE ZAMBIAN SPACE PROGRAM

This is one of those "truth is stranger than fiction" stories.
We think someone should make a movie about it.

In the late 1960s, Zambia—a small country in the heart of Africa—launched its own space program. Heading it was Edward Muka Nkoloso, the government's minister of space research. He labored long and hard to come up with a way to put a Zambian man on the moon…and he might have been successful if he hadn't run into a few insurmountable problems:

1. MONEY. "We are delaying our plans to plant the Zambian flag on the moon," Nkoloso told reporters in 1968 while decked out in his trademark red-and-green, superman-style cloak. "But this is only a temporary setback. A reply to my request to the United Nations for a loan of $19,600,000 and a further $1,900,000,000 from private foreign sources hasn't yet been received." It never was received. The only international financing the program ever got was a 10-rupee ($2.50) note sent in by a space-minded Indian schoolboy who had learned of the program on TV.

2. SUDDEN FAME. Egos became a major obstacle when Zambia's 10-person astronaut corps were catapulted from obscurity to fame overnight. "After the worldwide TV showing and press publicity of our astronauts in training I received thousands of letters from foreign countries," Nkoloso said at the time. "But my spacemen thought they were film stars. They demanded payment, and they refused to continue with our program of rolling down hills in oil drums and my special tree-swinging method of simulating space weightlessness. Two of my best men went on a drinking spree a month ago and haven't been seen since," he said. "Another of my astronauts has joined a local tribal song and dance group. He says he makes more money swinging from the top of a 40-foot pole."

3. BIOLOGY. Zambia's No. 1 space woman, Matha Mwamba, completed the full course of 50 hill rolls and tree swings…and then became pregnant. Shortly afterwards she returned to her parents, who talked her out of continuing her space training.

Though he was dejected, Nkoloso refused to abandon his plans to be first on the moon. His trials and trevails were covered by the world press, which generated widespread support for the space program. His office in the Zambian capital of Lusaka was filled with piles of letters from foreign well-wishers containing lots of advice …but no money (except the 10-rupee note). "Look at all those letters from every country in the world," he boasted shortly before the Apollo moon landings. "I've got the finest foreign stamp collection in Africa these days. If this space program doesn't work out, I may consider becoming an expert on stamp collecting."

Nkoloso continued in his efforts for several more years, despite requests from President Kenneth Kaunda of Zambia to take a more low profile approach. A proud nationalist, he was even willing to work with the space programs of other nations to achieve his goal. "Perhaps the Americans would like to join me in my space program," he said in 1969, "I'd be most happy. But let's get one thing straight I step on the moon and hoist the Zambian flag first."

*　　*　　*

MOON SHOTS
Three Apollo-related events

1. Ottowa television station CJOH-TV reported that they got 15 calls complaining about Apollo 11 pre-empting the regular program. The program they wanted to see: *Star Trek*.

2. David Thelfall, a London bookmaker, bet $24 in 1964 that a man would walk on the moon by 1971. The odds were 1,000 to 1. He was awarded a check for $24,000 on national television when the lunar module landed.

3. In Ghana, tribal chief Nagai Kassa VII listened to the Apollo saga on his short wave radio through the Voice of America. Reportedly, he was worried that the astronauts would fall off the moon, and was amazed that they were able to fit on it at all. "The moon is so small as I see it that I didn't think there would be enough room," he said.

THE COLA WARS

Some competitors have friendly rivalries, but not Coke and Pepsi.
These two have battled for most of this century, taking
no prisoners. And the Cola Wars continue today.

BEFORE THE BATTLES

To understand the bitterness between Coke and Pepsi, you have to go back a hundred years to the two pharmacists (both veterans of the Confederate army) who formulated the sticky-sweet brown liquids.

COKE BEGINNINGS

John Pemberton, a pharmacist in Atlanta, created Coca-Cola as a non-alcoholic "nerve medicine" in 1886.

• He came up with the first Coke syrup by boiling a batch of herbs, coca leaves, and kola nuts in his backyard.

• He mixed the syrup with tap water and sold it in his drugstore.

• It wasn't until a customer with an upset stomach specifically asked him to mix the syrup with fizzy water that he realized Coke's potential as a soft drink.

• Pemberton didn't live to see Coca-Cola become a success. Shortly after he created the drink, his health began to fail. He sold the rights to Coca-Cola to a group of druggists for about $350; he died in 1888.

THE NEW REGIME

Only one of Coca-Cola's new owners, Asa Candler, saw the drink's huge potential. By 1891, he had bought complete control of the company for $2,300, and he registered *Coca-Cola* as a trademark a few years later. Candler plowed nearly all of the company's early profits back into the business and kept costs to a minimum (one employee reported earning "$3 per week and lots of Coca-Cola").

Candler had an unmatched flair for promotion and began the company's tradition of giving away Coca-Cola clocks, fans, calendars, urns, scales, thermometers, and other premiums to storekeepers who ordered Coke syrup.

By 1892, he was selling more than 35,000 gallons of syrup a year, and by the turn of the century, Coca-Cola had become the best-known product in America.

EARLY COMPETITORS

Coca-Cola's meteoric rise inspired scores of imitators. Coke sued dozens of them for trademark infringement, including the Koke Company, Kola Koke, Coke-Ola, Koko-Cola, Koko-Kola, Ko-Kola, and Coca & Cola. The case against the Koke Company went all the way to the Supreme Court, and Coca-Cola won.

HITTING THE BOTTLE

According to legend, a mystery man walked into Coca-Cola's offices one day in 1891. He told Candler he knew a way to double the company's sales overnight, and would share his idea for $5,000 (or, some say, $50,000). Candler paid him. The man handed Candler a slip of paper which said, "Bottle it."

Regardless of whether the story is true, Candler resisted bottling Coca-Cola for a long time, fearing that pressurized bottles might explode and expose the company to legal liability. Eventually, a Mississippi candy store owner started bottling the liquid on his own. He had enormous success (and no lawsuits), and so five years later, Candler opened his first bottling plant.

At first, Coca-Cola's bottles were indistinguishable from those of other companies, but in 1915, the company hired an Indiana glass company to design a bottle that customers would recognize "even in the dark." Loosely adapting sketches of a cola nut they found in the *Encyclopedia Britannica*, the glassworkers designed the distinctive bottle that is still in use today.

Candler ran Coca-Cola until 1916, when he turned control of the company over to his sons. His wife's death in 1919 sent him into a deep depression; he tried to shake it off by taking a trip to Europe. While he was away, his sons sold the company to Robert Woodruff, an Atlanta entrepreneur, for $25 million.

PEPSI-COLA HITS THE SPOT

Meanwhile, back to 1893: In North Carolina, pharmacist Caleb Bradham decided he wanted to cash in on the success of Coca-Cola. At first, he called his imitation "Brad's Drink," but then decided to name it after *pepsin*, a digestive aid, hoping people would buy it as a stomach remedy. Like Pemberton, he didn't see Pepsi's potential as a soft drink until it became popular among people who *weren't* sick.

Bradham paid careful attention to advertising, and his sales grew to 100,000 gallons of syrup by 1898. Pepsi continued to grow until the end of World War I, when sugar prices shot up from 5 1/2 cents a pound to 22 1/2 cents a pound. To hedge against future shortages, Bradham stocked up on sugar at the higher price. But a few months later, sugar plummeted to 3 1/2 cents a pound, and the company went bankrupt. Bradham returned to his drugstore, leaving the soda world.

Roy C. McGargel bought the rights to Pepsi-Cola in 1920 and tried to put the company back on its feet. But he couldn't afford a large advertising budget, and the company faltered. It went bankrupt in 1925, reorganized, and went bankrupt again in 1931.

SKIRMISH #1: LOFTY GOALS

The day after Pepsi-Cola went bankrupt in 1931, Charles Guth, the president of the Loft Candy Store chain, bought it for $10,500. It didn't seem like a wise investment at the time, since Coca-Cola was already the industry giant and was getting bigger every year. But Guth wanted something more than mere money—he bought Pepsi to get *revenge*.

• Guth hated the Coca-Cola Company. Even though Loft's 115 candy stores sold 4 million servings of Coke every year, the company had refused to give him a quantity discount. When Guth bought Pepsi for himself, he dumped Coke from Loft stores.

• Coca-Cola was furious: Guth was one of its largest customers, and losing his business hurt. The company decided to fight back.

• It secretly sent its employees into Guth's stores to order "a Coke." On 620 occasions, they reported, they were served Pepsi instead. The company sued Guth, claiming he didn't have the right to serve Pepsi to customers asking for "a Coke." Coca-Cola fought the case for over 10 years, losing it in 1942. The bitterness between the two companies was just beginning.

SKIRMISH #2: "12 FULL OUNCES, THAT'S A LOT"

Two years after buying Pepsi, Guth had had enough. He couldn't expand sales beyond his own stores, and wanted to sell out. The logical buyer was Coke. Guth offered them the company at a bargain price...but they refused.

• Desperate to cut costs, Guth began bottling Pepsi in second-hand beer bottles, which held nearly twice as much soda as normal soft drink bottles. Guth saved money, and hoped the larger serving size would increase sales.

• It didn't. Nearly bankrupt, Guth took one last gamble to save his company: He cut Pepsi's price from 10 cents to a nickel, offering twice as much cola as Coke for half the price. The gamble paid off. By 1938, Pepsi was making $4 million a year and growing fast.

PALACE COUP

Guth won the battle, but lost it all in an internal power play. By 1935, he had spent so much of his attention and energy building up Pepsi that Loft Candy Stores was on the verge of bankruptcy. Loft's board of directors forced him to resign and hired the Phoenix Security Company to nurse the candy company back to health.

Guth still owned Pepsi-Cola outright; he said he had bought it with his own money. But audits showed that he had bought it using Loft's funds. Upon discovering this, Phoenix Securities hatched a scheme to take control of Pepsi itself. It bought up much of Loft's nearly worthless stock. Acting on behalf of the candy company, it then sued Guth for control of Pepsi. Phoenix won the suit in 1939. Their scheme had worked—for the bargain-basement price of a nearly bankrupt chain of candy stores, Phoenix Securities had taken control of the second most successful soft drink company in the nation.

SKIRMISH #3: A SMOKING GUN

Although Coca-Cola was still the undisputed leader of the cola companies, Pepsi-Cola's booming sales made it nervous. In 1934, it fired the next volley with a trademark-infringement suit against

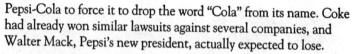

Pepsi-Cola to force it to drop the word "Cola" from its name. Coke had already won similar lawsuits against several companies, and Walter Mack, Pepsi's new president, actually expected to lose.

Everyone else thought Pepsi would lose, too. The widow of the president of Cleo-Cola, which had lost a similar lawsuit, visited Mack to commiserate. "My husband thought he was right, too," she said, "but they still put him out of business. And I still have a photograph of the check they gave him."

Check? What check? Purely by chance, she had given Mack an important piece of evidence proving that Coca-Cola had been bribing soft drink executives to deliberately lose the lawsuits it filed against them, in order to strengthen its trademark position for future cases.

Mack asked the widow for a copy of the check and introduced it as evidence in court. Caught red-handed, Coca-Cola asked for a two-day recess. The next day, Robert Woodruff, president of Coca-Cola, met with Mack in a New York hotel. He offered to withdraw the suit, and Mack agreed—but only after forcing Woodruff to sign a statement he had written out on the hotel's stationery: "I, Robert Woodruff, hereby agree that [Coca-Cola] will recognize the Pepsi-Cola trademark and never attack it in the United States."

Coke kept its word. It never again attacked Pepsi's trademark in this country. However, in other countries around the world, Coke has attacked Pepsi's trademark whenever and however possible.

SKIRMISH #4: BEG, BORROW & STEELE

By 1949, Pepsi was in trouble again. Coke had recaptured 84 percent of the U.S. soda market, and Pepsi was near bankruptcy. The problem: Pepsi's image. Its huge bottles and low price had made it popular during the Great Depression—but they also gave the brand a reputation as a "cheap" drink for people who couldn't afford Coke. Affluent post-war America was returning to Coke.

Luckily for Pepsi, a Coca-Cola vice president named Alfred Steele jumped ship. A former circus showman, Steele's flamboyant antics had been unpopular with the company, and his career had bottomed out. He quit and become president of Pepsi-Cola, taking 15 other top executives with him. For the second time in its history, Pepsi was run by a man bent on getting revenge on Coke.

In 1983, a Japanese artist made a copy of the Mona Lisa completely out of toast.

Steele was just what Pepsi needed. He reworked Pepsi's image, updating the company's logo to the familiar circular one used for decades and switching to fancy swirl bottles. He also launched a massive advertising campaign, which positioned Pepsi as a superior product, even a status symbol.

In 1955, Steele married actress Joan Crawford, a former Coca-Cola endorser, and she began appearing in Pepsi ads and publicity events. Her Hollywood glamour helped shake off the brand's "low class" image. Steele succeeded in breathing new life into Pepsi, and by the time he died in 1959, he had cut Coke's lead in half.

SKIRMISH #5: ICE-COLD WAR

During the 1950s, Pepsi was active in conservative politics. It was a big supporter of Senator Joseph McCarthy and his anti-Communist associate, Richard Nixon. In 1959, Vice President Nixon traveled to Moscow to attend an international trade show of American and Soviet products, including Pepsi-Cola. Soviet president Nikita Khrushchev was there, and while touring the Macy's kitchen exhibit, the two men got into a heated argument over the merits of communism and capitalism.

Pepsi officials asked Nixon to bring Khrushchev to their display to cool off after the debate. Nixon happily obliged, shoving a Pepsi into Khrushchev's hand. Photos of the scene were a public relations bonanza for Pepsi: at the height of the Cold War, the leader of the Communist world was photographed drinking a Pepsi. In one stroke, Pepsi's worldwide image and prestige had finally caught up with Coca-Cola's, and Donald Kendall, Pepsi's overseas operations chief, never forgot Nixon's gesture. A few years later, he got a chance to return the favor.

Nixon lost the presidential campaign in 1960, and the California gubernatorial race in 1962. Now unemployed, he was offered the presidency of several universities, considered for the chairmanship of Chrysler, and was even suggested as commissioner of baseball. But he decided to practice law so that he could stay active in politics. His wife, Pat, was too embarrassed by his defeat to stay in California, so they moved to New York.

Nixon hadn't practiced law for a long time and wasn't exactly a prestigious figure anymore, so he had a hard time finding a firm that would take him. Donald Kendall repaid the Moscow favor by presenting him with the Pepsi account, worth a considerable amount of money. And the job helped keep Nixon in the public eye. He traveled around the world, opening Pepsi bottling plants and stopping to meet world leaders. Coincidence: He was in Dallas making a Pepsi-related appearance on November 22, 1963, when JFK was killed.

Even after Nixon was elected President in 1968, his relationship with the company remained close. During his years in office, Pepsi was the only soft drink served at the White House. In 1972, Pepsi won the right to begin selling soft drinks in the USSR after Nixon personally asked the Soviets to "look favorably" on Pepsi's request. Pepsi had pull even when Nixon didn't intervene directly: foreign governments knew that giving Pepsi favorable treatment would score points with his administration.

SKIRMISH #6: COKE SHALL RISE AGAIN

In 1962, the same year Nixon became Pepsi's lawyer, a young Georgian named Jimmy Carter lost the Democratic nomination for the state senate. But Carter suspected election fraud and hired King & Spalding, Atlanta's most prominent law firm, to challenge the results. They succeeded: Carter was declared the Democratic nominee and went on to win the election.

The law firm got Carter together with officials from another of its clients: the Coca-Cola Company. Company officials saw immediately that he had potential as a national candidate. They introduced him to the inner circle of Georgia's corporate and industrial leaders, whose money and support would later prove crucial in Carter's campaigns for governor and president.

Carter remained close to Coca-Cola for the rest of his career. As governor, he often used the company's jets on official trips, and when his 1976 presidential campaign started losing steam, he turned to Coke's image makers to film his campaign commercials.

As early as 1974, he admitted to the company's role in developing his knowledge of foreign affairs: "We have our own built-in State Department in the Coca-Cola company. They provide me ahead of time with...penetrating analyses of what the country is, what its problems are, who its leaders are, and when I arrive there, provide me with an introduction to the leaders of that country."

Like Nixon, Carter returned the favor after being elected president. One of the first acts of his administration: removing the White House Pepsi-Cola machines and replacing them with Coke.

After Carter was elected, Portugal allowed Coke to be bottled and sold in the country—lifting a ban that was more than 50 years old. Not long afterward, the U.S. government approved a $300 million emergency loan to the country. And when China opened its markets to American companies during Carter's term, Coke got the nod over Pepsi.

SKIRMISH #7: PEPSICO STRIKES BACK

In the mid-1960s, the Pepsi-Cola Company (renamed Pepsico) began diversifying into the snack-food and restaurant business, eventually buying Kentucky Fried Chicken, Pizza Hut, and other popular chains—in part so they could switch their soda fountains over to Pepsi-Cola. Pepsico's diversification strategy worked: by 1979, the company had succeeded at the unthinkable—it had grown larger than Coca-Cola. While undiversified Coke still sold more soft drinks and had higher profits, Pepsi was gaining even there. And now Coke's own surveys were showing that younger drinkers preferred the taste of Pepsi. Coke decided to act.

A SHOT TO THE FOOT: NEW COKE

In 1985, the Coca-Cola company announced it was replacing the old Coke formula with one a new one. Extensive marketing tests indicated that people preferred New Coke over both the old product *and* Pepsi.

But the marketing tests didn't anticipate the huge negative reaction to tinkering with a beloved old product. It was a major embarrassment for Coca-Cola. Pepsi declared victory, consumers revolted, and within two months old Coke was back—in the form of "Classic Coke." Today, it outsells New Coke by a ratio of 4 to 1.

Today, the makers of the sweet liquids continue their bitter battle.

William Baldwin wrote the first English novel in 1553. Its title: *Beware the Cat.*

PRESIDENTIAL HEALTH SECRETS

If the president of the United States suddenly fell ill, do you think the public would be told? Here's a look at some of the best-kept health secrets in American history.

A PRESIDENTIAL DILEMMA

Suppose the president of the United States suffered a stroke, heart attack, or nervous breakdown in the midst of a national crisis. Should he go public with the illness...or keep it secret "for the good of the country"?

This may sound like the plot to a Tom Clancy thriller or an Oliver Stone movie, but it isn't. At numerous points in American history, presidents have hidden their own serious health problems from the public in the name of advancing the public good.

JOHN F. KENNEDY (1961-1963)

Background. Known for playing football on the White House lawn and advocating 50-mile hikes, JFK was seemingly one of the healthiest presidents—but he was probably one of the sickest people ever to serve in the White House. He nearly died from scarlet fever when he was three, and "nearly all his life," Rose Kennedy once remarked to a friend, "he had to battle against misfortunes of health," among them measles, German measles, whooping cough, chicken pox, diphtheria, malaria, asthma, jaundice, pneumonia, colitis, a dysfunctional gallbladder, urethritis, bladder and prostate disease, a spastic colon, and hemorrhoids. Kennedy also suffered from chronic back problems as a result of having a left leg that was nearly half an inch shorter than the right. "At least one half of the days that he spent on this Earth were days of intense physical pain," Bobby Kennedy recalled years later.

Addison's Disease. But Kennedy's worst illness by far was Addison's disease, a failure of the adrenal glands to produce the adrenaline and cortisone that the body needs to maintain the proper mineral levels in the bloodstream. Kennedy is believed to have contracted the condition in the mid 1940s, just as new drugs were being developed to treat it. Even so, JFK believed the illness would kill him. "The doctors say I've got a sort of slow-motion leukemia," the future president told a reporter in the 1950s, "but they tell me I'll probably last until I'm forty-five."

The 1960 Campaign. By the time JFK announced his candidacy for president in the late 1950s, Addison's disease had become fully treatable. But that didn't stop Senator Lyndon Johnson, Kennedy's rival for the Democratic nomination, from using it as an issue in the campaign. Kennedy had struck first, making an issue out of Johnson's 1955 heart attack, questioning whether Johnson was capable of being a "full-time" president. In retaliation, LBJ's campaign manager, John Connally, insisted that if Kennedy were elected, he "couldn't serve out the term," since because of the disease "he was going to die." The Kennedy campaign responded with outright denials. "John F. Kennedy does not now nor has he ever had an ailment described as classically as Addison's disease....Any statement to the contrary is malicious and false."

Kennedy's disease was one of the best-kept secrets of his presidency—even his doctors didn't admit he had it until 1966, and to this day his medical records at the Kennedy Library are sealed.

GROVER CLEVELAND (1885-1889; 1893-1897)

Background. In the spring of 1893, President Cleveland discovered a rough spot on the roof of his mouth about the size of a quarter. It was a tumor, it was cancerous, and it had to be removed immediately or he would die. The only problem: The "Panic of 1893" was sweeping the country—the stock market had crashed in May, and 600 banks and 16,000 businesses had already failed. "Not a syllable must be allowed to reach the press," Cleveland told his doctor. "Everyone knows we are in a financial crisis; and I am expected to lead the nation out of it. If the public knew of my condition, business failures and foreclosures would quadruple in a matter of days."

The "Pleasure" Cruise. Rather than risk exposure by checking into a hospital, Cleveland borrowed a yacht from a millionaire friend and set sail down New York's East River on what was supposed to be a "pleasure" cruise. It wasn't—Cleveland's companions were actually surgeons in disguise, and on July 1 they sat Cleveland up in a chair, strapped him to the mast below deck, and removed his upper left jawbone in a procedure lasting several hours. Sixteen days later they repeated the procedure, having failed to remove all of the cancer the first time around. For the rest of his life, Cleveland wore a prosthetic jawbone that enabled him to look and speak normally. The surgery was a success: he never got cancer again.

Rumors of the surgery abounded, but they were usually dismissed as partisan attacks or outright fantasy. Amazingly, the story wasn't confirmed until 1917, when Dr. W. W. Keen, one of Cleveland's doctors, described the incident in an article in the *Saturday Evening Post*. By then, Cleveland had been dead for over nine years.

WOODROW WILSON (1913-1921)

The year 1919 was a difficult one for President Wilson. Legislation to recognize his League of Nations was unpopular around the country...and was in jeopardy in the Republican-held Senate. But Wilson was determined to overcome the opposition. He embarked on an 8,000-mile, cross-country speaking tour, trying to drum up popular support for the League.

The Stroke. The trip was too much for him. On September 25, he collapsed from exhaustion after delivering a speech in Pueblo, Colorado, and was whisked back to Washington, D.C., aboard the presidential train. Two days later, he suffered a massive stroke—his entire left side was paralyzed, and his speech was garbled. White House usher Ike Hoover later described seeing him in the sickroom: "The president lay stretched out on the large Lincoln bed. He looked dead. There was not a sign of life....He was just gone." Rather than admit that the president might die at any minute, the White House released a statement that read, "The president had a fairly good night, but his condition is not at all good this morning."

The Coverup. Two days passed, and Wilson failed to make much improvement. Doctors felt he would never make a full recovery and wanted to make a full public statement on his condition, but First Lady Edith Wilson refused to let them. "Thus began," writes historian August Heckscher, "such a coverup as American history had not known before." Wilson was totally incapable of attending to his duties throughout the rest of 1919. During this time, First Lady Edith Wilson—who had only two years of formal education—virtually ran the White House.

While Vice President Thomas Marshall and Wilson's cabinet had been told that Wilson had suffered a stroke, the public was kept completely in the dark. And no one, not even the Wilson administration's highest officials, was allowed in to see the president. "Mrs. Wilson absolutely barred the door," Colonel Edward House, one of Wilson's closest advisers, later told the *Cleveland Plain Dealer*. "She alone decided what messages her husband would get."

Edith Wilson deferred as many decisions to Wilson administration officials as she could; the ones the president had to make she made herself. Although by the time his term expired in 1921 he had reassumed virtually all of the powers of the presidency, Wilson remained a shadow of a man.

The Aftermath. Although the coverup protected Wilson's presidency everyone knew he was suffering from *something* serious. Webb Garrison writes in *A Treasury of White House Tales*, "Rumors proliferated: zeal in campaigning for the League of Nations had caused the president to lose his mind; he had become the victim of venereal disease; marital strife had reached such a peak that Wilson had attempted suicide to escape his domineering wife." The true extent of his disability was not revealed until after he died in 1924.

FRANKLIN D. ROOSEVELT (1933-1945)

The Early Days. It was well known during Franklin Roosevelt's lifetime that he had suffered from polio, but only his inner circle knew just how disabled the disease had made him. The coverup began immediately after FDR was stricken in 1921, while vacationing with his family in Campobello, Maine: when it became clear that Roosevelt was not going to make a quick or full recovery, he was secretly taken to a New York hospital, where he received six weeks of treatment, and then to his home in Hyde Park, where he spent many more months in seclusion.

The Road to the White House. In 1932, "deeply concerned that the image of a 'permanently crippled man' seeking to lead a crippled nation out of the Depression would be damaging to his campaign, Roosevelt's aides made every effort to portray the Democratic nominee as a man who had conquered polio and who could walk," Robert Gilbert writes in *The Mortal Presidency*. "As he traveled across the country, his leg braces, without which he could not stand, had to be put on and locked into place before each campaign appearance....In getting on and off his campaign train, he was often seen 'walking' up and down a long, narrow ramp specially constructed with a strong hand railing which he could grip and use to pull himself forward."

His condition was subtly exploited by his opponents during his first campaign for president in 1932: more than one publicly congratulated him on his "great progress made toward full recovery," and President Herbert Hoover promoted himself as being "strong enough to step forward in manly fashion to lead the nation in its march up the road to economic recovery." Nevertheless, few people gathered the full extent of Roosevelt's disability and, despite the jibes, he trounced Hoover in the popular vote and won the electoral college by a margin of eight to one.

As President. The coverup continued into the White House years: FDR had his steel leg braces painted black to make them indistinguishable from his black trousers, socks, and shoes. At state banquets he was wheeled into the dining room and seated in a regular chair (the wheelchair was removed from the room) before other guests were allowed to enter. At many important White House speeches, the presidential podium—which was bolted to the floor so that he could lean his full weight against it—was set up just in front of a set of sliding doors, which were kept closed until the last minute. FDR would be wheeled up behind the doors and propped up on his feet; then the doors would be thrown open and he would amble up to the podium, grasping an aide's arm as he walked.

There was also an unspoken White House rule that no one photograph the president in his wheelchair or being assisted by his aides. Most of the reporters in the White House press corps were cooperative, but Secret Service agents, acting as enforcers, seized the cameras of any who weren't.

Final Years. Eventually, the strain of FDR's many years in office took their toll on his health. In March 1944, a physical exam revealed that in addition to a severe cough that had been lingering for months, Roosevelt was suffering from "moderately severe and well-advanced hypertension, obstructive pulmonary disease, and congestive heart failure." His cough was also filling his lungs with fluid, which, combined with his poor circulation, gave him a gray complexion with bluish lips and fingertips. According to Gilbert,

Dr. Howard Bruenn [a cardiologist] was deeply concerned by Roosevelt's physical decline. The report was dire in its ultimate judge-

---

If aircraft carriers ran on gasoline, they'd get about 6 inches to the gallon.

ment: The President might die at any moment. With proper treatment, he might live on for months, maybe even a year or two. Dr. McIntire [the White House physician] had ordered Bruenn to report his findings directly to him and to no one else....Neither Roosevelt nor his family were told of the disturbing facts.

Amazingly—and perhaps unknowingly—FDR decided to run for an unprecedented fourth term. As in the past, deception ruled the day, as the visibly deteriorating president struggled to prove he had the stamina for another four years. Perhaps because he was so ill, Roosevelt went to the greatest extremes of his career to prove that he wasn't; on one occasion he even rode in an open car through a rainstorm for more than four hours. Periodically along the route, Gallagher writes in *Splendid Deception,* the car would pull into heated garages, where

> Secret Service agents quickly lifted [him] from the car and stretched him out full length in blankets laid on the floor. They removed his clothes down to the skin. He was towelled dry and given a rubdown. He was redressed in dry clothes, brandy was poured down his throat and he was lifted back into the car.

Not everyone was convinced that the president would finish out his term, especially in the Democratic Party. Largely because of this, Vice President Henry Wallace, considered a "left-winger," was dumped from the ticket and Senator Harry S Truman of Missouri, a virtually unknown moderate, was nominated in his place. FDR was, of course, elected to a fourth term, but his health continued to fail. He died on April 12, 1945, not three months into the term.

Note: According to one 1979 report, near the end of FDR's third term his physician, Dr. Frank Leahy, discovered a cancerous tumor somewhere on the president's body, one that had metastasized and was spreading. He told FDR about the cancer and advised him not to run for a fourth term, but the president ignored his advice.

DWIGHT D. EISENHOWER (1953-1961)

Background. After Richard Nixon lost the 1960 presidential election to John F. Kennedy, observers wondered why Eisenhower didn't campaign harder for his vice president. Many assumed that Ike didn't particularly like Nixon, or that Nixon was too proud to ask Ike for help. In recent years, however, another reason for Ike's lackluster performance has become apparent. "We now know,"

In London, it's illegal to make love on a parked motorcycle.

Robert Gilbert writes in his book *The Mortal Presidency*, "that Eisenhower's health was a vital factor in limiting his involvement in the 1960 campaign. Indeed, at times during the campaign period, the President was actually in danger of death." Ike, who had had a heart attack in 1955 and a stroke in 1957, suffered repeated life-threatening health crises in 1960. He had to be hospitalized for several days in May after returning from a Paris peace conference and suffered episodes of erratic pulse and blood pressure in the fall.

The most serious episode came during a Nixon campaign appearance in Detroit, when Ike suffered a dangerous attack of ventricular fibrillation, a life-threatening condition in which the heart valves merely vibrate irregularly instead of pumping blood normally. By the end of October, his condition was so bad that his physician ordered him to "take extra oxygen" whenever he was at work. Historian Stephen Ambrose writes that Ike's deteriorating condition so worried Mamie Eisenhower that on October 30—only eight days before the election—the First Lady

> called Pat Nixon to say that she was distraught at the thought of her man taking on additional burdens, and told Mrs. Nixon she feared that Eisenhower "was not up to the strain campaigning might put on his heart." She tried to dissuade him, but could not, and therefore "begged" Pat Nixon to have her husband convince Eisenhower to change his mind, without letting Ike know she had intervened. The following morning, Dr. Snyder added his opinion, telling Nixon to "either talk him out of it or just don't let him do it—for the sake of his health."

Nixon consented, Ike relented...and Nixon lost the election to Kennedy by one vote per precinct, the narrowest defeat in American presidential history.

RONALD REAGAN (1981-1989)

Background. On November 5, 1994, Ronald Reagan announced to the world in a handwritten letter that he was suffering from Alzheimer's disease, a degenerative and irreversible brain disorder that robs the sufferer of memory and is ultimately fatal. Along with his letter, Reagan released a statement from his doctors that said the disease had been diagnosed the previous year.

Unanswered Question. Was Reagan really in the *early* stages of the disease, or had he been suffering from Alzheimer's for longer than his doctors were aware (or would admit)? Shortly after Reagan went public with his illness, Dr. Steven Miles, a professor of geriatric medicine at the University of Minnesota, published an article in the Minneapolis *Star Tribune* in which he said that he had suspected that Reagan was already in the early stages of Alzheimer's *during* his presidency. "We were concerned by the increasing vagueness of his presidency, his inability to speak lucidly outside of brief, tightly controlled settings," Miles wrote, adding that he and other geriatricians had even considered making a public appeal for an examination of Reagan to see if he was suffering from Alzheimer's—but that they ultimately decided not to, "given White House medical reports that all was well."

The Evidence. At one point in February 1987—during the depths of the Iran-Contra scandal—the White House brought in James Cannon to "clean house." One of the first things he did was interview top White House officials. "The overwhelming majority," he told the *Los Angeles Times* in 1988, expressed their concern that Reagan was no longer up to the job of being president. "They told stories about how inattentive and inept the president was....They said he wouldn't read the papers they gave him—even short position papers and documents. They said he wouldn't come to work—all he wanted to do was to watch movies and TV at the residence."

Cannon sent a memo to White House Chief of Staff Howard Baker outlining his concerns. The following day the two men carefully observed Reagan's behavior during a cabinet meeting...and decided nothing was wrong.

"What the hell is going on here?" Cannon recalls asking himself afterward. "The old fella looks just dandy."

"I didn't take Cannon's memo lightly," Baker said in 1988, "but from the first time I saw him (Reagan), he was fully in control, and I never had any question about his mental competence."

The Big Question. Is it possible that Reagan slipped into Alzheimer's disease while still president? Many experts say yes—the onset of the disease is so gradual that a person can have it for years before doctors or even family members recognize it for what it is. "Once a diagnosis is made, it's impossible to say how long a person has had it," says geriatrician Dr. Cheryl Woodson.

Given the history of health coverups in the presidency, we may never know.

At last count, 61 different languages are spoken in New York City.

THE LAST PAGE

FELLOW BATHROOM READERS:
The fight for good bathroom reading should never be taken loosely—we must sit firmly for what we believe in, even while the rest of the world is taking pot shots at us.

Once we prove we're not simply a flush-in-the-pan, writers and publishers will find their resistance unrolling.

So we invite you to take the plunge: Sit Down and Be Counted! by joining The Bathroom Readers' Institute. Send a self-addressed, stamped envelope to: BRI, 1400 Shattuck Avenue #25, Berkeley, CA 94709. You'll receive your attractive free membership card, a copy of the BRI newsletter (if we ever get around to publishing one), and earn a permanent spot on the BRI honor roll.

ᖓ ᖓ ᖓ

UNCLE JOHN'S NEXT BATHROOM READER IS IN THE WORKS!

Don't fret—there's more good reading on its way. In fact, there are a few ways *you* can contribute to the next volume:

1. Is there a subject you'd like to see us cover? Write and let us know. We aim to please.

2. Got a neat idea for a couple of pages in the new *Reader*? If you're the first to suggest it, and we use it, we'll send you a free copy of the book.

3. Have you seen or read an article you'd recommend as quintessential bathroom reading? Or is there a passage in a book that you want to share with other BRI members? Tell us where to find it, or send a copy. If you're the first to suggest it and we publish it in the next volume, there's a free book in it for you.

Well, we're out of space, and when you've gotta go, you've gotta go. Hope to hear from you soon. Meanwhile, remember:

Go With the Flow.